Data Structures
in ANSI C

Data Structures
in ANSI C

SAUMYENDRA SENGUPTA

Lecturer and Former Associate Professor in Computer Science
San Jose State University
and
Member of Technical Staff
Silicon Graphics, Incorporated

PAUL EDWARDS

Senior Software Engineer, OS Development
Unisys Corporation

ACADEMIC PRESS, INC.

Harcourt Brace Jovanovich, Publishers

San Diego   New York   Boston   London   Sydney   Tokyo   Toronto

ACADEMIC PRESS, INC.
San Diego, California 92101

United Kingdom Edition published by
Academic Press Limited
24–28 Oval Road, London NW1 7DX

Library of Congress Cataloging-in-Publication Data

Sengupta, Saumyendra.
    Data structures in ANSI C
  Saumyendra Sengupta, Paul Edwards.
      p.   cm.
    Includes bibliographical references.
    ISBN   0-12-636655-1
  1. C (Computer program language)   2. Data structures (Computer
  science)   I. Edwards, Paul, DATE.   II. ITitle.
  QA76.73.C15S44   1990
  005.7'3--dc20   90-32592
                                                            CIP

PRINTED IN THE UNITED STATES OF AMERICA
90 91 92 93   9 8 7 6 5 4 3 2 1

We dedicate this book to our fathers,
Santosh K. Sengupta and Paul Carroll Edwards, Jr.,
who pointed the way in life for us.

Contents

Preface xv

CHAPTER 1
Basic Concepts of Data Structure 1
  1.1 Computer Storage Model 1
  1.2 Definition of Data Structure 2
  1.3 From Data and Process Algorithms to Solution 3
  1.4 Abstract Data Structures 4
  1.5 Polymorphic Data Structures 6
  1.6 ANSI C 7
  1.7 A Coding Standard 7
     1.7.1 Indentation for Clarity 7
     Exercises 7

CHAPTER 2
Pointers and Structures in C 10
  2.1 The Concept of Pointers in C 10
  2.2 Pointer Arithmetic 11
  2.3 Pointers as Function Arguments 13
  2.4 Functions That Return Pointers and Pointers to Functions 13
  2.5 The Need for the Structure Construct 16
  2.6 Defining a Structure in C 16
  2.7 Accessing Components of a Structure in C 21
     2.7.1 Access Using a Period Operator 21
     2.7.2 Access Using a Pointer 22
  2.8 Initializing a Structure 22
  2.9 Structure Assignment 23

2.10 Pointers to Structures 23
2.11 Passing a Structure as a Function Argument 24
2.12 Passing a Pointer to a Structure as a Function Argument 25
2.13 Structure as a Return Value of a Function 26
2.14 Structure of Structures 26
2.15 Array of Structures 28
2.16 Entering Data into a Structure 28
2.17 Unions 28
2.18 Structures as Components of a Union 31
2.19 Bitfields 33
2.20 Complex Number Implementation Using Structures 34
2.21 Intervals Implemented with Structures 35
      Further Examples 37
      Exercises 56

CHAPTER 3
Arrays and Strings 57
3.1 One-Dimensional Arrays 57
3.2 Array Initialization 59
3.3 Address Translation 60
3.4 Passing Arrays as Function Arguments 61
3.5 The ADT Array 62
3.6 Multidimensional Arrays 64
3.7 Initializing Multidimensional Arrays 65
3.8 Passing Multidimensional Arrays as Function Arguments 66
3.9 Address Translation of Multidimensional Arrays 67
3.10 The Relationship between Arrays and Pointers 73
3.11 The Two-Dimensional ADT Array 76
3.12 Declaration and Access of Strings 78
3.13 Array of Strings 81
3.14 Array of Pointers to Strings 82
3.15 Interchange of Strings 83
3.16 The ADT String 83
3.17 Application: A Small Word Processor 86
      Exercises 89

CHAPTER 4
Recursion 93
4.1 Definition of Recursion 93
4.2 The C-Stack and Recursion 95
4.3 An Improved Recursive Function for Fibonacci Numbers 98
      Examples 99
      Exercises 104

CHAPTER 5
Lists 109
5.1 The Concept of ADT List 109
5.2 Array Implementation of Lists 110
5.3 Pointer Implementation of Lists 118
    5.3.1 The Singly Linked List Implementation 119
    5.3.2 The Doubly Linked List Implementation 130
5.4 Singly Linked Circular Lists 140
5.5 Circular Lists Using Double Links 157
5.6 Application: A Simple Database Using Doubly Linked Lists 158
    5.6.1 Schema of Parts Inventory Control System 159
    5.6.2 Database Implementation Approach 159
    5.6.3 Implementation Restrictions/Issues 161
    5.6.4 Parts Inventory Control Database Program 161
    Exercises 177

CHAPTER 6
Stacks and Queues 181
6.1 An ADT Stack 181
    6.1.1 Array Implementation of a Stack 183
    6.1.2 Linked List Implementation of a Stack 185
6.2 The ADT Double Stacks 187
6.3 Uses of Stacks: Reverse Polish Notation 188
    6.3.1 Postfix Evaluation 189
    6.3.2 Infix to Postfix Expression Conversion 192
6.4 The ADT Queue 196
    6.4.1 Array Implementation of a Queue 196
    6.4.2 Linked List Implementation of a Queue 199
6.5 An ADT Circular Queue 200
    6.5.1 Array Implementation of a Circular Queue 201
    6.5.2 Linked List Implementation of a Circular Queue 203
6.6 Uses of Queues 203
    6.6.1 Uses of FIFO Queues: Communication Buffer Queue 203
    6.6.2 Uses of Priority Queues: SSTF Disk Scheduling 207
    Further Examples 218
    Exercises 243

CHAPTER 7
Trees 247
7.1 Traversals of Binary Trees 248
7.2 The ADT Binary Trees 250
7.3 Binary Tree Implementation 250
    7.3.1 Array Implementation 250
    7.3.2 Linked List Implementation 254

7.4 The ADT Binary Search Tree 262

    7.4.1 Building a Binary Search Tree 266

    7.4.2 Deleting a Node from a Binary Search Tree 267

7.5 General Trees 269

    7.5.1 Implementation of a General Tree 270

    7.5.2 Traversal of the General Tree 272

    7.5.3 Building the General Tree 273

7.6 Search Path 279

7.7 AVL Trees 279

    7.7.1 The Concepts of the AVL Tree 280

    7.7.2 The ADT AVL Trees 281

    7.7.3 Pointer Implementation of an AVL Tree 282

    7.7.4 Inserting a Node in an AVL Tree 283

    7.7.5 Deleting a Node in an AVL Tree 288

    7.7.6 Rebalancing by Rotation 289

7.8 The B-Tree 290

    7.8.1 The ADT B-Tree 292

    7.8.2 Insertion in the B-Tree 292

    7.8.3 Deletion of a Node in the B-Tree 296

7.9 Application: Algebraic Expression Evaluation 299

    Further Examples 307

    Exercises 329

CHAPTER 8
Files 334

8.1 Raw I/O File Access 334

8.2 Streams I/O File Access 335

8.3 An Example of Streams I/O File Access 338

8.4 Data Structure Programming with Files 340

    Exercises 347

CHAPTER 9
Algorithms for Searching and Sorting 349

9.1 O Notation 349

9.2 Searching Algorithms 350

    9.2.1 Linear Search of an Array 351

    9.2.2 Linear Search of a Linked List 352

    9.2.3 Linear Search of an Ordered Array 353

    9.2.4 Linear Search of an Ordered List 354

    9.2.5 Binary Search of an Ordered Array 354

    9.2.6 Interpolation Search of an Ordered Array 355

9.2.7 Fibonacci Search 356

9.2.8 Searching a Binary Search Tree 357

9.2.9 Hash Search 360

9.3 Sorting Algorithms 378

9.3.1 Selection Sort 380

9.3.2 Bubble Sort 381

9.3.3 Insertion Sort 383

9.3.4 Insertion Sort for a Linked List 384

9.3.5 Quick Sort 385

9.3.6 Merge Sort 386

9.3.7 Concatenate Sort 390

9.3.8 Binary Search Tree Sort 391

9.3.9 The Heap Sort 391

Examples 400

Exercises 416

CHAPTER 10

The Object-Oriented Programming Approach 419

10.1 Classical Data Structures 419

10.2 The Object-Oriented Data Structure Concept 420

10.3 An Instance of Object-Oriented Programming 422

10.4 Application: A Singly Linked Circle Class 424

Exercises 439

CHAPTER 11

Applications for Simple Database Programming
Using B-Trees 442

11.1 Schema of Parts Inventory Control System 443

11.2 Database Implementation Approach Using B-Trees 443

11.3 Implementation Restrictions and Issues 448

11.4 A Small SQL Preprocessor 474

Exercises 476

CHAPTER 12

Applications for Science and Engineering 477

12.1 Engineering Application 477

12.2 Statistical Application 481

12.3 Least-Squares Application 484

Exercise 487

CHAPTER 13
Compiler and Editor Applications 488

13.1 Application: Compiler 488

    13.1.1 Overview of the Compilation Process 488

    13.1.2 The Lexical Analyzer 490

    13.1.3 The Parser 490

    13.1.4 The Parser Symbol Table 490

    13.1.5 The Code Generator 496

13.2 Application: A Small Editor 498

    13.2.1 Specification of a Small Line-Oriented Editor 498

    13.3.2 Source Code for the Small Editor 500

    Exercises 509

CHAPTER 14
Applications for Windowing 511

14.1 Stand-Alone Window Applications 512

    Examples 515

CHAPTER 15
Applications for Mathematics 539

15.1 ADT Complex Numbers and Implementations in C 539

    15.1.1 Static and Dynamic Implementations of
    Complex Numbers in C 539

    15.1.2 Implementations of Standard Operations on
    Complex Numbers 541

    15.1.3 Complex Function Evaluation 541

    15.1.4 Examples of Complex Arithmetic 542

15.2 Applications in Numerical Analysis in C 546

    15.2.1 C Code of Bisection Algorithm for Root Finding 547

    15.2.2 C Code of Newton–Raphson Algorithm for Root Finding ... 549

    15.2.3 C Code of Lagrange Interpolation 551

    15.2.4 C Code of Simpson Algorithm for Integration 553

    15.2.5 C Code of Runge–Kutta for a Differential Equation 554

    15.2.6 C Code of Gaussian Elimination for $Ax = b$ 556

    15.2.7 C Code of LU-Decomposition for $Ax = b$ 560

    15.2.8 C Code of Gauss–Seidel Iterative Method for $Ax = b$ 564

    Exercises 567

CHAPTER 16
Graphs 568

16.1 The Concept of a Graph 568

16.2 Graph Representations 570

16.2.1 Graph Representation Using Adjacency Matrix 570

16.2.2 Path Matrix and Transitive Closure 571

16.2.3 Graph Representation Using Linked Adjacency List 574

16.3 The Abstract Data Type Graph 576

16.4 Traversal of Graphs 578

16.4.1 Breadth-First Traversal 579

16.4.2 Depth-First Traversal 580

16.5 Graph Operations 581

16.6 Spanning Trees 585

16.6.1 Building a Spanning Tree of a Graph Using
Depth-First Traversal 585

16.6.2 Building a Spanning Tree of a Graph Using
Breadth-First Traversal 586

16.7 Application: Computing the Shortest Path 587

Example 590

Exercises 606

APPENDIX A
Important C-Language Information 611

A.1 Form of a Simple Program in C 611

A.2 28 Reserved Words in C 611

A.3 Special Characters Reserved in C 611

A.4 Built-in Data Types in C 612

A.4.1 Basic Integer Data Types in Standard C 612

A.4.2 Other Integer Types as Bitfields 612

A.4.3 Floating-Point Types 612

A.4.4 Enumeration Types 613

A.5 Casting in C 613

A.6 Identifiers in C 613

A.7 Arithmetic Operators in C 613

A.7.1 Standard Binary Operators 613

A.7.2 Auto Increment and Decrement Operators 614

A.8 Relational Binary Operators in C 614

A.9 Logical Operators in C 614

A.10 Bitwise Operators in C 614

A.11 Assignment Operators in C 614

A.12 Operators' Precedence and Associativity in C 615

A.13 Arrays in C 615

A.14 Records in C 615

A.15 Pointers in C 616

A.16 Statement Formats of Each Key Word in C 616

A.17 Input/Output Basics in C 617

A.18 File-Based Input/Output in C 617

A.19 Common Preprocessor Directives in C 618

A.20 Creating an Executable File for a C Program 618

    A.20.1 UNIX Environment 618

    A.20.2 IBM PC/MS–DOS Environment 618

APPENDIX B
Standard C Library Functions for Handling Strings 619

Bibliography 621

Index 623

Preface

This book offers coverage of the basic types and structured data types in ANSI C and the fundamental concepts of data structures and some applications in C programming. It is our intention to provide a text for an undergraduate course in Data Structures and Advanced Programming in C. We emphasize the abstract data structure (ADT) approach in order to describe the data structures in this book. We provide a terse reference for the C language and the standard string manipulation library in the appendixes; however, we assume that the reader is familiar with the C programming language.

Although programming in the newer languages and operating system environments has made increasing use of pointers and dynamic allocation of memory, use of static arrays is still relevant in such areas as operating system tables. Therefore, we present both array and pointer/dynamic memory implementations of data structures.

Each chapter is organized into discussion sections on various related topics, followed by the examples of the data structure definitions in C and the process algorithms as C functions. As much as possible, the code is presented in one place and then used throughout the rest of the book by cross-references to chapters, sections, examples, or exercises.

Chapter 1 is an introduction to the fundamental concepts of computer information organization and data structures.

Chapter 2 reviews the use of pointers and structures in C.

Chapter 3 discusses the use of arrays and strings.

Chapter 4 presents the notions of iterative and recursive processing, presents some examples, and prepares the way for the discussion of tree data structures and searching and sorting of data.

Chapter 5 is a discussion of lists and their uses.

Chapter 6 shows the construction of stacks and queues and the elementary processing of them.

Chapter 7 presents the data structures and their access algorithms for trees.

Chapter 8 covers the concept of files in C.

Chapter 9 is a discussion of searching and sorting.

Chapter 10 is a brief presentation of the object-oriented programming method of combining data structures and process algorithms into a unified structure.

Chapter 11 shows the use of data structures in database programming applications in B-trees.

Chapter 12 is a presentation of the use of data structures in several topics in physical science.

Chapter 13 shows some of the implementation details for a compiler (using stacks) and an editor (using buffers).

Chapter 14 discusses some windowing applications for stand-alone window functions.

Chapter 15 details solutions for problems in numerical analysis, matrix algebra, complex numbers, and linear algebra.

Chapter 16 presents the data structures and their access algorithms for graphs.

Appendix A is a terse reference of the C language.

Appendix B is a terse reference of the C library functions for handling strings.

We have been fortunate in the active interest shown by our colleagues and associates in the creation of this book. We are thankful for the material contributed by G. M. Harding, Jose Oliva, Luis Valle, Gabriel Jordan, Martin Moore, Frank E. Kretz, and Vasudha Bhaskara.

We have received many useful comments from reviewers from both the private sector and academic institutions. These reviewers include Robert Moody, G. M. Harding, Loan Nguyen, John Antia, Ed Bradford, Carl Held, Ron Green, and Joan Tomlinson of Unisys–Convergent; David Fenstemaker and Roger B. Dahl of Silicon Graphics, Inc.; Dr. Eldon R. Hansen, former Principal Scientist at Lockheed; Prof. Martin Billik, Prof. Vinh Phat, and Prof. Mary Rhodes of San Jose State University; Dr. Alpana Banerjee, formerly of San Jose State University; and Prof. Saroj Sabherwal of Mission College, Santa Clara, California.

We appreciate Prof. Vinh Phat for accepting and using this textbook for the Data Structure and Advanced Programming class and Prof. Mary Rhodes for using this text in the Advanced C class in the Mathematics and Computer Science Department, San Jose State University. We used this as a textbook for the Data Structure course at San Jose State University.

We also wish to express special thanks to Ron Green, Rudite Emir, Unisys–Convergent, and Silicon Graphics, Inc. for support and encouragement.

We are grateful for the support of our families in the effort of writing this book. Thanks to the Sengupta family: Prativa (mother); Saurendra and Nityananda (brothers); Snigdha, Bani, Arati, and Subhra (sisters); Juthika (wife); and Lopamudra and Ballori (daughters). Thanks to the Edwards family: Patricia (wife) and Matt and Joey (sons).

Frank E. Kretz has worked sincerely and diligently with one of the authors (S.S.) in producing the solutions manual for the selected exercises and programming projects.

We want to convey our special thanks to our numerous students, including Dr. Atila Mertol, Steve Colby, John Pliska, Michaelle Ann Barbaccia, Carl P. Korobkin, and Frank E. Kretz, for their helpful comments and suggestions.

Finally, we are indebted to Dean Irey and Bill LaDue of Academic Press for their helpful comments, encouragement, and excellent work toward expediting the publication process.

The code of complete programs in examples in this book has been compiled and tested using the Convergent Technologies CTIX (AT&T UNIX System V, 3.2) C and C++ compilers and the MicroSoft C and Turbo C compiler under DOS. The authors have made every effort to eliminate errors in the examples given.

CHAPTER 1

Basic Concepts
of Data Structure

Human activities often involve information that must be stored, transformed, and retrieved. The science and engineering disciplines require the collection and processing of large amounts of data. Companies keep many types of records and perform various analyses on them to aid in doing business. Manufacturers keep parts inventories and production schedules, use construction specifications that detail materials and measurements, and run machinery that uses the specifications. All these activities can be aided by the use of computers, which are useful for collection of information, computations on the data sets, storage and processing of records, and process controllers. The use of information requires a definition of its nature and how it will be processed.

1.1 Computer Storage Model

Computers have a fundamental information storage model. The basic units of storage are the binary bit and the machine word, a set of bits accessed in parallel. The storage is called *memory* and is composed of several parts: main memory, secondary storage, and peripheral I/O (input/output). Secondary storage is associated with disk drives and with the notion of a file system. Secondary storage is usually a bit stream organized into units (bytes) that are clustered into segments (blocks or sectors). The information in secondary storage is accessed bit-by-bit and then assembled into machine words. Peripheral I/O is associated with I/O registers or direct memory access (DMA) buffers. Main memory is organized into streams of words, so that an access of main memory is word-by-word.

All the machine storage types are composed of bits in parallel. The sizes vary with the type: bit, bitfield, byte, word, double word, single-precision floating point, double-precision floating point, and address. Figure 1-1 shows the usual machine storage types.

For further information, refer to Kernighan and Ritchie (1978). The actual sizes of machine types may vary from architecture to architecture. The details of how information is stored in the machine types also varies from machine to machine.

1

```
Machine                  Typical Size

Bit                      1 bit
Bitfield                 0 or more contiguous bits
Byte                     8 bits (1 byte)
Word                     2 bytes
Double word              4 bytes
Single float             4 bytes
Double float             8 bytes
Address                  4 bytes
```

Figure 1-1 Machine storage types and sizes

1.2 Definition of Data Structure

The concept of a data structure is used to represent a machine data process model in the programming language. The concept is also used to represent elements of the information involved in the problem to be handled by the machine. The problem defines the data structure used, so it is very useful to take the needed time to clarify the problem prior to constructing a solution. Often the problem definition–solution process is iterative or refined in hierarchical levels of detail.

A data structure is an ordered collection of data types, composed of basic unstructured types, structured types, or a mixture of unstructured and structured types, and a set of operations defined on the ordered data types.

In other words, a data structure will have three parts:

1. A set of operations
2. A storage structure specifying classes of related data and collection of variables
3. A set of algorithms, one for each operation

Each algorithm searches and modifies the storage structure to achieve the result defined for the operation.

A set of integer variables and the set of simple arithmetic operations (addition, subtraction, multiplication, division, negation, absolute value, etc.) on them are examples of a basic data structure.

Another example of a data structure is the reporting organization of a corporation. The data structure might be defined as the graph in Figure 1-2, with the names of the key managers as nodes, and the movement of information and orders as operations on the graph.

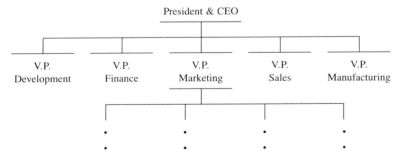

Figure 1-2 Corporate organization.

Up this graph (or tree), numerous people report to their respective vice president (V.P.). The structure in Figure 1-2 is not complete, but it conveys the basic concept involved. This organizational structure is an example of a general tree. It will be discussed later in this book.

Related to size of storage required, there are two classes of data structure:

Static: structures whose sizes and associated memory locations are fixed at compile time.

Dynamic: structures whose sizes expand or shrink as required during the program execution and their associated memory locations change.

1.3 From Data and Process Algorithms to Solution

The problem and the programming language used determine the design of the data structure. The definition of the data structure and its associated process algorithms represents a solution to the problem expressed in the chosen language.

For an example of an application, consider a landscape architect's files on plants. Suppose this architect has a file cabinet with file folders that contain information on each plant used. We want to set up a database. We define a data structure to hold the elements of the file folder.

The data structure has the following elements:

The common name of the plant
The technical name of the plant
The type of soil to use
The type of climate
Growth seasons
The type and amount of nutrient needed
The amount of watering needed
The dimensions at maturity
The local distributors

The operations on the data structure are:

Create a new entry in the database
Search for and retrieve entries that match the specification
Delete an entry from the database
Modify an entry

The algorithms associated with the operations are:

Create: obtain new space for the entry, and report error if there is none; obtain input for the fields of the new entry; insert it in the database
Retrieve: search through the database for entries that match the specification; return the location of each entry found; report error if none found
Delete: search for the specified entry; report an error if not found; otherwise remove it from the database and free its memory allocation
Modify: search for the specified entry; report an error if not found; otherwise apply the changes

The collection of data structures and access processes may be considered to form an object. This will be discussed further in the chapter on object-oriented programming (Chapter 10).

1.4 Abstract Data Structures

An *abstract data structure*—often referred to as an *abstract data type* (ADT)—is a
structure defined by its functional properties without regard for the machine representation of its internal data or operations.

An example is the set of alphanumeric characters and the set of string manipulation functions. How the characters are represented in machine code (ASCII,
EBCDIC, or whatever) is detail left to the string manipulation functions and macros
in the Standard C Library.

Abstract data structures provide modularity for programming. The external
interface remains the same, although the internal implementation details may change.

The use of ADT hides the data and puts emphasis on the operations (actions)
on the data. ADT hides the data like a capsule hides its ingredients. ADT provides
user interfaces via the functions that implement the operations on the ADT. The
concept of abstract data typing (encapsulating) is a fundamental concept in object-
oriented programming. Other aspects in object-oriented programming are inheritance, object identity, and binding. These aspects and their applications are discussed in Chapter 10.

The internal representation of data, storage, and the implementation of operations on the data are hidden from the users, who access and manipulate the data.
For example, we use the ADT integer arithmetic operations +, -, *, etc. without
knowing how the integer is internally represented in a computer system (e.g., 2's
complement).

The powers of data abstraction are:

1. We can use ADT without knowing and understanding its representation
   and implementation details.
2. We can modify or change implementation without affecting the usage and
   actions of the ADT.

A notation for defining an ADT is provided by the C++ class construct in the C++
programming language. The programs in C++ are organized into a set of abstract
data types.

We now want to define an ADT image as an example. Image processing is
becoming very popular and useful in such areas as commercial arts and medical
applications. In image processing, we deal with image objects. The data contained
in an ADT image object may be one or any combination of the following: text, human body, animal body, human face, car, flowers, space shuttle, building, machine,
computers, geometric drawings, or paintings.

The operations for an ADT image are:

1. Reading or scanning an image using a scanning device
2. Allocating space for an image in memory
3. Deallocating space for an image from memory
4. Storing an image from memory in a file on a disk [e.g., as a bit-mapped
   image in tagged image file format (TIFF)]
5. Loading an image from disk into memory
6. Getting the allocated depth of an image
7. Getting the allocated height of an image
8. Getting the allocated width of an image
9. Getting the size of an image

10. Defining the image rectangle
11. Setting the depth of an image rectangle
12. Setting the height of an image rectangle
13. Setting the width of an image rectangle
14. Setting the resolution of an image rectangle
15. Defining the size of an image envelope
16. Setting the depth of an image envelope
17. Setting the height of an image envelope
18. Setting the width of an image envelope
19. Modifying the allocated depth of an image
20. Modifying the allocated height of an image
21. Modifying the allocated width of an image
22. Deleting an image
23. Compressing an image [using facsimile (FAX) compression algorithms developed by CCITT] and placing it in the destination image
24. Decompressing the source image and placing it in a specified destination
25. Cropping an image (i.e., throwing away those parts of the image outside a rectangular envelope) according to specified factors
26. Cutting an image
27. Pasting an image with another image
28. Copying a source image to a destination (file or memory)
29. Translating an image that caused straight-line movement of the source image to the destination image
30. Rotating an image
31. Zooming an image or any part of an image
32. Highlighting any part of an image
33. Scaling (resizing) an image according to given factors, and placing it in a specified destination
34. Displaying an image on the screen
35. Printing an image
36. Scanning and displaying an image to a specified place, once the scanner is open
37. Scanning and scaling an image
38. Scanning, scaling, and displaying an image to a target field
39. Measuring distance between any two parts in an image

For another example, consider the representation and arithmetic processing of ADT complex numbers shown in Figure 1-3.

There are three main classes of data types:

1. *Atomic:* the set of basic types (signed and unsigned versions of char, short, long, int, float, double) and the basic operations on them (+, −, *, /, %, |, &, etc).
2. *Fixed-structured:* a structured type composed of a number of fixed atomic types and the basic operations, along with indexing (array or pointer).
3. *Variable-structured:* a structure with a varying set of subcomponents of atomic and fixed-structured types with the basic operations, indexing, and dynamic memory allocation and deallocation.

Elements of the atomic data class are used to compose the other types. Elements of the fixed-structured class are typically used for data buffers, system tables,

```
typedef  double  COMPLEX[2];
typedef  COMPLEX * pCOMPLEX;

double real( pCOMPLEX Z )
{
    return *Z;
}

double imaginary( pCOMPLEX Z )
{
    return *(++Z);
}

typedef  struct
{
    double  real;
    double  imag;;
} COMPLEX;

typedef  COMPLEX * pCOMPLEX;

double real( pCOMPLEX Z )
{
    return Z->real;
}

double imaginary( pCOMPLEX Z )
{
    return Z->imag;
}
```

Figure 1-3 Array and struct implementations of ADT complex numbers.

and matrix operations. Elements of the variable-structured class are used for list processing, stacks, queues, parsing trees, sorting, and searching.

1.5 Polymorphic Data Structures

Polymorphic data structures are structures that are nonspecific with respect to basic data types. They must be implemented by a dynamic memory allocation scheme, since the size of internal elements isn't known until run-time.

Polymorphic data structures allow processing independent of size, so:

1. The data structure never accesses data elements directly; instead, pointers are used, so a fixed size parameter (the pointer) refers to a variable-size data type. This requires the use of a generic pointer:

```
typedef char  *  GPOINTER;
```

2. Data structures used to implement polymorphism make no internal assumptions about data size, so all type-specific information must be passed to the access functions as parameters.
3. The data structures must use dynamic allocation of memory in order to arrange for storage of parameter and automatic variables.

4. Static variables cannot generally be used in access functions to store parameter values, because the next call to the function may involve parameters with quite different sizes.

1.6 ANSI C

We have chosen to present the examples of C code in the ANSI C format, because much new code has now been written for it. We have only used the function definition and declaration syntax.

If you have access to an older compiler, you will have to convert ANSI to K&R syntax. The process is simple, as shown in Figure 1-4.

```
ANSI                              K&R
_____               _____

char *                            char *
func(int i, char * cp)            func(i, cp)
{                                 int i;
    :                             char * cp;
    int funz(float f);           {
    :                                :
}                                     int funz();
                                     :
                                  }
```

Figure 1-4 Translation from ANSI to K&R syntax.

1.7 A Coding Standard

There are a number of books on good coding practices. We will follow several in this book.

1.7.1 Indentation for Clarity

We will use an indenting of four spaces to indicate structure:

```
main( int argc, char  *argv[] )
{
    int  i, A[10];
    for ( i = 0; i < 10; i++ )
        {
            A[ i ] = i * i;
        }
}
```

Exercises

1-1 Design an ADT string.

    (a) What operations would be desirable?
    (b) Think about C-style implementation.
    (c) Write functions implementing some operations.

1-2 Design an ADT set.

>   (a) What operations would be desirable?
>   (b) Think about C-style implementation.
>   (c) Write functions implementing some operations.

1-3 The natural numbers are characterized by Peano's axioms:

>   A1: 1 is a natural number.
>   A2: For any natural number n, the successor of n, successor(n), is a natural number.
>   A3: For any natural number n, 1 is not successor(n).
>   A4: If two natural numbers n and m, have the same successor, that is, successor(n) = successor(m), then $n = m$.
>   A5: (Principle of induction)
>   >   (i) A relation is true for $n = 1$, that is, R(1) = true.
>   >   (ii) If the assumption R(m) = true leads to R($m + 1$) = true for all natural numbers, then we can inductively conclude that the relation R(n) is true for all natural numbers n.

>   (a) Develop an ADT natural number using the axioms A1 through A5, together with the desirable operations.
>   (b) Define the function successor(n) so that any computer implementation of the positive integers will satisfy the axioms A1 through A5.

1-4 Rational numbers are ratios of the form a/b, where a and b are integers, and the denominator b is not zero. Design an ADT concept on the rational numbers.

>   (a) What operations would be desirable?
>   (b) Think about C-style implementation using a struct.
>   (c) Write functions implementing the operations.

1-5 Complex numbers are defined as $a + bi$, where a and b are rational numbers. The numbers a and b are called the real and imaginary parts of the complex number, respectively. Design an ADT concept on the complex numbers.

>   (a) What operations would be desirable?
>   (b) Think about C-style implementation using a struct.
>   (c) Write functions implementing the operations.

1-6 Interval numbers are defined as [a, b], where a and b are rational numbers, and $a \leq b$. Design an ADT concept on the interval numbers.

>   (a) What operations would be desirable?
>   (b) Think about C-style implementation using a struct.
>   (c) Write functions implementing the operations. You must include such operations as union and intersection of two intervals.

1-7 A matrix $[a_{ij}]$ is a rectangular array with m rows and n columns, and i ranges from 0 to $m - 1$, and j ranges from 0 to $n - 1$. The elements a_{ij} can be assumed to be integers. Design an ADT concept on the matrices.

(a) What operations would be desirable?

(b) Think about C-style implementation using an array.

(c) Write functions implementing the operations including equality of two matrices.

1-8 A file is a collection of program (source and executable codes), data, and related information defined by its creator. It is known and identifiable by a unique symbolic name. Design an ADT concept on the files.

(a) What operations would be desirable?

(b) Think about C-style implementation using a struct.

(c) From your known operating systems, for example, PC-DOS and Unix, show some examples of user-typed commands that implement some of those operations.

1-9 Design an ADT polynomial.

(a) What operations would be desirable?

(b) Think about C-style implementation.

(c) Write functions implementing some operations.

1-10 (*Advanced.*) The concept of a process is very fundamental in operating systems programming. A process is a program in execution; it is a continuous sequence of execution operation. It is identified by its entries in the table "process control block" (PCB) in operating systems. A process is an untyped, parameterless public procedure. Design an ADT concept on the processes together with their operations.

1-11 (*Advanced.*) Design an ADT window.

(a) What operations would be desirable?

(b) Think about C-style implementation.

(c) Write functions implementing some operations.

1-12 (*Advanced.*) Design an ADT window pop-up menu.

(a) What operations would be desirable?

(b) Think about C-style implementation. (*Hint:* General tree.)

(c) Write functions implementing some operations on pop-up menus.

CHAPTER 2

Pointers and Structures in C

In this chapter we review the pointers and structures in C. The concepts of these elements are fundamental to the development and implementation of such complex data structures as strings, lists, stacks, queues, and trees.

2.1 The Concept of Pointers in C

The concept of pointers arose from the use of CPU registers to reference memory locations. As CPU instruction sets became richer, the modes of address register reference expanded from simple register indirect (the register holds the address of a memory location of data) to such modes as register indirect with index (the register holds a base address to which is added a specified offset to produce the address of a location in memory), auto postincrement (reference the location and increment the address register) and auto decrement (reference the location and decrement the address register), or memory indirect (the register holds the address of a memory location that holds the address of a location in memory).

As computing evolved from programming in Assembly Language (machine instruction mnemonic syntax) to middle-level language (plain-text keyword syntax), features of the expanded instruction sets were incorporated into elements of the language. The register indirect became a pointer. The register indirect with an index became an array pointer with an array index. The memory indirect became a pointer to a pointer.

From an abstract data-type viewpoint, memory location becomes a variable (that holds a memory location), along with a set of operators on the variable. The base type (TYPE) of the variable determines the size of the location that it references and the size of the offset applied to it by increment or decrement. The operators are shown in Table 2-1.

Pointers are used to:

1. Pass variables (such as arrays, structs, and strings) to a function (called *reference by location*)
2. Process arrays easily
3. Return structured variables from a function

Table 2-1
Operators on Pointers

Operator	Meaning
&	Get the address of the referenced location
*	Get the contents of the referenced location
++	Increment the pointer by one unit of TYPE size
+=N	Increment the pointer by N units of TYPE size
--	Decrement the pointer by one unit of TYPE size
-=N	Decrement the pointer by N units of TYPE size
=	Assign a memory location to the pointer
TYPE *	Declare a pointer and its base type

4. Create such complex data types as list, queue, stack, and tree
5. Return pointers to allocated blocks of memory
6. Pass the name (and therefore the address of the first instruction) of a function to a function

2.2 Pointer Arithmetic

It is possible to use some arithmetic operators on pointers, but you must be careful about the restrictions:

1. Operators + and – may be used.
2. Operators *, /, and % may not be used.
3. Expressions of the type `ptr OP expr`, where OP is + or – and `expr` is an expression that evaluates to an integer type may be used. Expressions of the type `ptr OP (TYPE *) expr`, where OP is + or –, and TYPE is char, short, long, or int, may always be used.
4. Expressions of the type `expr OP ptr` may not be used.
5. Expressions of the type `ptr1 OP ptr2` may not be used, except when OP is –, but this construct should be avoided.
6. Assignments of the type `ptr1 = (base type of ptr1 *) ptr 2 OP (int *) expr` may always be used.
7. *Watch out:* the compiler will accept p + HUGE_INT. It may cause the resulting value to be wrapped around or truncated to the maximum unsigned int value.
8. *Watch out:* the compiler will accept p + ANY_INT. The resulting value may point to some unintended area of memory, like operating system space, and your program or the operating system will crash.

Pointer arithmetic is not number arithmetic. By this we mean:

In integer-number arithmetic: 'a++' means 'a = a + 1'
In pointer arithmetic: 'ptr++' means 'ptr = ptr + sizeof (base type)'

Pointer arithmetic is an alternative approach to memory indexing. This usage grew out of address register modes used in Assembly Language coding. The simplest pointer arithmetic, shown in Table 2-2, is increment and decrement. The use of pointer dereferencing with increment and decrement is shown in Table 2-3.

Table 2-2
Pointer Increment and Decrement

Operations on pointer	Meaning and effect
p++	Postincrement: get the value of p, then increment the pointer, p = p + sizeof (base type)
p--	Postdecrement: get the value of p, then decrement the pointer, p = p + sizeof (base type)
++p	Preincrement: increment the pointer, p = p + sizeof (base type), then get the value of p
--p	Predecrement: decrement the pointer, p = p + sizeof (base type), then get the value of p

Table 2-3
Pointer Increment and Decrement with Referencing

Operations on pointer	Meaning and effect
p	A pointer to a storage location
* (p++)	Get the value *p, then increment p
*p++	The same as * (p++) (remember, the operators are right-associative)
* (++p)	Preincrement p, then get the value at the new location [i.e., * (p + sizeof (base type)]
*++p	The same as * (++p) (right-associative)
(*p) ++	Get the value *p, then increment the value pointed to by p
++ (*p)	Increment the value pointed to by p
++*p	The same as ++ (*p)
* (p--)	Get the value *p, then decrement p
*p--	The same as * (p--) (remember, the operators are right-associative)
* (--p)	Predecrement p, then get the value at the new location [i.e., * (p - sizeof (base type)]
*--p	The same as * (--p) (right-associative)
(*p) --	Get the value *p, then decrement the value pointed to by p
-- (*p)	Decrement the value pointed to by p
--*p	The same as -- (*p)

There are several books with excellent treatments of pointers [see Holub (1987), Ward (1985), and Plum (1986)].

2.3 Pointers as Function Arguments

A pointer is passed to a function just as any other argument:

Example 2.1 A Pointer Passed to a Function

```
funcA ()
{
    int y, x = 4;
    int * p = &x;
    int modify(), modify_x();

    y = modify(p);
    /* at this point,  x == 4  and  y == 8  */

    y = modify_x(p);
    /* at this point,  x == 2  and  y == 1  */
}

int modify(int * ip)
{
    return *ip + 4;
}

int modify_x(int * ip)
{
    *ip = 2;
    return *ip / 2;
}
```

In this example, the value of x is not changed in modify (), because *ip
is used in an expression, but is not assigned to. The value of x is changed in the
second example, because *ip, which refers to the contents of x, is assigned the
value 2.

2.4 Functions That Return Pointers and Pointers to Functions

A function that returns a pointer allows access to memory locations by the calling
function. This is very useful for handling structured data types, such as arrays,
structs, and unions. The structured variable must exist outside the scope of the
called function; otherwise it will vanish with the other automatic variables when the
called function is exited. It is best to define the structured variable as global or static
to ensure its persistence. The use of a function that returns a pointer is shown in
Example 2.2.

Example 2.2 A Function That Returns a Pointer

```
struct SX
{
      int x;
      int y;
} X;

funcA ()
{
      struct SX * ip;
      struct SX * funcB ();

      ip = funcB ();
      /* ip == the address of X */

      ip->x = 8;
      ip->y = 4;
      /* X. x == 8 and X. y == 4 */
}

struct SX * funcB ()
{
      extern struct SX X;
      struct SX * Xp = &X;

      return Xp;
}
```

The concept of a pointer to function is easy to understand and use. The name of a function is actually the address of the first executable instruction within that function. A pointer to a function is the address of that first instruction. Example 2.3 shows how to use this concept.

Example 2.3 A Function That Returns a Pointer to a Function

```
int compare (int x, int y)
{
    return (x > y) ? 1 : 0;
}

int sum (int x, int y)
{
    return x + y;
}

int func ( int x, int y, int (* sfunc) ())
{
    return (* sfunc) (x, y);
}
```

```
caller()
{
    int  x = 1;
    int  y = 4;
    int  compare(),  sum();
    int  (* cfunc)();  /* the function pointer variable */

    /* Assign the address of compare() */
    cfunc = compare;
    printf("result = %d\n", func(x, y, cfunc));
                                 /* result = 0 */
    /* Assign the address of sum() */
    cfunc = sum;
    printf("result = %d\n", func(x, y, cfunc));
                                 /* result = 5 */
}
```

A pointer to a function can be used to implement a data structure called a *jump table*, used in operating system design. The jump table contains the addresses of service routines that are called to handle system device interrupts. Example 2.4 shows how the device jump table is set up and used.

Example 2.4 System Calls Implemented by a Pointer to a Function

```
extern struct sysent
{
    char  sys_arg;          /* number of arguments to
                               function */
    int   (* sys_call)();  /* the system call function */
} sysent[];

int diskclose();
int diskopen();
int diskread();
int diskwrite();

struct sysent syscall[4] =
{
    {1, diskclose},   /* syscall[0] == diskclose */
    {2, diskopen},    /* syscall[1] == diskopen  */
    {2, diskread},    /* syscall[2] == diskread  */
    {3, diskwrite}    /* syscall[3] == diskwrite */
};


/* openchannel():
 *    int    dev:      major number of device
 *    int    mode:     mode of access: RD, WR, etc.
 */
int openchannel(int dev, int mode)
{
    return (*syscall[2])(dev, mode);
}
```

2.5 The Need for the Structure Construct

The structure is the most powerful concept in data structure and in the C language. It is analogous to the record in the Pascal language. In Chapter 3 we will discuss organizing a collection of data objects as an array when they are of same type. When the data are not of same type, we can still organize them as a collection of one-dimensional arrays, but such organization will be complex and very inefficient. For example, in a car dealership we deal with for each car, a set of informative data: car model, car maker's name, year of manufacture, car owner, car owner's phone number, and type of service needed. We can organize each of these types as a one-dimensional array as follows:

```
                    Model   Maker   Year   Owner   Phone   Service
                   ____    ____    ____   ____    ____    ____
    car_1   [1]   |    |  |    |  |    | |    |  |    |  |    |
                  |----|  |----|  |----| |----|  |----|  |----|
    car_2   [2]   |    |  |    |  |    | |    |  |    |  |    |
                  |----|  |----|  |----| |----|  |----|  |----|
    car_3   [3]   |    |  |    |  |    | |    |  |    |  |    |
                  |----|  |----|  |----| |----|  |----|  |----|
    car_4   [4]   |    |  |    |  |    | |    |  |    |  |    |
                  |----|  |----|  |----| |----|  |----|  |----|
    car_5   [5]   |    |  |    |  |    | |    |  |    |  |    |
                  |----|  |----|  |----| |----|  |----|  |----|
      .     [.]   | .  |  | .  |  | .  | | .  |  | .  |  | .  |
                  |----|  |----|  |----| |----|  |----|  |----|
      .     [.]   | .  |  | .  |  | .  | | .  |  | .  |  | .  |
                  |----|  |----|  |----| |----|  |----|  |----|
      .     [.]   | .  |  | .  |  | .  | | .  |  | .  |  | .  |
                  |----|  |----|  |----| |----|  |----|  |----|
    car_n   [n]   | .  |  | .  |  | .  | | .  |  | .  |  | .  |
                  |____|  |____|  |____| |____|  |____|  |____|
```

In this organization, we will store information of car_1, car_2, car_3, . . . , car_n, respectively, in rows 1, 2, 3, . . . , n. But the difficulty, inefficiency, and complexity will arise when:

1. We write a program with many variables and indices
2. We start accessing, maintaining, and operating on these data
3. We cannot access them as a group or block of data
4. We reserve memory space for them
5. More different types of information are needed

In short, we want to conveniently, elegantly, efficiently, and collectively use such data objects of various types as a group. This is where the structure mechanism serves the purpose. Structures are very useful, not only because they contain different data types but also because they can form very complex data structures, such as linked lists, trees, graphs, and databases.

2.6 Defining a Structure in C

A structure is a collection of related but different data types, in which the number of data items is not limited. The C language provides us its powerful built-in type `struct` to define a structure. The type of each data item may be C-provided data types (int, char, float, struct, etc.) or user-defined data types.

The syntax in declaring a structure-type variable is given in many forms.

Form I

(Storage for variables `identifier_1` and `identifier_2` will be automatically allocated.)

```
       struct  < structure_name >
              {
                < member_type >    member1_name;
                < member_type >    member2_name;

                              . . .

                < member_type >    memberN_name;
              }   identifier_1, identifier_2;
```

Form II

```
struct  < structure_name >
      {
        < member_type >    member1_name;
        < member_type >    member2_name;

                      . . .

        < member_type >    memberN_name;
      };
/* Memory spaces for identifier_1 and identifier_2  will  be
 * allocated  only  after  the  declaration  in  the  following
 * line.
 */

struct  < structure_name >       identifier_1, identifier_2;
```

Form III

(This structure cannot be used later to declare more variables of this type because `structure_name` is omitted.)

```
       struct
              {
                < member_type >    member1_name;
                < member_type >    member2_name;

                              . . .

                < member_type >    memberN_name;
              }   identifier_1, identifier_2;
```

Form IV

(The `structure_type_name` has become a user-defined type replacing the future use of `structure_name`.)

```
typedef struct
      {
        < member_type >    member1_name;
        < member_type >    member2_name;

                      . . .
```

```
        < member_type >      memberN_name;
    } < structure_type_name >;

  < structure_type_name >   identifier_1, identifier_2;
                        /* Space is reserved now */
```

The structure_name is also called *tag*. It is not a variable name. It is simply a structure-type name that can be used later to declare more variables of this structure type. The members of a structure are also called *fields* or *components*. As a good programming practice it is advisable to give a name (i.e., *tag*) to a structure. At the identifier declaration, the computer allocates space for each identifier by calculating the size of the structure. It is not true that the size of a structure is the sum of the sizes of its individual members; it may be either larger or smaller.

Example 2.5

As described in the beginning for the car dealership, informative data for each car can be defined as the following structure:

```
    /* Allows naming a set */
    enum  Service  { repair, paint, maintenance };

    struct  car_record
        {
            char           Model_name[ 10 ];
            char           Maker_name[ 15 ];
            short          Year;
            char           Owner[ 20 ];
            char           Phone[ 10 ];
            enum   Service  service;

        } one_car, cars[ 100 ];
```

Note that by organizing our car-related data this way, we have only one array, cars of size 100, each element of the array being a structure car_record. As a result, we will deal with only one array index. From this example, we can note the following:

1. The structure car_record can be an individual data item of another structured data type, such as an array.
2. An individual component (e.g., Model_name) of a structure may be an array or even another record.
3. The identifier one_car is a structure of type car_record.

Example 2.6

In this example, our goal is to apply this structure concept in the context of Intel's 80386 microprocessor. Intel's iAPX-80386 microprocessor provides support to implement multitasking and virtual memory management with protection. The logical memory address space of the 80386 is inherently partitioned into segments. The segments are classified into three main groups:

1. Task (process/program) state segment (TSS) (only for privileged operating system programs)
2. Code segment (area for any executable program)
3. Data segment (area for program's data)

The 80386 architecture does not allow an application program to directly access a memory segment as a feature of its memory protection scheme. It defines a record, called *segment descriptor,* for each of the above three segments. The description for each segment is a structure containing:

1. Base (i.e., start) address of the segment in the linear address space
2. Limit (i.e, size) of the segment
3. Protection attributes (access rights) such as Writable(W), Accessed(A), DPL, etc.

For clarity, a data segment descriptor, as in Intel (1987), is:

```
  15                         7                         0
  +----------------------------------------------------+
  |  BASE Address 31-24  | G | B | 0 | AV | LIMIT 19-16 |
  |----------------------|-----------------------------|
  | P | DPL |1 |0 |E | W | A | BASE Address 23-16       |
  |----------------------------------------------------|
  |             BASE Address   15-0                     |
  |----------------------------------------------------|
  |                 LIMIT 15-0                          |
  |_____|
```

where:

```
  G    :   Granularity           B  :   Big       0  :   Must be 0
  AV   :   Available for OS use   P  :   Present   W  :   Writable
  EI   :   Expansion direction    A  :   Accessed
  DPL  :   Descriptor Privilege Level
```

Thus any user's program is allowed to access a memory location of a segment indirectly through the segment's descriptor upon validation. In C, one way we can define this segment descriptor as a structure is:

```
struct   segment_descriptor
{
   U32bits       base_address;     /* Unsigned 32 bits    */
   U20bits       limit;            /* Unsigned 20 bits    */
   access_bits   seg_protection;   /* field can be in bits */

}  data_seg;
```

Note that the user-defined data types U32bits, U20bits, and access_bits can be associated with individual members of a structure, as shown in Example 2.6. This example shows how to interpret these kinds of application using the structure concept. The structures tss_seg and code_seg can be defined in the same manner.

Example 2.7

The frequently used term *windowing system* deals with data (to be) displayed on a display screen, such as a video terminal. It is a facility to organize, position, paint, and partition the display screen, or even overlap with another set of data. Its basic function deals with screen data for the purpose of presentation. As presented in Gettys *et al.* (1986) on X-window, jointly developed by DEC and MIT, here is a sample structure on X-windows:

```
typedef   struct _WindowInfo
{
    short  width, height;      /* Width and height        */
    short  x, y;               /* x and y coordinates     */
    short  bdrwidth;           /* Border width            */
    short  mapped;             /* IsUnmapped, IsMapped,
                                  or IsInvisible          */
    short  type;               /* IsTransparent,
                                  IsOpaque, or IsIcon      */
    Window assoc_wind;         /* Associated icon or
                                  opaque Window            */
}   WindowInfo;                /* WindowInfo is struct
                                  type                     */
```

Note that this structure is defined to get various facts about a window. In Chapter 14 we will present applications based on stand-alone windowing. This shows how structure concept is instrumental in developing window applications.

Example 2.8

Suppose that a company needs to have an organized form of data for its employees. The data for each employee can be grouped in a record. Each record consists of the following:

First name: 10 chars long
Middle name: 10 chars
Last name: 10 chars
Social Security no.: 11 chars
Birth date: 10 chars
Marital status: char
Employee number: integer
Job title: 10 chars
Hiring date: 10 chars
Current salary: integer
Department number: integer

The employee record can be declared as the following structure:

```
typedef struct
    {
        char    empl_first_name[10];
        char    empl_middl_name[10];
        char    empl_last_name[10];
```

```
char      empl_ss_no[11];
char      empl_birth_dt[10];
char      empl_marital_stat;
int       empl_number;
char      empl_title[10];
char      empl_hiring_dt[10];
int       empl_currnt_salary;
int       dept_no;


} EMPL_STRUCT;
   /* EMPL_STRUCT is now a structure-type   */

EMPL_STRUCT   Joan;
     /* Joan is EMPL_STRUCT-type variable     */
```

2.7 Accessing Components of a Structure in C

2.7.1 Access Using a Period Operator

We now need to know how to access an individual component of a structure instead of the entire structure. In C, this can be accomplished by the form

```
< structure_identifier > . < component >
```

where the period operator (.) is used between the structure identifier (variable) and the variable's own component. Such form is not ambiguous because each structure identifier and component name in each structure are unique.

Example 2.9

In Example 2.8, as Joan is an EMPL_STRUCT-type variable, one of its components empl_number, say, can be identified by

```
Joan.empl_number
```

Example 2.10

The C language does not provide a built-in type declaration for the complex numbers. As a complex number may be viewed as a structured pair (a, b) data object, we will be able to define such structure-type data in a static form in C as the following:

```
/*  Static Representations of Complex Numbers in C   */

typedef struct _COMPLEX
   {
   float   real;        /* a for the complex number a + bi   */
   float   imaginary;   /* b for the complex number a + bi   */
   } COMPLEX;
```

```
/*
 *      main  ():   Add  two  complex  numbers
 *
 */

main()
{
    COMPLEX                 A,  B;
    COMPLEX         complex_add;   /* Storage struct for A + B */

    complex_add.real      =  A.real  +  B.real;
    complex_add.imaginary =  A.imaginary +  B.imaginary;

}
```

Note that real and imaginary components of both COMPLEX-type structures are individually identified and accessed without ambiguity. But they are not assigned any values yet.

2.7.2 Access Using a Pointer

When a pointer is used to address a structure, its components are indirectly accessed via that pointer. Such access is accomplished by the structure pointer operator -> (dash followed by a "greater than" sign) combined with the structure pointer name and the component name. Note that there should not be any spaces between the two symbols of the -> operator. The format is:

```
<pointer_to_structure_identifier> -> <component_name>
```

2.8 Initializing a Structure

Initializing a structure is actually initializing the components of the structure. So we must keep in mind the types and order of the components they were declared in the structure declaration. In this way the types and the values will match.

Like arrays, only static or extern structures can be initialized. Automatic structures cannot be initialized, but auto components can be assigned values.

Example 2.11

For the COMPLEX-type structure A in Example 2.10, the following statement

```
        static     COMPLEX A = { 2.0, 3.0 };
```

will implicitly initialize

```
            A.real      = 2.0
            A.imaginary = 3.0
```

Example 2.12

For the following structure:

```
struct  Machine
  {
    char      cpu_type;   /* M = Motorola, I = Intel   */
    int       cpu_no;     /* Number of CPU's           */
  };
```

the statement

```
    static  struct  Machine  mastermind = { 'M', 2 };
```

effectively sets

```
            mastermind.cpu_type = 'M';
            mastermind.cpu_no   = 2 ;
```

This example shows that 'M' is given first in the initialization statement because the corresponding component is char-type.

2.9 Structure Assignment

Structure assignment is an important feature of the C language. It is possible to assign value of one structure-type variable to another structure-type variable, provided both of them are of same structure type. This effectively assigns values of components of one structure variable to the corresponding components of the other structure variable.

Example 2.13

Using COMPLEX-type structure, suppose:

```
            static     COMPLEX A = { 2.0, 3.0 };
            COMPLEX    B;

            B = A;     /* Structure A is assigned to struct B */
  makes
                B.real      = 2.0
                B.imaginary = 3.0
```

2.10 Pointers to Structures

A pointer to a structure is a variable for holding the address of the structure. It is declared using either the detailed structure and variable declaration or the variable declaration. Once such a pointer is declared, it can be associated with a structure-type variable using the (&) operator:

```
<structure_pointer_name> = &<structure_variable_name>;
```

Each member of the structure will be accessed using the pointer notations * or –> as shown below:

```
( *<structure_pointer_name> ).<component_name>
```

or,

```
<structure_pointer_name> -> <component_name>
```

Failure to set a pointer using the (&) operator will cause run-time error.

2.11 Passing a Structure as a Function Argument

The C language allows passing of a structure as an argument to a function. Like passing a variable by "call by value," the structures are passed by value. In other words, copies of their components (members) are used as a local copy inside the function. All accesses, changes, and interchanges (i.e., swap) are made to the local copy, not to the original values of the structures. At the exit from the function, all these changes will be lost, and the original values of the structures that were passed to the function are unaltered. Note that any individual member can also be passed as an argument by "call by value." This concept will not be useful if we need to manipulate original values of the structures instead of their copies.

Here is an example of how to pass structures A and B to a function.

Example 2.14

```
/*
 * complex_mult (): A * B and returns 'struct'
 *       A * B = ( A_Real * B_Real  - A_imagn * B_Real,
 *                 A_Real * B_imagn + A_imagn * B_Real )
 */
COMPLEX  complex_mult ( COMPLEX A, COMPLEX B )
{
    COMPLEX   temp_complex; /* Temporary storage struct */

    temp_complex.real      =  A.real  * B.real
                             - A.imaginary * B.imaginary;
    temp_complex.imaginary =  A.real  * B.imaginary
                             + A.imaginary * B.real;
    return ( temp_complex );
}
```

2.12 Passing a Pointer to a Structure as a Function Argument

The C language allows passing of a pointer to a structure as an argument to a function. Like passing a variable by "call by reference," the structures are passed by their pointers (i.e., addresses). In other words, their original components (members) are indirectly used, being referenced by the pointers to their structures inside the function. All accesses, changes, and interchanges (i.e., swap) are made to the original values of the structures. At the exit from the function, all these changes will be restored. Note that any individual member can also be passed as an argument by "call by reference" (i.e., pointers). This approach is immensely useful.

Example 2.15 shows how to accomplish this in C. The variables A and B are COMPLEX_PTR-type arguments to complex number multiplication function com-plex_mult().

Example 2.15

```
/*
 * complex_mult (): A * B and returns COMPLEX_PTR pointer
 *                A * B = ( A_Real * B_Real  - A_imagn * B_Real,
 *                          A_Real * B_imagn + A_imagn * B_Real )
 */
COMPLEX_PTR     complex_mult ( COMPLEX_PTR A, COMPLEX_PTR B )
{
   COMPLEX_PTR   temp_complex,  create_Complex();

   temp_complex = create_Complex();
   temp_complex -> real  =   A -> real  * B -> real
                           - A -> imaginary * B -> imaginary;
   temp_complex -> imaginary =   A -> real  * B -> imaginary
                               + A -> imaginary * B -> real;
   free ( temp_complex );
   return ( temp_complex );
}

/*
 * create Complex() : Dynamically allocate memory for a
 * Complex number.  It will try to get a memory allocation to
 * store a Complex-type data and if successful, will return a
 * COMPLEX-type pointer.
 */
COMPLEX_PTR create_Complex ()
{
   COMPLEX_PTR          temp_complex;
   if ( (temp_complex =
      (COMPLEX_PTR) malloc ( sizeof (Complex_type) )) == NULL )
   {
      printf ("\n create_Complex: malloc failed for Complex\n");
      exit( 1 );
   }
```

```
    else
    return ( temp_complex );
}
```

Note that in this pointer approach, we must allocate memory before using the structure, and release the memory space if it is no longer needed.

2.13 Structure as a Return Value of a Function

This is very useful because C allows only one return value from a function. When we need to get more than one value returned from a function, we can form a structure consisting of those variables, and return them as one structure-type data. Then in the calling function we will simply access the individual components of the structure. In this case, we must declare the function as a structure type the same as the desired structure type it is returning to avoid a potential mismatch problem.

Example 2.16

In Example 2.14, the statement

```
        COMPLEX   complex_mult ( COMPLEX A,  COMPLEX B )
```

declares that `complex_mult` is a COMPLEX-type structured function.
       The statement

```
            return ( temp_complex );
```

returns the COMPLEX-type variable from this function.

2.14 Structure of Structures

In this section we want to mention that any component of a structure may be another structure, that is, a nested form of structures. The individual structure-type component (i.e., substructure) can be used and accessed in the same manner as ordinary components. In C, this can be done in many ways, for example:

   I. When using variable names for structure and substructure, the member
      identifier is

   `structure_name. component_name. sub_component_name`

   II. When using pointer to a structure and variable name of substructure(s),
       the member identifier is

   `structure_pointer_name -> component_name. sub_component`

   III. When using a pointer to a structure and pointer(s) to its substructure(s),
        the member identifier is

```
structure_pointer_name -> sub_structure_pointer_name -> sub_component
```

In form II, there is only one indirection, whereas there are two indirections (i.e., pointer to a pointer) in form III. This notion is like array of arrays. Thus, the abstract form of a nested structure in C will be

```
struct  <struct_name>
  {
    <type>                   component_1;
    struct <struct_name> component_2;
      . . .
    <type>                   component_n;
  };
```

Note that component_2 can even be a pointer to the same structure.

Example 2.17

Let us declare a structure date as

```
struct   date
  {
      int    month;
      int    day;
      int    year;
  };
```

Then the structure EMPL_STRUCT in Example 2.8 can be redefined as a structure of structures in the following form:

```
typedef struct
  {
      char          empl_first_name[10];
      char          empl_middl_name[10];
      char          empl_last_name[10];
      char          empl_ss_no[11];
      struct date   empl_birth_dt;
      char          empl_marital_stat;
      int           empl_number;
      char          empl_title[10];
      struct date   empl_hiring_dt;
      int           empl_currnt_salary;
      int           dept_no;

  } EMPL_STRUCT;   /* EMPL_STRUCT is now a structure-type  */

EMPL_STRUCT    Joan;
```

Then a member year, say, of the empl_hiring_dt structure in EMPL_STRUCT-type structure variable Joan (i.e, hiring year of employee Joan), can be accessed by

```
Joan.empl_hiring_dt.year
```

2.15 Array of Structures

This concept is like an array of integers in which each element is an int type. We can form an array of structures where all elements of the array are structure-type data. An array of structures is declared by

```
struct  <structure_name>   <array_name> [ <array_size> ];
```

For example, it can be declared as

```
EMPL_STRUCT   empl_db[ 100 ];
```

The array empl_db is an array of size 100, and each element of it is a structure of the type EMPL_STRUCT.

Accessing an individual component dept_no, of the 10th employee structure EMPL_STRUCT, is done by

```
empl_db[ 9 ].dept_no
```

where 9 indicates the 10th array index of the array empl_db. This form of design scheme is very useful in many applications.

2.16 Entering Data into a Structure

Now we want to know how to enter data into a structure, that is, into individual components of a structure. The basic methods are:

1. Through initialization   (as described in Section 2.8)
2. Value assignment to an individual component
3. During the program execution, read input from the keyboard for each component
3. Read input data from a disk file

Method 2 is very tedious and inefficient. Method 3 is an acceptable approach for an interactive program. Method 4 is advanced and most desirable. We used method 3 based on scanf () in developing our database application in this section. We will use scanf () and gets () in developing a part's database system in Chapter 5. Method 4 can be accomplished by calls to standard C library I/O routines fscanf () for reading and fprintf () for writing.

2.17 Unions

A union is like a structure variable except that it may store data objects, called *members,* of different types and of different sizes (at different occasions), but only one member object at a time. This means that all the members of a union variable share a common memory area, whose size is the size of the largest member of the same union variable. When different members are used or modified, the compiler does bookkeeping of size and alignment. Because of data overlay on the same memory location, it is important to note that a previously computed value of one union member will be overwritten by the value of another member of the same union variable. This indicates that if there is a need to reuse the value of one union variable, save it before using the same union variable. The size of a union variable is the size of its largest member type.

A union variable can be declared in C as

```
union   <union_name>
  {
    <member_type>       <member_1>;
                . . .
    <member_type>       <member_n>;

  }   <union_variable_name>,
      *<union_var_pointer_name>;
```

The declaration of a union variable reserves memory space only for its largest member type, but not for each individual member. Note that a structure variable declaration allocates memory space for all its members. Because a union is a derived type like a structure, the same rules on structures are applicable to unions. A member of a union variable can be accessed in the following manner:

```
<union_variable_name> . <union_member_name>
```

or

```
<union_var_pointer_name> -> <union_member_name>
```

In summary, the reasons for using union variables are:

1. To collectively access a number of different objects but not allocate space for each individual object
2. To save memory space by using the same memory space for different variables of different types and sizes
3. To port the same program over different machine architectures

Example 2.18

```c
/*
 * Program:   union.c
 * Purpose:   To demonstrate the use and size of union
 *            structured type data
 */
main()
{
    /* Declare a union variable, and a pointer to it */

    union   char_value_info
      {
        char    *word;
        int     integer_num;
        double  double_num;

      } a_union_var, *union_var_ptr;
```

```
    union_var_ptr = &a_union_var;        /* Assigned address to
                                            its pointer */

    printf("\n ** Example of Union type structured data ** \n");
    printf("\n Size of char    :   %3d  ", sizeof( char ) );
    printf("\n Size of int     :   %3d  ", sizeof( int  ) );
    printf("\n Size of double  :   %3d  ", sizeof( double));

    /* Assign an integer number to its component integer_num  */
    union_var_ptr -> integer_num = 10;

    printf("\n\n ** Effect after assigning 'integer_num' \
                                            member ** \n");
    printf("\n Integer member :  %5d   Size of Union Var : %d",
           union_var_ptr -> integer_num, sizeof( a_union_var ) );

/* Assign a floating point number to component float_num  */
union_var_ptr -> double_num = 11.2;

printf("\n\n ** Effect after assigning 'double_num' \
                                        member ** \n");
printf("\n double member  :  %5.2f   Size of Union Var : %d",
        union_var_ptr -> double_num, sizeof( a_union_var ) );
printf("\n Integer member :  %5d  ",
        union_var_ptr -> integer_num );

/* Assign a word to its component word  */
union_var_ptr -> word = "Union Demo";

printf("\n\n ** Effect after assigning 'word' member ** \n");
printf("\n Word member     :  %s   Size of Union Var : %d",
        union_var_ptr -> word, sizeof( a_union_var ) );
printf("\n double member  :  %5.2f ",
        union_var_ptr -> double_num );
printf("\n Integer member :  %5d \n",
        union_var_ptr -> integer_num );

}
```

Here is the output:

```
    ** Example of Union type structured data **

    Size of char    :      1
    Size of int     :      4
    Size of double  :      8

    ** Effect after assigning 'integer_num' member **

    Integer member :       10   Size of Union Var : 8

    ** Effect after assigning 'double_num' member **

    double member  :   11.20   Size of Union Var : 8
    Integer member :   1076258406
```

```
** Effect after assigning 'word' member **

Word member     :    Union Demo    Size of Union Var : 8
double member   :    0.00
Integer member :    592265
```

Analysis of this output shows that

1. The previous value of the 'integer_num' member is lost after 'double_num' assignment.
2. After 'word' member assignment, the previous values of the other members, 'integer_num' and 'double_num', are lost.

It is important to note that after first assigning member 'word', and then assigning either one of the other two members, any attempt to print the member 'word' will produce run-time error "Memory-fault".

2.18 Structures as Components of a Union

Like structures, unions can be constructed with structures as their members. In this case the structures that are members of the same union will share the common memory space with any other members of the union.

A union of structures can be declared in C as follows:

```
union   <union_name>
  {
     <member_type>            <member_1>;
     struct <struct_name>     <struct_type_var_1>;
     struct <struct_name>     <struct_type_var_2>;
            . . .
     <member_type>            <member_n>;

  } <union_var_name>,  *<union_var_pointer_name>;
```

As in the previous section, the size of the union variable will be the largest size of its members. A member of this type of union variable can be accessed in the following manner:

```
        <union_var_name> . <union_member_name>
```

or

```
        <union_var_pointer_name> -> <union_member_name>
```

or

```
<union_var_name> . <struct_var_member> . <member_struct_var>
```

or

```
<union_var_name> . <struct_var_pointer> -> <member_struct_var>
```

Example 2.18

This example is based on the concept of the Intel 8086 Microprocessor architecture. The iAPX-8086 has four 16-bit general-purpose registers (a register is a data holding device that the processor uses for calculation). These registers are:

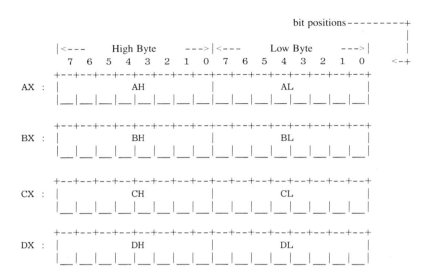

The registers AX, BX, CX, DX, SI (source index), and DI (destination index) are frequently used in the 8086 Assembly Language programming. Also the high and low byte (8-bit) registers AH, AL, BH, BL, CH, CL, DH, and DL are very useful in Assembly Language programming. In order to access these registers in C programming, we can treat the registers AX, BX, CX, DX, SI, and DI flags as unsigned int types, and the registers AH, AL, BH, BL, CH, CL, DH, and DL as unsigned char-type data. These registers can be structured as follows:

```
struct  _16BIT_WORD_REGS         /* 16-bit Word Registers   */
  {
    unsigned    int    ax;       /* Lowercase name for AX   */
    unsigned    int    bx;       /* Lowercase name for BX   */
    unsigned    int    cx;       /* Lowercase name for CX   */
    unsigned    int    dx;       /* Lowercase name for DX   */
    unsigned    int    si;       /* Lowercase name for SI   */
    unsigned    int    di;       /* Lowercase name for DI   */
    unsigned    int    flags;    /* Process Status Flag reg*/
  };

struct  _8BIT_BYTE_REGS          /* 8-bit Byte Registers    */
  {
    unsigned    char ah, al;     /* Names for regs AH, AL   */
    unsigned    char bh, bl;     /* Names for regs BH, BL   */
    unsigned    char ch, cl;     /* Names for regs CH, CL   */
    unsigned    char dh, dl;     /* Names for regs DH, DL   */
  };
```

```
union  _8086_REGISTERS
  {
    struct  _16BIT_WORD_REGS   x;  /* Size of variable x =16 */
    struct  _8BIT_BYTE_REGS    y;  /* Size of variable y =8  */

  } registers;
```

Note that the size of the union variable would be 16 bits long. Both member variables x and y will share the same 16-bit memory space.

The components, say, di and ch of the union variable registers, can be respectively identified by registers.x.di and registers.y.ch. This approach is very useful in making calls to IBM PC's ROM BIOS routines from a C program.

2.19 Bitfields

Bitfields are usually implemented as ints. There are some restrictions on bitfields:

1. Bitfields are not arrays and do not have addresses.
2. They may not overlap int boundaries.
3. Depending on implementation, they may be assigned left-to-right or right-to-left.
4. Bitfields are unsigned.
5. A field width of zero causes the next field to be started on a word boundary.

Bitfields are used mostly as flags. An example of bitfield definition and use is

```
        int  a:4;          /* a bitfield 4 bits wide */

        struct bits
        {
          int  a:2;
          int  b:6;
          int  c:4;
          int  d:12;
          int  e:8;
        } biteg;
```

The struct has five bitfields, with a total of 32 bits, so they are probably contained in one int:

```
                #define  OFF   0x01
                #define  ON    0x02
                #define  FAIL  0x10
                #define  OK    0x20

                biteg.a &= OFF;
                biteg.e ^= OK;
```

Example 2.19

In Example 2.6, we showed how we can define a segment descriptor as a structure, where we assumed and used user-defined types:

```
U32bits                  /* Unsigned 32 bits          */
U20bits                  /* Unsigned 20 bits          */
access_bits              /* Each field can be in bits */
```

We can define them as structures with bitfields:

```
typedef struct  _U32bits {
    unsigned   a: 32; /* Width of this field : 32 bits      */
    } U32bits;          /* U32bits is now a structured type  */

typedef struct  _U20bits {
    unsigned   a: 20; /* Width of this field : 20 bits      */
    } U20bits;          /* U20bits is now a structured type  */

typedef struct  _AccessBits {
    unsigned   G  : 1;  /* G   :  Granularity               */
    unsigned   B  : 1;  /* B   :  Big                       */
    unsigned   O  : 1;  /* O   :  Must be 0                 */
    unsigned   AV : 1;  /* AV  :  Available for OS use       */
    unsigned   P  : 1;  /* P   :  Present in memory          */
    unsigned   W  : 1;  /* W   :  Writable segment           */
    unsigned   EI : 1;  /* EI  :  Expansion direction        */
    unsigned   A  : 1;  /* A   :  Accessed                   */
    unsigned   DPL : 2; /* DPL :  Descriptor Privilege Level*/
    } access_bits;
```

2.20 Complex Number Implementation Using Structures

The C language does not provide a built-in-type declaration for the complex numbers. As a complex number may be viewed as a structured pair (a, b) data object, we will be able to define such structure-type data in a static or dynamic form in C as the following.

Static Representations of Complex Numbers in C

Form I

```
typedef struct          /* Define as a 'struct' */
    {
    float    real;       /* real part of a complex no. */
    float    imaginary; /* imaginary part of complex no. */
    } COMPLEX;           /* Define COMPLEX as a 'struct'type*/

COMPLEX    A ;          /* Declare complex identifiers */
```

A. real is used to access the real part of A, and A. imaginary is used to access
the imaginary part of A.

Dynamic Representation of Complex Numbers in C

Form II

```
typedef struct Complex_struct
   {
     float    real;
     float    imaginary;
   } Complex_type;

typedef struct Complex_struct *COMPLEX_PTR;

/* COMPLEX_PTR is defined as a pointer to the
   Complex_struct. */

COMPLEX_PTR    A;          /* Declare complex identifiers */
```

Note that A -> real is used to access the real part of A, and A -> imaginary is
used to access the imaginary part of A. In this case of dynamic representation, declaring identifiers does not allocate memory space. Before you use them we must
allocate memory using the system call malloc(), which returns a pointer to a
memory location to hold this complex data type; otherwise the function produces
a memory fault.

For detailed discussion, complete examples, and operations, see Chapter 15.

2.21 Intervals Implemented with Structures

Interval numbers play an important role in the applications of the sciences, engineering, and mathematics. An interval number is of the form

$$[a, b], \quad a <= b$$

where a and b are real numbers. The numbers a and b are respectively called *left*
and *right endpoints* of the interval number. In this section we will discuss how to
deal with interval-type data in the C language.

The C language does not provide a built-in type declaration for the interval
numbers. As an interval number may be viewed as a structured pair (a, b) data object, we will be able to define such structure-type data in a static or dynamic form in
C as the following.

Static Representations of Interval Numbers in C

Form I

```
typedef double INTERVAL[ 2 ];
/* Defined INTERVAL as an array, where
 * INTERVAL[ 0 ] = left end point,
```

```
     *  INTERVAL[ 1 ] = right end point.
     */
     INTERVAL A;      /* Declare interval identifiers      */
```

A[0] is used to access the left endpoint of A; A[1] is used to access the right endpoint of A.

    Form II

```
     struct INTERVAL
        {
           float      left_end_point;
                                /* a for the interval [ a, b ] */
           float      right_end_point;
                                /* b for the interval [ a, b ] */
        };
     struct INTERVAL    A;
```

Note that declaring interval identifiers automatically allocates memory space. A.left_end_point and A.right_end_point are used to access the left and right endpoints of A, respectively.

    Dynamic Representation of Interval Numbers in C

    Form III

```
     struct interval_struct
        {
           double     left_end_point;
           double     right_end_point;
        };

     typedef   struct interval_struct    interval_type;

     /* Define INTERVAL_PTR type as a pointer to the
      * interval_struct.
      */
     typedef   interval_type    *INTERVAL_PTR;

     INTERVAL_PTR    A;
```

A -> left_end_point, and A -> right_end_point are used to access the left and right endpoints of A, respectively.

    In this case of dynamic representation, declaring identifiers does not allocate memory space. Before we use them we must allocate memory using the system call malloc (), which returns a pointer to a memory location to hold this interval data type; otherwise the function produces a memory fault.

```
/*
 * create_interval():  Allocate memory space to store an Interval
 */
INTERVAL_PTR create_interval ()
{
     INTERVAL_PTR    temp_interval;
```

```
       temp_interval = (INTERVAL_PTR) malloc(sizeof(interval_type))
       if ( (temp_interval == NULL)
          {
            printf ("\n create_interval: malloc failed for Interval \
                                                        \n");

            exit( 1 );
          }
       else
          return ( temp_interval );
}

/*
 * free_interval(): Release the memory space acquired through
 * the 'malloc()' if we do not need that space pointed by
 * interval_pointer.  It uses the System Call 'free()' to
 * release the allocated memory space.
 */
free_interval (INTERVAL_PTR interval_pointer)
{
       free( interval_pointer );
}
```

Further Examples

Example 2-1

Code Section

```
/*
 *  Program: example01.c
 *  Purpose: To demonstrate simple usage of pointers in C
 */

demo1a()
{
   int a, b = 199, c;
   int *pointer_1;   /* Pointer to variable of integer type */

   /*  At this point, the pointer_1 does not have any
    *  content. The above statement allocates space for
    *  one 'pointer-sized' (as compared to int-sized) object.
    */

   printf("\n Enter a = ");
   scanf("%d", &a);

   /*  Put the address  of the variable 'a' (not the content
    *  of a) in pointer_1 using '&' operator.
    */

   pointer_1 = &a;

   printf("\n Content of a: %3d  Address of a: %d ",
           a, pointer_1);
   printf(" Content of Pointer to a: %d \n", pointer_1);
```

```c
    /* Assign some value to a using pointer_1 */
    *pointer_1 = - 200;

    printf ("\n Content of a: %3d  Address of a: %d ",
            *pointer_1, pointer_1);
    printf (" Content of Pointer to a: %d \n", pointer_1);

    /* Calculate c = a + b */
    c = a + b;
    pointer_1 = &c;   /* Assign address of c to pointer_1  */

    printf ("\n Content of c: %3d  Address of c: %d ",
            c, pointer_1);
    printf (" Content of Pointer to c: %d \n\n", pointer_1);

}

demo1b ()
{
    int a = 10,  b = 199,  c; /* value 10 of a is assigned here. */
    int *pointer_1;

    pointer_1 = &a;

    printf ("\n Content of a: %3d  Address of a: %d ",
            a, pointer_1);
    printf (" Content of Pointer to a: %d \n", pointer_1);

    /* Assign some value to a using pointer_1 */
    *pointer_1 = - 200;

    printf ("\n Content of a: %3d  Address of a: %d ",
            *pointer_1, pointer_1);
    printf (" Content of Pointer to a: %d \n", pointer_1);

    /* Calculate c = a + b */
    c = a + b;
    pointer_1 = &c;   /* Assign address of c to pointer_1  */

    printf ("\n Content of c: %3d  Address of c: %d ",
            c, pointer_1);
    printf (" Content of Pointer to c: %d \n\n", pointer_1);

}

main ()
{
    printf ("\n\n  ****** Usage of Pointers in C ****** \n\n");
    demo1a ();
    demo1b ();
}
```

Output Section

```
          ****** Usage of Pointers in C ******

          Enter a =
          Content of a:  19  Address of a: 25165592
          Content of Pointer to a: 25165592

          Content of a: -200  Address of a: 25165592
          Content of Pointer to a: 25165592

          Content of c:  -1  Address of c: 25165584
          Content of Pointer to c: 25165584


          Content of a:  10  Address of a: 25165592
          Content of Pointer to a: 25165592

          Content of a: -200  Address of a: 25165592
          Content of Pointer to a: 25165592

          Content of c:  -1  Address of c: 25165584
          Content of Pointer to c: 25165584
```

Example 2-2

Code Section

```
/*
 *  Program:  example02.c
 */


/*
 *  demo1a()
 *  Purpose:  1. To demonstrate the use of '*' & '++'
 *            2. Equivalency & difference between their usage
 *                   *pntr++
 *                   *(pntr++)
 *                   *(pntr)++
 */

demo1a()
{
    static int  array[10] = { 10, 20, 30, 40, 50,
                              60, 70, 80, 90, 100 };
    int    *pntr;
    int    i;

    printf("\n *** Example of Pointer arith: *pntr++  *** \n");
    printf("Memory Loc      Array Element      Content \n");

    for ( i = 0; i < 10; i++)
        printf("%d             array[%d]          %d\n",
               &array[i], i, array[i]);
```

```
        pntr = array;
        printf("\n ******* Note effect of '*pntr++'      ******* \n");
        printf("Before *pntr++    :  pntr = %15d      array = %d\n",
            pntr, array);
        printf("At *pntr++         : *pntr = %15d\n", *pntr++);
        printf("After *pntr++      : *pntr = %15d      pntr   = %d\n",
            *pntr, pntr);

        pntr = array;
        printf("\n ******* Note effect of '*(pntr++)'      ******* \n");
        printf("Before *(pntr++)   :  pntr = %15d      array = %d\n",
            pntr, array);
        printf("At *(pntr++)       : *pntr = %15d   \n", *(pntr++) );
        printf("After *(pntr++)    : *pntr = %15d      pntr   = %d\n",
            *pntr, pntr);

        pntr = array;
        printf("\n  ******* Note effect of '(*pntr)++'      ****** \n");
        printf("Before (*pntr)++   :  pntr = %15d      array = %d\n",
            pntr, array);
        printf("At (*pntr)++       : *pntr = %15d   \n", (*pntr)++ );
        printf("After (*pntr)++    : *pntr = %15d      pntr = %d\n\n",
            *pntr, pntr);
}

/*
 *    demo1b()
 *    Purpose:  1. To demo the use of '*' & '++'
 *              2. Equivalency & difference between their usage
 *                       *++pntr
 *                       *(++pntr)
 */

demo1b()
{
    static int  array[10] = { 10,  20,  30,  40,  50,
                              60,  70,  80,  90,  100 };
    int    *pntr;
    int    i;

    printf("\n**** Example on Pointer arith: %s  ****\n",
        "*++pntr++, *(++pntr)" );
    printf("Memory Loc        Array Element        Content\n");

    for (i = 0; i < 10; i++)
        printf("%d                 array[%d]             %d\n",
            &array[i], i, array[i]);

    pntr = array;
    printf("\n ***** Note the effect of '*++pntr'      ***** \n");
    printf("Before *++pntr   :  pntr = %15d      array = %d\n",
        pntr, array);
    printf("At     *++pntr   : *pntr = %15d   \n", *++pntr);
```

```
        printf("After *++pntr     : *pntr = %15d     pntr  = %d\n",
            *pntr, pntr);

        pntr = array;
        printf("\n ***** Note the effect of '*(++pntr)'  ***** \n");
        printf("Before *(++pntr) :  pntr = %15d     array = %d\n",
            pntr, array);
        printf("At       *(++pntr) : *pntr = %15d     \n", *(++pntr));
        printf("After   *(++pntr) : *pntr = %15d     pntr  = %d\n",
            *pntr, pntr);
}


/*
 *   demo1c()
 *   Purpose:  1.  To demo the use of '*' & '++'
 *             2.  Equivalency & difference between their usage
 *                      ++*pntr
 *                      ++(*pntr)
 */

demo1c()
{
        static int  array[10] = { 10,  20,  30,  40,  50,
                                  60,  70,  80,  90,  100 };
        int     *pntr;
        int     i;

        printf("\n Example of Pointer arith: ++*pntr, ++(*pntr)\n");
        printf("Memory Loc       Array Element        Content \n");

        for (i = 0; i < 10; i++)
            printf("%d                 array[%d]               \
                            %d\n", &array[i], i, array[i]);

        pntr = array;
        printf("\n *****  Note the effect of '++*pntr'    *****\n");
        printf("Before ++*pntr   :  pntr = %15d     array = %d\n",
            pntr, array);
        printf("At       ++*pntr   : *pntr = %15d     \n", ++*pntr);
        printf("After   ++*pntr   : *pntr = %15d     pntr  = %d\n",
            *pntr, pntr);

        pntr = array;
        printf("\n *****  Note the effect of '++(*pntr)'  ***** \n");
        printf("Before ++(*pntr) :  pntr = %15d     array = %d\n",
            pntr, array);
        printf("At       ++(*pntr) : *pntr = %15d     \n", ++(*pntr) );
        printf("After   ++(*pntr) : *pntr = %15d     pntr  = %d\n",
            *pntr, pntr);
}

/*
 *   demo1d()
```

```
 *   Purpose:   1. To demo the use of '*' & '++'
 *              2. Array of pointers:   *pntr[]
 */

demo1d()
{
    int   *ary_pntr[4];
    int   i, a, b, c, d;

    ary_pntr[0] = &a;
    ary_pntr[1] = &b;
    ary_pntr[2] = &c;
    ary_pntr[3] = &d;

    *ary_pntr[0] = 30;
    *ary_pntr[1] = 40;
    *ary_pntr[2] = 50;
    *ary_pntr[3] = 60;

    printf("\n **** Example on Array of Pointers   **** \n");
    printf("\n Memory Loc           Array Element              \
                  Content \n");

    for ( i = 0; i < 4; i++)
       printf(" %d                ary_pntr[%d]           %d \n",
              &ary_pntr[i], i, ary_pntr[i]);

    printf("\n *****  Note the effect of '*ary_pntr'  *****\n");

    printf("\n Memory Loc                Element       Content \n");
    printf(" %d                a                       %d \n", &a, a);
    printf(" %d                b                       %d \n", &b, b);
    printf(" %d                c                       %d \n", &c, c);
    printf(" %d                d                       %d \n", &d, d);
}

main()
{
    demo1a();
    demo1b();
    demo1c();
    demo1d();
}
```

Output Section

```
***  Example of Pointer arith: *pntr++   ***
Memory Loc        Array Element        Content
591936                array[0]             10
591940                array[1]             20
591944                array[2]             30
591948                array[3]             40
591952                array[4]             50
591956                array[5]             60
```

```
591960                 array[6]              70
591964                 array[7]              80
591968                 array[8]              90
591972                 array[9]             100
```

```
********** Note effect of '*pntr++'   **********
Before *pntr++   :  pntr =           591936     array = 591936
At *pntr++       :  *pntr =              10
After *pntr++    :  *pntr =              20     pntr  = 591940
```

```
********** Note effect of '*(pntr++)'  **********
Before *(pntr++)  :  pntr =          591936     array = 591936
At *(pntr++)      :  *pntr =             10
After *(pntr++)   :  *pntr =             20     pntr  = 591940
```

```
  ********** Note effect of '(*pntr)++'  **********
Before (*pntr)++  :  pntr =          591936     array = 591936
At (*pntr)++      :  *pntr =             10
After (*pntr)++   :  *pntr =             11     pntr  = 591936
```

```
**** Example on Pointer arith: *++pntr++, *(++pntr)   ****
Memory Loc         Array Element      Content
591848                 array[0]              10
591852                 array[1]              20
591856                 array[2]              30
591860                 array[3]              40
591864                 array[4]              50
591868                 array[5]              60
591872                 array[6]              70
591876                 array[7]              80
591880                 array[8]              90
591884                 array[9]             100
```

```
******** Note the effect of '*++pntr'   ********
Before *++pntr   :  pntr =           591848     array = 591848
At    *++pntr    :  *pntr =              20
After *++pntr    :  *pntr =              20     pntr  = 591852
```

```
******** Note the effect of '*(++pntr)'  ********
Before *(++pntr)  :  pntr =          591848     array = 591848
At    *(++pntr)   :  *pntr =             20
After *(++pntr)   :  *pntr =             20     pntr  = 591852
```

```
**** Example on Pointer arith: ++*pntr, ++(*pntr)   ****
Memory Loc         Array Element      Content
591840                 array[0]              10
591844                 array[1]              20
591848                 array[2]              30
591852                 array[3]              40
591856                 array[4]              50
591860                 array[5]              60
591864                 array[6]              70
591868                 array[7]              80
```

```
591872                 array[8]                90
591876                 array[9]                100


********* Note the effect of '++*pntr'   ******
Before ++*pntr   :  pntr  =            591840    array = 591840
At     ++*pntr   : *pntr  =            11
After  ++*pntr   : *pntr  =            11    pntr  = 591840

********* Note the effect of '++(*pntr)' ******
Before ++(*pntr) :  pntr  =            591840    array = 591840
At     ++(*pntr) : *pntr  =            12
After  ++(*pntr) : *pntr  =            12    pntr  = 591840

**** Example on Array of Pointers   ****

Memory Loc              Array Element           Content

25165576                ary_pntr[0]             25165568
25165580                ary_pntr[1]             25165564
25165584                ary_pntr[2]             25165560
25165588                ary_pntr[3]             25165556

********** Note the effect of '*ary_pntr'  *********

Memory Loc              Element    Content

25165568                a          30
25165564                b          40
25165560                c          50
25165556                d          60
```

Example 2-3

Code Section

```c
/*
 *  Program:     example03.c
 *  Purpose:     To demonstrate the use of a pointer of a pointer
 *               (i.e., double indirection) '**pntr'
 */

main()
{
 int x = 10;
 int *pntr_x;
 int **pntr_pntr_x;

 pntr_pntr_x = &pntr_x;
                    /* pntr_pntr_x holds address of pntr_x  */
 pntr_x = &x;
                    /* pntr_x holds address of x            */

 printf("\n * Example of using '**pntr_pntr_x'  *  \n\n");
```

```
printf("\n Before exec of '**pntr_pntr_x = -90' : \n");

printf("\n                x = %d                 \
                            Address of x = %d  \n", x, &x );
printf("\n          pntr_x = %d          *pntr_x = %d  \n",
        pntr_x, *pntr_x );
printf("\n   pntr_pntr_x = %d     *pntr_pntr_x = %d  \n",
        pntr_pntr_x, *pntr_pntr_x );
printf("\n **pntr_pntr_x = %d            \n", **pntr_pntr_x);

**pntr_pntr_x = -90;

printf("\n\n After exec of '**pntr_pntr_x = -90'  : \n");

printf("\n                x = %d           Address of x = %d  \n",
        x, &x );
printf("\n          pntr_x = %d               *pntr_x = %d  \n",
        pntr_x, *pntr_x );
printf("\n   pntr_pntr_x = %d     *pntr_pntr_x = %d  \n",
        pntr_pntr_x, *pntr_pntr_x );
printf("\n **pntr_pntr_x = %d            \n", **pntr_pntr_x);
}
```

Output Section

```
***** Example of using '**pntr_pntr_x'    *****

Before exec of '**pntr_pntr_x = -90' :

          x = 10            Address of x = 25165588

     pntr_x = 25165588             *pntr_x = 10

  pntr_pntr_x = 25165584     *pntr_pntr_x = 25165588

**pntr_pntr_x = 10

After exec of '**pntr_pntr_x = -90'  :

          x = -90           Address of x = 25165588

     pntr_x = 25165588             *pntr_x = -90

  pntr_pntr_x = 25165584     *pntr_pntr_x = 25165588

**pntr_pntr_x = -90
```

Example 2-4

Code Section

```
/*
 *  Program:  example04.c  ( Pointer version of matrix_ops.c:
 *                           ADT MATRIX operations. )
 */
```

```
#define   ROWS      4        /* in main() to initialize a matrix  */
#define   COLUMNS 4          /* in main() to initialize a matrix  */

typedef int            DATA_TYPE;
typedef DATA_TYPE   MATRIX [ROWS][COLUMNS]; /* Define MATRIX type */

/* Define MATRIX_PTR type as  pointer to each row of a matrix */
typedef int  *MATRIX_PTR [ ROWS ];

/*
 *   Assign_ptr_to_mat(): Assign array of pointers to rows of a
 *                         matrix A.
 */
Assign_ptr_to_mat( MATRIX A, MATRIX_PTR A_PTR, int rows )
{
    int    i;

    /* Assign rows of A to pointers A_PTR  */
    for ( i = 0; i < rows; i++ )

        /*  ---     *( A_PTR + i ) = *( A + i );    --- */
        *( A_PTR + i ) = &A[ i ][ 0 ];
}


/*
 *   matrix_add() :  C (m x n) = A (m x n)  + B (m x n)
 */
matrix_add( MATRIX_PTR A, MATRIX_PTR B, MATRIX_PTR C,
            int m, int n )
{
    int  i;      /* Used for row index, e.g. A[ i ][ j ] */
    int  j;      /* Used for col index, e.g. A[ i ][ j ] */
    int  temp1, temp2;

    for ( i = 0; i < m; i++)
       {
         for ( j = 0; j < n; j++ )
            {
             /*   C[ i ][ j ] = A[ i ][ j ] + B[ i ][ j ] */

             temp1  = *( *(A + i) + j );
             temp2  = *( *(B + i) + j );
             *( *(C + i) + j ) = temp1 + temp2;
            }
       }
}


/*
 *    matrix_mult():  C (m x p) = A (m x n) * B (n x p)
 */
matrix_mult( MATRIX_PTR A, MATRIX_PTR B, MATRIX_PTR C,
             int m, int n, int p )
{
    int  i;      /* Used for row index, e.g. A[ i ][ j ] */
```

```
      int     j;        /* Used for col index, e.g. A[ i ][ j ] */
      int     k;
      double sum;
      int     temp1, temp2;

      /*  C[i,j]  = Sum ( A[i,  k] * B[k,  j] ) for k = 0,  ..., n - 1
       *                where i = 0,  ..., m - 1  & j = 0,  ..., p - 1
       */

      for ( i = 0; i < m; i++)
         {
           for ( j = 0; j < p; j++ )
               {
                sum = 0;
                for ( k = 0; k < n ; k++ )
                   {
                    /* sum +=  (double) A[ i ][ k ] + B[ k ][ j ] */
                    temp1   = *( *(A + i) + k );
                    temp2   = *( *(B + k) + j );
                    sum    += (double) (temp1 * temp2 );
                   }

                   /*   C[ i ][ j ] =  sum;      */
                   *( *(C + i) + j )  =  sum;
               }
         }
}


/*
 *     print_matrix()  :  To print a matrix A ( m x n )
 */
print_matrix( MATRIX_PTR A, int m, int n, char *matrix_var_name)
{
      int                 i, j;
      printf("\n ====  Following Matrix: %s  ====\n\n",
             matrix_var_name );
      printf("        ");  /* To align row & column printing  */
      for (j = 0; j < n; j++)
         printf("    col %d", j);

      printf("\n");                          /* Print a new line  */
      for ( i = 0; i < m; i++ )
         {
            printf ("row %d  ", i );
            for  ( j = 0; j < n; j++ )
               printf (" %5d ", *( *(A + i) + j ) );
            printf("\n");
         }
}


/*
 *     main(): POINTER IMPLEMENTATION OF MATRIX OPERATIONS
 */
```

```
main()
{
    static int A[ ROWS ][ COLUMNS ] =
                { { 2,   -1,   7,   5 },   /* Row 0 of Matrix A   */
                  { 22,  10,   3,  -4 },   /* Row 1 of Matrix A   */
                  { 32,   1,  -7,   5 },   /* Row 2 of Matrix A   */
                  { 42,  11,  -5,   4 } };/* Row 3 of Matrix A   */

    static int B[ ROWS ][ COLUMNS ] =
                { { 5,   6,  -4,  0 },     /* Row 0 of Matrix B   */
                  { 7,   6,  10,  1 },     /* Row 1 of Matrix B   */
                  { 12,  9,   2,  2 },     /* Row 2 of Matrix B   */
                  { -5,  3,  -1,  3 } };   /* Row 3 of Matrix B   */

    MATRIX  C;
    MATRIX_PTR  A_PTR, B_PTR, C_PTR;

    printf("\n\n ===  POINTER IMPLEMENTATION OF %s === \n",
           "ADT MATRIX  OPERATIONS ");

    Assign_ptr_to_mat( A, A_PTR, ROWS );
    Assign_ptr_to_mat( B, B_PTR, ROWS );
    Assign_ptr_to_mat( C, C_PTR, ROWS );

    print_matrix( A_PTR, ROWS, COLUMNS, " A " );
    print_matrix( B_PTR, ROWS, COLUMNS, " B " );

    matrix_add( A_PTR, B_PTR, C_PTR, ROWS, COLUMNS );
    print_matrix( C_PTR, ROWS, COLUMNS, " C = A + B " );

    /* Reinitialize pointers to matrices A, B, & C */
    Assign_ptr_to_mat( A, A_PTR, ROWS );
    Assign_ptr_to_mat( B, B_PTR, ROWS );
    Assign_ptr_to_mat( C, C_PTR, ROWS );
    matrix_mult( A_PTR, B_PTR, C_PTR, ROWS, COLUMNS, COLUMNS );
    print_matrix( C_PTR, ROWS, COLUMNS, " C = A * B " );
}
```

Output Section

=== POINTER IMPLEMENTATION OF ADT MATRIX OPERATIONS ===

==== Following Matrix: A   ====

	col 0	col 1	col 2	col 3
row 0	2	-1	7	5
row 1	22	10	3	-4
row 2	32	1	-7	5
row 3	42	11	-5	4

==== Following Matrix: B   ====

	col 0	col 1	col 2	col 3
row 0	5	6	-4	0
row 1	7	6	10	1

```
row 2        12        9        2        2
row 3        -5        3       -1        3
```

```
====  Following Matrix:  C = A + B   ====

          col 0    col 1    col 2    col 3
row 0        7        5        3        5
row 1       29       16       13       -3
row 2       44       10       -5        7
row 3       37       14       -6        7
```

```
====  Following Matrix:  C = A * B   ====

          col 0    col 1    col 2    col 3
row 0       62       84       -9       28
row 1      236      207       22        4
row 2       58      150     -137        2
row 3      207      285      -72       13
```

Example 2-5

Code Section

```c
/*
 * Program Name: empl_db.c
 *
 *    Purpose:      To demonstrate the use of
 *                    1. 'struct' data type
 *                    2. organization of 'struct' data as an Array.
 *
 *       We will gradually develop an employee database with
 *       employee records:
 *
 *          empl_first_name:     10 chars long
 *          empl_middl_name:     10 chars long
 *          empl_last_name:      10 chars long
 *          empl_ss_no:          11 chars long
 *          empl_birth_dt:       10 chars long
 *          empl_marital_stat:   char
 *          empl_number:         integer
 *          empl_title:          10 chars
 *          empl_hiring_dt:      10 chars long
 *          empl_currnt_salary:  integer
 *          dept_no:             integer
 *
 */

/*  GLOBAL VARIABLES    */

typedef struct empl_record
   {
     char   empl_first_name[10];    /* 10 chars long */
     char   empl_middl_name[10];    /* 10 chars long */
     char   empl_last_name[10];     /* 10 chars long */
```

```
        char    empl_ss_no[11];              /* 10 chars long */
        char    empl_birth_dt[10];           /* 10 chars long */
        char    empl_marital_stat;           /* 1 character   */
        int     empl_number;                 /* integer       */
        char    empl_title[10];              /* 10 chars long */
        char    empl_hiring_dt[10];          /* 10 chars long */
        int     empl_currnt_salary;          /* integer       */
        int     dept_no;                     /* integer       */
    } EMPL_STRUCT;


EMPL_STRUCT   empl_db[50];
        /* Employee database is formed as an array */

int empl_total = 0;
int empl_number;
int db_index, index = 0;

/* Initialize the header */

char *header1    = "\n \t        PRATIVA Computers, Inc.";
char *header2    = "\n \t\t Employee DataBase ";

/* Initialize the menu  */

char *menu1    = "\n\n\t Add an employee              .... 1";
char *menu2    = "\n\t Delete an employee              .... 2";
char *menu3    = "\n\t Modify an employee record       .... 3";
char *menu4    = "\n\t Display an employee record      .... 4";
char *menu5    = "\n\t Exit                            .... 5";

/*
 * main(): EMPLOYEE DATABASE
 */
main()
{
    int forever = 1;

    while ( forever )
      {
            display_menu();
            process_choice(  );
      }
}

/*
 * display_menu(): EMPLOYEE DATABASE
 */
display_menu()
{
    system("clear");              /* Clear Display screen  */
    printf( header1 );
    printf( header2 );
    printf( menu1   );
    printf( menu2   );
```

```
        printf ( menu3    );
        printf ( menu4    );
        printf ( menu5    );
}


/*
 * process_choice():
 */
process_choice(  )
{
    int choice;

    do {
        printf ("\n\n Enter your choice ( 1 - 5 ): ");
        scanf ( "%d", &choice );
        } while ( choice < 1 || choice > 5 );

    switch ( choice )
       {
        case 1:
                add_empl();
                 /* Add an employee record in empl_db  */
                break;
        case 2:
                delete_empl();
                 /* Delete employee record in empl_db  */
                break;
        case 3:
                modify_empl();
                 /* Modify employee record in empl_db  */
                break;
        case 4:
                srch_display_empl();
                 /* Display employee record in empl_db */
                break;
        case 5:
        default:
                quit_db();
                 /* Exit from database empl_db          */
        }
}


/*
 * search_empl(): Search for an employee from empl_db
 *                employee number as key
 */
int search_empl( empl_number )
{
    int i;
    for (i = 0; i <= empl_total; i++)
        {
          if (empl_number == empl_db[i].empl_number)
          return( i );
        }
```

```
    /* Search failed at this point as no match found */

    printf("\n\n Search failed: No match found \n\n");
    return( -1 );
}


/*
 * add_empl(): Add a new employee in the empl_db database.
 * This version  does NOT check whether or not same employee
 * already exists.
 */
add_empl()
{
    print_menu_hdr( "ADD" );

    printf("\nEnter Employee's First name:   ");
    scanf("%s", empl_db[index].empl_first_name);

    printf("\nEnter Employee's Middle name:   ");
    scanf("%s", empl_db[index].empl_middl_name);

    printf("\nEnter Employee's Last name:   ");
    scanf("%s", empl_db[index].empl_last_name);

    printf("\nEnter Employee's Social Security Number:   ");
    scanf("%s", empl_db[index].empl_ss_no);

    printf("\nEnter Employee's Birth Date:   ");
    scanf("%s", empl_db[index].empl_birth_dt);

    printf("\nEnter Employee's Marital Status:   ");
    scanf("%s", &empl_db[index].empl_marital_stat);

    printf("\nEnter Employee's Number:   ");
    scanf("%d", &empl_db[index].empl_number);

    printf("\nEnter Employee's Hiring Date:   ");
    scanf("%s", empl_db[index].empl_hiring_dt);

    printf("\nEnter Employee's Current Salary:   ");
    scanf("%d", &empl_db[index].empl_currnt_salary);

    printf("\nEnter Employee's Department Number:   ");
    scanf("%d", &empl_db[index].dept_no);

    printf("\nEnter Employee's Job Title:   ");
    scanf("%s", empl_db[index].empl_title);

    index++;                 /* index = index + 1 */
    empl_total = index;
}

/*
 * delete_empl(): Delete an employee from empl_db database.
 */
```

```
delete_empl()
{
   print_menu_hdr( "DELETE" );
   printf("\n Menu2: Delete is not implemented yet");
}


/*
 * modify_empl(): Modify an employee record in empl_db database.
 */
modify_empl()
{
   print_menu_hdr( "MODIFY" );
   printf("\n Menu3: Modify is not implemented yet");
}


/*
 * srch_display_empl():
 *      Search an employee by employee number,
 *      and if successful, display that employee's
 *      record.
 */
srch_display_empl()
{
   int  db_index;   /* Assigned if search_empl() succeeds */
   char c;          /* Will be used to pause screen display */

   print_menu_hdr ( "DISPLAY" );
   printf("\n\n Enter employee number: ");
   scanf("%d", &empl_number);

   db_index = search_empl( empl_number );
   if (db_index == -1)
     {
       printf("\n display_empl: ERROR: Employee is not in \
                                Database \n");
       return;
     }
   /* Now display complete info for the employee */

   printf("\n Employee's First name:  %s",
          empl_db[db_index].empl_first_name);

   printf("\n Employee's Middle name: %s",
          empl_db[db_index].empl_middl_name);

   printf("\n Employee's Last name:  %s",
          empl_db[db_index].empl_last_name);

   printf("\n Employee's Social Security Number:  %s",
          empl_db[db_index].empl_ss_no);

   printf("\n Employee's Birth Date:  %s",
          empl_db[db_index].empl_birth_dt);
```

```
   printf("\n Employee's Marital Status: %c",
           empl_db[db_index].empl_marital_stat);

   printf("\n Employee's Number:  %d",
           empl_db[db_index].empl_number);

   printf("\n Employee's Hiring Date:  %s",
           empl_db[db_index].empl_hiring_dt);

   printf("\n Employee's Current Salary: %d",
           empl_db[db_index].empl_currnt_salary);

   printf("\n Employee's Department Number:  %d",
           empl_db[db_index].dept_no);

   printf("\n Employee's Job Title:  %s",
           empl_db[db_index].empl_title);

   printf("\n\n Hit y to continue ...   ");
   while ( (c = getchar()) != 'y' )
         ;
}

/*
 * quit_db()  :  Exit from database program
 */
quit_db()
{
   printf("\n Exiting from Employee DataBase ... \n\n");
   system("clear");          /* Clear screen   */
   exit(0);
}

/*
 * print_menu_hdr():  Print header of a menu
 */
print_menu_hdr ( header )
char    *header;
{
   system("clear");              /* Clear screen   */
   printf("\n\t\t\t ******************************** \n");
   printf("\t\t\t\t EMPLOYEE %s MENU \n", header );
   printf("\t\t\t ******************************** \n");
}
```

Here is the output of the above example:

```
                  PRATIVA Computers, Inc.
                    Employee DataBase

Add an employee                ....   1
Delete an employee             ....   2
Modify an employee record      ....   3
```

```
Display an employee record    ....  4
Exit                          ....  5


Enter your choice ( 1 - 5 ):
                    **********************************
                      EMPLOYEE  ADD  MENU
                    **********************************


Enter Employee's First name:
Enter Employee's Middle name:
Enter Employee's Last name:
Enter Employee's Social Security Number:
Enter Employee's Birth Date:
Enter Employee's Marital Status:
Enter Employee's Number:
Enter Employee's Hiring Date:
Enter Employee's Current Salary:
Enter Employee's Department Number:
Enter Employee's Job Title:
                PRATIVA Computers, Inc.
                  Employee DataBase


Add an employee               ....  1
Delete an employee            ....  2
Modify an employee record     ....  3
Display an employee record    ....  4
Exit                          ....  5


Enter your choice ( 1 - 5 ):
                    **********************************
                      EMPLOYEE  DISPLAY  MENU
                    **********************************


Enter employee number:
Employee's First name:  David
Employee's Middle name: R.
Employee's Last name:   Scharpf
Employee's Social Security Number:  543-22-6732
Employee's Birth Date:  02/03/1953
Employee's Marital Status: M
Employee's Number:  123
Employee's Hiring Date:  07/02/1982
Employee's Current Salary: 40000
Employee's Department Number:  5
Employee's Job Title:  4


Hit y to continue ...
                PRATIVA Computers, Inc.
                  Employee DataBase


Add an employee               ....  1
Delete an employee            ....  2
Modify an employee record     ....  3
```

```
Display an employee record    ....  4
Exit                          ....  5

Enter your choice ( 1 - 5 ):
          *********************************
                EMPLOYEE DISPLAY MENU
          *********************************

Enter employee number:

Search failed: No match found

display_empl: ERROR: Employee is not in Database

              PRATIVA Computers, Inc.
                 Employee DataBase

Add an employee               ....  1
Delete an employee            ....  2
Modify an employee record     ....  3
Display an employee record    ....  4
Exit                          ....  5

Enter your choice ( 1 - 5 ):
Exiting from Employee DataBase . . .
```

Because this program was executed on a Unix system and the output was captured using Unix's "tee" utility anything such as "choice" names typed on the keyboard (stdin) could not be captured. Any output printed by the program on the display (stdout) was captured by the tee utility.

Exercises

2-1 For the given example on Employee Database, implement the routine delete_empl() to delete an employee from the empl_db database.

2-2 For the given example on Employee Database, implement the routine modify_empl() to modify an employee's record in the empl_db database.

CHAPTER 3

Arrays and Strings

In Chapter 2, we reviewed the basic concepts of the pointers and structures in C. In this chapter, we first review the basic concepts of arrays and strings. Then we use the ADT approach to define ADT arrays in Sections 3.5 and 3.11 and strings in Section 3.13. We present a word processor application at the end. The concept of array-type data structure is available in almost all the languages. A language like FORTRAN supports the array-type data structure only. The uses of arrays are found in many such applications as the list of names, a table of symbols in compiler design, and a table of processes in operating system programming. The concept of strings is used in the string processing applications.

We have explained earlier that C supports three categories of data types: simple, structured, and pointer. The simple data type char, int, float, double, long double (and the signed version) represents a single data item. The array is a contiguous collection of the same type of data.

A single identifier can represent multiple data items. Such structure-type data objects can be accessed or manipulated collectively or individually, with elements being accessed by index.

3.1 One-Dimensional Arrays

A one-dimensional array can be viewed as a sequential list of data objects, all of the same type. These array objects are collectively referred to by the array identifier. Each individual data object can be selected by the array name with an index (or subscript). The brackets [and] are used to attach the array index. Thus, if ary is the name of a one-dimensional array containing n data objects, the individual data objects are

$$ary[\ 0\ ],\ ary[\ 1\ ],\ \ldots,\ ary[\ n\ -\ 1\ ]$$

Note that the index ranges from zero to one less than the size of the array. Here n is called the size of the array. Then the entire array ary can be as shown in Figure 3-1.

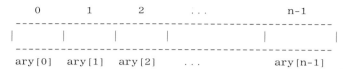

Figure 3-1 One-dimensional array.

The individual indexed variables ary[0], ary[1], ... can be used in any expression, like any ordinary nonstructured type. The index of any individual array element must be a nonnegative integer, either a constant, an expression, or a variable. Any array element can be accessed at random by its index.

A one-dimensional array is declared in C as

<type> <array_name>[<size>];

Example 3.1

```
int       ary[ 15 ];        /* Elements 0 to 14; Size = 15 */
double    number[ 500 ];    /* Numbers 0 to 499            */
char      name[ 10 ];       /* Space reserved for 9 chars  */

ary[ 5 ]     = 67;          /* Assign SIXTH element to 67  */
number[ 0 ] = 6.7;          /* Assign FIRST element to 6.7 */

ary[ 15 ]    = 10;          /* Out of range; Illegal ref;
                               A RUN-TIME ERROR will occur. */
```

Note that 15 consecutive memory locations are reserved for ary, one for each array element; 15 indexed variables ary[0], ary[1], ..., ary[14] are associated with them. The storage requirement for each element depends on the type. It is, in fact, the size of an int variable determined by sizeof(int).

Because the allocation of main memory spaces is fixed, a problem may arise in case the program needs to store more data than elements in the array ary (see Figure 3-2).

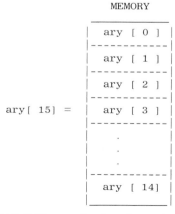

Figure 3-2 Memory allocation of array elements.

The following example shows how an ARRAY type can be defined using `typedef`.

Example 3.2

```
#define  SIZE  15;              /* Constant size = 15 */

typedef int   ARRAY[ SIZE ];   /* Type ARRAY is defined */

ARRAY            ary;  /* Variable 'ary' of ARRAY type*/

ary[ 5 ]    = 67;  /* Assign 67 to SIXTH element  */
```

3.2 Array Initialization

In C, arrays may be of storage class external (`extern`), static (`static`), or auto-matic (`auto`), but not register (`register`).

Static and external arrays may be initialized using an array initializer, that is, by declaring with a list of initial values enclosed in braces { } and separated by commas. For example,

```
static int  ary[6] = { - 4, 5, 3, 2, 0, 1 };
```

So:

```
ary[0] = -4;        ary[1] = 5;        ary[2] = 3;
ary[3] = 2;         ary[4] = 0;        ary[5] = 1;
```

When the list of initializing values is shorter than the size of the array, the remaining elements will be initialized to zero. For example,

```
static float f_ary[100] = { 20.1, -30.2, 55.6 };
```

So:

```
f_ary[0] = 20.1;    f_ary[1] = -30.2;
f_ary[2] = 55.6;    f_ary[3] = 0.0;
. . .
f_ary[98]= 0.0;     f_ary[99]= 0.0;
```

In the absence of explicit initialization for static and external arrays, the compiler automatically sets all elements of the array to zero.

If an automatic array is not initialized explicitly, its elements will have un-defined values.

If a sizeless static or external array is declared and is initialized to a set of values, the size of array will be implicitly the number of initializing values.

```
int  ary[ ] = { - 4, 5, 3, 2, 0, 1 };  /* Sizeless   */
int  ary[6] = { - 4, 5, 3, 2, 0, 1 };  /* Size = 6   */
```

are equivalent external declarations. To initialize a large array, use a `for` loop.

Example 3.3

```
int index;                /* Array index */
int array[ 1024 ];

for ( index = 0; index < sizeof(array); index++ )
    array[ index ] = 0;
```

3.3 Address Translation

The following demonstration shows the relationship between the base address of an array and the addresses of its elements.

Example 3.4

```
/*  Initialize, print addresses (i.e., Memory Locations)
 *  and contents of each address element.
 */
main()
{
   static int  array[10] = { 10, 20, 30, 40, 50,
                             60, 70, 80, 90, 100 };
   int    i;   /* Index */

   printf("\n== Example of Array Address Translation ===\n");
   printf("Memory Loc        Array Element        Content\n");

   for (i = 0; i < sizeof(array); i++)
   printf("%d                 array[%d]             %d\n",
           &array[i], i, array[i]);

}
```

This example, running on a computer using a Motorola 68020 CPU under Unix Sys5.3, yields the following output:

```
==== Example of Array Address Translation ====
Memory Loc          Array Element        Content
591660               array[0]             10
591664               array[1]             20
591668               array[2]             30
591672               array[3]             40
591676               array[4]             50
591680               array[5]             60
591684               array[6]             70
591688               array[7]             80
591692               array[8]             90
591696               array[9]             100
```

The 4-byte difference is the same as the size of an int in this system. Thus the address of any element can be calculated by

```
address of array[ i ]  = base address + i * sizeof ( int )
                       = &array[ 0 ] + i * element size
```

When the `array` is declared, the C compiler allocates a base address at load time and also allocates enough contiguous memory to store all the elements of the `array`. Note that the type (e.g., `int`) determines the location of the next element of the array.

3.4 Passing Arrays as Function Arguments

An array is passed to a function, by passing its base address (known as "call by name"). The elements of the array are not copied into another location. Let us consider the following demonstration.

Example 3.5

```
/*     To show the way and effect of passing an array as a
 *     function argument.
 */
main ()
{
    static int  score[10] = { 10, 20, 30, 40, 50,
                               60, 70, 80, 90, 100 };
    int    i;               /* Index */
    int    average;         /* average value */

    printf ("Memory Loc      Array Element      Content\n");

    for (i = 0; i < sizeof (score); i++)
    printf ("%d            score[%d]            %d\n",
            &score[i],      i,                  score[i]);

    average = compute_avrg( score, sizeof (score[0]) );
    printf ("\n Score Average = %d \n", average);
}


int    compute_avrg (int array, int size )
{
    int    index, sum;

    for ( index = 0, sum = 0; index < size; ++index )
        sum += array[ index ];  /* sum = sum + array[index] */
    return ( sum / size );      /* Return the average       */
}
```

The following is the output of Example 3.5:

Memory Loc	Array Element	Content
591752	score[0]	10
591756	score[1]	20
591760	score[2]	30
591764	score[3]	40
591768	score[4]	50
591772	score[5]	60
591776	score[6]	70

```
591780                  score[7]                80
591784                  score[8]                90
591788                  score[9]               100

Score Average = 55
```

Note that the base address, 591752, of the array `score` is passed to the function `compute_avrg`.

3.5 The ADT Array

An ADT array is a collection of data objects, a set of indices together with a set of operations:

1. Creating an array
2. Initializing an array
3. Storing a data object
4. Retrieving a data object
5. Inserting a data object
6. Deleting a data object
7. Updating a data object
8. Searching a data object
9. Sorting an array
10. Printing an array

The data objects, also called *elements,* must be of the same type (structured or non-structured). The array is homogeneous, but the data objects are heterogeneous.

If a member of the index set consists of a single index, for example, 20, the ADT array is one-dimensional. If it is *n*-tuple, for example, $(i_1, i_2, \ldots, i_n)$, the ADT array is *n*-dimensional. For a two-dimensional ADT array, a member of the index set is of the form [4, 10], where the first index value is 4 and the second index value is 10. For simplicity, each member of the index set is assumed to be an integer ranging between 0 and some positive integer, for example, $n - 1$. This determines the size (also called *dimension*) *n* of the array.

The specification of the data objects is as abstract as possible. It does not influence the structure of the ADT. Since the operations characterize the ADT, we now discuss the operations of the ADT array.

The `store` and `retrieve` operations are the most fundamental operations of an ADT array. Creating an ADT array is accomplished by its declaration in C:

```
int   Ary[20];
```

where `Ary` is an array of integers. Memory spaces for 20 data objects of integer type are automatically allocated by the compiler. However, the compiler does not initialize the array. For further discussion, see Section 3.1.

The function `init()` implements the initialization operation by assigning zero to all data objects of the array. That is,

```
Ary[i] = 0
```

for i = 0, . . . , $n - 1$. For details, see Section 3.2. This process accesses data objects of the array through address translation. As shown in Section 3.3, the indexing method takes one multiplication for each address translation:

address of Ary[i] = &Ary[0] + i * sizeof(int)

But if we use a pointer, `ary_ptr`, which points to Ary[0], no multiplication is needed to address the data object. For example,

```
int    i;
register int * ary_ptr;

for ( i = n, ary_ptr = (int *) Ary;
      --i >= 0;  *ary_ptr++ = 0 )
    ;
```

The latter approach, using a pointer and pointer arithmetic, is more efficient than the former approach.

The store operation implemented by the function

store(Ary, k, data)

uses parameter Ary for the name of an array, parameter k for the index value, and data for the data object to be stored in Ary[k]. It does the following steps:

1. Checks whether k is in the valid range between 0 and $n - 1$. If k is out of the valid range, it prints an error message and returns.
2. Otherwise, it executes the following assignment:

Ary[k] = data

The store operation defines the one-to-one correspondence between a data object and an index value.

The function retrieve(Ary, k) gets the data Ary[k] from the array and returns it. It does not destroy its value. The retrieve function may fail in the following two cases:

Case 1. The specified value of the array index k is not in the valid range for the array.
Case 2. The specified value of k is valid, but the value of the data object is not defined.

It is important to note that the value of a data object remains undefined until something is stored in it.

The function update(Ary, k, data) updates the value of the data object Ary[k]. Its function is the same as the function store(). It fails if the specified value of the index k is not within the valid range 0, . . . , $n - 1$. It then returns with an error message "Out of Bounds". For a valid index value, it overwrites A[k] with the specified data.

The function insert(Ary, k, where, data) inserts a data object into the array. It considers two cases:

1. If where indicates before the index k, the index value is k−1.
2. If where indicates after the index k, the index value is k+1.

First we must check whether the array is full, that is, whether all the *n* slots of the array Ary are occupied. If the array is full, the insertion operation fails, and returns with an error message "Array Overflow". Otherwise, in order to create room for the incoming data object data, it proceeds as follows:

   I. For the insert before the index k operation, shift data objects Ary[k] through Ary[last] (last <= n-2) to Ary[k+1] through Ary[last + 1]. Then Ary[k] = data

   II. For the insert after the index k operation, shift data objects Ary[k+1] through Ary[last] (last <= n-2) to Ary[k+2] through Ary[last + 1]. Then Ary[k + 1] = data

The function delete(Ary, k) deletes the data object of Ary[k]. However, this creates a hole at that slot in the array. To close the hole, we move all elements up and decrement last by 1. That is, move up the data objects Ary[k + 1] through Ary[last] (last <= n - 1) to Ary[k] through Ary[last - 1].

    The operation of searching for an item in an array looks for a match of item with the values of the data objects in the array Ary. If it is successful, it returns the index k such that Ary[k] matches item. Otherwise, it returns with an error message. Various search algorithms and implementations are presented in Chapter 9. The efficiency and type of the searching methods depend on whether the array is sorted in some order.

    The operation of sorting an ADT array rearranges its data objects in some predetermined order: ascending or descending. There are several sorting methods and implementations presented in Chapter 9.

3.6 Multidimensional Arrays

The C language provides for arrays of arrays, arrays of arrays of arrays, etc. We add another dimension to an array by adding another bracket pair [] to the array variable name.

    The two-dimensional array is the simplest form of the multidimensional array. A two-dimensional array consists of rows and columns. Each element will have two indices, the first index (i.e., the first dimension) indicating the row number and the second index (i.e., the second dimension) indicating the column number. For example, for the mathematical form of the two-dimensional array:

$$
A = \begin{array}{|llll|l}
 & A[0][0] & A[0][1] & \ldots & A[0][n-1] & (\text{Row } 0) \\
 & A[1][0] & A[1][1] & \ldots & A[1][n-1] & (\text{Row } 1) \\
 & \ldots & & & & \\
 & A[m-2][0] & A[m-2][1] & \ldots & A[m-2][n-1] & (\text{Row } m-2) \\
 & A[m-2][0] & A[m-1][1] & \ldots & A[m-1][n-1] & (\text{Row } m-1) \\
 & \wedge & \wedge & & \wedge &
\end{array}
$$

$$
\text{Column} \quad 0 \qquad\qquad 1 \qquad\qquad n-1
$$

in terms of its memory allocation it is represented as follows:

```
A[0][0]  ...  A[0][n-1] A[1][0]  ...   A[1][n-1]
<------ row 0 ------> <------ row 1 ------->

        ...  A[m-1][0]  ...   A[m-1][n-1]
             <-------- row m-1 ------->
```

The above two-dimensional array A has m rows and n columns. The individual array elements of A are A[0][0], A[0][1], ..., A[m-1][n-1]. In notation,

$$A = (A[i][j]), \quad i = 0, 1, \ldots, m - 1$$
$$j = 0, 1, \ldots, n - 1$$

where i = row index and j = column index.

All of the data objects in A will be collectively referred to by the single identifier A. Each individual element (e.g., A[4][3]) will be referred to by the array name A, followed by the appropriate values (e.g., 4 and 3) for the row and column indices each enclosed in square brackets []．

In C, a multidimensional array is, in fact, a one-dimensional array in which each element itself is a one-dimensional array and all of them are contiguous.

Examples of declarations	Meaning
Double A[200];	A one-dimensional array
Double B[200][100];	A two-dimensional array
Double C[200][100][300];	A three-dimensional array

Note that the array B will have 200 × 100 elements. The base address of the array B is the identifier B which is the same as &B[0][0]. At the declaration, starting at the base address of the array B, 20,000 cells for all the array elements of B will be contiguously allocated in memory. The size of each cell will be sizeof (double). This storage allocation of 20,000 cells is fixed, whether or not all of them are used.

The base address of the three-dimensional array C *is* &C[0][0][0]. Its elements can be referred to by

$$C[i][j][k] \quad \text{where} \quad i = 0, \ldots, 199$$
$$j = 0, \ldots, 99$$
$$k = 0, \ldots, 299$$

For all the above arrays A, B, and C, the elements are stored by the order: first row, second row, third row, and so forth. That is, the rightmost subscript varies faster than its immediate previous subscript as the elements are accessed in the memory. To access a given element of a two-dimensional array, the conventional rectangular calculation is used in consideration with the base address of the array identifier.

3.7 Initializing Multidimensional Arrays

Initializing multidimensional arrays can be done in the same manner as for the one-dimensional array. Storage classes of an array are static, auto, extern, but not register.

Example 3.6

```
static   int A[ 4 ][ 4 ] =
    { {   2,   -1,   7,   5 },      /* Row 0 of Matrix A */
      { 22,   10,   3,  -4 },      /* Row 1 of Matrix A */
      { 32,    1,  -7,   5 },      /* Row 2 of Matrix A */
      { 42,   11,  -5,   4 } };   /* Row 3 of Matrix A */
```

3.8 Passing Multidimensional Arrays as Function Arguments

When we use a multidimensional array as a formal argument in a function definition, we must specify the size of each dimension of the array, except the first in the declaration statement within the function.

This is required for the compiler to allocate the necessary space in the stack frame. For example:

```
int function_foo(int A[][10], int row_size)
{

}
```

Example 3.7

```
/*    Function to compute sum of all elements of the
 *    matrix A; return sum demonstrating the passing
 *    of a two-dimensional array as an argument.
 *    Note that row size of A is not specified.
 */

double   compute_sum ( double A[][10], int row_size )
{
  int    index_1,    /* Index for first array     */
         index_2;    /* Index for second array    */
  double  sum;       /* Computed sum              */

  sum = 0;            /* Initialize sum            */

  for ( index_1 = 0; index_1 < row_size; ++index_1 )
     for ( index_2 = 0; index_2 < 10; ++index_2 )
        sum += A[ index_1 ] [ index_2 ];
  return ( sum );
}
```

Example 3.8

```
/*    Function to compute sum of all elements
 *    of the 3-dimensional array A; return sum.
 *    This demonstrates the passing of a
```

```
 *      3-dimensional array as an argument.
 */

double  compute_sum ( double A[][10][15], int row_size )
{
   int    index_1,     /* Index for first array    */
          index_2,     /* Index for second array   */
          index_3;     /* Index for third array    */
   double sum;         /* Computed sum             */

   sum = 0;            /* Initialize sum           */

   for ( index_1 = 0; index_1 < row_size; ++index_1 )
      for ( index_2 = 0; index_2 < 10; ++index_2 )
         for ( index_3 = 0; index_3 < 15; ++index_3 )
            sum += A[ index_1 ] [ index_2 ] [ index_3 ];
   return ( sum );
}
```

In summary, for each dimension added to the existing array, additional changes in code are as follows:

1. We must add a dimension in [] in the declaration statement.
2. Additional index is required.
3. In case of passing this newly dimensioned array, we must specify the correct numerical value in the declaration statement within the function.

As an example of the use of multidimensional arrays for matrix operations (addition, multiplication) and for passing matrices as formal arguments of functions, a complete example with its output is given in Example 3.9.

3.9 Address Translation of Multidimensional Arrays

Example 3.9 demonstrates the relationship between the base address of a matrix and the addresses of its elements.

Example 3.9

```
/*
 * print_matrix() :  To print a matrix A ( m x n )
 */
print_matrix(int A[ ][4], int  m, int n, char *matrix_var_name)
{
    int  i, j;
    printf("\n ====  For the following Matrix: %s \n\n",
        matrix_var_name );
    printf("      ");          /* To align row & column printing */
    for (j = 0; j < n; j++)
       printf("   col %d", j); /* Print 'col' as header for each
                          column  */
```

```
    printf("\n\n");                  /* Print a new line    */
    for ( i = 0; i < m; i++ )
        {
            printf ("row %d  ", i );
            for  ( j = 0; j < n; j++ )
                printf (" %5d  ",  A[ i ][ j ] );
            printf("\n");    /* Print a new line after a row  */
        }
}


/*  Initialize, print addresses (i.e., Memory Locations)
 *  and contents of each matrix element.
 */

main ()
{
    static int A[  ][4 ] =         /* Assign values in Matrix A */
            { {   2,   -1,   7,   5 }, /* Row 0 of Matrix A      */
              { 22,   10,   3,  -4 }, /* Row 1 of Matrix A      */
              { 32,    1,  -7,   5 }, /* Row 2 of Matrix A      */
              { 42,   11,  -5,   4 } };  /* Row 3 of Matrix A    */

    int     i, j, m = 4, n = 4;

    printf("\n\n === BASE ADDRESS TRANSLATION OF %s \n",
            "MATRIX ELEMENTS    === ");
    print_matrix ( A, m, n, " A " );
    printf("\n==== Address Translation of above %s \n\n",
            "elements   ====");
    printf("Memory Loc        Matrix Element        Content\n\n");

    for ( i = 0; i < m; i++ )
        {
            for  ( j = 0; j < n; j++ )
            printf ("%5d           A[ %d ] [ %d ]        %d\n",
                    &A[i][j],   i, j, A[ i ][ j ] );
            printf("\n");
        }
}
```

The output of the above example is

```
===  BASE ADDRESS TRANSLATION OF MATRIX ELEMENTS    ===

====  For the following Matrix:   A

          col 0    col 1    col 2    col 3

row 0        2       -1        7        5
row 1       22       10        3       -4
row 2       32        1       -7        5
row 3       42       11       -5        4
```

```
==== Address Translation of above elements  ====

Memory Loc        Matrix Element         Content   Comment

591984            A[ 0 ][ 0 ]               2
591988            A[ 0 ][ 1 ]              -1        1st row
591992            A[ 0 ][ 2 ]               7
591996            A[ 0 ][ 3 ]               5


592000            A[ 1 ][ 0 ]              22
592004            A[ 1 ][ 1 ]              10        2nd row
592008            A[ 1 ][ 2 ]               3
592012            A[ 1 ][ 3 ]              -4


592016            A[ 2 ][ 0 ]              32
592020            A[ 2 ][ 1 ]               1        3rd row
592024            A[ 2 ][ 2 ]              -7
592028            A[ 2 ][ 3 ]               5


592032            A[ 3 ][ 0 ]              42
592036            A[ 3 ][ 1 ]              11        4th row
592040            A[ 3 ][ 2 ]              -5
592044            A[ 3 ][ 3 ]               4
```

Analysis of the above output shows:

```
Base address of Matrix A:   591984     (in decimal)

Location of A[ 0 ][ 0 ]:    591984
Location of A[ 0 ][ 1 ]:    591988    (Row 0, Column 1 )
Difference &A[0][1]   - &A[0][0]   = 4 bytes

Location of A[ 2 ][ 3 ]:    592028    (Row 2, Column 3 )
Location of A[ 2 ][ 3 ]  = 591984 + 44
                         = base address + ((2 * 4) + 3) * 4
```

In this output, the difference between two consecutive addresses is 4, the same as sizeof(int) on our system. When the matrix is declared, the compiler allocates a base address at load time, and also allocates enough contiguous memory to store the first row, the second row, and so on. The type plays an important role in locating the next element of the matrix.

The address of any TYPE element A[i][j] of a matrix A with n columns can be calculated by

```
address of A[ i ][ j ] = base address  + offset
              = &A[ 0 ][ 0 ]  + ( i * n + j ) * sizeof (TYPE)
```

This concept will be useful in the discussion of a pointer to matrices.

Example 3.10

```
/*   Program:     matrix_ops.c   (ADT MATRIX OPERATIONS)
 *
 *   Purpose:     1) To add two matrices A & B ( both m-rows &
 *                   n-columns ), the resultant matrix A + B will
 *                   have m-rows & n-columns.
 *
 *                2) Multiply two matrices A ( m x n ) & B
 *                   ( n x p ), and product is C ( m x p )
 *                   (i.e., m-rows & p-columns ).
 *
 *                This shows application of multi-dimensional
 *                array structure.
 */

#define ROWS     4 /* Used in main() to initialize a matrix     */
#define COLUMNS 4 /* Used in main() to initialize a matrix     */

/* Define data type and a type MATRIX in C   */
typedef   int          DATA_TYPE;
typedef   DATA_TYPE   MATRIX[ ROWS ][ COLUMNS ];

/*
 *   matrix_add() : C (m x n) = A (m x n)  + B (m x n)
 *
 *   Inputs:   Matrices A & B ;
 *             m        Number of rows in matrices A, B, & C
 *             n        Number of columns in matrices A, B, & C
 *   Output:  Matrix C with m rows and n columns
 */
matrix_add( MATRIX A, MATRIX B, MATRIX C, int m, int n )
{
    int    i;    /* Used for row index, e.g. A[ i ][ j ] */
    int    j;    /* Used for col index, e.g. A[ i ][ j ] */

    for ( i = 0; i < m; i++)
       {
       for ( j = 0; j < n; j++ )

           C[ i ][ j ] = A[ i ][ j ] + B[ i ][ j ];
       }
}

/*
 *   matrix_mult():  C (m x p) = A (m x n) * B (n x p)
 *   Inputs:   Matrices A & B ;
 *             m    Number of rows in matrices A, & C
 *             n    Number of cols in A, & number of rows in B
 *             p    Number of cols in matrices B, & C
 *   Output:  Matrix C with m rows and n columns
 */
```

```
matrix_mult ( MATRIX A, MATRIX B, MATRIX C,
              int m, int n, int p )
{
    int    i;    /* Used for row index, e.g. A[ i ][ j ] */
    int    j;    /* Used for col index, e.g. A[ i ][ j ] */
    int    k;
    double sum;

    /*
     *  C[i,j] = Sum ( A[i, k] * B[k, j] ) for k = 0, ..., n - 1
     *              where i = 0, ..., m - 1 &  j = 0, ..., p - 1
     */

    for ( i = 0; i < m; i++)
       {
          for ( j = 0; j < p; j++ )
             {
                sum = 0;
                for ( k = 0; k < n ; k++ )
                   /* Vector product for C[i][j] */
                   sum += (double)(A[ i ][ k ] * B[ k ][ j ]);

                C[ i ][ j ] =  sum;
             }
       }
}

/*
 *    print_matrix()  :  To print a matrix A ( m x n )
 */
print_matrix(MATRIX A, int m, int n, char *matrix_var_name )
{
    int  i, j;

    printf("\n ****  Following Matrix: %s \n\n",
        matrix_var_name );
    printf("      ");    /* To align row & column printing */
    for (j = 0; j < n; j++)
       printf("   col %d", j );

    printf("\n\n");   /* Skip a line  */
    for ( i = 0; i < m; i++ )
       {
          printf ("row %d  ", i );
          for  ( j = 0; j < n; j++ )
             printf (" %5d  ",  A[ i ][ j ] );
          printf("\n");   /* Print a new line after a row   */
       }

}

/*
 *    main(): MULTI-DIMENSIONAL ARRAY (MATRIX) OPERATIONS
 */
```

```
main()
{
    static   MATRIX   A =                     /* Assign values in Matrix A */
              { {  2,   -1,   7,   5 },      /* Row 0 of Matrix A      */
                { 22,   10,   3,  -4 },      /* Row 1 of Matrix A      */
                { 32,    1,  -7,   5 },      /* Row 2 of Matrix A      */
                { 42,   11,  -5,   4 } };    /* Row 3 of Matrix A      */

    static   MATRIX   B =                     /* Assign values in Matrix B */
              { {  5,   6,  -4, 0 },         /* Row 0 of Matrix B      */
                {  7,   6,  10, 1 },         /* Row 1 of Matrix B      */
                { 12,   9,   2, 2 },         /* Row 2 of Matrix B      */
                { -5,   3,  -1, 3 } };       /* Row 3 of Matrix B      */

    MATRIX      C;                            /* Output matrix          */

    printf("\n ***   ADT MULTI-DIMENSIONAL ARRAY ( MATRIX )   *** ");
    printf("\n        OPERATIONS & ARGUMENT PASSING          \n");

    print_matrix ( A, ROWS, COLUMNS, " A " );
    print_matrix ( B, ROWS, COLUMNS, " B " );

    matrix_add( A, B, C, ROWS, COLUMNS );
    print_matrix ( C, ROWS, COLUMNS, " C = A + B " );
    matrix_mult( A, B, C, ROWS, COLUMNS, COLUMNS );
    print_matrix ( C, ROWS, COLUMNS, " C = A * B " );
    printf("\n *** END OF ADT MATRIX OPERATIONS & %s \n",
           "ARGUMENT PASSING *** ");
}
```

Here is the output of Example 3.10:

```
    ***   ADT MULTI-DIMENSIONAL ARRAY ( MATRIX )   ***
          OPERATIONS & ARGUMENT PASSING

    ****   Following Matrix:   A

             col 0    col 1    col 2    col 3

    row 0       2       -1        7        5
    row 1      22       10        3       -4
    row 2      32        1       -7        5
    row 3      42       11       -5        4

    ****   Following Matrix:   B

             col 0    col 1    col 2    col 3

    row 0       5        6       -4        0
    row 1       7        6       10        1
    row 2      12        9        2        2
    row 3      -5        3       -1        3
```

```
****   Following Matrix:   C = A + B

         col 0    col 1    col 2    col 3

row  0       7        5        3        5
row  1      29       16       13       -3
row  2      44       10       -5        7
row  3      37       14       -6        7


****   Following Matrix:   C = A * B

         col 0    col 1    col 2    col 3

row  0      62       84       -9       28
row  1     236      207       22        4
row  2      58      150     -137        2
row  3     207      285      -72       13
```

*** END OF ADT MATRIX OPERATIONS & ARGUMENT PASSING ***

3.10 The Relationship between Arrays and Pointers

The array type doesn't really exist as a variable. In C, it is not possible to assign one array (and its contents) to another.

> Given: char a[8], b[8];
>   and b[i] initialized for i = 0 to 7;
>
> you can't write:
>   a = b;   or   a[] = b[];
>
> instead you must do:
>   for (i = 0; i < 8; i++)
>   a[i] = b[i];

The array variable name is, in fact, a pointer constant. Inside the scope of the array, it references a constant memory location, consisting of contiguous memory locations.

A pointer is a variable; it can have address values assigned to it.

> Given: int ivar;
>   ivar = 17;
>
> In an expression:
>   ivar   stands for the value of the variable, currently 17;
>   &ivar   stands for the location of the variable, for example the location
>   0x80000.
>
> Note that the following are syntax errors:
>   &12
>   &undeclared_var

```
Given: char    a[8];
       a       == &a[0];
       a + 1   == &a[1];
```

Be careful; a + 10 will be accepted by the compiler as &a[10], but reading or writing to &a[10] will produce unexpected results and likely cause quick termination of the program.

Declaring a pointer involves defining its base type, its name, and that it is a pointer. The symbol * is used to signal that it is a pointer. For the statement

```
char * cp;
```

the base type of the variable is char; * signals pointer; and the name of the variable is cp.

To access the contents of the location pointed to by a pointer, the *indirection* or *pointer dereferencing* operator * is used:

```
*cp = 'z';
```

Notice that the symbol * is a very overloaded symbol in C. Its meaning is context-dependent:

1. In the string /* ... */ it is part of the opening and closing terminators for comments.
2. In the expression a * b it is the operator for multiplication.
3. In the declaration char * cp; it is the signal that the variable is a pointer.
4. In the expression *cp = 'z' it is the pointer dereferencing operator.

Usually C compilers ignore the white space between * and the variable name in both contexts. We choose to clarify the meaning of * in the declaration context by putting a space between the pointer signal and the variable name.

The generic pointer in C may be defined by

```
typedef   char *   POINTER;
```

and used in declarations by

```
POINTER   cp;
```

The memory location sizes for the generic pointer and its related type are usually different:

```
sizeof(cp)    == 4   in a 32-bit system
sizeof(*cp)   == 1   in most cases
```

Note that the compiler replaces the string POINTER with the string char *. The compiler treats any similar type, for example, PTR (defined by typedef char * PTR;), as a separate type. Given

```
POINTER   cp;
PTR       ap;
```

the following assignment is permissible because the pointers have the same base type:

$$cp = ap;$$

Given:

```
char    ary[8];
char  * cp = ary;
short * sp = (short *) ary;
long  * lp = (long *) ary;
```

The variables have the following relationships:

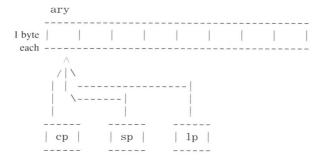

After the pointers are incremented, the variables have the following relationships:

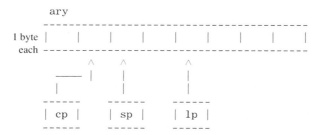

The concept of a pointer to a pointer can be shown by the following example.

Example 3.11 A Pointer to a Pointer

```
char    ca[8];
short  * cp0 = (short *) &ca[0],
short  * cp1 = (short *) &ca[2],
short  * cp2 = (short *) &ca[4],
short  * cp3 = (short *) &ca[6];
short ** cpp = &cp0;
```

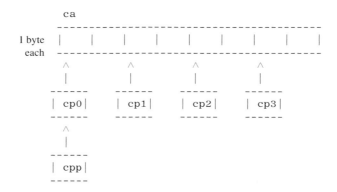

The address &ca is cast from "pointer to char" to "pointer to short" explicitly. Sometimes a compiler will allow an implicit cast, but it's better to be careful. The cast must be made to the base type of the variable assigned to. Given int * ip; and char * cp = 'm';, it is correct to write ip = (int *) cp;. It is not correct to write ip = (short *) cp; (which is a redeclaration of ip).

Each pointer to short is assigned the address of 2 bytes of the array of char's. The pointer to pointer is assigned the address of the pointer cp0.

There is a relationship between the pointer dereferencing operator and the address of operator:

1. TYPE ca;   TYPE * cp = &ca;
2. *cp == * (&ca)
3. *cp refers to the contents of the location of ca, that is *cp == ca
3. therefore * (&ca) == ca, in other words * (&var) == var
4. similarly *cp == ca so & (*cp) == &ca
5. &ca == cp
6. therefore & (*cp) == cp, in other words & (*var) == var

In the process of dereferencing a pointer to a pointer, the expression **cpp may be transformed by the following chain of substitutions:

1. TYPE ca;   TYPE * cp = &ca;   TYPE ** cpp = &cp;
2. **cpp   == * (*cpp)   associative grouping of the operators.
3. **cpp   == * (* (cpp))   associative grouping of the operators
4. **cpp   == * (* (&cp))   because cpp == &cp
5. **cpp   == * (cp)   because * (&cp) == cp
6. **cpp   == * (&ca)   because cp == &ca
7. **cpp   == ca   because * (&ca) == ca

8. *cp0 = 'z'   means   ca = 'z';
9. **cpp = 'z'   also means   ca = 'z';

3.11 The Two-Dimensional ADT Array

A two-dimensional ADT array is a collection of (1) data objects and (2) an index set, each member being [i, j], together with a set of operations:

1. Creating a two-dimensional array
2. Initializing a two-dimensional array
3. Storing a data object
4. Retrieving a data object
5. Inserting a data object
6. Deleting a data object
7. Updating a data object
8. Searching a data object
9. Sorting an array
10. Printing an array

As with the one-dimensional ADT array, the data objects are structured or nonstructured types. These are specified as abstract as possible.

A member of the index set is of the form [4, 10], where the first index value is 4 and the second index value is 10. For simplicity, each index set is assumed to be an integer ranging between 0 and a nonnegative integer, for example, $n - 1$. For details, see Section 3.6. We now discuss those operations that are different from those for the one-dimensional ADT array.

Creating a two-dimensional ADT array is accomplished by the following declaration in C:

$$\text{int} \quad \text{Ary\_2[20][15]};$$

Ary_2 is a two-dimensional array of integers. Memory spaces for 20*15 (i.e., 300) integer-type data objects are automatically allocated by the compiler. However, the compiler does not initialize the array. For further discussion, see Section 3.6.

The function init() implements the initialization operation by assigning zero to all data objects of Ary_2. That is,

$$\text{Ary\_2[i][j]} = 0 \quad \text{for} \quad \text{i} = 0, \ldots, \text{n-1},$$
$$\& \quad \text{j} = 0, \ldots, \text{m-1}.$$

For details, see Section 3.7.

As in a one-dimensional ADT array, we use pointers to initialize the two-dimensional ADT array as follows:

```
int   i,              /* index:  0 .. n*m  */
      tot_elements;   /* == n * m          */

register int * ary2_ptr;

tot_elements = n * m;

for ( i = tot_elements, ary2_ptr = (int *) Ary_2;
    --i >= 0;  *ary2_ptr++ = 0 )
   ;
```

In the above lines, we are treating Ary_2 as if it were a one-dimensional array. For a double-array index Ary_2[i][j], the C compiler requires three multiplications and two additions for each address translation:

$$address\ of\ Ary\_2[i][j]\ =\ Ary\_2\ +\ (i\ *\ m\ *\ sizeof(int))$$
$$+\ (j\ *\ sizeof(int))$$

where Ary_2 is the base address of the two-dimensional array, that is, &Ary_2[0][0]. For details, see Section 3.9. In this approach we are simply incrementing the pointer ary2_ptr, which does not require any multiplication. This code initializes the two-dimensional array very quickly.

The function store(Ary_2, k, p, data) does the storing of the specified value data in Ary[k][p] in the following steps:

Step 1. Checks whether k and p are in the valid ranges between 0 and $n - 1$, and between 0 and $m - 1$, respectively. If k or p is out of range, it returns printing an error message.

Step 2. Otherwise, it does the assignment:

$$Ary\_2[k][p]\ =\ data$$

The store operation defines the one-to-one correspondence between a data object and an index value (k, p).

The function retrieve(Ary_2, k, p) implements the operation of retrieving the data Ary_2[k][p]. As above, it does the following steps:

Step 1. Checks whether k and p are in the valid ranges between 0 and $n - 1$ and between 0 and $m - 1$, respectively. If k or p is out of range, it returns printing an error message.

Step 2. Otherwise, it returns the data:

$$return(\ Ary\_2[k][p]\ )$$

The function retrieve() does not check whether the data in Ary_2[k][p] is defined before retrieving it. Also, it does not destroy the value already stored in Ary_2[k][p].

3.12 Declaration and Access of Strings

A character string is an array of characters. An n-character string is a one-dimensional array of $n + 1$ chars, with a terminating NULL character '\0'. The compiler pads the string with the NULL character so that it can find the end of the string. To avoid the out-of-range condition, programs must check for the NULL character.

The following two ways of declarations are equivalent:

```
static char   header[ ] = "Program";   /* String constant   */
static char   header[ ] = {'P', 'r', 'o', 'g',
                           'r', 'a', 'm', '\0' };
                           /* Size = 7 characters plus \0 */
```

The base address of the string "Program" is the address &header[0]. A string can also be manipulated using pointers. To print such a string, use

```
printf( header );
```

Automatic character arrays cannot be initialized. Note that inclusion of size of array in the above initialization array will cause the compilation error "too many initializers".

Example 3.12

```
/*  Calculate the length of a string when the
 *  string is declared as an array of char's
 */
main ()
 {
    static char   header[ ] = "Program"; /* String init   */
    int    index      = 0;
    register int    count;                  /* Counter for chars */

    count = 0;
    /*  Do not count \0 as a part of the string; also \0
     *  is used to control the 'while' loop.
     */
    while ( header[ index++ ] != '\0' )
        ++count;                             /* count = count + 1 */

    printf (" === Example of a String as an Array  === \n");
    printf ("\n The given string:          ");
    printf ( header );
    printf ("\n The Length of the string: %d \n", count );

 }
```

In Example 3.12, after the execution of header[index++], the header still points to the start of the string. The output of Example 3.12 is

```
=== Example of a String as an Array  ===

The given string:          Program
The Length of the string: 7
```

Declaring and initializing a string can be also done using pointers:

```
char *s_ptr = "This section intends to focus on Strings";
char *t = s_ptr;
                /* t is assigned the value s_ptr. Then both
                   t and s_ptr points to the same string  */
```

Printing this string can be done by the following statement:

```
                printf (" %s ", s_ptr );
```

In order to discuss how we can use pointer arithmetic here, let us look into the memory storage of the above string in Figure 3-3.

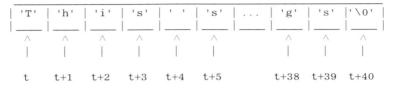

Figure 3-3 String memory storage.

The variables t, t+1, . . . , respectively point to the characters 'T', 'h', and so on. In other words,

$$*t == \text{'T'}, \; *(t+1) == \text{'h'}, \; *(t+2) == \text{'i'},$$
$$\ldots, \; *(t+40) == \text{'}\backslash0\text{'},$$

The string length is 41, including the NULL character '\0'. Because t points to the first character of the string, t + 1 (i.e., t++) points to the next character of the string. Thus the pointer t can be advanced to point to the next character using pointer arithmetic t++. The pointer version of the concept in Example 3.12 is given in Example 3.13.

Example 3.13

```
/*
 * strlen( s ) :        Calculates length of the string s
 *                      excluding '\0' and returns the
 *                      length which is an integer.
 */
int  strlen ( char * s )
{
   /*  Length is set to zero; Storage class 'register' is
    *  used for faster execution than normal.
    */
   register  int  length = 0;
   while ( *s != '\0' )
      {
          length++;        /* length = length + 1  */
          s++;             /* Pointer s advances to next char*/
      }
   return ( length );
}


main()    /* POINTER IMPLEMENTATION OF STRINGS               */
{
   STRING S = "Program"; /* String variables S & T declared
                             and  initialized.               */
   STRING T = "This section intends to focus on strings";

   printf("\n ***  POINTER IMPLEMENTATION OF STRINGS ***n");
   printf("\n For string S: %s\n  Length is: %d \n", S,
       strlen( S ) );
   printf("\n For string T: %s\n  Length is: %d \n", T,
       strlen( T ) );
}
```

The output of this example is:

```
***   POINTER IMPLEMENTATION OF STRINGS ***

For string S: Program
Length is: 7

For string T: This section intends to focus on strings
Length is: 40
```

3.13 Array of Strings

An array of strings can be defined as an array whose elements are strings. Because a string is an array of characters, an array of strings is then an array of arrays, that is, a two-dimensional array.

In C, an array of strings can be declared as

```
        char    error[ SIZE ][ String_length ]
```

where SIZE indicates the maximum size of the error message array, each element of the array error is a string of length strlen. This declaration automatically reserves memory spaces of SIZE × String_length bytes.

In C, an array of strings can be initialized as follows:

```
#define  SIZE    5                /* Number of Strings    */
#define  Length   23

static char error[ SIZE ][ Length ] =
    { "Line undefined",
      "Illegal indirection",
      "Illegal characters",
      "Syntax error",
      "Floating exception"
    };
```

The error[4][0-22] will be stored in the memory as shown in Figure 3-4. Note in the structure shown in Figure 3-4 that there are 5 rows and 23 columns, and all rows are not entirely filled with characters, even though spaces are statically allocated. This is because we declared each string as a one-dimensional array of fixed length 23.

```
              0 1 2 3 4 5 6 7 8 9    . . .                22

error[4]      |F|l|o|a|t|i|n|g| |e|x|c|e|p|t|i|o|n|\0| | | | |
              |_|_|_|_|_|_|_|_|_|_|_|_|_|_|_|_|_|_|__|_|_|_|_|
```

Figure 3-4 String memory storage.

Example 3.14

```
    /*
     * print_error(): Print error string
     */
```

```
print_str_ary ( char  error[ ][ 23 ], int    inx )
{
  printf ("%s \n ", error[inx] );
}
```

3.14 Array of Pointers to Strings

An array of strings is actually an array of constant pointers to a set of contiguous strings. In contrast, an array of pointers to strings is an array of variable pointers, not necessarily contiguous. One-dimensional arrays of pointers to strings are useful in dealing with the space wastage problem. This is also known as the *ragged array* structuring approach.

Declaration and initialization of an array of pointers to strings can be done as follows:

```
static char *error_ptr[ SIZE ] =
    { "Line undefined",
      "Illegal indirection",
      "Illegal characters",
      "Syntax error",
      "Floating exception"
    };
```

The *error_ptr [4] will be stored in the memory as shown in Figure 3-5. Note in the structure shown in Figure 3-5 that there are 5 rows, but the number of columns are not the same for each row because this number is implicitly determined by the length of each string. Comparing the storage structure in Figure 3-5 with that in the previous section, the pointer version uses less memory space.

Figure 3-5 String memory storage.

Note that

```
error_ptr[0]  == address of "Line undefined",
error_ptr[1]  == address of "Illegal indirection",
error_ptr[2]  == address of "Illegal characters",
error_ptr[3]  == address of "Syntax error"
error_ptr[4]  == address of "Floating exception"
```

The important reasons for using pointers to strings are

1. Efficient usage of memory space
2. String manipulation, such as sorting of strings
3. Passing pointers to strings to a function as arguments

Caution: The compiler will allow you to write a larger string than was in the originally defined storage, and your program will terminate abnormally.

Example 3.15

```
/*
 * print_error(): Print Strings through an array of
 *                Pointers to them. (POINTER Version)
 */
print_str_ptr ( char * error_ptr[ ], int inx )
{
    printf( " %s \n",  error_ptr[ inx ] );
}
```

3.15 Interchange of Strings

Swapping or interchange of strings is useful in operations like sorting of strings. If the strings are structured as arrays of strings (as in Section 3.10), swapping can be done as follows using strcpy():

```
char   temp[ Length ];

/* ***   Physically swap the strings   ***   */

strcpy( temp,                error[ index ]);
strcpy( error[ index ],    error[ index + 1 ]);
strcpy( error[ index + 1 ], temp);
```

The variable temp is a one-dimensional array used as a temporary storage. In this case, we need to physically move the strings to perform interchange. The library function strcpy() is used to copy the entire string to temp.

When we use pointers to strings, we can efficiently accomplish swapping of strings by simply interchanging pointers to those strings in the following manner:

```
char   *temp;

/* ***   Swap the pointers to strings   ***   */

temp                 = error_ptr[ index ];
error_ptr[ index ]   = error_ptr[ index + 1 ];
error_ptr[ index + 1] = temp;
```

Note in this approach that we do not require three calls of library routine strcpy() and the one-dimensional variable temp. Only the values of the pointer variables error_ptr are changed.

We discuss sorting algorithms in detail in Chapter 9.

3.16 The ADT String

An ADT string is a sequence of characters with operations several of which are presented in Figure 3-6. These are simple versions of the standard library functions.

ADT string operations	Description
1. Parse_Str(char *src, char *dest, char delim)	Parses a delimited string into its component strings
2. void Append_Str (char *to, char *from1, char *from2)	Form to string by appending from2 string after from1 string
3. int max_Str(char **string, int count)	Return maximum length of a string
4. int position_Str(char **string, char key, int count)	Return position of a key character in string; if it is not found, return -1
5. int numeric_compare(char *string1, char *string2)	Numerically compares two strings, and returns 1, 0, -1 if >, =, or < in value
6. int strlen(char * s)	Calculate length of the string s excluding \0, and return it

Figure 3-6 ADT string operations.

You may need to modify these routines in order to apply in your application.

Example 3.16

```
/*
 *  Program: string_ops.c      ADT STRING OPERATIONS
 */

/*
 * PROCEDURE Parse_Str() :
 *
 *  Input:   (1) SOURCE = string to parse
 *           (2) DELIM = delimiter character to parse the
 *                        string with
 *  Output: DESTIN = the destination string to store
 *                    result of parse
 *
 *  This procedure parses a string with delimiters into
 *  the first component string.
 */

Parse_Str( char *src, char *dest, char *delim)
{
  while ((*src != *delim) && *src != '\0' )
      *dest++ = *src++;
  *dest = '\0';
}

 /*
  *  Append_Str() : concatenate two strings together by
  *                 appending string2 after string1.
  *                 Appended string is 'to'.
  */
```

```
void Append_Str ( char *to, char *from1, char *from2)
{
  /*  copy the first string  */
  while (*from1) *to++ = *from1++;

  /*  now the second  */
  while (*from2) *to++ = *from2++;

  /*  and then tag on a terminator  */
  *to = '\0';

}

/*
 *  max_Str() : Count maximum length of a string
 */
int max_Str ( char  * *string, int   count )
{
  int max, i;

  for ( max = 0, i = 0; i < count; ++string, ++i)
     if ( strlen(*string) > max ) max = strlen( *string );

  return(max);
}

/*
 *  position_Str() : Return position of a character 'key'
 *                   in the input string 'string'. Return
 *                   -1 if key character is not in string
 */
int position_Str( char **string, char key, int  count )
{
  static  int position = 0;
  int     i;
  char    *ptr;

  for ( i = 0; i < count; ++i )
    {
       position = ++position % count;
       ptr = *( string + position );
       if ( *ptr == key )
          return( position );
    }
  return(-1);
}

/*
 * PROCEDURE numeric_compare()
 *
 *  Inputs: string1, and string2
 *  Output: Returns 1 if string1 is numerically > string2
 *                  0 if   "      "      "         =   "
 *                 -1 if   "      "      "         <   "
 *
```

```
 *   This procedure numerically compares two strings.
 */

int    numeric_compare( char   *string1, char   *string2 )
{
   float    string1_val,      /* To hold floating point
                                 value of String1          */
            string2_val;      /* To hold floating point
                                 value of String2          */

    /* Convert ASCII string1 & string2 to Float */
    string1_val = atof( string1 );
    string2_val = atof( string2 );

    if ( string1_val > string2_val )
        return( 1 );
    else if ( string1_val == string2_val )
        return( 0 );
    else                      /*  string1_val < string2_val  */
        return( - 1 );
}
```

3.17 Application: A Small Word Processor

Word processing is a common application of strings. The following is originally presented by Lafore (1987) as an example of a word processor. This small word processor has the following features:

1. *Insert:* To insert a character, the user simply moves the cursor to the desired position and starts typing.
2. *Delete:* To delete a character, the user hits the BACKSPACE key. This deletes the character to the left of the cursor. Any characters to the right of the deleted character will be shifted left to fill in the space.
3. *Underline:* Underline word(s). To start underlining, the user types the [Alt] [u] key combination; to stop underlining, the user types the [Alt] [u] key combination again.

The program design approach takes advantage of

1. dos.h: CPU registers are declared as a union of structures
2. int86(): Turbo C provided an interrupt service routine to access CPU registers, the addresses of which are defined in BIOS ROM.

This implementation gets characters from the terminal. It can be modified to do the following:

1. Get input from a string buffer.
2. Print the string.
3. Position cursor at the beginning of the string to perform insert, delete, and underline operations.

The C program (Lafore, 1987) of the small word processor is presented in Example 3.17.

Example 3.17

```
/*
 * Program:   Word_Procr.c
 * System:    MS-DOS plus Turbo C
 *
 * Purpose:   Develop a small Word Processor
 *            implementing the following operations:
 *                1) Insert    :   Insert a character
 *                2) Delete    :   Delete a character
 *                3) Underline :   Underline a word
 *
 * NOTE: This program uses dos.h and int86 interrupt
 *       routine.
 */

#include "dos.h"              /* for REGS definition */
union REGS regs;             /* for ROM BIOS calls */

/*
 *          GLOBAL VARIABLES  for WORDPROCESSOR PROGRAM
 */
#define COMAX   0x50          /* max number of columns (80) */
#define R_ARRO  0x4D          /* right arrow */
#define L_ARRO  0x4B          /* left arrow  */
#define BK_SPC  0x08          /* backspace   */
#define ATL_U   0x16          /* [Alt] and [u] keys */
#define VIDEO   0x10          /* video ROM BIOS service */
#define NORM    0x07          /* normal attribute */
#define UNDR    0x01          /* underline attribute */
#define CTRL_C  0x03          /* [Ctrl] [C] */

#define START   0xB0000000
#define CLEAR   0x700

int col = 0;                 /* cursor position */
int length = 0;              /* length of phrase */
int far *far_ptr;

/*
 *  main():   WORDPROCESSOR PROGRAM
 */
main()
{
   char ch, attr=NORM;

   far_ptr = (int far *) START;/* start of screen memory */
   clear_screen();              /* Clear screen          */
   cursor();                    /* position cursor       */
   while ((ch = getch()) != CTRL_C) /* exit on [Ctrl] [C]*/
     {
       if ( ch == 0 )            /* if char is 0          */
         {
           ch = getch();         /* read extended code    */
```

```
            switch ( ch )
            {
               case R_ARRO: if (col < length) ++col; break;
               case L_ARRO: if (col > 0)        --col; break;
               case ALT_U:
                          attr = (attr == NORM) ? UNDR : NORM;
            }
         }
      else
         switch( ch )
         {
            case BK_SPC: if (length > 0) delete(); break;
            default:     if (length < COMAX) insert(ch,attr);
         }
      cursor();
   }
}

/*
 *  cursor(): Move cursor to Row 0 and Column (input)
 *            in the screen
 */
cursor()
{
   regs.h.ah = 2;          /* 'set cursor pos' service */
   regs.h.dl = col;        /* column varies            */
   regs.h.dh = 0;          /* always top row           */
   regs.h.bh = 0;          /* page zero                */
   int86(VIDEO, &regs, &regs); /* call video interrupt */
}

/*
 *  insert(): Insert a character in the current
 *            cursor position
 *  Input: attr - Attribute such as NORMal, UNDERline
 */
insert(char ch, char attr)
{
   int j;
   for (j=length; j<col; j--) /* shift characters right*/
      *(far_ptr + j) = *(far_ptr +j -1);/* to make room*/
   *(far_ptr + col) = ch | attr<<8; /* insert character*/
   ++length;                        /* increment count */
   ++col;                           /* move cursor right*/
}

/*
 *  delete(): Delete a character at position one of
 *            current cursor
 */
delete()
{
   int j;
```

```
      for (j=col; j<=length; j++)          /* shift chars left */
         *(far_ptr + j - 1) = *(far_ptr + j);
      --length;                            /* decrement count  */
      --col;                               /* move cursor left */
   }

/*
 *   clear_screen (): Clear screen by inserting 0 at
 *                    every location.
 */
clear_screen()
{
   int j;

   for (j=0; j<200; j++)             /* fill screen memory   */
       *(far_ptr + j) = CLEAR;       /* with 0's (attr = 07) */
}
```

Exercises

3-1 Write a C program to implement a Pig Latin Generator that will accept a
     line of English text, and print out the corresponding Pig Latin text form.
     A Pig Latin word is constructed from an English word by shifting the first
     sound (usually the first letter) to the end of the word, and then adding the
     letter "a." For example, Pig Latin forms of "man" and "end" are re-
     spectively "anma" and "ndea." (*Hint:* A word of text can be viewed as a
     one-dimensional array of characters.)

3-2 Write a program that will read in values of the coefficients A, B, C, and D
     of a cubic polynomial $f(x) = Ax^3 + Bx^2 + Cx + D$, will print a
     graph of it, and will also print out values of x and $f(x)$ in tabular form.

3-3 Write a program to read a set of test scores, store them in a one-dimen-
     sional array, calculate the average score, and assign letter grades to each
     score, such as A if the score is greater than or equal to 90, B for a score
     between 80 and 90, C for a score between 60 and 80, D for a score be-
     tween 50 and 60, and F for a score less than 50. The program must print
     out the scores, the corresponding letter grade, and the average score.

3-4 Write a program to graphically display a random number generator in the
     form of a vertical histogram. The generator's domain is divided into equal
     subranges along the horizontal axis, and its histogram of the count of ran-
     dom numbers over each subrange is vertically displayed.

3-5 Write a program to graphically represent Pascal's triangle for the first 12
     rows, as follows:

```
                  1
               1     1
            1     2     1
         1     3     3     1
      1     4     6     4     1
```

     (*Hint:* Every row starts and ends with 1.)

3-6 Write a program that prints all input strings whose lengths are greater than 72.

3-7 Write a program that reverses and prints all input strings.

3-8 Write a program that counts the number of words in all input strings.

3-9 Write a string parsing program that parses all input strings in order to find the matching member of the following pairs:

    1. left and right braces
    2. left and right parentheses
    3. left and right brackets
    4. double quotes

in a string. The number of occurrences of the matching member may be more than one, and must be reported.

    The function parses the given input string for braces, parentheses, brackets, and quotes. The C syntax is followed:

    1. For every open (left) brace, parentheses, brackets, or quote, there should be a matching close (right). Number of open (left) = number of close (right)
    2. Before the innermost open brace or parentheses or bracket close, others cannot be closed. For example: { {[}] } is invalid, (] is invalid, {) is invalid.
    3. Braces can not be nested inside parentheses or brackets. For example : ([]{()}) is invalid
    4. After the open quote any char can follow any other character until the close quote. For example: `"abcdef{]{]]]]]"` is valid
    5. Quotes cannot be nested. For example: `"xyz("abc")"` is considered as two strings `"xyz("` and `")."`

3-10 Write a program that strips off all comment lines in a C program. Print the modified form of the C program.

3-11 Write a string-compression program that replaces all blank lines, blank spaces, and tabs in a string by special symbols. Print the modified form of the string. (*Note:* Remember the rules of using special symbols in order to perform decompression.)

3-12 Write a string-decompression program that converts all special symbols into corresponding blank lines, blank spaces, and tabs in a string. Print the string. (*Hint:* This is the reverse process of Exercise 3-11.)

3-13 [See Leestma and Nyhoff (1987).] Write a program with the following features:

    1. Reads first, middle, and last names
    2. Sorts them alphabetically by last name
    3. Prints the sorted list in the form:

    `Last_name, First_name Middle_name`

(*Hint:* Use `strcmp`.)

3-14 [See Holub (1987).] What does the following program print? Explain.

```
#include <stdio.h>

main()
{
  static int array[6][2] =
    {
      {' ', 's'}, {'d', 'r'}, {'a', 'w'},
      {'k', 'c'}, {'s', 'b'}, {'c', 'd'}
    };

  int    *p = (int *)(array + 4);

  for( ++p; p >= (int *)array; putchar( *p--) )
         ;
}
```

3-15 [See Holub (1987).] What does the following program print? What is an
   array (in words)? Draw a picture of it. Explain what's happening in all
   five arguments to printf() and why they evaluate to what they do.

```
main()
{
  static char *array[2][3] =
    {
      { "  c", "ng ", " no" },
      { "usi", "fun", "onf" }
    };

  printf("%s%s%s%s\n", **array, *(*(array+1)+2),
         *array[1], array[0][1] );
}
```

3-16 The word processing program gets characters as inputs from the terminal. Modify it to implement the following:

      1. Get input from a string buffer.
      2. Print the string.
      3. Position the cursor at the beginning of the string to perform in-
         sert, delete, and underline operations.

3-17 For a programming project, write a secured file system that implements
   its security from unauthorized users, and a command language interpreter (CLI). It allows 10 users, which are predefined as records containing the user's name and password. The users' records are stored in
   an array of structs. The security is implemented through the login
   (log-in) process. After the validity check, the program transfers control
   to its CLI part. The CLI parses the command line, and transfers control
   to the appropriate function to execute the command. It reports an error
   for an invalid command. The main features of the program are described
   below:

      1. When it is first invoked, it displays "SECURED FILE SYS-
         TEM V1.0" and prompts "login: ".

2. At the `login` prompt, it expects a user name (`user_id`). If the `user_id` is valid, it prompts "`Password:` "; when the user types the password, the password will not be echoed.

3. It allows three retries in case of invalid combination of the `user_id` and `Password`.

4. For the valid user, it prompts "`CLI> `".

5. At the `CLI>` prompt, it expects a line containing a valid command.

6. If the command is valid, and the syntax of the specified command is correct, it executes the command. The execution of the commands can be performed using the file system related commands of the host operating system. (*Hint:* In Unix, you can form the command line, and then call `system()` to execute it.)

The commands are stored in a table. The CLI is case-sensitive. The syntax and description of the commands are given below:

Command syntax	Description
`Copy_fl    <src_file>  <dest_file>`	Copy a file.
`Delete_fl  <target_fl>`	Delete a file.
`Display_fl <file_name>`	Display the content of a file to the terminal.
`Rename_fl  <src_file> <dest_file>`	Rename a file.
`Find_fl    <file_name>`	Find a file.
`Help       <command>`	Get help on the specified command.
`Show_date`	Show today's date.
`Exit`	Exit to the host operating system.

You can use your program name as the source file. The files are assumed to be in your current directory.

CHAPTER 4

Recursion

So far we have discussed the basic data types available in C. We have studied some straightforward operations on these data types.

Suppose we needed to do an iterative operation on some data, and the result of the operation were to be a part of the next operation.

If the number of iterations were small, we could write the steps in-line, but as the number of iterations grows, we would resort to a loop or a function call inside a loop. This would be a suitable solution for a simple problem, but suppose that the operations were such that some conditions required that the operation be executed again before the current operation was complete.

Let us consider, as an example, determining the meaning of a sentence. Suppose `meaning( char *string )` is the operation, `string` is at first the sentence, a sequence of characters, and the sentence is composed of phrases `phrase1`, `phrase2`, and `phrase3`. The function `meaning()` is to return the meaning. The call to `meaning( char *sentence )` decomposes the sentence to `phrase1`, . . . , `phrase3`. Now it must extract the meaning of each phrase, so it calls `meaning( phrase1 )`, which decomposes `phrase1` into words: `word1`, `word2`, . . . , `wordk`. Then `meaning()` is called for each word: `meaning( word1 )`, which returns a meaning, which is stored in some structure. When `phrase1` is exhausted, the call to `meaning( phrase1 )` returns with a value that represents the meaning of `phrase1`. The same sequence occurs for `phrase2` and `phrase3`. Finally, the meanings of the phrases are merged and the call to `meaning( sentence )` returns with a meaning for the whole sentence. This is a paraphrasing of a computer algorithm called *parsing*.

This type of operation is called *recursive*. It is a useful replacement for iteration whenever it is necessary to jump out of the current operation, keeping track of the current state of data, by calling the operation again.

4.1 Definition of Recursion

Recursion occurs when a function calls itself directly or indirectly. A function is directly recursive when it calls itself from within its own scope. A function is indirectly recursive when it calls a set of other functions that eventually calls this function.

Implementation of a recursive function requires five steps:

Step 1. Begin with the nonrecursive case as the terminating condition.
Step 2. Perform the next simplest case.
Step 3. Redefine and/or redo the next case in step 2 in terms of the previous case's returned values.
Step 4. If the termination criterion is not satisfied, call the function recursively to compute the next case. (The succeeding values of the function are calculated in terms of the previously defined values.)
Step 5. Return the value for the current case on returning from the recursive call. (The return values may be simple data type, or structured data types, e.g., `struct`, `pointer`, `array`.)

Steps 2 through 5 are called *inductive* steps.

Recursive functions must have a termination criterion also known as *anchor,* usually when the nonrecursive case is reached.

When implementing a recursive function, one must consider how its arguments are put into the stack. Each invocation gets a fresh copy of auto variables, totally independent of the previous set of values.

We will discuss several examples of recursion used for computing factorial, binomial coefficient, and power, and for creating, printing, and counting linked lists. Besides these, there are many examples of recursion in this book. A recursive function is more elegant and takes fewer variables to make the same calculations done than its iterative counterpart. In some cases, the use of the recursive method is inefficient. For some applications (e.g., linked lists, trees) recursive programming is easy to maintain, understand, and write. This is the major reason for using recursion.

For the recursive `factorial ()` function in Example 4-2 (in the Examples section at the end of this chapter), Figure 4-1 depicts the five levels of function calls generated by the initial call `factorial (4)`. (*Note:* ↓ means "calls to" and ↑ means "returns.") At the end of the fifth function call when the value of *n* reaches 0 (the terminating case value), no more function calls to `factorial ()` are generated. The value 1 is assigned to `factorial` in the fifth function call. The fifth function call is completed and it returns 1 to the preceding (fourth) function call in which the parameters are 1 and 1. Their product is 1 and is returned to the preceding (third) function call. The third function call computes the product of 2 and 1, and returns 2 to the preceding (second) function call. The second function call computes the product of 3 and 2, and returns 6 to the preceding (first) function call. Finally, the first function call computes the product of 4 and 6, and returns the product 24 to the expression originated from `main ()`.

We want to discuss the effects of iterative and recursive functions on stacks and function calls using the two versions of the `factorial ()` function. In the iterative implementation of Example 4-1, at the call of the `factorial ()` function in the `printf (..., factorial (n) )` statement in `main ()`, the address of this statement as its return address and the value 4 are pushed onto the C-stack. Then the `factorial ()` function begins execution. It obtains the value 4 from the C-stack frame and continues its calculation. At the completion it pops the return address of the calling function from the C-stack, and returns the computed result 24

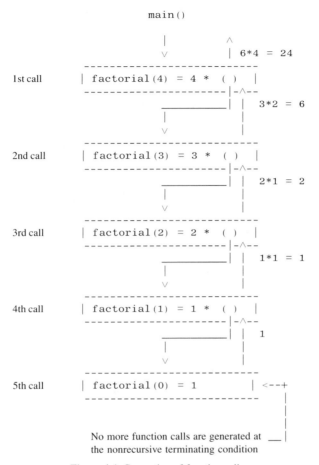

Figure 4-1 Generation of function calls.

and transfers control back to the calling function, main(). The call to an iterative function does not create excessive storage usage of the C-stack.

In the following section, we now turn our attention to recursive function calls and stack with the function's arguments in it.

4.2 The C-Stack and Recursion

To facilitate discussion, we will briefly sketch the recursive version of the fac-torial() function as detailed in the Example 4-2.

```
          .
          .
          .
int  factorial ( int  n )
{                  .
                   .
                   .
```

```
return address  Y -->  return( n * factorial( n - 1 ));
                          .
                          .
                          .


              } /*      END of factorial()    */

              main()
              {
                          .
                          .
                          .

return address  X -->  printf("\n\n Factorial of %d = %15d
                                \n\n", n, factorial(n) );
                          .
                          .
                          .

              }  /* END of main()    */
```

The state of the stack of the C compiler is shown in Figure 4-2. Note that there might be quite a bit of space between the elements in this stack frame. Notice that when the calling program main() calls the routine factorial(4), the value 4 for the argument and the address of the printf(. . . , factorial(n)) statement were pushed onto the C-stack. The stack frame is the working area for the C-compiler; it grows by push operations caused by function calls, and it shrinks by pop operations by function returns. Execution of the function factorial() is complete by the successive pop operations until the stack frame is empty. For more information on these operations, see Chapter 5. The call to a recursive function does create an additional burden on the CPU and storage requirement and usage of the C-stack.

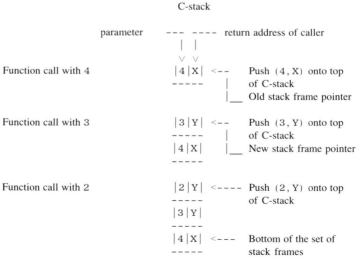

Figure 4-2 The C-stack.

```
Function call with 1            |1|Y|  <---- Push (1,Y) onto top
                                -----        of C-stack
                                |2|Y|
                                -----
                                |3|Y|
                                -----
                                |4|X|  <--- Bottom of the set of
                                -----       stack frames


Function call with 0            |0|Y|  <---- Push (0,Y) onto top
                                -----        of C-stack (this is
                                |1|Y|        the complete stack
                                -----        frame for the
                                |2|Y|        recursive function
                                -----        factorial() )
                                |3|Y|
                                -----
                                |4|X|  <--- Bottom of the set of
                                -----       stack frames


                                  --> 0 Y
                                   |
First function return           |1|Y|        Pop stack, taking out 0,
                                -----        and return to popped
                                |2|Y|        address Y
                                -----
                                |3|Y|
                                -----
                                |4|X|  <--- Bottom of the set of
                                -----       stack frames


                                  --> 1 Y
                                   |
Second function return          |2|Y|        Pop stack, taking out 1,
                                -----        and return to popped
                                |3|Y|        address y
                                -----
                                |4|X|  <--- Bottom of the set of
                                -----       stack frames


                                  --> 2 Y
                                   |         Pop stack, taking out 2,
Third function return           |3|Y|        and return to popped
                                -----        address Y
                                |4|X|  <--- Bottom of the stack
                                -----       frames


                                  --> 3 Y
                                   |
Fourth function return          -----        Pop stack, taking out 3,
                                |4|X|        and return to popped
                                -----        address Y


                                  --> 4 X
                                   |
Final function return           -----        Pop stack, taking out 4,
                                             popped address X
                                             (the stack frame for
                                             this function does
                                             not exist any more)
```

Figure 4-2 *(continued)*

4.3 An Improved Recursive Function for Fibonacci Numbers

We intend to present an improved version of a routine that calculates Fibonacci numbers. As in the first version of calculating Fibonacci numbers in Example 4-4, note the following sequence of execution to calculate the Fibonacci number F4:

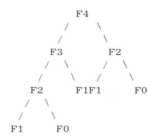

To calculate F4 we need to calculate F3, which needs F2, which needs F1, which is a nonrecursive stopping criterion. F2 also needs F0. It can be shown that in order to calculate a Fibonacci number Fn, this algorithm will require a total number of F (n+1) calculations.

Calculation of F3 depends on the two previous numbers, F2 and F1. In order to devise a faster recursive version of it, we will modify the first recursive approach as follows:

```
int Fibonacci_2 (int n, int Previous_1, int Previous_2)
{
    int next_Fib;
    if (n == 0)
        return (Previous_2);
    else if (n == 1)
        return (Previous_1);
    else
        next_Fib = Fibonacci_2 (n-1, Previous_1+Previous_2,
                                Previous_1);
        return (next_Fib);
}
```

To calculate Fibonacci number for n=4, the call to the above function Fibonacci_2 (4, 1, 0) will generate the following sequence of three successive recursive function calls:

```
                    Fibonacci_2 (3, 1, 1),
                    Fibonacci_2 (2, 2, 1),
                    Fibonacci_2 (1, 3, 2)
```

The last function call Fibonacci_2 (1, 3, 2) exhibits a nonrecursive stopping criterion. This returns 2, which is F4.

We first show how to write a factorial function in an iterative form (see Example 4-1). Its recursive implementation is shown in Example 4-2.

Examples

Example 4-1

Code Section

```
/*  Program Name: factorial.c (Iterative Version)
 *
 *  Purpose: To implement Factorial function
 *
 *      n! = n * ( n - 1 ) * ( n - 2 ) * . . . * 3 * 2 * 1
 *
 *      as an Iterative Function. The program requests
 *      input from user.
 */


/*
 * factorial(): Returns integer value n!   (Iterative
 *                 Version)
 */
int factorial( int n )
{
    int  i,  product;

    if ( n < 0 )
       {
         printf("\n\n Factorial: ERROR: %s \n\n",
                "input n is negative ");
         exit(1);
       }
    else if ((n == 0) || (n == 1))
        return (1);
    else if ( n > 1 )
       {
         product = 1;
         for ( i = n; i > 1; i-- )
            product *= i;       /* product = product * i  */
         return ( product );
       }
}


/*
 * main(): FACTORIAL FUNCTION (ITERATIVE IMPLEMENTATION)
 */
main()
{
    int n;

    printf("\n To iteratively calculate %s",
           "factorial, enter n = ");
    scanf("%d", &n);
    printf("\n\n Factorial of %d = %15d \n\n",
           n, factorial(n) );
}
```

Output Section

```
To iteratively calculate factorial, enter n = 4

Factorial of 4 =                    24
```

Example 4-2

Code Section

```c
/*  Program Name: factorial.c (Recursive Version)
 *
 *  Purpose: To implement the Factorial function
 *
 *                n! = n * ( n - 1 )!,
 *          with terminating cases:
 *              1! = 1, 0! = 1
 *          as a Recursive Function. The program requests
 *          input from the user.
 */

int factorial( int  n )
{
   if ( n < 0 )
     {
       printf("\n\n Factorial: ERROR: %s \n\n",
              "input n is negative ");
       exit(1);
     }
   else if (n == 0)
       return (1);
   else
       return ( n * factorial( n - 1 ) );
 }

main()
{
   int n;

   printf("\n To recursively calculate %s",
          "factorial, enter n = ");
   scanf("%d", &n);
   printf("\n\n Factorial of %d = %15d \n\n",
          n, factorial(n) );
}
```

Output Section

```
To recursively calculate factorial, enter n = 4

Factorial of 4 =                    24
```

Example 4-3

Code Section

```c
/*  Program Name: gcd.c
 *
```

```
 *   Purpose:   To recursively calculate the Greatest Common
 *              Divisor (GCD) of two integers a and b.
 */

/*
 * greatest_common_divisor():   Returns integer value for gcd
 */
int greatest_common_divisor( int a, int b )
{
    int    remainder;

    if ( (remainder = a % b) == 0)
        return (b);
    else
        return ( greatest_common_divisor( b, remainder ) );
}
main()
{
    int a = 20, b = 14;

    printf("\n\n %s a = %d  b = %d  is  %15d \n",
           "Greatest Common Divisor of",
           a, b, greatest_common_divisor(a, b) );
}
```

Output Section

```
    Greatest Common Divisor of a = 20  b = 14  is   2
```

Example 4-4

Code Section
```
/* Program Name: fibonacci.c   (Recursive Version)
 *
 * Purpose:   To recursively calculate the Fibonacci Numbers
 *              0, 1, 1, 2, 3, 5, 8, 13, 21, 34, ...
 *              that follow rule as shown below:
 *
 *                  fib_no[ 0 ] = 0
 *                  fib_no[ 1 ] = 1
 *
 *                  For n >= 2,
 *                    fib_no[ n ] = fib_no[ n - 2 ] +
 *                                  fib_no[ n - 1 ]
 */

/* No_Fibonacci_func_call is useful to check efficiency */
int  No_Fibonacci_func_call = 0;

/*
 * fibonacci_no(): Returns an integer value of
 *                 Fibonacci number
 */
```

```
int fibonacci_no( int n )
{
    ++No_Fibonacci_func_call;

    if ( n < 0 )
      {
        printf("\n\n fibonacci_no: ERROR: n must be >= 0 \n");
        exit( 1 );
      }
    else if ( n <= 1 )
          return ( n );
    else
          return ( fibonacci_no( n - 2 ) +
                     fibonacci_no( n - 1 ) );
}

/*
 * main(): Compute 26 FIBONACCI NUMBERS
 */
main()
{
  int  Number_of_times = 26,
       n;

  printf("\n\n Value of n   Value of Fibonacci_no( n ) ");
  printf(" No of Fib Func call");
  printf("\n --------------------------------");
  printf("---------------------------\n");

  for ( n = 0; n < Number_of_times; ++n)
     printf("\n %10d   %15d %25d", n,
             fibonacci_no( n ), No_Fibonacci_func_call );

   printf("\n\n Generation of Fibonacci numbers %s \n\n",
          "using Recursive method is complete ");
}
```

Output Section

```
Value of n   Value of Fibonacci_no( n )  No of Fib Func call
------------------------------------------------------------
```

Value of n	Value of Fibonacci_no(n)	No of Fib Func call
0	0	0
1	1	1
2	1	2
3	2	5
4	3	10
5	5	19
6	8	34
7	13	59
8	21	100
9	34	167
10	55	276
11	89	453
12	144	740

13	233	1205
14	377	1958
15	610	3177
16	987	5150
17	1597	8343
18	2584	13510
19	4181	21871
20	6765	35400
21	10946	57291
22	17711	92712
23	28657	150025
24	46368	242760
25	75025	392809

Generation of Fibonacci numbers using Recursive method is complete

Example 4-5

Code Section

```
/*  Program Name: binomial_coeff.c
 *
 *  Purpose:  To recursively calculate Binomial oefficients
 *          n
 *         C   or ( n | r )   ( n and r are positive integers)
 *          r
 *
 *            that follow following rule:
 *
 *              ( n | 0 ) = 1
 *              ( n | n ) = 1
 *
 *              For  0 < r < n,
 *              ( n | r ) = ( n - 1 | r - 1 ) + ( n - 1 | r )
 */


/*
 * binomial_coeff ():   Returns  n
 *                              C    or  ( n | r )
 *                               r
 */
float binomial_coeff( int n, int r )
{
   if ( n < 0  ||  r < 0  )
     {
       printf("\n binomial_coeff: ERROR: %s \n",
             "n & r must be positive ");
       exit(1);
     }
   else if ( n < r )
     {
        printf("\n binomial_coeff: ERROR: n must be >= r\n");
        exit(2);
     }
```

```
    else if ( r == 0 || r == n)
        return ( 1 );
    else
        return( binomial_coeff( n - 1, r - 1 ) +
                binomial_coeff( n - 1, r       )   );
}

/*
 * main():   BINOMIAL COEFFICIENT (RECURSIVE FUNCTION)
 */
main()
{
    int   n = 10,
          r = 7;

    printf("\n\n %s %d  & r = %d   is   %15f \n\n",
           "Binomial Coeff of n = ", n, r,
            binomial_coeff( n, r ) );
}
```

Output Section

```
Binomial Coeff of n = 10  & r = 7   is        120.000000
```

Exercises

4-1 A *palindrome* is an alphanumeric word that is the same when read from
    left to right or right to left (for example, "1234321," "TOOT,"
    "ATOYOTA," "STATS," "LEVEL," "ROTOR," "BUB," etc.). Write
    a recursive program to detect palindromes.

4-2 Write a recursive function to produce all $n!$ permutations of the n ele-
    ments $X[0]$, $X[1]$, . . . , $X[n\text{-}1]$.

4-3 The eight queens problem can be solved quite elegantly by the use of re-
    cursion. The problem is to place eight queens on a chessboard so that
    no queen is attacking another. Begin the program design by defining an
    8×8 array board:

```
int   board[8][8];
      board[i][j] is a square.
      board[i][j] == TRUE if there is a queen on the
                     square, else it is FALSE.
```

noattack() is a function that returns TRUE if no queen is attacking
another on the current board. It checks for attack at each queen/true
location:

                    1. On vertical axis
                    2. On horizontal axis
                    3. On southeast diagonal axis
                    4. On northwest diagonal axis
                    5. On southwest diagonal axis
                    6. On northeast diagonal axis

place() is the function that places queens on the board. It calls no-
attack() to check whether a placement is valid. The recursive func-

tion place() returns TRUE if it is possible to add queens in rows n through BDSIZE without attacking queens. place() returns FALSE if there is no solution. Write the function noattack() and run the program to show that the program produces a correct solution. If no-attack() returns FALSE or place(n + 1) returns FALSE, then board[n][i] is set to FALSE. This causes the program to backtrack and try board[n][i+1] (if i < BDSIZE) or board[n-1][i+1] (if i > BDSIZE). Here is a sample code of the program:

```
#define BDSIZE 8
#define FALSE   0
#define TRUE    ~FALSE
int      board[BDSIZE][BDSIZE];

int  noattack( int board[][BDSIZE] )
{
    /* Body of the function to be written */
}

/*  place(): Recursive function to place queens
 *           on a n x n board.
 */
int  place( int n )
{
    int result, i;

    if ( n >= BDSIZE )
        return( TRUE );
    else
    {
        result = FALSE;
        i = 0;
        while ( i < BDSIZE && result == FALSE )
        {
            board[n][i] = TRUE;
            if ( noattack( board ) && place( n + 1 ) )
                result = TRUE;
            else
            {
                board[n][i] = FALSE;
                i++;
            }
        }
        return( result );
    }
}

/*  print_board():
 *     Graphically display a board. Queens
 *     are indicated by displaying their
 *     horizontal and vertical position.
 *     Empty locations are displayed
 *     without a position.
 */
```

```
void  print_board ( int  board[][BDSIZE] )
{
    int i, j, result;

    for ( i = 0; i < BDSIZE; i++ )
       {
         printf("\n\n\t");
         for ( j = 0; j < BDSIZE; j++ )
            {
                if ( board[i][j] == TRUE )
                  printf(" [%D,%d] ", i, j );
                else
                  printf("[   ] " );
            }
         printf("\n");
       }
}


main()
{
    int i, j, result;

    /*  Initialize board */
    for ( i = 0; i < BDSIZE; i++ )
        for ( j = 0; j < BDSIZE; j++ )
                board[i][j] = FALSE;

    result = place( 0 );
    if ( result == TRUE )
    {
        printf("\n EIGHT QUEENS PROBLEM \n");
        printf("\n Success: \n\t");
        print_board( board );
    }
    else
      exit( FALSE );
}
```

Here is a sample solution:

```
[0,0] [   ] [   ] [   ] [   ] [   ] [   ] [   ]

[   ] [   ] [   ] [   ] [1,4] [   ] [   ] [   ]

[   ] [   ] [   ] [   ] [   ] [   ] [   ] [2,7]

[   ] [   ] [   ] [   ] [   ] [3,5] [   ] [   ]

[   ] [   ] [4,2] [   ] [   ] [   ] [   ] [   ]

[   ] [   ] [   ] [   ] [   ] [   ] [5,6] [   ]

[   ] [6,1] [   ] [   ] [   ] [   ] [   ] [   ]

[   ] [   ] [   ] [7,3] [   ] [   ] [   ] [   ]
```

4-4 The Hanoi trainyard has three tracks side-by-side that merge into the track leading out of Hanoi. On a particular morning there are 6 cars on track A, and tracks B and C are empty. The trainyard master wants to move the cars to track C in order to make some repairs to track A. The cars must end up in the same order on track C, so that the afternoon train can leave the yard without any delay. Unfortunately, the venerable train-yard engine is old and a little weak, so it can only pull one car at a time. Having heard of the famous Towers of Hanoi problem, the trainyard master decides to move the cars in such a way that no car originally behind another is in front of it at any time. Write a program to describe the movements of the cars. The program should recursively make the moves, printing out the current state of the cars on each track for each step. [*Hint:* Less than 20 lines of code, including declarations, are needed. See Tanenbaum (1987) for analysis of the Towers of Hanoi problem.]

4-5 Write a string parsing recursive program that parses all input strings in order to find matching member of the pairs (a) left and right braces, (b) left and right parentheses, (c) left and right brackets, and (d) double quotes in a string. The number of occurrences of the matching member may be more than one, and must be reported. Indicate the error by placing an up-arrow underneath that character. For more details, see Exercise 3-9.

4-6 Write a program to find all solutions to the eight queens problem.

4-7 To reinstill the backtracking concept, write a program modifying the eight queens problem in Exercise 4-3 that will deal with four queens. In this four queens problem, the board is a 4 × 4 square, and the rules are the same as in Exercise 4-3.

4-8 Write a program to find all solutions to the four queens problem.

4-9 *Maze problem:* The maze problem is of interest in problem solving and error debugging that use backtracking and tracing. Rats use backtracking when trying to traverse a maze. A maze can be simulated as a cell. We will use "U" to mean a cell is used and "V" to mean a cell is vacant. The maze in the following figure is a 6 × 6 square, partitioned into cells.

```
                        Columns
                 Start
                   |
                   V
                   0    1    2    3    4    5
                 ---------------------------
             0   | V  | U  | V  | U  | U  | U  |
                 |----|---|---|---|---|---|
             1   | V  | V  | V  | V  | U  | V  |
                 |----|---|---|---|---|---|
     Rows    2   | V  | U  | V  | U  | V  | U  |
                 |----|---|---|---|---|---|
             3   | U  | U  | V  | V  | U  | U  |
                 |----|---|---|---|---|---|
             4   | V  | U  | V  | V  | V  | U  |
                 |----|---|---|---|---|---|
             5   | U  | V  | U  | U  | V  | V  |
                 ---------------------------
                                         ^
                                         |_____   End of travel
```

In the above maze, the starting point of the travel is the cell at the top left corner (0,0), and the endpoint of his travel is the cell at the bottom right corner (5,5). While traveling through the maze, the rat may follow a path, which will encounter a dead end (caused by a cell, marked as U). Since some of the cells in the maze are used, one path of his travel from the cell at (0,0) to the cell at (5,5) includes the following adjacent cells (that is, cells with a common side) at

$$(0,0), (1,0), (1,1), (1,2), (2,2), (3,2),$$
$$(3,3), (4,3), (4,4), (5,4), (5,5).$$

(a) Write out any other paths from (0,0) to (5,5).
(b) Write algorithms for the following operations on an ADT maze:
    (i) Initialize a $n \times n$ maze
    (ii) Check whether two cells are adjacent
    (iii) Add a cell in the path
    (iv) Delete a cell from a path
    (v) Check whether the cell is a dead end
    (vi) Check whether you have tried the path in this direction, and have encountered a dead end
    (vii) Find a complete path from Start to End
    (viii) Print the maze
    (ix) Print a path

4-10 Write a recursive program using backtracking to search for a path from the start position to the end position through the 6×6 maze. The inputs are:

    (i) Initial state of the 6×6 maze specifying the used cells in the maze
    (ii) Start cell
    (iii) End cell

The output must display a path, or a message if there is no path through the maze. Enter three different sets of input data.

CHAPTER 5

Lists

In Chapter 3 we discussed a very basic data type using arrays. Because of its inherent limitations on structuring and accessing data, we now turn our attention to the ADT lists. The ADT list is a more general case of most ADTs, which we will discuss in this book.

In this chapter we shall discuss ADT lists, such as singly, doubly, and circularly linked lists, together with their implementations. The implementation of lists using arrays will be shown. However, because of its main drawbacks due to fixed allocation requirements and restrictions on accessing data, the array list is not used very frequently in real-world applications. Since C provides strong capabilities of pointer variables and dynamic storage allocation, we will emphasize the pointer implementation of the ADT lists and their associated operations.

Lists are used to order data and to implement such real-world events as a line of people waiting to be served by a bank teller, or a queue of airplanes waiting for a free runway in order to land or take off. The event that the runway is free is controlled and signaled by the airport's control tower. Some other applications of lists include editors, database management systems, window management, and process management in an operating system. For an editor application using a singly linked list, see Chapter 13. For a database application using a doubly linked list, see Chapter 5. For a window application using a doubly linked list, see Chapter 14.

The concept of lists is very fundamental to understanding and implementing ADTs like stacks, queues, trees, and many complex and useful applications, which will be discussed in the succeeding chapters. Their implementations are aided by the pointer variables and dynamic storage allocation facilities in C.

Linked lists are worth using because pointer variables and dynamic storage allocation alleviate any restrictions on such accessing as inserting and deleting data anywhere in the lists, regardless of the type of data.

5.1 The Concept of ADT List

An ADT list is a linear sequence of like data types with the following properties:

1. There is a first element (i.e., head) with a unique successor (i.e., next).
2. There is a last element (i.e., tail) with no successor.

3. Any other element has both one successor (i.e., next) and one predecessor (i.e., previous).

It also performs the following operations:

1. Creating an element
2. Creating a list
3. Checking for an empty list
4. Searching for an element
5. Searching for a predecessor of an element
6. Deleting an element
7. Inserting an element before a specified element
8. Inserting an element after a specified element
9. Retrieving an element
10. Updating an element
11. Sorting a list
12. Printing a list
13. Determining the number of elements in a list
14. Deleting a list
15. Checking whether there is space for another element

The data types can be considered very abstract. The main role in the ADT list structure is played by pointers. The elements in a list are tied together by their successor–predecessor relationship.

An ADT list can be implemented as static or dynamic data using (i) an array and index or (ii) pointers. We now discuss these implementations in detail in the succeeding sections.

5.2 Array Implementation of Lists

A list can be implemented as an array whose elements each consist of

1. Data
2. Key (optional)
3. Location (by index) in list

For elements in the list:

1. Array element [0] has no predecessor
2. Array element [LISTSIZE - 1] has no successor

Note that any other element in the list, with array index i, will have

1. Array element list [i - 1] holding its predecessor
2. Array element list [i + 1] holding its successor

The array implementation is static. Its size is fixed and allocated at compilation time. Thus a list can be conceptually implemented as an array as follows:

Array index	Element data	Predecessor index	Successor index
0	R	NIL	1
1	O	0	2
2	N	1	3
3	A	2	4
4	L	3	5
5	D	4	6
6	Allocated but not used		
. . .			
LISTSIZE - 1	not used	LISTSIZE - 2	NIL

The elements are sequentially stored in `list[0]`, `list[1]`,..., `list [ LISTSIZE - 1 ]`, where `list[0]` is the first element and `list [ LISTSIZE - 1 ]` is the last. The value `NIL` indicates no predecessor or successor element for the element. The elements `list[6]` through `list [ LISTSIZE - 1 ]` are allocated by the array declaration, but are not used. This is inefficient usage of memory space. Any element in the list array can be randomly accessed by its index. Because the elements are contiguously and sequentially stored (i.e., not scattered) in memory, the implementation of a list as an array does not require storing the indices of the predecessor and successor of each element. However, we might implement a list like:

where `FI` is the successor's index and `BI` is the predecessor's index.

In C, we can define such elements of a list as shown in the header file `"list_ary.h"`:

```
typedef   char    elt_data_type;   /* Define Element data type  */
#define   LISTSIZE   8              /* Array Size                */
#define   NIL        -1             /* Indicates no next or prev */
#define   HEAD       0  /* Index for first element in the List */

int       TAIL;          /* Index for last element in the list */

/* Define LIST_ARY as an array type for the list.             */
typedef elt_data_type   LIST_ARY [ LISTSIZE ];

/* Allocates memory spaces for all LISTSIZE number of
 * elements whether or not all of them will be used.
 */
LIST_ARY       list;
```

Note that in the array implementation:

1. Creating an element will not require the `malloc()` system call to allocate memory space.

2. As the size of the list is fixed, the list cannot grow in size if required during program execution.

Because insertion and deletion of an element in the array implementation of a list are most cumbersome and time-consuming, we will discuss them. Our goal is to arrive at some reasonable algorithm for them.

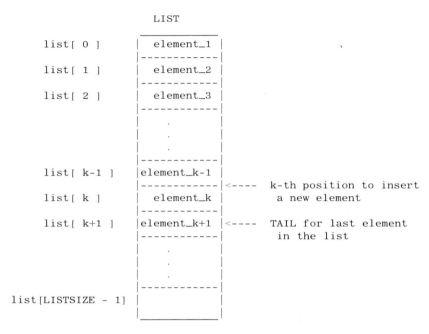

Assuming that `current_inx` is at the `k-th` (*k*th) position for `list[k-1]` element, to insert `new_elt` after `list[k-1]`, we perform the following:

Step 1. `temp_ inx = TAIL + 1`

Step 2. If `temp_inx > LISTSIZE - 1`, return with error message `"INSERT_ERROR: LIST OVERFLOW"`

Step 3. To make room for `new_elt` in `list[k]` position, we must shift elements `list[k]` through `list[last]` to respectively `list[ k + 1 ]` through `list[ TAIL + 1 ]`:

```
list[ TAIL + 1 ] = list[ TAIL ];
list[ TAIL ]     = list[ TAIL - 1 ];
. . .
list[ k + 2 ]    = list[ k + 1 ];
list[ k + 1 ]    = list[ k ];  /* (k+1)-th element
                                  is finally saved*/
```

Step 4. `list[k]    = new_elt;`

Step 5. `current_inx = k;`   /* `new_elt` is current element */

Step 6. `TAIL    = temp_inx;`   /* index of TAIL element after insertion */

Actual C code for the insertion will be left as an exercise.

When we delete an element, say list[k], of the list, it will create a gap in the array. We move all elements up and decrement TAIL by 1. The steps for deleting an element from a list as an array are:

Step 1. Move up elements list[k + 1] through list[TAIL_inx] to respectively list[k] through list[TAIL - 1].
More precisely,

```
list[ k ]          = list[ k + 1 ];
list[ k + 1 ]      = list[ k + 2 ];
. . .
list[ TAIL - 2 ] = list[ TAIL - 1 ];
list[ TAIL - 1 ] = list[ TAIL ];
```

Step 2. current_inx = k;   /* current element */
Step 3. TAIL   = TAIL - 1;   /* index of TAIL elt after deletion */

The C code of most common operations including the above deletion algorithm, is presented in Example 5.1. For the sake of simplicity, we assumed that the list in this example has only nonstructured data, or else assignments must change.

Example 5.1

Code Section

```
/*   Program Name:  list_ary.c
 *   Purpose:       Implement list as an array with
 *                  standard operations.
 */

typedef   char   elt_data_type;        /* Define Element data type  */

#define   NIL        -1                /* Indicates no next or prev */
#define   NOT_FOUND -2
#define   INVALID    -3
#define   LISTSIZE   8                 /* Array Size                */
#define   HEAD       0          /* Index for HEAD element in the List */

int       TAIL;     /* Counter and index for TAIL element in list */

int       current_inx;     /* Index for TAIL element in the list  */

/*    Define LIST_ARY as an array type for the list.               */
typedef elt_data_type   LIST_ARY [ LISTSIZE ];

/*   Allocates memory spaces for all LISTSIZE number of
 *   elements whether or not all of them will be used.
 */
LIST_ARY        list;

/*
 *   init_list(): Initialize  list by setting TAIL = NIL
 */
```

```
void init_list( int  *TAIL )
{
    *TAIL = NIL;
}

/*
 *  is_list_empty(): Return  true if TAIL = NIL
 */
int  is_list_empty( int TAIL )
{
    return ( TAIL == NIL );
}

/*
 *  is_list_full (): Return  true if TAIL = LISTSIZE - 1
 */
int  is_list_full ( int TAIL )
{
    return ( TAIL == (LISTSIZE - 1) );
}

/*
 *  delete_list (): Delete  an entire list
 */
delete_list( int  *TAIL )
{
    *TAIL = NIL;
}

/*
 *  search_elt ():   Search for an element with its key
 *                   value in a list.
 *                   Returns array index if found; otherwise
 *                   NOT_FOUND.
 *                   If successful, set current_inx to the
 *                   returned index in the calling function.
 */
int  search_elt( LIST_ARY list, int TAIL,
                 elt_data_type  element_key )
{
    int   i;
    for ( i = 0; i <= TAIL; i++ )
       {
          if ( element_key == list[ i ] )
             return ( i );      /* Return index of the element */
       }
    printf("\n search_elt: Failed; Element not found \n");
    return( NOT_FOUND );
}

/*
 *  search_prev():  Search for predecessor of an element with
 *                  its key value in a list.
 *                  Returns array index if found; otherwise
 *                  NOT_FOUND.
```

```
 *                      If successful, set current_inx to the
 *                      returned index in the calling function.
 */
int   search_prev( LIST_ARY list, int TAIL,
                   elt_data_type  element_key )
{
     int    srch_index;

     srch_index =  search_elt( list, TAIL, element_key );
     /* Is it the First element in the list ?   */
     if (( srch_index == 0 )   || (srch_index == NOT_FOUND))
        {
           printf("\n search_prev: Failed; %s \n",
                  "Has no Previous Element" );
           return( NOT_FOUND );
        }
     else
           return ( srch_index - 1 );
}


/*
 *  create_elt(): Create an element using Item; Calling function
 *                needs to put it in the list's desired position.
 *                This function will have significance in the
 *                pointer implementation of a list.
 */
elt_data_type create_elt( elt_data_type Item )
{
     return ( Item );
}


/*
 *  delete_elt():  Delete an element specified by its key from a
 *                 list. First search for the element with
 *                 its key value in a list.
 *                 If successful, deletes the element and moves
 *                 up the succeeding elements in the TAIL
 *                 to fill up the gap.
 *
 * Input: *current_inx:   Index of current element; will change
 *                        after delete.
 */
delete_elt ( LIST_ARY list, int *TAIL, int *current_inx,
             elt_data_type  element_key )
{
     int    srch_index, k;

     srch_index =  search_elt( list, *TAIL, element_key );
     if ( srch_index == NOT_FOUND )
        {
           return( srch_index );
        }
     else
        {
```

```
        for ( k = srch_index;  k < *TAIL;  k++ )
           list[ k ] = list[ k + 1 ];
        *current_inx = srch_index;
        --(*TAIL);
      }
}


/*
 *  insert_before():  Insert an element before the current
 *                    or specified element in a list
 */
insert_before( LIST_ARY list, int TAIL, int *current_inx,
              elt_data_type  element_key )
{
            /* Left as an Exercise            */
}


/*
 *  insert_after():   Insert an element after the current
 *                    or specified element in a list
 */
insert_after ( LIST_ARY list, int TAIL, int  *current_inx,
              elt_data_type  element_key )
{
            /* Left as an Exercise            */
}


/*
 *  retrieve_elt():  Retrieve an element from 'position' in
 *                   the list. 'position' allows flexibility. It can
 *                   be current.
 *                   Returns -1 if invalid position index.
 *                   Calling function must check whether the
 *                   return value is -1.
 */
elt_data_type   retrieve_elt ( LIST_ARY list, int TAIL,
                               int position )
{
   if ( (position < 0) || (position > TAIL) )
     {
       printf("\n retrieve_elt: Failed; %s \n",
             "Invalid position parameter" );
       return( INVALID );
     }
   else
      return( list[ position ] );
}


/*
 *  update_elt():  Update an element in a list by its new_value.
 */
update_elt ( LIST_ARY list, int TAIL, int position,
            elt_data_type  new_value )
{
```

```
    if ( (position < 0) || (position > TAIL) )
      {
        printf("\n update_elt: Failed; %s \n",
               "Invalid position parameter" );
        return( INVALID );
      }
    else
        list[ position ] = new_value;
}

/*
 * sort_list():  Sort a list
 */
sort_list( LIST_ARY list, int TAIL )
{
        /*  To be presented in a later chapter  */
}

/*
 *  print_list (): Print all elements list[0] through
 *                 list[TAIL] in the list.
 */
print_list ( LIST_ARY list, int TAIL, char *header )
{
    int   i;
    printf("\n  === List %s  is:  \n", header );
    for ( i = 0; i <= TAIL; ++i )
      printf(" %c ", list[ i ] );
    printf( "\n" );
}

/*
 *  count_elts ( list, TAIL ):  Determine number of elements
 *                              in a list.
 */
int  count_elts ( int TAIL )
{
    return ( TAIL + 1 );
}

/*
 *  main(): OPERATIONS ON ARRAY IMPLEMENTATION OF A LIST
 */
main()
{
   printf("\n === Example of ARRAY IMPLEMENTATION OF LIST === \n");
   init_list( &TAIL );
   list[ HEAD ] = create_elt( 'R' );
   ++TAIL;                          /* Added one element in list */
   list[ ++TAIL ] = create_elt( 'O' );
   list[ ++TAIL ] = create_elt( 'N' );
   print_list ( list, TAIL,  "before update");
```

```
    update_elt ( list, TAIL, 2, 'B' );
    print_list ( list, TAIL,  "after  update");
    delete_elt ( list, &TAIL, &current_inx, 'O' );
    print_list ( list, TAIL,  "after deleting O");
}
```

Output Section

```
    === Example of ARRAY IMPLEMENTATION OF LIST ===

     === List before update  is:
    R   O   N

     === List after  update  is:
    R   O   B

     === List after deleting O  is:
    R   B
```

In this array (static) implementation of a list, we notice the following drawbacks:

1. Memory storage space is wasted, because the list is often less than all the elements of the array as initially declared.
2. The growth of the list is restricted by the declared size of the array.
3. Some operations, such as insertion and deletion, are inefficient because of the need to move all data after the point of change.

5.3 Pointer Implementation of Lists

There are several types of linked list characterized by the number and nature of links used to connect each element of the list. The most common linked lists are:

1. Singly linked list
2. Doubly linked list
3. Circular list using single link
4. Circular list using double links

For the list elements (e.g., each being a character 'S', 'A', 'U', 'R', 'E', 'N'), we can conceptually form a structured list by connecting them using pointers, with head_ptr and tail_ptr respectively pointing to the first and last element of the list. The structures of the singly linked list and the doubly linked list are shown in Figures 5-1 and 5-2, respectively. The structures of the circular singly linked list and the circular doubly linked list are shown in Figures 5-3 and 5-4 (below).

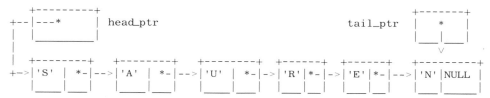

Figure 5-1 A singly linked list with head pointer.

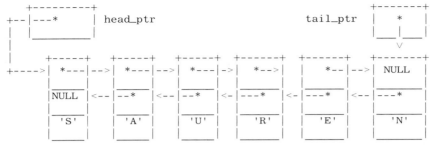

Figure 5-2 A doubly linked list with head and tail pointers.

5.3.1 The Singly Linked List Implementation

An ADT list can be implemented as a singly linked list having each of its elements consisting of

1. The data
2. One link pointing to the next element of the list

In view of ADT, the data could be of the simple or structured type. Considering the data as structured-type data, the element of the list can be, for example:

```
struct slist
    {
        union
        {
            char     ch[8];
            int      in[4];
            double   dbl;
        }
        struct   slist   *next;
    };
```

Thus the element of this singly linked list can be either double, a string of eight characters, or an array of four integers. But for the sake of simplicity, we will consider the simple data type.

Let us define a simple element of a singly linked list by structures of the form

```
typedef char    data_type;      /* Data type for list's element */

struct single_linked_list
  {
    data_type    data;          /* Data part of each element */
    struct single_linked_list   *next_elt;
  };

typedef struct single_linked_list ELEMENT;
typedef ELEMENT     *SINGLE_LINK_LIST;

SINGLE_LINK_LIST  head_ptr;   /* Pointer to First elt in list*/
SINGLE_LINK_LIST  tail_ptr;   /* Pointer to Last  elt in list*/
```

The single-link field `next_elt` is a pointer to the next element of the list. An element with NULL pointer value for `next_elt` will be the last element of the

list. Thus a singly linked list can be viewed as a chain of structs as illustrated in
Example 5.2. Initially, when the list is empty, the values of head_ptr, and tail
_ptr will be NULL. When the list has one element, all three pointers hold the
address of the same element. When the list has two elements, head_ptr points to
the first, and tail_ptr points to the second element.

Example 5.2

Code Section

```
/*
 *   Program Name:   single_lnk_lst.c
 *   Purpose:        Demonstrate a singly linked list by individually
 *                   connecting its elements by pointers.
 */
#define NULL    0
typedef char    data_type;          /* Data type for list's element */

struct slist_element
   {
        data_type    data;          /* Data part of each element    */
        struct  slist_element  *next_elt;
   };

typedef struct slist_element   ELEMENT;
typedef ELEMENT    *SINGLE_LINK_LIST;

main()
{
    ELEMENT    *current, *head,
               element_1,  element_2,  element_3,
               element_4,  element_5,  element_6;

    /*  Start from one element. Then connect (i.e. Link)
     *  the remaining elements together by assigning
     *  their addresses to the pointer next_elt as follows.
     */
    head    = &element_1;

    /* Assign address of element_2 */
    element_1.next_elt = &element_2;

    /* Assign address of element_3 */
    element_2.next_elt = &element_3;

    /* Assign address of element_4 */
    element_3.next_elt = &element_4;

    /* Assign address of element_5 */
    element_4.next_elt = &element_5;

    /* Assign address of element_6 */
    element_5.next_elt = &element_6;

    element_6.next_elt = NULL;
```

```
    /* Assign values to data of each element  */

    element_1.data = 'S';
    element_2.data = 'A';
    element_3.data = 'U';
    element_4.data = 'R';
    element_5.data = 'E';
    element_6.data = 'N';

    /* Print the entire string  */

    printf("\n ==== Example on how to %s \n",
           "form a Singly Linked List ====" );

    printf("\n The string is: ");
    current = head;
    while ( current != NULL )
      {
        printf(" %c -> ", current->data);
        current = current->next_elt;
      }
    printf("NULL");
    printf("\n\n This shows data retrieval %s \n",
           "starting from beginning ");
}
```

Output Section

```
    ==== Example on how to form a Singly Linked List ====

    The string is:  S ->  A ->  U ->  R ->  E ->  N -> NULL
```

This shows data retrieval starting from the beginning.

In the above example, the number of elements is fixed. This approach is not efficient to deal with a large list of elements. We will use pointer variables in that case. SINGLE_LINK_LIST is a pointer to ELEMENT, but its declaration does not reserve any memory space for an element. The entire list in a singly linked implementation can dynamically grow or shrink during the program execution. Thus to create and use an element, we must first allocate memory space by the malloc() system call, as shown in Example 5.3.

Example 5.3

```
/*
 *  Create an element of the list using 'Item' for data field
 */

SINGLE_LINK_LIST create_elt( data_type    Item )
{
    SINGLE_LINK_LIST    new_elt_ptr;

    /*  Allocate a memory space for the new node; if no space
     *  available return with error.
     */
```

```
    new_elt_ptr = (SINGLE_LINK_LIST) malloc(sizeof (ELEMENT))
    if ( new_elt_ptr == NULL )
      {
        printf("\n create_elt: malloc failed  \n\n");
        return ( NO_SPACE );              /* Define NO_SPACE = 0 */
      }
    else
      {
        new_elt_ptr -> data      = Item;  /* Item is input */
        new_elt_ptr -> next_elt = NULL;   /* No next node   */
        return( new_elt_ptr );
      }
}
```

Warning: When we delete an element, we must release the memory space it has held, by the free() system call. Otherwise we will soon run out of memory space, and this will eventually have the following impacts:

1. Performance degradation of the computer system may be caused because the system will be unable to allocate any more working buffer area in the memory in response to requests from programs. In such a situation, the system may be in a complete frozen state.
2. The system may crash with PANIC.

Example 5.4 shows how to release memory space after its use.

Example 5.4

```
/*  Dispose of the memory space held by the element
 *  pointed by 'element_ptr'. Return it to the free
 *  memory pool calling free() library routine.
 */

void   dispose_elt ( SINGLE_LINK_LIST  element_ptr )
{
    free ( element_ptr );
}
```

Here is the algorithm for creating a singly linked list in the following steps:

Step 1. Declare an element structure as shown above.
Step 2. Declare a head_ptr of type *SINGLE_LINK_LIST that will point to the first element of the list.
Step 3. Allocate memory space for an element and return its address.
Step 4. Set head_ptr = memory address.
Step 5. Create the first (i.e., head) element in steps 5.1 and 5.2.
Step 5.1. Set head_ptr -> data = element_value;.
Step 5.2. Allocate memory spaces for the next elements and set the returned memory addresses to head_ptr -> next_elt.
Step 6. Continue the process.

Use new_elt_ptr instead of head_ptr in the case of a nonrecursive implementation. These steps are implemented by the recursive function create_list() in Example 5.5.

Insertion Operation in a Singly Linked List

An element can be inserted in a singly linked list in four places:

1. At the beginning (i.e., head) as the first element
2. At the end (i.e., tail) as the the last element
3. After an element
4. Before an element

Cases 1 and 2 are special cases of 4 and 3, respectively.

Conceptually, given the following singly linked list, we want to insert `'U'` after `'A'`.

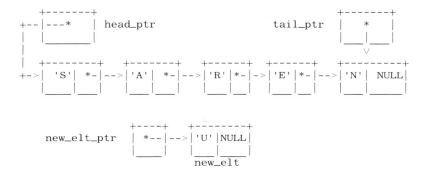

Insertion of `'U'` after `'A'` and before `'R'` can be done in the following steps:

Step 1. If the list is empty, return.

Step 2. Search for the element we want to insert after. If successful, perform steps 3 through 6.

Step 3. Create a memory space for element structure with data `'U '`; `new_elt_ptr` = address of this allocated space.

Step 4. `New_elt_ptr -> data = 'U'`.

Step 5. For the element with `'A'`, `new_elt_ptr -> next_elt = next_elt`.

Step 6. Set `next_elt` for the element with `'A'` to `new_elt_ptr`.

Note that in this insertion process, the data field of `new_elt` is not physically moved in memory. Instead, only the pointers are adjusted. This is the reason for efficiency in pointer implementation. In this singly linked implementation, difficulty arises in implementing the insert-before operation because an element does not have a link back to its previous element. The implementation of the above steps is left as an exercise.

Deletion Operation in a Singly Linked List

We show the states of the list before and after deletion as follows.

Singly linked list before deleting `'R'`:

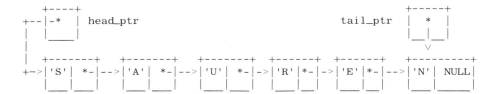

Singly linked list after deleting 'R':

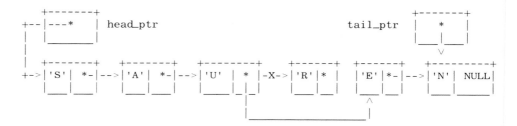

To describe the steps we wiLL use " elt_'R' -> next_elt " to mean the next_elt field of the element structure containing 'R' as its data field. The steps in deleting an element 'R' are:

Step 1. If the list is empty, return.

Step 2. Search for the element with key value 'R'. If search is successful, perform steps 3 through 5; otherwise, return with an error message.

Step 3. Save the pointer to the next element of 'R' temp_ptr = elt_ 'R' -> next_elt.

Step 4. Dispose of the memory space held by the element structure with 'R': free(elt_'U' -> next_elt).

Step 5. elt_ 'U' -> next_elt = temp_ptr.

Note that in this deletion process, elt_'U' indicates previous element of elt_ 'R', the element we wanted to delete. The elt_ 'R' stands by itself in the figure, but it is lost after the free() call. The function delete_elt() (implementing the above steps for deleting an element from a singly linked list) is left as an exercise.

We show some ADT Operations including the above creation, insertion, deletion, on a singly linked list as listed below. Example 5.5 contains the C code for these operations.

Operations on an ADT singly linked list	Function in C/comment
1. Initialize a list	init_list()
2. Check whether the list is empty	is_list_empty()
3. Create an element	create_elt()
4. Create a list	create_list()
5. Dispose of the memory space reserved for an element	dispose_elt()
6. Deleting a list	delete_list()
7. Search for an element with its key value in a list	search_elt
8. Search for predecessor of an element with its key value in a list	Exercise
9. Delete an element specified by its key from a list	Exercise
10. Insert an element before the current/specified element in a list	Exercise
11. Insert an element after the current/specified element in a list	Exercise
12. Retrieve an element from a list	retrieve_elt()
13. Update an element in a list	Exercise

14. Sort a list	To be presented in a later chapter.
15. Print a list	`print_list()`
16. Count elements in a list	`count_elt()`

Descriptions of these functions in Example 5.5 are provided below.

Description of Operations on Singly Linked Lists

`Init_list()` initializes a singly linked list by assigning NULL to three pointers of type SINGLE_LINK_LIST: `head_ptr`, `tail_ptr`, and `current_ptr`.

`Is_list_empty()` checks whether the list is empty. It returns TRUE or FALSE after comparing `head_ptr` to NULL.

`Create_elt()` expects `'Item'` as an input for node's data element. In order to allocate memory space for ELEMENT-type data, `create_elt()` uses the `malloc()` system call, which returns a pointer to char recast to a SINGLE_LINK_LIST pointer, `new_elt_ptr`. [`Malloc()` returns NULL if no memory space is available.] It then assigns `'Item'` to the data field of the ELEMENT structure pointed to by `new_elt_ptr`. Because this new element does not have any element following it, the function sets the `next_elt` pointer field to NULL. It returns `new_elt_ptr`, which can be used by the calling function. If no memory space is available, it prints an error message and returns a NULL pointer. The operation implemented by this function is the key to ADT lists. It dynamically allocates memory space for an element of the list.

`Dispose_elt()` disposes of the memory space held by an element, pointed to by `element_ptr`. It uses the `free()` library routine passing `element_ptr` as argument. This piece of memory space is then returned to the pool of free memory in the system. This routine allows the program to release unwanted and unused memory space.

`Create_list()` is a recursive function. It expects a string pointer as an input. It creates a list of characters using the input string. It calls the function `create_elt()` to create an element with one character of the string at a time as argument. It uses `next_elt`, the pointer of type SINGLE_LINK_LIST, to establish the link to the next element of the list. The last element of the list will have NULL for its field, `next_elt`. The function returns a pointer of type SINGLE_LINK_LIST, which points to the first element of the list.

`Delete_list()` implements the operation of deleting an entire list. It expects `list_ptr`, a pointer of type SINGLE_LINK_LIST as an input. `Delete_list` deletes the entire list if `list_ptr` is the same as `head_ptr`; otherwise it deletes a sublist. It calls the function `is_list_empty()` to check whether the list pointed to by `list_ptr` is empty. If the list is empty, it does nothing, otherwise, it saves the pointer to the element next to the current element pointed to by `list_ptr`, in a temporary pointer storage area, `next_ptr`. In order to release the current element pointed to by `list_ptr`, it calls the function `dispose_elt()`, passing `list_ptr` as the argument. In order to make the next element the current element, it sets `next_ptr` to `list_ptr`. Then it recursively calls itself, passing the current value of `list_ptr` as an argument. It deletes all the elements of the list until the list becomes empty. The `next_ptr` field of the last element is NULL, so the function `is_list_empty()` returns "empty" and the function `delete_list()` returns.

Here is another version of delete_list():

```
delete_list( SINGLE_LINK_LIST  list_ptr )
{
    if  ( ! is_list_empty( list_ptr ) )
        delete_list( list_ptr->next_elt );
    else
        return;
    dispose_elt( list_ptr );
}
```

Search_elt() is a recursive function. It searches for an element specified by its key value in a singly linked list. If the list is empty, the function prints a message, and returns a NULL pointer. When the list is not empty, the function looks for a match with the specified key value. It begins its search process in the forward direction, starting from the first element pointed to by head_ptr. If no match is found, it advances to the next element using the pointer, head_ptr -> next_elt. It continues its search process until all the list is exhausted or a match is found. If the match is found, the function returns a pointer of type SINGLE_LINK_LIST, which points to the element with the matching data.

Retrieve_elt() implements the operation of retrieving an element pointed to by current_ptr. It returns the value of the data field of the specified element. It does not check the validity of the current_ptr. It does not destroy the value of the data field of the specified element.

Count_elt() is implemented as a recursive function. It expects list_ptr as an input. When the sublist is empty, it returns zero. It returns the total number of elements in the single link list pointed to by list_ptr.

Print_list() uses list_ptr as an input. It is a recursive function. It prints a singly linked list in the forward direction, starting from the first element. Using the pointer, list_ptr -> next_elt, it traverses the list in forward direction. Using list_ptr allows us to print an entire list or any sublist.

Example 5.5

Code Section

```
/*
 *  Program Name:    sngl_lnk_lst_ops.c
 *  Purpose:         To implement a singly linked ADT List
 *                   with a simple data of 'char' type.
 */

#include <stdio.h>

typedef char    data_type;          /* Data type for list's element */

struct single_linked_list
{
        data_type    data;
        struct single_linked_list  *next_elt;
};
```

```
typedef struct single_linked_list ELEMENT;
typedef ELEMENT    *SINGLE_LINK_LIST;

SINGLE_LINK_LIST  head_ptr;    /* Pointer to First element in list */
SINGLE_LINK_LIST  tail_ptr;    /* Pointer to Last  element in list */
SINGLE_LINK_LIST  current_ptr; /* Pointer to Current elt in list */

/*
 *  init_list(): Initialize the Singly Linked list
 */
init_list()
{
     head_ptr    = NULL;
     tail_ptr    = NULL;
     current_ptr = NULL;
}

/*
 *  is_list_empty(): Return  true if the Singly Linked list empty.
 */
int  is_list_empty( SINGLE_LINK_LIST  head_ptr )
{
     return ( head_ptr == NULL );
}

/*
 *  create_elt(): Create an element using Item for its data field.
 *                Makes malloc() system call to get memory space.
 */
SINGLE_LINK_LIST create_elt( data_type  Item )
{
     SINGLE_LINK_LIST  new_elt_ptr;

     /*  Allocate a memory space for the new node; if no space
      *  available, return with error.
      */

     if ((new_elt_ptr = (SINGLE_LINK_LIST)malloc(sizeof (ELEMENT)))
             == NULL )
       {
          printf("\n create_elt: malloc failed  \n\n");
          return ( NULL );
       }
     else
       {
          new_elt_ptr -> data     =  Item;    /* Item is input */
          new_elt_ptr -> next_elt = NULL;    /* No Next elt   */
          return( new_elt_ptr );
       }
}

/*
 *  create_list(): Recursively create a singly linked list
 *                 from a String of variable length.
 */
```

```
SINGLE_LINK_LIST create_list( data_type   *string )
{
    SINGLE_LINK_LIST list_ptr;

    if ( *string == '\0' )        /* End of the string   */
       return( NULL );
    else
       {
          list_ptr              =  create_elt( *string++ );
          list_ptr -> next_elt = create_list( string );
          return( list_ptr );
       }
}

/*
 *  dispose_elt(): Dispose of memory space by the element pointed
 *                 to by element_ptr. Use 'free()' system call.
 */
void   dispose_elt ( SINGLE_LINK_LIST  element_ptr )
{
    free ( element_ptr );
}

/*
 *  delete_list(): Delete entire list and free up its memory
 *                 spaces (Recursive implementation).
 */
delete_list( SINGLE_LINK_LIST  *list_ptr )
{
    SINGLE_LINK_LIST  next_ptr; /* Temp ptr storage for next elt */

    if  ( ! is_list_empty( *list_ptr ) )
        {
          /* Save pointer to next elt */
          next_ptr = (*list_ptr)->next_elt;
          dispose_elt( *list_ptr );       /* Dispose of its space */
          *list_ptr = next_ptr;
          delete_list( list_ptr );
        }
}

/*
 *  search_elt():  Search for an element with its key value in
 *                 a list.
 *                 Return the pointer if found; otherwise NULL.
 *                 If successful, set current_ptr to the
 *                 returned pointer in the calling function.
 *                 (Recursive procedure)
 */
SINGLE_LINK_LIST  search_elt( SINGLE_LINK_LIST  list_ptr,
                              data_type          element_key )
{
    if ( ! is_list_empty( list_ptr ) )
       {
```

```
            if ( element_key == list_ptr -> data )
                return( list_ptr );
            search_elt( list_ptr -> next_elt, element_key );
        }
    else
        {
            printf("\n search_elt: Search failed; %s \n",
                   "Element is not found" );
            return( NULL );
        }
}

/*
 *  retrieve_elt(): Retrieve data field of an element pointed
 *                  to by current_ptr
 */
data_type  retrieve_elt( SINGLE_LINK_LIST  current_ptr )
{
    return( current_ptr -> data );
}

/*
 *  count_elt(): Recursively count elements in a Singly
 *               linked list.
 */
int count_elt( SINGLE_LINK_LIST  list_ptr )
{
    if ( list_ptr == NULL )
        return( 0 );
    else
        return( 1 + count_elt( list_ptr->next_elt) );
}

/*
 *  print_list(): Recursively print the singly linked
 *                list in the forward direction only.
 */
print_list( SINGLE_LINK_LIST  list_ptr )
{
    if (list_ptr == NULL)   /* NULL indicates last elt of list */
        printf("NULL \n");
    else
        {
          printf("%c -> ", list_ptr -> data );
          print_list( list_ptr -> next_elt );
        }
}

/*
 *  main(): SINGLY LINKED IMPLEMENTATION OF A LIST
 */
```

```
main()
{
    char    *string = "PRATIVA";       /* Input string    */
    SINGLE_LINK_LIST head_ptr;

    printf("\n === Example of SINGLY LINKED %s === \n",
           "LIST IMPLEMENTATION" );

    init_list();
    head_ptr  =  create_list( string );
    printf("\n The resulting list is: ");
    print_list( head_ptr );
    printf("\n %s in this list is: %d \n",
           "Number of elements",  count_elt( head_ptr ) );
    delete_list( &head_ptr );
    printf("\n The resulting list after %s",
           "delete_list operation is: ");
    print_list( head_ptr );
}
```

Output Section

=== Example of SINGLY LINKED LIST IMPLEMENTATION ===

The resulting list is: P -> R -> A -> T -> I -> V -> A -> NULL

Number of elements in this list is: 7

The resulting list after delete_list operation is: NULL

In the above example, head_ptr is reserved for the head of the list, and the list_ptr facilitates sublist processing.

A singly linked List implementation has the following drawback: We can traverse only in the forward direction, and we cannot easily access the immediately previous element. Such access will require traversing from the head of the list to a node whose next_elt pointer equals the current pointer. This makes singly linked list access inefficient.

5.3.2 The Doubly Linked List Implementation

A list can be implemented as an ADT doubly linked list having each of its elements consisting of three fields:

1. The data
2. One link pointing to the next element of the list
3. One link pointing to the previous element of the list

These two pointers will facilitate the traversal of the entire list in either direction, i.e., from beginning to end or from end to beginning, or changing traversal direction somewhere in between. As in a singly linked list, the data could be any simple or structured type.

For simplicity of data type, we define such elements of a doubly linked list by structures of the form

```
typedef char    data_type;

struct double_linked_list
    {
        data_type      data;
        struct double_linked_list  *next_elt;
        struct double_linked_list  *prev_elt;
    };

typedef struct double_linked_list ELEMENT;
typedef ELEMENT    *DOUBLE_LINK_LIST;

DOUBLE_LINK_LIST  head_ptr;
DOUBLE_LINK_LIST  tail_ptr;
```

The DOUBLE_LINK_LIST-type pointers next_elt and prev_elt point to
the next and previous elements in the doubly linked list, respectively. The head_
ptr and tail_ptr point to the first and last elements in the list.

Note that in a doubly linked list, the next_elt pointer field of the last element may be NULL (as in a singly linked list) or it may be the head pointer in a
circular list.

Initially, head_ptr and tail_ptr will have NULL value. When the list
has one element, these two pointers will point to the same first element. When the
list has two elements, the double linked list will be

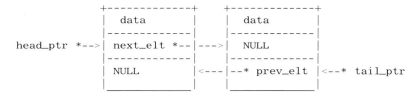

Our next goal is to discuss the standard operations on an ADT doubly linked list.

Insertion Operation in a Doubly Linked List

A doubly linked list before inserting 'P' after 'O':

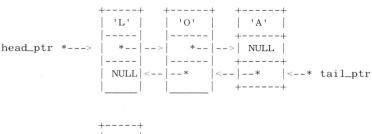

The doubly linked list after inserting 'P' after 'O':

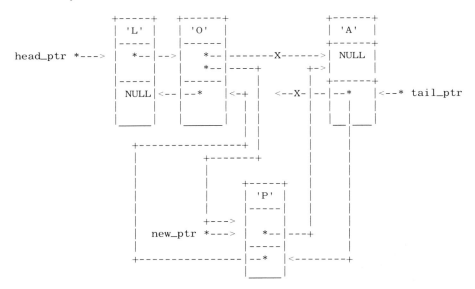

In the above figures, insertion is performed by simply adjusting the two pointers prev_elt and next_elt of three elements involved. Before insertion, the next_elt field of the elt_'O' pointed to the elt_'A'. After insertion, it points to the elt_'P'. Before insertion, the prev_elt field of the elt_'A' pointed to the elt_'O', but after insertion it points to the new elt_'P'. The next_elt and prev_elt fields of the new elt_'P' point to the elt_'A' and the elt_'O', respectively. (We used "elt_'O'" to mean the element containing 'O' as data.)

To write the steps of insertion, we will use list_ptr -> next_elt to mean the next_elt field of the element containing 'O' as its data field. The steps in inserting an element 'P' after 'O' are:

Step 1. If the list is empty, return.
Step 2. Search for the element we want to insert after; list_ptr points to the element searched for.
If successful, perform steps 3 through 6.
Step 3. Create a memory space for an element with data 'P'; set new_ptr to the address of this allocated space.
Step 4. new_ptr -> data = 'P'.
Step 5. new_ptr -> next_elt = elt_'O' -> next_elt; new_ptr -> prev_elt = elt_'O' -> next_elt -> prev_elt (i.e, address of elt with 'O').
Step 6. elt_'O' -> next_elt = new_ptr; new_ptr -> next_elt -> prev_elt = new_ptr.

A function implementing the above steps is left as an exercise.

Deletion Operation in a Doubly Linked List

The deletion operation in a doubly linked list is shown in the following figures.

The doubly linked list before deleting 'O' after 'L':

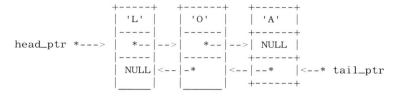

The doubly linked list after deleting 'O' after 'L':

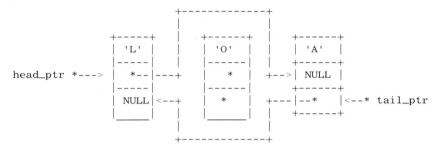

From this figure it is clear that the elt_'O' stands by itself after its deletion from the last. In fact, it is removed from the program area by relinquishing memory space held by it. After the deletion, the next_elt field of the elt_'L' points to the elt_'A', and the prev_elt field of the elt_'A' points to the elt_'L'. This is done by changing the values of these pointer variables. None of the elements in the list are moved physically.

To describe the steps of deletion we will use list_ptr -> next_elt to mean next_elt field of element structure containing 'L' as its data field. The steps in deleting an element 'O', say, are:

Step 1. Search for the element with key value 'O'; list_ptr points to the element searched for. If successful, perform steps 2 through 4.

Step 2. Save pointers to the next and previous elements of 'O' in a next_ptr and prev_ptr:

```
/* Address of next elt with 'A' */
next_ptr = elt_'O' -> next_elt
/* Address of prev_elt with 'L' */
prev_ptr = elt_'O' -> prev_elt
```

Step 3. Dispose of the memory space held by the element structure with 'O':

```
free( elt_'L' -> next_elt )
```

Step 4.   /* Address of next elt of 'O'   */
```
elt_'L' -> next_elt = next_elt
```

```
/* Address of prev elt of 'O'    */
elt_'A' -> prev_elt = prev_elt
```

Implementation of these steps for deleting an element from a doubly linked list, is left as an exercise.

In Example 5.6, we implement some basic operations on an ADT doubly linked list:

Operations on an ADT doubly linked list	Function in C/comment
1. Initialize a list	`init_list()`
2. Check whether the doubly linked list is empty	`is_list_empty()`
3. Create an element	`create_elt()`
4. Create a doubly linked list	`create_list()`
5. Dispose of the memory space reserved for an element	`dispose_elt()`
6. Delete a list	`delete_list()`
7. Search for an element with its key value in a list	`search_elt()`
8. Search for predecessor of an element with its key value in a list	Exercise
9. Delete an element specified by its key from a list	Exercise
10. Insert an element before the current/specified element in a list	Exercise
11. Insert an element after the current/specified element in a list	Exercise
12. Retrieve an element from a list	`retrieve_elt()`
13. Update an element in a list	Exercise
14. Count elements in a list	`count_elt()`
15. Print a list in forward direction	`forw_print_list()`
16. Print a list in backward direction	`rev_print_list()`

Descriptions of these functions in Example 5.6 are provided below.

Description of Operations on Doubly Linked Lists

Init_list() initializes a doubly linked list by assigning NULL to three pointers of type DOUBLE_LINK_LIST: head_ptr, tail_ptr, and current _ptr.

Is_list_empty() checks whether the list is empty. It returns TRUE or FALSE after comparing head_ptr to NULL.

Create_elt() expects Item as an input for node's data element. In order to allocate memory space for ELEMENT-type data, create_elt() uses the malloc() system call, which returns a pointer to char recast to a DOUBLE_LINK _LIST pointer, new_elt_ptr. [Malloc() returns NULL if no memory space is available.] It then assigns Item to the data field of the ELEMENT structure pointed to by new_elt_ptr. Because this new element does not have any element following it, and preceding it, the function sets the two pointer fields, next_ elt and prev_elt to NULL. It returns new_elt_ptr, which can be used by the calling function. If no memory space is available, it prints an error message and returns a NULL pointer. The operation implemented by this function is the key to ADT lists. It dynamically allocates memory space for an element of the doubly linked list.

Dispose_elt() disposes of the memory space held by an element, pointed to by element_ptr. It uses the free() library routine, passing element_ptr as the argument. This piece of memory space is then returned to the pool of free memory in the system. This routine allows the program to release unwanted and unused memory space.

Create_list() is a recursive function. It expects a string pointer and a tail pointer as inputs. It creates a list of characters using the input string. It calls the function create_elt() to create an element with one character of the string at a time as the argument. It uses next_elt, the pointer of type DOUBLE_LINK_LIST, to establish a link to the next element of the list. The last element of the list will have NULL for its next_elt field. The function returns a pointer of the type DOUBLE_LINK_LIST, which points to the first element of the list.

Delete_list() implements the operation of deleting an entire list. It expects list_ptr, a pointer of type DOUBLE_LINK_LIST, as an input. Delete_list deletes the entire list if list_ptr is the same as head_ptr; otherwise, it deletes a sublist. It calls the function is_list_empty() to check whether the list pointed to by list_ptr is empty. If the list is empty, it does nothing; otherwise, it saves the pointer, next_elt, to the element next to the current element pointed to by list_ptr, in a temporary pointer storage area, next_ptr. In order to release the current element pointed to by list_ptr, it calls the function dispose_elt(), passing list_ptr as the argument. In order to make the next element the current element, it sets next_ptr to list_ptr. Then it recursively calls itself, passing the current value of list_ptr as an argument. It deletes all the elements of the list until the list becomes empty. The next_ptr field of the last element is NULL, so the function is_list_empty() returns "empty" and the function delete_list() returns.

Search_elt() is a recursive function. It searches for an element specified by its key value in a doubly linked list. If the list is empty, the function prints a message, and returns a NULL pointer. When the list is not empty, the function looks for a match with the specified key value. It begins its search process in the forward direction, starting from the first element pointed to by head_ptr. If no match is found, it advances to the next element using the pointer, head_ptr -> next_elt. It continues its search process until all the list is exhausted or a match is found. If the match is found, the function returns a pointer of type DOUBLE_LINK_LIST, that points to the element with the matching data.

Retrieve_elt() implements the operation of retrieving an element pointed to by current_ptr. It returns the value of the data field of the specified element. It does not check the validity of the current_ptr. It does not destroy the value of the data field of the specified element.

Count_elt() is implemented as a recursive function. It expects list_ptr as an input. When the sublist is empty, it returns zero. It returns the total number of elements in the doubly linked list pointed to by list_ptr.

Forw_print_list() uses list_ptr of type DOUBLE_LINK_LIST as an input. It is a recursive function. It prints a doubly linked list in the forward direction, starting from the first element. Using the pointer list_ptr -> next_elt, it traverses the list in the forward direction. Using list_ptr allows us to print an entire list or any sublist.

Rev_print_list() uses tail_ptr of type DOUBLE_LINK_LIST as

an input. It is a recursive function. It prints a doubly linked list in the reverse direction, starting from the last element pointed to by `tail_ptr`. Using the pointer `tail_ptr -> prev_elt`, it traverses the list in the backward direction.

Example 5.6

Code Section

```
/*
 *   Program Name:    double_lnk_lst_ops.c
 *   Purpose:         To implement a Doubly Linked ADT List
 *                    with a simple data of 'char' type.
 */

#include <stdio.h>

typedef char    data_type;        /* Data type for list's element */

struct double_linked_list
  {
        data_type    data;
        struct double_linked_list  *next_elt;
        struct double_linked_list  *prev_elt;
  };

typedef struct double_linked_list ELEMENT;
typedef ELEMENT    *DOUBLE_LINK_LIST;

DOUBLE_LINK_LIST  head_ptr;        /* Pointer to First elt in list */
DOUBLE_LINK_LIST  tail_ptr;        /* Pointer to Last elt in list  */
DOUBLE_LINK_LIST  current_ptr;     /* Ptr to Current elt in list   */

/*
 *   init_list(): Initialize the Doubly Linked list
 */
init_list()
{
     head_ptr    = NULL;
     tail_ptr    = NULL;
     current_ptr = NULL;
}

/*
 *  is_list_empty(): Return  true if the Doubly Linked list empty.
 */
int  is_list_empty( DOUBLE_LINK_LIST  list_ptr )
{
     return ( list_ptr == NULL );
}

/*
 *   create_elt(): Create an element using Item for its data field.
 *                 Calls 'malloc()' to get memory space.
 */
```

```
DOUBLE_LINK_LIST create_elt( data_type   Item )
{
    DOUBLE_LINK_LIST            new_elt_ptr;

    /*  Allocate a memory space for the new node;
     *  if no space available, return with error
     */

    if ( (new_elt_ptr = (DOUBLE_LINK_LIST)
                        malloc (sizeof(ELEMENT) )) == NULL )
      {
        printf("\n create_elt: malloc failed  \n\n");
        return ( NULL );
      }
    else
      {
        new_elt_ptr -> data      =   Item;
        new_elt_ptr -> next_elt  =   NULL;
        new_elt_ptr -> prev_elt  =   NULL;
        return( new_elt_ptr );
      }
}


/*
 *  create_list(): Create a doubly linked list by recursion from a
 *                 String
 */
DOUBLE_LINK_LIST create_list( data_type  *string,
                            DOUBLE_LINK_LIST tail )
{
    DOUBLE_LINK_LIST  list_ptr;
    extern DOUBLE_LINK_LIST  tail_ptr;

    if ( *string == '\0' )         /* End of the string
     */
        return( NULL );
    else
      {
        list_ptr               =  create_elt( *string++ );
        list_ptr->prev_elt = tail;
        tail_ptr               = list_ptr;
        list_ptr->next_elt = create_list( string, list_ptr );
        return( list_ptr );
      }
}


/*
 * dispose_elt(): Dispose of memory space by the element
 *                pointed to by element_ptr. Use the
 *                'free()' system call to return it the
 *                free memory pool.
 */
```

```
void    dispose_elt ( DOUBLE_LINK_LIST  element_ptr )
{
    free ( element_ptr );
}


/*
 * delete_list(): Delete entire list and free up its entire
 *                memory space. (Recursive implementation)
 */
delete_list( DOUBLE_LINK_LIST  *list_ptr )
{
    DOUBLE_LINK_LIST  next_ptr;              /* Temp ptr storage */

    if  ( ! is_list_empty( *list_ptr ) )
       {
        /* Save pointer to next elt */
        next_ptr = (*list_ptr)->next_elt;
        /* Dispose of the space held by the current element */
        dispose_elt( *list_ptr );
        *list_ptr = next_ptr;
        delete_list(  list_ptr );
       }
}


/*
 * search_elt():
 *     Search for an element with its key value in a list
 *     Returns pointer if found; otherwise NULL.
 *     If successful, set current_ptr to the returned
 *     pointer in the calling function. (Recursive proc).
 */
DOUBLE_LINK_LIST  search_elt( DOUBLE_LINK_LIST  list_ptr,
                              data_type         element_key )
{
    if ( ! is_list_empty( list_ptr ) )
       {
        if ( element_key == list_ptr -> data )
           return( list_ptr );
        search_elt( list_ptr -> next_elt, element_key );
       }
    else
       {
        printf("\n search_elt: Element not found \n");
        return( NULL );
       }
}


/*
 * retrieve_elt(): Retrieve data field of an element
 *                 pointed to by current_ptr
 */
```

```
data_type  retrieve_elt( DOUBLE_LINK_LIST  current_ptr )
{
    return( current_ptr -> data );
}


/*
 * count_elt(): Recursively count elements in a Double
 *              linked list.
 */
int count_elt( DOUBLE_LINK_LIST  list_ptr )
{
    if (list_ptr == NULL)
        return( 0 );
    else
        return( 1 + count_elt( list_ptr -> next_elt) );
}


/*
 * forw_print_list(): Recursively print the doubly linked
 *                    list in in the forward direction
 *                    starting from the head of the list.
 */
forw_print_list( DOUBLE_LINK_LIST list_ptr )
{
    /* NULL indicates last element of list  */
    if (list_ptr == NULL)
        printf("NULL \n");
    else
      {
        printf("%c -> ", list_ptr -> data );
        forw_print_list( list_ptr -> next_elt );
      }
}


/*
 * rev_print_list():  Recursively print the doubly linked
 *                    list in in the reverse direction
 *                    starting from the tail of the list.
 */
rev_print_list( DOUBLE_LINK_LIST tail_ptr )
{
    if (tail_ptr == NULL)
        printf(" NULL \n");
    else
      {
        printf(" %c ->", tail_ptr -> data );
        rev_print_list( tail_ptr -> prev_elt );
      }
}


/*
 *  main(): DOUBLY LINKED IMPLEMENTATION OF AN ADT LIST
 */
```

```
main()

{
    char  *string = "PRATIVA";            /* Input string    */
    DOUBLE_LINK_LIST          head_ptr;
    extern   DOUBLE_LINK_LIST  tail_ptr;

    printf("\n === Example of DOUBLY LINKED %s === \n",
           "LIST IMPLEMENTATION" );

    init_list();
    head_ptr  =  create_list( string, tail_ptr );
    printf("\n The resulting list is: ");
    forw_print_list( head_ptr );
    printf("\n The resulting reverse list is: \n\n");
    rev_print_list( tail_ptr );
    printf("\n %s in this list is: %d \n",
           "Number of elements",  count_elt( head_ptr ) );
    delete_list( &head_ptr );
    printf("\n The resulting list after %s ",
           "delete_list operation is: ");
    forw_print_list( head_ptr );
}
```

Output Section

=== Example of DOUBLY LINKED LIST IMPLEMENTATION ===

The resulting list is: P -> R -> A -> T -> I -> V -> A -> NULL

The resulting reverse list is:

A -> V -> I -> T -> A -> R -> P -> NULL

Number of elements in this list is: 7

The resulting list after delete_list operation is: NULL

5.4 Singly Linked Circular Lists

Figure 5-3 shows a circular list using a single link. From Figure 5-3, it is clear that
its implementation does not require `tail_ptr`. The last element in a singly linked

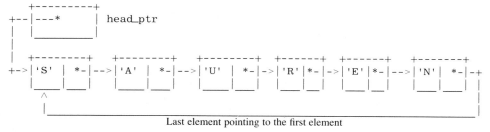

Last element pointing to the first element

Figure 5-3 A circular list with head pointer using a single link.

circular list will point to the first element. That is, the `next_elt` part of the last element created will have the same value as `head_ptr`. Besides this difference, implementation of this list is very similar to that of a singly linked list. To create a circular singly linked list, we can use the same header file and declarations as those for the singly linked list. One advantage of a circular list is that you can traverse the entire list using only one pointer.

One potential problem is that an infinite loop may arise while processing a circular singly linked list. To avoid such a problem, the `head_ptr` is used. The list is empty if the `head_ptr` is NULL or points to itself.

In Example 5.7, we implemented some operations that are necessary to work with an ADT circular singly linked list.

Operations on an ADT circular singly linked list	Function in C/comment
1. Initialize a circular list	`init_list()`
2. Check whether the list is empty	`is_list_empty()`
3. Create an element	`create_element()`
4. Create a list	`cir_create_list()`
5. Delete a list	`cir_delete_list()`
6. Search for an element with its key value in a list	`search_element()`
7. Search for predecessor of an element with its key value in a list	`search_previous()`
8. Delete an element specified by its key from a list	`delete_element()`
9. Insert an element before the current/specified element in a list	`insert_before()`
10. Insert an element after the current/element in a list	`insert_after()`
11. Update an element in a list	`modify_element()`
12. Sort a list	To be presented in a later chapter.
13. Print a list	`print_list()`
14. Count elements in a list	`count_element()`
15. Enter a character string from keyboard to circular list	`input_string()`
16. Find a string's predecessor and display results	`search_string_predecessor()`
17. Delete a string element and display results	`delete_string_element()`
18. Insert a string element before a specified element and display results	`insert_string_before()`
19. Insert a string element after a specified element and display	`insert_string_after()`
20. Modify a string element and display results	`modify_string_element()`
21. Display menu as a test driver	`display_menu()`
22. Main test driver	`main()`

Description of Operations on Circular Singly Linked Lists

`Init_list()` initializes a circular singly linked list. The address of `head_ptr` is passed to the function. The function initializes the list by setting `head_ptr` to NULL.

Is_list_empty() is used to check if a circular singly linked list is empty. If head_ptr, which must be passed to the function, is equal to NULL, YES is returned to the calling function. Otherwise, NO is returned to the calling function.

Create_element() allocates memory for a new element in a circular singly linked list. The function calls malloc() to obtain a pointer to allocate memory for the new element. If NULL is returned by malloc(), the function prints an error message to the screen and the program is terminated. The function initializes new element data with new_data of type DATA_TYPE, which must be passed to the function, and initializes the new element's next pointer to NULL. A pointer to the new element is returned to the calling function.

Cir_create_list() creates a circular singly linked list from a string using recursion. The address of the string and an initialized NULL head_ptr must be passed to the function. The recursive loop ends when the string character is NULL. At this time, the head pointer is returned and set equal to the last element in the list's next pointer to complete the circular link. The remaining next pointers are updated as recursion terminates at each level. A pointer to the head of the list is returned to the calling function. It is called by the test function, input_string().

Cir_delete_list() deletes the entire circular singly linked list and frees up the unwanted memory spaces. It is a nonrecursive function. Head_ptr must be passed to the function. If head_ptr is equal to NULL, control is returned to the calling function. A while loop is used to delete individual elements. The loop terminates when the next pointer of the current element points to head_ptr indicating the end of the list (circular connection). Inside the loop, list_ptr traverses linearly through the list and memory is returned to the system as list_ptr is updated.

Search_element() locates data in a circular singly linked list. Data to search for and head_ptr are passed to the function. The function iteratively searches for the value in the list using a while loop that terminates when the next pointer of the current element points to head_ptr, indicating the end of the list (circular connection). If the data is located, a pointer to the element containing the data is returned to the calling function; otherwise NULL is returned.

Search_previous() locates data in a circular singly linked list and returns a pointer to the previous element of where the data is found. Data to search for and head_ptr are passed to the function. The function iteratively searches for value in list using a while loop that terminates when the next pointer of the current element points to head_ptr indicating the end of the list (circular connection). If the data is located, a pointer to the element previous to the one containing the data is returned to the calling function; otherwise NULL is returned.

Delete_element() deletes an element in a circular singly linked list given its data. Data to search for and head_ptr must be passed to the function. If head_ptr is to be deleted, the end of the list is found and the pointer to the next pointer is updated to contain the new head pointer in the list to complete the circular connection. The old head_ptr memory is then returned to the system and the new head pointer is returned to the calling function. Otherwise, search_previous() is called to find the previous pointer of the element containing search data. The previous next pointer is then updated, released memory is returned to the system, and head_ptr is returned to the calling function.

Insert_before() inserts an element before a specified element in a circular singly linked list. Data to insert before, new data to insert, and head_ptr are passed to function. Memory is allocated to hold the new data element. If new data is to be inserted at the head of the list, the end of the list is found and the pointer to next is updated to contain the address of the new element to complete the circular connection. The new element next pointer is set to the old head_ptr and the new element is returned to the calling function as the new head_ptr. Otherwise, search_previous () is called to find the previous pointer of the element containing the data to insert before. The previous next pointer and the new next pointer are then updated to complete insertion and head_ptr is returned to the calling function.

Insert_after () inserts an element after a specified element in a circular singly linked list. Data to insert after, new data to insert, and head_ptr are passed to the function. Memory is allocated to hold the new data element. Search_element () is called to find a pointer to the element containing the data to insert after. The element next pointer and the new next pointer are then updated to complete insertion and head_ptr is returned to the calling function.

Modify_element () modifies data in a circular singly linked list. Old data to be modified, new data, and head_ptr must be passed to the function. Search _element is called to find the pointer to the element containing the data to modify. If the element is found, old data is modified with new data.

Print_list () prints a circular singly linked list in the forward direction from head to tail. Head_ptr must be passed to the function. The function iteratively prints values in the list using a while loop that terminates when the next pointer of the current element points to head_ptr indicating the end of the list (circular connection).

Count_element () counts the number of elements in a circular singly linked list. The function iteratively counts each element in the list using a while loop that terminates when the next pointer of the current element points to head_ ptr indicating the end of the list (circular connection). An integer count is returned to the calling function.

Example 5.7

Code Section

```
/*
 *   Program Name:   cirlist.c
 *   Purpose:        To implement an ADT Circular singly
 *                   linked list using simple data of
 *                   type 'char' to test functions.
 */

#include <stdio.h>
#include <conio.h>

#define    MALLOC(x)    (  (x *) malloc ( sizeof (x) )  )
#define    FOREVER     1
#define    ESC         27    /*  ascii code for esc key  */
#define    BELL      "\007"  /*  ascii code for tone  */

enum { NO, YES };    /*  used by is_list_empty function  */
```

```c
typedef char    DATA_TYPE;

struct cir_linked_list
{
  DATA_TYPE                 data;
  struct cir_linked_list    *next;
};

typedef struct cir_linked_list    ELEMENT;
typedef ELEMENT                   *PTR_ELEMENT;

/*
 * init_list():
 * Function to initialize circular linked list.  Address
 * of head pointer must be passed to function.
 */

void    init_list ( PTR_ELEMENT    *head_ptr )
{
  *head_ptr = NULL;
}

/*
 * is_list_empty():
 * Function to check if circular linked list is empty.
 * Head pointer must be passed to function.
 */
int    is_list_empty ( PTR_ELEMENT    head_ptr )
{
  if ( head_ptr == NULL )
    return ( YES );
  else
    return ( NO );
}

/*
 * create_element():
 * Function to create a new element in a circular linked
 * list containing new data.  A pointer to the new element
 * is returned if memory is available, otherwise an error
 *  message is printed and the program is halted.
 */

PTR_ELEMENT    create_element ( DATA_TYPE    new_data )
{
  PTR_ELEMENT    new_element_ptr;

  /*
   *  allocate memory for new element if available,
   *  otherwise print error message and exit program.
   */
  if ( ( new_element_ptr = MALLOC ( ELEMENT ) ) == NULL )
  {
```

```
      printf ("\n\nERROR:  System Memory Not Available!\n");
      exit ();
   }

   new_element_ptr->data = new_data;
   new_element_ptr->next = NULL;
   return ( new_element_ptr );
}

/*
 * cir_create_list():
 * Function to create a circular linked list from a
 * string using recursion.  Pointer to beginning of list
 * is returned.  Address of string and an initialized NULL
 * head pointer must be passed to function.
 */

PTR_ELEMENT   cir_create_list ( DATA_TYPE   *string,
                                PTR_ELEMENT head_ptr )
{
   PTR_ELEMENT   list_ptr;

   if ( *string == '\0' )   /*  end of string  */
     return ( head_ptr );   /*  complete circular link  */
   else
   {
     list_ptr = create_element ( *string );
     if ( head_ptr == NULL )  /*  initialize head_ptr  */
       head_ptr = list_ptr;

     list_ptr->next = cir_create_list ( ++string, head_ptr );
     return ( list_ptr );
   }
}

/*
 * cir_delete_list():
 * Function to delete entire circular linked list and
 * free up memory given head pointer.
 */

void   cir_delete_list ( PTR_ELEMENT   head_ptr )
{
   PTR_ELEMENT   list_ptr = head_ptr, temp_ptr;

   if ( head_ptr == NULL )   /*  check for empty list  */
     return;

   while ( list_ptr->next != head_ptr )   /*  check for wrap around  */
   {
     temp_ptr = list_ptr;
     list_ptr = list_ptr->next;
     free ( temp_ptr );   /*  delete element  */
   }
```

```
    free ( list_ptr );
}


/*
 * search_element():
 *   Function to search forward for an element in a
 *   circular singly linked list given its data.  Pointer
 *   to element is returned if element is found, otherwise
 *   NULL is returned.
 */

PTR_ELEMENT    search_element ( DATA_TYPE    search_data,
                                PTR_ELEMENT    head_ptr )
{
  PTR_ELEMENT    list_ptr = head_ptr, temp_ptr;

  if ( head_ptr == NULL )    /*  check for empty list  */
    return ( NULL );

  while ( list_ptr->next != head_ptr )    /*  check for wrap around *
  {
    if ( list_ptr->data == search_data )
      return ( list_ptr );

    list_ptr = list_ptr->next;
  }

  if ( list_ptr->data == search_data )
    return ( list_ptr );
  else
    return ( NULL );
}


/*
 * search_previous():
 *   Function to search for an element in a circular singly
 *   linked list given its data and to return a pointer to
 *   previous element if found.  Null returned if data is
 *   not found.
 */

PTR_ELEMENT    search_previous ( DATA_TYPE    search_data,
                                 PTR_ELEMENT    head_ptr )
{
  PTR_ELEMENT    list_ptr = head_ptr, temp_ptr;

  if ( head_ptr == NULL )    /*  check for empty list  */
    return ( NULL );

  while ( list_ptr->next != head_ptr )    /* check for wrap around */
  {
    if ( list_ptr->next->data == search_data )
      return ( list_ptr );
```

```
      list_ptr = list_ptr->next;
    }

    if ( list_ptr->next->data == search_data )
      return ( list_ptr );
    else
      return ( NULL );
}


/*
 * delete_element():
 *  Function to delete an element in a circular singly
 *  linked list given its data.  Pointer to head of list
 *  is returned.
 */

PTR_ELEMENT   delete_element ( DATA_TYPE   search_data,
                              PTR_ELEMENT   head_ptr )
{
  PTR_ELEMENT   element_ptr, previous_ptr;

  if ( head_ptr == NULL )   /*  check for empty list  */
    return ( NULL );

  /*  check to see if element is first one in the list  */
  if ( head_ptr->data == search_data )
  {
    previous_ptr = head_ptr;
    while ( previous_ptr->next != head_ptr )   /* find end of list */
      previous_ptr = previous_ptr->next;

    element_ptr = head_ptr->next;   /*  delete first element  */
    previous_ptr->next = element_ptr;
    free ( head_ptr );
    return ( element_ptr );
  }

  if ( ( previous_ptr = search_previous ( search_data, head_ptr ) )
          != NULL )
  {
    element_ptr = previous_ptr->next;   /*  delete element  */
    previous_ptr->next = element_ptr->next;
    free ( element_ptr );
  }

  return ( head_ptr );
}


/*
 * insert_before():
 *  Function to insert an element before specified
 *  element in a circular singly linked list given data
```

```
 *   to insert and data to insert before.  Pointer to
 *   head of list is returned.
 */

PTR_ELEMENT    insert_before ( DATA_TYPE    search_data,
                DATA_TYPE    new_data, PTR_ELEMENT    head_ptr )
{
  PTR_ELEMENT    new_ptr, previous_ptr;

  if ( head_ptr == NULL )    /*  check for empty list  */
    return ( NULL );

  /*  check to see if element is first one in the list  */
  if ( head_ptr->data == search_data )
  {
    previous_ptr = head_ptr;
    while ( previous_ptr->next != head_ptr )    /* find end of list
      previous_ptr = previous_ptr->next;

    new_ptr = create_element ( new_data ); /* insert first element
    new_ptr->next = head_ptr;
    previous_ptr->next = new_ptr;
    return ( new_ptr );
  }

  if ( ( previous_ptr = search_previous ( search_data, head_ptr )
        != NULL )
  {
    new_ptr = create_element ( new_data );    /*  insert element  *
    new_ptr->next = previous_ptr->next;
    previous_ptr->next = new_ptr;
  }

  return ( head_ptr );
}

/*
 * insert_after ():
 *   Function to insert an element after specified
 *   element in a circular singly linked list given data
 *   to insert and data to insert after.  Pointer to head
 *   of list is returned.
 */

PTR_ELEMENT    insert_after ( DATA_TYPE    search_data,
                DATA_TYPE    new_data, PTR_ELEMENT    head_ptr )
{
  PTR_ELEMENT    new_ptr, element_ptr;

  if ( ( element_ptr = search_element ( search_data, head_ptr ) )
        != NULL )
  {
    new_ptr = create_element ( new_data );    /*  insert element  *
```

```
      new_ptr->next = element_ptr->next;
      element_ptr->next = new_ptr;
   }

   return ( head_ptr );
}

/*
 * modify_element():
 *   Function to modify the an element in a circular singly
 *   linked list given the old data and new data.
 */

void   modify_element ( DATA_TYPE   old_data, DATA_TYPE   new_data,
                        PTR_ELEMENT   head_ptr )
{
   PTR_ELEMENT   element_ptr;

   if ( ( element_ptr = search_element ( old_data, head_ptr ) )
        != NULL )
      element_ptr->data = new_data;
}

/*
 * print_list():
 *   Function to print a circular linked list in the forward
 *   direction from head to tail given head pointer.
 */

void   print_list ( PTR_ELEMENT   head_ptr )
{
   PTR_ELEMENT   list_ptr = head_ptr;

   printf ("\nThe current circular linked list is:\n");
   if ( head_ptr == NULL )    /*  check for empty list  */
   {
      printf ("NULL");
      return;
   }

   while ( list_ptr->next != head_ptr )    /* check for wrap around */
   {
      printf ("%c -> ", list_ptr->data );
      list_ptr = list_ptr->next;
   }

   printf ("%c -> Head", list_ptr->data );
}

/*
 * count_element():
 *   Function to count number of elements in a circular
 *   singly linked list.
 */
```

```c
int    count_element ( PTR_ELEMENT   head_ptr )
{
  PTR_ELEMENT    list_ptr = head_ptr;
  int            count = 0;

  if ( head_ptr == NULL )
    return ( 0 );

  while ( list_ptr->next != head_ptr )
  {
    ++count;
    list_ptr = list_ptr->next;
  }

  return ( ++count );
}

/*
 * key_to_continue():
 *  Function to continue if any key is pressed.
 */

void   key_to_continue ()
{
  printf ("\n\n            Press any key to continue!\n\n");
  if ( getch () == 0 )    /*  read extended ascii code  */
    getch ();
}

/*
 * display_menu():
 *  Function to display main operator interface menu.
 */

void   display_menu ()
{
  clrscr ();
  printf ("\n\n");
  printf ("\nADT Circular Singly Linked List Test Program");
  printf ("\nEnter Choice or ESC to Quit!");
  printf ("\n");
  printf ("\n0.  Check if List is Empty");
  printf ("\n1.  Create a List from a Character String");
  printf ("\n2.  Delete List");
  printf ("\n3.  Count Number of Items in List");
  printf ("\n4.  Print List");
  printf ("\n5.  Search for Predecessor of an Element");
  printf ("\n6.  Delete an Element");
  printf ("\n7.  Insert an Element before Specified Element");
  printf ("\n8.  Insert an Element after Specified Element");
  printf ("\n9.  Update an element in List");
  printf ("\n\n");
}
```

```
/*
 * check_if_list_empty ():
 *  Function to determine if list is empty and print results.
 */

void   check_if_list_empty ( PTR_ELEMENT   head_ptr )
{
  clrscr ();
  if ( is_list_empty ( head_ptr ) == YES )
    printf ("\n\n\n\n\n          List is Empty.");
  else
    printf ("\n\n\n\n\n          List is Not Empty.");
  key_to_continue ();
}

/*
 * input_string ():
 *  Function to enter a character string from keyboard to
 *  circular singly linked list and display results.  Pointer
 *  to head of list is returned.
 */

PTR_ELEMENT   input_string ( PTR_ELEMENT   head_ptr )
{
  char    string[81];

  clrscr ();
  printf ("\n\n");
  if ( is_list_empty ( head_ptr ) == NO )
  {
    printf ("\n\nList is Not Empty - %s ",
            "Delete List before Continuing.");
    key_to_continue ();
    return ( head_ptr );
  }

  printf ("\nEnter a character string of unique %s \n\n",
          "characters to test list:" );
  gets ( string );
  if ( string[0] == '\0' )    /*  nothing entered  */
    return ( NULL );

  head_ptr = cir_create_list ( string, head_ptr );
  printf ("\n\nThe Entered List is:\n");
  print_list ( head_ptr );
  key_to_continue ();
  return ( head_ptr );
}

/*
 * search_string_predecessor ():
 *  Function to find a strings predecessor and display results.
 */
```

```
void   search_string_predecessor ( PTR_ELEMENT   head_ptr )
{
  PTR_ELEMENT    current_ptr;
  char           search_ch;

  clrscr ();
  printf ("\n\n\n\nThe Current List is:\n");
  print_list ( head_ptr );
  printf ("\n\nEnter character to find predecessor of:   ");
  search_ch = getche ();
  if ( ( current_ptr = search_previous ( search_ch,
                       head_ptr ) ) != NULL )
    printf ("\n\nPredecessor of \"%c\" is \"%c\".",
            search_ch, current_ptr->data);
  else
    printf ("\n\n%c was not found.", search_ch);

  key_to_continue ();
}

/*
 * delete_string_element ():
 *   Function to delete a string  element and display results.
 *   A pointer to the head of the list is returned.
 */

PTR_ELEMENT   delete_string_element ( PTR_ELEMENT   head_ptr )
{
  char    search_ch;

  clrscr ();
  printf ("\n\n\n\nThe Current List is:\n");
  print_list ( head_ptr );
  printf ("\n\nEnter character to delete:   ");
  search_ch = getche ();
  head_ptr = delete_element ( search_ch, head_ptr );
  printf ("\n\nThe Current List is now:\n");
  print_list ( head_ptr );
  key_to_continue ();
  return ( head_ptr );
}

/*
 * insert_string_before ():
 *   Function to insert a string element before a specified
 *   element and display results. Function to head of list
 *   is returned.
 */

PTR_ELEMENT   insert_string_before ( PTR_ELEMENT   head_ptr )
{
  char    search_ch, data_ch;

  clrscr ();
  printf ("\n\n\n\nThe Current List is:\n");
```

```
    print_list ( head_ptr );
    printf ("\n\nEnter character to insert:  ");
    data_ch = getche ();
    printf ("\n\nEnter character to insert before:  ");
    search_ch = getche ();
    head_ptr = insert_before ( search_ch, data_ch, head_ptr );
    printf ("\n\nThe Current List is now:\n");
    print_list ( head_ptr );
    key_to_continue ();
    return ( head_ptr );
}

/*
 *  insert_string_after ():
 *  Function to insert a string element after a specified
 *  element and display results.  Pointer to head of list
 *  is returned.
 */

PTR_ELEMENT   insert_string_after ( PTR_ELEMENT   head_ptr )
{
    char    search_ch, data_ch;

    clrscr ();
    printf ("\n\n\n\nThe Current List is:\n");
    print_list ( head_ptr );
    printf ("\n\nEnter character to insert:  ");
    data_ch = getche ();
    printf ("\n\nEnter character to insert after:  ");
    search_ch = getche ();
    head_ptr = insert_after ( search_ch, data_ch, head_ptr );
    printf ("\n\nThe Current List is now:\n");
    print_list ( head_ptr );
    key_to_continue ();
    return ( head_ptr );
}

/*
 *  modify_string_element ():
 *  Function to modify a string element and display results.
 */

void   modify_string_element ( PTR_ELEMENT   head_ptr )
{
    char    old_ch, new_ch;

    clrscr ();
    printf ("\n\n\n\nThe Current List is:\n");
    print_list ( head_ptr );
    printf ("\n\nEnter character to modify:  ");
    old_ch = getche ();
    printf ("\n\nEnter new character:  ");
    new_ch = getche ();
    modify_element ( old_ch, new_ch, head_ptr );
    printf ("\n\nThe Current List is now:\n");
```

```
    print_list ( head_ptr );
    key_to_continue ();
}

/*
 *  main ():
 *    Implement ADT Circular Singly Linked List.
 */

main ()
{
  PTR_ELEMENT    head_ptr;
  char    ch;

  init_list ( &head_ptr );    /*  initialize head pointer to NULL  *

  while ( FOREVER )
  {
    display_menu ();

    switch ( getch () )
    {
      case 0:            /*  read extended code  */
        getch ();
        printf ( BELL );
        break;

      case '0':    /*  Check if List is Empty  */
        check_if_list_empty ( head_ptr );
        break;

      case '1':    /*  Create a list from a character string  */
        head_ptr = input_string ( head_ptr );
        break;

      case '2':    /*  Delete list  */
        clrscr ();
        cir_delete_list ( head_ptr );
        init_list ( &head_ptr );
        printf ("\n\n\n\nThe Current List has been Deleted.");
        key_to_continue ();
        break;

      case '3':    /*  count number of items in list  */
        clrscr ();
        printf ("\n\n\n\nThere are %d Items in List:\n",
                                count_element ( head_ptr ) );
        print_list ( head_ptr );
        key_to_continue ();
        break;

      case '4':    /*  print list  */
        clrscr ();
        printf ("\n\n\n\nThe Current List is:\n");
        print_list ( head_ptr );
```

```
      key_to_continue ();
      break;

    case '5':   /*  Search for Predecessor of an Element  */
      search_string_predecessor ( head_ptr );
      break;

    case '6':   /*  Delete an Element  */
      head_ptr = delete_string_element ( head_ptr );
      break;

    case '7':   /*  Insert an Element before Specified Element  */
      head_ptr = insert_string_before ( head_ptr );
      break;

    case '8':   /*  Insert an Element after Specified Element  */
      head_ptr = insert_string_after ( head_ptr );
      break;

    case '9':   /*  Modify an Element  */
      modify_string_element ( head_ptr );
      break;

    case ESC:   /*  quit  */
      clrscr ();
      exit ();
      break;

    default:
      printf ( BELL );
      break;
    }
  }
}
```

Output Section

```
ADT Circular Singly Linked List Test Program
Enter Choice or ESC to Quit!

0.   Check if List is Empty
1.   Create a List from a Character String
2.   Delete List
3.   Count Number of Items in List
4.   Print List
5.   Search for Predecessor of an Element
6.   Delete an Element
7.   Insert an Element before Specified Element
8.   Insert an Element after Specified Element
9.   Update an element in List


1


Enter a character string of unique characters to test list:

STRONG
```

The Entered List is:

The current circular linked list is:
S -> T -> R -> O -> N -> G -> Head

Press any key to continue!

ADT Circular Singly Linked List Test Program
Enter Choice or ESC to Quit!

0.   Check if List is Empty
1.   Create a List from a Character String
2.   Delete List
3.   Count Number of Items in List
4.   Print List
5.   Search for Predecessor of an Element
6.   Delete an Element
7.   Insert an Element before Specified Element
8.   Insert an Element after Specified Element
9.   Update an element in List

3

There are 6 Items in List:

The current circular linked list is:
S -> T -> R -> O -> N -> G -> Head

Press any key to continue!

ADT Circular Singly Linked List Test Program
Enter Choice or ESC to Quit!

0.   Check if List is Empty
1.   Create a List from a Character String
2.   Delete List
3.   Count Number of Items in List
4.   Print List
5.   Search for Predecessor of an Element
6.   Delete an Element
7.   Insert an Element before Specified Element
8.   Insert an Element after Specified Element
9.   Update an element in List

9

The Current List is:

The current circular linked list is:
S -> T -> R -> O -> N -> G -> Head

Enter character to modify: O

Enter new character: I

```
The Current List is:

The current circular linked list is:
S -> T -> R -> O -> N -> G -> Head

          Press any key to continue!

ADT Circular Singly Linked List Test Program
Enter Choice or ESC to Quit!

0.   Check if List is Empty
1.   Create a List from a Character String
2.   Delete List
3.   Count Number of Items in List
4.   Print List
5.   Search for Predecessor of an Element
6.   Delete an Element
7.   Insert an Element before Specified Element
8.   Insert an Element after Specified Element
9.   Update an element in List

ESC
```

5.5 Circular Lists Using Double Links

Figure 5-4 shows a circular list using double links. From Figure 5-4, it is clear that its implementation does not require `tail_ptr`. The last element, unlike in a standard doubly linked list, will point to the first element, and the `prev_elt` of the first element will point to the last element. That is, to implement a circular doubly linked list, the following two modifications in standard doubly linked list implementation will be necessary:

1. The `next_elt` part of the last element created will have the same value as `head_ptr`.

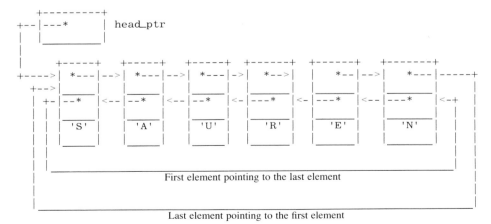

Figure 5-4 A circular list with head pointer using double links.

2. The `prev_elt` part of the first element will be the address of the last element.

Besides these differences, its implementation is very similar to that of the doubly linked list. To create a circular doubly linked list, we can use the same header file and declarations for the doubly linked list.

The circular list is known as a *ring*. The ring concept is used in structuring computer networks, for example, the *token ring network*.

We now conclude this chapter by noting the following issues and considerations in structuring a set of data objects as a list:

1. The array implementation of a list is simple but inefficient because of its static nature.
2. Although singly linked list implementation allows the list to grow or shrink dynamically, it is difficult to implement operations like `insert_before`, `delete`, and `find_previous`.
3. Doubly linked list implementation allows dynamic memory usage, and it is efficiently suited for most operations.
4. The type of list to be designed depends significantly on what operations will be performed on its elements.
5. Because of the use of the forward and backward pointers in a doubly linked list and in a circular doubly linked list are so varied, these lists have considerable advantages over their singly linked counterparts in most operations, including forward and backward traversals. However, one extra storage for the second pointer variable is required in a doubly linked list.
6. In the worst-case performance, search time is $O(n)$, where n is the number of elements in the array, singly, doubly, or circular lists. This is explicitly discussed in Chapter 9.
7. Lists are the building tools for the complex data structures—stacks, queues, and trees.

5.6 Application: A Simple Database Using Doubly Linked Lists

In this section we discuss and develop a small database application. This presentation will show the uses of many of the data structure concepts: structure, array, pointers, files, doubly linked lists, dynamic memory allocation, relocatable loading, search, and character I/O. The development of a database using an advanced structure, B-Trees, is provided in Chapter 11.

A database is an organized collection of groups of related data (usually called *records*). The data can be collectively implemented as a structure. The most common operations on a database are:

1. Enter a record
2. Update a record
3. Retrieve a record
4. Delete a record
5. Search or select a record
6. Display a record

7. Sort records by a special key
8. Store a record/database in a database on a disk
9. Load a database from disk into memory

We will present a simple database management program. It is a template to be used for an expanded version. We will show an example of such expansion and present other expansions as exercise problems.

5.6.1 Schema of Parts Inventory Control System

The following is the specification of our database application program. Write a database application for a Parts Inventory Control System for Eutopia Computers, Inc. The schema for each part's record will contain the following fields:

Field name	Field length
part_name	15 chars long
part_rev_level	4 chars long
part_serial_no	10 chars long
part_vendor_name	11 chars long
part_vendor_phone	12 chars long
part_quantity	Integer
part_description	20 chars
part_unit_price	Decimal number (e.g., 4.95)

The user interface of the application will be menu-driven, permitting the following operations:

1. Add a new part
2. Delete a part
3. Modify a part record
4. Search and display a part record
5. Store a database on disk
6. Load a database from disk
7. Exit

5.6.2 Database Implementation Approach

As the information fields for each part can be collectively viewed as a record, we can define the fields as components in the following structure:

```
struct part_record
   {
   char                      part_name[ 15 ],
                             part_rev_level[ 4 ],
                             part_serial_no[ 10 ],
                             part_vendor_name[ 11 ],
                             part_vendor_phone[ 12 ],
                             part_description[ 60 ];

   int                       part_quantity;
   float                     part_unit_price;
```

```
      struct part_record  *next;        /* Pointer to next part
                                            record              */
      struct part_record  *previous;    /* Pointer to previous
                                            part record          */
   };

/* Part record Variable in the database */
typedef struct part_record  *PART_PTR;
struct part_record  PART_RECORD;

/* Pointer to first part record in database */
PART_PTR first  = PART_NULL;
/* Pointer to last part record in database */
PART_PTR last   = PART_NULL;
/* Pointer to current part record in database */
PART_PTR current = PART_NULL;
```

In this structure definition we use two fields, next and previous, each of type
pointer to part_record structure. Using these next (i.e., forward) and previous
(i.e., backward) links, we will tie together all the records in the Parts Inventory
Control database. We will use two additional part_record pointers first and
last to respectively point to the first and last records of the database. Initially they
are set to PART_NULL because the database is empty. The structure of the Parts
Inventory Control database will be constructed as a double linked list with each part
record as an element in the following manner:

```
                Part Record          Part Record          Part Record
                    1                    2                    3

   first      -------------- next --------------        --------------
   *---->  |      *------|------> |      *------|------> | PART_NULL  |
           -------------- link --------------        --------------
           | Name       |        |            |        |            |
           --------------        --------------        --------------
           | Rev Level  |        |            |        |            |
           --------------        --------------        --------------
           | Serial No  |        |            |        |            |
           --------------        --------------        --------------
           | Vendor Name|        |            |        |            |
           --------------        --------------        --------------
           | Vendor Phon|        |            |        |            |
           --------------        --------------        --------------
           | Description|        |            |        |            |
           --------------        --------------        --------------
           | Quantity   |        |            |        |            |
           --------------        --------------        --------------
           | Unit Price |        |            |        |            |
           -------------- prev --------------        --------------
           | PART_NULL  | <------|------*  | <------|------*      |
           -------------- link --------------        --------------
                                                          ^
                                                          |
                                                          * last
```

We must note that we are not initially allocating physical memory space for the database, unlike an array of structures implementation. The database will dynamically grow or shrink during the execution of the application program. When we add a new part, we allocate memory using the `malloc()` system call. When we delete a record, we must release the memory space using the `free()` system call. Because of the double-link list structure of the database, operations like creating and inserting a part's record, deleting a part's record, or searching for a part's record will simply follow the same steps as their counterparts in the doubly linked list described earlier in the chapter.

5.6.3 Implementation Restrictions/Issues

In the above implementation of the Parts Inventory application system, we will use the following limitations:

1. Saving and loading the database are based on Character-by-Character I/O. This is definitely a primitive approach, not taking the full advantage of C-language-based libraries and the computer system's data bus bandwidth. Character I/O has very slow performance. The most efficient approach would be to use Block I/O, performing transfer of data records in blocks. In the exercises we are suggesting to rewrite and improve the `"save_db _to_disk()"` and `"load_db_from_disk()"` routines using disk block (i.e., record) I/O calls `fread()` and `fwrite()`. Note that even system low-level I/O routines `read()` and `write()` are useful.
2. "Delete" and "update" functions are not intentionally implemented.
3. A very basic and somewhat inefficient search operation is used.
4. Names are defined as an array of characters. Storage can be saved if pointers are used instead.
5. There is no checking for the following situations:

   (a) When a user tries to load the database from disk into memory more than once.
   (b) When a user tries to save data from the memory buffer into the database file on disk.

The C-language implementation of the database as specified above is given below. The disk copy of the database file name is `"parts_db_fl"`. The file is opened to read the records in it to the database manager's memory buffer by the `load_db_ from_disk()` routine. To show the content of the database file `"parts_db_ fl"` after the program execution, its octal dump is provided in the output section.

5.6.4 Parts Inventory Control Database Program

Code Section

```
/* ****************************************************************** *
 *              PARTS INVENTORY CONTROL DATABASE PROGRAM             *
 *                                                                   *
 * Program Name:   parts_db.c                                        *
 *                                                                   *
 * ****************************************************************** */
```

```c
#include  <stdio.h>

/* *************************************************************** *
 * GLOBAL VARIABLES : PARTS INVENTORY CONTROL DATABASE PROGRAM  *
 * *************************************************************** */

int    part_total = 0; /* Total number of parts in the database */

struct part_record
    {
      char                    part_name[15],
                              part_rev_level[4],
                              part_serial_no[10],
                              part_vendor_name[11],
                              part_vendor_phone[12],
                              part_description[60];

      int                     part_quantity;
      float                   part_unit_price;
      struct part_record  *next;
      struct part_record  *previous;

    };

/* Part record Variable in the database */
typedef struct part_record  *PART_PTR;

struct  part_record  PART_RECORD;
#define PART_NULL      (PART_PTR) NULL

/* Pointer to first part record in the database  */
PART_PTR  first  = PART_NULL;
/* Pointer to last part record in the database  */
PART_PTR  last   = PART_NULL;
/* Pointer to current part record in the database  */
PART_PTR  current = PART_NULL;

 /* Initialize the header */

 char *header1   = "\n\n \t\t        EUTOPIA Computers, Inc.";
 char *header2   = "\n \t\t PARTS INVENTORY CONTROL DATABASE ";

 /* Initialize the menu  */

 char *menu1  = "\n\n\t Add a part               .... a";
 char *menu2  = "\n\t Delete a part            .... d";
 char *menu3  = "\n\t Modify a part record     .... m";
 char *menu4  = "\n\t Display a part record    .... p";
 char *menu5  = "\n\t Store a Database on Disk .... s";
 char *menu6  = "\n\t Load a Database from Disk .... l";
 char *menu7  = "\n\t Exit                     .... e";
```

```c
/* *************************************************************** *
 * main(): PARTS INVENTORY CONTROL DATABASE                      *
 * *************************************************************** *** */
main()
{
   int   forever = 1;

   while ( forever )
     {
        display_menu();
        process_choice(   );
     }

}

/* **************************************************************** *
 * display_menu(): PARTS DATABASE                                 *
 * **************************************************************** */
display_menu()
{
   system("clear");             /* In UNIX, Clear Display screen    */
   printf( header1 );
   printf( header2 );
   printf( menu1   );           /*  Menu: ADD a Part Record         */
   printf( menu2   );           /*  Menu: DELETE a Part Record      */
   printf( menu3   );           /*  Menu: MODIFY a Part Record      */
   printf( menu4   );           /*  Menu: DISPLAY a Part Record     */
   printf( menu5   );           /*  Menu: STORE a Database on Disk  */
   printf( menu6   );           /*  Menu: LOAD a Database from Disk */
   printf( menu7   );           /*  Menu: EXIT                      */

}

/* **************************************************************** *
 * process_choice():  Get first letter (upper or lower case) of   *
 *                    menu and transfer control to the routine    *
 *                    based on the choice.                        *
 * **************************************************************** */
process_choice(   )
{
   char   choice;

   printf("\n\n Enter your choice : ");
   scanf( "%c", &choice );

   switch ( choice )
     {
       case 'a':
       case 'A':
               add_part();
               break;
       case 'd':
       case 'D':
               delete_part();
               break;
```

```
              case 'm':
              case 'M':
                      modify_part();
                      break;
              case 'p':
              case 'P':
                      srch_display_part();
                      break;
              case 's':
              case 'S':
                      save_db_to_disk();
                      break;
              case 'l':
              case 'L':
                      load_db_from_disk();
                      break;
              case 'e':
              case 'E':
                      exit_db();
              default:
                      printf("\n\n Unknown choice !!!\n");
                      pause_screen();

      }   /* End of switch  */

}

/* *********************************************************** *
 * create_part_record(): Dynamically allocate memory space for *
 *                       each part record calling 'malloc()".   *
 * *********************************************************** */
PART_PTR    create_part_record()
{
   PART_PTR   new_part_ptr;

   if ( (new_part_ptr = (PART_PTR) malloc( sizeof( PART_RECORD )))
                    == PART_NULL )
     {
        error("create_part_ecord: Memory allocation failed");
        return( PART_NULL );
     }
   else
        return( new_part_ptr );
}

/* *********************************************************** *
 * search_part(): Search for a part from part_db database by the *
 *                part number as key. If successful, returns a    *
 *                pointer to that part's record, otherwise         *
 *                return PART_NULL.                                *
 *                It uses Linear Search Algorithm.                 *
 * *********************************************************** */
PART_PTR   search_part( char part_name[15] )
{
   PART_PTR   srch_ptr;
```

```
    srch_ptr = first;              /* Start searching from beginning  */
    while ( srch_ptr != PART_NULL )
       {
         if ((strncmp( part_name, srch_ptr -< part_name, 15) == NULL))
            {
              current = srch_ptr;        /* This becomes current part */
              return( srch_ptr );
            }
         else
             srch_ptr = srch_ptr -< next;
       }
    /* Search failed at this point as no match found         */
    error("search_part: Search failed; No match found");
    return( PART_NULL );
}

/* ************************************************************** *
 * add_part(): Add a new part in the part_db database.  This     *
 *             version does NOT check whether or not same part   *
 *             already exists.                                   *
 * ************************************************************** */
add_part()
{
    PART_PTR   new_part;

    /* Allocate memory for a new Part Record using 'malloc()' */

    if ( (new_part = create_part_record()) == PART_NULL )
       {
         error("add_part: No more memory space ");
         return(-2);
       }
    else
       {
         print_menu_hdr ( "ADD" );
         get_input( " Enter Part's name ",
                    new_part -> part_name, 15 );

         get_input( " Enter Part's Revision Level ",
                    new_part -> part_rev_level, 4 );

         get_input( " Enter Part's Serial Number ",
                    new_part -> part_serial_no, 10 );

         get_input( " Enter Part's Vendor Name ",
                    new_part -> part_vendor_name, 11 );

         get_input( " Enter Part's Vendor Phone Number ",
                    new_part -> part_vendor_phone, 12 );

         get_input( " Enter Part's Description ",
                    new_part -> part_description, 20 );

         printf("\n  Enter Part's Quantity:   ");
         scanf( "%d", &new_part -> part_quantity );
```

```
      printf("\n  Enter Part's Unit Price ($):  ");
      scanf("%f", &new_part -> part_unit_price );

      /*  Now insert this new part in the parts
       *  Linked list structure.
       */

      if ( first == PART_NULL )    /* part_db is empty     */
        {
          first                = new_part;
          first -> next        = PART_NULL;
          first -> previous    = PART_NULL;
          last                 = first;
          current              = first;
        }
      else                /* Append it at the end of the list    */
        {
          last -> next          = new_part;
          new_part -> previous = last;   /* last becomes
                                             prev to new_part */
          last                  = new_part;
          last -> next          = PART_NULL;
          current               = new_part;
        }
      part_total++;      /* part_total = part_total + 1 */
    }
}

/* ***************************************************************** *
 * get_input(): Get input from user. It ignores any more than      *
 *              the expected size of the string ( specified by     *
 *              string_length                                      *
 * ***************************************************************** */
get_input( char  *prompt, char  *string, int  string_length )
{
   char   input_string[ 30 ];

   do
     {
        fflush( stdin );      /* UNIX system call to flush buffer */

        printf( "\n %s ( %d long) :  ", prompt, string_length );
        gets( input_string );
        if ( strlen( input_string ) > string_length )
            printf( "\n Input too long \n");
     } while ( strlen( input_string ) > string_length );

   strncpy( string, input_string, string_length );
}

/* ***************************************************************** *
 * delete_part(): Delete a part record from part_db database.      *
 * ***************************************************************** */
delete_part()
{
```

```
    print_menu_hdr ( "DELETE" );
    printf("\n Menu2: Delete is not implemented yet \n");
    pause_screen();
}

/* ************************************************************* *
 * modify_part(): Modify a part record in part_db database.    *
 * ************************************************************* */
modify_part()
{
    print_menu_hdr ( "MODIFY" );
    printf("\n Menu3: Modify is not implemented yet \n");
    pause_screen();
}

/* ************************************************************* *
 * srch_display_part(): Search a part by part name, and if     *
 *                      successful, display that part's record *
 * ************************************************************* */
srch_display_part()
{
    PART_PTR    part_ptr;
                        /* Assigned if search_part() succeeds  */
    char c;             /* Will be used to pause screen display */
    char part_name[15]; /* Will be used to search for this part */

    print_menu_hdr ( "DISPLAY" );

    get_input(" Enter part name to find : ", part_name, 15 );

    part_ptr = search_part( part_name  );
    if ( part_ptr == PART_NULL )
      {
        error("display_part: Part is not in Database ");
        return(-2);
      }
    /* Now display complete info for the entire part record    */

    printf("\n Part's name:   ");
    printf("%s", part_ptr -> part_name);

    printf("\n Part's Revision Level:   ");
    printf("%s", part_ptr -> part_rev_level);

    printf("\n Part's Serial Number:   ");
    printf("%s", part_ptr -> part_serial_no);

    printf("\n Part's Vendor Name:   ");
    printf("%s", part_ptr ->    part_vendor_name);

    printf("\n Part's Vendor Phone Number:   ");
    printf("%s", part_ptr -> part_vendor_phone);

    printf("\n Part's Description:   ");
    printf("%s", part_ptr ->  part_description);
```

```
        printf("\n Part's Quantity:   ");
        printf("%d", part_ptr -> part_quantity);

        printf("\n Part's Unit Price ($):   ");
        printf("%10.2f", part_ptr -> part_unit_price   );

        pause_screen();
}

/* ************************************************************ *
 * user_confirm(): Get user's confirmation                     *
 * ************************************************************ */
int  user_confirm( char  *prompt )
{
        char   reply;

        printf("\n\n Are you sure to %s (y/n) ?   ", prompt);
        scanf("%c", &reply );
        if ((reply == 'Y') || (reply == 'y') )
                return( 1 );
        else
                return( 0 );
}

/* ************************************************************ *
 * exit_db(): Exit from database program                       *
 * ************************************************************ */
exit_db()
{
        if ( user_confirm( "exit" ) == 1 )
          {
                printf("\n Exiting from Parts DataBase ... \n\n");
                /* UNIX system call to Clear screen */
                system("clear");
                exit(0);
          }
}

/* ************************************************************ *
 * print_menu_hdr(): Print header of a menu                    *
 * ************************************************************ */
print_menu_hdr ( char  *header )
{
        system("clear");
        printf("\n\n\t\t ******************************** \n");
        printf("\t\t\t PARTS %s MENU \n", header );
        printf("\t\t ******************************** \n\n");
}
```

```
/* **************************************************************** *
 * save_db_to_disk(): Save database from memory buffer into a      *
 *                    file "parts_db_fl" on a disk. This           *
 *                    routine uses Character-by-Character I/O.      *
 * **************************************************************** */
save_db_to_disk()
{
   register   int          i, part_rec_size;
   PART_PTR   part_ptr;
   char       *char_ptr;
   FILE       *fd_db;                /* Database File descriptor */

   /* Open a file "parts_db_fl" in Write only mode on disk */

   if ( ( fd_db = fopen( "parts_db_fl", "w") ) == NULL )
     {
       error("save_db_to_disk: Cannot open parts_db_fl file ");
       return( -1 );
     }
   else
     {
       printf("\n Saving database %s parts_db_fl ... \n",
              "buffer into disk file" );

       part_rec_size = sizeof( PART_RECORD );
       part_ptr      = first;          /* Start from first record */

       while ( part_ptr != PART_NULL )
          {
            char_ptr  = (char *) part_ptr; /* Convert it to
                                              character pointer */
            for ( i = 0; i < part_rec_size; ++i )

            /*  Save one character at a time into "parts_db_fl" */
                putc( *char_ptr++, fd_db );

            part_ptr = part_ptr -> next; /* Point to next record */
          }

       /*  Put an End of File marker in parts_db_fl    */
       putc( EOF, fd_db );
       /* Close the database file "parts_db_fl"         */
       fclose( fd_db );
     }

}

/* **************************************************************** *
 * load_db_from_disk(): Load database "parts_db_fl" from disk      *
 *                    into memory buffer. This routine uses        *
 *                    Character-by-Character I/O.                  *
 * **************************************************************** */
load_db_from_disk()
{
```

```
register    int         i, part_rec_size;
PART_PTR    part_ptr, temp_ptr;
char        *char_ptr;
FILE        *fd_db;              /* Database File descriptor */

/* Open a file "parts_db_fl" in Read only mode on disk */

if ( ( fd_db = fopen( "parts_db_fl", "r") ) == NULL )
  {
    error("load_db_frm_disk: Cannot open parts_db_fl file ");
    return( -1 );
  }
else
  {
    printf("\n Loading database %s into memory ...    \n",
           "parts_db_fl from disk" );

    part_rec_size = sizeof( PART_RECORD );

    /* Allocate mem for 1st record */
    first  = create_part_record();

    if ( first == PART_NULL )
      {
        error("load_db_frm_disk: Failed, no memory space ");
        return(-2);
      }

    part_ptr  = first;            /* Start from first record  */
    /* Convert it to character pointer  */
    char_ptr  = (char *) part_ptr;

    while ( ( *char_ptr++ = getc( fd_db ) ) != EOF )
      {
        for ( i = 0; i < part_rec_size - 1; ++i )
          /* Get one character at a time from parts_db_fl */
            *char_ptr++  = getc( fd_db );

          /* Get mem for next part */
        part_ptr -> next = create_part_record();
        if ( part_ptr -> next == PART_NULL )
          {
            error("load_db_frm_disk: Failed, no memory space");
            return(-2);
          }
        temp_ptr              = part_ptr;
        part_ptr              = part_ptr -> next;
        part_ptr -> previous = temp_ptr;

        /* Convert it to character pointer */
        char_ptr  = (char *) part_ptr;
      }
    free( temp_ptr -> next );       /* Free up unused memory */
    temp_ptr -> next  = PART_NULL;
```

```
         last            = temp_ptr;
         current         = last;
         first -> previous = PART_NULL;

         fclose( fd_db );      /* Close the database "parts_db_fl" */
      }
}

/* ***********************************************************  *
 * pause_screen(): Pause screen display. Continue display after  *
 *                 user hits any key.                            *
 * ***********************************************************  */
pause_screen()
{
   printf("\n\n Hit any key to continue ...   ");
   getchar();
}

/* ***********************************************************  *
 * error(): Print error message                                 *
 * ***********************************************************  */
error( char * msg )
{
   fprintf(stderr, "\n %s \n", msg );
}
```

Output Section

Here is the output of the first run on Unix System 5.2.

```
                  EUTOPIA Computers, Inc.
             PARTS INVENTORY CONTROL DATABASE

      Add a part               ....  a
      Delete a part            ....  d
      Modify a part record     ....  m
      Display a part record    ....  p
      Store a Database on Disk  ....  s
      Load a Database from Disk ....  l
      Exit                      ....  e

Enter your choice : a

         **********************************
                  PARTS ADD MENU
         **********************************

 Enter Part's name   ( 15 long) :  iAPX-80386
 Enter Part's Revision Level   ( 4 long) :  A-234
Input too long

 Enter Part's Revision Level   ( 4 long) :  A-23
 Enter Part's Serial Number  ( 10 long) :  iSN-1234
 Enter Part's Vendor Name  ( 11 long) :  Intel Corpn
 Enter Part's Vendor Phone Number  ( 12 long) :  408-987-8080
```

```
Enter Part's Description  ( 20 long) : 32-Bit Processor
Enter Part's Quantity: 2300
Enter Part's Unit Price ($): 159.95
```

                    EUTOPIA Computers, Inc.
                PARTS INVENTORY CONTROL DATABASE

```
        Add a part                  .... a
        Delete a part               .... d
        Modify a part record        .... m
        Display a part record       .... p
        Store a Database on Disk    .... s
        Load a Database from Disk   .... l
        Exit                        .... e
```

Enter your choice : a

```
            **********************************
                       PARTS ADD MENU
            **********************************
```

```
 Enter Part's name  ( 15 long) : M-68020
 Enter Part's Revision Level  ( 4 long) : B-19
 Enter Part's Serial Number  ( 10 long) : mSN-1011
 Enter Part's Vendor Name  ( 11 long) : Motorola
 Enter Part's Vendor Phone Number  ( 12 long) : 408-227-2020
 Enter Part's Description  ( 20 long) : 32-Bit Processor
 Enter Part's Quantity: 3550
 Enter Part's Unit Price ($): 180.00
```

                    EUTOPIA Computers, Inc.
                PARTS INVENTORY CONTROL DATABASE

```
        Add a part                  .... a
        Delete a part               .... d
        Modify a part record        .... m
        Display a part record       .... p
        Store a Database on Disk    .... s
        Load a Database from Disk   .... l
        Exit                        .... e
```

Enter your choice : s
Saving database buffer into disk file parts_db_f1 ...

                    EUTOPIA Computers, Inc.
                PARTS INVENTORY CONTROL DATABASE

```
        Add a part                  .... a
        Delete a part               .... d
        Modify a part record        .... m
        Display a part record       .... p
        Store a Database on Disk    .... s
        Load a Database from Disk   .... l
        Exit                        .... e
```

Enter your choice : p

```
***********************************
        PARTS DISPLAY MENU
***********************************
```

 Enter part name to find :   (15 long) :   M-68020
Part's name: M-68020
Part's Revision Level: B-19
Part's Serial Number: mSN-1011
Part's Vendor Name: Motorola
Part's Vendor Phone Number: 408-227-2020
Part's Description: 32-Bit Processor
Part's Quantity: 3550
Part's Unit Price ($):   180.00

Hit any key to continue ...

```
              EUTOPIA Computers, Inc.
          PARTS INVENTORY CONTROL DATABASE

      Add a part                 ....   a
      Delete a part              ....   d
      Modify a part record       ....   m
      Display a part record      ....   p
      Store a Database on Disk   ....   s
      Load a Database from Disk  ....   l
      Exit                       ....   e
```

Enter your choice : p

```
***********************************
        PARTS DISPLAY MENU
***********************************
```

 Enter part name to find :   (15 long) :   iAPX-80386
Part's name: iAPX-80386
Part's Revision Level: A-23
Part's Serial Number: iSN-1234
Part's Vendor Name: Intel Corpn
Part's Vendor Phone Number: 408-987-8080
Part's Description: 32-Bit Processor
Part's Quantity: 2300
Part's Unit Price ($):   159.95

Hit any key to continue ...

```
              EUTOPIA Computers, Inc.
          PARTS INVENTORY CONTROL DATABASE

      Add a part                 ....   a
      Delete a part              ....   d
      Modify a part record       ....   m
      Display a part record      ....   p
```

```
        Store a Database on Disk   ....   s
        Load a Database from Disk  ....   l
        Exit                       ....   e


Enter your choice : k

Unknown choice !!!

Hit any key to continue ...

                EUTOPIA Computers, Inc.
           PARTS INVENTORY CONTROL DATABASE

        Add a part                 ....   a
        Delete a part              ....   d
        Modify a part record       ....   m
        Display a part record      ....   p
        Store a Database on Disk   ....   s
        Load a Database from Disk  ....   l
        Exit                       ....   e


Enter your choice : m

        *********************************
                PARTS MODIFY MENU
        *********************************

Menu3: Modify is not implemented yet

Hit any key to continue ...

                EUTOPIA Computers, Inc.
           PARTS INVENTORY CONTROL DATABASE

        Add a part                 ....   a
        Delete a part              ....   d
        Modify a part record       ....   m
        Display a part record      ....   p
        Store a Database on Disk   ....   s
        Load a Database from Disk  ....   l
        Exit                       ....   e


Enter your choice : d

        *********************************
                PARTS DELETE MENU
        *********************************

Menu2: Delete is not implemented yet

Hit any key to continue ...
```

```
                    EUTOPIA Computers, Inc.
                PARTS INVENTORY CONTROL DATABASE

        Add a part                    . . . .   a
        Delete a part                 . . . .   d
        Modify a part record          . . . .   m
        Display a part record         . . . .   p
        Store a Database on Disk      . . . .   s
        Load a Database from Disk     . . . .   l
        Exit                          . . . .   e


Enter your choice : e

Are you sure to exit (y/n) ? y
Exiting from Parts DataBase ...
```

Output Section

The output of the second run is presented below. During the first run of the program, the database file "parts_db_fl" was saved in a disk by the "Store a Database on Disk" menu. This output is included to demonstrate the working features "Store a Database on Disk", "Load a Database from Disk", and "Search invoked by Display menu" of the program.

```
                    EUTOPIA Computers, Inc.
                PARTS INVENTORY CONTROL DATABASE

        Add a part                    . . . .   a
        Delete a part                 . . . .   d
        Modify a part record          . . . .   m
        Display a part record         . . . .   p
        Store a Database on Disk      . . . .   s
        Load a Database from Disk     . . . .   l
        Exit                          . . . .   e


Enter your choice : l
Loading database parts_db_fl from disk into memory ...
```

```
                    EUTOPIA Computers, Inc.
                PARTS INVENTORY CONTROL DATABASE

        Add a part                    . . . .   a
        Delete a part                 . . . .   d
        Modify a part record          . . . .   m
        Display a part record         . . . .   p
        Store a Database on Disk      . . . .   s
        Load a Database from Disk     . . . .   l
        Exit                          . . . .   e


Enter your choice : p
```

```
*********************************
        PARTS  DISPLAY  MENU
*********************************


 Enter part name to find :   ( 15 long)  :   M-68020
Part's name:  M-68020
Part's Revision Level:   B-19
Part's Serial Number:   mSN-1011
Part's Vendor Name:  Motorola
Part's Vendor Phone Number:   408-227-2020
Part's Description:   32-Bit Processor
Part's Quantity:  3550
Part's Unit Price ($):        180.00


Hit any key to continue ...

            EUTOPIA Computers, Inc.
        PARTS INVENTORY CONTROL DATABASE

        Add a part                  . . . .   a
        Delete a part               . . . .   d
        Modify a part record        . . . .   m
        Display a part record       . . . .   p
        Store a Database on Disk     . . . .   s
        Load a Database from Disk  . . . .   l
        Exit                        . . . .   e

Enter your choice : p


        *********************************
                PARTS  DISPLAY  MENU
        *********************************


 Enter part name to find :   ( 15 long)  :   M-68000

search_part: Search failed; No match found

display_part: Part is not in Database


            EUTOPIA Computers, Inc.
        PARTS INVENTORY CONTROL DATABASE

        Add a part                  . . . .   a
        Delete a part               . . . .   d
        Modify a part record        . . . .   m
        Display a part record       . . . .   p
        Store a Database on Disk     . . . .   s
        Load a Database from Disk  . . . .   l
        Exit                        . . . .   e

Enter your choice :

Are you sure to exit (y/n) ? y
Exiting from Parts DataBase ...
```

Output Section

To show the content of the database file `"parts_db_fl"`, it is possible to use Unix's octal dump `'od -c'` utility, which yields the following octal dump form of `"parts_db_fl"`:

```
0000000   i   A   P   X   -   8   0   3   8   6  \0  \0  \0  \0
         \0   A
0000020   -   2   3   i   S   N   -   1   2   3   4  \0  \0   I
          n   t
0000040   e   l       C   o   r   p   n   4   0   8   -   9   8
          7   -
0000060   8   0   8   0   3   2   -   B   i   t       P   r   o
          c   e
0000100   s   s   o   r  \0  \0  \0  \0  \0  \0  \0  \0  \0  \0
         \0  \0
0000120  \0  \0  \0  \0  \0  \0  \0  \0  \0  \0  \0  \0  \0  \0
         \0  \0
*
0000160  \0  \0  \b 374   C 037 363   3  \0  \t 034 360  \0  \0
         \0  \0
0000200   M   -   6   8   0   2   0  \0  \0  \0  \0  \0  \0  \0
         \0   B
0000220   -   1   9   m   S   N   -   1   0   1   1  \0  \0   M
          o   t
0000240   o   r   o   l   a  \0  \0  \0   4   0   8   -   2   2
          7   -
0000260   2   0   2   0   3   2   -   B   i   t       P   r   o
          c   e
0000300   s   s   o   r  \0  \0  \0  \0  \0  \0  \0  \0  \0  \0
         \0  \0
0000320  \0  \0  \0  \0  \0  \0  \0  \0  \0  \0  \0  \0  \0  \0
         \0  \0
0000360  \0  \0  \r 336   C   4  \0  \0  \0  \0  \0  \0  \0  \t
034   1
0000400 377  \0
0000401
```

Note that the first column in each row indicates the starting location of the first character in the second column, and the remaining columns show the actual data in ASCII. One interesting thing to note is that the NULL (\0) characters are padded for those fields of the `part_record` that are declared as an array of characters. This is definitely a wastage of space. From the discussion on pointers to strings in chapter 2, we probably could have avoided this wastage if we were to define those fields by `(char *)`-type pointers.

Exercises

5-1 For a polynomial of degree *n:*

$$P(x) = P_n x^n + P_{n-1} x^{n-1} + \cdots + P_2 x^2 + P_2 x^1 + P_0$$

(a) Represent this equation as a simple linked list.
(b) Write a program to add two polynomials.
(c) Print the sum in the symbolic form.

5-2 For a polynomial

$$P(x,y) = P_m x^m + P_{m-1} x^{m-1} y + \cdots + P_1 xy^{n-1} + P_0 y^n$$

(a) Represent this as a doubly linked list.
(b) Write a program to add two polynomials.
(c) Print the sum in symbolic form (i.e., with x, y, and their powers)

[*Hint:* A term of a polynomial can be viewed as a structure containing (coefficient, power of x, power of y).]

5-3 Write algorithms for the following operations on a sparse matrix:

(a) Read in inputs for the entries of a sparse matrix, and form a double circular linked list.
(b) Addition of two sparse matrices.
(c) Subtraction of two sparse matrices.
(d) Multiplication of two sparse matrices.
(e) Deletion of a sparse matrix.
(f) Print sparse matrices (in matrix form).

5-4 *Programming project.* In this project, we will implement a sparse matrix, in which many or most of the entries are zero. Because allocating memory spaces for all entries of the matrix will be wasteful, we intend to allocate memory space only for nonzero entries.

(a) Represent a sparse matrix as a doubly linked circular list schematically (with a figure).
(b) Write a program to perform the following operations:
   (i)   Read in inputs for the entries of a sparse matrix, and form a double circular linked list.
   (ii) Addition of two sparse matrices
   (iii) Subtraction of two sparse matrices
   (iv) Multiplication of two sparse matrices
   (v)   Deletion of a sparse matrix
   (vi) Print sparse matrices (in matrix form)

(*Hint:* Each entry of a sparse matrix can be viewed as a structure of the form

```
-----------------------------------
|  row-index  |  column-index  |  value  |
-----------------------------------
|   next-row      |    next-column     |
|   (i.e., down)  |    (i.e., right)   |
-----------------------------------
```

5-5 For a list implemented as an array in the given example, write functions to implement the following operations:

(i) `Insert_before()` to insert an element before the current or specified element in a list,
(ii) `Insert_after()` to insert an element after the current or specified element in a list,

5-6 For a singly linked list ADT in the given example, write functions to implement the following operations:

   (i)   Search for the precedessor of an element with its key value in a list.
   (ii) Delete an element specified by its key from a list.
   (iii) Insert an element before the current/specified element in a list.
   (iv) Insert an element after the current/specified element in a list.
   (v)   Update an element in a list.

5-7 For a doubly linked ADT list, write functions to implement the following operations:

   (i)   Insert an element anywhere in the list.
   (ii) Search forward and backward.
   (iii) Delete an element specified by its key from a list.
   (iv) Print forward and backward.

   (*Hint:* See Example 5.6.)

5-8 For a circular doubly linked ADT, write functions to implement the following operations:

   (i)   Initialize it.
   (ii) Create it.
   (iii) Check whether it is empty.

5-9 Write a function to search for the predecessor of an element with its key value in a circular doubly linked list.

5-10 Write a function to delete an element specified by its key from a circular doubly linked list.

5-11 Write a function to insert an element before the current/specified element in a circular doubly linked list.

5-12 Write a function to insert an element after the current/specified element in a circular doubly linked list.

5-13 Write a function to update an element in a circular doubly linked list.

5-14 Write a function to count the length of a circular list.

5-15 Write a program to invert a singly linked list. It can be done using three list pointers. When using a `while` loop, the computing time is $O(n)$, $n >= 1$.

5-16 Write a program to concatenate two singly linked lists. Print out the two lists, and the concatenated list.

5-17 Write an "overhead transparency generator," an interactive program that draws on the screen geometric objects specified by the user. You should offer the user a menu of options like points, lines, circles, rectangles, and text. When the user has chosen an object, ask for the required information, which will be different for each type of object. For example, for a circle, you need the coordinates of the center and the radius. When the user has specified as many objects as desired, display them on the screen. If possible, store information about a particular object in a structure tailored to that object. Create a node that can hold any object. Store object descriptions in a doubly linked list. (*Hint:* Use some C libraries capable of drawing the figures mentioned above.)

5-18 Implement `"update_part()"` in the given Parts Inventory Control Database.

5-19 Implement `"delete_part()"` in the given Parts Inventory Control Database.

5-20 (*Advanced.*) In the given example, rewrite and improve the `"save_db_to_disk()"` routine using disk `Block` (i.e., record) `I/O call fwrite()`. (*Hint:* Refer to Chapter 8.)

5-21 (*Advanced.*) In the given example, rewrite and improve the `"load_db_from_disk()"` routine using disk `Block` (i.e., record) `I/O call fread()`. (*Hint:* Refer to Chapter 8.)

5-22 In the given example, add a menu, `"Move data from one part record to another"`, and the associated routine.

CHAPTER 6

Stacks and Queues

Since stacks and queues are not provided as standard data types by the C language, we will develop abstract data type (ADT) versions of stacks and queues in this chapter. In the previous chapter we discussed lists with emphasis on their implementations using pointer variables and dynamic storage allocation. Since the stacks and queues are special cases of lists, it will be relatively easy to discuss their ADT structures and operations.

Stacks and queues are very useful in computer science. These are explicitly or implicitly used by compilers and operating systems. The stack concept is applied in the evaluation of reverse polish notation (RPN), in parsing an expression by recursion by a compiler, memory management in operating systems, a stack of windows with operations like push and pop, and stacks of cards where each card may contain text attributes (color, highlight), a pointer to a text buffer, etc.

Applications of queues can be found in such areas as the arrival of planes at an airport, bus passengers waiting for a ticket agent, and many business applications requiring processing of customers' phone calls, orders, and jobs in the order of their arrivals. Some other applications of queues include CPU scheduling, printer spooling, tape scheduling, disk scheduling, message queueing in interprocess communication and in computer networks, and window scheduling, etc.

The list of applications of stacks and queues is enormous; we demonstrate RPN as an application of stacks, and simulate a process manager as an application of queues.

6.1 An ADT Stack

An ADT stack is a data structure in which data objects or elements are stored and retrieved in a *last-in–first-out* (LIFO) order, with the following most common operations:

Operation	Description
is_stk_empty()	Checks whether the stack is empty; returns true if it is.
is_stk_full()	Checks whether the number of data objects in the stack has reached the maximum allowable size of the stack; returns true if it has.
init_stk()	Initializes a stack.

Operation	Description
create_stk()	Creates a stack.
clear_stk()	Clears a stack.
get_top()	Gets a copy of the top data object of the stack and does not destroy its existence in the stack.
push(x)	Stores x onto the stack if the stack is not full; if full, reports error, "stack overflow occurred".
pop()	Retrieves data object at the top of the stack if the stack is not empty.
print_stk()	Prints the entire stack.

The data in a stack may be simple or structured. The main interest in dealing with an ADT stack is to perform the above operations regardless of the type of data.

In a stack, the last data object stored in is the first data object to be retrieved. A stack can be viewed as a collection of process sequential data objects, where the order indicates when the data object arrived to be added into the stack. The most recently arrived data object will be the first one to depart from the stack.

A stack has only one end for data access, commonly called the "top" of the stack. As previously noted, the data objects may be of any language-definable type. The store and retrieval operations for a stack are respectively called *push* and *pop*.

A stack can be implemented as a special type of list in which one end is designated as the top of the stack, and access to the data objects is done only through this end of the list.

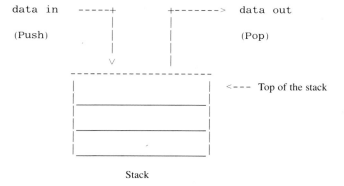

Stack

For example, a pile of plates is a stack. To store a plate in that pile, lay the new plate on the plate currently at the top of the pile. The new plate is the current top of the pile. This is the *push* operation. Repeated push operations may cause an overflow, if the pile of plates reaches the ceiling. The next attempt to push will fail. Such a situation is called *stack overflow*. To retrieve a plate from the pile, take out the plate currently at the top of the pile. Then the plate stored immediately below that one will be at the top of the pile. This is the *pop* operation. Repeated pop (i.e., retrieval) operations may exhaust the pile of plates. This is the *empty* state of the stack. The next attempt to pop will fail. This is called *stack underflow*.

Note that in the above list of stack operations with the exception of init_stk() and create_stk() all operations require the existence of a stack as a precondition. A stack can be implemented as one of the following data structures: (1) array or (2) linked list. The rationale in selecting an appropriate data structure for a stack depends considerably on the requirement of the operations to be performed on its data objects. However, we will discuss both implementations.

6.1.1 Array Implementation of a Stack

A stack may be implemented by an array and the use of an index counter to access the stack locations. The stack bounds are defined by constants that bound the index. Notice that the stack is growing in some direction, either from a high to a low location or from a low to a high location.

A stack may be implemented by an array and pointers to the array. The stack bounds are set by the starting address of the array and by the address of the last element of the array. The variable `top_stk` is an index to an element of the stack array and is assumed to range from 0 to `Stk_Size - 1`, which is the maximum size of the stack. At the initial state when the stack is empty, the variable `top_stk` is set to NULL. The stack becomes full if `top_stk` reaches its maximum element `&stack[Stk_Size - 1]`. Again the stack is assumed to be growing in the direction from STACK[0] to STACK[`Stk_Size - 1`]. The stack as an array can be sketched as shown in Figure 6-1.

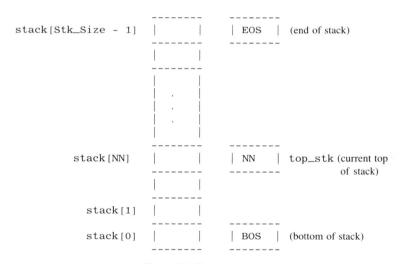

Figure 6-1 The stack as an array.

Beginning with an empty state of stack, a sequence of three push operations followed by one pop operation will yield the states of the array stack and the changing values of `top_stk` shown in Figure 6-2.

For simplicity, we assumed data of a stack to be char-type. A stack implemented as an array is defined in the following manner:

```
#define   Stk_Size   128              /* Stack Limit   */
#define   BOS        0
#define   EOS        Stk_Size - 1
```

```
After Push 'X':
                        --------
stack[Stk_Size-1]  |        |
                        --------
                        |   .    |
                        |   .    |
                        |   .    |
                        --------
        stack[2]   |        |
                        --------
        stack[1]   |        |
                        --------        --------
        stack[0]   |   X    |       |   0    | top_stk
                        --------        --------


After Push 'Y':
                        --------
stack[Stk_Size-1]  |        |
                        --------
                        |   .    |
                        |   .    |
                        |   .    |
                        --------
        stack[2]   |        |
                        --------        --------
        stack[1]   |   Y    |       |   1    | top_stk
                        --------        --------
        stack[0]   |   X    |
                        --------


After Push 'Z':
                        --------
stack[Stk_Size-1]  |        |
                        --------
                        |   .    |
                        |   .    |
                        |   .    |
                        --------        --------
        stack[2]   |   Z    |       |   2    | top_stk
                        --------        --------
        stack[1]   |   Y    |
                        --------
        stack[0]   |   X    |
                        --------


After Pop:
                        --------
stack[Stk_Size-1]  |        |
                        --------
                        |   .    |.
                        |   .    |
                        |   .    |
                        --------
        stack[2]   |        |
                        --------        --------
        stack[1]   |   Y    |       |   1    | top_stk
                        --------        --------
        stack[0]   |   X    |
                        --------
```

Figure 6-2 Stack states after successive push and pop operations.

```
typedef   char   data_type;                  /* Define stack data */
/* Define STACK as an array of Stk_Size  */
typedef   data_type   STACK [ Stk_Size ];

STACK        stack;              /* STACK-type variable     */
int          top_stk;           /* This is top of the stack */
```

The init_stk() function sets top_stk to −1.

The push() function implements the push operation in the following three steps:

    Step 1. Check whether the stack is full. If true (i.e., if it is full), print an error message; return an error value. Otherwise, proceed to step 2.

    Step 2. Increment top_stk by 1:

$$top\_stk++;$$

    Step 3. Store the new element in the stack array with index value of top_stk as follows:

$$stack[\ top\_stk\ ]\ =\ new\_elt;$$

The pop() function implements the pop operation as follows:

    Step 1. Check whether the stack is empty. If true, print an error message; return an error value. Otherwise, proceed to step 2.

    Step 2. Take out the element at the top of the stack array with index value of top_stk as follows:

$$element\ =\ stack[\ top\_stk\ ];$$

    Step 3. Decrement the top_stk index by 1 to make the element next to the stack[top_stk] the current top of the stack:

$$top\_stk\ =\ top\_stk\ -\ 1;$$

For a detailed implementation of these operations, see Example 6-1 in the Further Examples section (at the end of the chapter).

The disadvantage of the array implementation of a stack is that the memory storage space is of fixed size by allocation of the array declaration statement. Some memory space will be wasted if the stack does not need all the space it was initially allocated. Conversely, the stack could run out of space and the allocation and use of further array space would be cumbersome.

6.1.2 Linked List Implementation of a Stack

To avoid the space problems of an array implementation, a stack may be implemented as a linked list. The stack bounds are now determined by the use of a NULL pointer for the bottom of the stack and by running out of heap space for the upper bound. A general form of a singly linked stack can be as shown in Figure 6-3.

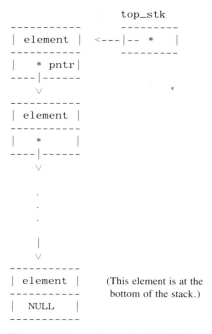

Figure 6-3 The stack as a singly linked list.

To illustrate, after three successive push operations as done in case of an array stack, the singly linked stack will be as illustrated in Figure 6-4.

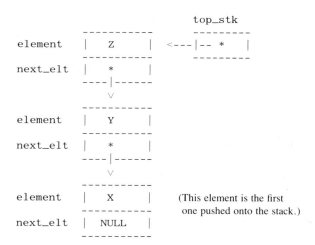

Figure 6-4 The stack after three push operations.

The stack element described above has one data field and one list pointer.

```
typedef   char   data_type;            /* Define stack data      */
struct elt_struct                      /* Define ELEMENT struct  */
    {
        data_type    element;          /* 'data' field           */
```

```
            struct elt_struct   *next_elt; /* Pointer to next
                                              STACK_TYPE element of
                                              the stack          */
        };
typedef   struct elt_struct    STACK_TYPE;
typedef   STACK_TYPE  *STACK_PTR;        /* Define type STACK_PTR */

STACK_PTR  top_stk;                       /* Variable: top of stack*/
```

The function `create_elt()` will obtain memory space for a new stack element using the `malloc()` system call, and return the pointer to the new element or return the NULL pointer, if the system memory heap is out of space. When the `push()` function is called, it calls the `create_elt()` function to dynamically allocate memory space for the new element to be pushed onto the stack.

When the `pop()` function is called, it pops the top element of the stack and calls the function `free()` that returns the memory space allocated to the stack's currently popped element to the system memory heap. Notice that the order of stack elements is now random, in contrast to the sequential implementation of a stack. The advantage of this implementation is that it allows the stack to dynamically grow or shrink as needed during the execution of the program. One disadvantage is that in addition to the stack data element, space for a pointer (in the case of a singly linked list; two pointers in the case of a doubly linked list) is needed. See Example 6-2 for most common operations on a singly linked list structure of a stack.

6.2 The ADT Double Stacks

The ADT double-stack concept is sometimes used to save space by having two stacks that share the same area. Two stacks are stored in one array, allowing one stack to grow "down" from the top of the array, and the other stack to grow "up" from the bottom of the array. The data objects in both stacks are of the same data type. The double-stack operations are:

1. `is_stk_empty(stack_no)`
2. `is_stk_full(stack_no)`
3. `create_stks()`
4. `init_stk(stack_no)`
5. `push(item, stack_no)`
6. `pop(item, stack_no)`
7. `print(stack_no)`

Two stacks coexisting one array can be conceived in Figure 6-5.
Potential concerns and issues in implementing double stacks coexisting in one array are:

1. While one stack is growing, its push operation cannot cross over the current top of the other stack. Otherwise, it will overwrite the other stack's data area. This indicates a boundary check is necessary during push operations for either stack.
2. The array space is fully used up when the tops of the two stacks are adja-

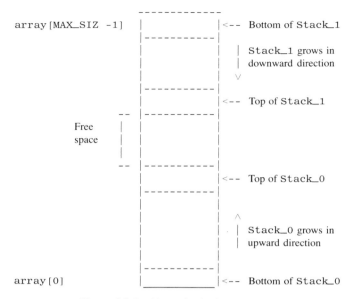

Figure 6-5 Double stacks sharing one array.

cent, that is, next to each other. The `Stack Overflow` condition occurs for both stacks. Note that the two tops are indices of the same array.

3. In the case of stack overflow, neither stack can grow until one of the stacks does some pop operations and thereby releases locations in the array. This implies a mechanism for holding off until space is freed up.

The `create_stks ()` function can be done in the following manner:

1. Set `top_stk_0 = -1`.
2. Set `top_stk_1 = MAX_SIZ`.

Detailed implementations of double-stack array implementation and the six operations are left as an exercise.

6.3 Uses of Stacks: Reverse Polish Notation

Stacks may be used to process or transform expressions. Expressions are usually written with infix notation, with the operator written between operands: A op B. In many instances (compilers, calculator programs, etc.), infix expressions must be converted by the program to postfix notation, with the binary or unary operator after operands (e.g., ABop, B-).

Infix operations often need parentheses to clarify operator binding. Postfix expression don't require parentheses:

Infix: `(a+b) /c`
Postfix: `ab+c/`

Postfix notation is also called reverse polish notation (RPN). In RPN the expression

6 3 - 4 2 / *

evaluates to

$$6$$

A stack machine (such as an RPN calculator) can be used to process RPN expressions, as shown in Example 6.1.

Example 6.1

```
6  3  -  4  2  /  *  (EOE)

1. read 6;  push 6
2. read 3;  push 3
3. read -;  pop 3;  pop 6;  subtract 3 from 6;
   push resulting 3
4. read 4;  push 4
5. read 2;  push 2
6. read /;  pop 2;  pop 4;  divide 2 into 4;
   push resulting 2
7. read *;  pop 2;  pop 3;  multiply 2 times 3;
   push resulting 6
8. read EOE;  pop 6;  output 6
```

where EOE means *end of expression,* usually appearing at the end of the line.

6.3.1 Postfix Evaluation

The following example of postfix evaluation demonstrates the algorithm for RPN expression evaluation. Define the term TOKEN to be a constant, variable, or operator (binary or unary) symbol.

Algorithm

1. Obtain the expression.
2. Repeat until the end of the expression.
   2.1. Read the next TOKEN.
   2.2. If TOKEN is an operand (constant or variable), push it onto the stack.
   2.3. If the TOKEN is an operator (op), do the following:
      2.3.1. Pop a TOKEN from the stack (B).
      2.3.2. Pop a second TOKEN (A) (stack underflow is an error if the operator is binary).
      2.3.3. Evalute A op B.
      2.3.4. Push the result onto the stack.
3. Pop the stack to obtain the result of the expression.

Example 6.2

```
#include <math.h>

/*  Include Example 6-1 without main() for
 *  pop(), push(), and data_type must be defined float:
 *       typedef float          data_type;
 */
#include "ary_stk.c"
```

```
#define    BLANK_SPACE    ' '
#define    Stk_Size       80

enum    answer { NO, YES };


/* =============================================================  *
 * answer(): Function that determines if a character is a        *
 *           numeric character or a decimal point.               *
 * =============================================================  */
enum answer    is_numeric ( char    check )
{
    if ( ( check >= '0' && check <= '9' ) || check == '.' )
        return ( YES );
    else
        return ( NO );
}


/* =============================================================  *
 * Evalute_Postfix(): Function that evaluates a string of        *
 *                    postfix notation (RPN) and returns the     *
 *                    result.                                    *
 * =============================================================  */

data_type    Evaluate_Postfix ( char    *ptr_string )
{
    data_type    operand_1, operand_2;
    data_type    operand_stk[Stk_Size];
    int          operand_stk_top = 0;    /* Initialize stack's top */
    char         number_buffer[20], *ptr_number_buffer;

    /*  parse string until the end of the RPN expression
     *  is found.
     */
    while ( *ptr_string != '\0' )
    {
        /*  ignore blank spaces  */
        if ( *ptr_string != BLANK_SPACE )
        {
            if ( is_numeric ( *ptr_string ) == YES )
              {
                /*  read numeric value, convert to floating
                 *  point, and push stack.
                 */
                ptr_number_buffer = &number_buffer[0];
                while ( is_numeric ( *ptr_string ) == YES &&
                        *ptr_string != '\0' )
                    *ptr_number_buffer++ = *ptr_string++;

                *ptr_number_buffer = '\0';
                push ( operand_stk, &operand_stk_top,
                       atof ( number_buffer ) );
              }
```

```
               else
               /*  pop stack twice and do requested operation  */
               {
                  operand_2 = pop ( operand_stk,
                                       &operand_stk_top ) ;
                  operand_1 = pop ( operand_stk,
                                       &operand_stk_top ) ;
                  switch ( *ptr_string++ )
                  {
                    case '+':
                      push ( operand_stk, &operand_stk_top,
                             operand_1 + operand_2 ) ;
                      break;
                    case '-':
                      push ( operand_stk, &operand_stk_top,
                             operand_1 - operand_2 ) ;
                      break;
                    case '*':
                      push ( operand_stk, &operand_stk_top,
                             operand_1 * operand_2 ) ;
                      break;
                    case '/':
                      push ( operand_stk, &operand_stk_top,
                             operand_1 / operand_2 ) ;
                      break;
                    default:
                      printf ("\n\nUnexpected Parameter\n") ;
                      /* End program on an unexpected parameter */
                      exit () ;

                  }    /*  End of switch  */
               }
            }
         else
              ++ptr_string;

      }   /*  End of while   */

      /*  Get the result stored in top of the stack  */
      return ( pop ( operand_stk, &operand_stk_top ) ) ;

}   /*  End of procedure  */

main ()
{
 char    buffer[81] ;

 printf ("\n\nEnter a RPN expression to be evaluated: \n") ;
 gets ( buffer ) ;
 printf ("\n\nThe result of RPN expression: \n%s\nis:   %5.2f\n",
         buffer, Evaluate_Postfix ( buffer ) ) ;
}
```

Here is the output of Example 6.2:

```
Enter a RPN expression to be evaluated:
32 54 + 67 57 - *

The result of RPN expression:
32 54 + 67 57 - *
is:   860.00
```

6.3.2 Infix to Postfix Expression Conversion

We now concentrate on the conversion process from the correctly formed infix expression into a postfix RPN. No error checking on the correct form, that is, syntax of the infix expression, is done in this program. However, it is given as an exercise.

Some issues and considerations in designing infix–postfix coversion procedure must be noted as follows:

1. When an operator is encountered in the input string, it is pushed on the stack because the second operand has yet to be read.
2. Define "priority," that is, precedence of an arithmetic operator when there are no parentheses. By the precedence of an operator, we mean an operator with higher priority on the stack will be executed or evaluated before the operators with lower priority on the stack.
3. When parentheses are present in an infix expression, the left parenthesis " (" encountered first when scanning the expression from left to right must immediately go on the stack. This is because of the lack of information on its scope at this point. This implies that a left parenthesis always takes higher priority over any operator on the top of the operand stack. When a right parenthesis ") " is found in the input string, we need to send (pop) all operators on the stack, down to (but not inclusive of) its matching left parenthesis for immediate evaluation. The right parenthesis is never pushed onto the stack. When an infix expression has nested parentheses, we must determine which left parenthesis correctly matches the encountered right parenthesis. While scanning an infix expression from left to right, any left parenthesis that is encountered before a right parenthesis is pushed on the stack. The "last" left parenthesis on the stack will be the correct match of encountered right parenthesis.

The precedence table influences the flow control of the infix–postfix conversion algorithm. Remember that the infix expression is obtained as a string of characters. Define TOKEN to be a constant, variable, or operator symbol.

1. Obtain an infix expression.
2. Repeat until EOE.
   2.1. Read next TOKEN.
   2.2. If TOKEN is a left parenthesis, push it.
   2.3. If it is an operand, pass it through.
   2.4. If it is an operator:
        2.4.1. Repeat. If the stack is empty or TOKEN has a higher precedence than the top of stack token (left parenthesis has precedence), push TOKEN and end the repeat.

2.4.2. Or else pop an operator and pass it on through; continue to repeat.

2.5. If TOKEN is a right parenthesis, then pop and pass through stack items until a left parenthesis is reached. Pop it and discard it and the right parenthesis.

3. Pop to obtain the result.

Example 6.3

```
/*
 *   Include Example 6.1 without main() in order to use push()
 *   and pop() functions. The data is of type char.
 */
#include "ary_stk.c"

#ifdef DOS
#include <stdio.h>
#endif

#define  BUF_SIZ   128
#define  STK_SIZ   256

typedef  char   EXPR[ BUF_SIZ ];
typedef  char   *EXPR_PTR;
typedef  char   TOKEN;
typedef  char   EXSTACK[ STK_SIZ ];

EXSTACK  estack;
int      estack_top = 0;

#define  PRIORITY0          0
#define  PRIORITY1          1
#define  PRIORITY2          2
#define  EMPTY              0
#define  BLANK_SPACE        ' '
#define  EOL                '\0'

/* ============================================================ *
 * priority(): Function to determine the priority of operators  *
 * ============================================================ */
int   priority ( char   op )
{
    switch (op)
      {
        case '(': return PRIORITY0;
        case '+':
        case '-': return PRIORITY1;
        case '*':
        case '/': return PRIORITY2;
      }
}
```

```
/* ================================================================ *
 * in_to_post(): Function to convert a Infix expression to RPN      *
 * ================================================================ */

void    in_to_post ( EXPR_PTR    expr, EXPR_PTR    postexpr )
{
    TOKEN    token, retoken;

    while ( ( token = *expr++ ) != EOL )
      {
        if ( token == BLANK_SPACE )
           continue;
        else
          switch ( token )
            {
              case '(':
                   push ( estack, &estack_top, token );
                   break;
              case ')':
                   while ( ( retoken = pop ( estack,
                           &estack_top ) ) != '(' )
                     {
                       *postexpr++ = BLANK_SPACE;
                       *postexpr++ = retoken;
                     }
                   break;
              case '+':
              case '-':
              case '*':
              case '/':
                   while ( estack_top != EMPTY )
                     {
                       retoken = pop ( estack, &estack_top );

                       if ( priority ( token ) <=
                            priority ( retoken ) )
                         {
                           *postexpr++ = BLANK_SPACE;
                           *postexpr++ = retoken;
                         }
                       else
                         {
                           push ( estack, &estack_top,
                                  retoken );
                           break;
                         }
                     }
                   push ( estack, &estack_top, token );
                   *postexpr++ = BLANK_SPACE;
                   break;
              default:
                   *postexpr++ = token;
                   break;
            }   /* end of switch */
      }   /* end of while   */
```

```
    while ( estack_top != EMPTY )
      {
          *postexpr++ = BLANK_SPACE;
          *postexpr++ = pop ( estack, &estack_top );
      }
    *postexpr = '\0';
}

main()
{
    EXPR     inbuf, obuf;
    char     reply;

    do
    {
      printf ("\n\n Enter an Infix expression %s \n",
              "to be converted into RPN:");
      gets ( inbuf );

      in_to_post ( inbuf, obuf );
      printf ("\n\n The %s: \n %s \n is: \n %s \n",
              "converted RPN expression of",
        inbuf, obuf);

      printf("\n Do you have another one (y/n)? ");

    } while ( (reply = getchar() ) == 'y' );
}
```

Here is the output of Example 6.3:

```
    Enter an Infix expression to be converted into RPN:
    (32 + 54) * (67 - 57)

    The converted RPN expression of:
    (32 + 54) * (67 - 57)
    is:
    32 54 + 67 57 - *

    Do you have another one (y/n)? y

    Enter an Infix expression to be converted into RPN:
    ((A - B) / (D - C)) * (E + F)

    The converted RPN expression of:
    ((A - B) / (D - C)) * (E + F)
    is:
    A B - D C - / E F + *

    Do you have another one (y/n)? n
```

196   *6. Stacks and Queues*

6.4 The ADT Queue

A queue is an ADT that is conceptually very similar to the stack, but complex in its implementation. In this section we provide its definition with an ADT approach, its array and list implementations, and show its usage with several examples. In a queue, which is a list with a head and a tail, the elements are added at the tail; elements are removed from the head.

An ADT queue is defined as a collection of data objects (items) that have a process-sequential order, with the following set of operations:

1. `qinit`: Initializes a queue
2. `qcreate`: Creates a queue
3. `qempty`: Checks whether a queue has any item
4. `qadd`: Adds an item at one end, called the *rear,* of a queue; also called the `"enqueue"` operation
5. `qremove`: Removes or deletes an item from the other end, called the *front,* of a queue; also called the `"dequeue"` operation
6. `qdelete`: Deletes the entire queue

The items in a queue may be simple or complex structure-type data objects.

The oldest item is stored (added) at the front of the queue, and the youngest item is stored at the rear of the queue. Each new data item is stored at the back of the structure, and the oldest data item is retrieved from the front of the structure. This type of data access is called first-in–first-out (FIFO). In day-to-day life, we see examples of queues such as waiting lines of customers in banks and stores.

As an illustrative approach, let us consider a simple implementation of a queue as a character array. The data in the array is a string of characters terminated by a null character. The first character is at the front of the array, and the terminating character is at the rear of the string. When the string is processed, the first character is read, then the second one, and so on, until the terminating character is read. If another character were to be added before the terminating character was reached, the new character would be added after the null character.

If we propose an infinite character array, we could simply continue on adding new characters and retrieving characters from the front of the queue. We would have to keep track of the location of the front item and the location of the rear item.

A computer has finite storage space, so we must adapt the model to a finite sequence of items.

6.4.1 Array Implementation of a Queue

A queue may be implemented by an array and the use of an index counter to access the queue head and tail locations. The queue bounds are defined by constants that bound the index.

If the queue is assumed to be ordered in the direction from queue [0] to queue [MAXQUEUE – 1] , the queue as an array can be sketched as in Figure 6-6.

We can implement a queue as an array by defining its data type in the following manner:

```
#define   MAXQUEUE      128

typedef   int          data_type;
typedef   data_type    *IPOINTER;

typedef   int     QINDEX;   /* Range:  0 ...  MAXQUEUE */

#define   QNULL    (QINDEX)  0

struct   QUEUE
{
    QINDEX     qfront;
    QINDEX     qrear;
    data_type  item[ MAXQUEUE ];
};

typedef struct QUEUE   AQUEUE;

AQUEUE   arq;                /* arq is AQUEUE-type variable */
```

In this form, a `data_type` variable is an int; it is the item placed on the queue.
However, `data_type` may be a structured-type data. The array-based QUEUE is
composed of queue indices, `qfront` and `qrear`, and the stored items in the
array item.

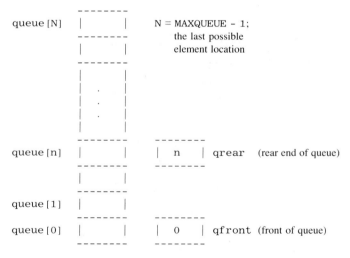

Figure 6-6 The queue as an array.

The queue bounds are set by the starting address of the array and by the address of
the last element of the array. The two variables `'qrear'` and `'qfront'` in the
QUEUE-type structure are indices of the queue array assumed to be ranging from 0
to MAXQUEUE − 1, where MAXQUEUE is the maximum size of the queue. At the
initial state when the queue is empty, the two variables `'qrear'` and `'qfront'`

are set to QNULL. The queue becomes full if 'qrear' reaches its maximum size, MAXQUEUE - 1.

The qinit () function, which implements the queue initialization operation, sets qrear and qfront to QNULL.

The qadd () function implements the enqueue operation in the following three steps:

Step 1. Check whether the queue is full by testing

$$qrear \;==\; \text{MAXQUEUE}$$

If true, print an error message "QUEUE OVERFLOW OCCURRED"; return an error value. Otherwise, proceed to step 2.

Step 2. Increment qrear by 1:

$$qrear \;=\; qrear \;+\; 1;$$

Step 3. Store the new element in the queue array with index value of qrear as follows:

$$queue[\; qrear \;]\;=\; new\_elt;$$

The qremove () function is the dequeue operation and follows the steps:

Step 1. Check whether the queue is empty by testing

$$qfront \;==\; qrear$$

If true, print an error message "QUEUE UNDERFLOW"; return an error value. Otherwise, proceed to step 2.

Step 2. Take out the queue item at the front of the array queue with index value of qfront as follows:

$$element\;=\; queue[\; qfront \;];$$

Step 3. Shift down all the rest of the queue items in the array queue.
Step 4. Decrement qrear index by 1:

$$qrear \;=\; qrear \;-\; 1;$$

For a detailed implementation of these operations, see Example 6-4 in the Further Examples section.

The disadvantages of the array implementation of a queue are that the size of the memory storage space is fixed by the array declaration statement, and the dequeue operation requires physical shifting of the items in the physical memory, which is time-consuming. Because of the static allocation, the queue's growth is limited by the size of the array. The memory space will be wasted if the queue does not need all the spaces it was initially allocated.

6.4.2 Linked List Implementation of a Queue

A queue may be implemented as a linked list. The queue bounds are now determined by the use of a NULL pointer for the rear of the queue; see Figure 6-7.

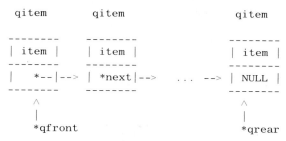

Figure 6-7 Queue as a singly linked list.

For example, the two integers 450 and 654 enqueued in sequence to form a queue as follows:

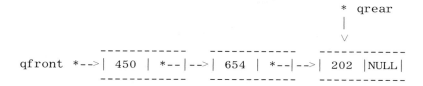

Enqueuing an integer 202 yields the queue as follows:

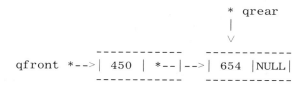

Dequeueing yields the following queue:

```
                                        *  qrear
                                        |
                                        V
                  ------------     ------------
     qfront  *-->| 654   | *--|-->| 202  |NULL|
                  ------------     ------------
```

In the queue shown above as a singly linked list, the queue item is composed of the item and a pointer for the links. The singly linked list uses one pointer, qnext, for forward linking. We define this queue as follows:

```
typedef  int  data_type;

struct qitem
    {
```

```
        struct qitem   *qnext;
        data_type       item;
    };

typedef struct qitem QITEM;
typedef struct qitem *IPOINTER;

#define  QNULL   (IPOINTER) 0

struct queue
    {
        IPOINTER  qfront;
    };

typedef  struct  queue  QUEUE;

QUEUE      lq;  /* Pointer variable lq.qfront points
                    to the front of the queue */
```

The queue list is composed of the pointers to the front and rear of the queue. The pointer variable `lq.qfront` points to the front of the queue.

The `qinit()` function implements queue initialization in the following steps:

Step 1. Allocate memory space enough to hold QUEUE-type structure using `malloc()`. If space is available, `malloc()` returns a QUEUE-type pointer. Otherwise, stop the initialization.

Step 2. Set `qfront` to QNULL and return.

When the `qadd()` function is called to enqueue a new item in the queue, it calls the `malloc()` function to dynamically allocate memory space for the item to be added in the queue. When the `qremove()` function is called to dequeue an item from the queue, it removes the item at `qfront` from the queue, and calls the `free()` function to return the memory space to the system memory heap. The advantage of this implementation is that it allows the queue to dynamically grow or shrink as needed during the execution of the program. One disadvantage is that in addition to the space needed for the queue element, we need one pointer in case of a singly linked list or two pointers in case of a doubly linked list for list links in each queue element.

For implementations of most common operations on a singly linked list version of a queue, see Example 6-4 in the Further Examples section.

6.5 An ADT Circular Queue

A circular queue is a special form of an ADT queue. In this section we consider its definition with an ADT approach, its sequential implementation, and show its usage with several examples. A circular queue is used to avoid shifting data when the array implementation is chosen.

An ADT circular queue is defined as a collection of data objects (items) that have a process-sequential order, with the following set of operations:

1. `qinit`: Initializes a queue
2. `qcreate`: Creates a queue
3. `qempty`: Checks whether a queue has any item
4. `qfull`: Checks whether a queue contains the maximum number of items
5. `qadd`: Adds an item to the rear of a queue (the `enqueue` operation)
6. `qremove`: Removes an item from the front of a queue (the `dequeue` operation), and returns the item
7. `qdelete`: Deletes the entire queue

As with queues, the items in a circular queue may be simple or complex structured-type data objects. The causes of underflow and overflow are the same as those for a simple queue. One application of a circular queue is in the message-passing mechanism between processes implemented in an operating system. This concept is also heavily used in the computer networking environment, where computers exchange data or messages between each other.

In the following subsections, we will discuss the implementations of an ADT circular queue using (1) an array and an index and (2) a singly linked list. Note that an array implementation of a circular queue is used to avoid the shifting of data. When data is deleted from such a queue, a hole is created. Usually it is required to shift the remaining data in the array to fill in the gap. In an array version of a circular queue, the data can be inserted in any empty or unused slot.

6.5.1 Array Implementation of a Circular Queue

A circular queue may be implemented by an array and the use of an index counter to access the queue locations. The queue bounds are defined by constants that bound the index.

We can implement a Circular Queue as an array by defining its data structure in the following manner:

```
#define   MAXQUEUE   64

typedef   int    ITEM;   /* An ITEM variable is an int;
                            it is the item placed on the queue*/
typedef   ITEM   *IPOINTER;

typedef   int    QINDEX; /* A QINDEX variable has values
                            from 0 to MAXQUEUE - 1        */

struct   QUEUE
    {
         QINDEX      qfront;
         QINDEX      qrear;
         QINDEX      ovflag;
         ITEM        item[ MAXQUEUE ];
    };
typedef struct QUEUE   AQUEUE;

typedef   AQUEUE   *QPOINTER;

AQUEUE   arq;             /* arq is AQUEUE-type variable */
QPOINTER  q = &arq;       /* q is QPOINTER-type variable */
```

In this structured data type, an ITEM variable is an int; it is the item placed on the queue. A QINDEX variable has values from 0 to MAXQUEUE − 1. A QPOINTER variable is used to pass the AQUEUE-type structure to functions that will access it.

The array-based circular queue is composed of queue indices, qfront and qrear, and the stored items in the array aqueue. The flag ovflag is used to keep track of the current ordering of qfront and qrear in the queue. The queue indices wrap around modulus MAXQUEUE, so we must change the overflow test from qrear >= qfront to qrear < qfront when qrear has wrapped around and is now less than qfront, and change the underflow test from qrear > qfront to qrear < qfront. Once qfront wraps around, the normal ordering is restored. Thus we use the MAXQUEUE locations item[0], ..., item [MAXQUEUE − 1] allocated for a circular queue.

The term "circular" signifies that the queue item item[0] follows behind item [MAXQUEUE − 1]. In other words, the queue item item [m + 1] is ahead of the queue item item [m].

To initialize a circular queue, the qinit() function sets the variables qfront and qrear to QNULL, and ovflag to QTAIL_BEHIND.

The qadd() function implements the enqueue operation in the following four steps:

Step 1. Check whether the circular queue is full by testing ovflag and the equality of qfront and qrear variables. If true, print an error message: "QUEUE OVERFLOW OCCURRED"; return. Otherwise, proceed to step 2.

Step 2. Store the new element in the queue array with the index value of qrear as follows:

```
q -> item[ q -> qrear ] = new_elt;
```

Step 3. Increment qrear by 1, that is,

```
q -> qrear = q -> qrear + 1;
```

Step 4. If qrear has reached the maximum array size MAXQUEUE, perform the 'modulus' operation by setting:

```
q -> qrear   = QNULL;
q -> ovflag = QTAIL_BEHIND;
```

To implement the dequeue operation in a circular queue, the steps taken by the qremove() function are:

Step 1. Check whether the queue is empty by testing

```
qfront == qrear
```

If true, print an error message: "QUEUE UNDERFLOW"; return. Otherwise, proceed to step 2.

Step 2. Take out the queue item at the front of the queue with the index value of qfront:

```
element = q -> item[ q -> qfront ];
```

Step 3. Increment qfront by 1:

$$q \; \text{->} \; qfront = q \; \text{->} \; qfront + 1;$$

Step 4. If qfront has reached the maximum array size MAXQUEUE, perform the 'modulus' operation by setting

$$q \; \text{->} \; qfront = QNULL;$$
$$q \; \text{->} \; ovflag = QTAIL\_AHEAD;$$

For a detailed implementation of these operations, see Example 6-5 in the Further Examples section.

6.5.2 Linked List Implementation of a Circular Queue

A circular queue may be implemented as a linked list. The queue bounds are now determined by the amount of system heap space available.

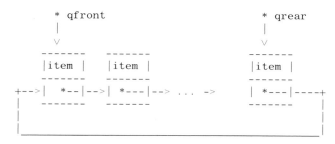

Figure 6-8 The circular queue as a singly linked list.

In the circular queue shown in Figure 6-8 as a singly linked list, the circular queue item is composed of the item and a pointer for the links. The singly linked list uses one pointer, qnext, for forward linking. Its implementation and operations are given as exercises.

6.6 Uses of Queues

In this section we show applications of queues, one using the standard FIFO queues, and the other on disk scheduling with SSTF (shortest seek time first) policy using the priority queues.

6.6.1 Uses of FIFO Queues: Communication Buffer Queue

Communication buffers make extensive use of queues. Messages from one computer to another are generally created asynchronously to actual delivery. Messages must be buffered in a queue until the receiving computer is ready for data transmission. In addition, messages must be sent to the receiving computer in the same order that they are created (FIFO). Since the number of messages that can be queued is usually fixed, a simple array implementation of queues is possible.

A pointer to keep track of the position in the array to insert a new message (bottom of buffer) is required. A pointer to keep track of the position in the array to remove a message (top of buffer) is also required. To reduce array manipulation overhead as messages are randomly inserted and removed from the queue buffer, messages remain fixed in the array while only top and bottom pointers are updated to track messages. When the end of the queue is reached, new messages "wrap around" and are written over old messages that have previously been sent. The buffer is empty (all messages have been sent) when the insert or bottom pointer is equal to the remove or top pointer. The buffer is full (no room for new messages) when the insert pointer is one less than the remove pointer.

Example 6.4 implements a communication buffer queue with messages of type char. For an actual application, the presented functions could be used with messages of type struct or type array. The function insert_queue () inserts a message into a queue at the appropriate pointer location. The function checks for queue boundaries and rolls over the insert pointer if appropriate. The function also checks to see if the queue is full. The function remove_queue () removes a message from the top of the queue. The function checks to see if the queue is empty. The function also checks for queue boundaries and rolls over the remove pointer if appropriate. This example uses the following user interface to add in, and remove a message from, the message buffer queue:

```
Enter "I" to Insert Message in Queue.
Enter "R" to Remove Message from Queue.
Enter "E" to Exit.
```

Example 6.4

```c
/* Example on Communication Buffer Queue */

#define    NULL             0
#define    MAX_QUEUE_SIZE   10
#define    FOREVER          1
#define    BELL             "\007"  /*  ascii code for tone  */

enum    status { OK, FULL };    /*  used by insert_queue ()  */

/*  define queue data type and a queue array of data types  */
typedef char        DATA_TYPE;
typedef DATA_TYPE    QUEUE[MAX_QUEUE_SIZE];

/*  define pointers to queue insert and queue remove positions */
struct    queue_pointer_def
{
  int    insert_position;
  int    remove_position;
};

typedef struct queue_pointer_def    QUEUE_POINTER;

/* =============================================================== *
 * insert_queue():                                                 *
 * Function to insert a message into a queue at requested          *
 * location.  Function automatically rolls insert position         *
 * pointer to 0 if end of queue is reached.  OK is returned        *
 * if successful. FULL is returned if queue insert position        *
 * pointer has caught up with queue remove position pointer.       *
 * =============================================================== */
```

```
enum status   insert_queue ( QUEUE    queue, QUEUE_POINTER
                              *queue_pointer, DATA_TYPE    message )
{
  int   new_position;

  if ( ( new_position = queue_pointer->insert_position + 1 ) >=
                  MAX_QUEUE_SIZE )
    new_position = 0;   /*  roll pointer  */

  if ( new_position == queue_pointer->remove_position )
    return ( FULL );   /*  queue is full  */

  /* increment queue insert position pointer and store message */
  queue_pointer->insert_position = new_position;
  queue[queue_pointer->insert_position] = message;
  return ( OK );
}


/* ============================================================ *
 *   remove_queue():                                            *
 *   Function to remove a message from queue at requested       *
 *   location. NULL is returned if queue is empty. Function     *
 *   automatically rolls remove position pointer to 0 if end of *
 *   queue is reached.                                          *
 * ============================================================ */

DATA_TYPE remove_queue ( QUEUE           queue,
                         QUEUE_POINTER *queue_pointer )
{
  DATA_TYPE   message;

  if ( queue_pointer->remove_position ==
       queue_pointer->insert_position )
    return ( NULL );   /*  queue is empty  */

  /*  increment queue remove position pointer and get message  */
  if ( ( queue_pointer->remove_position += 1 ) >= MAX_QUEUE_SIZE )
    queue_pointer->remove_position = 0;   /*  roll pointer  */
  message = queue[queue_pointer->remove_position];

  return ( message );
}

main ()
{
  QUEUE           queue;
  QUEUE_POINTER   queue_pointer;

  /*  initialize queue position pointers  */
  queue_pointer.insert_position = 0;
  queue_pointer.remove_position = 0;

  while ( FOREVER )
  {
    printf ("\n\nEnter \"I\" to Insert Message in Queue.");
```

```
        printf ("\nEnter \"R\" to Remove Message from Queue.");
        printf ("\nEnter \"E\" to Exit.\n\n");

#ifdef  DOS
    switch ( getch () )
#else
    switch ( getchar () )
#endif

    {
      case   'i':
      case   'I':
        printf ("Enter Message to Queue\n\n");

#ifdef  DOS
        if ( insert_queue ( queue, &queue_pointer, getche() )
             == FULL )
#else
        if ( insert_queue ( queue, &queue_pointer, getchar() )
             == FULL )
#endif
          printf ("\nQueue Full - Message not Accepted!" );
        break;
      case   'r':
      case   'R':
        printf ("Removed Message is:   %c",
                 remove_queue ( queue, &queue_pointer ) );
        break;
      case   'e':
      case   'E':
        exit ();
      default:
        printf ( BELL );
        break;
    }
  }
}
```

Here is the output of Example 6.4:

```
        Enter "I" to Insert Message in Queue.
        Enter "R" to Remove Message from Queue.
        Enter "E" to Exit.

        I

        Enter Message to Queue.

        R

        Enter "I" to Insert Message in Queue.
        Enter "R" to Remove Message from Queue.
        Enter "E" to Exit.

        I
```

```
           Enter "I" to Insert Message in Queue.
           Enter "R" to Remove Message from Queue.
           Enter "E" to Exit.

           Enter Message to Queue.

           A

           Enter "I" to Insert Message in Queue.
           Enter "R" to Remove Message from Queue.
           Enter "E" to Exit.

           I

           Enter Message to Queue.

           M

           Enter "I" to Insert Message in Queue.
           Enter "R" to Remove Message from Queue.
           Enter "E" to Exit.

           R

           Removed Message is:  R

           Enter "I" to Insert Message in Queue.
           Enter "R" to Remove Message from Queue.
           Enter "E" to Exit.

           R

           Removed Message is:  A

           Enter "I" to Insert Message in Queue.
           Enter "R" to Remove Message from Queue.
           Enter "E" to Exit.

           R

           Removed Message is:  M

           Enter "I" to Insert Message in Queue.
           Enter "R" to Remove Message from Queue.
           Enter "E" to Exit.

           E
```

6.6.2 Uses of Priority Queues: SSTF Disk Scheduling

Queues are useful for disk-drive management. In the following simulation example, the disk management scheduling policy is "shortest seek time first" (SSTF),
which is handled easily by a priority queue data structure. A priority queue is a
variant of standard queues (see Exercise 6-6). In the following paragraphs, we de-

scribe the address of a disk block, why disk scheduling is necessary, the SSTF algorithm, and its implementation.

In a multiprogramming computer system, system performance (and response time) are strongly dependent on rotational disk storage devices.

The disk's physical characteristics are:

1. For external storage, most computer systems have one or more disk drives. Each disk drive may have one or more disks. Each disk has two surfaces.
2. The disk is a round flat aluminum plate, covered with magnetic recording material.
3. To organize data on a disk, each surface is divided into concentric circles, called *tracks,* and each track is divided into sectors.
4. Data is stored by recording it magnetically as a stream of bits in a specified sector of a track under the read–write head of the disk drive. The data is usually stored as bytes.
5. A disk drive can have for each surface either fixed heads, one for each track, or one head that moves over all the tracks.
6. The address of data on a disk is:

```
--------+---------+-------+--------+--------+--------
| Drive | Surface | Track | Sector | Sector | Count |
| no.   | no.     | no.   | no.    | offset |       |
--------+---------+-------+--------+--------+--------
```

where "Drive no." specifies the target disk drive (applicable in case of multiple disk drives) and "Count" specifies the size of the data.
7. In a moving-head disk, the total time to access (read or write) data on a disk is:

$$\text{Data access time} = \text{track seek time} + \text{latency time} + \text{transmission time}$$

"Track-seek time" is the time spent in moving the read–write head from the current track position to the target track, specified in the data address field; it depends on the distance between the current position of the read–write head and the target track. The *average seek time* is the time needed to move the head over one half the total number of tracks on one surface. "Latency time," also called *rotational time,* is the time taken to rotate the disk until the read–write head is over the specified sector. The *average latency time* is the time for one half a rotation of the disk. "Transmission time" is the time spent in transferring data from the read–write head to the system through the system data path.

In a multitasking environment, many executing programs (usually called *processes*) reside in the main memory simultaneously, but the central processing unit (CPU) executes only one process at any time. Each process may produce requests for reading and writing disk data, which arrive at random. Because the CPU is faster than the disk drive, and the requests might arrive more quickly than the disks can serve them, the requests are placed in a service queue. A scheduling policy is required to manage this request queue. The policy determines the scheduling algorithm.

In the "first-come–first-served" (FCFS) policy, requests are placed on the queue as they arrive. The request that is at the front of the queue is removed from the queue and served. FCFS may yield very long waiting times for requests because the disk addresses of the requests are usually in random sequence and the read–write head must swing back and forth across the disk surface to serve the requests. FCFS is simple, but not efficient, because FCFS does not attempt to optimize the head movement.

The goal of SSTF is to minimize head seek time. It is a better scheduling policy than FCFS. It examines positional relationships among new and pending requests in the request queue. It rearranges the order of the requests to service the closest track first. The steps of SSTF algorithm are:

Step 1. Get the current position of the read–write (R/W) head.
Step 2. Find the smallest track-distance among the (pending and new) requests in the request queue, relative to the current head position.
Step 3. Move the R/W head to the track found in step 2. Serve the request with the smallest track-distance, and delete it from the queue.
Step 4. Repeat steps 1 through 3 until the request queue is empty.

The request queue is handled by using the priority of the associated process. The priority of each request is determined by the smallest track-distance. The smallest track-distance yields the smallest seek time. The SSTF algorithm requires knowledge of the current R/W head position. A continuous flow of requests close to each other may cause indefinite postponement; a request in the queue may stay in the queue for an indefinite period of time waiting for service. This is the disadvantage of the SSTF algorithm.

Main() is the test driver for SSTF disk scheduling simulation. To initialize the process request queue, it calls init(), passing the address of seed process number, se_no = 1. Then it calls sstf_disk_sched().

Random() calculates the random number using the *linear congruence method*. It does not expect any input. Its output is a random number, which is an integer less than MAXTRACKS, the maximum number of tracks. It is assumed that the tracks are numbered from 1 to N from innermost track to outermost track.

Find_sstf_track() finds a process in the input process queue with the minimum seek time from the current process's track. It is of type TRACK, and expects c_track of type TRACK, the current track number as the input. It scans the processes' waiting queue proc_queue[] (which is implemented as an array), and compares c_track with the tracks of each process in this queue. It selects the process number, say k, in proc_queue with the smallest track distance from the current track c_track. The priority is given to the process k for servicing its request. Then the function puts the process k in the output queue ord_proc[]. The process k is assumed (simulated) to be serviced and is removed from the waiting process queue, proc_queue. The function prints the numbers of the processes that are serviced in the current sweep. It returns the track number of the process k, which will be used as the current track for the next sweep. The function sstf_scan() is called by sstf_disk_sched().

Sstf_disk_sched() implements the SSTF disk scheduling simulation. It expects the address of a process number. It services the waiting process queue, proc_queue, using the process in proc_queue[0] as the first process. The servicing of the requests of the processes in proc_queue is continued until the queue is empty. The queue is empty when it has no process with the non-NULL process number. Within the while loop, the function calls print_q() to print the queue of requests before SSTF, and calls find_sstf_track() to select and service the process satisfying the SSTF criterion; then if the process number is less than MAX_TRIALS, and if the process queue is empty, it creates a new process, whose number is the increment of the last process number, and the track number is a random number. The random number is used to simulate the random arrival pattern of the track requests. The creation of a new process is done to simulate the arrival of a new process during and after a sweep. This new process is put into the waiting queue, proc_queue. The function sstf_disk_sched() calls print_q() to print the queue of requests, including the new requests that arrived during the sweep. This repeating process of scheduling and servicing is terminated when the process queue proc_queue becomes empty. This function is called by main().

Init_q() initializes the input process queue proc_queue and the output queue ord_queue. It expects the address of the last process. It sets NULL to the process number and track number in the two queues proc_queue and ord_queue. Then it creates five processes 1 through 5, and their respective track numbers are created by the random number generator, random(). Random() is used to simulate the randomness in track numbers. The function puts the process number and track number for each of these five processes in the waiting queue, proc_queue. It returns the process number that was created last. This number will be used as an input to the disk scheduler, sstf_disk_sched(). The test driver main() calls init_q() and then sstf_disk_sched().

Analysis of the output shows that the processes arrived in the order 1, 2, 3, 4, 5, 6, 7, 8. But they are serviced based on the priority, which is determined by the SSTF criterion. The order in which the requests are serviced is:

Process number	Track number
1	97
4	94
7	91
6	62
2	51
8	27
5	12
3	2

The code and output of the above functions are given in Example 6.5.

Example 6.5

Code Section

```
/*
 *  Program:   Disk Scheduling Simulation using
 *             SSTF policy.
 */

#include <stdio.h>
#ifdef DOS
#include <stdlib.h>
#endif

/*  Maximum number of tracks on the disk. */
#define  MAXTRACKS   99
```

```
/*  Define MULTIPLIER, INCREMENT, MODULUS
 *  in random number generation.
 */
#define   MULTIPLIER   40
#define   INCREMENT    3641
#define   MODULUS      729

/* Define Number of times each algorithm is called. */
#define   MAX_TRIALS   8

typedef   int   TRACK;
typedef   int   PROCESS_NO;

/*
 *  Define a request queue stores process number and
 *  track number of each process.
 */
typedef struct proc
   {
     PROCESS_NO    proc_no;
     TRACK         track_no;
   } proc_q;

proc_q proc_queue[MAX_TRIALS + 10]; /* Input process queue. */
proc_q ord_proc[MAX_TRIALS + 10];    /* output process queue. */
proc_q ord_procin[MAX_TRIALS + 10];

/* output process queue in SCAN during inward sweep. */

int seed = 5;            /* used in random number generation. */
int se_no = 1;           /* To store processes serial number. */

/*
 *  random():
 */
int random(void)

/*  PURPOSE: Calculate random number using
 *           'linear congruence method'.
 *  INPUT: some number called as seed.
 *  OUTPUT: Random number.
 */

{
  int   randval ;    /* storage for random number */
  do
  {
    randval = (MULTIPLIER * seed + INCREMENT) % MODULUS;
    seed = randval;         /* for the next calculation. */

  } while( seed < 0 );
  /*  Get a value less than MAXTRACK  */
  while (randval > MAXTRACKS)
```

```
  randval = randval % MAXTRACKS;
   return(randval);
}

/*
 *   find_sstf_track():
 */

TRACK find_sstf_track ( TRACK c_track )

/*   PURPOSE: Find a process in the input process queue
 *            with the minimum seek time from the current
 *            process (track).
 *   INPUT:   The current track number.
 *   OUTPUT:  The track number closest to the current track.
 */
{
    int   i, j,              /* counters */
          min_dist, dist;

    /*  Calculate the distance between the current process
     *  and the waiting processes.
     */
    TRACK   min_track_no = 0,
            min_track;       /* Track number closest to the
                                current track. */

    min_dist = c_track - proc_queue[0].track_no;
    /*  Get absolute distance between tracks */
    if ( min_dist < 0 )
        min_dist = - min_dist;
    /*  Get process number with the minimum seek
     *  distance from the current track.
     */
    for ( i = 1; proc_queue[i].proc_no != '\0'; i++ )
      {
          dist = (c_track - proc_queue[i].track_no);
          if ( dist < 0 )
            dist = - dist;
          if ( dist < min_dist )
            {
               min_dist = dist;
               min_track_no = i;
            }
      }
    /* Put it in the output queue. */
    for ( i = 0; ord_proc[i].proc_no != '\0'; i++ )
      ;
    ord_proc[i].proc_no =  proc_queue[min_track_no].proc_no;
    ord_proc[i].track_no = proc_queue[min_track_no].track_no;
    min_track = proc_queue[min_track_no].track_no;
    printf("The process number that is serviced %s ",
          "in the current sweep is:");
    printf("  %d\n", proc_queue[min_track_no].proc_no);
```

```
    /*  Remove the serviced process from the input queue.
     *  The queue is organized as an array.
     */
    i = min_track_no;
    j = i + 1;
    do
    {
        proc_queue[i].proc_no = proc_queue[j].proc_no;
        proc_queue[i].track_no = proc_queue[j].track_no;
        i++;
    } while ( proc_queue[j++].proc_no != '\0' );
    return ( min_track );
}

/*
 *  print_q():
 */

void print_q ( proc_q *queue )

/*  PURPOSE:   Print the process queue with process
 *             number and track number.
 *  INPUT:     queue to be printed.
 *  OUTPUT:    queue is printed on the output terminal.
 */
{
    int  i;
    if ( queue[0].proc_no == '\0' )   /* if queue is empty. */
      {
        printf("\nAll requests are serviced, %s \n\n",
                "the queue is empty.");
        return;
      }
    printf("Process#      Track#\n");
    for ( i = 0; queue[i].proc_no != '\0'; i++ )
        printf(" %d              %d\n", queue[i].proc_no,
                queue[i].track_no);
    return;
}

/*
 *  sstf_disk_sched():
 */

void sstf_disk_sched ( PROCESS_NO * p_no )

/*  PURPOSE: Implement SSTF disk scheduling algorithm.
 *  INPUT:   Process number(ID) of the last request.
 *  OUTPUT:  Processes in the input queue are serviced
 *           according to the SSTF algorithm.
 */
{
    TRACK  cur_track = proc_queue[0].track_no;
    int    i;
```

```
      /*  Repeat servicing the requests as long as
       *  input queue is not empty.
       */
      while ( proc_queue[0].proc_no != '\0' )
        {
          printf("\n\nThe current track is: %d.\n",
                 cur_track);
          printf("The queue  of requests before SSTF:\n");
          print_q( proc_queue );

          /*  Call find_sstf_track() to find the track that
           *  satisfies the minimum seek time criterion.
           */
          cur_track = find_sstf_track ( cur_track );
          /*  Add a new process in the request to simulate
           *  arrival of new process' requests
           */
          if ( *p_no < MAX_TRIALS )
            {
              for ( i = 0; proc_queue[i].proc_no != '\0'; i++ )
                ;
              proc_queue[i].proc_no = ++(*p_no);
              proc_queue[i].track_no = random();
            }
          printf("The queue of requests after SSTF (the %s %s \n",
                 "new requests which arrived \nduring the",
                 "sweep, are also included):");
          print_q ( proc_queue );
        }
      printf("The order in which requests are serviced:\n" );
      print_q ( ord_proc );       /* print output queue. */
}


/*
 *  init_q():
 */

void init_q ( int *p_no )
/*  PURPOSE: Initialize the input process queue.
 *  INPUT:   The process id of the last process received.
 *  OUTPUT:  Initialized input process  queue.
 */
{
    int  i;

    /*  Initialize the process queues by putting '\0'
     *  in the places for process numbers and track
     *  numbers.
     */
    for ( i = 0; i < MAXTRACKS; i++ )
        {
          proc_queue[i].proc_no = '\0';
          proc_queue[i].track_no = '\0';
```

```
            ord_proc[i].proc_no = '\0';
            ord_proc[i].track_no = '\0';
        }
    /*  Initially create processes 1 through 5,
     *  and their track numbers are generated by
     *  a random number generator, random().
     */
    for ( i = 0; i < 5; i++ )
        {
            proc_queue[i].proc_no = i + 1;
            proc_queue[i].track_no = random();
        }
    *p_no = i;
}


/*
 *  main():   Main test driver for SSTF disk scheduling
 *            simulation.
 */

void main( void )
{
    PROCESS_NO se_no = 1;

    init_q ( &se_no );
    printf("\n ** Disk Scheduling Simulation Using %s \n\n",
            "SSTF Algorithm  **");
    sstf_disk_sched ( &se_no );
}
```

Output Section

```
  ** Disk Scheduling Simulation Using SSTF Algorithm  **

The current track is: 97.
The queue  of requests before SSTF:
Process#        Track#
 1               97
 2               51
 3               2
 4               94
 5               12
The process number that is serviced in the current sweep is:    1
The queue of requests after SSTF (the new requests which arrived
during the sweep, are also included):
Process#        Track#
 2               51
 3               2
 4               94
 5               12
 6               62


The current track is: 97.
The queue  of requests before SSTF:
```

```
Process#        Track#
   2              51
   3              2
   4              94
   5              12
   6              62
```
The process number that is serviced in the current sweep is: 4
The queue of requests after SSTF (the new requests which arrived
during the sweep, are also included):
```
Process#        Track#
   2              51
   3              2
   5              12
   6              62
   7              91
```

The current track is: 94.
The queue of requests before SSTF:
```
Process#        Track#
   2              51
   3              2
   5              12
   6              62
   7              91
```
The process number that is serviced in the current sweep is: 7
The queue of requests after SSTF (the new requests which arrived
during the sweep, are also included):
```
Process#        Track#
   2              51
   3              2
   5              12
   6              62
   8              27
```

The current track is: 91.
The queue of requests before SSTF:
```
Process#        Track#
   2              51
   3              2
   5              12
   6              62
   8              27
```
The process number that is serviced in the current sweep is: 6
The queue of requests after SSTF (the new requests which arrived
during the sweep, are also included):
```
Process#        Track#
   2              51
   3              2
   5              12
   8              27
```

The current track is: 62.
The queue of requests before SSTF:

Process#   Track#
  2   51
  3   2
  5   12
  8   27

The process number that is serviced in the current sweep is: 2
The queue of requests after SSTF (the new requests which arrived during the sweep, are also included):

Process#   Track#
  3   2
  5   12
  8   27

The current track is: 51.
The queue of requests before SSTF:
Process#   Track#
  3   2
  5   12
  8   27

The process number that is serviced in the current sweep is: 8
The queue of requests after SSTF (the new requests which arrived during the sweep, are also included):

Process#   Track#
  3   2
  5   12

The current track is: 27.
The queue of requests before SSTF:
Process#   Track#
  3   2
  5   12

The process number that is serviced in the current sweep is: 5
The queue of requests after SSTF (the new requests which arrived during the sweep, are also included):

Process#   Track#
  3   2

The current track is: 12.
The queue of requests before SSTF:
Process#   Track#
  3   2

The process number that is serviced in the current sweep is: 3
The queue of requests after SSTF (the new requests which arrived during the sweep, are also included):

All requests are serviced, the queue is empty.

The order in which requests are serviced:
Process#   Track#
  1   97
  4   94
  7   91
  6   62
  2   51
  8   27

5   12
3   2

Further Examples

Example 6-1

Code Section

```
/*  Program:  ary_stk.c   (ARRAY IMPLEMENTATION OF ADT STACKS)
 *
 *  Purpose:  Implement an ADT Stack as an Array
 *            with operations implemented by the following
 *            functions:
 *
 *                 1.   is_stk_empty()
 *                 2.   create_elt()
 *                 3.   create_stk()
 *                 4.   clear_stk()
 *                 5.   push()
 *                 6.   pop()
 *                 7.   get_top()
 *                 8.   print_stk()
 *
 *  Note: In this case, the top of the stack, 'top_stk', is
 *        merely an index of the STACK array, ranging from
 *        index 0 through Stk_Size - 1. In other words, the
 *        stack will grow from STACK[0] to STACK[ Stk_Size - 1]
 *        at its maximum.
 */

#define  NULL       0
#define  Stk_Size   8                   /* Stack Limit           */

typedef  int   BOOLEAN;                  /* Define BOOLEAN type */
#define  FALSE  0
#define  TRUE   ~FALSE

typedef  char  data_type;               /* Define stack data    */
typedef  data_type   STACK [ Stk_Size ]; /* STACK defined as an
                                           array of Stk_Size    */
/* ===========================================================
 * is_stk_empty(top_stk): Returns TRUE if empty, else FALSE
 * ===========================================================*/
BOOLEAN  is_stk_empty( int top_stk )
{
    return ( top_stk == -1 );
}

/* ===========================================================
 * init_stk(top_stk ):Initialize the stack by setting top_stk = -1
 * ===========================================================*/
init_stk( int * top_stk )
{
    *top_stk = -1;
}
```

```
/* ============================================================ *
 * clear_stk( stack, size ) :                                   *
 *   Clear the entire stack by setting each element of Stack    *
 *   array to null.                                             *
 * ============================================================ */
void clear_stk( STACK  stack, int size, int * top_stk )
{
    int    i;
    for ( i = 0; i < size; i++ )
        stack[ i ] = '\0';
    init_stk(top_stk);
}


/* ============================================================ *
 * push( stack, top_stk, size, new_elt ) :                      *
 *   Creates a memory space for  'elt_struct' to hold 'new_elt' *
 *   as its data field. Finally, make it 'top' element of the   *
 *   stack by simply adjusting the Pointers.                    *
 * ============================================================ */
void push ( STACK  stack, int  *top_stk, int size, data_type new_elt )
{
    /* Check whether stack is full  */
    if ( *top_stk == size - 1 )
        {
          printf("\n push: ERROR: Stack Overflow occurred !!! \n");
          exit ();
        }
    ++*top_stk;
    stack [ *top_stk ] = new_elt;
}


/* ============================================================ *
 * pop( stack, top_stk ) :                                      *
 *   Pop (i.e., take out) the element at the top of the stack,  *
 *   and put it in 'element'. Make the element next to the 'top'*
 *   previous to 'pop' operation the 'current top' of the stack.*
 *   Free the memory space held by the element just popped out.  *
 * ============================================================ */
data_type  pop( STACK  stack, int  *top_stk )
{
    data_type  element;

    if ( is_stk_empty ( *top_stk ) )
        {
          printf("\n pop: fails, Stack is empty. \n");
          exit ();
        }
    else            /* Stack has at least one element   */
        {
          element = stack[ *top_stk ];
          --*top_stk;                   /* top_stk = top_stk - 1 */
          return ( element );
        }
}
```

```
/* ==============================================================  *
 * get_top( stack, top_stk ) :                                    *
 *   Return a copy of element at the top of the stack without     *
 *   destroying it.                                               *
 * ==============================================================  */
data_type  get_top( STACK  stack, int  *top_stk )
{
    if ( is_stk_empty ( *top_stk ) )
        printf("\n get_top: fails, Stack is empty. \n");
    else
      return ( stack[ *top_stk ] );
}


/* ==============================================================  *
 * print_stk ( stack, top_stk ):                                  *
 *   Print the entire 'stack' starting from its element at        *
 *   'top of the stack' to bottom.                                *
 * ==============================================================  */
void print_stk ( STACK  stack, int  top_stk )
{
    int     stk_index;

    if ( is_stk_empty ( top_stk ) )
        printf("\n print_stk: Stack is empty. \n");
    else
      {
        for ( stk_index = top_stk; stk_index >= 0; stk_index-- )
            printf(" %c --> ", stack[ stk_index ] );
        printf(" NULL \n ");
      }
}


/* ==============================================================  *
 * create_stk (string[ ], stack, size, *top_stk )                 *
 *   Create/build a stack from a string of chars. Return the      *
 *   top of the stack.                                            *
 * ==============================================================  */
void create_stk ( data_type string[ ], STACK  stack,
                  int size, int  *top_stk )
{
    int    i;
    int    temp_stk_index =  *top_stk;

    if ( string[ 0 ] == '\0' )
        printf("\n create_stk: String is empty. \n");
    else
      {
        /*  Note string[0] will be at the bottom of stack  */
        for ( i = 0; string[ i ] != '\0'; ++i )
            push ( stack, &temp_stk_index, size, string[i] );
        *top_stk = temp_stk_index;
      }
}
```

```
/* =================================================================   *
 *  main(): STACK OPERATIONS WHEN IT IS STRUCTURED AS AN ARRAY         *
 *  =================================================================  */
main()
{
    static char string[ ] = "PRATIVA";   /* Input String              */
    int         top_stk;
    STACK       stack;

    printf("\n == ADT STACK OPERATIONS IN ITS %s \n",
            "SEQUENTIAL IMPLEMENTATION == ");
    printf("\n Original String: " );
    printf( string );

    /* Represent string as a stack    */
    init_stk( &top_stk );                        /* Initialize the stack */
    create_stk ( string, stack, Stk_Size, &top_stk );

    printf("\n\n Stack representation of %s: \n",
            "above string after Push operation" );
    print_stk ( stack, top_stk );
    printf("\n \/\ \n");
    printf(" |_____   Top of this Stack \n");
    printf("\n == End of ADT STACK OPERATIONS Example == \n");
}
```

Output Section

```
== ADT STACK OPERATIONS IN ITS SEQUENTIAL IMPLEMENTATION ==

Original String: PRATIVA

Stack representation of above string after Push operation:
A --> V --> I --> T --> A --> R --> P --> NULL

/\
|_____   Top of this Stack

== End of ADT STACK OPERATIONS Example ==
```

Example 6-2

Code Section

```
/*  Program: lnk_stk_ops.c   (LINKED LIST IMPLEMENTATION OF ADT
 *                            STACKS)
 *
 *  Purpose: Implement an ADT Stack as a Singly Linked List with
 *           the following operations on it:
 *
 *              1.   is_stk_empty()
 *              2.   create_elt()
 *              3.   create_stk()
 *              4.   clear_stk()
```

```
*                   5.   push()
*                   6.   pop()
*                   7.   get_top()
*                   8.   print_stk()
*/

#define  NULL   0
typedef  int    BOOLEAN;                            /* Define BOOLEAN type*/

typedef  char  data_type;                           /* Define stack data */
typedef  struct elt_struct
    {
        data_type   element;
        struct elt_struct  *next_elt;
    };
typedef  struct elt_struct    STACK_TYPE;
typedef  STACK_TYPE  *STACK_PTR;            /* Define type STACK_PTR */

/* ================================================================ *
 * is_stk_empty(top_stk): Returns TRUE is empty, else FALSE         *
 * ================================================================ */
BOOLEAN  is_stk_empty( STACK_PTR  top_stk )
{                                    /* Stack is empty if top_stk = 0    */
    return ( top_stk == NULL );
}


/* ================================================================ *
 * init_stk(top_stk ):Initialize the stack by setting top_stk = NULL
 * ================================================================ */
void init_stk( STACK_PTR  *top_stk )
{
    *top_stk = NULL;
}


/* ================================================================ *
 * create_elt (): Allocate mem space and pointer to that           *
 *                memory space                                     *
 * ================================================================ */
STACK_PTR create_elt ()
{
    STACK_PTR new_elt_ptr;    /* Will be returned after malloc     */

    /*  Allocate a memory space for the new element; if no space
     *  available, return with error
     */

    if ( (new_elt_ptr = (STACK_PTR) malloc ( sizeof(STACK_TYPE) ) )
            == NULL )
      {
          printf("\n create_elt: malloc failed  \n\n");
          return ( NULL );
      }
```

```
      else
          {   /*  Initialize this element   */
              new_elt_ptr -> element  =  NULL;
              new_elt_ptr -> next_elt = NULL;
              return( new_elt_ptr );
          }
}


/* =============================================================  *
 * push( top_stk, new_elt ) :                                     *
 *    Creates a memory space for   'elt_struct' to hold 'new_elt' *
 *    as its data field. Finally, make it 'top' element of the    *
 *    stack by simply adjusting the Pointers.                     *
 * =============================================================  */
void push ( STACK_PTR  *top_stk, data_type   new_elt )
{
      STACK_PTR   temp_elt_ptr;

      /* Allocate memory space to hold 'elt_struct' using malloc() */
      temp_elt_ptr = create_elt();
      /* Put new element on top */
      temp_elt_ptr -> element = new_elt;
      temp_elt_ptr -> next_elt = *top_stk;

      /* top_stk becomes next to top elt of the stack */
      *top_stk = temp_elt_ptr;
}


/* =============================================================  *
 * pop( top_stk ) :                                               *
 *  Pop (i.e., take out) the element at the top of the stack,     *
 *  and put it in 'element'. Make the element next to the 'top'   *
 *  previous to 'pop' operation the 'current top' of the stack.   *
 *  Free the memory space held by the element just popped out.    *
 * =============================================================  */
data_type  pop( STACK_PTR *top_stk )
{
      data_type   element;
      STACK_PTR   temp_elt_ptr = *top_stk;

      if ( is_stk_empty ( temp_elt_ptr ) )
          printf("\n pop: fails, Stack Underflow. \n");
      else
        {  /* Stack has at least one element   */
           element = temp_elt_ptr -> element;
           /* Top of the stack now points to next elt */
           *top_stk = temp_elt_ptr -> next_elt;
           free( temp_elt_ptr );
           return ( element );
        }
}
```

```
/* ================================================================ *
 * get_top( top_stk ) : Get a copy of element at the top of the *
 *                      stack without destroying it.            *
 * ================================================================ */
data_type  get_top( STACK_PTR  top_stk )
{
    if ( is_stk_empty ( top_stk ) )
        printf("\n get_top: fails, Stack is empty. \n");
    else
        return ( top_stk -> element );
}


/* ================================================================ *
 * print_stk (): Print contents of a stack.                     *
 * ================================================================ */
void print_stk ( STACK_PTR   top_stk )
{
    STACK_PTR  temp_elt_ptr;
    temp_elt_ptr =   top_stk;

    if ( is_stk_empty ( temp_elt_ptr ))
        printf("\n print_stk: Stack is empty. \n");
    else
      {
        while ( temp_elt_ptr != NULL )
          {
            printf(" %c --> ", temp_elt_ptr -> element );
            temp_elt_ptr = temp_elt_ptr -> next_elt;
          }
        printf(" NULL \n");
      }
}


/* ================================================================ *
 * create_stk(): Create/build a stack from a string of chars.   *
 *               Return the top of the stack.                   *
 * ================================================================ */
void create_stk ( data_type  string[ ], STACK_PTR *top_stk )
{
    int    i;
    STACK_PTR  temp_elt_ptr;
    temp_elt_ptr =  *top_stk;

    if ( string[ 0 ] == '\0' )              /* End or Null delimiter */
        printf("\n create_stk: String is empty. \n");
    else
      {
        for ( i = 0; string[ i ] != '\0'; ++i )
            push ( &temp_elt_ptr, string[i] );
        *top_stk = temp_elt_ptr;
      }
}
```

```
/* ================================================================ *
 * clear_stk( top_stk ) : Takes out all elements in the stack      *
 *                        calling 'pop()' that frees spaces.        *
 * ================================================================ */
void clear_stk( STACK_PTR *top_stk )
{
   while ( ! is_stk_empty( *top_stk ) )
     pop( top_stk );
}


/* ================================================================ *
 * main(): STACK OPERATIONS IN ITS SINGLE LINKED STRUCTURE         *
 * ================================================================ */
main()
{
    static char string[ ] = "PRATIVA";   /* Input String         */
    STACK_PTR  top_stk = NULL;            /* Initialize the stack */

    printf("\n == STACK OPERATIONS IN ITS %s == \n",
           "SINGLY LINKED IMPLEMENTATION" );
    printf("\n Original String: " );
    printf( string );

    /* Represent string as a stack */
    create_stk ( string, &top_stk );

    printf("\n\n Stack representation of the above : \n",
           "string after Push operation" );
    print_stk ( top_stk );
    printf("\n \/\ \n");
    printf(" |_____   Top of this Stack \n");
    printf("\n == End of STACK OPERATIONS Example == \n");
}
```

Output Section

```
== STACK OPERATIONS IN ITS SINGLY LINKED IMPLEMENTATION ==

Original String: PRATIVA

Stack representation of the above string after Push operation:
A --> V --> I --> T --> A --> R --> P --> NULL

/\
|_____   Top of this Stack

== End of STACK OPERATIONS Example ==
```

Example 6-3

Code Section

```
/*
 * Program: aryQueOps.c   (ARRAY IMPLEMENTATION OF ADT QUEUES)
 */
```

```
#include <stdio.h>
#define  FALSE     0
#define  TRUE      ~FALSE
#define  MAXQUEUE  16

/*
 *  An ITEM variable is an int; it is the item placed on the queue.
 */
typedef  int   ITEM;
typedef  ITEM  *IPOINTER;

/*
 *  A QINDEX variable has values from 0 to MAXQUEUE - 1
 */
typedef  int   QINDEX;
#define  QNULL  (QINDEX) 0

/*
 * The array-based queue is composed of queue indices,
 * qfront and qrear, and the stored items in the array
 * item.
 */
struct  QUEUE
{
    QINDEX     qfront;
    QINDEX     qrear;
    ITEM       item[MAXQUEUE];
};
typedef struct QUEUE  AQUEUE;

/*
 *  A QPOINTER variable is used to pass the queue structure
 *  to functions that will access it.
 */
typedef  AQUEUE  *QPOINTER;

/*
 *  main for array implementation of queues
 */

main()
{
    QINDEX  qadd( QPOINTER, ITEM ),
            qremove( QPOINTER, IPOINTER );
    int  qinit( QPOINTER ), qempty( QPOINTER );
    int      getinput();
    ITEM     item;
    AQUEUE   arq;
    QPOINTER  q = &arq;
    QINDEX    qinx;
    int    c;
    char      ch;
```

```
    qinit(q);

    /*
     *   Create a Queue   reading characters from
     *   terminal input
     */
    while ((c = getinput()) != EOF)
    {
        switch (c)
        {
            case 'q':
                printf("\nGoodbye\n");
                exit (0);
                break;
            case 'a':
                printf("\nInput a queue item value + <RETURN>: ");
                scanf("%d", &item);
                getchar(ch);
                printf("%d\n", item);
                if ((qinx = qadd(q, item)) == MAXQUEUE)
                    qerror("Queue full; do some removes");
                break;
            case 'r':
                if (qempty(q) == TRUE)
                    qerror("Queue empty; do some adds");
                else
                    qinx = qremove(q, &item);
                    printf("item: %d", item);
                break;
            case 'p':
                for (qinx = 0; qinx < q->qrear; qinx++)
                {
                    printf("item[%d] = %d\n", qinx, q->item[qinx]);
                }
                break;
            default:
                qerror("Invalid input");
                break;
        }
    }
}

int getinput()
{
    char   ch[5];

    printf("\nInput menu:\n");
    printf("\ta = add an item to the queue\n");
    printf("\tr = remove an item from the queue\n");
    printf("\tp = print the queue\n");
    printf("\tq = quit\n");
    printf("Please input selection: ");
```

```
    if ((gets(ch)) == (char *) 0)
    {
      printf("\n");
      return(EOF);
    }
    else
    {
      printf("%c\n", ch[0]);
      return((int) ch[0]);
    }
}
/*
 *  array implementation of queue operations
 */

int       qinit( QPOINTER  q )
{
    q->qfront = QNULL;
    q->qrear  = QNULL;
}

int        qempty( QPOINTER   q )
{
    return((q->qrear == q->qfront) ? TRUE : FALSE);
}

QINDEX     qadd( QPOINTER   q, ITEM  item )
{
    int  qerror();

    if (q->qrear < MAXQUEUE)
    {
        q->item[q->qrear] = item;
        q->qrear += 1;
        return (q->qrear);
    }
    else
    {
        qerror("queue overflow");
        return (MAXQUEUE);
    }
}

QINDEX     qremove( QPOINTER   q, IPOINTER   ip )
{
    QINDEX     qinx;
    int        qerror();

    if (q->qrear > q->qfront)
    {
        /*
         * Get the queue item from the front of the queue
         */
```

```
        *ip = q->item[q->qfront];
        /*
         * Now all the rest of the queue items must be shifted down
         */
        for (qinx = q->qfront; qinx < q->qrear; qinx++)
            q->item[qinx] = q->item[qinx+1];
        q->qrear -= 1;
        return (q->qrear);
    }
    else
    {
        qerror("queue underflow");
        return (QNULL);
    }
}

int qerror( char * msg )
{
    fprintf(stderr, "\nError: %s\n", msg);
}
```

Output Section

```
            Input menu:
             a = add an item to the queue
             r = remove an item from the queue
             p = print the queue
             q = quit
            Please input selection: a
            Input a queue item value + <RETURN>: 0

            Input menu:
             a = add an item to the queue
             r = remove an item from the queue
             p = print the queue
             q = quit
            Please input selection: a
            Input a queue item value + <RETURN>: 1

            Input menu:
             a = add an item to the queue
             r = remove an item from the queue
             p = print the queue
             q = quit
            Please input selection: a
            Input a queue item value + <RETURN>: 2

            Input menu:
             a = add an item to the queue
             r = remove an item from the queue
             p = print the queue
             q = quit
```

```
Please input selection: p
qitem[0] = 0
qitem[1] = 1
qitem[2] = 2

Input menu:
 a = add an item to the queue
 r = remove an item from the queue
 p = print the queue
 q = quit
Please input selection: a
Input a queue item value + <RETURN>: 3

Input menu:
 a = add an item to the queue
 r = remove an item from the queue
 p = print the queue
 q = quit
Please input selection: r
item: 0

Input menu:
 a = add an item to the queue
 r = remove an item from the queue
 p = print the queue
 q = quit
Please input selection: p
qitem[0] = 1
qitem[1] = 2
qitem[2] = 3

Input menu:
 a = add an item to the queue
 r = remove an item from the queue
 p = print the queue
 q = quit
Please input selection: q
Goodbye
```

Example 6-4

Code Section

```c
/*
 *  Program: lstQueOps.c   (SINGLY LINKED LIST IMPLEMENTATION OF ADT
 *  QUEUES)
 */
#include  <stdio.h>
#include  <malloc.h>

#define  FALSE   0
#define  TRUE    ~FALSE
```

```
/*
 *   An ITEM variable is an int
 *   it is the item placed on the queue.
 */
typedef   int   ITEM;

/*
 *   In a linked list implementation, the queue item is composed
 *   of the item and a pointer for the links.  The singly linked
 *   list uses one pointer, qnext, for a forward linking.
 */
struct qitem
{
    struct qitem   *qnext;
    ITEM           item;
};

typedef struct qitem QITEM;
typedef struct qitem *IPOINTER;
#define   QNULL   (IPOINTER)  0

/*
 * The queue list is composed of the pointer to the front of
 * the queue.
 */
struct queue
{
    IPOINTER   qfront;
};

typedef   struct   queue   QUEUE;

/*
 *   main for list implementation of queues
 */

main ()
{
    IPOINTER    qadd( QUEUE,  ITEM );
    ITEM        qremove( QUEUE );
    int         qinit( QUEUE ),  qempty( QUEUE );
    int         getinput ();

    ITEM        item;
    QUEUE       lq, *q;
    IPOINTER    ip;
    int         c;
    char        ch;

    q = &lq;
    qinit(q);
    while ((c = getinput()) != EOF)
    {
```

```
        switch (c)
        {
            case 'q':
                printf("\nGoodbye\n");
                exit (0);
                break;
            case 'a':
                printf("\nInput a queue item value + <RETURN>: ");
                scanf("%d", &item);
                getchar(ch);
                printf("%d\n", item);
                if ((qadd(q, item)) == QNULL)
                    qerror("Queue space exhausted; do some removes");
                break;
            case 'r':
                if (qempty(q) == TRUE)
                    qerror("Queue empty; do some adds");
                else
                    {
                        item = qremove(q);
                        printf("item: %d", item);
                    }
                break;
            case 'p':
                if (q->qfront != QNULL)
                    for (ip = q->qfront; ip != QNULL; ip = ip->qnext)
                        {
                            printf("item = %d\n", ip->item);
                        }
                break;
            default:
                qerror("Invalid input");
                break;
        }
    }
}

int getinput()
{
    char  ch[4];

    printf("\nInput menu:\n");
    printf("\ta = add an item to the queue\n");
    printf("\tr = remove an item from the queue\n");
    printf("\tp = print the queue\n");
    printf("\tq = quit\n");
    printf("Please input selection: ");
    if ((gets(ch)) == (char *) 0)
    {
      printf("\n");
      return(EOF);
    }
    else
    {
```

```
            printf("%c\n", ch[0]);
            return((int) ch[0]);
    }
}


/*
 *  The list implementation of queue operations
 */

int        qinit( QUEUE  *q )
{
    char   *malloc();

    if ((q = (QUEUE *) malloc(sizeof(QUEUE))) == 0)
    {
        printf("qinit: no memory available\n");
        exit(-1);
    }
    else
        q->qfront = QNULL;
}

int        qempty( QUEUE  *q )
{
    return((q->qfront == QNULL) ? TRUE : FALSE);
}

IPOINTER  qadd( QUEUE    *q, ITEM     newitem )
{
    int          qerror();
    char         *malloc();
    IPOINTER     newp, ip;

    if ((newp = (IPOINTER) malloc(sizeof(QITEM))) != 0)
    {
        /*
         * find the rear of the queue
         */
        if (q->qfront == QNULL)
            q->qfront = newp;
        else
        {
          for (ip = q->qfront; ip->qnext != QNULL; ip = ip->qnext)
                ;
          ip->qnext = newp;
        }

        /*
         * insert the new queue item
         */
        newp->qnext = QNULL;
        newp->item = newitem;
        return (newp);
    }
```

```
        else
        {
            printf("queue memory space overflow\n");
            return (QNULL);
        }
    }

ITEM        qremove( QUEUE    *q )
{
    ITEM          qdata;
    IPOINTER      oldqfront = q->qfront;
    int           qerror();
    void          free();

    if (q->qfront != QNULL)
    {
        /*
         * Get the queue item from the front of the queue
         */
        qdata = q->qfront->item;
        /*
         * shift qfront to the next item in the queue
         */
        q->qfront = q->qfront->qnext;
        /*
         * free the space held by the discarded item
         */
        free((char *) oldqfront);
        /*
         * and return the data item
         */
        return (qdata);
    }
    else
    {
        qerror("queue underflow");
        return (0);
    }
}

int  qerror( char   *msg )
{
    printf(stderr, "\nError: %s\n", msg);
}
```

Output Section

```
            Input menu:
            a = add an item to the queue
            r = remove an item from the queue
            p = print the queue
            q = quit
            Please input selection: a

            Input a queue item value + <RETURN>: 0
```

```
Input menu:
 a = add an item to the queue
 r = remove an item from the queue
 p = print the queue
 q = quit
Please input selection: a

Input a queue item value + <RETURN>: 1

Input menu:
 a = add an item to the queue
 r = remove an item from the queue
 p = print the queue
 q = quit
Please input selection: a

Input a queue item value + <RETURN>: 2

Input menu:
 a = add an item to the queue
 r = remove an item from the queue
 p = print the queue
 q = quit
Please input selection: a

Input a queue item value + <RETURN>: 3

Input menu:
 a = add an item to the queue
 r = remove an item from the queue
 p = print the queue
 q = quit
Please input selection: a

Input a queue item value + <RETURN>: 4

Input menu:
 a = add an item to the queue
 r = remove an item from the queue
 p = print the queue
 q = quit
Please input selection: p
item = 0
item = 1
item = 2
item = 3
item = 4

Input menu:
 a = add an item to the queue
 r = remove an item from the queue
 p = print the queue
 q = quit
Please input selection: a
```

```
Input a queue item value + <RETURN>:  5

Input menu:
 a = add an item to the queue
 r = remove an item from the queue
 p = print the queue
 q = quit
Please input selection:  r
item:  0
Input menu:
 a = add an item to the queue
 r = remove an item from the queue
 p = print the queue
 q = quit
Please input selection:  r
item:  1
Input menu:
 a = add an item to the queue
 r = remove an item from the queue
 p = print the queue
 q = quit
Please input selection:  r
item:  2
Input menu:
 a = add an item to the queue
 r = remove an item from the queue
 p = print the queue
 q = quit
Please input selection:  p
item = 3
item = 4
item = 5

Input menu:
 a = add an item to the queue
 r = remove an item from the queue
 p = print the queue
 q = quit
Please input selection:  q

Goodbye
```

Example 6-5

Code Section

```
/*
 *  Program: caryQueOps.c   (ARRAY IMPLEMENTATION OF CIRCULAR QUEUES)
 */
#include <stdio.h>

#define  FALSE      0
#define  TRUE       ~FALSE
#define  MAXQUEUE   6
```

```
/*
 *  An ITEM variable is an int; it is the item placed on the queue.
 */
typedef   int    ITEM;
typedef   ITEM   *IPOINTER;

/*
 *  A QINDEX variable has values from 0 to MAXQUEUE - 1
 */
typedef   int    QINDEX;

/*
 *   The array-based circular queue is composed of queue indices,
 *   qfront and qrear, and the stored items in the array aqueue.
 *   The flag ovflag is used to keep track of the current ordering
 *   of qfront and qrear in the queue.  The queue indices wrap around
 *   modulus MAXQUEUE, so we must change the overflow test from
 *   qrear >= qfront  to qrear < qfront when qrear has wrapped around
 *   and is now less than qfront, and change the underflow test from
 *   qrear > qfront to qrear < qfront.  Once qfront wraps around, the
 *   normal ordering is restored.
 */

struct   QUEUE
{
    QINDEX        qfront;
    QINDEX        qrear;
    QINDEX        ovflag;
    ITEM          item[MAXQUEUE];
};
typedef struct QUEUE   AQUEUE;

#define   QNULL           (QINDEX)  0
#define   QTAIL_BEHIND    (QINDEX)  1
#define   QTAIL_AHEAD     (QINDEX)  2
#define   OVERFLOW        0
#define   ADDOK           1
#define   UNDERFLOW       (ITEM)    0

/*
 *  A QPOINTER variable is used to pass the queue structure to
 *  functions that will access it.
 */
typedef   AQUEUE   *QPOINTER;

/*
 *  main for array implementation of Circular Queues
 */

main()
{
    ITEM          qremove();
    int           qinit(), qempty(), qfull(), qadd();
    int           getinput();
```

```
ITEM       item;
AQUEUE     arq;
QPOINTER   q = &arq;
QINDEX     qinx;
int        c;
char       ch;

qinit(q);
while ((c = getinput()) != EOF)
{
    switch (c)
    {
        case 'q':
            printf("\nGoodbye\n");
            exit (0);
            break;
        case 'a':
            if (qfull(q) == FALSE)
            {
              printf("\nInput a queue item value + <RETURN>: ")
                scanf("%d", &item);
                getchar(ch);
                printf("%d\n", item);
                qadd(q, item);
            }
            break;
        case 'r':
            if (qempty(q) == FALSE)
                item = qremove(q);
                printf("item: %d\n", item);
            break;
        case 'p':
            if (qempty(q) == FALSE)
            {
                qinx = q->qfront;
                printf("item[%d] = %d\n", qinx, q->item[qinx]);
                if (qinx == MAXQUEUE - 1)
                    qinx = QNULL;
                else
                    qinx += 1;
                while (qinx != q->qrear)
                {
                    printf("item[%d] = %d\n", qinx,
                            q->item[qinx]);
                    if (qinx == MAXQUEUE - 1)
                        qinx = QNULL;
                    else
                        qinx += 1;
                }
            }
            break;
        default:
            printf("\nInvalid input\n");
```

```
                         break;
                }
        }
}

int getinput()
{
        char   ch[4];

        printf("\nInput menu:\n");
        printf("\ta = add an item to the queue\n");
        printf("\tr = remove an item from the queue\n");
        printf("\tp = print the queue\n");
        printf("\tq = quit\n");
        printf("Please input selection: ");
        if ((gets(ch)) == (char *) 0)
        {
          printf("\n");
          return(EOF);
        }
        else
        {
          printf("%c\n", ch[0]);
          return((int) ch[0]);
        }
}
/*
 *   array implementation of queue operations
 */

int        qinit( QPOINTER   q )
{
    q->qfront = QNULL;
    q->qrear  = QNULL;
    q->ovflag = QTAIL_AHEAD;
}

int         qempty( QPOINTER    q )
{
    return((q->ovflag == QTAIL_AHEAD &&
             q->qrear == q->qfront) ? TRUE : FALSE);
}

int         qfull( QPOINTER    q )
{
    return((q->ovflag == QTAIL_BEHIND &&
             q->qrear == q->qfront) ? TRUE : FALSE);
}

int         qadd( QPOINTER    q, ITEM    item )
{
    int  qerror();
```

```
    if (q->ovflag == QTAIL_BEHIND && q->qrear == q->qfront)
    {
        qerror("queue overflow");
        return (OVERFLOW);
    }
    else
    {
        q->item[q->qrear] = item;
        q->qrear += 1;
        if (q->qrear == MAXQUEUE)
        {
            q->qrear = QNULL;
            q->ovflag = QTAIL_BEHIND;
        }
        return (ADDOK);
    }
}

ITEM        qremove( QPOINTER   q )
{
    ITEM     item;
    int      qerror();

    if (q->ovflag == QTAIL_AHEAD && q->qfront == q->qrear)
    {
        qerror("queue underflow");
        return (UNDERFLOW);
    }
    else
    {
        /*
         * Get the queue item from the front of the queue
         */
        item = q->item[q->qfront];
        q->qfront += 1;
        if (q->qfront == MAXQUEUE)
        {
            q->qfront = QNULL;
            q->ovflag = QTAIL_AHEAD;
        }
        return (item);
    }
}

int qerror( char  *msg )
{
    fprintf(stderr, "Error: %s\n", msg);
}
```

Output Section

```
        Input menu:
        a = add an item to the queue
        r = remove an item from the queue
```

```
  p = print the queue
  q = quit
Please input selection: a
Input a queue item value + <RETURN>: 0

Input menu:
  a = add an item to the queue
  r = remove an item from the queue
  p = print the queue
  q = quit
Please input selection: a
Input a queue item value + <RETURN>: 1

Input menu:
  a = add an item to the queue
  r = remove an item from the queue
  p = print the queue
  q = quit
Please input selection: a
Input a queue item value + <RETURN>: 2

Input menu:
  a = add an item to the queue
  r = remove an item from the queue
  p = print the queue
  q = quit
Please input selection: a
Input a queue item value + <RETURN>: 3

Input menu:
  a = add an item to the queue
  r = remove an item from the queue
  p = print the queue
  q = quit
Please input selection: p
item[0] = 0
item[1] = 1
item[2] = 2
item[3] = 3

Input menu:
  a = add an item to the queue
  r = remove an item from the queue
  p = print the queue
  q = quit
Please input selection: a
Input a queue item value + <RETURN>: 4

Input menu:
  a = add an item to the queue
  r = remove an item from the queue
  p = print the queue
  q = quit
```

```
Please input selection: a
Input a queue item value + <RETURN>:  5

Input menu:
 a = add an item to the queue
 r = remove an item from the queue
 p = print the queue
 q = quit
Please input selection:  r
item:  0

Input menu:
 a = add an item to the queue
 r = remove an item from the queue
 p = print the queue
 q = quit
Please input selection:  r
item:  1

Input menu:
 a = add an item to the queue
 r = remove an item from the queue
 p = print the queue
 q = quit
Please input selection:  a
Input a queue item value + <RETURN>:  6

Input menu:
 a = add an item to the queue
 r = remove an item from the queue
 p = print the queue
 q = quit
Please input selection:  a
Input a queue item value + <RETURN>:  7

Input menu:
 a = add an item to the queue
 r = remove an item from the queue
 p = print the queue
 q = quit
Please input selection:  p
item[2] = 2
item[3] = 3
item[4] = 4
item[5] = 5
item[0] = 6
item[1] = 7

Input menu:
 a = add an item to the queue
 r = remove an item from the queue
 p = print the queue
 q = quit
```

```
Please input selection: r
item: 2

Input menu:
  a = add an item to the queue
  r = remove an item from the queue
  p = print the queue
  q = quit
Please input selection: r
item: 3

Input menu:
  a = add an item to the queue
  r = remove an item from the queue
  p = print the queue
  q = quit
Please input selection: r
item: 4

Input menu:
  a = add an item to the queue
  r = remove an item from the queue
  p = print the queue
  q = quit
Please input selection: p
item[5] = 5
item[0] = 6
item[1] = 7

Input menu:
  a = add an item to the queue
  r = remove an item from the queue
  p = print the queue
  q = quit
Please input selection: q
Goodbye
```

Exercises

6-1 Using stacks as a singly linked list, write a program to check whether a given string is a palindrome.

6-2 Using a linked list implementation of a stack, write a program to reverse a string.

6-3 Write programs to implement the following operations on an ADT queue when it is implemented as a doubly linked list:

       (a) qinit ()
       (b) qcreate ()
       (c) qempty ()
       (d) qadd ()
       (e) qremove ()

6-4 Write programs to implement the following operations on an ADT circular queue when it is implemented as a singly linked list:

(a) `qinit()`
(b) `qcreate()`
(c) `qempty()`
(d) `qadd()`
(e) `qremove()`

6-5 For ADT double stacks implemented as an array, write programs to implement following operations:

(a) `is_stk_empty (stack_no)`
(b) `is_stk_full (top_stk_1, top_stk_2)`
(c) `create_stk`
(d) `init_stk (stack_no)`
(e) `push (item, stack_no)`
(f) `pop (item, stack_no)`

6-6 The *priority queue* is a variant of standard queues. Instead of considering time arrival of the elements, the priority value is considered for data retrieval and removal. An element with the highest priority value can be retrieved or removed only from the priority queue. The priorities must be, for example, integer, from some ordered set to determine the highest value. When an element is enqueued, it can be placed in any position of the queue. But for convenience, it may be worthwhile to keep the queue ordered based on the priority key. A priority queue can have elements with the same priority value. Such queues are widely used by process scheduling algorithm in operating systems. When a priority queue is implemented as a singly linked list, its elements can be defined by:

```
typedef   char   data_type;
typedef   int    PRIORITY;

typedef struct   _pqueue
{
     data_type        element;
     PRIORITY         priority;
     struct _pqueue   *next;
} PQUEUE;
```

For an ADT priority queue, write functions to implement the following operations:

(a) `PQ_init()`
(b) `is_PQ_empty ()`
(c) `PQ_create()`
(d) `PQ_enqueue()`
(e) `PQ_retrieve()`
(f) `PQ_remove_elt()`

6-7 Write a function to pop at least three elements in a stack. This must check the existence of three elements in the stack. This may be useful in the evaluation of RPN.

6-8 Convert the following infix expressions to RPN form:

      (a) A * (B - C) / D
      (b) (A + B / C) / (D - E * F)
      (c) ((A - B) + (D - C)) * (E - F)
      (d) A / B * (C - F) + D

6-9 Convert the following RPN expressions to infix form:

      (a) A B / C +
      (b) A B C D - * +
      (c) A B - C D + *
      (d) A B - C + D E / *

6-10 Write a function to check the correct syntax of an infix expression.

6-11 Prefix notation is used in LISP programming language. It is an alternative to RPN expression. In a prefix expression, each operation precedes the operands. It does not require parentheses. For example,

Infix form	Prefix form
A * B - C	- * A B C
A * (B - C)	* A - B C

      Convert each of the infix expressions in Exercise 6-8 to prefix form.

6-12 For prefix notation, write functions to:

      (a) Convert infix expressions to prefix
      (b) Evaluate prefix expressions containing integers
      (c) Convert prefix expressions to infix

6-13 Convert the following prefix expressions to infix form:

      (a) + - A + B C D
      (b) + + + A B C D
      (c) / - * A B C + D E
      (d) * - A B + C D

6-14 Convert each of the postfix expressions in Exercise 6-9 to prefix form.

6-15 For prefix notation, write functions to:

      (a) Convert postfix expressions to prefix
      (b) Convert prefix expressions to postfix

6-16 The C programming language has no exponentiation operator. Write a function power (x, n), where x may be a real number or an integer, and n is an integer. The function returns the value of x to the power n. Use the concept of an ADT stack.

6-17 A deque (double-ended queue) is an ADT list in which insertion and deletion are allowed at either the front or the rear. Thus an ADT deque contains the features of both stacks and queues. To insert and delete elements in a doubly linked deque, write the following functions:

(a) Front_enqueue ( )

(b) Rear_enqueue ( )

(c) Front_dequeue ( )

(d) Rear_dequeue ( )

6-18 For the disk scheduling simulation, write

(a) An algorithm for FCFS method

(b) A function implementing FCFS

(c) A test program

See discussions in Section 6.6.2, and use a random number generator to produce track numbers.

6-19 Example 6.5 implements the SSTF disk scheduling simulation using an array-type priority queue. Implement it using a singly linked priority queue.

6-20 The disk scheduling using SSTF policy favors process requests that have the shortest track distance from the current read–write head position. The requests that do not satisfy this criterion, will have to wait in the queue for an indefinite period of time. An improvement of SSTF policy is the SCAN method, also called the "elevator" method. The disk scheduling using SCAN policy is mostly used in applications. It works like SSTF, using preferred direction and some modification of SSTF. The steps of SCAN disk scheduling are:

(a) Get the information about the current position and movement direction of the read–write head.

(b) Choose the shortest seek distance in the current direction considering all requests that are:

(i) Pending in the current direction

(ii) Arriving in front of the read–write head, and after the current sweep began

(c) Save requests arriving behind the read–write head and after the current sweep began. These requests would be considered in the next sweep.

(d) Change direction if you encounter the last track or there are no further requests pending in the current direction.

(e) Repeat steps (a) through (d) until the request queue is empty and if the direction of the sweep is changed.

The disk scheduling using SCAN policy uses a priority queue and random track numbers, as described in Example 6.5.

Write a program to implement and test the disk scheduling simulation using the SCAN algorithm. You may use the appropriate declarations and functions in Example 6.5.

6-21 *Maze problem revisited:* Do Exercise 4-10 using stacks.

CHAPTER 7

Trees

In the earlier chapters we discussed ADT strings, lists, stacks, and queues. To solve the problem of inserting an element into a linear linked list, we use an ADT tree. In this chapter we will develop ADT trees.

The concept of trees is one of the most fundamental and useful concepts in computer science. Trees are used in such applications as compiler construction and expression evaluation, database design and efficient data retrieval, graphs, sparse matrix implementation, decision trees, pop-up menus as in menu-driven window applications, hierarchical process (that is, program in execution) systems, and hierarchical file systems in operating system programming.

Trees have many variations and implementations, and many more applications. Because of having the grace of powerful pointer variables and dynamic memory allocation facilities in C, we will intensively discuss pointer implementations of trees and such variants as binary, binary search, and general trees. We will implement some basic ADT operations on them and their nodes. Finally an application of evaluating the algebraic expression will be presented.

Trees are categorized into (1) binary trees, (2) binary search trees, and (3) general trees. In the following sections we will discuss their concepts, implementations, and operations in C.

Let us first define tree-related terms such as node, root, child, leaf, subtree, level, height, and leftmost and rightmost leaf nodes.

A tree is a finite collection of data objects called *nodes*. A node can contain any information depending on an application. In a database application of customers, a node may contain such information as name, address, and phone number.

A tree is either empty or contains a single unique data object called the "root" of the tree and whose remaining data objects, that is, the nodes are partitioned into any collection of subtrees, each of which is also a tree. Any node is the root of a subtree, and the entire tree is itself a subtree.

The nodes in a tree have a parent–child (predecessor–successor) relationship. The root of the entire tree does not have a "parent," but the nodes immediately following (that is, immediate successor of) another node are called *children* of that node, which is called the *parent*. A node that has no children (subtree) is called a *leaf;* that is, a leaf node is the last node in the (sub)tree.

To illustrate, let us consider the tree shown in Figure 7-1. Figure 7-1 depicts a tree, whose root node is node_A. Node_A has two children, node_B and node_C. Node_B is the root of the subtree containing node_D and node_E as the left and right children, respectively. Node_C is the right child of the root node, node_A. The nodes node_C, node_D, and node_E are all leaf nodes. Node_D and node_C are called the *leftmost* and *rightmost* leaf nodes of the root node_A, respectively.

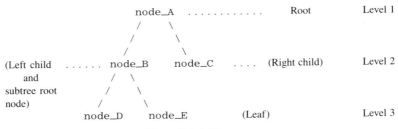

Figure 7-1 A binary tree.

The tree in Figure 7-1 is a binary tree. By definition, a binary tree is a finite collection of nodes such that it is either empty or contains a root node and the remaining nodes are partitioned into two disjoint collections of subtrees. The root node has at most two subtrees, and each subtree root node is either empty or has at most two subtrees. These two subtrees are called the *left* and *right* branches or children.

Binary trees are special cases of general trees. By the term "level" of a node in a binary tree, we mean one plus the total number of ancestors of that node in the tree. In Figure 7-1, node_A, the root of the entire tree, has level 1 because it does not have any ancestors. The nodes node_B and node_C are in level 2, and the nodes at level 3 are node_D and node_E.

By the term "height" of a binary tree, we mean the number of different levels of its nodes. The height of a tree is the maximum of the levels of nodes. In other words, the height of a tree is the length of the longest path from the root node to any given leaf node. For example, the height of a binary tree containing only the root is one. The height of the tree in Figure 7-1 is three.

7.1 Traversals of Binary Trees

Traversing a binary tree is movement through the tree. It is useful in many applications. It involves "visiting" all nodes of a tree. Visiting a node involves obtaining the node's data and using it. The use may be comparison, or sorting, or printing the data contained in the node, or updating its data contents or pointer links. Since a tree is a finite collection of nodes, a node is visited exactly once.

The fundamental steps in a binary tree traversal are:

1. Search for the first node in the tree.
2. Search for the next node in the tree.
3. Determine whether the (sub)tree is empty (i.e., contains no more nodes).
4. Perform operations (i.e., print, update, etc.).

In some cases, it may be necessary to visit the nodes in some specific sequence. The sequence in which we can traverse the binary tree categorizes various forms of tree traversals.

Visiting each node of a binary tree exactly once, we write the recursive steps of the various traversal methods as follows:

Preorder or depth-first order

Step 1. Visit the root node	(N)
Step 2. Traverse the left subtree	(L)
Step 3. Traverse the right subtree	(R)

Inorder or symmetric order:

Step 1. Traverse the left subtree	(L)
Step 2. Visit the root node	(N)
Step 3. Traverse the right subtree	(R)

Postorder manner:

Step 1. Traverse the left subtree	(L)
Step 2. Traverse the right subtree	(R)
Step 3. Visit the right node	(N)

Other possible sequences:

NRL
RNL
RLN

The preorder traversal can also be referred to as the NLR method.

For illustration purposes, we will consider the preorder traversal. Consider the binary tree shown in Figure 7-2.

Figure 7-2 A binary tree.

In Figure 7-2, P is the data contained in the root node of the binary tree. The root nodes of the left and right subtrees of the tree's root P are R and A, respectively.

For the preorder traversal, we start at the root P. We visit it and print P. Then we must traverse the left and right subtrees of P. We now visit the left subtree of P, whose root is R, and print R. We then visit the left subtree of R, whose root is T, and print T. Then the root of the left subtree of T is visited, and nothing is printed because T is a leaf node. This completes the traversal of the left subtree of R. Next, we traverse the right subtree of R, whose root is I. Visiting it we print I. Since I is a leaf node, traversal of the right subtree of I is completed.

As the visit of the entire left subtree of P is done, we now visit the root of the right subtree of P, which is A. We print A. Since it does not have a left subtree, we traverse the right subtree of A. Visiting its root, we print A. Traversing the left sub-tree of A, we visit its root and print V. Since V is a leaf node, and A has no right subtree, the preorder traversal of the entire tree is complete. Thus the result of the preorder traversal is PRTIAAV.

It is important to note that if the inorder traversals of two binary trees are different even though their preorder and postorder traversals are the same, it suffices to claim that the two binary trees are different.

7.2 The ADT Binary Trees

An ADT binary tree has atmost two disjoint binary subtrees with the simple or structured-type nodes and the following operations on them:

1. Create a node.
2. Create a tree.
3. Check whether a tree is empty (contains no root node).
4. Search for a node of a tree from parent to descendants.
5. Delete a node (or a subtree) of a tree.
6. Sort a tree.
7. Add/insert a node in a tree as a left or right child.
8. Update a node.
9. Print a node.
10. Print a (sub)tree.
11. Search from child to ancestors.
12. Retrieve a node.
13. Determine tree attributes (height, size, total path length).

7.3 Binary Tree Implementation

A binary tree can be implemented as either (1) an array of nodes or (2) a linked list. The data contained in a node may be simple or structured-type. The abstraction of data and how efficiently it can be performed depend significantly on implementation of the tree structure and operations.

7.3.1 Array Implementation

A binary tree can be implemented as an array in which each node consists of a struct with the following elements:

1. Left child array index "linx" (array[linx] holds its left child node)
2. Right child array index "rinx" (array[rinx] holds its left child node)
3. Node data

Note that this array implementation has a fixed number of nodes for the tree. Thus a binary tree can conceptually be implemented as an array as in the following:

Array index	Node data	Left child index (linx)	Right child index (rinx)
0	E	1	2
2	L	3	LEAF
3	D	LEAF	4
4	O	LEAF	LEAF
5	N	LEAF	LEAF

Array[0] can be assumed to be the root of the binary tree. The term LEAF indicates no subtree(child). The nodes array[5] is allocated by the array declaration, but is not used. The above form can also be visualized as the binary tree shown in Figure 7-3.

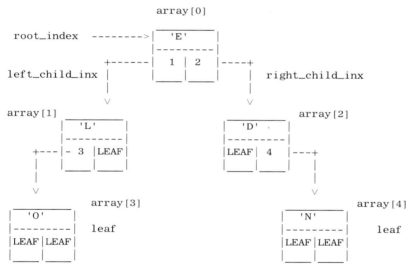

Figure 7-3 Binary tree implementation.

We can define such nodes of a binary tree by structures as in the following header file "tree_ary.h":

```
typedef  char   node_data_type;   /* Define Node data type   */
struct node_struct                /* Define tree node struct */
   {
       int    left_child_inx;    /* Index of the array contain-
                                    ing its left child      */
       int    right_child_inx;   /* Index of the array contain-
                                    ing its right child     */
       node_data_type node_data;
   };
```

```
#define   TREESIZE   6              /* Array Size              */
#define   LEAF       -1             /* Indicates no child      */
#define   ROOT       0              /* root of the binary tree */

/* Define BTREE_ARY as an array type for the binary tree. */
typedef struct node_struct   BTREE_ARY [ TREESIZE ];

/*  Allocates memory spaces for all TREESIZE number
 *  of nodes whether or not all of them used.
 */
BTREE_ARY       binary_tree;
```

In the array implementation:

1. Creating a node will not require the malloc () system call to allocate memory space.
2. As the size of the tree is fixed, the tree cannot grow to its full size if required during the program execution.

Creating a node and a binary tree as an array is given in Example 7.1.

Example 7.1

```
/*
 *  Purpose:        Implement an ADT binary tree as an array
 */
#include "tree_ary.h"              /* Header file shown above  */

/* ******************************************************** *
 * create_node() : Create an node with 'Item' as its node   *
 *                 value. In this case, no memory           *
 *                 allocation is necessary.                 *
 * ******************************************************** */
struct node_struct create_node( node_data_type   Item )
{
    struct  node_struct new_node;

    new_node.node_data  =  Item;
    new_node.left_child_inx  = LEAF;   /* No left child yet */
    new_node.right_child_inx = LEAF;   /* No right child yet*/

    return( new_node );
}


/* ******************************************************** *
 * create_binary_tree(): Calls create_node, and puts        *
 *                       nodes sequentially in the array.   *
 * ******************************************************** */
create_binary_tree( BTREE_ARY   binary_tree )
{
    int   i;

    for ( i = 0; i <= TREESIZE - 1; i++ )
        {
```

```
                binary_tree[ i ] = create_node( 'P' );
                binary_tree[ i ].left_child_inx = i + 1;
            }

        binary_tree[ TREESIZE - 1].left_child_inx  = LEAF;
        binary_tree[ TREESIZE - 1].right_child_inx = LEAF;
}

/* ******************************************************** *
 * print_binary_tree (): Print data in ALL nodes of a binary *
 *                       tree, implemented as an array.      *
 * ******************************************************** */
print_binary_tree( BTREE_ARY  binary_tree )
{
    int   i;

    for ( i = 0; i < TREESIZE; i++ )
        {
          printf("\n\n node[ %d ].data = %2c", i,
                      binary_tree[ i ].node_data );

            printf("     node[ %d ].left = %2d", i,
                      binary_tree[ i ].left_child_inx);

            printf("     node[ %d ].right = %2d", i,
                      binary_tree[ i ].right_child_inx);
        }
      printf("\n\n End of the Binary Tree   \n\n");
}

/* ******************************************************** *
 * main():  Create a  node with 'Item' as its node value.   *
 *          In this case, no memory allocation is necessary *
 * ******************************************************** */
main()
{
    printf("\n ===  Array Implementation %s  === \n",
           "of a Binary Tree");

    create_binary_tree( binary_tree );
    print_binary_tree();
}
```

The output of Example 7.1 is:

```
===  Array Implementation of a Binary Tree  ===

node[ 0 ].data = P    node[ 0 ].left = 1    node[ 0 ].right = -1

node[ 1 ].data = P    node[ 1 ].left = 2    node[ 1 ].right = -1

node[ 2 ].data = P    node[ 2 ].left = 3    node[ 2 ].right = -1

node[ 3 ].data = P    node[ 3 ].left = 4    node[ 3 ].right = -1
```

```
node[ 4 ].data = P      node[ 4 ].left = 5      node[ 4 ].right = -1

node[ 5 ].data = P      node[ 5 ].left = -1     node[ 5 ].right = -1
```

End of the Binary Tree

Note that every node in the tree has a left child only. The value −1 indicates that the right child is a leaf.

This is one way of implementing the binary tree as an array. Its drawbacks are inherited from the static data structure. Insertion of a node may require shifting another to make room for the node. Deletion of a node will create a gap, and it will be expensive to fill that gap.

7.3.2 Linked List Implementation

A binary tree can be implemented as a multiply linked list in which each node consists of

1. One link pointing to its left child (subtree or node)
2. One link pointing to its right child (subtree or node)
3. Node data

For simplicity, assuming character-type node data, we can define such nodes of a binary tree by structures of the form

```
typedef  char   node_data_type;              /* Node data type */

struct node_struct                           /* Node structure */
   {
      struct node_struct *left_child_ptr;    /* Pointer to its
                                                Left Child  */
      struct node_struct *right_child_ptr;   /* Pointer to its
                                                Right Child */
      node_data_type      node_data;
   };

typedef struct node_struct   Tree_Node;
typedef Tree_Node           *BTREE_PTR;
BTREE_PTR                    root_ptr;    /* Root of the tree */
```

The two link fields left_child_ptr and right_child_ptr are respectively pointers to the nodes representing the left and right subtrees. A node with NULL pointer values for left_child_ptr and right_child_ptr is a "leaf." Such a node can be viewed as

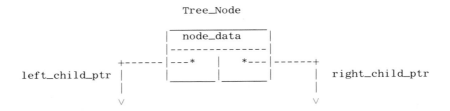

Thus a binary tree can be represented as a set of linked lists of structs:

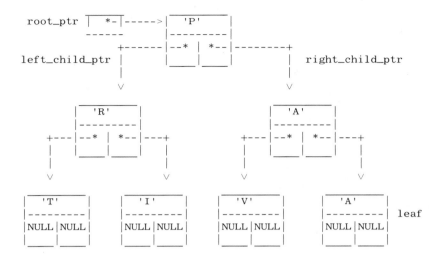

The BTREE_PTR declaration does not reserve any memory space for a node. To dynamically create and use a node, we must first allocate memory space by the malloc() system call, as shown in Example 7.2. The entire binary tree in a linked list implementation can dynamically grow or shrink during the program execution.

Example 7.2

```
/*  Create a node using 'Item' as node data.   */

BTREE_PTR create_node( node_data_type    Item )
{
    BTREE_PTR          new_node_ptr;

    /*  Allocate a memory space for the new node;
     *  if no space available, return with error.
     */

    if ( (new_node_ptr = (BTREE_PTR) malloc(sizeof (Tree_Node)))
              == NULL )
      {
        printf("\n create_node: malloc failed  \n\n");
        return ( NULL );
      }
    else
      {
        new_node_ptr ->node_data =  Item;       /* Item is input */
        new_node_ptr ->left_child_ptr  = NULL; /* No left child */
        new_node_ptr ->right_child_ptr = NULL; /* No right child*/
        return( new_node_ptr );
      }
}
```

Warning: When we delete a node, we must release the memory space it has held, using the free () system call. Otherwise we will soon run out of memory space.

How to release memory space after its use is shown in Example 7.3.

Example 7.3

```
void    dispose_node ( BTREE_PTR   node_ptr )
/*
 *  Dispose the memory space held by the node pointed to
 *  by 'node_ptr'.
 */
{
     free ( node_ptr );
}
```

Let us now describe how we can build a binary tree using the following steps:

Step 1. Declare a node structure as shown above.
Step 2. Declare a root_ptr of type BTREE_PTR that will point to the root of the binary tree.
Step 3. Call create_node () to allocate a memory space for a node and set root_ptr equal to the returned address of the first node.
Step 4. Call create_node () to allocate memory spaces for the left and right children of the root and set the returned memory addresses to root_ptr -> left_node_ptr and root_ptr -> right_node_ptr.
Step 5. Continue the process for each subtree.

In doing binary tree traversals, the rule is to always traverse the left subtree before the right subtree.

To see the process of tree traversal, consider the following binary tree:

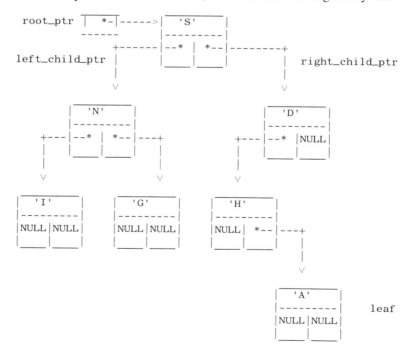

The preorder, inorder, and postorder traversals visit the nodes of the above binary tree in the following sequences:

Traversal	Sequence	Started from node	Ended at node
Preorder	S N I G D H A	Root of the tree	Rightmost leaf node
Inorder	I N G S H A D	Leftmost leaf node	Rightmost leaf node
Postorder	I G N A H D S	Leftmost leaf node	Root of the tree

These three traversals are implemented as recursive functions shown in Example 7.4.

Example 7.4

```
/*
 *      Visit each node of a tree exactly once in one of the
 *      most common ways:
 *          InOrder,  PostOrder, PreOrder
 */


/* *********************************************************** *
 * Traverse_Inorder(): Inorder Traversal of the binary        *
 *                     tree pointed to by root_ptr.           *
 *                     (Recursive Implementation )            *
 * *********************************************************** */
Traverse_InOrder( BTREE_PTR  root_ptr )
{
    if ( root_ptr != NULL )
      {
        /*  Recursively  Traverse the Left subtree  */
        Traverse_InOrder ( root_ptr -> left_child_ptr );
        /*  Visit root by printing it  */
        printf(" %c ", root_ptr -> node_data );
        /*  Recursively  Traverse the right subtree  */
        Traverse_InOrder ( root_ptr -> right_child_ptr );
      }
}

/* *********************************************************** *
 * Traverse_Postorder(): Postorder Traversal of the binary    *
 *                     pointed to by the root_ptr.            *
 *                     (Recursive method)                     *
 * *********************************************************** */
Traverse_PostOrder( BTREE_PTR  root_ptr )
{
    if ( root_ptr != NULL )
      {
        /*  Recursively Traverse the Left subtree */
        Traverse_PostOrder ( root_ptr -> left_child_ptr );
        /*  Recursively Traverse the Right subtree */
        Traverse_PostOrder ( root_ptr -> right_child_ptr );
        /*  Visit root by printing it  */
```

```
        printf (" %c ", root_ptr -> node_data );
    }
}

/* ********************************************************* *
 * Traverse_PreOrder ():   PreOrder Traversal of the binary  *
 *                         pointed to by the root_ptr.        *
 *                         (Recursive method)                 *
 * ********************************************************* */
Traverse_PreOrder ( BTREE_PTR  root_ptr )
{
    if ( root_ptr != NULL )
    {
        /* Visit root by printing it */
        printf (" %c ", root_ptr -> node_data );
        /* Recursively Traverse the Left subtree */
        Traverse_PreOrder ( root_ptr -> left_child_ptr );
        /* Recursively Traverse the Right subtree */
        Traverse_PreOrder ( root_ptr -> right_child_ptr );
    }
}
```

Note the similarity and simplicity of these traversal functions. The recursive implementation necessitates substantial stack storage, so the above recursive functions may not be efficient with respect to space and time.

Example 7-1 in the Further Examples section provides C implementations of the most common operations on a multiply linked binary tree.

Operations on an ADT binary tree	Our implementations in C
1. Check whether the binary tree is empty	`is_tree_empty ()`
2. Create a binary tree node	`create_node ()`
3. Initialize a binary tree	`init_tree ()`
4. Update a node's data	`update_node ()`
5. Retrieve a node's data	`retrieve_node ()`
6. Insert a node in a binary tree	`insert_node ()`
7. Search for the parent node	`search_parent ()` Exercise
8. Delete the entire tree	`delete_tree ()`
9. Delete a binary subtree	`delete_subtree ()`
10. Inorder traversal of tree	`Traverse_InOrder ()`
11. Postorder traversal of tree	`Traverse_PostOrder ()`
12. Preorder traversal of tree	`Traverse_PreOrder ()`

Descriptions of these functions in Example 7-1 are provided below.

Description of Operations on an ADT Binary Tree

`Is_tree_empty ()` is a Boolean function that checks whether an ADT binary tree is empty. It accepts a BTREE_PTR type `root_ptr` that points to the root node of a binary tree. `Is_tree_empty ()` checks whether the tree is empty by testing the equality of `root_ptr` with NULL. It returns TRUE or FALSE.

Create_node() is a function returning a pointer of type BTREE_PTR. It calls malloc() in order to allocate memory space for a new node of type Tree_Node. If no space is available, it prints an error message and returns a NULL pointer. Otherwise, the pointer returned by malloc() is recast as a pointer of type BTREE_PTR, which points to the memory space for the new node. Because this node does not have any data, nor any left and right child subtrees yet, the function initializes the data field, node_data, and the child pointer fields, left_child _ptr and right_child_ptr, of the tree node. It sets these three fields to NULL. It returns new_node_ptr. It is called by the functions init_tree() and insert_node().

Init_tree() implements the operation of initializing an ADT binary tree. It calls the function create_node(). It returns a pointer of type BTREE_PTR. This pointer is set to root_ptr, which points to the root node of the binary tree.

Update_node() takes as input current_node_ptr of type BTREE_ PTR, which points to the current node. Using the current_node_ptr, the function copies its second input new_data to the node_data field of the current node.

Retrieve_node() is a function that returns a value of type node_data _type. It accepts as input current_node_ptr of type BTREE_PTR. It retrieves and returns the data contained in the current node, which is pointed to by current_node_ptr. It neither checks the validity of current_node_ptr (left as an exercise) nor destroys the value of the node's data.

Insert_node() implements the operation of inserting a node into an ADT binary tree. It is a function that returns a pointer of type BTREE_PTR. It takes four inputs: BTREE_PTR-type pointers root_ptr and current_node_ptr, new _data of node_data_type type, and where of type position. The possible values of where are: root, left_child, right_child, and parent. A new node with 'new_data' will be inserted in the binary tree in one of these four positions. It calls the function create_node() to allocate memory space for the new node. If memory space is available, the returned BTREE_PTR-type pointer is non-NULL, and it is set to temp_node_ptr. It sets new_data to the data field of the new node pointed to by temp_node_ptr. Based on the position (root, left_child, or right_child) specified by the value of 'where', it sets temp_node_ptr to the root_ptr, or to the current node's left_child _ptr or right_child_ptr, respectively. It fails to insert the node at the 'parent' position. It exits with an error message "Unknown place to insert" if the specified value of where is not one among those four. If the insertion operation succeeds, it makes the new node as the current node, and returns the pointer to this new node (i.e., temp_node_ptr). If the insertion fails, it releases the memory space using the free() library routine; it prints an error message, and returns a NULL pointer.

Search_parent() implements the operation of searching the parent of the current node pointed to by current_node_ptr. The root node of the binary tree is pointed by root_ptr. If it is successful, it returns a BTREE_PTR-type pointer pointing to the parent of the specified node. Otherwise, it returns a NULL pointer. It is called by the function delete_subtree(). Here is the iterative version of the algorithm for finding the parent of a given child:

Search_parent (BTREE_PTR   root_ptr,   BTREE_PTR   node_ptr)

The steps in this procedure are:

Step 1. Create a stack which will hold the visited subtree node data.

Step 2. Check whether the root_ptr equals node_ptr. If it is equal, return a NULL pointer. (The node pointed to by node_ptr does not have any parent; it is at the root of the tree.) If it is not equal, do the following steps.

Step 3. Push the root_ptr data into the stack; and using temp_ptr to traverse along the tree, repeat the following steps until the parent node is found, or the stack is empty. If the stack becomes empty before finding the parent, then the data is not in the tree; print error message, and return a NULL pointer.

Step 3.1. Check left and right children to find whether they point to the specified data. If one of them does, then the parent is found, and return temp_ptr, which points to the parent; otherwise, proceed to step 3.2.

Step 3.2. Move the pointer to the left child:

```
temp_ptr = temp_ptr -> left_child_ptr
```

Step 3.3. Push the pointer to the node into the stack:

```
head_ptr = push( temp_ptr )
```

Step 3.4. Repeat steps 3.1 through 3.3 until the parent is found or the leaf node is encountered. If the parent is found, then return temp_ptr. If the leaf node is encountered, perform steps 3.5 through 3.9.

Step 3.5. Pop the pointer to the node from the stack:

```
head_ptr = pop( temp_ptr )
```

Step 3.6. Repeat step 3.5 until

```
head_ptr -> right_child_ptr != NULL
```

Step 3.7. Repeat step 3.5 until

```
head_ptr -> right_child_ptr != temp_ptr
```

(This step checks whether we are coming back from the right child; if it is the case, then both the left and the right child were visited without success.)

Step 3.8. Move to the right child:

```
temp_ptr = head_ptr -> right_child_ptr
```

Step 3.9. Repeat steps 3.1 through 3.8 until the parent is found or the stack is empty.

Search_parent () is left as an exercise.

Delete_tree() implements the operation of deleting the entire ADT binary tree whose root node is pointed to by root_ptr. It is a recursive function. It takes BTREE_PTR root_ptr as an input. It uses the postorder traversal method to delete each node of the tree. If the tree is empty, it returns with a message "Tree is already empty". If the tree is nonempty, it proceeds as follows. It calls itself to traverse along the left subtrees. Then it calls itself to traverse along the right subtrees. After traversals and deletions of the left and right subtrees of a node, it visits the root node of the subtree, and uses the free() library routine to dispose of the memory space for the root node. It continues such traversals until all subtrees are deleted. It is called by the function delete_subtree().

Delete_subtree() implements the operation of deleting all nodes of a subtree whose root node is pointed to by current_node_ptr. It accepts BTREE_PTR pointers, current_node_ptr and root_ptr, as inputs. It calls the function search_parent() in order to find the parent of the current_node_ptr. If it finds the parent node, it returns parent_ptr pointing to the parent node. It tests whether the current node is the left or right child of its parent node. If the current node is the left or right child of its parent, make the parent disown the current node by breaking the links to the left or right child. This is done by setting the parent node parent_ptr->left_child_ptr or parent_ptr->right_child_ptr to NULL. Then in either case, or in the case it does not find the parent node, it calls the function delete_tree() with the input current_node_ptr in order to delete all the nodes in the subtree. It returns this value of the current node pointer.

Traverse_InOrder() is a recursive function. It takes the BTREE_PTR pointer root_ptr as an input, which points to the root node of a binary tree. If the tree is empty, it does nothing. If the tree is nonempty, it uses the inorder traversal method:

1. To recursively traverse the left subtree, it calls itself by passing root_ptr->left_child_ptr, the pointer to the root node of its left subtree.
2. It visits the root node of each subtree, and prints it.
3. To recursively traverse the right subtree, it calls itself by passing root_ptr->right_child_ptr, the pointer to the root node of its right subtree.

Traverse_PostOrder() is a recursive function. It takes the BTREE_PTR pointer root_ptr as an input, which points to the root node of a binary tree. If the tree is empty, it does nothing. If the tree is nonempty, it uses the postorder traversal method:

1. To recursively traverse the left subtree, it calls itself by passing root_ptr->left_child_ptr, the pointer to the root node of its left subtree.
2. To recursively traverse the right subtree, it calls itself by passing root_ptr->right_child_ptr, the pointer to the root node of its right subtree.
3. It visits the root node of each subtree, and prints it.

Traverse_PreOrder() is also a recursive function. It takes the BTREE_PTR pointer root_ptr as an input, which points to the root node of a binary tree. If the tree is empty, it does nothing. If the tree is nonempty, it uses the preorder traversal method:

1. It visits the root node of each subtree, and prints it.
2. To recursively traverse the left subtree, it calls itself by passing `root_ptr->left_child_ptr`, the pointer to the root node of its left subtree.
3. To recursively traverse the right subtree, it calls itself by passing `root_ptr->right_child_ptr`, the pointer to the root node of its right subtree.

7.4 The ADT Binary Search Tree

Although the binary tree structure is useful in applications like compiler construction, there are some difficulties in a binary tree:

1. There is no logical way of inserting a node in the tree,
2. When a node is deleted from the binary tree, the fate of the subtree hanging off the node to be deleted is not well defined.
3. There is no ordering among the nodes in the tree,
4. Searching for a node will require traversing the entire tree with worst-case time complexity $O(\log_2 n)$. See Chapter 9 for further explanation of "Big oh" notation.

If you choose to perform the insertion, deletion, and search operations in a frequent manner, the binary tree will not be a suitable data structure for your application. To overcome the above difficulties, a binary search tree is useful.

A binary search tree (BST) is a binary tree with the following property: *The data objects in the left subtree nodes are of a value less than the data object in the subtree root node, and the data objects in the right subtree nodes are of a value greater than the subtree root nodes' data object.*

For an example, see Figure 7-4.

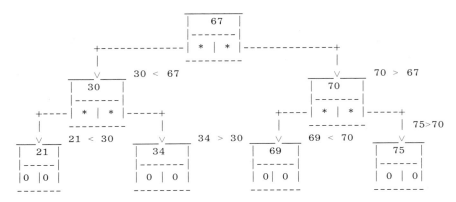

Figure 7-4 A binary search tree.

In Figure 7-4, the nodes with zero left and right pointer values mean these nodes are the "leaves" of the BST.

A BST is implemented as follows:

```
typedef int        data_type;            /* Define Node data type */

typedef  struct node_struct              /* BST node structure     */
  {
    struct node_struct       *left_child_ptr;
    struct node_struct       *right_child_ptr;
    data_type       node_data;
  } Tree_Node;

typedef Tree_Node    *BSTREE_PTR;   /* Define BSTREE_PTR type */

BSTREE_PTR    root_ptr;              /* root of the BST        */
/*  Current subtree root node of BST */
BSTREE_PTR    current_ptr;
```

In this pointer implementation of BST, the left_child_ptr and right_child_ptr are used to point to the current subtree's left and right children, respectively. Note that root_ptr and current_ptr are initially set to NULL. In its implementation, we had to pass pointers to the pointers root_ptr and current_ptr as arguments to functions in order to capture changes to the values of these pointers. This turned out to be a very serious issue in this implementation. The implementation approach for inserting a node in a BST is little different from that in a binary tree.

There is no set of standard operations for an ADT binary search tree.

In Example 7-2 (in the Further Examples section), we implement the following operations on an ADT multiple linked BST:

Operations on an ADT binary search tree (BST)	Our implementations in C
1. Check whether the BST is empty	is_BST_empty()
2. Create a BST node	create_node()
3. Initialize a BST tree	BSTinit_tree()
4. Update a node's data	BSTupdate_node()
5. Retrieve a node's data	BSTretrieve_node()
6. Insert a node in a BST	BST_Insert_node()
7. Create a BST from an array	BST_Create()
8. Search for an item in BST	BST_Search()
9. Search for the parent node	BSTsearch_parent() (Exercise)
10. Delete the entire BST	BSTdelete_tree()
11. Delete the BST's subtree	BST_subtree()
12. Inorder traversal of BST	BST_InOrder()
13. Postorder traversal of BST	BST_PostOrder()
14. Preorder traversal of BST	BST_PreOrder()

Descriptions of these functions in Example 7-2 are provided below.

Description of Operations on an ADT Binary Search Tree

For an ADT BST, the functions is_BST_empty(), create_node(), BSTinit_tree(), BSTupdate_node(), BSTretrieve_node(),

`BSTdelete_tree()`, `BST_InOrder()`, `BST_PostOrder()`, and `BST_PreOrder()` are included in Example 7-2 for completeness. The operations implemented by these functions are exactly the same as those of their counterpart functions for the binary tree in Example 7-1. We describe only those functions in Example 7-2 that are different from their counterparts in Example 7-1. The function `BST_delete_node()` implements the operation of deleting a node in a BST. Its description is presented in Section 7.4.2. Its implementation is left as an exercise.

The function `BST_Search()` implements the operation of searching for a node with the specified key value in a binary search tree. It expects a BSTREE_PTR pointer, `root_ptr`, and `'Item'` of type `data_type` as inputs. The root node of the BST is pointed to by `root_ptr`. It is implemented as an iterative function because recursive search in a BST would require a lot of stack space. It first checks whether the tree is empty by calling `is_BST_empty()`. If it is empty, it prints an error message `"Empty Binary Search Tree"`, and returns a NULL pointer. Otherwise, it sets `root_ptr` to `Search_ptr`, a BSTREE_PTR pointer. It starts its search process beginning with the root node of the BST. It performs the following steps:

Step 1. `Search_ptr = root_ptr`

Step 2. If `Search_ptr` is not NULL, do steps 3 through 5, or else return NULL.

Step 3. If `Item` is less than the data value of the node pointed to by the present value of `Search_ptr`, set:

    Search_ptr = Search_ptr->left_child_ptr

Then repeat step 2, that is, search for thematch in the left subtree until all of its subtrees are exhausted.

Step 4. If `Item` is greater than the data value of node pointed to by the present value of `Search_ptr`, set:

    Search_ptr = Search_ptr->right_child_ptr

Then repeat step 2; that is, search for the match in the right subtree until all of its subtrees are exhausted.

Step 5. If the test conditions in steps 3 and 4 are false, the item has been found. Return the present value of `Search_ptr`, pointing to the node that matches the `Item` in value.

Step 6. Otherwise, print a message `"Item is not found"` and return a NULL pointer.

The recursive version of the above function `BST_Search()` is given below. The main drawback of this recursive version is that it may require a large stack space.

```
/*
 *   BSTREE_PTR BST_Search( root_ptr, Item ):
 *
 *   RECURSIVE VERSION:
 *
 *   Search for Item in the Binary Search Tree with root
 *   pointed to by root_ptr. If successful, it returns a
```

```
*   pointer to the node that contains the specified Item.
*   If not successful, it returns a NULL pointer.
*
*   If  Item < root's data, search in the left subtree.
*   If  Item > root's data, search in the right subtree.
*   If  Item = root's data, search is successful.
*/

BSTREE_PTR BST_Search( BSTREE_PTR root_ptr, data_type  Item )
{
    BSTREE_PTR Search_ptr; /* Used as a Search pointer in BST*/

    /*  Is the binary search tree empty ?   */
    if ( root_ptr != NULL )
      {
        /* Start searching from root */
        Search_ptr = root_ptr;

        /*  Perform search recursively.  */
        if ( Item < Search_ptr -> node_data )
          /* Continue search in the Left subtree */
          BST_Search( Search_ptr ->left_child_ptr, Item);
        else if ( Item > Search_ptr -> node_data )
          /* Continue search in the Right subtree*/
          BST_Search( Search_ptr -> right_child_ptr, Item);
        else
          return ( Search_ptr );
      }
    /*  Search is not successful. */
    return( NULL );
}
```

The worst-case performance for the BST search is between $O(\log_2 n)$ and $O(n)$. See Chapter 9 for a detailed analysis.

The BST_Insert_node () accepts a BSTREE_PTR pointer, *subtree_ptr, and new_data of type data_type as inputs. It is a recursive function. It implements the ADT operation of inserting the value new_data in the BST pointed to by subtree_ptr, such that the resulting tree remains a BST. If the subtree is empty, it calls the function create_node (), in order to allocate a memory space for the new node. If space is available, it puts new_data in the data field of the root node of this subtree, and makes subtree_ptr point to the new node. This is the anchor case of this recursive function. When the subtree is non-empty, it compares new_data with the data field, for example X, of the root node of the current subtree. If they are equal in value, that is, the same data already exists in the BST, it simply returns (because of this, this search could have been done before creating a node). If new_data is less than *X,* then new_data must be inserted in the left subtree. To do this, it recursively calls itself by passing left_child_ptr as the pointer to the root node of the left subtree of the current subtree pointed to by *subtree_ptr, that is, by passing *subtree_ptr->left_child_ptr. If new_data is greater than *X,* then new_data must be inserted in the right subtree. To do this, it recursively calls itself passing *subtree_ptr->right_child_ptr as an input. This input points to the root node of the right subtree of the current subtree pointed to by *subtree_ptr. This recursive approach ultimately reaches the anchor case in which the root node of a subtree has a NULL data field. For further illustrative explanation, see Section 7.4.1.

The BST_Create() function implements the ADT operation of creating a BST from an array of integers. Each integer will be contained in only one node of the BST. It expects BSTREE_PTR type *subtree_ptr, data_array of integers, and array_size as inputs. Array_size is the size of data_array. In order to insert the integer elements of data_array, it calls the function BST_Insert_node(), passing integer data from the data_array for the array_size number of times. Further illustrative description of it is given in Section 7.4.1.

7.4.1 Building a Binary Search Tree

In this section we will demonstrate the building process of a binary search tree from a set of data. To illustrate the process, consider the set of integers

$$\{ 67, 30, 70, 21, 34, 69, 75 \}.$$

The function BST_create() is called to create the BST from this data set. It takes as arguments a pointer to the root node and a pointer to the data set array. It loops through the data set calling BST_Insert_node() for each item.

The BST_Insert_node() function takes as arguments a pointer to the pointer to the current subtree node and the current data item from the data set array. The first time it is called with the pointer to a pointer to a root node, which has the value NULL. The node is created; the data item value 67 is stored in the node; and the root node pointer is set to the address of the pointer to the new node. Thereafter BST_Insert_node() is called twice for each data item processed by BST_create(). The first pass through, the subtree_ptr, is not NULL, so the if false part of the function is executed, which calls BST_Insert_node() again with a subtree_ptr value that is NULL; so the if true part of the function is executed, a new node is created, the data item stored, and the subtree_ptr value updated.

The second data item is 30 when BST_create() calls BST_Insert_node(). *subtree_ptr points to the root node (and therefore is non-NULL), new data (== 30) is not == (equal) to subtree node_data (== 67), so a test is done to see if new_data < node_data. Since it is true, BST_Insert_node(subtree_ptr->left_child_ptr, new_data) is called. Subtree_ptr->left_child_ptr is NULL, so now the "top half" of the function is executed, and the second node is inserted as shown in Figure 7-5.

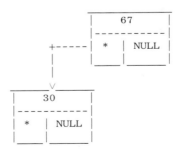

Figure 7-5 BST tree after second data item is processed.

For the third data item 70, as before the BST_Insert_node () compares it with 67, and because 70 > 67, it inserts 70 in the BST as the right child of the root node 67. Continuing the same process until all data items are exhausted, the BST looks like Figure 7-6.

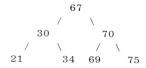

Figure 7-6 The BST.

For simplicity, Figure 7-6 is drawn without the pointer symbols. For the code, see Example 7-2 in the Further Examples section.

The structure of the BST will be different from that in Figure 7-6 when the elements in data set, for example,

$$\{ 69, 21, 75, 67, 30, 70, 34 \}$$

are inserted in the BST. For this set, the BST is as shown in Figure 7-7.

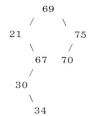

Figure 7-7 The BST with different ordering.

Thus for the same set of elements, the BSTs will differ from each other according to the order of their insertions in the BST.

7.4.2 Deleting a Node from a Binary Search Tree

Deleting a node, for example x, from a BST, is complex. The complexity arises because the tree must remain a binary search tree after the deletion of the node x.

First we search for the target node x in the BST. If the BST is empty, or the node x is not found in the nonempty BST, we cannot delete the node x. If the node x is found in the BST, we need to consider four possible cases depending on the location of x in the BST. The search must at least provide the pointer to the parent (predecessor) of the node x. In essence, the overall objective in deleting the node x is to replace x by the value of a second node in the BST, and then remove the second node from the BST by releasing its memory space. Since the BST is implemented as a linked list, we accomplish this by resetting the values of the appropriate pointers.

To discuss the four cases listed below, consider the BST shown in Figure 7-8.

Case 1. Node x is a leaf, such as nodes A, C, R, or Z in Figure 7-8. This case is simple. First free (that is, release the memory space of) the node x, and then set its parent–child pointer to it to NULL. (*Caution:* If it

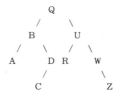

Figure 7-8 A BST before deleting any node.

is done in the reverse order, the memory space allocated to the node
x would not be released.)

Case 2. Node x has an empty right child, but a nonempty left child, such as
D. Replace D by its left child C Because D is the right child of B, this
is done by first saving and then resetting the right child pointer of its
parent B to D's left child pointer that points to C. Use the saved
pointer value to release the memory space occupied by D.

Case 3. Node x has an empty left child, but a nonempty right child, such as
W. Move the right child Z in place of W as in case 2.

Case 4. Node x has nonempty left and right children, that is, two subtrees,
such as U or Q. There are many possible solutions, such as replacing
x by its predecessor or by its successor under inorder traversal. The
best solution would be to minimize the height of the resulting BST,
which would in turn minimize search time.

The best solution to case 4 is to replace x by the node with the largest value in the
left subtree of x. The node with the largest value is the rightmost node in the left
subtree of x. This node is, in fact, the predecessor of x under inorder traversal. The
predecessor will be D if Q is deleted, and R if U is deleted. Since this is the predecessor under inorder traversal, it is greater than everything (in value) in the left subtree
of x, and since it is a node in the left subtree of x, it is, by default, less than any
node (in value) in the right subtree of x. Thus this becoming the root of the subtree
replacing x, will ensure that the properties of a BST are still satisfied. For this solution, the rightmost node in the left subtree of x must have at least one empty subtree.

The alternative solution is to replace x by the node with the smallest value in
the right subtree of x. The node with the smallest value is the leftmost node in the
right subtree of x. This node is, in fact, the successor of x under inorder traversal.

To illustrate, suppose the node Q is deleted from the BST in Figure 7-8. Then
using the rightmost node D in the left subtree of Q, the content of the node Q is
replaced by the content of the node D. The node containing C, which was the left
child of D prior to this replacement, is moved to the position where it becomes the
right child of the node B. The resulting BST takes the form shown in Figure 7-9.

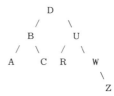

Figure 7-9 The BST after deleting the node Q.

The code for this deleting a node from a BST is left as an exercise.

7.5 General Trees

In previous sections, we discussed binary trees, where any node has a relationship with at most two children nodes. If we are dealing with a set of data objects where one data object may have a relationship with more than two children data objects, the general tree is useful in structuring these data objects.

A *general tree,* also called a *hierarchical tree,* has either of the following properties: (1) It is empty or (2) it contains a node called the "root" that has pointers to any "unrestricted" number of disjoint general (sub)trees. In this case, one node may have relationship with many children nodes.

For an example, see Figure 7-10.

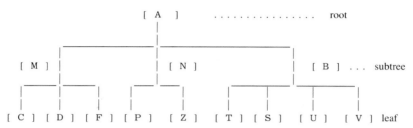

Figure 7-10 General tree natural diagram.

The uses of general trees are in many such applications as telephone networks, computer networks, company organization, computer file systems, window pop-up menu systems.

Figure 1-2 is an example of the general tree, displaying the organizational tree for a corporation. The root node of the general tree is represented by "President & CEO." Each node in this general tree represents the position of a person in the corporation. The parent–child relationship is the boss–subordinate relationship as represented by the hierarchical position. In Figure 1-2, the node containing VP of Development is a child of the root node containing President and Chief Executive Officer (CEO) because the Vice President (VP) of Development reports directly to the President and CEO in the organization. The leaf node in this hierarchical structure contains a person to whom no one else reports.

As another example of a general tree, the computer file system can be structured as a general tree. In such a hierarchical file system, the root directory is the root node. Any number of files or subdirectories are contained in the root directory. A subdirectory may contain files or subdirectories. Such a containment relationship can be construed as the parent–child relationship in a general tree. The leaf node is an ordinary file or empty directory:

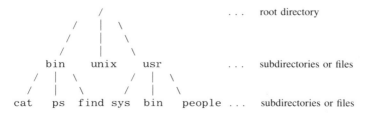

In this hierarchical file system, the root directory, denoted by / (forward slash), contains children nodes: bin, unix, and usr. The children bin and usr are sub-

directories, and unix is an ordinary file. The subdirectory 'bin' is the root of the
subtree containing the files: cat, ps, etc. The subdirectory usr contains the subdirectories: sys, bin, people, etc. The above structure is not complete, but it
conveys the basic concept involved in structuring the hierarchical file system.

Another interesting example of a general tree is the window pop-up menu system. The main menu is the root of the general tree. The main menu contains submenus or simple actions. A submenu can be regarded as the root of a subtree that
contains submenus or simple actions. A leaf node in this hierarchical menu system
is a simple action or an empty submenu. One instance of such a menu system is as
follows:

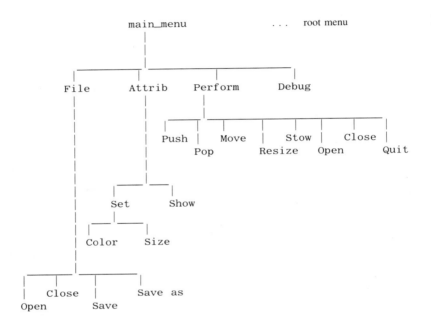

7.5.1 Implementation of a General Tree

This instance of a general tree is implemented by having a pointer to a child
node which has its pointer pointing to a a list of sibling nodes. The tree has a root
node with a pointer to the list of its immediate children. Traversal of the tree is
accomplished by moving down the chain of descendants and along the sibling list.
The siblings have the same parent node, and will be implemented as a single linked
list. The diagram of the general tree in Figure 7-10 uses downward arrows to indicate child relationships and rightward arrows to indicate sibling relationships, as
shown in Figure 7-11.

In Figure 7-11, children of the nodes containing N and B are not drawn for
simplicity. The zero value means NULL pointer value. Another figure of a general
tree implemented in this manner is shown in Figure 7-12.

The following header file describes the general tree:

```
/*
 * gentree.h
 */
```

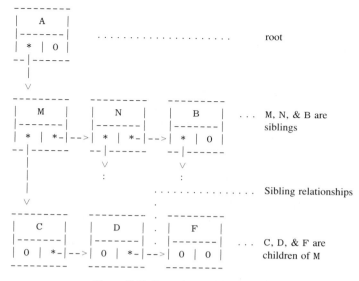

Figure 7-11 General tree with siblings.

```
#define   NULL   0
typedef   int    data_type;

struct   NODE
{
  data_type   node_data;
  struct NODE *sibling;
  struct NODE *child;
};

typedef struct NODE T_NODE;
typedef T_NODE      *T_POINTER;
T_POINTER  gtree; /* gtree points to the root of the tree */
```

The following functions create a node:

```
    T_POINTER   make_tnode()
    {
      /* Caution: The malloc() does not set the individual
       *          members of the T_NODE structure to zeros.
       */
      return((T_POINTER) malloc(sizeof(T_NODE)));
    }

    T_POINTER   init_tnode(data_type  data,
                           T_POINTER  sibling,
                           T_POINTER  child )
    {
      T_POINTER  gt;

      gt = make_tnode();
      gt->node_data = data;
```

```
   gt->sibling    = sibling;
   gt->child      = child;
   return(gt);
}
```

The following statements create an instance of a general tree:

```
gtree = init_tnode(0, NULL, NULL);
gtree->child = init_tnode(1, NULL, NULL);
gtree->child->sibling = init_tnode(2, NULL, NULL);
gtree->child->sibling->sibling = init_tnode(3, NULL, NULL);
gtree->child->child = init_tnode(4, NULL, NULL);
gtree->child->child->sibling = init_tnode(5, NULL, NULL);
gtree->child->child->sibling->sibling = init_tnode(6, NULL, NULL);
gtree->child->child->sibling->sibling->sibling = init_tnode(7,
                                                 NULL, NULL);
gtree->child->child->child = init_tnode(8, NULL, NULL);
```

This produces the tree shown in Figure 7-12.

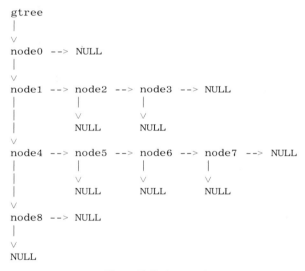

Figure 7-12 A general tree.

In Figure 7-12, gtree points to node0. The vertically downward lines indicate "child of" and the horizontal lines represent "sibling of" relationships. Thus, node1 is the child of node0, and the nodes node2 and node3 are the siblings of node1. The NULL means no more nodes are in the chain.

7.5.2 Traversal of the General Tree

Traversal of the tree is accomplished by searching along the sibling lists (horizontal motion with respect to the figure) and down the descendant chains (vertical motion). The preorder, postorder, and inorder traversal orderings are easily adapted to this tree structure.

For example, postorder:

```
t_postorder ( T_POINTER gt )
{
  T_POINTER   t = gt;

  if ( t -> sibling != NULL)   t_postorder ( t -> sibling );
  if ( t -> child   != NULL)   t_postorder ( t -> child );
  printf ("%d\n", t -> node_data );
}
```

The use of recursion allows easy processing of each subtree.

7.5.3 Building the General Tree

The set of statements used to build the general tree in Figure 7-10 is simple, but it is awkward and becomes cumbersome if the tree has more than 8 nodes. The tree can be initially built by passing a sibling specification in the form of an array of ints that specify how many descendants each node has in relation to a build function, gt_build(), which returns a pointer to the root node. However, because of its above-mentioned limitations, we will abandon this approach. Keeping the general tree in Figure 7-10 as the goal of our implementation, we will proceed to build the tree as follows.

In order to conveniently build a general tree, we use a set of data. We first discuss creating specifications of such a data set. Using the natural diagram of a general tree (Figure 7-10), we specify the input data set so as to read the tree in terms of its children and siblings (Figure 7-11). We will use the right-hand side specifying its children and siblings as we progress.

```
                                3
Begin at the root node. Represent it by a numeral equal to the number of its      3
children, say 3. If that number is zero, we are done; or else draw a child link    |
downward. The current subtree node is the root. Move down the tree to the          2
leftmost child of the subtree. Represent it by the number of its children, say     |
2. If that number is not zero, draw a child link downward. Continue until a        3
node is reached with zero children.                                                |
                                                                                   2
                                                                                   |
                                                                                   0
```

```
                                                                    3
Draw a sibling link to the right. If the node above has more childen,  |
place the number of children of its next child at the right of the sib-  2
ling chain. This sibling is the new current subtree node. Continue       |
until all nodes in the subtree of the first child of the root node are 0-2
handled.                                                                 |
                                                                       0-0
```

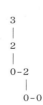

```
                                                                    3
If the root node has more children, draw a sibling link to the right   |
of the previous child or root, and place the number of children of   2-0-3
this child node at the end of the sibling chain, and process that    |   |
subtree. Continue until all nodes of the tree are processed.         |  0-0-0
                                                                   0-2
                                                                     |
                                                                   0-0
```

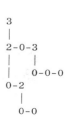

We now present the above process of representing a general tree in some concise form of a data set. The root node is the current subtree node. Write an opening brace, the number of children of the root, and a comma. Descend the child links to the left. The node's leftmost child is now the current subtree node. Write down its number of children and a comma. Continue down the left edge until a node is encountered with no child link.

{3,

{3,2,

    Now move over one sibling to the right (if there is one). Write the number of its children and a comma. It becomes the current subtree node. Continue to process the root's first child subtree. Return to the first child and follow its sibling link. Continue until all nodes are written. Finish the string with a closing brace.

{3,2,0

{3,2,0,2,

{3,2,0,2,0,0,

    This process produces the structure shown in Figure 7-13.

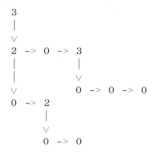

Figure 7-13 General tree child diagram.

To build the specification array, `init_set [ ]`, used by `Build_Tree ()`, follow the above child diagram, starting from the root node. Form the string of characters that represents the arrays initialization as follows:

$$\text{init\_set [ ]} = \{ 3, 2, 0, 2, 0, 0, 0, 3, 0, 0, 0 \}.$$

We now discuss the tree building function, `Build_Tree ()`. The tree building function uses a stack to keep track of the number of children nodes yet to be processed in each subtree.

    The function uses a node data type of int's, but other data types could be substituted. The use of the `calloc ()` library routine ensures that the data portion is initialized to zeros. The function does not include the ability to assign initial nonzero values of data to the nodes. This enhancement is left as an exercise.

    Note that if all nodes have no more than two children, then the general tree is a binary tree. The implementations are not equivalent, however, because the tree scanning algorithms are different and the general tree is less efficient for implementing a binary search tree. Notice in Figure 7-14 that it takes one more step to reach node K in a general tree. The corresponding binary tree is also shown in Figure 7-14.

    The code for building a general tree is given in Example 7.5.

Example 7.5

Code Section

```
/*
 * Program: gentree.c
```

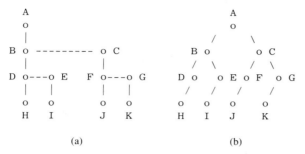

Figure 7-14 A binary tree in two forms: (a) children and siblings; (b) normal.

```
 *   Purpose: To create a General tree.
 */

#include <stdio.h>
#include <ctype.h>

typedef char  DATA;

struct  tnode
   {
     DATA    data;
     struct tnode *child;
     struct tnode *sibling;
   };

typedef struct tnode TNODE;
typedef TNODE * T_POINTER;

#define TNULL   (T_POINTER) NULL

struct stackitem
   {
     int        nchildren; /* Number of children */
     T_POINTER  curnode;    /* Current working node */
   };

typedef struct stackitem STACKITEM;
typedef STACKITEM * S_POINTER;
#define SNULL   (S_POINTER) NULL

S_POINTER stack[ 250 ];     /* Stack of pointers to items */
int        top_stk = 0;

/* Define some macros */
#define GETNODE         (T_POINTER) calloc(1, sizeof(TNODE))
#define GETSTACKITEM    (S_POINTER) calloc(1, sizeof(STACKITEM))

/* State of tree build   */
#define FINISHED    0               /* Back to root node */
#define BACKUP      1               /* Back up to parent */
#define ONWARDS     2               /* Process Sibling */
```

```
/* fatal conditions     */
#define NODATA      1          /* No data in init_set */
#define NOTNODES    2          /* No space for tree nodes */
#define NOSNODES    3          /* No space for stack nodes */
#define STKOVFLOW   4          /* Stack overflow */
#define STKUNDFLOW  5          /* Stack underflow */

int init_set[] = {3, 2, 0, 2, 0, 0, 0, 3, 0, 0, 0 };
int NNODES   = sizeof(init_set)/sizeof(int);

/*
 *  pop() : Pops an element of type S_POINTER from the stack
 */

S_POINTER pop()
{
    return( stack[ --top_stk ] );
}

/*
 *  push() : Pushes an element of type S_POINTER into the stack
 */

S_POINTER push( S_POINTER  item )
{
   stack[ top_stk++ ] = item;
   return( stack[ top_stk - 1 ] );
}

/*
 *   Handle_Leaf() :
 *     It determines whether a leaf node of a general tree has
 *     any siblings by checking the number of children of its
 *     parent, and takes the appropriate action. It adjusts the
 *     stack by pushing and popping the elements of type S_POINTER.
 *     It releases the memory space that was previously allocated
 *     by GETSTACKITEM, but is no longer needed.
 */

*/

int Handle_Leaf ( T_POINTER rnp )
{
    S_POINTER  sp;

    if ( ( sp = pop() ) == SNULL )
        fatal("Handle_Leaf: stack underflow", STKUNDFLOW);
    if ( ( --(sp -> nchildren)) == 0 )
    {
       if ( sp -> curnode == rnp )
       {
           free( sp );
           return( FINISHED );
       }
    }
```

```
        else
        {
            push( sp );
            return( BACKUP );
        }
    }
    if ( push( sp ) != sp )
        fatal("Handle_Leaf: stack overflow", STKOVFLOW);
    return( ONWARDS );
}

/*
 *  Build_Tree() : Function to build a general tree.
 */

T_POINTER Build_Tree( int node_set[] )
{
    T_POINTER   rnp = TNULL,     /* Root node pointer */
                cnp;             /* Current node pointer */
    S_POINTER   sp;              /* Current stack item pointer */

    int         inx, backup;

    static DATA nodename = 'A';

    if ( NNODES == 0 )
        fatal("No data", NODATA);

    for ( inx = 0; inx < NNODES; inx++, nodename++ )
    {
        if ( inx == 0 )
        {
            if (( cnp = GETNODE ) == TNULL )
                fatal("Build_Tree: Out of free space for nodes",
                        NOTNODES);
            else
                rnp = cnp;
        }
        cnp -> data = nodename;

        if (( sp = GETSTACKITEM ) == SNULL )
            fatal("Build_Tree: Out of free space for nodes",
                    NOSNODES);
        sp -> nchildren = node_set[inx];
        sp -> curnode = cnp;

        if ( push( sp ) != sp )
            fatal("Build_Tree: stack overflow", STKOVFLOW);

        if ( node_set[ inx ] == 0 )
        {
            sp = pop();
            free( sp );
```

```
            while (( backup = Handle_Leaf ( rnp )) == BACKUP )
            {
                if ( ( sp = pop() ) == SNULL )
                    fatal("Build_Tree: stack underflow",
                          STKUNDFLOW);
                cnp = sp -> curnode;
                free( sp );
            }
            if ( backup == FINISHED )
                return( rnp );
            cnp -> sibling = GETNODE;
            cnp = cnp -> sibling;
        }
        else
        {
            cnp -> child = GETNODE;
            cnp = cnp -> child;
        }
    }
    return( rnp );
}

/*
 * fatal() - prints error message and exits program
 */

int fatal( char * string, int error )
{
    fprintf( stderr, "%s \n", string );
    exit(error);
}

/*
 * Print_Tree() - prints the general tree
 */

Print_Tree ( T_POINTER  rnp )
{
    T_POINTER cnp = rnp;

    if ( cnp != TNULL)
      {
        if (isalnum( cnp -> data ))
            printf(" %c ", cnp -> data);
        Print_Tree(cnp -> child);
        Print_Tree(cnp -> sibling);
      }
}

/*
 * main() - a test driver for the general tree builder
 */
```

```
main()
{
    T_POINTER rnp;

    rnp = Build_Tree( init_set );
    printf("\n ADT GENERAL TREE \n\n" );
    Print_Tree( rnp );
    printf("\n\n");
}
```

Output Section

                ADT GENERAL TREE

        A   B   C   D   E   F   G   H   I   J   K

The output simply shows that the nodes have been correctly stored and a listing of
children at each node. It would be nice to get the output to do something like the
following diagram:

```
            A
            |
            v
            B  -> G -> H
            |         |
            v         v
            C  -> D   I -> J -> K
                  |
                  v
                  E -> F
```

The code to produce the above output is left as an exercise.

7.6 Search Path

To access a data of a node in any tree, it may be useful to note the search path. The
search path may be specified in two ways:

  1. *Absolute Path:* starts from the root of the tree.
  2. *Relative Path:* starts from the root of the subtree in which the current node
     resides.

For example, to search for node [P] from the current node [D] in the above
general tree structure,

            Absolute Path: node_A / node_N
            Relative Path: node_M /node_A / node_N

7.7 AVL Trees

In previous sections, we discussed binary, binary search, and general trees. For a
binary search tree, the search time is $O(\log_2 n)$ in the best case (where the BST is
bushy), and $O(n)$ in the worst case (where the BST is degenerate). Performance of

searching for a node in a tree has a significant impact on performance of an application using trees. The more uniform the shape of a tree, the more quickly it can be traversed during searches. The use of AVL trees is aimed at reducing the average search length (and time) by reducing the height of the tree. In this section, we will first discuss the concepts of the AVL trees; then we will discuss ADT operations on AVL trees.

An AVL (or balanced binary search tree) is one in which the heights of the two subtrees of any node never differ by more than one. For a balanced tree of height h, all the leaf nodes are at levels h or $h - 1$. The balance of a subtree is defined as the difference between the height of its left subtree and the height of its right subtree:

$$Balance = height(right\ subtree) - height(left\ subtree)$$

The relation between the number of nodes n and the height of the tree h is

$$n = 2^h - 1$$

or

$$h = \log_2 (n + 1) = O(\log_2 n)$$

So the effort to search for a node, traversing the full height of the AVL tree from the root node to a leaf node, is $O(\log_2 n)$.

The height of an ordinary binary tree can become $O(n)$, if the tree has degenerated to one long branch. The effort of searching a node in such a tree is $O(n)$. As n becomes larger, the performance of searches in such a tree increasingly degrades compared to that of a binary tree with height $O(\log_2 n)$, the number of traversal steps.

The balance of the AVL tree is maintained after insertion and deletion of nodes. The effort of inserting a node into or deleting a node from an AVL tree is at most $O(\log_2 n)$.

In the following sections, we discuss basic concepts, an ADT definition, pointer implementation, and the two major operations of insertion and deletion of a node in an AVL tree.

For further details of the origination of AVL trees, see Adel'son-Vel'skii and Landis (1962).

7.7.1 The Concepts of the AVL Tree

An AVL tree is a height-balanced binary search tree, that is, the difference in height between the left and the right subtrees of every node in the tree is at most one and the nodes of the tree are ordered.

For a brief illustration, consider a set of the integers { 1, 2, 3, 4, 5 }. Figure 7-15 shows trees produced from this set.

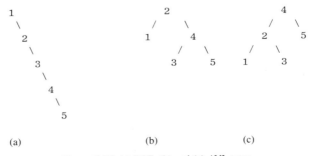

Figure 7-15 (a) BST; (b) and (c) AVL trees.

The tree in Figure 7-15(a) is degenerate, and its height is 5. The trees in Figure 7-15(b) and (c) are AVL trees with height 3. Note that the height of each of the AVL trees is at a minimum and is only 60% of the height of the degenerate tree. Forming an AVL tree is discussed later.

Some non-AVL trees are shown in Figure 7-16.

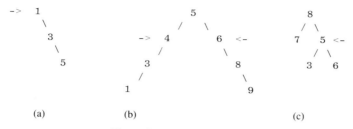

(a)   (b)   (c)

Figure 7-16 Non-AVL trees.

In Figures 7-16(a) and 7-16(b), the nodes indicated by arrows violate the balance requirement. In Figure 7-16(c), the node indicated by the arrow violates the binary search tree requirement.

7.7.2 The ADT AVL Trees

An ADT AVL tree has nodes with an abstract data type and the following operations defined on it:

1. Create a node.
2. Create an AVL tree.
3. Initialize an AVL tree.
4. Check whether an AVL tree is empty.
5. Search for a node specified by a key.
6. Insert a node in an AVL tree.
7. Delete a node.
8. Retrieve a node.
9. Update a node.
10. Delete a subtree.
11. Delete the entire tree.
12. Print a node.
13. Print the entire tree in its original form.
14. Print the entire tree horizontally, where the tree grows from left to right.
15. Determine the tree attributes (height, size, total and average path lenghts).
16. Perform preorder traversal.
17. Perform postorder traversal.
18. Perform inorder traversal.

The node data may be of simple or structured type, and are abstract.   The operations defined on the tree are able to handle data of any type, given information about the type of the data.

All the above operations except insert and delete are similar to those in a binary search tree. The operations of inserting and deleting a node require the resultant tree must remain an AVL tree. We will consider these operations later. A complete example of operations on an ADT AVL tree is given in Example 7-3 (in the Further Examples section).

7.7.3 Pointer Implementation of an AVL Tree

The pointer implementation of is accomplished by defining the structure of its nodes in `avltree.h` as follows:

```
typedef   int    data_type;
typedef   int    balance;

typedef struct _avl_node
    {
        struct       _avl_node  *left_child_ptr;
        struct       _avl_node  *right_child_ptr;
        data_type  node_data;
        balance     height;


    }
AVL_NODE;

typedef AVL_NODE    * AVLTREE_PTR;
#define TNULL         (AVLTREE_PTR)  NULL

AVLTREE_PTR   root_ptr;
```

The data type may be a basic data type (e.g., int, char), structure or any abstract form. The pointer fields `left_child_ptr` and `right_child_ptr` are used to point to the subtrees of the nodes. For each node, the field "height" is of type "balance" with the following meanings:

Height $= -1$ means the height of its left subtree is one higher than that of its right subtree.

Height $= 0$ means the node is balanced.

Height $= +1$ means the height of its right subtree is one higher than that of its left subtree.

The root node of an AVL tree will be pointed to by the AVLTREE_PTR-type pointer `root_ptr`. Initially, the value of `root_ptr` is NULL.

Here is the function `create_node()` that creates memory space for an AVL node. It returns a pointer of type AVLTREE_PTR. It is called by the function `AVL_Insert()`.

```
/*
 *   create_node():
 *      Allocate mem space and pointer to that space
 */
AVLTREE_PTR create_node()
{
    AVLTREE_PTR new_node_ptr;

    /*  Allocate a memory space for the new node;
     *  If no space available, return with error
     */

    new_node_ptr = (AVLTREE_PTR) malloc(sizeof(AVL_NODE))
    if (new_node_ptr == TNULL )
      {
```

```
                printf("\n create_node: malloc failed  \n\n");
                return ( TNULL );
        }
    else
        {    /*  Initialize this node   */
            new_node_ptr -> node_data =  NULL;
            new_node_ptr -> left_child_ptr  = TNULL;
            new_node_ptr -> right_child_ptr = TNULL;
            new_node_ptr -> height = NULL;
            return( new_node_ptr );
        }
}
```

7.7.4 Inserting a Node in an AVL Tree

The operation of inserting a node into an ADT AVL tree might cause the tree to become unbalanced anywhere between the root node and the grandparent of the new node. If it is unbalanced after the insertion, the tree is rebalanced as part of the insertion.

The insertion first allocates a memory space for the new node. It next determines the path, called the *search path,* from the root node to the location of the node where the new node will be inserted. The node is inserted just as described in Section 7.4.1. If necessary, the heights are then adjusted to recreate an AVL tree. The insertion is skipped if the new node is found in the AVL tree. The steps of the insert operation are:

Step 1. In order to insert the new node into an AVL tree, call the function `BST_Insert_node()`. (See Example 7-2 in the Further Examples section.)

Step 2. Search the node which is not balanced (i.e., "height" field is not 0), and which is closest to the new node. Call it the "balancing node."

Step 3. Adjust the newly formed tree so that each of its nodes is height-balanced, and it is an AVL tree.
Consider the three possible cases:
Case 1. There is no balancing node.
Case 2. The new node is inserted into the subtree of the "balancing node," which is lower in height.
Case 3. The new node is inserted into the subtree of the "balancing node," which is higher in height.

In case 1, simply assign new balance values to the field "height" of each node on the search path. This is because each node on the search path is balanced. For illustration, see Figure 7-17.

```
          25  (0)                     25   (+1)
         /    \                      /    \
    (0) 15     35 (0)           (0) 15     35  (+1)
                                               \
                                                99  (0)

          (a)                          (b)
```

Figure 7-17 (a) AVL tree before inserting 99; (b) AVL tree after inserting 99

In order to indicate the values of the "height" field of each node in figures, we use −1, 0, and +1.

In case 2, change the value of the field "height" of each node on the search path beginning with the "balancing node." For illustration, see Figures 7-18 and 7-19. We want to insert 10 into the AVL tree in Figure 7-18:

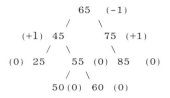

Figure 7-18 AVL tree before inserting 10.

After inserting 10 as the left child of the pivot node containing 25, there is no need of rebalancing. It yields the AVL tree shown in Figure 7-19.

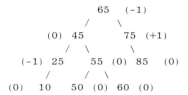

Figure 7-19 AVL tree after inserting 10.

We determine the balances of each node in Figures 7-18 and 7-19 in the following table:

	Before insertion of 10			After insertion
Node	Height of left subtree	Height of right subtree	Balance	Balance
65	4	3	3 − 4 = −1	Same (−1)
45	2	3	3 − 2 = +1	3 − 3 = 0
25	1	1	1 − 1 = 0	1 − 2 = −1
55	2	2	2 − 2 = 0	Same (0)
50	1	1	1 − 1 = 0	Same (0)
60	1	1	1 − 1 = 0	Same (0)
75	1	2	2 − 1 = +1	Same (+1)
85	1	1	1 − 1 = 0	Same (0)
10	—	—	—	1 − 1 = 0

In case 3, rebalance the tree by either a single or a double rotation. For illustration, see Figures 7-20 through 7-22.

Before inserting 10, the AVL tree is as shown in Figure 7-20.

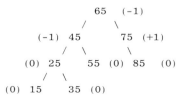

Figure 7-20 AVL tree before inserting 10.

After inserting 10, and before rebalancing with rotation, the tree is as shown in Figure 7-21.

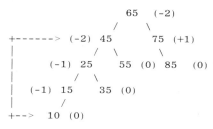

```
                              65    (-2)
                            /    \
        +------>  (-2)  45        75  (+1)
        |              /   \           \
        |       (-1)  25     55  (0)  85   (0)
        |            /  \
        |    (-1)  15     35  (0)
        |         /
        +-->   10  (0)
```

Figure 7-21 AVL tree after inserting 10 and before rotation.

Figure 7-21 shows an intermediate state of the tree after insertion. The tree is unbalanced because the pivot node containing 45 has a tall subtree. This requires an adjustment of the tree's structure using the right rotation. The nodes involved in this rotation are indicated by the arrows.

We determine the balances of each node in Figures 7-20 and 7-21 in the following table:

| Node | Before insertion of 10 | | | After insertion |
	Height of left subtree	Height of right subtree	Balance	Balance
65	4	3	$3 - 4 = -1$	$3 - 5 = -2$
45	3	2	$2 - 3 = -1$	$2 - 4 = -2$
25	2	2	$2 - 2 = 0$	$2 - 3 = -1$
15	1	1	$1 - 1 = 0$	$1 - 2 = -1$
35	1	1	$1 - 1 = 0$	Same (0)
55	1	1	$1 - 1 = 0$	Same (0)
75	1	2	$2 - 1 = +1$	Same (+1)
85	1	1	$1 - 1 = 0$	Same (0)
10	—	—	—	$1 - 1 = 0$

Because the balance of the pivot node containing 45 is -2 (less than -1), rotate the left subtree of the pivot node to the right.

After inserting 10 and rebalancing with a single right rotation, the tree in Figure 7-21 takes the balanced form of the AVL tree in Figure 7-22.

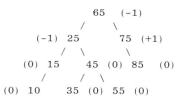

```
                    65    (-1)
                  /    \
        (-1)  25        75  (+1)
             /   \          \
       (0)  15     45  (0)  85   (0)
           /      /   \
     (0)  10   35  (0)  55  (0)
```

Figure 7-22 AVL tree after inserting 10 and after rotation.

The search path for inserting 10 contains the nodes with values 65, 45, 25, and 15. The node with value 45 is the balancing node, also called the *pivot node*.

Note that before the insert operation in Figure 7-20, the values 15 and 35 are respectively the left and right child of the node containing 25, whose parent, called the *balancing node*, has the value 45.

After inserting 10 as the left child of the node containing 15 in Figure 7-22, the node with 10 becomes the left child of the node with value 25, whose right child is the balancing node with value 45. The node with value 35, the right child of node 25 in Figure 7-20, becomes the left child of the node with value 45 in Figure 7-22. The node with value 55, the right child of the node with value 45 in Figure 7-20, has an unchanged parent, but a grandparent with value 25 in Figure 7-22. The key note is that the balancing node has been changed to the right child of its former left child, which was the root node of the left subtree the new node is added to.

The following function AVL_Insert () performs the insertion of a node in an AVL tree:

```
/*
 *   AVL_Insert() :   Insertion of a node in an AVL Tree
 */

AVLTREE_PTR AVL_Insert ( AVLTREE_PTR tree,  AVLTREE_PTR new )
{
    AVLTREE_PTR   p   = tree,
                  y   = p,        /* y points to the youngest ancestor *
                  v   = TNULL,    /* v points to the parent of y */
                  s   = TNULL,    /* s points to the parent of p */
                  q   = TNULL;    /* q points to the new node location
    balance       imbal;

    /* Part I : search for the new data slot */
    if ( tree == TNULL )
        return( new );
    while ( p != TNULL)
      {
        if ( p->node_data == new->node_data )
            return( new );
        else
          {
            if ( new->node_data < p->node_data )
                q = p->left_child_ptr;
            else
                q = p->right_child_ptr;
            if ( q != TNULL && q->height != 0 )
              {
                v = p;
                y = q;
              }
            s = p;
            p = q;
          }
      }

    q = new;
    q->height = 0;

    if ( p == TNULL && s == TNULL )
        return (q);
```

```
if ( new->node_data < s->node_data)
    s->left_child_ptr = q;
else
    s->right_child_ptr = q;
/*  the balance in all nodes between node y and node q
 *  must be changed to 0
 */
if ( new->node_data < y->node_data )
    p = y->left_child_ptr;
else
    p = y->right_child_ptr;
s = p;
while ( p != q )
  {
    if ( q->node_data < p->node_data )
      {
        p->height = 1;
        p = p->left_child_ptr;
      }
    else
      {
        p->height = -1;
        p = p->right_child_ptr;
      }
  }
/* Part II */
if ( q->node_data < y->node_data )
    imbal = 1;
else
    imbal = -1;
if ( y->height == 0 )   /* another level has been added to */
    y->height = imbal; /* and the tree remains balanced  */
else if ( y->height != imbal )
    /*  The added node was placed in the opposite
     *  direction from the imbalance, so the tree
     *  is still balanced.
     */
    y->height = 0;
else
  {
    /*  Part III:
     *  y and s have been unbalanced in the same
     *  direction.
     */
    if ( s->height == imbal )
      {
        p = s;
        if ( imbal == 1 )
            Rotate_Right(y);
        else
            Rotate_Left(y);
        y->height = 0;
        s->height = 0;
      }
```

```
         else
           { /* y and s are unbalanced in the opposite direction */
             if ( imbal == 1 )
                {
                  p = s->right_child_ptr;
                  Rotate_Left(p);
                  y->left_child_ptr = p;
                  Rotate_Right(y);
                }
             else
                {
                  p = s->left_child_ptr;
                  Rotate_Right(s);
                  y->right_child_ptr = p;
                  Rotate_Left(y);
                }
             if ( p->height == 0 )
                {
                  y->height = 0;
                  s->height = 0;
                }
             else if ( p->height == imbal )
                {
                  y->height = -imbal;
                  s->height = 0;
                }
             else
                {
                  y->height = 0;
                  s->height = imbal;
                }
             p->height = 0;
           }
      if ( v == TNULL )
         tree = p;
      else if ( y == v->right_child_ptr )
         v->right_child_ptr = p;
      else
         v->left_child_ptr = p;
   }
   return(q);

}   /*  end of AVL_Insert()  */
```

7.7.5 Deleting a Node in an AVL Tree

The operation of deleting a node from an ADT AVL tree must keep the resultant tree balanced.

The deletion operation determines the search path, from the root node to the location of the parent node whose left or right child is the node that will be deleted. The node deletion follows the procedure described in Section 7.4.2. The operation then adjusts,if necessary, the heights of some nodes to re-create an AVL tree. The deletion is skipped if no node contains the data searched for. The implementation of the delete operation is left as an exercise.

7.7.6 Rebalancing by Rotation

During insertion or deletion, it might be necessary to restructure the AVL tree in order to regain balance. This restructuring is done by rotation. Often we need to use the double rotation. A double rotation is composed of the left and right rotations, for example, the left rotation followed by a right rotation.

The functions for left and right rotations are given below. The pointer to the AVL tree root node is `tree_ptr`.

```
Rotate_Left( AVLTREE_PTR  tree_ptr )
{
    /*  Rotate right child tree_ptr to the left
     *  child tree_ptr.
     */
    AVLTREE_PTR  hold_ptr;    /* Temp ptr storage */

    hold_ptr = tree_ptr;
    tree_ptr = tree_ptr -> right_child_ptr;
    hold_ptr -> right_child_ptr = tree_ptr -> left_child_ptr;
    tree_ptr -> left_child_ptr = hold_ptr;
}

Rotate_Right( AVLTREE_PTR  tree_ptr )
{
    /*  Rotate left child tree_ptr to the right
     *  child tree_ptr.
     */
    AVLTREE_PTR  hold_ptr;    /* Temp ptr storage */

    hold_ptr = tree_ptr;
    tree_ptr = tree_ptr -> left_child_ptr;
    hold_ptr -> left_child_ptr = tree_ptr -> right_child_ptr;
    tree_ptr -> right_child_ptr = hold_ptr;
}
```

Figures 7-23(a) and 7-23(b) show left and right rotation. The working pointer to the root node is `hold_ptr`.

The important points for an AVL tree are:

1. What values of the balance factor indicate the need of a left rotation or a right rotation or both?
2. In order to assure the balance of the entire tree, the balance must be checked from the pivot node on the search path to the root of the tree.
3. Checking of balance must be done after a new node is inserted, if the difference of heights of any two subtrees of a node is greater than one.
4. The advantage of the AVL tree over the BST is that time is less required for searches. Since an AVL tree is guaranteed to be balanced, the search time is $O(\log_2 n)$ for nodes.
5. The AVL tree will never degenerate to $O(n)$ search time as the BST possibly can.

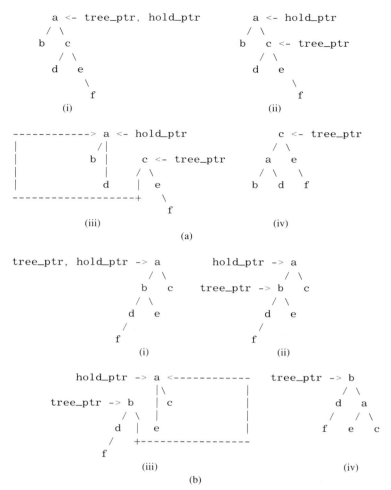

Figure 7-23 (a) Left rotation: (i) Tree before left rotation; (ii) and (iii) intermediate states; (iv) tree after left rotation. (b) Right rotation: (i) Tree before right rotation; (ii) and (iii) intermediate states; (iv) tree after right rotation.

7.8 The B-Tree

The B-tree is known as the *balanced sort tree,* which is useful for external sorting. There are strong uses of B-trees in a database system as pointed out by D. Comer (1979): "While no single scheme can be optimum for all applications, the technique of organizing a file and its index called the B-tree is, de facto, the standard organization for indexes in a database system."

The file is a collection of records. The index refers to a unique key, associated with each record. An application of a parts inventory control database system using the B-tree is shown in Chapter 11. One application of B-trees is found in IBM's Virtual Storage Access Method (VSAM) file organization. Many data manipulation tasks require data storage only in main memory. For applications with a large database running on a system with limited memory, the data must be stored as records on secondary memory (disks) and be accessed in pieces. The size of a record can be quite large, as shown below:

```
struct DATA
  {
     int   ssn;
     char  name[80];
     char  address[80];
     char  school[76];
     struct DATA * left;      /* main memory addresses */
     struct DATA * right;     /* main memory addresses */
     d_block d_left;          /* disk block address */
     d_block d_right;         /* disk block address */
  };
```

There are two sets of pointers in the struct DATA. The main memory pointers, left and right, are used when the children of the node are in memory and the disk addresses, d_left and d_right, are used to reference the children on disk. The size of DATA is 256 bytes.

Data is moved by block transfer into main memory for manipulation; however, the disk access is slow (tens of milliseconds) compared with a main memory move (tens of microseconds), so we want to minimize the disk accesses. One method is to make the data nodes even fractions ($\frac{1}{2}$, $\frac{1}{4}$, etc.) or multiples (1, 2, etc.) of the disk sector size.

Another method is to expand the capacity of the node for storage of data. A binary tree node contains one key or data element and has pointers to two children. We can construct a tree with nodes that have more than two possible children and more than one key. The tree has a property called *order,* the maximum number of children for any given node. If the maximum is N children, then the order of the tree is N. A tree of order 4 is shown in Figure 7-24. The symbol

```
o
|
=
```

is used to denote a null pointer.

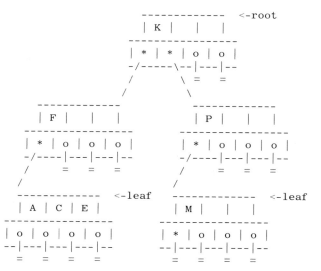

Figure 7-24 A B-Tree of Order 4.

7.8.1 The ADT B-Tree

To reduce disk accesses, several conditions of the tree must be true: the height of the tree must be kept to a minimum; there must be no empty subtrees above the leaves of the tree; the leaves of the tree must all be on the same level; and all nodes except the leaves must have at least some minimum number of children (perhaps half of the maximum). The root alone may have no children, if the tree has only one node. Otherwise it may have as few as two and as many as the maximum number of children. The keys in the tree should have some defined ordering (numerical, lexical, or some other relationship). A tree that has these properties is called a *balanced sort tree* (a B-tree). The B-tree properties are listed below.

An ADT B-Tree of order N is a tree in which:

1. Each node has a maximum of N children and a minimum of $N/2$ children. The root may have no children or any number from 2 to the maximum.
2. Each node has one fewer keys than children with a maximum of $N - 1$ keys.
3. The keys are arranged in a defined order within the node. All keys in the subtree to the left of a key are predecessors of the key, and all keys in the subtree to the right of a key are successors of the key.
4. When a new key is to be inserted into a full node, the node is split into two nodes, and the key with the median value is inserted in the parent node. In case the parent node is the root, a new root node is created.
5. All leaves are on the same level. There is no empty subtree above the level of the leaves.

These properties are combined with the following operations:

1. Creating a node
2. Inserting a new key into a B-tree
3. Deleting a node from a B-tree
4. Searching for a node in a B-tree
5. Modifying a node in a B-tree
6. Printing a B-tree

7.8.2 Insertion in the B-Tree

The insertion of a new key into a B-tree begins with the search for a match. If a match is found for the key, then the insertion operation takes some action (an error message is sent or a count is incremented, etc.) and returns an error indication to the caller. If no match is found, then the key is simply added to a leaf, unless the leaf is full. If the leaf is full then it is split into two nodes (requiring creation of a new node and the copying of half of the old nodes keys and pointers to the new node) and the median value key is inserted into the parent of the node. If the parent was also full, the split and key push up ripples upward. The ordering of the keys is maintained, and the ordering of keys among subtrees is maintained.

The tree tends to become more balanced with subsequent insertions. The B-tree is like a crystal in its growth: upward and outward from its base, the leaf level. To illustrate the insertion process, we will build a B-tree of order 5 by inserting the following data:

{D, H, K, Z, B, P, Q, E, A, S, W, T, C, L, N, Y, M}

The key ordering is ascending lexical. We keep track of the pointers by number-
ing them.

    D: First the root node is created (+) , then key D is inserted into it.

```
        --- (+)
        |D|
        -----
        |o|o|
        -|-|-
        = =
```

    H, K, Z: the keys are searched for match; if match not found, they are simply
       inserted.

```
        ---------
        |D|H|K|Z|
        ----------
        |o|o|o|o|o|
        -|-|-|-|-|-
        = = = = =
```

    B: The node is full, so it must be split; of the keys, B, D, H, K, and Z, key H
       is the median value key, so it promotes to the parent, but this is the root
       node so we must create a new node (+) .

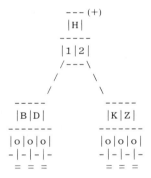

    P, Q, E, A: Each key is simply inserted.

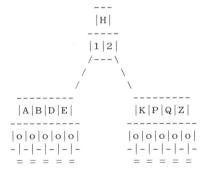

S: The node is full, so it must be split. A new node at the leaf level is created
(*). Of the keys, K, P, Q, S, and Z, key Q is the median value.

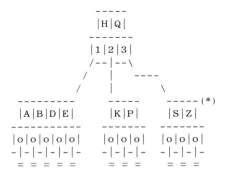

W, T: The keys are simply inserted.

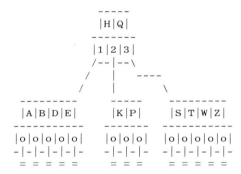

C: The node is full, so it must be split. A new node at the leaf level is created
(*). Of the keys, A, B, C, D, and E, key C is the median value.

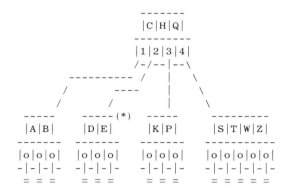

L, N: The keys are simply inserted.

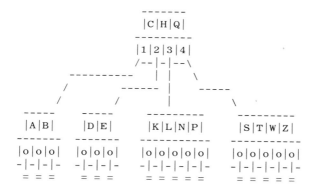

Y: The node is full, so it must be split. A new node at the leaf level is created (*). Of the keys, S, T, W, Y, and Z, key W is the median value.

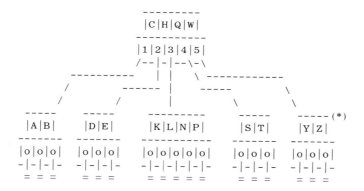

M: The node is full, so it must be split. A new node at the leaf level is created (*). Of the keys, K, L, M, N, and P, key M is the median value.

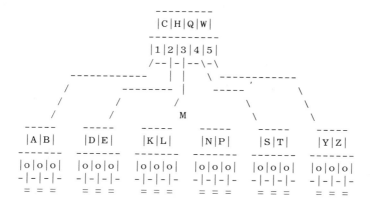

The root node is also full, so it is split. A new root node is created (+) . Of the keys, C, H, M, Q, and W, the key M is the median key. It is inserted into the new root.

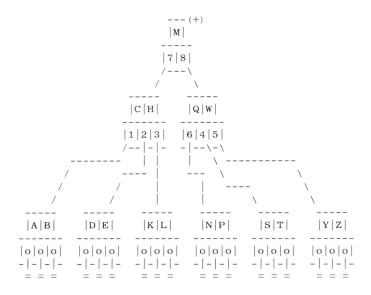

Note how the balance has been maintained throughout the insertions. A node split prepares the way for a number of simple insertions. If the number of keys in a node is large, the time before the next split (involving node creation and data transfer into the new node) will be fairly long.

The code for inserting a new key in a B-tree is given in the Parts Inventory Control Database system using B-tree in Chapter 11.

7.8.3 Deletion of a Node in the B-Tree

Deletion of a key is somewhat the reverse of insertion. If the key is found in a leaf, the deletion is fairly straightforward. If the key is not in a leaf, then the key's successor or predecessor must be in a leaf, because the insertion is done starting at a leaf. If the leaf is full, the median value key is pushed upward, so the key closest in value to a key in a nonleaf node must be in the root. The requirement that there be a minimum number of keys in a node also plays a part, as we shall see.

If the key is found in a leaf node and the node has more than the minimum number of nodes, then the key is simply deleted and the other keys in the node adjusted in position. If the node has only the minimum number of keys, then we must look at the immediately adjacent leaf nodes. If one of nodes has more than the minimum number of keys, the median key in the parent node is moved down to replace the deleted key and one of the keys from the adjacent leaf node is moved into the parent node in place of the median key.

To demonstrate this deletion, we use the B-tree of order 5 shown in the section on insertion. We will delete the key P from the tree after the insertion of the key S.

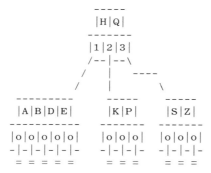

P: Its leaf node is at minimum key count, and the adjacent node with keys A, B, D, and E has more than the minimum key count. We can replace P with the median key H in the parent node. We then replace H with the key closest to it in value, key E.

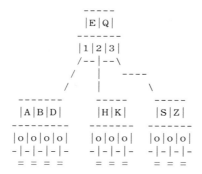

If both of the adjacent nodes have only the minimum number of keys, one of the adjacent nodes can be combined with the node that held the deleted key, and the median key from the parent node that partitioned the two leaf nodes is pushed down into the new leaf node. We will use the tree from the last example with keys A and B deleted.

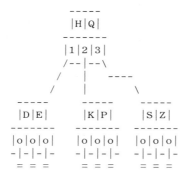

P: Its leaf node is at minimum key count, and the adjacent nodes also have minimum key count. We push H down into the combined node.

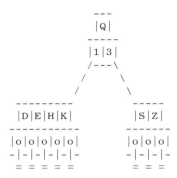

The code for deleting a node from a B-tree is given in the Parts Inventory Control Database system using the B-tree in Chapter 11.

A final word about the structure of the B-tree node is that it is best constructed with an array to hold the keys and an array to hold the pointers to children. Restricting our attention to the in-memory pointers, the definition of the node for the B-tree of order 5 is shown below.

```
#define  BTORDER  5
#define  KEYMAX   BTORDER - 1
#define  KEYMIN   KEYMAX / 2

struct  BTnode
   {
    int count;   /* number of keys held currently */
    DATATYPE  key[ KEYMAX ];
    struct BTnode * pointer[ BTORDER ];
   };
```

A key in a nonleaf node is the median value key between all keys in the adjacent subtrees. Suppose `btptr` is a pointer to a nonleaf node, `inx` is a key position with a value between 0 and KEYMAX, and the tree ordering is ascending numerical. The value of `btptr->key[inx]` will be greater than that of any key in the subtree pointed to by `btptr->pointer[inx]` and will be less than that of any key in the subtree pointed to by `btptr->pointer[inx+1]`. Note that in the Parts Inventory Control Database, we used "elements" and "children" in place of "key" and "pointers," respectively.

We summarize the key features of a B-tree as follows:

1. There is no redundant storage of search key values. That is, B-tree stores each search key value in only one node, which may contain other search key values.
2. The B-tree is inherently balanced, and is ordered by only one type of search key.
3. The insertion and deletion operations are complex with the time complexity $O(\log_2 n)$.

4. The search time is $O(\log_2 n)$.
5. The number of keys in the nodes is not always the same. The storage management is only complicated if you choose to create more space for pointers and keys, otherwise the size of a node is fixed.
6. The B-tree grows at the node as opposed to the binary tree, BST, and AVL trees.
7. For a B-tree of order N with n nodes, the height is $\log n$. The height of a B-tree increases only because of a split at the root node.

There are several variations of B-tree, including B^+-tree and B^*-tree. The B^+-tree indices are similar to B-tree indices. The main difference between the B^+-tree and B-tree are:

1. In a B^+-tree, the search keys are stored twice; each of the search keys is found in some leaf nodes.
2. In a B-tree, there is no redundancy in storing search-key values; the search key is found only one in the tree. Since search-key values that are found in nonleaf nodes are not found anywhere else in the B-tree, an additional pointer field for each search key is kept in a nonleaf node.
3. In a B^+-tree, the insertion and deletion operations are complex and $O(\log_2 n)$, but the search operation is simple, efficient, and $O(\log_2 n)$.

For a detailed discussion on B-tree and B^+-tree, see Comer (1979).

7.9 Application: Algebraic Expression Evaluation

Expression (or algebra) trees are useful applications of binary trees. This application does not need the tree to be a binary search tree. The expression trees are closely related to parse trees, used by the parser of compilers and other language translators.

An expression tree is a tree that has operators as the root nodes of subtrees and operands as the leaf nodes.

A general tree can be used to hold a general expression, containing operators that have single operands to operators that have many operands. For example, a function $f(x, y, z)$ would have a subtree:

```
f            . . . . . . . . . .   root
|
v
x -> y -> z     . . . .   operands
```

If $x = g(i, k)$, then the function $f[g(i, k), y, z]$ would have the following tree:

```
f
|
v
g -> y -> z
|
v
i -> k
```

A binary tree can be used to store and evaluate an algebraic expression containing only binary and unary operators. For example, the expression X * Y has the subtree:

Note the convention that the unary operator, for example, negation, cube root, will have an empty right subtree. Thus the expression (X + Y / Z) * (-W) will be represented as

The expression tree structure contains the grouping and precedence of the expression operators using parentheses, and traversal of the tree produces an unambiguous evaluation of the tree.

Given an expression tree:

Preorder traversal produces: + * A B C (prefix notation)

Inorder traversal produces: A * B + C (infix notation—*caution:* grouping is lost)

Postorder traversal produces: A B * C + (postfix notation)

Postorder traversal produces an expression similar to the keypad entry of a handheld calculator based on reverse polish notation (RPN). In Chapter 6, we discussed the evaluation of the RPN using a stack. We can also evaluate the RPN using the expression binary tree. The use of a tree rather than a stack (as in the RPN example) allows the expression to be stored and reaccessed.

The program shown in Example 7.6 will demonstrate the evaluation of an algebraic expression using an expression tree. This program also demonstrates a simple recursive descent parser. In the following paragraphs, we describe this program.

The program prompts for input of an expression, builds a binary expression tree, prints out the tree structure, and prints the result. The program recognizes parentheses used for grouping. The program uses a function `Create_Expr_Node()` to allocate a tree node, using the library routine `calloc()`, and returns a pointer to it. The `calloc()` initializes the fields `Item`, `Left_Operand`, and `Right_Operand` of the EXPR_NODE structure.

The function `Expression()` builds the expression tree. It calls the function `token()` to obtain a term of the expression. It tests the using the global variable `glbl_symbol` for the + or – operators and if found, creates a new node and calls the function token() to evaluate a new term. It returns the pointer to the first term subtree. It is a simple recursive descent parser.

The function token() obtains a factor in the current term. It calls the function parentheses() to check for an opening parenthesis. It tests, using the global glbl_symbol, for the * or / operators, and if found, creates a new node, and calls parentheses() to convert the operand from character string to number. Token() returns a pointer to the subtree created by parentheses().

The function parentheses() tests for open parenthesis (. If it is found, it skips over the left parenthesis, and calls Expression() to get another token. This is the heart of the recursive descent logic of this algorithm. On return, it tests for closing parenthesis,), and if it is not found, it exits with an error message. If it finds the right parenthesis as expected, it skips it to get another token. If the (is not found, then parentheses() calls convert() to convert the current character stream to a number, calls Create_Expr_Node(), and stores the number in it. The function parentheses() returns a pointer to a subtree.

The function convert() obtains a string of characters with values 0 through 9, keeps a running sum of the numerical equivalent of the string of characters. It terminates at the first nondigit character, and returns the string as a number.

The function hPrint_Tree() prints the binary expression tree horizontally. The root node will appear on the left side with its left and right subtrees to its right. The level parameter is used to print the subtree at that level. The function uses Inorder traversal to print the expression tree.

The function Evaluate() evaluates the expression tree considering the cases for the +, -, *, and / operators. It returns an integer number.

Here is an example expression for the expr_tree.c example, which steps through generation of the tree, and then does postorder traversal evaluation. Corresponding to the expression

$$(3+5) * (9 - (4*2))$$

the expression binary tree is

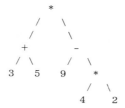

The postfix expression is: 3 5 + 9 4 2 * - *

The evaluation steps are:

```
3  5  +          does  3  +  5  =  8
8
8  9  4  2  *    does  4  *  2  =  8
8  9  8
8  9  8  -       does  9  -  8  =  1
8  1
8  1  *          does  8  *  1  =  8
8
```

The result is 8.

Here is the code for the expression tree evaluation.

Example 7.6

Code Section

```
/*
 * PROGRAM:    expr_tree.c
 * PURPOSE:    To evaluate an algebraic expression using
 *             Binary Tree. It is a simple recursive descent parser.
 */

#include <stdio.h>

#define   PLUS        '+'
#define   MINUS       '-'
#define   TIMES       '*'
#define   DIVIDE      '/'

#define   LEFT_PAREN    '('
#define   RIGHT_PAREN   ')'

typedef   struct   node
{
      int      Item;
      struct   node *Left_Operand;
      struct   node *Right_Operand;
} EXPR_NODE;

typedef EXPR_NODE   *EXPR_BTREE_PTR;

int  glbl_symbol;        /* Global symbol for next character */

EXPR_BTREE_PTR    Create_Expr_Node   (   )
{
   /*  PURPOSE:  Create a new node of the expression tree.
    *  RETURNS:  A EXPR_BTREE_TYPE Pointer
    */
   EXPR_BTREE_PTR   etp;      /* Expression tree pointer */

   etp = (EXPR_BTREE_PTR) calloc (1, sizeof (EXPR_NODE));
   if ( etp == NULL )
     {
       error("Create_Expr_Node: No more memory space");
       exit (1);
     }
   return (etp);
}

int convert()
{
   /*  PURPOSE:  Convert a string of digit characters
    *            to a number.
```

```
    *  RETURNS:   integer
    */

    int result;

    if ( glbl_symbol < '0' || glbl_symbol > '9' )
      {
        error("\n Convert: Number Expected");
        exit(1);
      }
    result  = glbl_symbol - '0';
    while ( ( glbl_symbol = getchar() ) >= '0' &&
              glbl_symbol <= '9' )

          result = 10 * result + glbl_symbol-'0';
    return ( result );
}


EXPR_BTREE_PTR   parentheses (   )
{
    /*  PURPOSE:   Checks to find either an operand or
     *             left parenthesis.
     *  RETURNS:   EXPR_BTREE_PTR type pointer pointing
     *             to the root of an expression tree
     */

    extern    EXPR_BTREE_PTR  Expression();

    EXPR_BTREE_PTR etp;   /* creates the tree after digit is found */
    int  digit;           /* holds the value returned from convert() */

    if ( glbl_symbol == LEFT_PAREN   )
      {
        glbl_symbol = getchar();

        etp  =  Expression ();
        if ( glbl_symbol != RIGHT_PAREN )
          {
            error("parentheses: Right Parenthesis Expected");
            exit(1);
          }
        glbl_symbol  = getchar();
      }
    else
      {
        digit = convert();
        etp  = Create_Expr_Node ();
        etp -> Item = digit ;
      }
    return ( etp );
}


EXPR_BTREE_PTR   token ()
{
```

```
    /*  PURPOSE:   To obtain a term of the expression
     *  RETURNS:   EXPR_BTREE_PTR type pointer pointing
     *             to the expression tree
     */

    EXPR_BTREE_PTR  etp,    /* creates right subtree */
                    Left;   /*    "     left      "   */

    Left = parentheses ();
    while ( glbl_symbol == TIMES || glbl_symbol == DIVIDE )
       {
          etp = Create_Expr_Node ();
          etp -> Item = glbl_symbol ;
          etp -> Left_Operand = Left ;

          glbl_symbol = getchar ();

          etp -> Right_Operand = parentheses ();
          return ( etp );
       }
    return ( Left );
}

EXPR_BTREE_PTR  Expression ()
{
    /*  PURPOSE:   Create the expression tree
     *  RETURNS:   EXPR_BTREE_PTR type pointer pointing
     *             to root of the expression tree
     */

    EXPR_BTREE_PTR  etp, /* expression tree pointer */
             Left;       /* contains left subtree from token() */

    Left = token ();

    while ( glbl_symbol == PLUS || glbl_symbol == MINUS )
       {
          etp  = Create_Expr_Node ();
          etp -> Item = glbl_symbol;
          etp -> Left_Operand = Left;

          glbl_symbol = getchar ();

          etp -> Right_Operand = token ();

          if (glbl_symbol != PLUS || glbl_symbol != MINUS )
             return ( etp );
       }
    return ( Left );
}

int   Evaluate ( EXPR_BTREE_PTR  etp )
{
```

```
    /*  PURPOSE:   Evaluate the expression binary tree
     *  RETURNS:   Integer result
     */

    int  Result = 0;   /* Result for the expression  */

    if ( etp -> Item == TIMES || etp -> Item == DIVIDE ||
         etp -> Item == PLUS  || etp -> Item == MINUS )

      switch ( etp -> Item )
      {
        case PLUS :
                Result = Evaluate ( etp ->Left_Operand ) +
                         Evaluate ( etp -> Right_Operand);
                break;
        case MINUS :
                Result = Evaluate ( etp ->Left_Operand ) -
                         Evaluate ( etp -> Right_Operand);
                break;
        case TIMES :
                Result = Evaluate ( etp ->Left_Operand ) *
                         Evaluate ( etp -> Right_Operand);
                break;

        case DIVIDE :
                Result = Evaluate ( etp ->Left_Operand ) /
                         Evaluate ( etp -> Right_Operand);
                break;
      }
    else
          Result = etp -> Item;
    return ( Result );
}

hPrint_Tree  ( EXPR_BTREE_PTR  etp, int level )
{
    /*    PURPOSE:  Horizonatally print the binary
     *              tree using Inorder (LNR) traversal.
     */

    int  i;

    if ( etp != NULL )
      {
        hPrint_Tree ( etp -> Left_Operand, level + 1 );
        for ( i = 0; i <= level;  i++ )
          printf ("    " );

        if ( etp -> Item == TIMES || etp -> Item == DIVIDE ||
             etp -> Item == PLUS  || etp -> Item == MINUS )
          printf ("%c \n ", (char) etp -> Item );
        else
          printf ("%d \n", etp -> Item);
```

```
      hPrint_Tree ( etp -> Right_Operand, level + 1 );
   }
}

error( char * string )
{
   /*  PURPOSE:  Print error message
    */
   fprintf( stderr, "\n %s \n", string );
}

main (   )
{
  EXPR_BTREE_PTR  Expr_Tree = NULL;  /* expression tree   */
  int    Result;                /* Result for the expression */

  printf("\n *** EVALUATE EXPRESSION USING BINARY TREE *** \n");
  printf ("\n Input an expression in %s \n\n",
          "integers without spaces: ");

  glbl_symbol = getchar();

  Expr_Tree = Expression ();

  printf("\n  Expression Binary Tree is: \n");
  hPrint_Tree (Expr_Tree, 1);
  Result = Evaluate (Expr_Tree );

  printf ("\n\n The evaluation of the given expression = %d \n ",
          Result);
}
```

Output Section

```
        *** EVALUATE EXPRESSION USING BINARY TREE ***

        Input an expression in integers without spaces:

        (11+4)-33

          Expression Binary Tree is:
                        11
              +
                        4
            -
              33

        The evaluation of the given expression = -18
```

Further Examples

Example 7-1

Code Section

```
/*  Program Name: binary_tree_ops.c  (ADT Binary Tree)
 *  Purpose:       Implement following operations on an ADT
 *                 binary tree when it is implemented as a
 *                 Multiple Linked List with the following
 *                 operations:
 *
 *      1.   Create a node
 *      2.   Create a tree
 *      3.   Check whether the binary tree is empty
 *      4.   Search for a node of a tree
 *      5.   Delete a node (or a subtree) of a tree
 *      6.   Preorder Traversal
 *      7.   Inorder Traversal
 *      8.   Postorder Traversal
 *      9.   Add/insert a node in a tree as a left
 *           or right child
 *      10.  Update a node
 *      11.  Print a node
 *      12.  Print a (sub)tree
 *      13.  Find a parent node
 *      14.  Obtain the data from a node
 */


#define   NULL        0
#define   FALSE    0              /* BOOLEAN False  */
#define   TRUE     ~FALSE         /* BOOLEAN True   */
typedef   int      BOOL;

/* 'position' will be used in insert_node() */
enum  position  { root, left_child, right_child, parent };

/*  Define Node data type        */
typedef   char    node_data_type;

struct node_struct
   {
      node_data_type      node_data;
      struct node_struct  *left_child_ptr;
      struct node_struct  *right_child_ptr;
   };

typedef struct node_struct      Tree_Node;
typedef Tree_Node               *BTREE_PTR;

BTREE_PTR    root_ptr;           /* root of the binary tree    */
```

```
/* ********************************************************* *
 * is_tree_empty(): Check whether the tree is empty.         *
 * ********************************************************* */
BOOL is_tree_empty( BTREE_PTR root_ptr )
{
   return( root_ptr == NULL ? TRUE : NULL );
}


/* ********************************************************* *
 * create_node(): Allocate mem space and pointer to that     *
 * ********************************************************* */
BTREE_PTR create_node ()
{
   BTREE_PTR new_node_ptr;

   /*  Allocate a memory space for the new node; if no space
    *  available, return with error
    */

   if ((new_node_ptr = (BTREE_PTR) malloc(sizeof(Tree_Node)))
               == NULL )
     {
       printf("\n create_node: malloc failed  \n\n");
       return ( NULL );
     }
   else
     {   /*  Initialize this node   */
       new_node_ptr -> node_data =  NULL;
       new_node_ptr -> left_child_ptr  = NULL;
       new_node_ptr -> right_child_ptr = NULL;
       return( new_node_ptr );
     }
}


/* ********************************************************* *
 * init_tree(): Initialize the binary tree by getting a      *
 *              pointer for its root. It calls create_node() *
 * ********************************************************* */
BTREE_PTR   init_tree ()
{
   return ( create_node() );
}


/* ********************************************************* *
 * update_node():    Update node's data field by new_data    *
 * ********************************************************* */
update_node ( BTREE_PTR       current_node_ptr,
              node_data_type  new_data )
{
     current_node_ptr -> node_data = new_data;
}
```

```
/* ************************************************************ *
 * retrieve_node():                                            *
 *      Retrieve node's data in the current node               *
 * ************************************************************ */
node_data_type retrieve_node ( BTREE_PTR   current_node_ptr )
{
    node_data_type      data;
    data = current_node_ptr -> node_data;
    return ( data );
}


/* ************************************************************ *
 * insert_node():                                              *
 *      Insert 'new_data' in the binary tree based on the      *
 *      intended position (i.e., 'where'). The possible of     *
 *      'where' are root, left_child, right_child, or parent.  *
 *      If successful, returns TRUE. Otherwise, returns        *
 *      FALSE. Note that insertion will fail if there is       *
 *      already a a node at 'where' position.                  *
 * ************************************************************ */

BTREE_PTR    insert_node ( BTREE_PTR        root_ptr,
                           BTREE_PTR        current_node_ptr,
                           node_data_type   new_data,
                           enum             position   where )
{
    BTREE_PTR    temp_node_ptr;

    /*  Use local var 'insert' as a flag to check success
     *  or failure.
     */
    int  insert = TRUE;

    temp_node_ptr = create_node();
    temp_node_ptr -> node_data = new_data;

    switch ( where )
     {
      case root:
        if ( root_ptr -> node_data == NULL )
            root_ptr = temp_node_ptr;
        else
            insert = FALSE;
        break;

      case left_child:
        if ( current_node_ptr -> left_child_ptr == NULL)
           current_node_ptr -> left_child_ptr = temp_node_ptr;
        else
        insert = FALSE;
        break;
```

```
        case right_child:
          if ( current_node_ptr -> right_child_ptr == NULL)
             current_node_ptr -> right_child_ptr = temp_node_ptr;
          else
             insert = FALSE;
          break;

        case parent:
          insert = FALSE;        /* Cannot insert at parent node */
          break;
        default:
          printf("\n insert_node: Unknown place to insert \n");
          exit ( 1 );
        }
        if ( insert == TRUE )
        {
           current_node_ptr = temp_node_ptr;
           return( temp_node_ptr );
        }
        else
        {                              /* Inserting the node failed. */
           free( temp_node_ptr );
           printf("\n insert_node: %s  %c \n",
                  "Failed to insert node data");
           return ( NULL );     /* Return NULL pointer          */
        }
}


/* ********************************************************* *
 * search_parent () :                                        *
 *      Searches for parent of the current node. If          *
 *      successful, returns BTREE_PTR to its parent node.    *
 *      Otherwise, returns NULL ptr.                         *
 * ********************************************************* */

BTREE_PTR    search_parent ( BTREE_PTR   root_ptr,
                             BTREE_PTR   current_node_ptr )
{
   /*  Algorithm is provided, but coding is
    *  left as an exercise.
    */
}


/* ********************************************************* *
 * delete_tree():                                            *
 *      Delete all nodes of the tree whose root (i.e.,       *
 *      parent) is the current_node; Release all memory      *
 *      spaces occupied by the nodes of this tree. It calls  *
 *      'PostOrder' Traversal'                                *
 * ********************************************************* */

delete_tree( BTREE_PTR   root_ptr )
{
```

```
      if ( root_ptr != NULL )
        {
          delete_tree( root_ptr -> left_child_ptr );
          delete_tree( root_ptr -> right_child_ptr );
          free ( root_ptr );
        }
}

/* **************************************************** *
 * delete_subtree(): Delete all nodes of the subtree whose  *
 *                    root (i.e., parent) is the current_node *
 * **************************************************** */

BTREE_PTR    delete_subtree( BTREE_PTR    *current_node_ptr,
                             BTREE_PTR    root_ptr )
{
    BTREE_PTR    parent_ptr;      /* Retuned from get_parent() */

    /* Find the parent of the current node
     * pointed to by current_node_ ptr
     */
    if ( (parent_ptr = search_parent( *current_node_ptr ))
            != NULL)
      {  /* Test whether the current node is left or
         * right child of its parent.
         */
        if (parent_ptr ->left_child_ptr == *current_node_ptr)
            /* yes, break the link now */
            parent_ptr -> left_child_ptr = NULL;
        else
            /* The current node is the right child
             * of its parent. Break the link.
             */
            parent_ptr -> right_child_ptr = NULL;
      }
    /* Delete all nodes in the subtree headed by
     * current_node_ptr
     */
    delete_tree( *current_node_ptr );
    /* Let root become the current node */
    *current_node_ptr = root_ptr;
    return ( current_node_ptr );
}

/* **************************************************** *
 * Traverse_InOrder(): InOrder Traversal of the binary  *
 *                    tree pointed to by root_ptr.        *
 *                    (Recursive Implementation )         *
 * **************************************************** */
Traverse_InOrder( BTREE_PTR  root_ptr )
{
    if ( root_ptr != NULL )
      {
```

```
                    /*  Recursively  Traverse the Left subtree  */
                    Traverse_InOrder ( root_ptr -> left_child_ptr );
                    /*  Visit root by printing it  */
                    printf(" %c ", root_ptr -> node_data );
                    /*  Recursively  Traverse the right subtree  */
                    Traverse_InOrder ( root_ptr -> right_child_ptr );
                }
}

/* ******************************************************* *
 * Traverse_PostOrder(): PostOrder Traversal of the binary *
 *                       pointed to by the root_ptr.       *
 *                       (Recursive method)                *
 * ******************************************************* */
Traverse_PostOrder( BTREE_PTR  root_ptr )
{
    if ( root_ptr != NULL )
        {
            /*  Recursively Traverse the Left subtree */
            Traverse_PostOrder ( root_ptr -> left_child_ptr );
            /*  Recursively Traverse the Right subtree */
            Traverse_PostOrder ( root_ptr -> right_child_ptr );
            /*  Visit root by printing it  */
            printf(" %c ", root_ptr -> node_data );
        }
}

/* ******************************************************* *
 * Traverse_PreOrder():  PreOrder Traversal of the binary  *
 *                       pointed to by the root_ptr.       *
 *                       (Recursive method)                *
 * ******************************************************* */
Traverse_PreOrder( BTREE_PTR  root_ptr )
{
    if ( root_ptr != NULL )
        {
            /*  Visit root by printing it */
            printf(" %c ", root_ptr -> node_data );
            /*  Recursively Traverse the Left subtree */
            Traverse_PreOrder ( root_ptr -> left_child_ptr );
            /*  Recursively Traverse the Right subtree */
            Traverse_PreOrder ( root_ptr -> right_child_ptr );
        }
}

void print( char * header )
{
    printf("\n\n %s \n", header);
}
```

```
/* ************************************************************ *
 *  main(): Operations on an ADT  Binary Tree                  *
 * ************************************************************ */
main()
{
    BTREE_PTR    root_ptr = NULL;   /* Root of the Binary tree */
    BTREE_PTR    current_node_ptr = NULL;
    BTREE_PTR    temp;

    root_ptr =  init_tree();

    /*  Building the binary tree from a string of characters */

    root_ptr -> node_data = 'P';
    current_node_ptr =  root_ptr;

    if ((temp = insert_node( root_ptr, current_node_ptr,
         'R',left_child)) != NULL )
        current_node_ptr =  temp;

    if ((temp = insert_node( root_ptr, current_node_ptr,
         'A',right_child)) != NULL )
        current_node_ptr =  temp;

    if ((temp = insert_node( root_ptr, current_node_ptr,
         'T',right_child)) != NULL )
        current_node_ptr =  temp;

    if ((temp = insert_node( root_ptr, current_node_ptr,
         'I',right_child)) != NULL )
        current_node_ptr =  temp;

    if ((temp = insert_node( root_ptr, current_node_ptr,
         'V',right_child)) != NULL )
        current_node_ptr =  temp;

    if ((temp = insert_node( root_ptr, current_node_ptr,
         'A',right_child)) != NULL )
        current_node_ptr =  temp;

    print(" ***  Example of BINARY TREE Operations ***");
    print("The Binary tree when traversed by InOrder():");
    Traverse_InOrder( root_ptr );

    print("The Binary tree when traversed by PostOrder():");
    Traverse_PostOrder( root_ptr );

    print("The Binary tree when traversed by PreOrder():");
    Traverse_PreOrder( root_ptr );

    print(" *** End of example of BINARY TREE Operations ***");
}
```

Output Section

```
    ***   Example of BINARY TREE Operations ***

The Binary tree when traversed by InOrder():
R   A   T   I   V   A   P

The Binary tree when traversed by PostOrder():
A   V   I   T   A   R   P

The Binary tree when traversed by PreOrder():
P   R   A   T   I   V   A

    *** End of example of BINARY TREE Operations ***
```

Example 7-2

Code Section

```c
/*   Program Name: BSTree_ops.c   (ADT Binary Search Tree)
 *   Purpose:         Implement following operations on an ADT
 *                    Binary Search Tree (BST) when it is
 *                    implemented as a Multiple Linked List
 *                    with the following operations:
 *
 *           1.   Create a node
 *           2.   Create a tree
 *           3.   Initialize a BST
 *           4.   Check whether the BST is empty
 *           5.   Search for a node of a tree
 *           6.   Delete a BST
 *           7.   Delete a subtree) of a tree
 *           8.   Delete a node (or a subtree) of a tree
 *                (Exercise)
 *           9.   Preorder Traversal
 *          10.   Inorder Traversal
 *          11.   Postorder Traversal
 *          12.   Add/insert a node in a tree as a left
 *                or right child
 *          13.   Update a node's data
 *          14.   Print a node (Exercise)
 *          15.   Print a (sub)tree (using traversals)
 *          16.   Search for a parent node (Exercise)
 *          17.   Retrieve a node
 */

typedef   int      BOOL;
#define   FALSE    0                   /* BOOLEAN False    */
#define   TRUE     ~FALSE              /* BOOLEAN True     */

#define   NULL     0
typedef   int      data_type;    /* Define Node data type */
```

```
typedef   struct node_struct
    {
      data_type        node_data;
      struct node_struct      *left_child_ptr;
      struct node_struct      *right_child_ptr;
    } Tree_Node;

typedef Tree_Node      *BSTREE_PTR;   /* Define BSTREE_PTR type */

BSTREE_PTR    root_ptr;                  /* root of the binary tree */

/* ********************************************************* *
 * is_BST_empty(): Check whether the BST is empty.          *
 * ********************************************************* */
BOOL   is_BST_empty( BSTREE_PTR root_ptr)
{
   return( root_ptr == NULL ? TRUE : FALSE );
}


/* ********************************************************* *
 * create_node(): Allocate mem space and pointer to that.   *
 * ********************************************************* */
BSTREE_PTR create_node()
{
   BSTREE_PTR new_node_ptr;

   /*  Allocate a memory space for the new node;
    *  If no space available, return with error
    */

   if ( (new_node_ptr = (BSTREE_PTR) malloc(sizeof(Tree_Node)))
              == NULL )
     {
        printf("\n create_node: malloc failed  \n\n");
        return ( NULL );
     }
   else
     {   /*  Initialize this node   */
        new_node_ptr -> node_data  =  NULL;
        new_node_ptr -> left_child_ptr  = NULL;
        new_node_ptr -> right_child_ptr = NULL;
        return( new_node_ptr );
     }
}


/* ********************************************************* *
 * BSTinit_tree(): Initialize the Binary Search Tree by     *
 *                 getting a pointer for its root. It calls  *
 *                 create_node()                             *
 * ********************************************************* */
BSTREE_PTR    BSTinit_tree()
{
   return ( create_node() );
}
```

```
/* *********************************************************** *
 * BSTupdate_node(): Update node's data field by new_data      *
 * *********************************************************** */
BSTupdate_node ( BSTREE_PTR   current_node_ptr,
                 data_type    new_data )
{
    current_node_ptr -> node_data = new_data;
}


/* *********************************************************** *
 * BSTretrieve_node(): Retrieve node's data in the current     *
 *                     node pointed to by current_node_ptr.    *
 * *********************************************************** */
data_type BSTretrieve_node ( BSTREE_PTR   current_node_ptr )
{
    data_type      data;
    data = current_node_ptr -> node_data;
    return ( data );
}


/* *********************************************************** *
 * BST_Insert_node ( subtree_ptr, new_data ):                  *
 *                                                             *
 *    Insert an element new_data into a BST pointed by         *
 *    subtree_ptr. Compare new_data with root ( root of each   *
 *    subtree ) and move to a left or right subtree depending  *
 *    on whether the new_data is less than or greater than     *
 *    the root of each subtree. If successful, sets Pointer    *
 *    to that node with 'new_data' to the subtree_ptr. It      *
 *    simply returns if there is a node with the same          *
 *    'new_data'.  ( Recursive Implementation )                *
 * *********************************************************** */

BST_Insert_node ( BSTREE_PTR    *subtree_ptr,       /* Input */
                  data_type     new_data )          /* Input */
{
   BSTREE_PTR    new_node_ptr;

   if (*subtree_ptr == NULL )
     {
       new_node_ptr = create_node();
       /* Put new data in root   */
       new_node_ptr -> node_data = new_data;
       /* 'subtree_ptr' points to the current subtree root */
       *subtree_ptr = new_node_ptr;
     }
   else
     {
       if ( new_data == (*subtree_ptr) -> node_data )
          /* Data already exists */
          return;
       else if ( new_data < (*subtree_ptr) -> node_data )
          /* Must be inserted in the left subtree */
          BST_Insert_node ( &(*subtree_ptr) -> left_child_ptr,
                            new_data );
```

```
            else if ( new_data > (*subtree_ptr) -> node_data )
               /* Must be inserted in the right subtree */
               BST_Insert_node ( &(*subtree_ptr) -> right_child_ptr,
                                 new_data ) ;
         }
}


/* *********************************************************** *
 * BST_Create(): Creates a BST from an array of elts calling *
 *               BST_Insert_node(). Elements are integers.    *
 * *********************************************************** */

BST_Create( BSTREE_PTR    *subtree_ptr,
            data_type     data_array[ ],
            int           array_size)
{
    int  i;
    for ( i = 0; i < array_size; i++ )
       BST_Insert_node ( subtree_ptr, data_array[ i ]);
}


/* *********************************************************** *
 * BSTREE_PTR BST_Search( root_ptr, Item )                    *
 *                                                            *
 *  Search for Item in the Binary Search Tree with root       *
 *  pointed to by root_ptr. If successful, it returns a       *
 *  pointer to the node that contains the specified Item.     *
 *  If not successful, it returns a NULL pointer.             *
 *  ( Iterative implementation ; This is more advantageous    *
 *     than its Recursive counterpart with respect to time.   *
 * *********************************************************** */

BSTREE_PTR BST_Search( BSTREE_PTR   root_ptr, data_type Item )
{
    BSTREE_PTR Search_ptr; /* Used as a Search pointer in BST*/

    /*  Is the binary search tree empty ?  */
    if ( root_ptr == NULL )
      {
        printf("\n BST_Search: Empty Binary Search Tree \n");
        return( NULL ) ;
      }
    else
      {
        Search_ptr = root_ptr;  /* Start searching from root */

        /*  Perform search iteratively, because recursive
         *  search in BST will require a lot of stack space.
         */
        while (  Search_ptr != NULL  )
          {
             if ( Item < Search_ptr -> node_data )
               /* Continue search in the Left subtree */
                 Search_ptr = Search_ptr -> left_child_ptr;
```

```
            else if ( Item > Search_ptr -> node_data )
                /* Continue search in the Right subtree*/
                   Search_ptr = Search_ptr -> right_child_ptr;
            else
                   return ( Search_ptr );
            }
        printf("\n BST_Search: Item %d  not found \n", Item);
        return ( NULL );

      } /* End of 'else' when BST is nonempty  */
}

/* ************************************************************ *
 * BSTsearch_parent():                                         *
 *    Searches for parent of the current node. If successful,  *
 *    returns BSTREE_PTR to its parent node. Otherwise,        *
 *    returns a NULL pointer.  ( Both Iterative and Recursive  *
 *    versions given as Exercises)                             *
 * ************************************************************ */

BSTREE_PTR   BSTsearch_parent ( BSTREE_PTR current_node_ptr )
{
    /* Left as an exercise  */
}

/* ************************************************************ *
 * BSTdelete_tree():                                           *
 *    Delete all nodes of the entire tree whose root  (i.e.,   *
 *    parent) is the current_node. Release all memory spaces   *
 *    occupied by the nodes of this tree.  It uses 'PostOrder'*
 *    Traversal method to traverse the BST.                    *
 * ************************************************************ */

BSTdelete_tree( BSTREE_PTR  root_ptr )
{
    if ( root_ptr != NULL )
      {
        BSTdelete_tree( root_ptr -> left_child_ptr );
        BSTdelete_tree( root_ptr -> right_child_ptr );
        free ( root_ptr );
      }
}

/* ************************************************************ *
 * BSTdelete_subtree(): Delete all nodes of the BST subtree    *
 *                      whose root (i.e., parent) is the       *
 *                      current_node. After the deletion,      *
 *                      current_node_ptr is set to root.       *
 *                      It calls BSTsearch_parent().           *
 *                      ( Recursive implementation )           *
 * ************************************************************ */
BSTdelete_subtree( BSTREE_PTR   *current_node_ptr,
                   BSTREE_PTR    root_ptr )
{
    BSTREE_PTR    parent_ptr;  /* Returned from search_parent() */
```

```
   /*  Find the parent of the current node pointed by
    *  current_node_ptr because current_node will no
    *  longer left or child of its parent.
    */

   if ( (parent_ptr = BSTsearch_parent( *current_node_ptr ))
         != NULL )
     {
       /*  Test whether the current node is left or
        *  right child of its parent.
        */
       if (parent_ptr -> left_child_ptr == *current_node_ptr )
          /* Break the link now */
          parent_ptr -> left_child_ptr = NULL;

       else
          /*  The current node is the right child of its
           *  parent. Break link now.
           */
          parent_ptr ->right_child_ptr = NULL;
     }

   /*  Delete all nodes in the subtree headed by
    *  current_node_ ptr
    */
   BSTdelete_tree( *current_node_ptr );

   /*  Let root become the current node  */
   *current_node_ptr = root_ptr;
}

/* ********************************************************* *
 * BST_InOrder(): Inorder Traversal of the Binary Search    *
 *                Tree pointed to by the root_ptr.          *
 *                (Recursive Implementation )               *
 * ********************************************************* */

BST_InOrder( BSTREE_PTR  root_ptr )
{
   if ( root_ptr != NULL )
     {
       /* Recursively  Traverse the Left BST subtree  */
       BST_InOrder ( root_ptr -> left_child_ptr );
       /* Visit root by printing it  */
       printf(" %d ", root_ptr -> node_data );
       /* Recursively  Traverse the right BST subtree  */
       BST_InOrder ( root_ptr -> right_child_ptr );
     }
}
```

```
/* ************************************************************ *
 * BST_PostOrder(): Postorder Traversal of the BST pointed   *
 *                  to by the root_ptr (Recursive method).   *
 * ************************************************************ */

BST_PostOrder( BSTREE_PTR   root_ptr )
{
    if ( root_ptr != NULL )
      {
          /* Recursively Traverse the Left BST subtree */
          BST_PostOrder ( root_ptr -> left_child_ptr );
          /* Recursively Traverse the Right BST subtree*/
          BST_PostOrder ( root_ptr -> right_child_ptr );
          /* Visit root by printing it  */
          printf(" %d ", root_ptr -> node_data );
      }
}


/* ************************************************************ *
 * BST_PreOrder(): Preorder Traversal of the BST pointed to  *
 *                 by the root_ptr. (Recursive Procedure)    *
 * ************************************************************ */

BST_PreOrder( BSTREE_PTR   root_ptr )
{
    if ( root_ptr != NULL )
      {
          /* Visit root by printing it */
          printf(" %d ", root_ptr -> node_data );
          /* Recursively Traverse the Left BST subtree */
          BST_PreOrder ( root_ptr -> left_child_ptr );
          /* Recursively Traverse the Right BST subtree*/
          BST_PreOrder ( root_ptr -> right_child_ptr );
      }
}

void print( char * header )
{
    printf("\n\n %s \n", header);
}


/* ************************************************************ *
 *  main(): Operations on an ADT  Binary Search Tree (BST)   *
 *          (Linked List form)                               *
 * ************************************************************ */
main()
{
    BSTREE_PTR    root_ptr = NULL;           /* Root of the BST */
    BSTREE_PTR    current_node_ptr = NULL; /* Ptr to Cur node */

    /* For the following set of nodes, root = 67   */
    static int  A[] = { 67, 30, 70, 21, 34, 69, 75 };
    int no_data = sizeof( A )/sizeof( data_type );
```

```
                 /* ****  Building the Binary Search Tree  ****  */
                 BST_Create( &root_ptr, A, no_data );

                 print(" *** Example of BINARY SEARCH TREE Operations ***");

                 print("The Binary Search Tree when traversed by InOrder() :");

                 BST_InOrder( root_ptr );

                 print("The Binary Search Tree when traversed by PostOrder():");
                 BST_PostOrder( root_ptr );

                 print("The Binary Search Tree when traversed by PreOrder():");
                 BST_PreOrder( root_ptr );

                 if ( (current_node_ptr = BST_Search( root_ptr, 70 )) != NULL )
                      printf("\n\n The data item: %d is found in the BST\n",
                                current_node_ptr -> node_data );
                 print("*** End of example of BINARY SEARCH TREE Operations ***");
        }
```

Output Section
```
        *** Example of BINARY SEARCH TREE Operations ***

    The Binary Search Tree when traversed by InOrder() :
    21   30   34   67   69   70   75

    The Binary Search Tree when traversed by PostOrder():
    21   34   30   69   75   70   67

    The Binary Search Tree when traversed by PreOrder():
    67   30   21   34   70   69   75

    The data item: 70 is found in the BST

    *** End of example of BINARY SEARCH TREE Operations ***
```

Example 7-3

Code Section
```
/*
 *  avltree.c  :  Implement operations on an ADT AVL tree
 */

#include <stdio.h>

typedef   int   data_type;
typedef   int   balance;

typedef struct _avl_node
      {
          struct     _avl_node *left_child_ptr;
```

```
if ( new->node_data < y->node_data )
   p = y->left_child_ptr;
else
   p = y->right_child_ptr;
s = p;
while ( p != q )
  {
    if ( q->node_data < p->node_data )
      {
        p->height = 1;
        p = p->left_child_ptr;
      }
    else
      {
        p->height = -1;
        p = p->right_child_ptr;
      }
  }
/* Part II */
if ( q->node_data < y->node_data )
   imbal = 1;
else
   imbal = -1;
if ( y->height == 0 )   /* another level has been added to */
   y->height = imbal; /* and the tree remains balanced  */
else  if ( y->height != imbal )
   /*  The added node was placed in the opposite
    *  direction from the imbalance, so the tree
    *  is still balanced.
    */
   y->height = 0;
else
  {
    /*  Part III:
     *  y and s have been unbalanced in the same
     *  direction.
     */
    if ( s->height == imbal )
      {
        p = s;
        if ( imbal == 1 )
           Rotate_Right(y);
        else
           Rotate_Left(y);
        y->height = 0;
        s->height = 0;
      }
    else
      { /* y and s are unbalanced in the opposite direction */
        if ( imbal == 1 )
          {
            p = s->right_child_ptr;
            Rotate_Left(p);
```

```
                        y->left_child_ptr = p;
                        Rotate_Right(y);
                    }
                else
                    {
                        p = s->left_child_ptr;
                        Rotate_Right(s);
                        y->right_child_ptr = p;
                        Rotate_Left(y);
                    }
                if ( p->height == 0 )
                    {
                        y->height = 0;
                        s->height = 0;
                    }
                else if ( p->height == imbal )
                    {
                        y->height = -imbal;
                        s->height = 0;
                    }
                else
                    {
                        y->height = 0;
                        s->height = imbal;
                    }
                p->height = 0;
            }
        if ( v == TNULL )
            tree = p;
        else if ( y == v->right_child_ptr )
            v->right_child_ptr = p;
        else
            v->left_child_ptr = p;
    }
    return(q);
}


/*
 * AVL_Create () : Creates a AVL from an array of elts calling
 *                 AVL_Insert_node(). Elements are integers.
 */

AVLTREE_PTR AVL_Create( data_type  data_array[ ],
                        int        array_size )
{
    AVLTREE_PTR    temp_ptr,     /* temporary pointer */
                   root_ptr,     /* tree root pointer */
                   new_ptr;      /* current new pointer */
    int   i;
    AVLTREE_PTR create_node( void );
    int print( char * string );

    if (array_size <= 0)
        return(TNULL);
```

```
                struct      _avl_node  *right_child_ptr;
                data_type  node_data;
                balance    height;

          } AVL_NODE;

typedef AVL_NODE  * AVLTREE_PTR;

#define  TNULL      (AVLTREE_PTR) NULL

/*
 *  create_node(): Allocate memory space and pointer
 *                 to that space. If no space available,
 *                 return a NULL pointer.
 */
AVLTREE_PTR create_node()
{
   AVLTREE_PTR new_node_ptr;

   if ( (new_node_ptr = (AVLTREE_PTR) calloc(1,
                       sizeof(AVL_NODE))) == TNULL )
      printf("\n create_node: calloc failed\n");
   return( new_node_ptr );
}

/*
 *  Rotate_Right(): Rotate left child tree_ptr to the
 *                  right child tree_ptr.
 */

Rotate_Right( AVLTREE_PTR  tree_ptr )
{
   AVLTREE_PTR  hold_ptr;    /* Temp ptr storage */

   hold_ptr = tree_ptr;
   tree_ptr = tree_ptr -> left_child_ptr;
   hold_ptr -> left_child_ptr = tree_ptr -> right_child_ptr;
   tree_ptr -> right_child_ptr = hold_ptr;
}

/*
 *  Rotate_Left(): Rotate right child tree_ptr to the
 *                 left child tree_ptr.
 */

Rotate_Left( AVLTREE_PTR  tree_ptr )
{
   AVLTREE_PTR  hold_ptr;    /* Temp ptr storage */

   hold_ptr = tree_ptr;
   tree_ptr = tree_ptr -> right_child_ptr;
```

```
      hold_ptr -> right_child_ptr = tree_ptr -> left_child_ptr;
      tree_ptr -> left_child_ptr = hold_ptr;
}

/*
 *  AVL_Insert() :   Insertion of a node in an AVL Tree
 */

AVLTREE_PTR AVL_Insert( AVLTREE_PTR tree, AVLTREE_PTR new )
{
      AVLTREE_PTR  p  = tree,
                   y  = p,      /* y points to the youngest ancestor */
                   v  = TNULL,  /* v points to the parent of y */
                   s  = TNULL,  /* s points to the parent of p */
                   q  = TNULL;  /* q points to the new node location   */
      balance        imbal;

      /* Part I : search for the new data slot */
      if ( tree == TNULL )
          return( new );
      while ( p != TNULL)
        {
          if ( p->node_data == new->node_data )
              return( new );
          else
            {
              if ( new->node_data < p->node_data )
                  q = p->left_child_ptr;
              else
                  q = p->right_child_ptr;
              if ( q != TNULL && q->height != 0 )
                {
                  v = p;
                  y = q;
                }
              s = p;
              p = q;
            }
        }

      q = new;
      q->height = 0;

      if ( p == TNULL && s == TNULL )
          return (q);

      if ( new->node_data < s->node_data)
          s->left_child_ptr = q;
      else
          s->right_child_ptr = q;
      /*  the balance in all nodes between node y and node q
       *  must be changed to 0
       */
```

```
    root_ptr = TNULL;
    for ( i = 0;  i < array_size;  i++ )
        {
          if ((new_ptr = create_node()) == TNULL)
             {
               printf("AVL_Create: failed to obtain new node. Truncate
               input.\n");  break;
             }
          new_ptr -> node_data = data_array[i];
          if ( i == 0 )
              root_ptr = new_ptr;
          if ( (temp_ptr = AVL_Insert( root_ptr, new_ptr )) != new_ptr
              root_ptr = temp_ptr;
        }
    return( root_ptr );
}


/*
 * AVLdelete_tree(): delete the entire tree
 */

AVLdelete_tree( AVLTREE_PTR   root_ptr )
{
    if ( root_ptr != TNULL )
       {
         AVLdelete_tree( root_ptr -> left_child_ptr );
         AVLdelete_tree( root_ptr -> right_child_ptr );
         free ( root_ptr );
       }
}


/*
 * AVL_Inorder(): Inorder Traversal of the AVL Tree
 *                pointed to by the root_ptr.
 *                (Recursive Implementation )
 */

AVL_InOrder( AVLTREE_PTR   root_ptr )
{
    if ( root_ptr != TNULL )
       {
         /* Recursively  Traverse the Left AVL subtree  */
         AVL_InOrder ( root_ptr -> left_child_ptr );
         /* Visit root by printing it  */
         printf(" %d ", root_ptr -> node_data );
         /* Recursively  Traverse the right AVL subtree  */
         AVL_InOrder ( root_ptr -> right_child_ptr );
       }
}


/*
 * AVL_PostOrder(): Postorder Traversal of the AVL pointed
 *                  to by the root_ptr (Recursive method)
 */
```

```
AVL_PostOrder ( AVLTREE_PTR   root_ptr )
{
    if ( root_ptr != TNULL )
      {
          /* Recursively Traverse the Left AVL subtree */
          AVL_PostOrder ( root_ptr -> left_child_ptr );
          /* Recursively Traverse the Right AVL subtree*/
          AVL_PostOrder ( root_ptr -> right_child_ptr );
          /* Visit root by printing it  */
          printf (" %d ", root_ptr -> node_data );
      }
}

/*
 * AVL_PreOrder(): Preorder Traversal of the AVL pointed to
 *                 by the root_ptr. (Recursive Implementation)
 */

AVL_PreOrder ( AVLTREE_PTR   root_ptr )
{
    if ( root_ptr != TNULL )
      {
          /* Visit root by printing it */
          printf (" %d ", root_ptr -> node_data );
          /* Recursively Traverse the Left AVL subtree */
          AVL_PreOrder ( root_ptr -> left_child_ptr );
          /* Recursively Traverse the Right AVL subtree*/
          AVL_PreOrder ( root_ptr -> right_child_ptr );
      }
}

/*
 *  print(): print a string
 */

print ( char * string )
{
    printf ("\n\n %s \n", string);
}

/*
 *  hPrint_AVLtree(): Print AVL tree in its horizontal form
 *                    using Inorder traversal.
 */

hPrint_AVLtree  ( AVLTREE_PTR  root_ptr, int level )
{
  int  i;

  if ( root_ptr != NULL )
    {
      hPrint_AVLtree ( root_ptr -> right_child_ptr, level + 1 );
      for ( i = 0; i <= level;  i++ )
        printf ("       " );
```

```
        printf ("%d \n", root_ptr -> node_data );
        hPrint_AVLtree ( root_ptr -> left_child_ptr, level + 1 );
    }
}


/*
 *   AVL_Demo (): Demonstrate an ADT AVL Tree
 */

AVL_Demo ( AVLTREE_PTR root_ptr )
{
    print("  *** Demonstration of the ADT AVL TREE ***");
    print("The AVL Tree when traversed by InOrder () :");
    AVL_InOrder ( root_ptr );
    print("The AVL Tree when traversed by PostOrder ():");
    AVL_PostOrder ( root_ptr );
    print("The AVL Tree when traversed by PreOrder ():");
    AVL_PreOrder ( root_ptr );
    print("Horizontal form of the AVL Tree: \n");
    hPrint_AVLtree ( root_ptr, 0 );
    print("\n *** End of Demonstration of the ADT AVL TREE ***\n");
}


/*
 *   main (): Demonstrations of an ADT AVL Tree
 *            (Pointer implementation).
 */
main ()
{
    AVLTREE_PTR    root_ptr = TNULL;    /* Root of the AVL */

    /* For the following set of nodes, root = 67  */
    static data_type  A[] = { 67, 30, 70, 21, 34, 69, 75 };
    int num_data = sizeof ( A )/sizeof ( data_type );

    /* ****  Building the AVL Tree  ****  */
    root_ptr = AVL_Create ( A, num_data );
    AVL_Demo ( root_ptr );
}
```

Output Section

```
      *** Demonstration of the ADT AVL TREE ***

   The AVL Tree when traversed by InOrder () :
   21   30   34   67   69   70   75

   The AVL Tree when traversed by PostOrder ():
   21   34   30   69   75   70   67

   The AVL Tree when traversed by PreOrder ():
   67   30   21   34   70   69   75
```

Horizontal form of the AVL Tree:

```
                        75
              70
                        69
    67
                        34
              30
                        21
```

*** End of Demonstration of the ADT AVL TREE ***

Exercises

7-1 Write a function that deletes the root of a binary tree and to replace the root by the leftmost leaf node.

7-2 Write a program for binary trees to:

(a) Print contents of the tree
(b) Determine the total number of nodes
(c) Determine the total number of occurrences of a node with the same value, say, *j*

7-3 Write a function to calculate maximum level leaf node of a general tree.

7-4 Write a function to transform a binary tree into a general tree that uses sibling chains.

7-5 Write two functions to copy a binary tree into another one:

(a) Iteratively
(b) Recursively

7-6 Write a function that checks a binary tree to determine whether it is a binary search tree.

7-7 Write a function to convert a binary tree into a binary search tree.

7-8 Write a function that will create a binary tree from a given binary tree where each node of the new binary tree will have an additional link to its parent. Print both the trees.

7-9 Write a function to delete a node in a BST.

7-10 Write a function `search_parent ()` that searches for the parent of the current node in an ADT binary tree. If successful, it returns a pointer to the parent node; otherwise NULL. How could you change the structure of the node to make this task easier? Implement the function

(a) Iteratively
(b) Recursively

(*Hint:* You need to traverse the tree down to the parent, and test for a child.)

7-11 Write a nonrecursive function to traverse a binary tree in "double order," defined recursively as in the following steps:

Step 1. Visit (print, say) the root for the first time.
Step 2. Traverse the left subtree in double order.

Step 3. Visit (print, say) the root for the second time.

Step 4. Traverse the right subtree in double order.

7-12 [Refer to Reingold and Hansen (1983).] Let T be a binary tree in which, associated with each edge (FATHER (v) , v) , there is a nonnegative capacity c (FATHER (v) , v) , the amount of water that can flow from FATHER (v) to v. We assume that an infinite supply of water is available at the root of T. A flow in T is a nonnegative function f on the set of edges such that

$$f \text{ (FATHER (v) , v)} \le c \text{ (FATHER (v) , v)}$$

and

$$f \text{ (FATHER (v) , v)} = f \text{ (v, LEFT (v))} + f \text{ (v, RIGHT (v))}$$

The value of a flow is defined as the total flow through the root. A flow f is a maximum flow if its value is the largest possible.

(a) Explain why the value of f is the summation of f (FATHER (v) , v) for v, a leaf.

(b) Devise an algorithm to compute the value of a maximum flow f for a binary tree T with its associated capacity function. (*Hint:* Base your algorithm on a traversal).

(c) Devise an algorithm to compute the values f (FATHER (v) , v) for a maximum flow.

7-13 A bank needs to maintain records of its customers. It is decided to create a database as a binary search tree. The order is based on the key and the Social Security number of each customer. Each record contains the following information:

Name	(25 characters)
Social Security number	(long)
Street address	(20 characters)
City	(10 characters)
State	(10 characters)
Zip	(long)
Date of birth	
Marital status	(character)
Account number	(long)
Account type	(F: fixed, PB: savings, C: checking)

A database management system needs to be designed to provide menu-driven facilities to its users. The facilities are:

I: Insert the record for a new customer into the BST

F: Find and display the record for a customer specified by name or by Social Security number

U: Update the record of a customer already in the BST

D: Delete the record of a customer from the BST

Q: Quit from the menu.

Any option other than these must be prompted to the user as an invalid selection. Write a program to implement this. (*Note:* Because the above BST is structured on the basis of the search key "Social Security number," the search process by the key "name" cannot take advantage of the present form of the customer BST.)

7-14 Enhance the program for evaluating an algebraic expression in Example 7.6 in order to allow the following:

(a) The % operator

(b) At least one blank space between the operators and operands

7-15 Write a function to print a binary tree vertically, like the trees shown in Figures 7-1 and 7-2. The fundamental issues to consider are:

(a) The printer does not scroll back; it prints in the vertically downward direction only.

(b) Finding the position of each node in the tree.

(c) Avoiding overprinting of the node data, and defining appropriate spacing between the nodes.

7-16 (a) Write an algorithm to find the successor and the predecessor of any given node in a binary tree.

(b) Write a function implementing the algorithm in part (a).

7-17 For the expression tree in Example 7.6, write the following functions to display the algebraic expression in

(a) Infix form

(b) Prefix form

(c) Postfix form

7-18 Write a nonrecursive version of preorder traversal of a binary tree.

7-19 Write a nonrecursive version of postorder traversal of a binary tree. You must not use `goto`.

7-20 Write a function to determine the number of occurrences of various characters in a text, using a binary tree. Each node may be comprised of a character and the number of occurrences for that character. The counting process disregards the difference between upper- and lower-case characters.

7-21 Write a function to determine the number of occurrences of various words in a text, using a binary tree. Each node may be composed of a word and the number of occurrences for that word. The counting process disregards the difference between the upper- and lower-case characters.

7-22 Write a function that checks a binary tree to determine whether it is an ADT AVL tree.

7-23 Write a function that implements the operation of deleting an element from an ADT AVL tree.

7-24 Write a function that creates an ADT AVL tree whose elements are integers. Use a random-number generator to create the elements.

7-25 Write a function that prints a general tree in Example 7.5 like the following diagram:

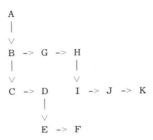

This diagram shows a child–siblings relationship.

7-26 The general tree building functions could have used the stack implicit in the use of recursion rather than an explicit stack. Rewrite the functions to use the recursion stack to keep track of ancestor nodes.

7-27 Construct a B-tree for the set of key values:

$$10, 15, 78, 6, 22, 30, 80, 45, 90, 99, 55$$

with the order

(a) 3
(b) 4
(c) 5

Assume that the tree is initially empty, and values are inserted in ascending order. Show the form of the tree after each insertion.

7-28 Show the form of the B-tree after deleting the node with the key value 22.

7-29 (*Advanced.*) Construct a B^+-tree for the set of key values

$$10, 15, 78, 6, 22, 30, 80, 45, 90, 99, 55$$

with the order

(a) 3
(b) 4
(c) 5

Assume that the tree is initially empty, and values are inserted in ascending order. Show the form of the tree after each insertion.

7-30 Show the form of the B^+-tree after deleting the node with the key value 22.

7-31 (a) Write an algorithm to search for a node in a general tree.
     (b) Implement the algorithm as a function.
     (c) Estimate the worst-case performance of the searching algorithm for a general tree.

7-32 Suppose we want to keep the organizational structure of a corporation as a general tree (see Figure 1-2). The record for each employee in the corporation contains the name, address, Social Security number, employee number, title, and department. Write an interactive program that

(a) Accepts inputs from the keyboard or a file
(b) Builds the general tree
(c) Prints the Social Security number for each employee in the form of a general tree with child–siblings relationship (see Exercise 7-25)
(d) Searches for an employee specified by the name, and prints all of the fields of the record, each on a separate line.

CHAPTER 8

Files

Most operating systems allow user access to files and devices (devices are treated, for the most part, as simple files) in one of two modes, colloquially known as "raw" and "cooked." In raw mode, the system imposes little or no filtering between the application and the data, and allows maximum control over the input or output. Raw-mode reads and writes are fast, because they are handled by operating system primitives with very little software overhead. The cooked mode imposes an additional layer of software overhead, but in return provides full buffering of the data. This allows an application for treating data linearly, in what is called "stream" format. The advantages of stream I/O will become more apparent as we proceed.

8.1 Raw I/O File Access

Raw-mode I/O is particularly well suited to data in fixed-length records, because it readily adapts to the record size, allowing us to step through the data one record at a time. The procedure is straightforward. Suppose we have a data file containing daily temperature information. To read it, the code in Figure 8-1 might be used.

By an analogous process using the `write()` system call, we might output the data to a new file, perhaps after modifying it in memory. Note that the `open()`, `read()`, and `close()` system calls return integer values, which programmers may, at their peril, ignore. If `open()` returns `-1`, there has been an error of some sort, and an error routine should be invoked. The `read()` system call returns the number of bytes actually read, or `-1` on an end-of-file condition. [Thus, it would actually have been more informative to test for `(read() == sizeof(struct temp))` in the example.] The `close()` system call returns `-1` on error; its value can be safely ignored when the `close()` occurs at the end of a program, but as a matter of prudent engineering we can use it as the return value of the `main()` function. This causes the value to be preserved as the program's exit status, which in turn is made available for the use of other programs.

Note the advantages and disadvantages of manipulating data structures in this way. The code is elegant, the I/O is fast, and the data image is compact; however, nothing is portable, except for the source code itself. If a program like this one were used to create a data file on one machine, there would be no guarantee that that data

```
#include <fcntl.h>

#define NSITES 100

static struct temp          /* Data on disk looks like this */
    {
       char      site[24];
       float     low,
                 high;
    }
Data[NSITES];

int
main()
{
    register struct temp *j;
    register int fd;

    fd = open("datafile",O_RDONLY);

    for (j = Data; read(fd,j,sizeof(struct temp)) > 0; ++j)
       ;

    return (close(fd));
}
```

Figure 8-1 A raw-mode data-read program.

file could be read on any other machine, because floats (and even chars) have little
meaning in C except with regard to a specific implementation.

Another point to be considered is that the code in Figure 8-1 requires that the
name of the data file be known, so that it can be opened for reading. In particular,
the program cannot easily read its data from a pipe, which is frequently a useful
thing to do. [Some versions of Unix allow named pipes, and, for all the program
knows, "data file" might be a named pipe, but the essential point is that its name
must be known in order to execute the open() call.]

Still another drawback to the raw-mode approach is that it virtually forces the
programmer to use fixed record lengths. In the example, if the actual site names to
be read averaged six characters in length, there would be a great deal of wasted
storage to accommodate a few long names.

8.2 Streams I/O File Access

The alternative to raw reading and writing is to process data as a stream. Streams are
manipulated by calls to library functions, which in turn are responsible for calling
system primitives such as open() and read(). This additional layer of software
gives the programmer much finer control over I/O formatting, and also greatly en-
hances the portability of code and data. Refer to Figure 8-2.

A file named "stdio.h" will be found on almost every system that supports
C programming. Its actual content will vary somewhat from system to system, even
between different Unix implementations; Figure 8-2 is reasonably typical, but
should be regarded as illustrative only. The whole idea of the file, in fact, is to pro-

```
/* Stream buffer size (installation-specific) */
#define BUFSIZ   512

/* Maximum number of simultaneously open files per process */
/* (implementation-specific) */
#define _NFILE    20

extern struct _iobuf    /* Data structure for stream I/O */
{
   char *_ptr;
   int  _cnt;
   char *_base;
   char _flag;
   char _file;
};

_iob[_NFILE];


#define stdin   (&_iob[0])     /* Standard input stream */
#define stdout  (&_iob[1])     /* Standard output stream */
#define stderr  (&_iob[2])     /* Standard error stream */

#define NULL    (char *)(0)    /* The invalid pointer value */

#define FILE    struct _iobuf  /* Could also be a typedef */

#define EOF     (-1)           /* Value returned on EOF */

#define getc(p)      (--(p)->_cnt >= 0 ? \
                       *(p)->_ptr++ & 0377 : \
                       _filbuf(p))

#define getchar()    getc(stdin)

#define putc(x,p)    (--(p)->_cnt >= 0 ? \
                     ((int)(*(p)->_ptr++ = (unsigned)(x))) : \
                     _flsbuf((unsigned)(x),p))

#define putchar(x)   putc(x,stdout)

#define feof(p)      (((p)->_flag & _IOEOF) != 0)

#define ferror(p)    (((p)->_flag & _IOERR) != 0)

#define fileno(p)    p->_file

FILE *fopen(), *fdopen(), *freopen();
long ftell();
```

Figure 8-2 A typical <stdio.h> file.

mote portability by encouraging programmers to use standard constructs in their
source code; they can do this with confidence because they know that, by including
stdio.h, their standard constructs will be automatically translated to system-
specific usage prior to compilation. Programs which include this file can, by virtue
of its definitions, declarations, and data structures, perform stream-mode I/O on a
multitude of systems. Let's examine its elements in more detail.

The first entries in the file are two manifests, BUFSIZ and _NFILE. ("Manifest" is the technical term for a symbolic constant. It derives from the usage "manifest constant," in which the word "manifest" has its dictionary meaning of "self-evident.") BUFSIZ is seldom of practical interest to the application programmer; it gives the number of characters buffered by the stream library routines, which is generally the same as the number of bytes in a file system data block. [Bear in mind that the stream library functions must execute read() and write() system calls, and the most efficient way to do so is in multiples of file system block size.] _NFILE gives the maximum number of files that a process may have open at once. This number is typically 20, although newer implementations allow it to be configured into the system at boot time. In any case, the standard input, output, and error files are counted in this total, which means that only (_NFILE−3) files may be opened unless the standard files are closed.

The next entry in stdio.h is a declaration of an array of data structures, one for each possible open file. Note that the maximum number of open files per process is a system-imposed constant, having nothing to do with whether a process performs raw I/O or uses the stream access model. If a programmer elects to perform stream-based I/O, the only effect is that a data structure in the array named "_iob" is associated with each file opened. (The actual storage for this array is allocated in one of the stream library functions, which must be linked into the program after compilation.) The structures in the array contain buffering and redirection information for each open stream; this information can actually be accessed by the application programmer, although in practice this is never necessary and seldom desirable.

Next we have three definitions that associate symbolic names with the streams reserved for the standard input, output, and error files. These files exist regardless of whether there are streams associated with them; on Unix systems, by definition, they are assigned file descriptors zero, one, and two, respectively, and are opened automatically by the system whenever a process is spawned. If stream I/O is used, the descriptor of an open file is also its index into _iob[]. Note that one of the fields in the _iobuf structure is named "_file". This field exists to support redirection of input and output by allowing elements in the _iob array to point to each other. The field may not exist at all on systems that do not offer the Unix redirection feature, which is one excellent reason to avoid writing code that accesses the individual fields of stream buffers.

The names "FILE" and "NULL" are seen frequently in stream-based applications. Most stream arguments are expected to be of type "pointer to FILE," so FILE can actually be a typedef. Many of the stream library functions return a value of this type, so it is necessary to have some way of flagging invalid pointers; hence "NULL." It is worth noting that NULL is not guaranteed to be zero-valued. NULL is a constant of the implementation; its actual value is typically zero, and in any event can always be found in the stdio header file, but the programmer must make no assumptions about it. In particular, a program is nonportable if it expects invalid pointers to behave as if they were logically false. Moreover, any program that must deal with pointer values in a portable manner should use the value NULL from the system's stdio.h file, whether the program performs stream-based I/O or not.

When data is read as a stream, the application issues sequential requests for characters, each of which is returned as an integer until end-of-file is reached. On EOF, the integer value −1, which cannot be a valid character, is returned. The implementation must guarantee that programs can "push back" at least one character onto any input stream between successive reads from that stream; this is done via the ungetc() call, subject to the restriction that EOF cannot be unread. Four macros are available for use by applications in controlling I/O streams. The macros getc() and putc() actually increment and decrement the stream buffer pointers, calling the low-level library functions _filbuf() and _flsbuf() as necessary to fill or flush the buffers; these functions in turn call read() and write(). The macros getchar() and putchar() are more frequently seen; they are synonyms for getc(stdin) and putc(stdout), respectively.

The whole idea behind stream I/O is that files can be regarded as ordered sequences of characters, which programs may process in sequential order. On input, for example, as each character is read, the application can decide what to do with it based on its value. (As a minimum, of course, it will almost always be compared against EOF, so that the program can decide when to exit.) The power and elegance of this model are evidenced by the fact that the C compiler's front end uses nothing else for source file input: stream I/O underlies all of the compiler's sophisticated parsing algorithms.

A simple yet powerful extension to this basic idea is the gets() function in the standard C library. Gets() simply copies bytes from its standard input (which may be a file, a pipe, or even a raw device) to a caller-supplied buffer until a newline is encountered in the stream. This newline is replaced by a zero byte, which, under a convention observed by all of the C-library routines, signals the end of a character string. The caller's buffer then contains a full line of text from the input stream, suitable for processing by a parsing routine such as sscanf().

8.3 An Example of Streams I/O File Access

To see how this all fits together in practice, consider a program to process monthly sales figures for the branch offices of a hypothetical company, CPU Corporation. To facilitate human editing (not to mention portability), the data is maintained in an ASCII file. Suppose that the file contains these entries:

```
Atlanta $81609.23
Chicago $93772.82
Dallas $88617.76
Denver $75975.60
Houston $79820.11
Indianapolis $72831.56
Kansas City $82321.45
Los Angeles $96970.97
Minneapolis $77488.02
New York $90826.19
Pittsburgh $88600.37
St. Louis $84408.93
San Francisco $89826.89
```

A program for reading this file into memory and calculating the total monthly sales figure is shown in Figure 8-3.

This program is considerably more involved than the raw input program of Figure 8-1. However, it does many more things. To run it, the text of the data file

```
#include <stdio.h>

#define NOFFICES  20
#define NAMESIZE  24
#define BUFFSIZE 256

static struct sales
    {
        char  office[NAMESIZE + 1];
        double amount;
    }
Sales[NOFFICES];

static char
Buffer[BUFFSIZE];

extern double fabs();
extern char *gets(), *strcpy();
extern int printf(), sscanf(), strlen();

int main()
{
    register struct sales *j;
    double d, total = 0.0;
    char c[BUFFSIZE];

    for (j = Sales; gets(Buffer) != NULL; ++j)
        {
        sscanf(Buffer, "%[^$]$%LF", c, &d);
        if (strlen(c) > NAMESIZE)
            c[NAMESIZE] = '\0';
        strcpy(j->office, c);
        if ((d = fabs(d)) > 1e6)
            d = 1e6;
        j->amount = d;
        }

    printf("SUMMARY: \n");

    while (--j >= Sales)
        {
        total += j->amount;
        printf("%-30s%10.21f\n", j->office, j->amount);
        }

    printf("%-30s%10.21f\n", "TOTAL SALES: ", total);

    return (0);
}
```

Figure 8-3 A stream-based data-read program.

must be redirected to the standard input of the program. When this is done, the following output results:

```
SUMMARY:
San Francisco                         89826.89
St. Louis                             84408.93
```

Pittsburgh	88600.37
New York	90826.19
Minneapolis	77488.02
Los Angeles	96970.97
Kansas City	82321.45
Indianapolis	72831.56
Houston	79820.11
Denver	75975.60
Dallas	88617.76
Chicago	93772.82
Atlanta	81609.23
TOTAL SALES:	1103069.90

Several things about this program, and its output, merit further discussion. For example:

1. The stream-mode program does not have to open its input file by name. Instead, it simply calls the library function gets(), which reads from standard input and hence does not care whether its input is a file, a pipe, or a device. Gets() automatically returns an entire line of input, regardless of length; thus, stream mode frees us from the requirement that all input records be of fixed length. Also, since stream-mode data files are typically text files, complete portability of code and data can be achieved.

2. Since input records need not be of uniform length, we can save considerable disk space by not blank-padding strings. The parsing function sscanf(), from the standard library, looks at each input line in turn and extracts office names based on the occurrence of a dollar sign in the input. Because we told sscanf() that the dollar sign effectively delimits the office name, we need not worry about blanks in some of the names.

3. Stream mode makes it easy to perform sanity checks on the input. For example, before transferring an office name to an in-memory name array, we can check its length and truncate if necessary. [We could have used scanf(3s) to read data from the input stream directly into the data array, but chose to test it first, at the cost of some extra code. Note the way in which we guard against wildly excessive numeric inputs. In a real application, these tests would be much more sophisticated, and would undoubtedly issue warnings on the standard error output as appropriate.]

8.4 Data Structure Programming with Files

We conclude this chapter with an example of data-structure programming that approaches real-world complexity. The sales offices of large companies typically report to regional sales offices, which in turn report to the corporate headquarters. It is important to track sales by regions, not just by individual offices. Moreover, some local offices are so large that they have branch offices, and it is important to track the performance of the branches. What we have, in short, is a hierarchical structure, which must somehow be modeled in software. Here are the monthly sales figures for CPU Corporation, broken down by region, by local office, and by branch, with indentation used to reflect the hierarchical structure:

```
Corporate Headquarters::0:22650.44:King
 Northeast Region:NY:33116.24:17222.09:Hansen
  New York:NY:51622.80:11490.93:Lewis
   Brooklyn:NY:43993.72:6109.46:Gregg
   Paterson:NJ:46832.47:6098.08:Vucacich
  Pittsburgh:PA:88600.37:9891.26:Bingham
 Midwest Region:IL:24890.79:13716.82:Wallace
  Chicago:IL:93772.82:10102.24:Paulsen
  Indianapolis:IN:72831.56:9237.57:Benham
  Kansas City:KS:82321.45:8725.78:Wilton
  Minneapolis:MN:77488.02:8520.48:Morton
  St. Louis:MO:84408.93:8814.03:Piper
 Southern Region:TX:29260.84:12812.49:Dean
  Atlanta:GA:81609.23:9692.80:Switzer
  Dallas:TX:88617.76:9914.96:Phelan
  Houston:TX:79820.11:9108.20:Garza
 Western Region:CA:38180.19:16581.10:Muro
  Denver:CO:75975.60:8992.36:Wolf
  Los Angeles:CA:43212.19:11480.12:Lee
   Sepulveda:CA:44450.32:5162.39:Vela
   Orange:CA:52520.65:5980.16:Reed
  San Francisco:CA:49826.89:9897.77:Fenton
   Oakland:CA:39368.42:6138.30:Burley
   Cupertino:CA:41127.66:6964.82:Oakes
```

Clearly, this is a much more complicated data file than the one used in the previous example. Records consist of colon-separated fields, containing, from left to right, the name of the office, its state (for tax purposes), gross sales, cost of sales, and manager's surname. Regional offices are indented by one space, local offices by two spaces, and branch offices by three spaces; a subordinate office reports to the next-higher office that immediately precedes it in the file. Note that local offices and regional offices have some direct sales (i.e., sales not handled by a subordinate office).

Despite the complexity of this data file, it retains the benefits associated with stream-mode I/O: it can be maintained with no tools other than a standard text editor, and it is highly portable. (Indeed, without adding more fields, it is hard to imagine how this data could be represented in fixed-length records at all.) These advantages are so compelling that they almost always outweigh the small improvement in efficiency that can be obtained by the use of fixed-length, binary data files. From its inception, in fact, Unix itself has used text files almost exclusively for system administration: the password file, the group file, and the configuration master file are well-known examples of this philosophy. The few exceptions, such as utmp and wtmp, tend to be highly dynamic and of purely local interest.

What kind of program is required to process the above data file? Whenever data is structured hierarchically, recursion is the access technique that naturally suggests itself. In fact, recursion is the only efficient way to process nested data of any complexity.

It is often remarked that the C language supports recursion, but it is more precise to say that C allows self-referent function calls within the scope of a function's local variable set. This feature is what allows C to deal so elegantly with tree-structured data. Refer to Figure 8-4.

```
/* * * * * * * * * * * * * * * * * * * * * * * * * * * * *
 *                                                        *
 * Program to process tree-structured data files read from *
 * the standard input stream.                             *
 *                                                        *
 * * * * * * * * * * * * * * * * * * * * * * * * * * * * */

#include <stdio.h>          /* Useful definitions/declarations */

#define BUFFSIZE 256        /* Size of the main input buffer   */
#define MAXNODES  50        /* Maximum tree nodes available    */
#define MAXSUBS    6        /* Maximum subordinate offices     */
#define NAMSIZ_M  16        /* Maximum manager name length     */
#define NAMSIZ_O  24        /* Maximum office name length      */

static struct salesdat
{
    char    office[NAMSIZ_O+1];      /* Name of the office   */
    char    state[3];                /* State abbreviation   */
    double  sales;                   /* Actual sales amount  */
    double  costs;                   /* Cost of sales        */
    double  total;                   /* Holds total of subs  */
    char    manager[NAMSIZ_M+1];     /* Name of the manager  */
    struct salesdat *sub[MAXSUBS];   /* Ptrs to subordinates */
} Salesdat[MAXNODES];

static char
Buffer[BUFFSIZE];           /* Text from stdin is buffered here */

extern int  fprintf();      /* Function to format stream output */
extern char *gets();        /* Function to get line from stdin  */
extern int  printf();       /* Function to format stdout stream */
extern int  sscanf();       /* Function to parse memory string  */
extern char *strcat();      /* Function to concatenate strings  */

static int Nestlev( register char *p )
{
    /*  Return an office's nesting level.
     *  We want this routine to be FAST.
     */

    register char *q = p;

    while (*p == ' ')
        ++p;

    return (p - q);
}


static struct salesdat *
Nalloc()                    /* Allocate, initialize a tree node */

{
    static struct salesdat *p = Salesdat;
    register struct salesdat *q;
    register int i;
```

Figure 8-4 A full-featured, recursive data-read program.

```
        q = p++;

        if ((q - Salesdat) >= MAXNODES)
        {
            fprintf(stderr,"\070Out of tree space!\n");
            exit(-1);
        }

        q->office[0] = '\0';            /* Initialize the node values */
        q->state[0] = '\0';
        q->sales = q->costs = q->total = 0.0;
        q->manager[0] = '\0';
        for (i = 0; i < MAXSUBS; ++i)
            q->sub[i] = NULL;

        return (q);
}

/*
 +----------------------------------------------
 | This function is the heart of the program's
 | input logic. It reads text data, one line at
 | a time, from the standard input stream; con-
 | verts the text to internal form by means of
 | a library parsing function; and recursively
 | fills the in-memory data tree based on the
 | hierarchy implicit in the indentation of the
 | input lines. For the sake of brevity, NO
 | SANITY OR OVERFLOW CHECKS ARE PERFORMED ON
 | THE INPUT.
 +----------------------------------------------
 */

static struct salesdat * Filltree()
{
    register struct salesdat *p = Nalloc();
    int level = Nestlev(Buffer);
    register int i;

    sscanf(Buffer,"%[^:]:%[^:]:%LF:%LF:%s",
            p->office, p->state, &p->sales,
            &p->costs, p->manager);

    if (gets(Buffer) == NULL)
    {
        Buffer[0] = '\0';
        return (p);
    }

    if (Nestlev(Buffer) <= level)
        return (p);

    for (i = 0; i < MAXSUBS; ++i)
    {
        p->sub[i] = Filltree();
```

Figure 8-4 *(continued)*

```
        if (Nestlev(Buffer) <= level)
            return (p);
    }

    fprintf(stderr,"\07Too many subs!\n");
    exit(-1);

    /* NOTREACHED */
}

/*
  +----------------------------------------------
  | This function walks the tree, hierarchically
  | summing all sales and costs and placing the
  | result in the "total" field of each node.
  +----------------------------------------------
*/

static void Sumtree( register struct salesdat *p )
{
    register int i;

    p->total = p->sales;
    p->total -= p->costs;

    for (i = 0; i < MAXSUBS; ++i)
    {
        if (p->sub[i] == NULL)
            break;
        Sumtree(p->sub[i]);
        p->total += p->sub[i]->total;
    }
}

/*
  +----------------------------------------------
  | This function recursively outputs net sales
  | results for all offices.
  +----------------------------------------------
*/

static void Dumptree( register struct salesdat *p )
{
    static int level = -1;
    register int i;
    char c[256];

    ++level;

    c[0] = '\0';

    for (i = 0; i < level; ++i)
        strcat(c,"   ");

    strcat(c,p->office);

    printf("%-40s%10.21f\n",c,p->total);
```

Figure 8-4 *(continued)*

```
    for (i = 0; (i < MAXSUBS) && (p->sub[i] != NULL); ++i)
        Dumptree(p->sub[i]);

    --level;
}


/*
+---------------------------------------------
| This is the program main routine. It does
| little more than define the correct sequence
| for calling the working routines. Its only
| additional task of any consequence is to
| ensure that the input file is not empty. In
| the process, it seeds the input buffer with
| the first line of text, which is necessary
| because the Filltree() function requires one
| line of look-ahead during each invocation.
| A suitable output header is also printed
| prior to dumping the tree.
+---------------------------------------------
*/

int main()
{
    register struct salesdat *root;

    if (gets(Buffer) == NULL)       /* Seed the input buffer */
    {
        fprintf(stderr,"\07No input!\n");
        return (-1);
    }

    root = Filltree();

    Sumtree(root);

    printf("%-40s%10s\n", "OFFICE", "NET SALES");
    printf("%-40s%10s\n", "------", "--- -----");
    Dumptree(root);

    return (0);
}
```

Figure 8-4 *(continued)*

When the nested data file with colon-separated fields is read as the standard input of the program in Figure 8-4, the following output results:

```
OFFICE                                     NET SALES
------                                     --- -----
Corporate Headquarters                     1118544.38
        Northeast Region                    213353.78
                New York                    118750.52
                    Brooklyn                 37884.26
                    Paterson                 40734.39
                Pittsburgh                   78709.11
```

```
Midwest Region                              376596. 65
    Chicago                                  83670. 58
    Indianapolis                             63593. 99
    Kansas City                              73595. 67
    Minneapolis                              68967. 54
    St. Louis                                75594. 90
Southern Region                             237779. 49
    Atlanta                                  71916. 43
    Dallas                                   78702. 80
    Houston                                  70711. 91
Western Region                              313464. 90
    Denver                                   66983. 24
    Los Angeles                             117560. 49
        Sepulveda                            39287. 93
        Orange                               46540. 49
    San Francisco                           107322. 08
        Oakland                              33230. 12
        Cupertino                            34162. 84
```

The reader may wish to verify these figures with pencil and paper. Verification of software with short, sample data runs is generally prudent, and in this case presents no great difficulty because so few offices are involved. Once the logic is verified, the program can deal with an arbitrary number of offices, nested to arbitrary depth, by making appropriate adjustments to the manifests MAXNODES and MAXSUBS. Failure to make these adjustments will generally result in nothing worse than a few harmless diagnostics, although it is possible for programs to crash if nesting is carried to an extreme degree. This seldom happens in practice, and when it does, it almost always results from a programmer's failure to ensure that recursively called functions will eventually return. The problem is that most implementations of C do not generate code to perform run-time checks of the position of the subroutine stack pointer with respect to allocated dynamic memory. Thus, the stack can, in principle, overwrite memory allocated for other uses, with potentially chaotic consequences.

The code in Figure 8-4 is intended to exemplify sound software engineering practices, including error handling and diagnostics; however, in the interest of brevity, it performs no sanity or overflow checks on its input. A real-world program should always make such checks; in working software, the checks tend to evolve over time until, in some cases, they become so sophisticated as to constitute a program in their own right.

Observe how tree nodes are painlessly allocated by doling out chunks of a predefined array. This technique, which is useful whenever the items to be allocated are of fixed size, allows us to avoid the dangerous shoals of malloc(), on which so many programs have come to grief. In the example, allocation is simplified by the fact that deallocation is never required; however, deallocation can be implemented if needed without any major changes to the scheme. The standard Unix C compiler uses this method of allocating tree nodes.

Finally, since this chapter is dedicated to real-world programming, a practical observation must be made: Financial applications are seldom coded using floating-point logic, for the simple reason that round-off errors are intolerable in a program dealing with money. In fact, if the programs in Figure 8-3 and Figure 8-4 are re-coded using floats rather than doubles, they will exhibit round-off error on many systems. One of the often overlooked strengths of C is its suitability for scientific and engineering work, but there are few financial applications for which C is usable.

Exercises

8-1 "Whereas software consists largely of variables, hardware consists al-most exclusively of constants." Give some examples of components that might be considered hardware "variables."

8-2 Give an example of software written to take advantage of a particular ma-chine cycle time, and suggest ways of enhancing its portability.

8-3 Modify the program in Figure 8-1 so that it reads its input, converts all temperatures from Fahrenheit to centigrade, and saves the converted data in a new file.

8-4 (a) A peculiarity of the stream-input program (Figure 8-3) is that its out-put reverses the order of its input. Clearly, this could be avoided by performing the output as part of the input loop. However, in pro-grams of this sort, it is often undesirable to mix input with output. Why?

   (b) Given that input and output are not to be mixed, is there a way to preserve input ordering without resorting to the inelegance of an ad-ditional variable?

8-5 (a) "There are few financial applications for which C is usable." Can you give an example of one?

   (b) How might one go about writing a financial application in C if it were necessary to do so?

8-6 *Programming project:* Add a provision for taxes to the recursive data in-put program. The following data file, which the program must open, read, and parse, contains the tax rates for the various states:

```
CA: 0. 17*25000. 0 : 0. 275*50000. 0 : 0. 3275
CO: 0. 225
GA: 0. 1875*57500. 0 : 0. 29375
IL: 0. 1295*10500. 0 : 0. 2295*62750. 0 : 0. 3795
IN: 0. 0725*10000. 0 : 0. 1705*100000. 0 : 0. 4275
KS: 0. 1266*27500. 0 : 0. 2725*72575. 0 : 0. 395
MN: 0. 2225*38150. 0 : 0. 3795*115750. 0 : 0. 44575
MO: 0. 1195*47620. 0 : 0. 2015*85290. 0 : 0. 325
NJ: 0. 1995*51650. 0 : 0. 2975*127500. 0 : 0. 4195
NY: 0. 205*61250. 0 : 0. 375*119675. 0 : 0. 425
PA: 0. 1715*33500. 0 : 0. 2825*66500. 0 : 0. 3715
TX: 0. 2475
```

All taxes are assessed against net, rather than gross, sales by all of the company's offices in the state. The fields in the tax-rate file are interpreted as follows. First is the state abbreviation, followed by one or more colon-separated fields containing the rates for each bracket. For example, the tax in California is 17% of the first $25,000, plus 27.5% of the next

$50,000, plus 32.75% of the remaining net. Two states, Colorado and Texas, have a flat rate on all net sales. Formatting of the output is left to the discretion of the programmer, provided that all tax amounts are clearly identified by state in order to facilitate the calculation of federal taxes. This exercise, dismal as it is, only begins to hint at the complexities of real-world application programming. Nevertheless, those who complete it will be well-grounded in the basic techniques of practical software engineering.

CHAPTER 9

Algorithms for Searching and Sorting

In previous chapters we discussed various methods for structuring data objects as arrays, stacks, queues, linked lists, and trees. In this chapter we will use these structures either to search for an element in a collection of data or to sort the collection of data in some order.

In a searching process, we seek one data object from a collection of data objects, and finally retrieve it if it is found in that collection. It is useful as a tool of some other process, or a main objective. It is very useful in a database application. For example, in order to know the filing status of a particular taxpayer, search the database by the Social Security number of that taxpayer.

In a sorting process, we order a collection of data objects in an ascending or descending order based on a key value. Sorting is useful in such applications as customer names and grades of students. It is also useful to enhance the performance of a search process in an ordered list.

We now discuss several search and sort algorithms.

9.1 O Notation

In order to select the best and appropriate searching and sorting algorithm, we need to analyze the computational efficiency of each algorithm using $O(n)$ ("Big Oh") notation. The notation $O(n)$ means "On the Order of n." So $O(n^2)$ means "on the order of n-square" or "proportional to n-square."

"O notation" is a way of measuring the order of magnitude of a mathematical expression. The order of magnitude is dominated by the term with highest exponent. Given the expression

$$n^4 + 3\,n^2 + 10 = f(n)$$
$$O(\,n^4 + 3\,n^2 + 10\,) = O(n^4)$$

Let $g(n) = n^4$; then the order of $f(n)$ is $O[g(n)]$. Thus $f(n) = O[g(n)]$ if there exist some positive constants c and k such that

$$f(n < c\,g(n) \qquad \text{for all values of} \quad n \geq k$$

That is, for a sufficiently large number n ($n \geq k$) of input data, the growth rate of $f(n)$ over $g(n)$ will be contained within a constant. For small values of n, $g(n)$ does

349

not accurately represent $f(n)$, because the above relationship between $f(n)$ and $g(n)$ will not necessarily be true for small n.

For various expressions, $f(n)$, the O notation function, $g(n)$, and the O notation expression, $O[g(n)]$, are given below:

$f(n)$	$g(n)$	$O[g(n)]$
35	1	$O(1)$
$25n$	n	$O(n)$
$n^3 + 70,000\,n^2 - 16$	n^3	$O(n^3)$
$\frac{1}{2}n^2 + \frac{1}{2}n$	n^2	$O(n^2)$
$[n(n+1)/2]^2$	n^4	$O(n^4)$

The main drawback of O notation is that it ignores constants of terms with lower exponent. Such a constant may be a significant contributing factor to a term. For example, for small values of n, the coefficient 70,000 of the n-square term will be significant, but $g(n)$, being n cube, ignores that value. However, O notation is universally used to measure efficiency by comparing execution times of several methods.

For the size n of a problem, some arithmetic rules of "Big Oh" are:

1. $O(n) + k = O(n)$ (k is a constant)
2. $O(kn) = O(n)$ (k is a constant)
3. $O(n) + O(m) = \begin{cases} O(n) & \text{if } m \le n \\ O(m) & \text{if } m \ge n \end{cases}$
4. $O(n) + O(m) = O(m) + O(n)$

9.2 Searching Algorithms

In this section, we will discuss and implement techniques for searching for a data object in a collection of objects. A search in general consists of the following steps:

Step 1. Moving from object to object, examine the entire collection of objects for a match of a data object specified by some value.

Step 2. If match is found, return SUCCESS. If no match is found, return FAILURE.

In this section we will first study searching algorithms for data objects structured as an array. The efficiency of each of these algorithms depends on the form of the structure of the data objects. If the list of data objects is already sorted (ordered), the searching method will be very efficient. For example, we can quickly find a name in the phone book, because the phone book (list) is alphabetically sorted.

The most common search algorithms are:

I. Simple search algorithms
1. Linear search of an array
2. Linear search of a linked list
3. Linear search of an ordered array
4. Linear search of an ordered list
II. Advanced search algorithms
1. Binary search of an ordered array
2. Interpolation search of an ordered array

   3. Fibonacci search
   4. Searching a binary search tree
   5. Search using hash function

Since there are many search algorithms, no one is best. However, some may be best for a particular application than other algorithms, but may be worst for another application. Thus some considerations and issues in selecting a search method include:

   1. Performance in the light of speed.
   2. Space requirement.
   3. Size of the search list.
   4. Whether the list is static or dynamic. Does it grow its size dynamically because of insertion and deletion processes.
   5. Do we allow duplicate data, that is, data with the same key value. This may be considered an error in some applications.

In order to compare and to analyze computational performance of the above algorithms, we will use O ("Big Oh") notation.

To search a key item in an array A [n] of integers (random ordered or sorted), the number of comparisons required by each search algorithm are given below.

	Worst case (random ordered)	Best case (sorted)
Linear search	$O(n)$	$O(n)$
Binary search	—	$O(\log_2 n)$
Interpolation search	—	$O(\log_2 \log_2 n)$

The searching methods with $O(\log_2 \log_2 n)$ or $O(\log_2 n)$ performance are computationally are more efficient, but are harder to understand and to program.

9.2.1 Linear Search of an Array

   In this section we will assume data objects structured as an array A [0] , A [1] , . . . , A [n-1] of n elements. The array is assumed to be not ordered. The objective of sequential search to find a key Item in the array is accomplished in the following manner:

   1. First compare Item with A [0]. If it is equal, Item is found at A [0] with index 0; stop the process. Otherwise, proceed to the next step.
   2. Compare Item with A [1]. If it is equal, Item is found at A [1] with index 1; stop the process. Otherwise, proceed to the next step.
   3. Continue comparing each element A [3] , . . . , A [n-1] with Item until an equality is encountered. In this process, we will have one of the two cases: (a) find an index i such that A [i] = Item or (b) reach the end of the array without finding any element equal to Item.

Note that this search approach requires comparing with each element of the array until all elements are used if match is not found in earlier comparison.

   For the C program and its output run, see Example 9-1 (in the Examples section at the end of the chapter).

Analysis

The function linear_srch() in Example 9-1 implements the linear search of a list of *n* elements. The list is implemented as an array. The elements are not assumed to be ordered. We analyze the computing performance of this algorithm in the best case and in the worst case. The best case is not as informative as the worst case.

The function begins its search by comparing the specified item with the first element array[0] of the list. If there is no match, it compares the item with the next element array[1] of the list. The function continues this comparison process within the for loop until all the list is exhausted or a match is encountered.

The best case for the linear search algorithm occurs when the specified item is found at array[0]. In this case, the total number of comparisons required is one. Then the best-case performance of the linear search is O(1).

The worst case for the linear search algorithm occurs when the specified item is not an element of the array. In this case, the function performs the comparison of the specified item and each element of the array sequentially within the for statement. Because the array has *n* elements, the total number of comparisons required, is *n*. Hence, the worst-case performance of the linear search algorithm is O(*n*).

On the average, it will take *n*/2 steps to find the match. For large *n*, *n*/2 is still O(*n*).

9.2.2 Linear Search of a Linked List

In this section we will assume that data objects are structured as a singly linked list. The number of elements in such a list is not fixed. The linked list is assumed to be unordered. In this implementation, an element of the list is as follows:

```
typedef   int data_type;
typedef   struct _element
{
        data_type         data;
        struct _element   *next_elt;
} ELEMENT;

ELEMENT   *head_ptr, *tail_ptr;
```

Recall the structure of a singly linked list as shown in Figure 9-1.

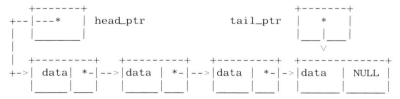

Figure 9-1 List using a single link.

The sequential search to find a match of the Item in the singly linked list can be accomplished in the following manner:

Step 1. If the list is nonempty, proceed to step 2. Otherwise, print message "empty list" and return (NULL).

Step 2. Compare Item with data field of the first list element pointed to by head_ptr. If it is equal, return (head_ptr). Otherwise, proceed to the next step.

Step 3. Compare Item with data field of the next element pointed to by head_ptr -> next_elt. If it is equal, return (head_ptr -> next_elt). Otherwise, proceed to the next step.

Step 4. Continue comparing Item with data field until a match is encountered or the NULL value of the pointer next is reached (that is, the last element of the linked list is used). Return (element pointer).

More precisely,

```
1. Set     search_ptr  =  head_ptr      /* Start of Linked List */
2. while  (search_ptr <> NULL)          /* Continue until end    */
   do
       if search_ptr -> data = Item
          "Item is found"; return ( search_ptr )
       else
          search_ptr = search_ptr -> next_elt
   done
3. Reached the end of the list;
   "Item is not found in the list";  return ( NULL )
```

For the C program and its output run, see Example 9-2 in the Examples section.

Analysis

The recursive function search_elt() in Example 9-2 performs a linear search for an item in a list of *n* elements. The list is organized as a singly linked list (it can also be a doubly linked list), and it is not ordered. The first element of the list, also called the *head,* is pointed to by head_ptr.

The best case occurs when the list is empty (that is, the value of head_ptr is NULL), or the specified item is found as the first element of the list. The best-case performance is O(1).

The worst case occurs when the list is not empty and the specified item is not in the list. The function compares the key value of the specified item with the first element of the list. If there is no match, it linearly advances to the next element of the list using the link, head_ptr -> next_elt. It continues advancing and comparing until it reaches the last element of the list. This is done within a while loop. The last element has NULL as the value of the pointer, next_ptr. For a list of *n* elements, the comparison statement within the while loop is executed *n* number of times. Thus, the worst-case performance of the linear search of an unordered linked list is O(*n*). The performance of order *n* means the search time linearly increases as the number *n* of elements in the list increases. This algorithm is simple, but very inefficient for large *n*.

9.2.3 Linear Search of an Ordered Array

In an earlier section we noticed that when the list of elements is not ordered, unsuccessful linear search continues its process until the last element is encountered. This indicates wastage of computer time in case of an unsuccessful linear search. We may improve this aspect if the list is an ordered one. Keeping a list in some normal order numerically or alphabetically (lexicographically) is possible in many situations. The linear search in an ordered list is very much like that in an unordered list except that search may be found unsuccessful even before using all elements in the list.

Assuming search for the key `Item` in the ascending ordered list `A[0]`, `A[1]`, ..., `A[n-1]`, the linear search procedure can be stated as follows:

Step 1. `If ((Item < A[0]) or Item > A[n-1]))`
             `"Item is not found";` return `(-1)`
Step 2. Set i = 0.
Step 3. `while ( i < n )`
              `do`

                `if ( Item = A[i] )`
                    `"Item is found in list";` return (i)
                `else`
             `done`
                `i = 1`
                    `"Item is not found in the list";` return (-1)

The C program of this search is assigned as an exercise. Analysis of this algorithm is left as an exercise.

9.2.4 Linear Search of an Ordered List

In this section, the linear search assumes the list is maintained in an ascending order, the first element in the linked list is of highest order. One version of its algorithm can be given as follows:

Step 1. Set `search_ptr = head_ptr`   `/* Start of Linked List */`
Step 2. Continue search until the end of the linked list:

        `while ( (search_ptr <> NULL ) AND`
                `(item > search_ptr->data) )`
          `do`
            `search_ptr = search_ptr->next`

            `if search_ptr->data = item`
                `"Item is found",` return (search_ptr)
          `done`

Step 3. `"Item is not found in the list";` return (NULL)

The C program of this search is assigned as an exercise. Analysis of this algorithm is left as an exercise.

9.2.5 Binary Search of an Ordered Array

In the method of linear search in an ordered list, our search starts from the beginning of the list. The essence of the binary search procedure is to take advantage of the sorted order of the list as well as to improve the linear search method by starting the search for the key Item at the middle of the ascending ordered list in the following manner:

if Item < A[mid],   then it cannot be in A[mid+1], ..., A[n-1]; Continue search only among A[0], ..., A[mid - 1]

if Item > A[mid],   then it cannot be in A[0], ..., A[mid - 1]; Continue search only among A[mid + 1], ..., A[n-1]

Restating the purpose of the binary search in the array A[0], A[1], ..., A[n-1], ordered in ascending order, for a given Item, note that the array elements and the item are of same type. The step-by-step algorithm is given below:

Step 1. Set First = 0; Last = n - 1
Step 2. Calculate Mid_index = (First + Last) / 2
Step 3. Compare A[Mid_index] with item. If equal, return Mid_index, the index of the found item.

If A[Mid_index] < Item, search for Item in the second half, repeating steps 1 through 3, while

First <= Last

If A[Mid_index] > Item, search for item in the first half, repeating steps 1 through 3, while

First <= Last

Step 4. Otherwise, if First > Last, the subarray to be searched is empty. The search is not successful in finding a match of the Item. Return the out-of-range value for index.

This method is based on dividing the array into two halves, and continues the search for Item in one half or the other. In short, it uses the "divide-and-conquer" policy. In this way it reduces the search time. Note that the binary search algorithm is very complex and time-consuming when the list of elements is implemented as a linked list. This is because a binary search requires random access to all elements of the list (which is allowed by a list implemented as an array).

For the C program and its output run, see the Examples section. Analysis of this algorithm is left as an exercise.

9.2.6 Interpolation Search of an Ordered Array

The objective of an interpolation search is the same as that of a binary search. Instead of searching from the middle of the list as a binary search does, it starts its search from a location nearer to the expected location of the target key Item. This starting search location, which would be the index of the array of ordered elements A[0], ..., A[n-1], is calculated using the following interpolation formula:

$$\text{Interpolate} = \text{low} + \frac{(\text{Item} - A[\text{low}])\ (\text{high} - \text{low} - 1)}{A[\text{high}] - A[\text{low}]}$$

Search_index = interpolate (rounded down to the nearest integer value)

Initially, low = 0, and high = $n - 1$. The search process continues while "high – low > 1." Use this search_index in place of Mid_index in the binary search algorithm. See Reingold and Hansen (1983) for more information. Note that this method requires more calculation of the next index per search step than the binary search process.

An algorithm for an interpolation search of an ordered list is given below:

Step 1. Set low = 0 and high = $n - 1$.

Step 2. Calculate search index rounded to the lowest integer

$$\text{low} + \frac{(\text{Item} - A[\text{low}])\ (\text{high} - \text{low} - 1)}{A[\text{high}] - A[\text{low}]}$$

Step 3. If A[search index] = Item, then return index.

If A[search index] < Item, set low = search index + 1 and return to step 2 if high - low > 1.

If A[search index] > Item, set high = search index - 1 and return to step 2 if high - low > 1.

Step 4. If high - low ≤ 1, item was not found. Return an out-of-range value for search index. If search index becomes less than low or greater than high, Item was not found.

The C program of this search is assigned as an exercise.

Analysis

Without strong mathematical discussion, it is not easy to calculate $O(\log_2 \log_2 n)$ performance of interpolation search.

This is beyond the level of this book.

For small n number of input data, interpolation search is slower than binary search. For large value of n, interpolation search is much faster than binary search, because $\log_2 \log_2 n$ grows much less rapidly than $\log_2 n$ as n grows.

9.2.7 Fibonacci Search

This search approach is a modified form of binary search using the concept of Fibonacci numbers.

Fibonacci numbers are defined as follows:

```
F[ 0 ] = 0,
F[ 1 ] = 1,
F[ i ] = F[ i - 1 ] + F[ i - 2 ], i > 1
```

In particular, each Fibonacci number being the addition of the two previous numbers, the first few Fibonacci numbers are:

$$0, 1, 1, 2, 3, 5, 8, 13, 21, 34, \ldots .$$

The Fibonacci search method replaces the division by 2 used in a binary search. Note that a binary search divides the given list into two halves, that is, two sublists in each step. If the size of the list to be used for the search is a Fibonacci number, for example, 34, the Fibonacci search will divide the list into two sublists with sizes 13 and 21 (these being the previous two Fibonacci numbers forming 34). Then the search continues for the key Item in each sublist and if necessary subdivides a sublist of size, say 21, into two sublists whose sizes are also Fibonacci numbers (8 and 13), and so on. This essentially divides a large problem into short problems.

Because the calculation of Fibonacci numbers is based on addition and subtraction operations, the Fibonacci search is suitable for computers that do not have division supported in the hardware.

However, division by 2 as required by a binary search can be accomplished by shifting the register right by 1 bit, and the right-shift operation is provided by most computers. This indicates one way of using binary search method for computers with no hardware divide operation.

An algorithm for a Fibonacci search of an ordered list is given below:

Step 1. Set offset = 0 and n = MAX_SIZE – 1.
Step 2. Set Fibonacci low = 0 and Fibonacci high = 1. Calculate Fibonacci split of array until offset + Fibonacci low + Fibonacci high > n.
Step 3. Position to search in array = offset + Fibonacci low.

If A[position] = Item, return position.

If A[position] < Item, set n = position and return to step 2 if Fibonacci low > 1.

If A[position] > Item, set offset = position and return to step 2 if Fibonacci low > 1.

Step 4. If Fibonacci low > 1, search last items in array until offset > n. If item is not found, return an out-of-range value for search index.

The C program of this search is assigned as an exercise.

Analysis of the worst-case performance of this search is left as an exercise.

9.2.8 Searching a Binary Search Tree

The search for a key Item contained in the data component of a node (called the *target node*) in a binary search tree takes advantage of the structure of a binary search tree.

As described in a previous chapter, a binary search tree (BST) is a special form of a binary tree in which the location of each node is suggested by the value of its key data component.

That is, for each node's data component, say X, of a BST, we must have both (1) left child of X < X and (2) right child of X > X. In other words, the key value of any node in right subtree is "greater than" that of any node in the left subtree. For example,

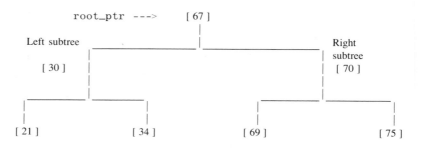

Because of the unique structure of a binary search tree, inorder traversal yields the elements in the normal ascending order. Making use of the embedded ordering relationship, a brief description of the search in a BST is

```
while (there are more nodes to search)
do
    if (the target node < current node)
        search the left subtree

    else if (the target node > current node)
        search the right subtree
    else
        return ("Item is found")
done
return ("Item is not found")
```

The detailed version of this algorithm for searching a target node with the key item is described below:

Step 1. Check whether the BST tree is empty.
        If so, the search fails;
           Item is not in the BST; return error.
        Else, proceed to step 2.

Step 2. Prepare for search from the root of the BST by setting:

$$Search\_ptr = root\_ptr$$

Step 3. Perform search iteratively:

```
while   ( there are more nodes in BST to search )
   do

      if ( Item < Search_ptr->node_data )
```

           item cannot be in the right subtree. Continue search in the left subtree by setting:

```
                    Search_ptr = Search_ptr->left_child_ptr
       else
          if ( Item > Search_ptr->node_data )
```

Continue search in the right subtree by setting:

```
                    Search_ptr = Search_ptr->right_child_ptr
       else
              "Item is found"; return (Search_ptr)
    done
```

Step 4. "Item is not found in the binary search tree.";
return (NULL)

Because recursive search in BST will require a lot of stack space, it is recommended to use an iterative search approach. For the C program and its output run, see the Examples section.

Analysis

The worst-case performance for the BST search is between $O(\log_2 n)$ and $O(n)$. We will deduce these using illustrations.

Since the worst case occurs when the search key is not in the BST, or it appears in the leaf node, we need to consider it in two cases: (1) The BST is balanced; (2) the BST is degenerate.

Case 1. The BST is balanced. Suppose the following BST contains 15 nodes:

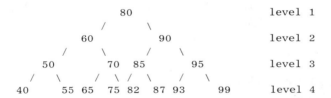

```
                        80                       level 1
                      /    \
                  60         90                  level 2
                /    \      /   \
            50        70  85      95             level 3
          /    \    /  \ /  \    /  \
        40      55 65  75 82 87 93      99       level 4
```

Suppose we want to search for a node containing 75, we want to calculate the total number of comparisons.

Comparison	Level	Number of nodes	Number of comparisons
Is 75 = 80? No 75 < 80	1	$2^0 = 1$	1
Is 75 = 60? No 75 > 60	2	$2^1 = 2$	1
Is 75 = 70? No 75 > 70	3	$2^2 = 4$	1
Is 75 = 75? Yes	4	$2^3 = 8$	1

Thus, total number of comparisons $= 4$
$$= \log_2 (2^4)$$
$$\sim \log_2 (15) , n = 15$$
$$= \log_2 (n)$$

Case 2. For a degenerate BST of size 4:

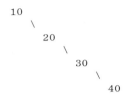

suppose we are searching for 50. In this case we will have to linearly traverse the tree until we reach the leaf node, which takes four comparisons, O(n).

9.2.9 Hash Search

In previous sections, we discussed binary search methods. A binary search in a list requires that the list be ordered. For a binary search tree, the elements are distinct, and the operations are insert, delete, and search. The search in a binary search tree is done by a sequence of comparisons. Hash search is an alternative method to these search techniques.

The use of arrays for storage and retrieval of structs has the advantage of fast random access by way of index, but the disadvantage of fixed size. The use of lists has the advantage of almost no size constraint, and ease of reference using pointers, but the disadvantage of relatively slow access by way of sequential list traversal. A useful merge of the two methods is the hash table and hash chains. Hashing algorithms calculate the location of a particular array element. A hashing algorithm is used to arrange the array, and to search for a specified key. In this section we will discuss the hash table, various hash functions, overflow and collision handling methods using buckets and chaining, hash search, and performance of the hash search.

Hash Tables

In hashing, the elements are stored in a table, called the *hash table*. The hash table is organized as an array. The hash table contains the elements, or pointers to the lists of elements. The latter part will be discussed in the section on collision handling. However, the address or location of an element must be determined for the operations of insert, delete, search, and retrieve. The address of an element specified by its key k is calculated by a function H(k). The function H(k) is called the *hash function,* and the value of H(k) for some k is called the *hash of* k. In other words, the hash function yields the address of an element specified by k in the hash table. The addresses or hashes of all the elements are kept in the hash table. When the hash table, htable, is structured as an array htable[0], ..., htable[n-1], the hash value is an index of the array (hash table) ranging from 0 to $n - 1$. Thus, the hash value must be a positive integer:

$$H(k) = \text{address of an element specified by the key } k,$$
$$\text{in the hash table } htable[]$$

A hash table can be implemented in two ways:

1. An array of buckets, each bucket holding one or more slots for data elements. (See discussion on collision resolution using buckets.)
2. An array of pointers to lists of elements. (See discussion on collision resolution using chaining.)

We now want to discuss how to determine n, the size of the hash table htable[]. For a list of m elements, htable[0], ..., htable[n-1] are buckets, each bucket holds p number of elements, where $m = np$. The number p is also referred to as the *number of slots*. For example, consider a list of 120 elements. Each element represents a student's record. If each bucket contains four slots, corresponding to the hash function H(k), the hash table is as shown in Figure 9-2.

Hash table (Student_List)

Figure 9-2 Hash table with 30 buckets and four slots per bucket.

In Figure 9-2, htable[] is an array of 30 buckets, and each bucket has 4 slots for data elements. The data elements may be records of the following type:

```
#define TSIZE    30
#define SLOTS    4

typedef char    DATA_TYPE;
typedef unsigned short   KEY_TYPE;

typedef struct _hash_elt
   {
     KEY_TYPE         key;
     DATA_TYPE        data;
     ELEMENT          data1; /* ELEMENT is of given type */

   } HASH_ELEMENT;

typedef  HASH_ELEMENT  BUCKET[ SLOTS ];

typedef  BUCKET        HASH_TABLE[ TSIZE ];
```

When hash chaining is used (see discussion on chaining), the hash table can be an array of pointers to lists (see Figure 9-6). A list is selected by indexing into the table, and the list is accessed by traversal. The selection of element nodes to be placed on a particular list is done by a hashing function. The hashing algorithm is efficient if the nodes are evenly distributed over all the table entries, so that the list traversals are kept to a minimum.

For example, in case of hash chaining, the following elements, defined in hash. h, are given:

```
#define   NULL    0
#define   TSIZE   30

typedef char            DATA_TYPE;
typedef unsigned short  KEY_TYPE;

typedef struct _node
    {
       KEY_TYPE        key;
       DATA_TYPE       data;
       ELEMENT         data1;
       struct  _node * next;

    } NODE;

typedef   NODE   * NODE_PTR;

typedef   NODE_PTR   HASH_TABLE[ TSIZE ];

#define   HNULL   ( NODE_PTR ) NULL

HASH_TABLE   htable;
```

ELEMENT is of any given type. The header file might contain a list of possible data types indicated by name:

```
typedef   int   DT_INT;
    :
typedef   struct ITNODE DT_ITNODE;
    :
```

where struct ITNODE might be defined as

```
struct ITNODE
{
    KEY_TYPE           key;
    int                datatype;
    int                data;
    struct ITNODE *  left;
    struct ITNODE *  right;
};
```

ITNODE is the structure of a node in a binary tree.

Another method is to use flags, which avoids having to define array sizes in typedef statements:

```
#define   DT_INT        0x01    /* type int */
#define   DT_FLOAT      0x02    /* type float */
   :
#define   DT_ITNODE     0x40    /* type tree node with int data */
```

Hash Functions

The choice of hash table size and hash function are crucial to success. Table size is somewhat defined by the function, but the order of magnitude depends on how many nodes you estimate must be stored at any one time. A chain depth of 4 to 8 is optimal for fast processing.

In practice, an ideal hash function will put the elements uniformly in a hash table. The hash function determines the location in the hash table, where the element should be stored. Since there is no general form of a hash function, we will present numerous hashing functions. The uses of these functions will depend on your application.

The hash function can be as simple as the operation

$$\% \text{ <table size>} \quad \text{(modulo the table size)}$$

That is, the hash function $H(k) = k \% TSIZE$ returns the hash values $0, \ldots,$ $TSIZE - 1$, which are the remainders of the division of k by $TSIZE$. Its code is

```
int  H( KEY_TYPE k, int n )

/*  H(k, n):
 *     It is a hash function that returns the remainder
 *     (0, ..., n - 1) as the hash value, when  the
 *     (unsigned short) key k is divided by n;
 *            H(k, n) = k % n
 */
{
    int   hash;

    hash = k % n;
    return( hash );
}
```

Note that the hash key k is declared as an unsigned short, because the hash value cannot be a negative integer.

In the simplest case of hashing, the hash table holds the nodes themselves. The table is made large enough to hold all the nodes that might be stored at any given time. The hash function might be, given data I of type `int`:

$$key = I / TSIZE$$
$$\text{where} \quad TSIZE == sizeof(htable) / sizeof(int)$$

If data item I can be greater than the hash table size, then hashing collision (that is, for two distinct key values $H(p) = H(q)$ can occur. A good hash function minimizes such collisions by spreading the hashed keys uniformly over the table. For the simplest types of hash table, collision resolution is necessary. The problem corresponding to collision for the hash chain type of table is that of clustering, where some of the chains grow much longer than others. For this problem, cluster resolution is necessary to improve performance, but with chaining there need not be a loss of data.

Early versions of hashing used an array that stored the data, of some basic type. The method of storage was called "scatter storage." Later versions allowed structured data with a key and some complex data type, such as a string array or a multidimensional array.

The hashing functions were variations of manipulations of the bits in the key or input data. Only heuristic rules exist for the design of hash functions. We now present a hash function using digit analysis. This method is useful in processing a static file where all the keys are known in advance. A few sets of digits are used to determine an address in the hash table. There are four basic techniques, used individually or in combination: (1) extraction, (2) compression, (3) division, and (4) multiplication. The key (or data) is converted into a string of bits; for example:

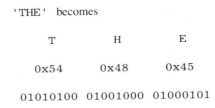

```
'THE'   becomes

      T            H            E

    0x54         0x48         0x45

   01010100  01001000  01000101
```

Extraction is simple. A few scattered bits are picked out of the bit string, say the 3rd, 4th, 11th, 14th, 19th, and 23rd. In the example string, the extraction would produce:

```
MSBit                         LSBit
|                               |
01010100  01001000  01000101        produces hashed key  110001
-    -      -   -         --
1    1      0   0         01
```

where MSBit and LSBit respectively represent most significant bit and least significant bit. This technique is used when the data set is well known and the bits to extract are carefully chosen. The result depends on only a small subset of the bits in the data. The technique is generally collision-prone.

The preceding observation leads to a guiding principle: *Use all of the information contained in the input data.*

Compression reduces the number of bits to the number required for the table address. Usually the data is broken into some fixed length and then the bits of the pieces are combined by logical SUMing or EXCLUSIVE ORing. For example:

```
'THE'   becomes

      T            H            E

   01010100  01001000  01000101
```

```
     10100       01000       00101        10100
                                       XOR 01000
                                           -------
                                           11100
                                       XOR 00101
                                           -------
                                           11001    the hashed key
```

The problem with compression is that XOR and SUM are commutative so hash('THE') == hash('ETH') == hash('TEH'), etc. This observation leads to a second guiding principle: *Break up naturally occurring clusters of elements.*

Sometimes this can be accomplished only by experimentation.

The third method is *division*, typically by use of the modulus operator: hash(x) = x % M. This is usually much faster and simpler than the first two methods. This observation leads to a third guiding principle: *The hash function should be very quick and very simple to code.*

The value of M must be chosen carefully. Usually M should be a prime number or should have no small prime factors. For hashing of data composed of the lower-case letters (a–z), the radix of the set must be 26 or greater, and is usually chosen as 32. Then M should be a value greater than 32, perhaps 37. There are many published studies of this technique.

The last technique is *multiplication*. Some real number is chosen, perhaps $Z = 0.6125423371$. The hash function is

$$\text{hash}(x) = (\text{ integer part of } (x * Z)) \% M$$

where M is the table size, on which the hash function is less dependent. The value of Z should be far away from 0.0 and 1.0, or small values of the data will cluster around the endpoints. Values of Z derived from:

$$Z = (\text{ SQUAREROOT}(5) - 1) / 2 \quad \text{or}$$

$$Z = 1 - ((\text{ SQUAREROOT}(5) - 1) / 2)$$

produce uniform distribution.

On the average, with 365 table slots and 23 data items, there is a 50% chance of a collision. This means that the performance of the collision-resolution algorithm is a major factor. The usual resolution is to find another slot by applying a secondary hash function to the first result. This rehashing technique is called *linear probing*. Any rehashing function that relies solely on the produced hashed key will cause clustering or further collisions.

A recently developed class of hash functions is called the *bloom filters*. It uses double division:

$$\text{hash}_{c,d}(x) = ((c * x + d) / p) / m$$

where p is a large prime number, m is a power of 2, and $0 < c < p$ and $0 <= d < p$. The class is the set of hash functions determined by the values of c and d, given values for p and m. The performance of this class is analyzed by Ramakrishna (1989).

Insertion in a Hash Table

Given the datatype == DT_INT and the data == 43, the program sequence that adds the new data to the hash table structure looks like:

```
NODE_PTR     tmp;
tmp = ( NODE_PTR ) create_node(datatype, &data);
tmp->key = tmp->data % TSIZE;
addlist(tmp, tmp->key);

TSIZE == 30, so tmp->key == 13 <--- 43 % 30
```

The function addlist() places tmp at the front of the hash chain pointed to by htable[12]. Notice the resemblance of the hash chain to a queue. This is the basis for priority queues in operating systems. When hashing with chaining is used, the complete code for inserting a node is shown later.

Figure 9-3 shows an example of a hash function and hash table. The result of the hash function is called "the hash of the key" or "the hashed key."

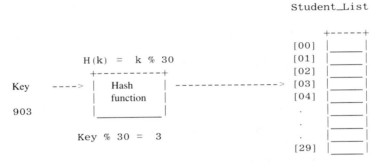

Figure 9-3 Using a hash function to determine the location of the item in the array Student_List.

In Figure 9-3, the hash function, H(k) = k % 30, yields the hash value 3 for the key value 903. The hash value 3 will be used to search, insert, delete, update, or retrieve the element specified by its key 903.

When adding a new record, it is inserted into the first empty place with the array index calculated by H(k), as shown in Figure 9-4.

In Figure 9-3, the hash function, H(k) = k % 30, yields the hash value 3 for the key value 903. The hash value 3 will be used to search, insert, delete, update, or retrieve the element specified by its key 903.

Overflow and Collision Handling

In Figure 9-4, suppose we want to insert a record with key 32. For k = 32, we calculate the hash value H(32) = 32 % 30 = 2. If we assume that each of htable[0], ..., htable[29] holds only one record (that is, only one slot), we find that htable[02] already holds the record with key 692. Then the record with key 32 can not be inserted in that slot. This situation causes overflow, and collision. By collision, we mean that for any two distinct keys p and q, H(p) = H(q) occurs for some hash function H(k). One way to deal with the overflow and colli-

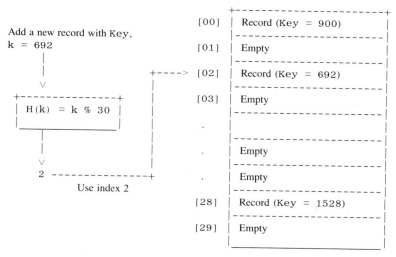

Hash table (htable[])

Figure 9-4 Search and insertion using a hash function.

sion in the case where there is only one slot per one hash value, is done by the following linear search algorithm:

Step 1. For the given key k, and for some hash function H (k, n), compute the hash value:

$$hash\_val = H(k)$$

Step 2. If htable[hash_val] is empty, return hash_val.

Step 3. If htable[hash_val] is not empty, treat the hash table as circular to find an empty slot.

Step 4. Perform searching for an empty slot starting from htable[hash_val].

Step 5. If no empty slot is found, return with an error message "The hash table is full".

The code for the above linear search algorithm that deals with an overflow and collision is

```
int    Hash_Linear_Search ( ELEMENT  htable[],
                            int n,   int (*H) (),
                            KEY_TYPE k )
{
    int  hash_val, roll_inx;

    /*  Compute the hash value for the element specified
     *  by its key, k.
     */
    hash_val = (*H) ( k, n );
    roll_inx = hash_val;
```

```
/*  Search for an empty slot treating the hash table
 *  as a circular list.
 */

while ( ( htable[ roll_inx ]. key != k ) &&
        ( htable[ roll_inx ] != EMPTY ) )
  {
     roll_inx = ( roll_inx + 1 ) % n;
     /*  Check whether we came back to the starting
      *  position, hash_val.
      */
     if ( roll_inx == hash_val )
       {
          printf("\n Hash_Linear_Search: %s \n",
                 "Hash Table is full" );
          return( -1 );
       }
  }
  return( roll_inx );
}
```

The function Hash_Linear_Search performs a linear search for the element specified by its key k, in the hash table htable[0], ..., htable[n-1]. If it finds a match in the hash table, it returns the index, roll_inx. If it is not successful in finding an empty slot, it prints an error message, and returns −1. The term EMPTY can be defined by zero or '\0', if we choose to initialize all the slots of htable[] by zero or null. The hash table htable[] is an array of type ELEMENT:

```
typedef   char              DATA_TYPE;
typedef   unsigned short    KEY_TYPE;

typedef   struct _element
  {
     KEY_TYPE   key;
     DATA_TYPE  data;

  } ELEMENT;
```

When the above Hash_Linear_Search() is used to resolve overflows, elements appear to form clusters. The contiguous clusters approach to compact. This causes the increase in the search time.

The collision for different key values of k occurs when their corresponding values of H (k) are the same. We can resolve collisions by using either (1) buckets or (2) chains. The collision resolution using buckets forms an array of arrays for the same value of the hash function. The bucket is formed by an array of records, each record will have its unique key but the same bucket (hash function) value. The size of a bucket is equivalent to the number of slots for holding records.

In Figure 9-5, in order to insert a new record specified by its key, k = 1802, we first calculate the bucket value 1802 % 30 (i.e., 2). Using the bucket value 2, we find there is a collision between the record with key 692, and the new record with

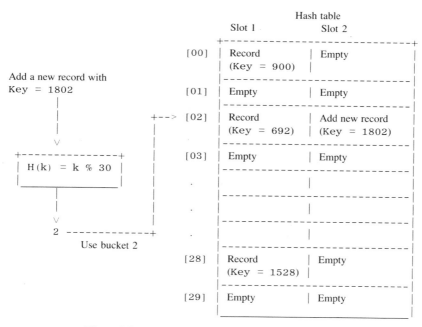

Figure 9-5 Resolving collisions by hashing with buckets.

key 1802. Because bucket corresponding to htable[02] contains more than one slot, for example, p = 2, we insert the new record in the first empty slot in the hash table htable[02]. Although this resolves the collision problem, we still may face the overflow problem. The overflow occurs when we try to insert the next record with its key 62. The following method using chaining will handle both over-flow and collision very efficiently.

The second method is called *hashing with chaining*. This method uses the hash table as an array of pointers, which will point to the first element of the singly linked list. Each element (record) of the same list will have same hash function value. The hash function value determines the chain (that is, the index of the pointer array).

In Figure 9-6, we resolve collisions by hashing with chaining. In order to in-sert a new record specified by its key 1802, we first compute its chain value. Using the hash function, H(k) = k % 30, we get 2 for the chain value. Then we check whether htable[02] has a NULL pointer value. If it is not NULL, htable[02] points to the head of the singly linked list. We can either add the new record at the beginning or at the end of the list. In this case, the limit on the number of records per chain is imposed by the available memory space.

When hashing with chaining is used, we implement the following operations:

1. Initializing a hash table
2. Creating a hash node
3. Inserting a node in the hash table
4. Deleting a node from the hash table
5. Searching for a node in the hash table

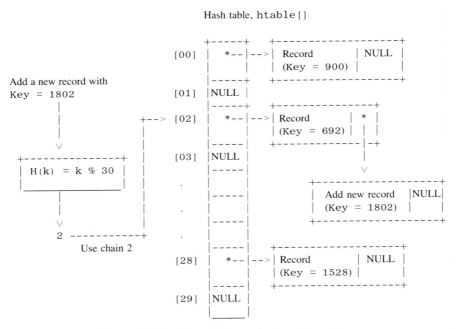

Figure 9-6 Resolving collisions by hashing with chaining.

To implement these operations, we use the following simple header file "hash_chain.h":

```
#define  NULL    0
#define  TSIZE   30

typedef  char             DATA_TYPE;
typedef  unsigned short   KEY_TYPE;

typedef  struct  _node
   {
     KEY_TYPE          key;
     DATA_TYPE         data;
     struct  _node * next;

   } NODE;

typedef   NODE   * NODE_PTR;

typedef   NODE_PTR   HASH_TABLE[ TSIZE ];

#define  HNULL   ( NODE_PTR ) NULL

HASH_TABLE   htable;
```

When hashing with chaining is used, the following steps perform search for an element specified by a key k, in the hash table htable[0], ..., htable[n-1].

Algorithm

Step 1. Compute the chain number for the specified key k using the hash function H (k) :

$$hash\_chain = H(k)$$

The hash value i is the index of the hash table, array `htable[]`.

Step 2. Get the `list_ptr`, the pointer to the head of the singly link list corresponding to the hash chain i. Since the list head is stored in the `htable[hash_chain]`,

$$list\_ptr = htable[hash\_chain]$$

Step 3. Check whether the list is empty by comparing `list_ptr` with NULL. If the list is empty, the specified element is not found; otherwise, proceed to step 4.

Step 4. Perform linear search for k starting from the head of the list pointed to by `list_ptr`. Do the search by comparing k and the key field of an element, `list_ptr->key`.

Step 5. Continue the search process until a match is found, or all the elements in the list are exhausted. If a match is found, return the pointer to the element containing the key that matches with the specified key, k. If no match of k is found, return NULL pointer.

The function Hash_Chain_Search() for the hash search using chaining is

```
NODE_PTR   Hash_Chain_Search ( HASH_TABLE htable,
                                int n, int (*H) (),
                                KEY_TYPE  k )
/*  Perform hash search with chaining for the element
 *  specified by its key k, in the hash table
 *  htable[0], ..., htable[n-1].
 *  Either htable[ H(k, n) ] = HNULL,
 *  or, htable[ H(k, n) ] = list_ptr, that points to
 *  the head of the list associated with the hash
 *  chain H(k, n).
 *  If the search is successful, it returns a pointer
 *  to the element containing the specified k;
 *  otherwise, it returns HNULL pointer.
 */
{
    int        hash_chain;
    NODE_PTR   list_ptr;

    /*  Compute the hash chain for the element specified
     *  by its key, k.
     */
    hash_chain = (*H) ( k, n );

    /*  Get list_ptr, the pointer pointing to the head of
     *  the list associated with the hash_chain. It is
     *  stored in htable[ hash_chain ].
     */
    list_ptr = htable[ hash_chain ];
```

```
    /* Check whether the list is empty. */
    if ( list_ptr == HNULL )
      {
        printf("\n Hash_Chain_Search: List is empty \n");
        return( HNULL );
      }
    /* Associated list is not empty. Perform linear search
     * iteratively.
     */
    while ( list_ptr != HNULL )
      {
          if ( list_ptr -> key == k )
              return( list_ptr );
          else
              list_ptr = list_ptr -> next;
      }
    /* Search is not successful  */
    return( HNULL );

  }  /* End of Hash_Chain_Search() */
```

When the hash search using chaining is used, the hash table htable is of type
HASH_TABLE. It is an array of pointers to lists (chains). The htable is initialized
by setting each element of htable[] to HNULL. Here is the code:

```
    Hash_Chain_Init( HASH_TABLE htable, int table_siz )
    {
        int  i;

        for ( i = 0; i < table_siz; i++ )
              htable[ i ]  = HNULL;
    }
```

Here is the code for creating a node element when hashing with chaining is used:

```
/*
 *  Create_Hash_Node(): Create a new node for the
 *                      hash chain. Allocate memory
 *                      space.
 */

NODE_PTR  Create_Hash_Node( KEY_TYPE k, DATA_TYPE new_data )
{
    NODE_PTR  new_node_ptr;

    /*
     *  Allocate a memory space for the new node;
     *  If no space is available, return with error.
     */
    new_node_ptr = (NODE_PTR) calloc( 1, sizeof( NODE ));
```

```
      if  ( new_node_ptr  != HNULL )
        {
            new_node_ptr  ->  key = k;
            new_node_ptr  ->  data =   new_data;
            new_node_ptr  ->  next =   HNULL;
        }
      return ( new_node_ptr );
}
```

Here is the code for inserting an element in the hash table when hashing with chaining is used:

```
Hash_Chain_Insert ( HASH_TABLE htable,  int n,
                    int  (*H) (),  KEY_TYPE k,
                    DATA_TYPE    new_data )
{

    int        hash_chain;
    NODE_PTR   list_ptr, new_node_ptr;

    /*
     *  Compute the hash chain for the specified
     *  by its key,  k.
     */
    hash_chain = (*H)  ( k,  n );

    /*
     *  Get list_ptr, the pointer pointing to the
     *  head of the list associated with the
     *  hash_chain. It is stored in htable[ hash_chain ].
     */
    list_ptr = htable[ hash_chain ];

    /*  Allocate memory space for the new element  */
    new_node_ptr = Create_Hash_Node ( k, new_data );
    if ( new_node_ptr == HNULL )
      {
          printf("\n Hash_Chain_Insert: No memory space \n");
          exit( 1 );
      }
    /*  Check whether the list is empty.  */
    if ( list_ptr != HNULL )
       /*
        *  The list is nonempty. Insert the new element
        *  at the front of the list.
        */
      new_node_ptr -> next = list_ptr;
    htable[ hash_chain ] = new_node_ptr;

}   /*  End of Hash_Chain_Insert ()  */
```

Here is the code for deleting an element specified by a key k, in the hash table when hashing with chaining is used:

```
Hash_Chain_Delete( HASH_TABLE htable, int n,
                   int (*H)(), KEY_TYPE k,
                   DATA_TYPE   new_data )
{

    int       hash_chain;
    NODE_PTR  list_ptr, tmp_ptr;

    /*
     *  Compute the hash chain for the specified
     *  by its key, k.
     */
    hash_chain = (*H) ( k, n );

    /*
     *  Get list_ptr, the pointer pointing to the
     *  head of the list associated with the
     *  hash_chain. It is stored in htable[ hash_chain ].
     */
    list_ptr = htable[ hash_chain ];

    /*  Check whether the list is empty.   */
    if ( list_ptr == HNULL )
        return;

    /*
     *  The list is nonempty. Is it the first
     *  element in the list?
     */
    if ( list_ptr -> key == k )
      {
        htable[ hash_chain ] = list_ptr -> next;
        free( list_ptr );
        return;
      }

    /*
     *  Find the element in the corresponding chain,
     *  and delete it.
     */

    /*  while ( list_ptr -> next -> next != HNULL )   */
    while ( list_ptr -> next != HNULL )
    {
       if ( list_ptr -> next -> key == k )
         {
           tmp_ptr = list_ptr -> next;
           list_ptr -> next = tmp_ptr -> next;
           /*  Release the memory space   */
           free( tmp_ptr );
```

```
                return;
          }
     else
                list_ptr = list_ptr -> next;
     }

}        /* End of Hash_Chain_Delete() */
```

Here are the ideal and real hashing schemes for 120 students:

Ideal plan:

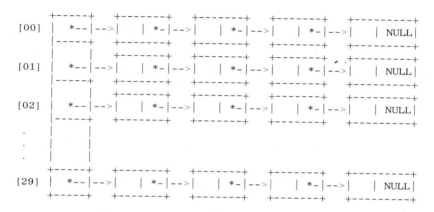

In this scheme, there are 30 chains and 4 records per chain. This scheme will hold records for 30 × 4 = 120 students. The singly linked list corresponding to each chain contains 4 elements. So, the search time will be O(4). However, in reality, the worst case occurs when the key values for all the 120 student records belong to the same chain:

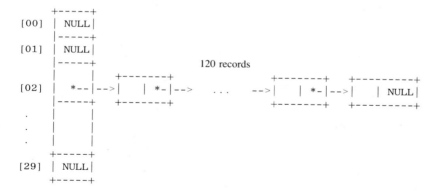

In this case, the total search time is O(120). Thus, for a list of *n* elements, the worst-case performance of the hash search algorithm using chaining is O(*n*).

The hash table entries could be a structure containing a pointer to the front and a pointer to the back of a chain. Then the tail of the chain (the oldest member) can be accessed quickly, allowing hashed process run and sleep queues.

If the original list of data is 1024 nodes long and the hash function is efficient, then the longest chain in a hash table with 31 slots has 34 nodes. If traversing the next node takes about as long as the hash function calculation and comparing the node data is five times as long as the list traversal step, then the total time to scan the longest hash chain is:

$$1 \text{ hash function} + 34 \text{ list traversal steps} + 34 \text{ data compares} =$$
$$1 + 34 + 34 \times 5 = 205 \text{ time units}$$

The time to traverse the 1024 node list is

$$1024 \text{ list traversal steps} + 1024 \text{ data compares} =$$
$$1024 + 1024 \times 5 = 6144 \text{ time units}$$

$$\frac{205}{6144} = 3\% \text{ of the list search time}$$

Given that the node will be found on the average in the middle of the list, the average list search is 3072 time units, so:

$$\frac{205}{3072} = 7\% \text{ of the list search time}$$

This is still a remarkable savings. Hash tables and hash chaining are your friends!!

As a final word, consider the combination of hash table and heap in the application of *interval analysis*. The data are real numbers in some range that are to be grouped as members of some interval within the range. The intervals are represented by the hash table slots, the numbers within the interval by nodes in a heap pointed to by the hash table entry. Use of a heap for the interval members allows for dynamic allocation of storage and for ordering of the members within the interval. The structure is shown in Figure 9-7.

Hash Table Structure for Interval Analysis Application

When hashing is used for interval numbers, the data structure of the hash table is as follows:

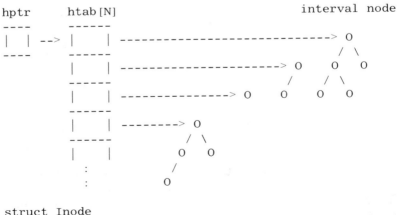

```
struct Inode
    {
        double   nval;
```

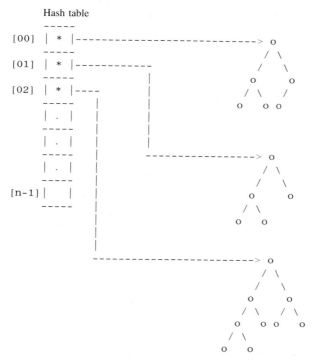

Figure 9-7 Hash table with heaps as node data.

```
    struct   Inode * left;
    struct   Inode * right;
  };

typedef   struct Inode   * pInode;
#define   TABSIZE   10

struct htentry
  {
     double   lower;      /*  Left endpoint of interval  */
     double   upper;      /*  Right endpoint of interval */
     pInode   head;
  };

typedef   struct htentry  HTABENT;
typedef   HTABENT  * PHTABENT;
HTABENT   htab[TABSIZE];
PHTABENT  htp = &htab[0];
```

Here are several of the data structure operations. The function `init_table()`
constructs a simple set of 10 equal and contiguous intervals from 0 to 10. It sub-
tracts EPSILON from upper to indicate that the right endpoint is not closed. In
actual applications, the interval boundaries would have negative as well as positive
values, and the intervals would be discontinuous. The function `init_table()`
would then be changed to accept pairs of interval boundaries:

```
void init_table( PHTABENT htp )
{
    double  EPSILON = 1.0e-100;
    short   inx;

    for (inx = 0; inx < TABSIZE; inx++)
      {
        htp[inx]->lower = 0.0 + inx;
        htp[inx]->upper = 1.0 + inx-EPSILON;
        htp[inx]->head  = NULL;
      }
}

/* fd is a global variable holding a valid file descriptor */

pInode enter_data( PHTABENT htp)
{
    pInode   new;
    int      interval;

    if (( new = (pInode)calloc(1, sizeof(struct Inode)) == NULL)
        error("out of memory");
    else
      {
        fscanf(fd, "%g\n", &new->nval);
        interval = floor(new->nval);
        Heap_insert(htp[interval], new);
      }
    return(new);
}
```

In summary, we must note the following key points for hashing:

1. Hashing methods translate addresses of elements via the use of a hash function H ( )
2. Choose a hashing function that

    (a) Uniformly distributes the hashing values in the hash table
    (b) Efficiently handles overflow conditions
    (c) Minimizes the number of collisions

3. Organize elements using a hash table
4. A hash table is an array of either

    (a) Buckets containing elements
    (b) Pointers to the list of elements

5. Hash search starts by translating the specified key to a hash value, which is the location in the hash table. It then performs search in the associated bucket, or in the associated chain list.

9.3 Sorting Algorithms

In this section we will discuss and implement techniques in rearranging data in sorted order. The sorting criteria (equality with the key) may be based on the numeric or alphabetic (lexicographic) value of the data objects. Although we are not structuring data in this section, we must be aware of the size and storage media of the list of data to be sorted. If the list of data is sufficiently small, it may be stored in physical memory (internal storage). If the list of data is very large, requiring a large amount of physical memory, it may be stored on secondary storage (such as a disk). The type of data storage essentially categorizes two sorting techniques:

1. Internal storage sorting
2. External storage sorting

In this section we will primarily emphasize internal storage sorting algorithms. The merge sort algorithm will be discussed for external storage sorting. The efficiency of each of these algorithms depends on the structure of the data objects to which the algorithm is applied. A sort, in general, consists of the following steps:

Step 1. Examine the entire collection of objects to find a maximum (or minimum) among data objects specified by their key values.
Step 2. Swap data or pointer links to form an ascending or descending order.
Step 3. Continue steps 1 and 2 until no more swapping is required.
Step 4. The list is now sorted.

The most common sort algorithms are:

I. Simple sort algorithms
  1. Selection sort
  2. Bubble sort
  3. Insertion sort
  4. Insertion sort for a linked list
II. Advanced sort algorithms
  1. Quick sort
  2. Merge sort
  3. Binary search tree sort
  4. Heap sort
  5. Shell sort

To sort an array A[n] of integers (random ordered; sorted), the number of comparisons required by each sort algorithm are:

	Worst case (random ordered)	Best case (sorted)
1. Selection sort	$O(n^2)$	$O(n^2)$
2. Bubble sort	$O(n^2)$	$O(n)$
3. Insertion sort	$O(n^2)$	$O(n)$
4. Insertion sort (linked list)	$O(n^2)$	$O(n)$
5. Quick sort	$O(n^2)$ (depends on order/split)	$O(n \log_2 n)$
6. Merge sort	$O(n \log_2 n)$	$O(n \log_2 n)$
7. Heap sort	$O(n \log_2 n)$	$O(n \log_2 n)$

Since the function $\log_2 n$ grows less rapidly than n or n-square as the number n of input data increases, such sort algorithms as quick, merge, or heap sorts will be more efficient than others.

9.3.1 Selection Sort

To arrange a list A[0], A[1], ..., A[n-1], use the following linear sort method:

Step 1. Search for the smallest number among A[0], A[1], ..., A[n-1] and obtain its corresponding indexed location, say k. Swap positions of A[0] and A[k].

Step 2. Search for the smallest number among A[1], A[2], ..., A[n-1] and obtain its corresponding indexed location, say k. Swap positions of A[1] and A[k].

Step 3. Continue searching for the smallest number and perform swap in the remaining list until the remaining list contains only one element.

Step 4. The list is sorted in an ascending order.

To illustrate the above steps, let us consider the following elements:

$$-23 \quad 10 \quad 4 \quad 5 \quad -2 \quad 56 \quad 2 \quad 300 \quad 199$$

After the first pass [find the smallest number (−23), and swap its position (1st) with the 1st element], it will be

$$\underline{-23} \quad 10 \quad 4 \quad 5 \quad -2 \quad 56 \quad 2 \quad 300 \quad 199$$

After the second pass [find the smallest number (−2) among 2nd through 9th, and swap its position (5th) with the 2nd element], the list will be

$$-23 \quad \underline{-2} \quad 4 \quad 5 \quad \underline{10} \quad 56 \quad 2 \quad 300 \quad 199$$

After the third pass [find the smallest number (2) among 3rd through 9th, and swap its position (7th) with the 3rd element], the list will be

$$-23 \quad -2 \quad \underline{2} \quad 5 \quad 10 \quad 56 \quad \underline{4} \quad 300 \quad 199$$

After the fourth pass [find the smallest number (4) among 4th through 9th, and swap its position (7th) with the 4th element], the list will be

$$-23 \quad -2 \quad 2 \quad \underline{4} \quad 10 \quad 56 \quad \underline{5} \quad 300 \quad 199$$

After the fifth pass [find the smallest number (5) among 5th through 9th, and swap its position (7th) with the 5th element], the list will be

$$-23 \quad -2 \quad 2 \quad 4 \quad \underline{5} \quad 56 \quad \underline{10} \quad 300 \quad 199$$

After the sixth pass [find the smallest number (10) among 6th through 9th, and swap its position (7th) with the 6th element], the list will be

$$-23 \quad -2 \quad 2 \quad 4 \quad 5 \quad \underline{10} \quad \underline{56} \quad 300 \quad 199$$

After the seventh pass [find the smallest number (56) among 7th through 9th, and swap its position (7th) with the 7th element], the list will be

$$-23 \quad -2 \quad 2 \quad 4 \quad 5 \quad 10 \quad \underline{56} \quad 300 \quad 199$$

After the eighth pass [find the smallest number (199) among 8th through 9th, and swap its position (9th) with the 8th element], the list will be

$$-23 \quad -2 \quad 2 \quad 4 \quad 5 \quad 10 \quad 56 \quad \underline{199} \quad \underline{300}$$

Then the sorted list will be

$$-23 \quad -2 \quad 2 \quad 4 \quad 5 \quad 10 \quad 56 \quad 199 \quad 300$$

Note the following drawbacks in this method:

1. On each pass through the sublist, only one element is placed in its correct sorted position.
2. It always requires $n - 1$ number of passes.
3. It does not check whether the list is already sorted to stop the process.

The C program and its output are given in the Examples section.

Analysis

In each pass i, there are at most $n - i$ number of comparisons. For $n - 1$ number of passes, the total number of comparisons is:

$$(n - 1) + (n - 2) + \cdots + [n - (n - 1)]$$
$$= n(n - 1) - [1 + 2 + \cdots + (n - 1)]$$
$$= n(n - 1)/2$$
$$= n^2/2 - n/2$$
$$= O(n^2)$$

9.3.2 Bubble Sort

In this section, our goal is to sort a list of n elements organized as an array A[0], ..., A[n-1] in an ascending order. The goal of the bubble sort algorithm is to improve performance of the selection sort algorithm. It does multiple swappings in one pass. The algorithm can be described as follows:

Step 1. For the elements A[0], A[1], ..., A[n-1], compare each consecutive pair from left to right, and swap members of the pair if they are found to be out of order. [The largest numbers will "bubble-up" to the right (end) of the list, and the smaller numbers will be placed to the left (beginning) of the list.]

Step 2. If no swapping (exchange/interchange) occurred in step 1, the list is already sorted. Otherwise, proceed to step 3.

Step 3. For the elements A[0], A[1], ..., A[n-2] repeat steps 1 and 2 until no swapping is necessary.

The detailed form of the algorithm is shown below:

Step 1. Set exchange = TRUE   /* Flag   */
              pass = 0
Step 2. Continue steps 3 through 4 for pass ranging from 0 through n while exchange = TRUE   /* n = arraysize */
Step 3. For i ranging from 0 through $(n - \text{pass})$,

```
           If A[ i ] > A[ i + 1 ]
           then
                1. Swap them by:
                      store       = A[ i ]
                      A[ i ]      = A[ i + 1 ]
                      A[ i + 1 ] = store
                2. Set exchange = TRUE
           else
                1. Set exchange = FALSE
```

Step 4. Increment pass by 1, i.e., pass = pass + 1.

Step 5. The list is sorted in an ascending order.

The number of comparisons between the elements of the array performed by the bubble sort algorithm is directly proportional to the "square of n." Thus, it is computationally very inefficient, due to the "only one position at a time" movements of its elements. This algorithm heavily relies on the swapping of consecutive elements. Its performance can be improved by interchanging elements that are far away from each other.

Examples of C program implementation and its output are given in the examples section. For the same set of elements as in the previous section, the bubble sort algorithm takes five passes, compared to nine passes by the selection sort method.

Analysis

The function bubble () in Example 9-6 implements the bubble sort algorithm for an array of n elements, sorted in an ascending order. It consists of one outer loop and one inner loop. The outer loop is the for statement with pass as the loop counter, and it continues until there are no exchanges of the elements. The loop counter ranges from 0 to $(n - 1)$. The inner loop is the for statement with inx as the loop counter that ranges from 0 to $(n - \text{pass} - 1)$. At each step of the outer loop, comparison of $(n - \text{pass})$ elements is done inside the inner loop. Sometimes the inner loop performs an exchange. Let sorted_pass denote the number of executions of the outer loop before there are no exchanges, that is, the elements become sorted. The total number of times the inner loop is executed, is:

$$(n - 1) + (n - 2) + \cdots + (n - \text{sorted\_pass})$$
$$= (2n - \text{sorted\_pass} - 1)(\text{sorted\_pass})/2$$

When sorted_pass = 1, the original elements are sorted, and there are no exchanges. The total number of comparisons is

$$(2n - 1 - 1)(1)/2 = n - 1 = O(n)$$

and the total number of exchanges = 0. This is the best-case performance of the bubble sort algorithm.

When sorted_pass = $(n - 1)$, the original elements are not sorted. The total number of comparisons is

$$(2n - n + 1 - 1)(n - 1)/2 = n(n - 1)/2 = O(n^2),$$

and the total number of exchanges is $n(n - 1)/2$. This is the worst-case performance of the bubble sort algorithm.

The drawbacks of the bubble sort algorithm are:

1. The inner loop requires swapping the elements physically, so it has very poor performance for structured data.
2. One element is swapped with its adjacent element; that is, it is moved to its adjacent place.

Only an additional space for a temporary swapping variable is needed. The implementation can be improved by using pointers.

9.3.3 Insertion Sort

Insertion sort is an efficient sorting technique for a small list of data items. The algorithm repeatedly inserts a single item in an already sorted list so that the final list will still remain sorted. In order to describe this method, assume a list of n items represented as an array A [0] , A [1] , . . . , A [n-1] to be rearranged in an ascending order. Before writing the steps of this algorithm, let us show two approaches to insertion sort, one starting from the front of the list, the other starting from the back. At each pass i, we continually insert an item, say A [i] , into its previously sorted i - 1 items. There will be changes in positions of the items in the list. The changed form of the list at each pass is given below in both approaches.

The arrow originating from an item means that the item is inserted in that position in the next pass.

Approach I. Begin insertion with the first item, A [0] :

Start/initial		Pass 1		Pass 2		Pass 3		Pass 4
A[0]	520	520	--->	−20		−20		−20
A[1]	670	---> 670		520	--->	90	--->	30
A[2]	−20	−20		670		520		90
A[3]	90	90		90		670		520
A[4]	30	30		30		30		670

Approach II. Begin insertion with the last item, A [n-1] :

Start/initial		Pass 1		Pass 2		Pass 3		Pass 4
A[0]	520	520		520		520 ---		−20
A[1]	670	670		670 ---		−20		30
A[2]	−20	−20	--->	−20		30		90
A[3]	90 ---	30		30		90	|-->	520
A[4]	30	|--> 90		90	|-->	670		670

Notice that the resulting list is in ascending order and is the same in both approaches. The steps of the insertion sort algorithm are given below based on the first approach:

Step 1. Begin with the first item A [0] . Note that it is already sorted because there is no previously sorted item.

Step 2. Item A [1] is to be inserted into the one-item sorted sublist A [0] based on comparing A [1] with A [0] :

If A [1] < A [0] , insert A [1] previous to A [0] . Otherwise, proceed to step 3.

Step 3. Item A [2] is to be inserted into the two-item sublist containing A [0] and A [1] . Place A [2] among these two items according to its value. For example, first save A [2] .

If A [2] < A [0] , place A [2] before A [0] and A [1] by moving A [1] to the position of A [2] , A [0] to that of A [1] , and finally the saved value of A [2] to the position of A [0] .

If $A[0] < A[2] < A[1]$, place $A[2]$ before $A[1]$ by moving $A[1]$ to the position of $A[2]$, and the saved value of $A[2]$ to the position of $A[1]$.

Step 4. Repeat the process until the last item $A[n-1]$ is inserted into the $(n - 1)$-item sorted sublist.

Step 5. The list $A[0], \ldots, A[n-1]$ is now sorted in an ascending order.

For the C code and its output, see Example 9-7 in the Examples section.

Analysis

The function `insert_sort()` in Example 9-7 implements the insertion sort algorithm. It arranges an array of n elements in an ascending order. It contains an outer loop and an inner loop. In `insert_sort()`, the outer loop is executed by the `for` statement with the loop counter j, which ranges from $(n - 2)$ to 0. This means it is executed $n - 1$ times. The inner loop is implemented by the `while` loop whose looping depends on the outer loop counter j and on how the elements are ordered. In the best case when the elements are sorted, the inner loop is never executed. In the worst case when the elements are not sorted, the inner loop is executed the following number of times:

$$(n - 1) + (n - 2) + \cdots + 2 + 1 = n(n - 1)/2 = O(n^2)$$

Because the interchange of the array elements is done in the inner loop, the total number of exchanges is $n(n - 1)/2$, that is, $O(n^2)$. In In the worst case, the insertion sort needs $O(n^2)$ comparisons and $O(n^2)$ exchanges. In the best case, the insertion sort needs $(n - 1)$ comparisons and $2(n - 1)$ exchanges. It takes advantage of partial ordering.

Regarding the performance and improvement of the insertion sort algorithm, we can quote Stubbs and Webre (1985): "Because of its low overhead and favorable performance for nearly sorted data, insertion sort will be combined with quick sort to produce the best general purpose internal sorting algorithm known at this time."

9.3.4 Insertion Sort for a Linked List

In this section we would like to implement the insertion sort algorithm with the data items in the list structured as a doubly linked list. This method can also be applied for a singly linked list structure with a bit more work because of the non-availability of the "back link" that points to the item previous to each item in the list.

As described regarding the data structure of each item in Chapter 6, let us recall the following structure of a doubly linked list:

```
+-----+                                 +-----+
|  *  | head_ptr          tail_ptr |  *  |
|__|__|                                 |__|__|
   V                                       V
+-------+    +-------+               +-------+
| item  |    | item  |               | item  |
|       |    |       |      . . .     |       |
|  *--- |-->|  *--- |-->    . . . -->| NULL  |
|       |    |       |               |       |
| NULL  |<--|   *   |<----  . . . <--|--*    |
|       |    |       |               |       |
```

Note the following aspects of a doubly linked list structure:

1. If the value of head_ptr is NULL, the list is empty.
2. If head_ptr = tail_ptr, the list has only one element (which is already sorted).
3. The last item in the list can be determined by the tail_ptr or by the NULL value of the next pointer field in the item's structure.
4. Each pass of the insertion sort requires the insertion of an item into the list. This was easily done in the case of array implementation by using an array index. In this case, we will have to do this by adjusting both previous (i.e., back) and next (i.e., forward) links, and we will have to search for the position of the item to be inserted by keeping track of these previous and next pointers.
5. Each pass will also require moving items around within the list. This can be performed by only manipulating pointers.

The programming part for this linked version is assigned as an exercise.

The materials in the following two sections are credited to Leetsma and Nyhoff (1987).

9.3.5 Quicksort

Quicksort is one of the fastest internal sort techniques. ("Internal" means that the items to be sorted are all stored in main memory.) The basic approach is the divide-and-conquer strategy: "Divide" the problem into simpler subproblems until subproblems are found that are "conquered," that is, all items are sorted.

If the items to be sorted are: A[0], A[2], ..., A[n - 1], then one step of the quicksort procedure would reorganize the items, yielding three sublists in the following order:

Sublist 1: A[0], A[1], ..., A[k-1]
Sublist 2: A[k]
Sublist 3: A[k+1], A[k+2], ..., A[n - 1]

with the following properties:

1. Each item of the sublist 1 is < A[k].
2. A[k] is in its sorted position.
3. Each item of sublist 2 is > A[k].

Sublists 1 and 2 need to be sorted in the next step. In essence, each step of the quicksort technique replaces the problem of sorting a large list by the problem of sorting two small sublists.

If the data items are stored in a file on disk, and if the file size fits into the available physical memory, the quicksort algorithm performs very well in many situations.

The steps of the quicksort algorithm are described below:

Step 1. Select one item in the list to be properly positioned.
Step 2. Rearrange the list so that this item is in its proper position: All preceding items are less than it, and all following items are greater than it.

Step 3. Repeat steps 1 and 2 with the left sublist.

Step 4. Repeat steps 1 and 2 with the right sublist.

The quicksort algorithm's efficiency is largely dependent on an efficient sublist dividing algorithm. One efficient form of the "dividing" algorithm is given below:

Step 1. Select an item (the first one).

Step 2. Repeat steps 3 through 5 (in this list; below) until the two search "pointers" meet or cross.

Step 3. Search from the right for an item less than the selected one.

Step 4. Search from the left for an item greater than or equal to selected one.

Step 5. Interchange these two items.

Step 6. Interchange the selected item and the item found from the right search.

Quicksort computing time is on the order of $n \log_2(n)$, where n is the size of the list. This time is the best possible order of computing time for any sorting scheme that uses only comparisons and interchanges.

Possible improvements in the above algorithm can be made as follows:

1. Don't always sort the left sublist first; sort the smaller sublist.
2. Switch to a faster sorting scheme when the sublist is small; for example, use insertion sort if the length is less than 20.
3. Select the item to be positioned differently in an attempt to produce more uniform dividing, e.g., randomly, or use the "median-of-three" rule. This latter technique should work better if the list is already partially sorted.

Analysis

The function `quick_sort ()` in Example 9-8 arranges an array of n elements in an ascending order. Its worst-case performance is $O(n^2)$. The detailed analysis is left as an exercise.

The quicksort algorithm is not efficient in practice for files residing on external devices such as magnetic disk. This is because fetching the file from the disk into the physical memory will be very time-consuming.

9.3.6 Merge Sort

Merge sort is an external sorting method; the items to be sorted are stored in a file and the collection is usually too large to be stored in main memory all at once. Merging two sorted files F1 and F2 to produce a sorted file F is the basis for merge sort.

The steps of one version of merge sort presented in many books is a "binary" scheme:

Step 1. Copy elements of file F one at a time alternately to files F1 and F2.

Step 2. Merge corresponding 1-element subfiles in F1 and F2; write them back to F.

Step 3. Copy elements of F two at a time alternately to F1 and F2.

Step 4. Merge corresponding 2-element subfiles in F1 and F2; write them back to F.

Step 5. Copy elements of F four at a time alternately to F1 and F2.

Step 6. Merge corresponding 4-element subfiles in F1 and F2; write them back to F.

Step 7. Continue until the number of elements (a power of 2) to be copied reaches or exceeds the length of F.

These steps can be illustrated as follows:

```
F:   15,  1,  7,  12,  3,  2,  4,  9,  13,  5,  10,  6,  8,  14,  11
     --   -   -   --   -   -   -   -   --   -   --   -   -   --   --
                      |
                      V
F1:  15,  7,  3,  4,  13,  10,  8,  11
     --   -   -   -   --   --   -   --
F2:  1,  12,  2,  9,  5,  6,  14
     -   --   -   -  -   -   --
                 |
                 V
F:   1,  15,  7,  12,  2,  3,  4,  9,  5,  13,  6,  10,  8,  14,  11
     -----    -----    ----    ----    -----    -----    -----    --
                 |
                 V
F1:  1,  15,  2,  3,  5,  13,  8,  14
     -----    ----    -----    -----
F2:  7,  12,  4,  9,  6,  10,  11
     -----    ----    -----    --
                 |
                 V
F:   1,  7,  12,  15,  2,  3,  4,  9,  5,  6,  10,  13,  8,  11,  14
     ------------    ----------    ------------    ---------
                 |
                 V
F1:  1,  7,  12,  15,  5,  6,  10,  13
     ------------    ------------
F2:  2,  3,  4,  9,  8,  11,  14
     ----------    ---------
                 |
                 V
F:   1,  2,  3,  4,  7,  9,  12,  15,  5,  6,  8,  10,  11,  13,  14
     ----------------------    -----------------------
                 |
                 V
F1:  1,  2,  3,  4,  7,  9,  12,  15
     ----------------------
F2:  5,  6,  8,  10,  11,  13,  14
     ----------------------
                 |
                 V
F:   1,  2,  3,  4,  5,  6,  7,  8,  9,  10,  11,  12,  13,  14,  15
     -----------------------------------------------------
```

Note that in some cases, subfiles being copied or merged may not have the same number of elements as other subfiles. This approach does not take advantage of the fact that parts of the file may already be in order.

We will now consider "natural merge" sort. Note the "natural" sorted sub-files ("runs") in the original file F above:

```
F:  15,  1,  7,  12,  3,  2,  4,  9,  13,  5,  10,  6,  8,  14,  11
    --  ---------  -  -----------  -----  --------  --
```

If we do not require that the subfiles being copied have the same number of elements (a power of 2), we can improve upon the binary merge sort. Repeat the following until F contains only one run. First, copy runs from F alternately to F1 and F2. Then merge corresponding runs from F1 and F2, writing them back to F:

```
F1:  15,  3,  5,  10,  11
     --  ------------
F2:  1,  7,  12,  2,  4,  9,  13,  6,  8,  14
     --------  -----------  --------
                     |
                     V
```

(Note that some runs have combined to form larger ones in F1)

```
                     |
                     V
F:  1,  7,  12,  15,  2,  3,  4,  9,  13,  5,  6,  8,  10,  14,  11
    -----------  --------------  ---------------  --
                     |
                     V
F1:  1,  7,  12,  15,  5,  6,  8,  10,  14
     -----------  ---------------
 F2:  2,  3,  4,  9,  13,  11
      --------------  --
                     |
                     V
F:  1,  2,  3,  4,  7,  9,  12,  13,  15,  5,  6,  8,  10,  11,  14
    --------------------------  -------------------
                     |
                     V
F1:  1,  2,  3,  4,  7,  9,  12,  13,  15
     -----------------------------
 F2:  5,  6,  8,  10,  11,  14
      ------------------
                     |
                     V
F:  1,  2,  3,  4,  5,  6,  7,  8,  9,  10,  11,  12,  13,  14,  15
    --------------------------------------------------------
```

How can the end of a run in F be determined?
    Use the "look-ahead" property of the file:

1. $n = 1$
2. While NOT eof(F), do the following:
    2.1. EndOfRun = false
    2.2. While NOT EndOfRun, do the following:
        2.2.1. Read x from F
        2.2.2. Write x to file n
        2.2.3. EndOfRun = (F->Key < x.Key) OR eof(F)
    2.3. n = 3-n /* switch files for next run */

A possible modification is to copy n items from F into an array. Sort these items with a good internal sort (e.g., quicksort). Write these to F1. Now copy the next n items into the array, sort them but write them to F2, and so on, alternating between F1 and F2. Finally, merge F1 and F2 back into F; continue until F is sorted.

Here is a simple and brief version of the merge sort algorithm:

Step 1. Divide the array of n elements in half.
Step 2. Sort the left half.
Step 3. Sort the right half.
Step 4. Merge the two sorted halves into one sorted array.

The recursive form of `Merge_sort ()` implementing the above steps is:

Step 1. Divide the array of n elements in half.
Step 2. Call `Merge_sort ()` for the left half.
Step 3. Call `Merge_sort ()` for the right half.
Step 4. Merge the two sorted halves into one sorted array by calling the function `concat_ordr ()` (see Example 9-9).

The implementation of this merge sort algorithm is given as an exercise.

Analysis

Because the merge sort uses a "divide-and-conquer" strategy, it goes through the left half and then the right half, and thus, the entire array each pass it is called. During each pass, it takes $O(n)$ steps to move all of n elements. During the phase of merging two sorted subarrays, it takes $n/2$ or $n - 1$ comparisons for a subarray of size one or of size greater than $n/2$, respectively.

The worst case for merge sort occurs when the elements of the array are in reverse order. Because we divide arrays and subarrays into halves, the partitioned subarrays are of sizes 1, 2, 4, 8, and so on. For an array of n elements, the merge sort procedure requires $\log_2 n$ passes of partitioning and merging operations. In each pass, it examines each of the n elements in each of them.

Pass	Number of partitions	Partitioned array	Order
0	$2^0 = 1$		$O(n)$
1	$2^1 = 2$		$O(n)$
2	$2^2 = 4$		$O(n)$
3	$2^3 = 8$		$O(n)$
.			
.			
.			
$\log_2 n$	n		$O(n)$

Thus the total number of comparisons is between $(n/2) \log_2 n$ and $n \log_2 n$. The total number of moves is $n \log_2 n$.

Thus in the worst case, the performance of merge sort is $O(n \log_2 n)$.

One drawback of the merge sort algorithm is that it needs two arrays of the same size and of the same type in order to perform the merging step. To sort an array of n elements, it needs a holding area for $2n$ elements.

9.3.7 Concatenate Sort

This sorting technique is very useful for internal merge sorting. The objective of this sort is as follows. Given two sorted arrays A[m] and B[n] of the same type, sort and concatenate them into an ascending ordered array C[] . As the sizes of A[] and B[] are respectively m and n, the size of array C must be at least $m + n$ to ensure enough holding storage space. The size of C may be less than $m + n$ in case A[] and B[] have some common elements.

The approach described below is based on comparing pairs of elements from each array, A and B, until one of the arrays is exhausted, then copy the rest of the other array into C[] .

Step 1. Compare A[0] and B[0].
    If   A[0] <= B[0],   set C[0] = A[0]
    else   set C[0] = B[0]

    Assume   A[0] < B[0] &   C[0] = A[0].
    Then if A[1] > B[0], set C[1] = B[0]
    If   A[1] > B[1], set C[2] = B[1]
    If   A[1] < B[2], set C[3] = A[1]
    If   A[2] > B[2], set C[4] = B[2]
    . . .

Step 2. Continue step 1 until all elements in one of the arrays are copied into C[] .

Step 3. Append the remaining uncopied elements in the other array to the sorted array C.

To illustrate the algorithm for concatenate sort, consider the two sorted arrays A and B:

```
        +---+---+---+----+                +---+---+---+
A:      | 1 | 4 | 9 | 12 |        B:      | 3 | 6 | 8 |
        ------------------                ------------
```

The final sorted list C is created step by step as follows:

```
                                        +---+
1 < 3, so move 1 from A to C;    C:      | 1 |
                                        -----
```

```
                                        +---+---+
3 < 4, so move 3 from B to C;    C:      | 1 | 3 |
                                        ---------
```

```
                                        +---+---+---+
4 < 6, so move 4 from A to C;    C:      | 1 | 3 | 4 |
                                        ------------
```

6 < 9, so move 6 from B to C;   C:

8 < 9, so move 8 from B to C;   C:

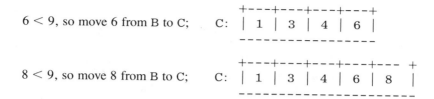

Now array B is empty, so move all the remaining elements of A to C. The final sorted list C is

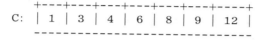

The function `concat_ordr()` in Example 9-9 implements the algorithm for concatenate sort.

9.3.8 Binary Search Tree Sort

The objective is to sort the items of an array A[0], ..., A[n-1] in an ascending order using a binary search tree (BST). Binary search tree sort, also called the "Treesort" procedure, consists of the following steps:

Step 1. Initialize an empty BST.

Step 2. Create a BST by inserting n items of the array into the BST. That is, for i ranging from 0 to n − 1, insert A[i] into the BST.

Step 3. Retrieve items from the binary search tree by inorder traversal and put the items back into the array. This is done in steps 4 through 6.

Step 4. Set array index i to 0.

Step 5. While doing inorder traversal of the BST, visit a node with the following operations:

Step 5.1. Place the currently visiting node in the array item A[i].

Step 5.2. Increase i by 1.

Step 6. Continue inorder traversal until all nodes in the BST are visited, retrieved, and put back into the array.

Step 7. If the BST is no longer needed, delete the BST by freeing the memory spaces allocated for its nodes.

Step 8. The items in the array A are now sorted in an ascending order.

This shows how we can use a binary search tree to sort an array of items. Note that this approach requires extra internal memory space to store the BST, which is in fact used as a temporary work area.

The C implementation of this sorting method is left as an exercise. The detailed analysis of the binary search tree sort is left as an exercise.

9.3.9 The Heap Sort

In this section, we will first discuss the concept of a heap, and then a sorting method using a heap.

Choosing the right data structure for an application needs careful consideration of the requirements and knowledge of the trade-offs. There are several good sources (Sedgewick 1983; Gonnet 1984), but nothing surpasses the experience of solving problems.

The heap[1] is a useful data structure. It provides one of the fastest methods of sorting an arbitrary collection of data. The heap is a special form of either an array or a binary tree, in which the following conditions hold:

1. Each node's key (often the data field of the node) preserves some form of specified ordering (for example, that each node's key is less than the key of either of its children).
2. The tree is fully balanced. The subtrees of any node differ in height by at most 1.
3. Each level is filled from left to right, allowing both tree and array implementations.

A fixed-size heap can be implemented by an array, because condition 3 assures that the ordering can be maintained with a simple indexing scheme. The children of a node indexed by i are nodes indexed by $2*i$ and $2*i+1$. The array can hold the data field of the node, if the data is one of the basic types, or the array can hold pointers to data nodes of some structured type. We will look at the array implementation in parallel with that of the tree.

An auxiliary property of the heap, with N nodes, is that any node is at most $\log_2(N)$ levels from the root, which means that the maximum number of necessary search steps is a minimum. Some effort is required to maintain the heap properties, but this is outweighed for large N by the small search path.

An array-based instance of a heap is shown in Figure 9-8(a) and a tree-based instance, in Figure 9-8(b).

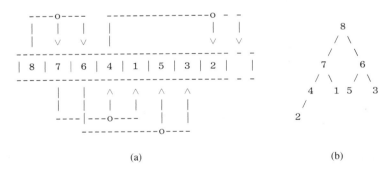

(a)   (b)

Figure 9-8 A heap stored in (*a*) an array and (*b*) a tree.

Converting an unordered collection of nodes into a heap involves rearranging the nodes, working from the top to the bottom of the heap. Consider an array A [N] , with N even. To convert A into a heap with node key less than that of its children, the following steps are taken:

1. Set x = 1.
2. Exit if x is greater than or equal to N.

---

[1] Another use of the term "heap" is for unallocated memory available for a user program.

3. Set i = x and j = i / 2 (so A[j] is the parent of A[i]).
4. If A[i] is not the same as A[0] and A[j] is greater than or equal to A[j], then:
    (a) Swap A[i] and A[j].
    (b) Set i = j and j = i / 2.
    (c) Loop back to 4.
5. Set x = x + 1 and loop back to 2.

The algorithm for creating a heap depends on two operations: comparison of data elements and swap of data elements. In the above simple algorithm, we used an array holding one of the basic unstructured types. The comparison and swap functions are the built-in relationship and assignment operators. For simple applications this is sufficient. For most applications, however, we must resort to trees and pointers, and the comparison and swap functions must handle those data types. In order to develop an ADT version of the heap data structure, we must have our top-level functions handle any data type, using pointers to the nodes and to data-type-specific functions. Each class of comparison functions and of swap functions must have a common interface. The set of pointers to functions of each class can be kept in a table and can be called by a symbolic index.

```
/*
 *    Comparison and swap function table symbolic indices
 */
#define    BYTE_FOR_BYTE      0
#define    NODE_FOR_NODE      1
#define    PTR_FOR_PTR        2

int (* compare[]) () = {
    bcompare,
    ncompare,
    pcompare,
       :
       :
};

int (* swap[]) () = {
    bswap,
    nswap,
    pswap,
       :
       :
};
```

The call for a comparison might look something like this:

```
int functioncall;
   :
   :

functioncall = NODE_FOR_NODE;
   :
   :

compare[functioncall] (data1, data2, sizeof(data1));
```

Another form of call might be of the form

```
Create_Heap ( ELEMENT * hptr, int heapsize,
              int (* compare) (), int (* swap) ()) ;
```

An interesting viewpoint about this usage is that the low-level functions have become, effectively, data (function call arguments) for higher level functions. For comparisons, we would define symbols for less than, equal to, and greater than:

```
#define   LESSTHAN      -1
#define   EQUALTO        0
#define   GREATERTHAN    1
```

The comparison functions can be written in several ways. The first shown is byte-for-byte:

```
/*
 *  bcompare() - a byte-for-byte comparison
 *  called by: bcompare(&data1, &data2, sizeof(data1))
 */
int  bcompare (char * p1, char * p2, int size)
{
    while (size-- != 0)
      {
        if (*p1 > *p2)
            return (GREATERTHAN) ;
        else if (*p1 < *p2)
            return (LESSTHAN) ;
      }
        return (EQUALTO) ;
}
```

This might fail for comparison of structs with holes that contain undefined residue values. The use of calloc() (which zeros the allocated memory—and therefore takes longer to run) rather than malloc() will mitigate this, but it is still an unsafe programming practice to assume anything about how structured data types are stored by the C compiler and the operating system.

Another comparison might be done on nodes that contain a struct with a data field that is one of the basic data types (the field name for the class of struct comparisons must be generic, for example, data):

```
/*
 *  ncompare() - a node-for-node comparison
 *  called by: ncompare(&data1, &data2, sizeof(data1))
 */
int  ncompare (char * p1, char * p2, int size)
{
    if (*p1->data > *p2->data)
        return (GREATERTHAN) ;
    else if (*p1->data < *p2->data)
        return (LESSTHAN) ;
```

```
      return (EQUALTO) ;
}
```

The first swap function presented assumes that the node data fields are composed of contiguous memory. It simply swaps data byte-for-byte using the size of the data element as a countdown-to-zero counter. The second swap function assumes that the nodes are linked elements, so it swaps pointers:

```
/*
 * bswap() - a byte-for-byte swap
 * called by: bswap(&data1, &data2, sizeof(data1))
 */
int  bswap (char * p1, char * p2, int size)
{
    char tmp;
    while (size-- != 0)
      {
          tmp   = *p1;
          *p1++ = *p2;
          *p2++ = tmp;
      }
}

/*
 *  pswap() - a pointer-for-pointer swap
 *  called by: bswap(&&data1, &&data2, sizeof(data1))
 */
int  bswap (char ** p1, char ** p2, int size)
{
    char * tmp;
    tmp = *p1;
    *p1 = *p2;
    *p2 = tmp;
}
```

The swap function might also be a node-for-node swap.

```
/*
 *  nswap() - a node-for-node swap
 *  called by: bswap(&node1, &node2, sizeof(node1->data))
 */
int nswap (char * p1, char * p2, int size)
{
    char * tmp;
    tmp        = p1->left;
    p1->left   = node2->left;
    p2->left   = tmp;
    tmp        = p1->right;
    p1->right  = node2->right;
    p2->right  = tmp;
}
```

The swap function can be added as a function argument:

```
int  (* swap) () ;
   :
   :
swap = nswap;
   :
   :
Adjust_Heap (char * hptr, int heapsize,
             int (*compare) () , int (*swap) () ) ;
```

The function to create a heap from a set of unordered elements is shown below. It follows from the algorithm described above. For this version we assume a heap built as an array of pointers to elements. The ordering is for node data to be greater that that of its children:

```
/*
 *  Create_Heap ()
 */
int  Create_Heap (char * hptr, int heapsize,
                  int (*compare) () , int (*swap) () )
{
    int x, i, j;
    int check;
    int size = sizeof (hptr [0] ->data) ;

    for (x = 1; x < heapsize; x++)
      {
        i = x;
        j = i/2;   /* hptr[j] is the parent of hptr[i] */
        while ((compare(hptr[i], hptr[0], size) != EQUALTO)
              && ((check = compare(hptr[j], hptr[i],
                   size)) == LESSTHAN || check == EQUALTO))
          {
            swap(hptr[j], hptr[i], size);
            i = j;
            j = i/2;
          }
      }
}
```

Once the heap is created, it may be sorted. The sort uses a function, Adjust_ Heap () , built on the following algorithm and based on a heap constructed from an array of pointers to heap elements. This algorithm ripples the smallest node downward until the heap ordering property is restored.

1. Set i = 0 and j = 1. (A [i] is the parent of A [j] .)
2. If the heapsize is greater than or equal to 3 (so the root node has two children) and the data of A [1] is less than that of A [2] , then set j = 2 (the larger child).
3. While j is within the array index range and the data of A [i] is less than that of A [j] , do the following:
   (a) Swap A [i] and A [j] .

(b) Set i = j and j = 2*i + 1.

(c) If j + 1 is within the array index range and the data of A[j] is less than that of A[j+1], then set j = j + 1.

(d) Loop back to 3.

The function Adjust_Heap() is

```
/*
 *   Adjust_Heap()
 *   called by: Adjust_Heap(&heap, heapsize, &compare(),
 *                              &swap())
 */
int Adjust_Heap (char * hptr, int heapsize,
                 int (*compare)(), int (*swap)())
{
    int i = 0, j = 1;
    int size = sizeof(hptr[0]->data);
    int check;

    if (heapsize > = 3 && ((check = compare(hptr[1],
        hptr[2], size)) == LESSTHAN || check == EQUALTO))
        j = 2;
    while (j < heapsize && (check = compare(hptr[i],
            hptr[j], size)) == LESSTHAN || check ==
            EQUALTO))
    {
        swap(hptr[i], hptr[j], size);
        i = j;
        j = i*2 + 1;
        if (j+1 < heapsize && ((check = compare(hptr[j],
            hptr[j+1], size)) == LESSTHAN ||
            check == EQUALTO))
            j++;
    }
}
```

Figure 9-9 illustrates the creation of a heap, represented as a tree, given the set of data

$$\{25, 57, 48, 37, 12, 92, 86, 33\}$$

In this figure and Figure 9-10, a "//" or a "\\" means that the elements have been swapped.

The heap sort algorithm comprises the following steps:

1. If the heapsize is less than or equal to 1, then return; otherwise:

   (a) Swap the root node with the last node.

   (b) Set heapsize = heapsize − 1.

   (c) Adjust the reduced data set to regain the heap ordering property.

   (d) Loop to 1.

2. Print the elements of the original structure from last to first element.

Taking the heap of Figure 9-9, we will go through the first pass of the heap sort algorithm. In the figure, "=" means that the element has been removed from the current heap.

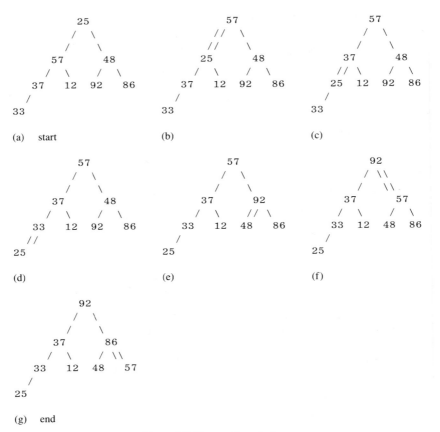

Figure 9-9 The creation of a heap.

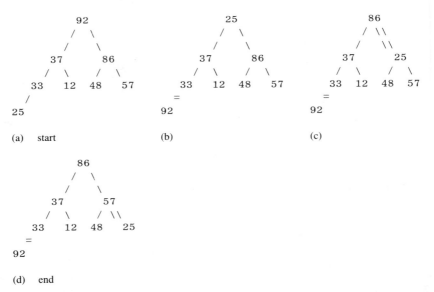

Figure 9-10 The first pass of sort of a heap.

The heap sort function is shown below. Heap_Sort () assumes that the following steps have already occurred:

1. An array of pointers has been initialized.
2. The type of data element has been defined, and the auxiliary functions for compare, swap, and data element printout are assigned.
3. Each data item input has had a node created, the data copied into the node data field, and the next available heap pointer in the array set to the node's location.
4. A counter has been kept of the total number of data items obtained and stored. This is the heapsize.

The heap sort function is called with the location of the first heap array pointer, the total number of items counter, and the locations of the required auxiliary functions. The function printheap () is left as an exercise.

```
/*
 *  Heap_Sort ()
 */
int Heap_Sort (char * hptr, int heapsize, int (*compare) (),
               int (*swap) (), int (*printheap) ())
{
    int i;
    int holdsize = heapsize;
    int size = sizeof (hptr [0] ->data) ;

    Create_Heap (hptr, heapsize, (*compare) (), (*swap) ()) ;
    while (heapsize > 1)
        {
        swap (hptr [0], hptr [heapsize-1], size) ;
        heapsize--;
        Adjust_Heap (hptr, heapsize, (*compare) (),
                (*swap) ()) ;
        Heap_Sort (hptr, heapsize, (*compare) (),
                (*swap) ()) ;
        }
    for (i = holdsize; i >= 0; i--)
        (*printheap) (hptr [i]) ;
}
```

The progression of the sort phase of Heap_Sort () is shown in Figure 9-11. The start of the sequence is the same as the end of the heap creation, shown in Figure 9-9(g). The elements are shown as a set or list of items, in order to save space on the page. All elements to the left of the vertical line are in the current heap. Curly braces, "{ . . }," indicate that the collection is a heap. Square brackets, "[. .]," indicate that the collection requires adjustment to return to heap properties. The array-to-tree translation is simple (because of heap property 3):

Notice that as the sort progresses, the collection as a linear array is becoming ordered from least to greatest value. The final output of sorted data is therefore done from back to front of the collection.

```
{ 92, 37, 86, 33, 12, 48, 57, 25 |}

[ 25, 37, 86, 33, 12, 48, 57 | 92 ]

[ 86, 37, 25, 33, 12, 48, 57 | 92 ]

{ 86, 37, 57, 33, 12, 48, 25 | 92 }

[ 25, 37, 57, 33, 12, 48 | 86, 92 ]

[ 57, 37, 25, 33, 12, 48 | 86, 92 ]

{ 57, 37, 48, 33, 12, 25 | 86, 92 }

[ 25, 37, 48, 33, 12 | 57, 86, 92 ]

{ 48, 37, 25, 33, 12 | 57, 86, 92 }

[ 12, 37, 25, 33 | 48, 57, 86, 92 ]

[ 37, 12, 25, 33 | 48, 57, 86, 92 ]

{ 37, 33, 25, 12 | 48, 57, 86, 92 }

[ 12, 33, 25 | 37, 48, 57, 86, 92 ]

{ 33, 12, 25 | 37, 48, 57, 86, 92 }

{ 25, 12 | 33, 37, 48, 57, 86, 92 }

{ 12 | 25, 33, 37, 48, 57, 86, 92 }

{| 12, 25, 33, 37, 48, 57, 86, 92 }
```

Figure 9-11 The sort of a heap.

In the summary, the selection of any one sorting algorithm is based on the following factors:

1. The data structure of the items to be sorted
2. The size of the list of data items
3. The requirement and availability of core memory
4. The requirement and availability of secondary memory

Examples

Example 9-1

Code Section

```
/*  Program:  linear_search.c  (ARRAY IMPLEMENTATION)
 *
 *  Purpose:  Search the array A[0], A[1], ..., A[n-1]
```

```
 *                     for a given 'Item'. The array elements
 *                     and the Item are of same type.
 */


/*
 *  linear_srch(): LINEAR SEARCH array A whose size is
 *                     no_elements.
 *              If search is successful, returns the 'index' of the
 *              matching array element. Otherwise, returns -1.
 */

int  linear_srch(int A[], int no_elements, int Item)
{
    int  i;                             /* Index of the array  */

    for ( i = 0; i < no_elements; i++ )
       {
          if ( A[ i ] == Item )
                                        /* Found match          */
                 return ( i );     /* Return the index 'i'       */
       }
    /*  Could not find a match with 'Item'                   */
    printf("\n linear_srch: %d not found in the array %s \n",
                         Item, "A" );
    return ( -1 );
}


/*
 * main() :          LINEAR SEARCH - Implemented for an ARRAY
 */
main()
{
    static  int  A[ ] = { 4, 5, 56, 32, 92, 100, -10, -23 };
    int     n = 8;       /* Number of elements in the array       */
    int     index;       /* index of the matching array element */
    int     Item = 75;  /* Searching for this element in A[ ]    */

    printf("\n ===  EXAMPLE ON LINEAR SEARCH ALGORITHM  === \n");
    printf("\n ===  Searching for %d in the following Array \n",
                                              Item);
    for ( index = 0; index < n; index++ )
      printf(" %d  ", A[ index ] );

    if ( (index = linear_srch( A, n, Item )) != -1 )
      printf("\n Item = %d  is  found as A[ %d ] \n",
                                              Item, index );
}
```

Output Section

```
        ===  EXAMPLE OF LINEAR SEARCH ALGORITHM  ===

        ===  Searching for 5 in the following Array
        4   5   56   32   92   100   -10   -23
        Item = 5  is  found as A[ 1 ]
```

Output Section

```
===  EXAMPLE OF LINEAR SEARCH ALGORITHM  ===

===  Searching for 75 in the following Array
4    5    56    32    92    100    -10    -23
linear_srch: 75 not found in the array A
```

Example 9-2

Code Section

```
/*
 *  search_elt() :  Perform linear search for an element
 *                  in a list, that is structured as a
 *                  a singly linked list. The element is
 *                  specified by its key value. If the
 *                  element is found, it returns a pointer;
 *                  otherwise, NULL.
 *
 *  NOTE:  For data types, see Example 5.5.
 */

SINGLE_LINK_LIST  search_elt( SINGLE_LINK_LIST  list_ptr,
                              data_type          element_key )
{
    while ( list_ptr != NULL )
      {
          if ( element_key == list_ptr -> data )
            return( list_ptr );
          /*  Advance to the next element  */
          list_ptr = list_ptr -> next_elt;
      }
    printf("\n search_elt: Element is not found \n");
    return( NULL );
}
```

Output Section

When the function search_elt() is called in Example 5.5 (in Chapter 5) to
search for an element specified by key value T, the following output is produced:

```
=== Example of SINGLE LINKED LIST IMPLEMENTATION ===

The resulting list is: P -> R -> A -> T -> I -> V -> A -> NULL

Number of elements in this list is: 7

Searched element T is found

The resulting list after delete_list operation is: NULL
```

Example 9-3

Code Section

```
/*  Program:  binary_search.c   (ARRAY IMPLEMENTATION)
 *
```

```
 *  Purpose:   Binary Search the array A[0], A[1], ..., A[n-1],
 *             ordered in Ascending order, for a given Item.
 *             The array elements and the Item are of same type.
 */

#define    FALSE  0
#define    TRUE   ~FALSE

/*
 * binary_srch() : BINARY SEARCH IN AN ORDERED LIST (ARRAY)
 * If search is successful, returns the 'index' of the matching
 * array element. Otherwise, returns -1.
 */

int binary_srch(int A[], int First_index, int Last_index, int Item )
{
    int  Mid_index;  /* Index of the middle element the array  */
    int  Found = FALSE;

    while (( First_index <= Last_index ) && !Found )
      {
         /* Calculate Mid_index = ( First_index + Last_index ) div 2 */
         Mid_index = (int) (( First_index  +  Last_index ) / 2
                          - ( First_index  +  Last_index ) % 2);

         if ( Item ==   A[ Mid_index ])
           { Found = TRUE;                /* Found match          */
             return ( Mid_index );   /* Return the 'Mid_index'*/
           }
         else if ( Item >  A[ Mid_index ] )
             {
         /* Set First_index = Mid_index + 1; Item in Second half*/
             First_index = Mid_index + 1;
               binary_srch( A, First_index, Last_index,  Item );
             }
         else  /*   Item <  A[ Mid_index ]      */
             {
         /* Set Last_index = Mid_index - 1; Item in Second half */
             Last_index = Mid_index - 1;
               binary_srch( A,  First_index,  Last_index,  Item );
             }

      }  /* End  while ( )      */

    /*  Could not find a match with 'Item' */
    return ( -1 );
}

/*
 *  main() : BINARY SEARCH IN AN ORDERED LIST (ARRAY)
 */
main()
{
    static  int  A[ ] = { -23, -10, 4, 5, 32, 56, 92, 100 };
    int  n = 8;        /* Total number of elements of array A */
```

```
int   index;          /* index of the matching array element */
int   First_index = 0; /* Index of First element of array */
int   Last_index  = n; /* Index of Last element of array  */
int   Item =  -999;   /* Searching for this element in A[] */

printf ("\n ===  EXAMPLE OF BINARY SEARCH ALGORITHM   === \n");
printf ("\n ===  Searching for %d in the following Array \n",
                                              Item);
for ( index = 0; index < n; index++ )
  printf (" %d  ", A[ index ] );

if ((index = binary_srch( A, First_index,
                     Last_index, Item )) != -1)
  printf ("\n Item = %d  is  found as A[ %d ] \n",
          Item, index );
else
    printf ("\n binary_srch: %d not found in the array %s \n",
                         Item, "A" );
}
```

Output Section

```
===  EXAMPLE OF BINARY SEARCH ALGORITHM  ===

===  Searching for -999 in the following Array
-23   -10   4   5   32   56   92   100
binary_srch: -999 not found in the array A

===  EXAMPLE ON BINARY SEARCH ALGORITHM  ===

===  Searching for 4 in the following Array
-23   -10   4   5   32   56   92   100   399
Item = 4   is  found as A[ 2 ]
```

Example 9-4

Code Section

For the data structure, related routines and complete program including main ()
for a binary search tree, see Further Examples section of Chapter 7.

```
/*
 *  BSTREE_PTR BST_Search( root_ptr, Item )
 *
 *  Search for Item in the Binary Search Tree with root
 *  pointed by root_ptr. If successful, it returns a
 *  pointer to the node that contains the specified Item.
 *
 *  If not successful, it returns a NULL pointer.
 *    ( Iterative implementation )
 */
BSTREE_PTR BST_Search (BSTREE_PTR root_ptr, node_data_type Item )

{
    BSTREE_PTR Search_ptr;  /* Used as a Search pointer in BST*/
```

```
      /*   Is the binary search tree empty ?   */
      if ( root_ptr == NULL )
        {
           printf("\n BST_Search: Empty Binary Search Tree \n");
           exit( 1 );
        }
      else
        {
           Search_ptr = root_ptr;      /* Start searching from root */

           /*   Perform search iteratively, because recursive
            *   search in BST will require a lot of stack space.
            */
           while (  Search_ptr != NULL  )
   {
              if ( Item < Search_ptr -> node_data )
                    /* Continue search in the Left subtree */
                 Search_ptr = Search_ptr -> left_child_ptr;

              else if ( Item > Search_ptr -> node_data )
                    /* Continue search in the Right subtree */
                 Search_ptr = Search_ptr -> right_child_ptr;
              else
                 {
                    return ( Search_ptr );
                 }
   } /*   End of while ( !Found && (Search_ptr != NULL)) */

           printf("\n BST_Search: Item %d  not found \n", Item);
           return ( NULL );
        }
}
```

Output Section

   *** Example of BINARY SEARCH TREE Operations ***

 BST_Search: Item 31 not found

 The Binary Search Tree when traversed by InOrder():
 21   30   34   67   69   70   75

 *** End of example of BINARY SEARCH TREE Operations ***

Output Section

   *** Example of BINARY SEARCH TREE Operations ***

 Searched data item is 70

 The Binary Search Tree when traversed by InOrder():
 21   30   34   67   69   70   75

 *** End of example of BINARY SEARCH TREE Operations ***

Example 9-5

Code Section

```
/*
 *  Program:   select_sort.c    (ARRAY IMPLEMENTATION)
 *  Purpose:   Perform 'Selection Sort' on the elements
 *                  A[0], ..., A[n-1]
 *             of an array  A, whose size is 'n'.
 *             The sorted form is in ascending order.
 *
 * To Compile:  cc -O select_sort.c -DDEBUG -o select_sort
 */

typedef    int  array_type[ ];        /* Define array_type   */
typedef    int  array_member;         /* Define array_member */

/*
 *  select_sort(): SELECTION SORT of an Array whose size is
 *                  'arraysize'
 */

void select_sort(array_type array, int arraysize)
{
    int i, j,
        index_small_elt,
        temp;          /* Temporary storage needed for swapping */
    void print_ary( array_type, int, int );

    /* Does  the list array[ ] has more than one element?   */
    if ( arraysize > 0 )
      {
        for ( i = 0; i < arraysize - 1; i++ )
          {
            index_small_elt = i;
            for ( j = i + 1; j < arraysize; j++ )
                if ( array[ j ] < array[ index_small_elt ])
                    index_small_elt = j;

        /* Interchange array[ i ] and array[ index_small_elt ] */
            temp  = array[ index_small_elt ];
            array[ index_small_elt ] = array[ i ];
            array[ i ] = temp;

#ifdef  DEBUG
            print_ary( array, arraysize, i );
#endif
          }
      }
}

/*
 *  print_ary ( A, n, pass_number ):
 *    Print the array the array A[ n ] for each pass_number
 */
```

```
void print_ary (array_type A, int n, int pass_number )
{
    int  index;                              /* Array index */

    printf ("\n      Pass #  %d : ", pass_number );
    for ( index = 0; index < n; index++ )
        printf (" %d  ", A[ index ] );
}

/*
 * main ()  :  SELECTION SORT (ARRAY IMPLEMENTATION)
 */
main ()
{
    static int  A[ ] = { 10, 100, 20, -5, -20, 200, 67, 89, -400 };
    int  n = 9;           /* Total number of elements of array A */
    int  index;           /* index of the matching array element */

    printf ("\n === EXAMPLE OF SELECTION SORT ALGORITHM  === \n");
    printf ("\n ===  Sorting the following %s \n",
            "List in Ascending Order ");
    for ( index = 0; index < n; index++ )
        printf (" %d  ", A[ index ] );
    printf ("\n");

    select_sort ( A, n );

    printf ("\n\n === Sorted form of the above List \n");
    for ( index = 0; index < n; index++ )
        printf (" %d  ", A[ index ] );

    printf ("\n === End of EXAMPLE OF %s \n",
            "SELECTION SORT ALGORITHM  === ");
}
```

   Output Section

```
=== EXAMPLE OF SELECTION SORT ALGORITHM  ===

=== Sorting the following List in Ascending Order
10   100   20   -5   -20   200   67   89   -400

    Pass #  0 :  -400   100   20   -5   -20   200   67   89   10

    Pass #  1 :  -400   -20   20   -5   100   200   67   89   10

    Pass #  2 :  -400   -20   -5   20   100   200   67   89   10

    Pass #  3 :  -400   -20   -5   10   100   200   67   89   20

    Pass #  4 :  -400   -20   -5   10   20   200   67   89   100

    Pass #  5 :  -400   -20   -5   10   20   67   200   89   100
```

```
    Pass #  6 :    -400    -20    -5    10    20    67    89    200    100

    Pass #  7 :    -400    -20    -5    10    20    67    89    100    200
```

```
===  Sorted form of the above List
-400    -20    -5    10    20    67    89    100    200
===  End of EXAMPLE OF SELECTION SORT ALGORITHM   ===
```

Example 9-6

Code Section

```
/*
 *  Program:   bubble_sort.c
 *  Purpose:   Perform 'Bubble Sort' on the elements
 *                 A[0],  ...,  A[n-1]
 *             of an array  A, whose size is 'n'.
 *             The sorted form is in ascending order.
 *
 * To Compile:   cc -O bubble.c -DDEBUG -o bubble
 */


#define    FALSE   0
#define    TRUE    ~FALSE

typedef    int   array_type[ ];       /* Define array_type        */
typedef    int   array_member;        /* Define array_member      */

/*
 *  bubble(): BUBBLE SORT of an Array whose size is 'arraysize'
 */
void bubble(array_type array, int arraysize)
{
    int             exchange;       /*  Will be used as a flag    */
    array_member    store;          /*  Temporary storage         */
    int             pass, inx;
    void print_ary (array_type, int, int );

    exchange = TRUE;

    for (pass = 0; pass < arraysize  &&  exchange == TRUE; pass++)
    {
        exchange = FALSE;
        for (inx = 0; inx < arraysize - pass; inx++)
            if ( *(array + inx) > *(array + inx + 1) )
                {                      /* Perform swap using Pointer  */
                exchange = TRUE;
                store = *(array +  inx);
                *(array + inx) = *(array + (inx + 1) );
                *(array + (inx + 1) ) = store;
                }

#ifdef  DEBUG
        print_ary( array, arraysize, pass );
```

```
#endif
      }
}

/*
 *   print_ary ( A, n, pass_number ):
 *        Print the array A[n] for each pass_number
 */

void print_ary (array_type A, int n, int pass_number )
{
    int  index;

    printf ("\n      Pass #  %d : ", pass_number );
    for ( index = 0; index < n; index++ )
       printf (" %d   ", A[ index ] );
}

/*
 *   main()   :   BUBBLE SORT of an Array whose size is 'arraysize'
 */
main ()
{
    static  int  A[ ] = { -23,  10, 4, 5, -2, 56, 2, 300, 199 };
    int   n = 9;          /* Total number of elements of array A */
    int   index;          /* index of the matching array element */

    printf ("\n ===  EXAMPLE OF BUBBLE SORT ALGORITHM  === \n");
    printf ("\n === Array before Bubble Sort ===  \n" );
    for ( index = 0; index < n; index++ )
       printf (" %d   ", A[ index ] );
    printf (" \n ");

    bubble ( A, n );

    printf ("\n\n ===  Array after  Bubble Sort ===   \n" );
    for ( index = 0; index < n; index++ )
       printf (" %d   ", A[ index ] );
    printf ( "\n" );
}
```

Output Section

```
===  EXAMPLE OF BUBBLE SORT ALGORITHM  ===

===  Array before Bubble Sort ===
-23   10   4   5   -2   56   2   300   199

      Pass #  0 :  -23    4    5   -2   10    2   56   199   300
      Pass #  1 :  -23    4   -2    5    2   10   56   199   300
      Pass #  2 :  -23   -2    4    2    5   10   56   199   300
      Pass #  3 :  -23   -2    2    4    5   10   56   199   300
      Pass #  4 :  -23   -2    2    4    5   10   56   199   300

===  Array after  Bubble Sort ===
-23   -2   2   4   5   10   56   199   300
```

Example 9-7

Code Section

```
/*
 *  Program:   insert_sort.c     (ARRAY IMPLEMENTATION)
 *  Purpose:   Perform 'Insertion Sort' on the elements
 *                A[0], ..., A[n-1]
 *             of an array A, whose size is 'n'.
 *             The sorted form is in ascending order.
 *
 * To Compile:  cc -O insert_sort.c -D DEBUG -o insert_sort
 */

typedef    int   array_type[ ];        /* Define array_type   */
typedef    int   array_member;         /* Define array_member */

/*
 *  insert_sort(): INSERTION SORT of an Array whose size is
 *                 'arraysize'
 */
void insert_sort(array_type array, int arraysize)
{
    int              i, j, start_index;
    array_member     store;
    void print_ary (array_type , int , int );

    /*  Begin insertion process starting with the last
     *  item array[n-1], where n = arraysize.
     *  First, we will insert array[n-2] before or after
     *  array[n-1].
     */

    start_index = arraysize - 2;
    for ( j = start_index; j >= 0; j-- )
       {
           i = j + 1;
           store =   array[ j ];
           array[ arraysize + 1 ] = store;

    /*  Insert array[j] in its sorted position among
     *  array[j+1], array[j+2], ..., array[n-1]
     */

           while ( store > array[ i ] )
              {
                 array[ i - 1 ] = array[ i ];
                 i++;
              }
           array[ i - 1 ] = store;

#ifdef   DEBUG
           print_ary( array, arraysize, j );
#endif
       }
}
```

```
/*
 *   print_ary ( A, n, pass_number ):
 *      Print the array the array A[ n ] for each pass_number.
 */

void print_ary (array_type A, int n, int pass_number )
{
    int  index;

    printf("\n      Pass #  %d : ", pass_number );
    for ( index = 0; index < n; index++ )
      printf(" %3d  ", A[ index ] );
}


/*
 *   main() :   INSERTION SORT (ARRAY IMPLEMENTATION)
 */
main()
{
    static int  A[ ] = { 10, 100, 20, -5, -20, 200, 67, 89, -400 };
    int  n = 9;           /* Total number of elements of array A */
    int  index;           /* index of the matching array element */

    printf("\n === EXAMPLE OF INSERTION SORT ALGORITHM  === \n");
    printf("\n === Sorting the following List %s \n",
           "in Ascending Order ");
    for ( index = 0; index < n; index++ )
      printf(" %d  ", A[ index ] );
    printf(" \n " );

    insert_sort ( A, n );

    printf("\n\n === Sorted form of the above List \n");
    for ( index = 0; index < n; index++ )
       printf(" %d  ", A[ index ] );

    printf("\n === End of EXAMPLE OF %s \n",
           "INSERTION SORT ALGORITHM  === ");
}
```

Output Section

```
=== EXAMPLE OF INSERTION SORT ALGORITHM  ===

=== Sorting the following List in Ascending Order
10   100   20    -5    -20   200   67   89    -400

    Pass #  7 :   10   100   20    -5    -20   200    67   -400    89
    Pass #  6 :   10   100   20    -5    -20   200  -400    67    89
    Pass #  5 :   10   100   20    -5    -20  -400    67    89   200
    Pass #  4 :   10   100   20    -5   -400   -20    67    89   200
    Pass #  3 :   10   100   20  -400   -20    -5    67    89   200
    Pass #  2 :   10   100 -400   -20    -5    20    67    89   200
    Pass #  1 :   10  -400  -20    -5    20    67    89   100   200
    Pass #  0 : -400   -20   -5    10    20    67    89   100   200
```

```
=== Sorted form of the above List
-400   -20   -5   10   20   67   89   100   200
=== End of EXAMPLE OF INSERTION SORT ALGORITHM   ===
```

Example 9-8

Code Section

```c
/*
 *  Program:   quick_sort.c
 *  Purpose:   Perform 'Quick Sort' on the elements A[0], ...,
 *             A[n-1] of an array  A, whose size is 'n'.
 *
 *  NOTE:   The number of comparisons between the elements of
 *          array, performed by the Quick sort algorithm, is
 *          directly proportional to the 'square of n'.
 *
 *  To Compile:   cc -O quick_sort.c -o quick_sort
 */

typedef   int   array_type[ ];
typedef   int   array_member;

/*
 *  quick_sort1():   does the sorting work
 */

void quick_sort1(array_type array, int lower, int upper)
{
    int  j, k;
    array_member   amem, temp;

    if  ( lower < upper )
    {
        amem = array[ lower ];
        j = lower;
        k = upper;

        while ( j < k )
        {
            while ( array[ j ] <= amem && j < upper)
                j += 1;

            while ( array[ k ] >= amem && k > lower)
                k -= 1;
            if ( j < k )
            {                                /* Swap  */
                temp     = array[ j ];
                array[ j ] = array[ k ];
                array[ k ] = temp;
            }
        }
        /* Swap A[lower] and A[ k ]  */
        temp     = array[ lower ];
```

```
                array[ lower ] = array[ k ];
                array[ k ] = temp;

                quick_sort1(array, lower, k - 1);
                quick_sort1(array, k + 1, upper);
        }
}


/*
 *  quick_sort():   QUICK SORT of an Array whose size is
 *                  'arraysize'
 */

void quick_sort(array_type array, int arraysize)
{
    void quick_sort1(array_type , int , int );

    quick_sort1(array, 0, arraysize - 1);
}


/*
 *   main():   QUICKSORT IMPLEMENTATION   ON AN ARRAY
 */

main()
{
    static  int  A[ ] = { -23,  10, 4, 5, -2, 56, 2, 300, 199 };
    int   n = 9;         /* Total number of elements of array A */
    int   index;         /* index of the matching array element */

    printf("\n === EXAMPLE OF QUICK SORT ALGORITHM  === \n");
    printf("\n === Array before QUICK Sort ===  \n" );
    for ( index = 0; index < n; index++ )
      printf(" %d  ", A[ index ] );
    printf(" \n ");

    quick_sort( A, n );

    printf("\n\n === Array after  QUICK Sort ===  \n" );
    for ( index = 0; index < n; index++ )
        printf(" %d  ", A[ index ] );
    printf( "\n" );
}
```

Output Section

```
        ===  EXAMPLE OF QUICK SORT ALGORITHM  ===

        ===  Array before QUICK Sort ===
        -23    10    4    5    -2    56    2    300    199

        ===  Array after  QUICK Sort ===
        -23    -2    2    4    5    10    56    199    300
```

Example 9-9

Code Section

```
/*
 *   Program:    concat_ordr.c
 *
 *   Purpose:    Given two Sorted arrays A[m] and B[n] of the same
 *               type, sort and concatenate them into an Ascending
 *               ordered array C[]. The sizes of A[] and B[] being
 *               respectively m and n, the size of the array C must
 *               be at least m + n to ensure enough holding storage
 *               space. The size of C may be less than m + n in
 *               case A[] and B[] have some common elements.
 *
 *               The approach is based on comparing pairs of
 *               elements from each array A and B until no more
 *               elements in one of the arrays to be copied into C[]
 *               For step-by-step discussion, see Section 9.3.7.
 */

typedef int  array_type[ ];                /* Define an array type */

/*
 *   concat_ordr(): Takes two ordered arrays A and B;
 *                  Concatenates them into another sorted array
 *                  C; returns size of C[]
 */

int  concat_ordr (array_type A, array_type B,
                  array_type C, int m, int n )
{
   int  i = 0, j = 0, k = 0; /* Temporary variables for indices */

   while (( i < m ) && ( j < n ))
     if ( A[ i ] >= B[ j ] )
       C[ k++ ] = B[ j++ ];          /* Put B[j] in C[k], and
                                         j = j + 1, k = k + 1       */
     else                            /* A[i] is smaller than B[j]  */
       C[ k++ ] = A[ i++ ];          /* Put A[i] in C[k], and
                                         i = i + 1, k = k + 1       */
   /*  Append the remaining uncopied elements in the other
       array to the sorted array C.                                */

   while ( j < n )        /* The array B is not completely used up */
     C[ k++ ] = B[ j++ ];             /* Put B[j] in C[k], and
                                         j = j + 1, k = k + 1       */

   while ( i < m )                    /* Means: The array A is not
                                          completely used up        */
         C[ k++ ] = A[ i++ ];         /* Put A[i] in C[k], and
                                         i = i + 1, k = k + 1       */

   return ( k );                      /* Return the size of C[]     */
}
```

```
/*
 *  main()   :   CONCATENATE SORT of two Arrays
 */
main()
{
   static   int   A[ ] = { -23, -10, 4, 5, 32, 56, 92, 99, 199 };
   static   int   B[ ] = { -13,   0, 4, 7, 22, 46, 52, 80, 111,
                           120, 220};
   int   m = 9,        /* Total number of elements of array A      */
         n = 11,       /* Total number of elements of array B      */
         index,        /* index of an array                        */
         C_size,       /* size of array C[] returned by concat_sort*/
         C[ 20 ];      /* Output: Concatenated & Ascending ordered */

   printf("\n === EXAMPLE OF CONCATENATE SORT ALGORITHM  === \n");
   printf("\n === The Ascending Ordered Array A[]: \n" );
   for ( index = 0; index < m; index++ )
     printf(" %d  ", A[ index ] );

   printf("\n\n === The Ascending Ordered Array B[]: \n" );
   for ( index = 0; index < n; index++ )
      printf(" %d  ", B[ index ] );

   C_size = concat_ordr ( A, B, C, m, n );

   printf("\n\n === %s Array C[]: \n",
          "The Ascending Ordered Concatenated" );
   for ( index = 0; index < C_size; index++ )
      {
        if ( index % 10 == 0 )
           printf("\n ");   /* Print only 10 elements per line  */
        printf(" %d  ", C[ index ] );
      }
   printf("\n\n === End of EXAMPLE OF %s \n",
          "CONCATENATE SORT ALGORITHM  === ");
}
```

Output Section

```
=== EXAMPLE OF CONCATENATE SORT ALGORITHM  ===

=== The Ascending Ordered Array A[]:
-23   -10   4   5   32   56   92   99   199

=== The Ascending Ordered Array B[]:
-13   0   4   7   22   46   52   80   111   120   220

=== The Ascending Ordered Concatenated Array C[]:

 -23   -13   -10   0   4   4   5   7   22   32
  46    52    56  80  92  99 111 120 199  220

=== End of EXAMPLE OF CONCATENATE SORT ALGORITHM  ===
```

Exercises

9-1 Write a program on linear search in an ordered list. See the algorithm in the text.

9-2 Write a program on linked list search in an ordered list. See the algorithm in Section 9.2.4.

9-3 For interpolation search in an ordered list as described in the text, write

    (a) A program implementing the algorithm

    (b) A test program to test the above program

9-4 For Fibonacci search in an ordered list as described in the text, write

    (a) A program implementing the algorithm

    (b) A test program to test the above program

9-5 Write a program to implement a recursive Linear Search for a specified Item in an array of n items.

9-6 [Refer to Stubbs and Webre (1985).] *Shell sort:* The speed of quicksort is attributed to three aspects of the algorithm:

    (a) The simplicity of its inner loop

    (b) Its ability to move elements long distances

    (c) Its use of insertion sort to mop up short sublists

Both insertion sort and bubble sort are particularly deficient with respect to item 2. They both plod along, moving items (elements) from one position to an adjacent position. An approach that can be used to modify either of these algorithms is often called "shell sort." Shell sort attempts to move items (elements) through long distances. It does this by breaking the sort process into a sequence of subsorts, which we will call "*k*-sorts." For example, if there are the following 10 array components to sort:

```
A[0],  A[1],  A[2],  ...,  A[9]
```

then a 3-sort would be to sort the following three sublists:

```
A[0],  A[3],  A[6],  A[9]
A[1],  A[4],  A[7]
A[2],  A[5],  A[8]
```

Any technique can be applied to sort sublists. Shell sort consists of a sequence of *k*-sorts such that the last value of *k* is 1. The hope is that by the time *k* is 1 all items will be near their sorted position. A sequence of *k* values that seems to work well is

$$\ldots, 364, 121, 40, 13, 4, 1$$

Write a program implementing shell sort. (*Hint:* Modification of the insertion sort algorithm will produce the shell sort algorithm.)

9-7 Write a program to implement the merge sort method.

9-8 Write a program to implement the insertion sort method for a doubly linked list.

9-9 Write a program to implement the selection sort method for a doubly linked list.

9-10 Write a program to implement the BST sort method for an array of elements.

9-11 Given a two-dimensional matrix, if each column is arranged into ascending order and then each row is arranged into ascending order, do the columns still stay sorted into ascending order? Write a program to answer this.

9-12 Analyze worst-case performance of linear search algorithm for an ordered array.

9-13 Analyze worst-case performance of the linear search algorithm for an ordered list.

9-14 Analyze worst-case performance of the binary search algorithm for an ordered array.

9-15 Analyze worst-case performance of the Fibonacci search algorithm.

9-16 Analyze worst-case performance of the searching algorithm in a BST sort.

9-17 Analyze best-case and worst-case performances of the quick sort algorithm (see Example 9-8).

9-18 (a) Write an algorithm to delete an element specified by its key p from a hash table with buckets, and one slot per bucket. The hash table uses a hash function H() and one slot per bucket to resolve the collision.

(b) If deletion is permitted, show the modification of the linear search function Hash_Linear_Search() in Section 9.2.9.

9-19 When a hash table htable[] uses buckets with p slots per bucket, write

(a) An algorithm to implement bucket search for an element specified by a key k.

(b) A function implementing the bucket search that resolves collision.

9-20 Write a nonrecursive version of the function binary_srch() in Example 9-2.

9-21 Write an iterative version of the function quick_sort() in Example 9-7.

9-22 List_Insertion_Sort: Write a program to sort a list of *n* names in alphabetical order. Use insertion sort for a singly linked list. Perform sorting by comparing and inserting each name into the singly linked list immediately after each name is read from a file or the keyboard. Print the sorted list.

9-23 Tree_Insertion_Sort: Write a program to sort a list of *n* names in alphabetical order. Use insertion sort for a binary tree. Perform sorting by comparing and inserting each name into the singly linked list immediately after each name is read from a file or the keyboard. Print the sorted list.

9-24 For the given set of key values:

23, 56, 78, 99, 120, 305, 40, 1254, 39

construct a hash table with buckets containing 3 slots for the hash function:

(a) H(k) = k % 5
(b) H(k) = k % 8
(c) H(k) = k % 15

9-25 Redo Exercise 9-23 for hashing with chaining.

The Object-Oriented Programming Approach

The main appeal in object-oriented programming is that it provides better concepts and tools to model and represent real-world problems as closely (directly) as possible. It has been pointed out that object (oriented) programming allows a more direct representation of the real mode in the code. The result is that the normal radical transformation from system requirements (defined in user's terms) to system specification (defined in computer terms) is greatly reduced.

Object-oriented programming is used in such applications as operating systems programming, intelligent database, window, computer-aided system engineering (CASE) tools, HyperCard, HyperMedia, HyperText, etc.

In this chapter, we want to present the basic concept in object-oriented programming, followed by a couple of applications in C++. For rigorous discussions, refer to Lippman (1989), Stroustrup (1986), and Wiener and Pinson (1989).

10.1 Classical Data Structures

The data structure concepts that we have presented in this book might be called "classical," in the sense that they have been in use for some time and are based on the idea of a collection of defined data variables (nonstructured and structured) and the operations defined on them. The classical programming languages [of the FORTRAN–ALGOL (ALGOrithmic Language) family] have been closely concerned with the representation and use of basic machine storage types. Thus the array (of contiguous, homogeneous machine memory spaces) and the record (a unit of contiguous, nonhomogeneous memory spaces) were the first data structures derived from the basic machine types.

Consider as an example of the classical data structure the stack. Its definition is a sequence-ordered set of identical stored objects, the most recently stored being at the stack top (which is the only position that can be accessed), the top of stack (an index or pointer), and a set of functions (push, pop, stack full, stack empty, top of stack) to access the stack. If the stack is implemented as an array of ints, the stack would be defined and a set of functions declared in a header file, and the functions would be defined in a source file:

```
/*
 *   stack.h
 */
typedef  int  STACK[ STACK_SIZE ];
void init_stack();
void push();
int  top_of_stack(), pop();
void stack_full(), stack_empty();

/*
 *   stack.c
 */

void  init_stack()
{
      /* etc.....;  */
}

void  push( int   item )
{
      /* etc.....;  */
}
```

There are problems with this approach. The data structure is not well protected from misuse by other functions within the program that creates and uses the resource. The creation and deletion of data items may not be well controlled. The same structures may be implemented over and over again by programmers, even within the same development group. The set of operation functions and data variables may be available in a library of compiled sources, and thus be available to many different programmers, but it may be difficult to change the "shape" of the data structure easily. (This has lead to the use of levels of abstraction and decomposition of data and operations to small bits, but this can cause large processing overhead due to excessive function calls.) And finally, the data and function declarations can become so complex (try a quick tour through the Unix operating system source code) that programmer errors are made as a result of confusion about usage.

The stack is one of the most used data structures. We have seen quite a few examples of it in earlier chapters. The stack is a central element of operating system and compiler construction. To achieve reasonable performance, one part of the stack definition is violated. The operating system, and programs build by the C compiler use the notion of "frame pointer" to access areas within the stack. If the frame pointer is corrupted, the program or even the operating system will quickly crash. If an incorrect type of variable is pushed on the stack, data will be corrupted and wonderfully bizarre events begin to occur (or worse yet, undetected errors create worm holes in data files).

10.2 The Object-Oriented Data Structure Concept

The object-oriented approach to data structures is to design by defining a set of objects, their interrelationships, and their access operations. Objects can represent abstractions of such physical entities as manufacturing processes, mechanical models, and the stars of a galaxy, or abstractions of such programming entities as system resources, databases, and graphical windows.

The most fundamental aspects of object-oriented programming are:

1. *Abstract data typing (encapsulation) and modularization:* Abstract data typing allows hiding of the internal representation of the datum (object unit) and implementation of internal operations (actions) and the user interface to the outside world. The users who access and manipulate the objects, do not see nor know the internal representation details, data structure, storage used to implement the objects of abstract data types and operations on them. The information-hiding is accomplished by two means:

    (a) Objects have private (hidden) abstract data structures, storage, and implementations of operations on them,
    (b) Objects have public interfaces, whose implementations are made private.

    The C++ class construct provides both facilities. Modularization allows generation and compilation of code as indepenedent units, and it provides better abstraction.

2. *Inheritance:* It is inheritance that distinguishes object-oriented programming from classical programming, and from programming languages such as Modula-2 and Ada. It allows sharing and reusing of data and code among modules and interface routines belonging to the same object class. Any member in the class or any subclass will inherit the privilege of sharing variables and interfaces and varying implementations. Inheritance is unique and the most powerful concept in object-oriented programming. Reiterating the power of inheritance, we must note:

    (a) Share interfaces, and vary implementations.
    (b) Share code using interfaces among different object classes.

    The C++ language provides a means of implementing inheritance via constructs: class, base, subclass, friend, etc.

3. *Object identity:* Object identity is a powerful concept in object-oriented programming. It is a characteristic unique to an object that distinguishes it from other objects. An identity of an object stays with it during its life time and during state transitions, independent of any data structure that is user-modifiable. For example, a person is identified by a black mole on the right cheek. An address-based identity in a programmimg language is implemented via pointers. For detailed discussion, see Parsaye *et al.* (1989).

4. *Dynamic binding:* Besides inheritance, dynamic binding characterizes object-oriented programming. The dynamic binding is implemented through virtual functions. For details, see Lippman (1989) and Stroustrup (1986).

In object-oriented programming, it is important to remember the following key points:

1. Everything is considered as an object.
2. There are no static variables.

3. There are no static functions.
4. There are some global objects.
5. The global variables are defined within a class construct.

An instance of a class is a state of an object. It is created by the constructor, which calls the "new" operator on the class. The instance is destroyed by the destructor, which calls the "delete" operator on the class.

Objects are used to solve problems. In the design and implementation of a program, a concrete representation of the ideas of the design is created. The structure of the program should reflect the ideas as directly as possible. Two key concepts aid in this cognitive process—class and object:

1. A class is an abstract data type. It specifies how objects of its type behave, are created and deleted, and are accessed.
2. An object is an instance of a class; it is used during program execution.

A class does nothing; it is used to build objects. Something that can be thought of as a separate idea is a class. Data concepts that are not easily represented as fundamental data types or functions without associated static data are good candidates for becoming a class. Something that is accessed is an object. The key to a good program is to create classes that each clearly represent a single concept. If questions about how the object of a class is created, used, and deleted have vague answers, then the class needs redefinition.

Assuming an initial library of classes, the following design steps are taken:

1. Decompose the problem into objects and their interactions. Move the elements of the problem around until the connections between functions (caller and called) and between data and operations (access) are the fewest and least complex. Natural divisions of elements become apparent.
2. Scan the library for reusable object definitions.
3. Where classes are lacking, design new ones. If two classes have significant elements in common, create a new base class.
4. Define the interactions between objects in the program.
5. Construct the program.
6. After the program is completed, install the new (and proven) classes in the library.

10.3 An Instance of Object-Oriented Programming

The C++ language is an instance of object-oriented programming. Refer to Stroustrup (1986) for a complete description. C++ contains the notions of class and object. We will use the stack data structure as an example.

A class is defined with two parts: a private section holding data and operations that can only be used internally, and a public section that holds the interface operations. In other words, the definition of a class consists of the following:

1. The name of the class
2. The internal representation of data structure and storage

3. The internal implementation of the interface
4. The external operations for accessing and manipulating the instances of the class

A class defines an ADT, and the elements belonging to the set of objects described by the class, are called "instances" of the class (see Figure 10-1).

```
//   Definition of the class stack
class stack {
    int * stk;
    int * top;
    int   size;
public:
    //   stack initialization
    stack(int sz)      { top = stk = new int[size=sz]; }
    //   stack destruction
    ~stack()           { delete stk; }
    void  push(int i)  { *top++ = i; }
    int   pop();       { return *-top; }
    int   top_of_stack();
};

int stack::top_of_stack()
{
    return *top;
};
```

Figure 10-1 Stack defined as a class.

```
//   Example of function using stack objects
int anyfunction()
{
    stack registers(1028);   // an object of class stack
    stack scratch(512);      // another object of class stack
    int   bio_status;
    int   iflag;

    //  ...

    register.push(bio_status);
    return iflag = scratch.pop();
};
```

Figure 10-2 Use of stack objects defined by class stack.

A push operation (Figure 10-2) to the object register is simply handled by a call to its push operation. A push to the object scratch can be done only through its interface routine, `scratch.push`. One must take care not to misuse the object (stack under/overflow); attempts to push the wrong type of data or to reference the stack with some rogue pointer will result in trapping and reports of error.

Although C++ retains some of the characteristics of C, and although early versions of C++ were a front-end translator of C++ code to standard C, C++ provides the means of organizing data structures in an elegant way suitable for object-oriented programming.

10.4 Application: A Singly Linked Circle Class

In this section, our goal is to construct a class for ADT circle objects and organize these circle objects in class of singly linked circle objects. We want to perform ADT operations on these circle objects, and provide the user interface to access and manipulate these circle objects.

The user interface is menu-driven and provides only one selection at a time, from the following choices:

Insert a circle object at front	. . .	i
Append a circle object at end	. . .	a
Delete a circle object	. . .	d
Count circle objects in the list	. . .	c
Print the list of circle objects	. . .	p
Exit	. . .	e

The display of this menu is done in the function `display_menu()`.

Once the selection (i, a, d, c, p, or e) is made by the user, it is processed by the function, `process_menu()`. The function, `user_interface()`, calls `display_menu()`, and then calls `process_menu()`. For example, to process the choice for add, `'a'`, it calls the function `get_input()` to get input for the coordinates of the center of the circle, *x* and *y,* and for the radius *r.* Then it calls the `Circle_List`-type member interface, `c.insert_obj()`, where the instance `'c'` is a global circle object belonging to the class `Circle_List`. The main test driver, `main()`, calls `user_interface()` continuously within a `while` loop.

Let us turn our attention to the internal representation of the circle objects class. In this application, we have intentionally defined two classes, `Circle_Obj` and `Circle_List`. This is to demonstrate the ways of establishing the communication protocol between the two different classes through the "public" interfaces (routines). This application can be alternatively done by combining the two classes into one.

Since the shape of a circle can be described by its center (*x, y*), and the radius *r,* and since we need one link to the next circle object, we define the `Circle_Obj` class as follows:

```
class  Circle_Obj
{
  private:
    COORD           _x;
    COORD           _y;
    RADIUS          _r;
    Circle_Obj * _next;

  public:
    Circle_Obj ( COORD x, COORD y, RADIUS r );

    COORD  x()            { return _x; }
    COORD  y()            { return _y; }
    RADIUS r()            { return _r; }
    Circle_Obj * next()   { return _next; }
```

```
                Circle_Obj * set_next( Circle_Obj * new_next )
                {
                    _next = new_next;
                    return _next;
                }
        }
```

In the class `Circle_Obj`, "`private:`" is used to protect the fields, `_x`, `_y`, `_r`, and `_next`, from corruption and unauthorized access. The interface to this class for all other classes are declared under "`public:`". `Circle_Obj ()` is the constructor function that dynamically allocates a circle object. In order to update the link to the next circle object, the public interface, `set_next ()`, will be necessary. This operation will be called (that is, shared) by the interface routines in the class `Circle_List`, which is different from the class `Circle_Obj`.

We now define the `Circle_List` class that contains the `Circle_Obj`'s as a singly linked list, and some operations that will be the interfaces to the outside world. Because the function `process_menu ()` needs to use the interface routines, and is not a member function of the class `Circle_List`, we declare the interface routines in the class `Circle_List`, as public. In order to serve the requirements of the user interface shown above as a menu, we define the `Circle_List` as follows:

```
class   Circle_List
{
    private:
        Circle_Obj *head_ptr;      // Pointer to first object
        Circle_Obj *tail_ptr;      // Pointer to last  object

    public:
        Circle_List();             // Constructor function
        ~Circle_List();            // Destructor function

        void init_list()     { head_ptr = 0;  }
        int  is_list_empty() { return head_ptr == 0;  }

        void insert_obj( COORD x,  COORD y,  COORD r );
        void append_obj( COORD x,  COORD y,  COORD r );
        void delete_obj( COORD x,  COORD y,  COORD r );
        Circle_Obj * search_obj( COORD x,  COORD y,  COORD r );
        Circle_Obj * search_previous( COORD x,  COORD y,  COORD r,
                                        Circle_Obj * list_ptr );
        Circle_Obj * get_obj( Circle_Obj * );
        void print_list();
        int  count_circle_objs(  );
};
```

The member fields, `head_ptr` and `tail_ptr`, are pointers to the first and last object in the class `Circle_Obj`, respectively. These are considered global variables to all the interface functions in the class `Circle_List`.

The operation, `Circle_List ()`, with the same name as the type `Circle`

_List, is called the *constructor*. It is automatically called when a class variable of type Circle_List is declared and allocated. For example,

$$\texttt{Circle\_List} \quad \texttt{c;}$$

implicitly calls the constructor function, Circle_List(). This dynamically allocates memory storage for Circle_Obj by calling the new operator:

$$\texttt{Circle\_Obj} \quad \texttt{*} \quad \texttt{head\_ptr;}$$

$$\texttt{new Circle\_Obj(0, 0, 0);}$$

Note that the analogous action in C is the use of the system calls malloc() or calloc().

The operation, ~Circle_List(), is the destructor function. It is called to destroy the entire singly linked list. It traverses the list using the next pointer, and deallocates the memory space by calling the delete operator.

$$\texttt{Circle\_Obj} \quad \texttt{*} \quad \texttt{tmp\_ptr;}$$

$$\texttt{delete tmp\_ptr;}$$

Implementations of the interface operations listed below follow the algorithms for an ADT singly linked list, described in Chapter 5. So we omit their detailed descriptions:

```
init_list(),   is_list_empty(),
insert_obj(),  append_obj(),          delete_obj(),
search_obj(),  search_previous(),  get_obj(),
print_list(),  count_circle_objs()
```

Init_list() initializes the list of the circle objects.

Is_list_empty() checks whether the list of the circle objects is empty.

Insert_obj() adds a new circle object to the front of the list.

Append_obj() adds a new circle object to the end of the list.

Delete_obj() deletes a specified circle object in the list.

Search_obj() searches for a specified circle object in the list.

Search_previous() searches for the previous circle object in the list.

Print_list() prints the entire list of objects for an instance of the class Circle_List.

Count_circle_objs() counts the number of objects for an instance of the class Circle_List.

Since the interfaces, insert_obj(), append_obj(), and delete_obj() are of class Circle_List, and also require to update the field, _next, of another class Circle_Obj, we must use the public interface function, set_next().

Warning: Without the interface, set_next() as public, any attempt to update _next, for example, in insert_obj(),

$$\texttt{new\_obj\_ptr->\_next = head\_ptr;}$$

caused the compilation error _next undefined. This is because it looks for the
member _next in the class Circle_List.
    The complete code and its output are given below.

Code Section

```
//  Program Name:  circle.c++
//  Purpose:       Define and implement the class Circle
//                 as a singly linked list.

//  Include the header files for standard input stream
//  (cin), standard output stream (cout), standard error
//  output stream (cerr), exit, and stream classes.

#include <stream.h>        // For Stream I/O Facilities
#include <stdlib.h>

//  Define types for coordinates and radius.

typedef   int   COORD;
typedef   int   RADIUS;

//  Now define the Circle_Obj class.

class  Circle_Obj
{
  private:
    COORD          _x;
    COORD          _y;
    RADIUS         _r;
    Circle_Obj  * _next;    // pointer to next object

  public:
    Circle_Obj ( COORD x, COORD y, RADIUS r );
                           // Constructor function

  //  Define the following functions as public in order to
  //  allow access of the components _x, _y, _r, & _next.

    COORD  x ()            { return  _x;  }
    COORD  y ()            { return  _y;  }
    RADIUS r ()            { return  _r;  }

    Circle_Obj * next ()   { return  _next;  }
    Circle_Obj * set_next ( Circle_Obj * new_next )
    {
      _next = new_next;
      return  _next;
    }

};

//  Now define the Circle_List class that contains
//  Circle_Obj's as a singly linked list, and
```

```
//   some necessary operations on these objects.
//   The functions for these operations will be
//   public.

class  Circle_List
{
  private:
     Circle_Obj *head_ptr;      // Pointer to first object
     Circle_Obj *tail_ptr;      // Pointer to last  object

  public:
     Circle_List();             // Constructor function
     ~Circle_List();            // Destructor function

     void init_list()      { head_ptr = 0;  }
     int  is_list_empty()  { return head_ptr == 0;  }

     void insert_obj( COORD x, COORD y, COORD r );
             //  Function to add at the head of list
     void append_obj( COORD x, COORD y, COORD r );
             //  Function to add at the tail of list
     void delete_obj( COORD x, COORD y, COORD r );
     Circle_Obj * search_obj( COORD x, COORD y, COORD r );
     Circle_Obj * search_previous( COORD x, COORD y, COORD r,
                                   Circle_Obj * list_ptr );
     Circle_Obj * get_obj( Circle_Obj * );
             //  Get and remove from head of the list.
     void print_list();
     int  count_circle_objs(  );
};

//  Declare a global Circle_List object.

Circle_List  c;

//  Implement the interface operations.

Circle_List::Circle_List()
{
   //  Allocate memory space for a new Circle_Obj object,
   //  whose _x = 0, _y = 0, _r = 0, & _next = 0.
   //  This constructor function is automatically
   //  called by the declaration of an object of the
   //  class Circle_List.

   new Circle_Obj( 0, 0, 0 );

}

//  Destroy the entire singly linked list of circle objects

Circle_List::~Circle_List()
{
   Circle_Obj  *tmp_ptr, *next_ptr;
```

```
      tmp_ptr = head_ptr;

      while ( tmp_ptr != 0 )
         {
           next_ptr = tmp_ptr->next();
           delete tmp_ptr;              //  free memory space
           tmp_ptr = next_ptr;
         }
      delete head_ptr;
}

//  Add the circle object to the front (head) of the list.

void  Circle_List::insert_obj( COORD x, COORD y, RADIUS r )
{
      int  head_ptr_state = 0;          //  State of head_ptr
      Circle_Obj * new_obj_ptr;

      new_obj_ptr = new Circle_Obj( x, y, r );
      if ( new_obj_ptr == 0 )
          return;

      else
         {
             //  Link the new object with the object currently
             //  at the head position of the list.
             //  That is, new_obj_ptr->_next = head_ptr
             //            head_ptr = new_obj_ptr;

             new_obj_ptr->set_next( head_ptr );

             if ( head_ptr == 0 )
                head_ptr_state = 1;

             //  The new object is now at the haed of the list
             head_ptr = new_obj_ptr;

             //  If this is the first time we are inserting
             //  a circle object, i.e., head_ptr = 0, set this
             //  new value of head_ptr to tail_ptr

             if ( head_ptr_state == 1 )
                 tail_ptr = head_ptr;
         }
}

//  Add the circle object to the end of the list.
//  The last object is pointed to by tail_ptr.

void  Circle_List::append_obj( COORD x, COORD y, RADIUS r )
{
      Circle_Obj * new_obj_ptr;
```

```
    new_obj_ptr = new Circle_Obj ( x, y, r );
    if ( new_obj_ptr == 0 )
        return;

    else
      {
          // Is the list empty?
          if ( is_list_empty() )
            {
                head_ptr = new_obj_ptr;
                tail_ptr = new_obj_ptr;
            }
          else
            {
                // Link the object after the object currently
                // at the last position of the list, i.e.,
                //    tail_ptr->next() = new_obj_ptr;
                //    tail_ptr = new_obj_ptr;

                tail_ptr->set_next ( new_obj_ptr );
                tail_ptr = new_obj_ptr;
            }
      }
}

// Search for a circle object, specified by (x, y),
// and r, in the list pointed to by head_ptr.

Circle_Obj * Circle_List::search_obj ( COORD x, COORD y,
                                       RADIUS r )
{
    Circle_Obj * search_ptr;    // search pointer

    search_ptr = head_ptr;

    while ( search_ptr != 0 )
      {
          if ( search_ptr->x() == x  &&
               search_ptr->y() == y  &&
               search_ptr->r() == r  )
               return ( search_ptr );

          search_ptr = search_ptr->next();
      }
    // Specified circle object is not found
    return ( 0 );
}

// Search for the previous to a circle object, specified
// by (x, y), and r, in the list pointed to by head_ptr.

Circle_Obj * Circle_List::search_previous ( COORD x, COORD y,
                                            RADIUS r,
                                            Circle_Obj * list_ptr )

{
```

```
   while ( list_ptr != 0 )
     {
       if ( list_ptr->next()->x() == x  &&
            list_ptr->next()->y() == y  &&
            list_ptr->next()->r() == r  )
            return( list_ptr );

       list_ptr = list_ptr->next();
     }
   //  Specified circle object is not found
   return( 0 );
}


//  Delete a circle object, specified by (x, y),
//  and r, from the list pointed to by head_ptr.

void  Circle_List::delete_obj( COORD x, COORD y, RADIUS r )
{
   Circle_Obj * search_ptr,    // search pointer
              * prev_obj_ptr;

   //  Check to see if the object to be deleted
   //  is the first one in the list.

   if ( ( head_ptr != 0 ) &&
        ( head_ptr->x() == x   &&
          head_ptr->y() == y   &&
          head_ptr->r() == r ) )
     {
        search_ptr = head_ptr;
        head_ptr = head_ptr->next();

        //  Free up the memory space
        delete search_ptr;
        return;
     }

   // Search for the circle object to be deleted
   search_ptr = search_obj( x, y, r );
   if ( search_ptr == 0 )
     {
       cerr << "\n Circle object to be deleted is not found \n";
       return;
     }

   //  Search for the previous object of the object to
   //  be deleted.

   prev_obj_ptr = search_previous( x, y, r, head_ptr );

   //  Drop the link
   prev_obj_ptr->set_next( search_ptr->next() );

   delete  search_ptr;          // free memory space
}
```

```
//  Get an object from the front of the list, and then
//  remove it from the list, pointed to by head_ptr.
//  Return a pointer to the object. Remember to delete
//  it after its use in the calling function.

Circle_Obj * Circle_List::get_obj ( Circle_Obj * head_ptr )
{
   Circle_Obj * tmp_ptr;

   //  Check whether the list is empty
   if ( is_list_empty () )
       return ( 0 );
   else
     {
        tmp_ptr = head_ptr;
        head_ptr = head_ptr->next ();
        return ( tmp_ptr );
     }
}

//  Print the center and radius of each circle object
//  in the list.

void  Circle_List::print_list ()
{
   Circle_Obj * tmp_ptr;

   tmp_ptr = head_ptr;

   if ( tmp_ptr == 0 )
      cout << "\n   The list of circle objects is empty! \n";
   else
     {
       cout << "\n   Centers and radii of Circles are: \n\n";
       while ( tmp_ptr != 0 )
          {
            cout << "   x = " << tmp_ptr->x ()  << ", y = "
                 << tmp_ptr->y ()  << ", r = "
                 << tmp_ptr->r () << "\n";
            tmp_ptr = tmp_ptr->next ();
          }
     }
}

//  Count circle objects in the list (Iterative implementation).

int Circle_List::count_circle_objs ()
{
   int   count = 0;
   Circle_Obj * tmp_ptr;

   tmp_ptr = head_ptr;
   for  ( ; tmp_ptr != 0; tmp_ptr = tmp_ptr->next (),
                            ++ count )
       ;
```

```
        return( count );
}

Circle_Obj::Circle_Obj( COORD x, COORD y, RADIUS r )
{
    _x   =  x;
    _y   =  y;
    _r   =  r;
    _next  =  0;
}


//  Get an integer from standard input.
//  If the input is not an intger, print
//  an error message, and exit.

int  get_input()
{
    int  i;

    if  ( !(cin >> i ) )
      {
          cerr << "\n   get_input(): Input is not an integer \n";
          exit( 1 );
      }
    return ( i );
}


//  display_menu():  Display menu for the menu-driven user
//                   interface

void display_menu()
{
    cout << "\n\n Test Program for Singly Linked Circle Class";
    cout << "\n\n   Insert a Circle Object at Front   ...  i ";
    cout << "\n   Append a Circle Object at End      ...  a ";
    cout << "\n   Delete a Circle Object             ...  d ";
    cout << "\n   Count Circle Objects in the list  ...  c ";
    cout << "\n   Print the list of Circle Objects  ...  p ";
    cout << "\n   Exit                               ...  e ";
    cout << "\n\n   Enter choice: ";
}


//  process_choice():  Process user's choice (i, a, d, c, p, or e)

void process_choice()
{
    COORD       x, y;
    RADIUS      r;
    char        ch;

    cin >> ch;
    switch ( ch )
    {
      case 'I':
      case 'i':
```

```
                          cout << "\n    Input x-coord of center:  ";
                          x = get_input();
                          cout << "    Input y-coord of center:  ";
                          y = get_input();
                          cout << "    Input radius:  ";
                          r = get_input();
                          c.insert_obj( x, y, r );
                          break;
            case 'A':
            case 'a':
                          cout << "\n    Input x-coord of center:  ";
                          x = get_input();
                          cout << "    Input y-coord of center:  ";
                          y = get_input();
                          cout << "    Input radius:  ";
                          r = get_input();
                          c.append_obj( x, y, r );
                          break;
            case 'D':
            case 'd':
                          cout << "\n    Input x-coord of center:  ";
                          x = get_input();
                          cout << "    Input y-coord of center:  ";
                          y = get_input();
                          cout << "    Input radius:  ";
                          r = get_input();
                          c.delete_obj( x, y, r );
                          break;
            case 'C':
            case 'c':
                          cout << "\n    Number of Circle objects is:  "
                               << c.count_circle_objs();
                          break;
            case 'P':
            case 'p':
                          c.print_list ();
                          break;
            case 'E':
            case 'e':  exit( 0 );

            case ' ':
            case '\n':
            case '\t':
                          //   Ignore blank space, new line, and tab
                          break;
            default:  cout << "\n    Unknown choice !!! \n";
                          break;
      }
}

//   user_interface(): User interface
```

```
void user_interface()
{
        display_menu();
        process_choice();
}

// main():  Main test driver for singly linked Circle class

void main()
{
    int FOREVER = 1;

    while ( FOREVER )
    {
        user_interface();
    }
}
```

Output Section

```
        Test Program for Singly Linked Circle Class

            Insert a Circle Object at Front    ...  i
            Append a Circle Object at End      ...  a
            Delete a Circle Object             ...  d
            Count Circle Objects in the list   ...  c
            Print the list of Circle Objects   ...  p
            Exit                               ...  e

        Enter choice: p

        The list of circle objects is empty!

        Test Program for Singly Linked Circle Class

            Insert a Circle Object at Front    ...  i
            Append a Circle Object at End      ...  a
            Delete a Circle Object             ...  d
            Count Circle Objects in the list   ...  c
            Print the list of Circle Objects   ...  p
            Exit                               ...  e

        Enter choice: c

        Number of Circle objects is: 0

        Test Program for Singly Linked Circle Class

            Insert a Circle Object at Front    ...  i
            Append a Circle Object at End      ...  a
            Delete a Circle Object             ...  d
            Count Circle Objects in the list   ...  c
            Print the list of Circle Objects   ...  p
            Exit                               ...  e
```

```
Enter choice: i

Input x-coord of center: 1
Input y-coord of center: 2
Input radius: 3

Test Program for Singly Linked Circle Class

    Insert a Circle Object at Front    ...   i
    Append a Circle Object at End      ...   a
    Delete a Circle Object             ...   d
    Count Circle Objects in the list   ...   c
    Print the list of Circle Objects   ...   p
    Exit                               ...   e

    Enter choice: p

    Centers and radii of Circles are:

    x = 1, y = 2, r = 3

Test Program for Singly Linked Circle Class

    Insert a Circle Object at Front    ...   i
    Append a Circle Object at End      ...   a
    Delete a Circle Object             ...   d
    Count Circle Objects in the list   ...   c
    Print the list of Circle Objects   ...   p
    Exit                               ...   e

    Enter choice: a

Input x-coord of center: 5
Input y-coord of center: 6
Input radius: 8

Test Program for Singly Linked Circle Class

    Insert a Circle Object at Front    ...   i
    Append a Circle Object at End      ...   a
    Delete a Circle Object             ...   d
    Count Circle Objects in the list   ...   c
    Print the list of Circle Objects   ...   p
    Exit                               ...   e

    Enter choice: p

    Centers and radii of Circles are:

    x = 1, y = 2, r = 3
    x = 5, y = 6, r = 8
```

```
Test Program for Singly Linked Circle Class

    Insert a Circle Object at Front    ...   i
    Append a Circle Object at End      ...   a
    Delete a Circle Object             ...   d
    Count Circle Objects in the list   ...   c
    Print the list of Circle Objects   ...   p
    Exit                               ...   e


    Enter choice: c

    Number of Circle objects is: 2

Test Program for Singly Linked Circle Class

    Insert a Circle Object at Front    ...   i
    Append a Circle Object at End      ...   a
    Delete a Circle Object             ...   d
    Count Circle Objects in the list   ...   c
    Print the list of Circle Objects   ...   p
    Exit                               ...   e


    Enter choice: i

    Input x-coord of center: 3
    Input y-coord of center: 6
    Input radius: 9

Test Program for Singly Linked Circle Class

    Insert a Circle Object at Front    ...   i
    Append a Circle Object at End      ...   a
    Delete a Circle Object             ...   d
    Count Circle Objects in the list   ...   c
    Print the list of Circle Objects   ...   p
    Exit                               ...   e


    Enter choice: p

    Centers and radii of Circles are:

    x = 3, y = 6, r = 9
    x = 1, y = 2, r = 3
    x = 5, y = 6, r = 8

Test Program for Singly Linked Circle Class

    Insert a Circle Object at Front    ...   i
    Append a Circle Object at End      ...   a
    Delete a Circle Object             ...   d
    Count Circle Objects in the list   ...   c
    Print the list of Circle Objects   ...   p
    Exit                               ...   e
```

```
Enter choice: c

Number of Circle objects is: 3

Test Program for Singly Linked Circle Class

    Insert a Circle Object at Front    ...   i
    Append a Circle Object at End      ...   a
    Delete a Circle Object             ...   d
    Count Circle Objects in the list   ...   c
    Print the list of Circle Objects   ...   p
    Exit                               ...   e

    Enter choice: d

    Input x-coord of center: 1
    Input y-coord of center: 2
    Input radius: 3

Test Program for Singly Linked Circle Class

    Insert a Circle Object at Front    ...   i
    Append a Circle Object at End      ...   a
    Delete a Circle Object             ...   d
    Count Circle Objects in the list   ...   c
    Print the list of Circle Objects   ...   p
    Exit                               ...   e

    Enter choice: p

    Centers and radii of Circles are:

    x = 3, y = 6, r = 9
    x = 5, y = 6, r = 8

Test Program for Singly Linked Circle Class

    Insert a Circle Object at Front    ...   i
    Append a Circle Object at End      ...   a
    Delete a Circle Object             ...   d
    Count Circle Objects in the list   ...   c
    Print the list of Circle Objects   ...   p
    Exit                               ...   e

    Enter choice: c

Number of Circle objects is: 2

Test Program for Singly Linked Circle Class

    Insert a Circle Object at Front    ...   i
    Append a Circle Object at End      ...   a
    Delete a Circle Object             ...   d
```

```
Count Circle Objects in the list  ...  c
Print the list of Circle Objects  ...  p
Exit                              ...  e

Enter choice: e
```

Exercises

10-1 Define and implement the class Matrix. The elements of the matrix are integers, and the operations are addition, multiplication, transpose, printing, etc. See Example 2.4 on the ADT matrix for the public interface functions.

10-2 Define and implement the class String together with the operations for parsing, appending, finding the length, and numerically comparing, etc. See Example 3.16 on the ADT strings for the public interface functions of a String class object.

10-3 Define and implement the class Complex. The real and imaginary parts of the object, complex, are are double, and the operations are addition, subtraction, negation, multiplication, division, printing, etc. See Example 15.1 on the ADT complex for the public interface functions.

10-4 Define and implement the class Singly Linked List. The objects are of type char. See Example 5.5 on the ADT singly linked list for the public interface functions.

10-5 Define and implement the class Triangle as a singly linked list.

10-6 Define and implement the class Rectangle as a singly linked list.

10-7 Write a function to draw the shape of a rectangular object. You need to redefine the class Rectangle as done in Exercise 10-6.

10-8 Define and implement the class Hexagon as a singly linked list.

10-9 Define and implement the class Polygon as a singly linked list.

10-10 Define and implement the class Polynomial as a singly linked list.

10-11 Define and implement the class Doubly Linked List. The objects are of type char. See Example 5.6 on the ADT doubly linked list for the public interface functions.

10-12 Define and implement the class Triangle as a doubly linked list.

10-13 Define and implement the class Rectangle as a doubly linked list.

10-14 Write a function to draw the shape of a rectangle object. You need to redefine the class Rectangle as done in Exercise 10-13.

10-15 Define and implement the class Circle as a doubly linked list.

10-16 Define and implement the class Hexagon as a doubly linked list.

10-17 Define and implement the class Polygon as a doubly linked list.

10-18 Define and implement the class Polynomial as a doubly linked list.

10-19 Define and implement the class Circular Singly Linked List. The objects are of type char. You must include the public interface functions.

10-20 Define and implement the class Triangle as a circular singly linked list. You must include the public interface functions.

10-21 Define and implement the class Rectangle as a circular singly linked list.

10-22 Write a function to draw the shape of a rectangle object. You need to redefine the class Rectangle as done in Exercise 10-21.

10-23 Define and implement the class Circle as a circular singly linked list.

10-24 Define and implement the class Hexagon as a circular singly linked list.

10-25 Define and implement the class Polygon as a circular singly linked list.

10-26 Define and implement the class Polynomial as a circular singly linked list.

10-27 Define and implement the class Circular Doubly Linked List. The objects are of type char. You must include the public interface functions.

10-28 Define and implement the class Triangle as a circular doubly linked list. You must include the public interface functions.

10-29 Define and implement the class Rectangle as a circular doubly linked list.

10-30 Write a function to draw the shape of a rectangle object. You need to redefine the class Rectangle as done in Exercise 10-29.

10-31 Define and implement the class Circle as a circular doubly linked list.

10-32 Define and implement the class Hexagon as a circular doubly linked list.

10-33 Define and implement the class Polygon as a circular doubly linked list.

10-34 Define and implement the class Polynomial as a circular doubly linked list.

10-35 Define and implement the class Sparse Matrix as a circular doubly linked list. See Exercises 5-3 and 5-4.

10-36 Implement the class Stack as a singly linked list. You must include the public interface operations. See Section 10.3.

10-37 (a) Define a class RPN expression for storing, converting from infix to RPN form, evaluating the RPN, and printing the infix and RPN. The RPN expression contains integers as operands and the operators +, -, *, %, and /.

   (b) Implement and test the operations using stacks. See Section 6.3 on the RPN.

10-38 (a) Define a class Queue of characters together with constructors, destructors, and other public interface operations that are independent of representation. Refer to the ADT queue in Section 6.4.

   (b) Implement the class Queue as an array. Refer to Example 6.3 on an array implementation of ADT queues.

10-39 Define and implement the class Queue as a singly linked list. Refer to Example 6.4 on the singly linked implementation of the ADT queues.

10-40 Define and implement the class Queue as a doubly linked list.

10-41 (a) Define a class Circular Queue of characters together with the necessary public operations.

   (b) Implement the class Circular Queue as an array. See Example 6.5 on an array implementation of the ADT circular queues.

10-42 Define and implement the class Circular Queue as a singly linked list.

10-43 Define and implement the class Circular Queue as a doubly linked list.

10-44 Define and implement the class Binary Tree as a linked list. See Example 7-1 on the ADT binary tree for the public interface functions.

10-45 Define and implement the class Binary Expression Tree as a linked list. The expression is in the infix form allowing the binary operators +, -, *, and /. The binary expression tree has operators as the root nodes of subtrees and operands as the leaf nodes. The member functions of the class must include evaluating, printing, etc. See Example 7.6 on the binary expression tree for the public interface functions.

10-46 Define and implement the class Binary Search Tree as a linked list. See Example 7-2 on the ADT binary search tree for the public interface functions.

10-47 Define and implement the class AVL Tree as a linked list. See Example 7-3 on the ADT AVL tree for the public interface functions.

10-48 Define and implement the class B-Tree.

10-49 Define and implement the class Maze. Refer to the description of the Maze problem in Section 4.5.

10-50 Design the class Spreadsheet that is organized as a stack. Must specify the operations. The implementation of the operations is not required.

10-51 Write a program to implement the bank customer class as in the database described in Exercise 10-13. Redo Exercise 10-13 using the object-oriented programming approach.

10-52 *Programming project:* A computer company likes to maintain records of its employess by the following (derived) classes:

```
President, Vice_President, Director, Manager,
Technical_staff, NonTechnical_staff, Others.
```

Each record in the base class, Employee, contains the following information:

```
Name,  Social Security Number,
Address (Street, City, Zip),
Date of birth, Marital Status, Date of Hire,
Job Title, Highest Degree, Current Annual Salary,
Employee Number, Department Number, etc.
```

The class Manager contains the Employee data as a member, and a pointer to a group of Employee class objects.

Design and implement an employee database class, Empl_db, as a binary search tree. The search will be performed by the key, and Social Security number. The public member functions of the class empl_db, include inserting, finding and displaying, updating, deleting, and error-handling. (*Hint:* Use the concept of derived classes.)

Applications for Simple Database Programming Using B-Trees

In this chapter we discuss and develop a small and efficient database application. This presentation will show the uses of many of the data structure concepts we learned in the previous chapters: structure, array, pointers, files, B-trees, dynamic memory allocation, relocatable loading, search, and block I/O using `fread()` and `fwrite()`.

A database is an organized collection of groups of related data (usually called *records*). The data can be collectively implemented as a structure. The most common operations on a database are:

1. Enter a record
2. Update a record
3. Retrieve a record
4. Delete a record
5. Search or select a record
6. Display a record
7. Sort records by a special key
8. Print a record
9. Store a record/database in a database on disk
10. Load a database from disk into memory

In Chapter 5, we presented the Parts Inventory Control System using doubly linked lists, and noted the deficiencies of this implementation. As pointed out by Comer (1979), "B-trees have become, de facto, a standard for file organization." We will design and develop a Parts Inventory Control database using B-trees. For the B-tree structured parts database, the search, insert, delete, retrieve, and update operations will be efficient.

11.1 Schema of Parts Inventory Control System

Here is the specification of our database application program:

Write a database application for a Parts Inventory Control System for Eutopia Computers, Inc. The schema for each part's record will contain the following fields:

Field name	Field length
part_name	15 chars long
part_rev_level	4 chars long
part_vendor_name	11 chars long
part_vendor_phone	12 chars long
part_description	20 chars
part_quantity	Integer
part_unit_price	Decimal number (e.g., 4.95)
part_number	long

The search key is the part number.

The user interface of the application will be menu-driven, permitting the following operations:

```
Parts Inventory Control Database Program
Enter Choice or ESC to Quit!
A. Add a Part to Database
E. Erase a Part from Database
M. Modify a Part in Database
D. Display a Part in Database
S. Save Database to Disk
R. Read Database from Disk
P. Print Part Numbers in Database
```

11.2 Database Implementation Approach Using B-Trees

As the information fields for each part together, with the search key, key, can be collectively viewed as a record (henceforth, we will refer to each part record as "element"), we can define the fields as components in the following structure:

```
typedef   long            KEY_TYPE;

struct element_def
   {
   KEY_TYPE               key;                /* Part number */
   char                   part_name[ 15 ],
                          part_rev_level[ 4 ],
                          part_vendor_name[ 11 ],
                          part_vendor_phone[ 12 ],
                          part_description[ 60 ];
```

```
    long                        part_quantity;
    float                       part_unit_price;
};
```

```
/* ELEMENT as Part record Variable in the database */
```

```
typedef struct element_def     ELEMENT;
```

A unique key, the part number, is assigned to each part record of type ELEMENT. "Key" will be used to insert into, delete, retrieve from, and search for all parts in the parts database file, PartTree.dat, a collection of part records.

As discussed in Chapter 7, a typical node in a B-tree of order N contains $2N$ search-key values and $2N + 1$ pointers, and is of the form

```
+----+-------+----+-------+----+-----+-----+--------+--------+
| P₁ | Key 1 | P₂ | Key 2 | P₃ | ... | P₂ₙ | Key 2N | P₂ₙ₊₁  |
+----+-------+----+-------+----+-----+-----+--------+--------+
```

For $1 \leq i \leq 2N$, the pointer P_i points to the subtree for records with search-key values less than the key i, and the pointer P_{2N+1} points to the subtree for records with search-key values greater than the key $2N$.

We model the parts database as a B-tree of order 2 with part number as the search key, and will call it "BTree." For the part records with the part numbers 50, 100, 25, 75, and 125, the structure of the parts tree, BTree, as a B-tree is as shown in Figure 11-1.

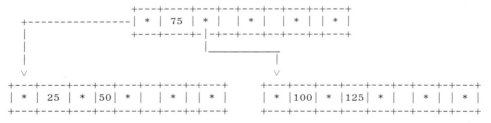

Figure 11-1 Parts B-tree of order 2.

In Figure 11-1, the star (*) indicates the place for pointers, and its adjacent (vacant) place indicates the holding area for the search key. For this parts B-tree of order 2 containing 5 search keys, the height is $\log_2 5$, which is approximately 2.

The BTree is a parts tree structure containing nodes of data (part record) placed such that a search for any key item requires a single path from the root node to the search node, similar to a BST, but with the additional property that a BTree always remains perfectly balanced. Each BTree node contains an array of ordered elements. Size of the array is determined by the chosen order of the BTree. Each node, other than the root, must contain at least an order number of elements and no more than twice the order number of elements. For example, if the order is chosen as 2, then each node must contain at least 2 elements but must contain no more than 4 elements. The root node is defined to contain between one element and twice the order number of elements. Each node has a second array containing pointers to its children. The number of children pointers required is one more than the current number of elements in the node for a maximum of twice the order plus one. A child exists for keys less than the smallest key in the node, a child exists for keys greater than the largest key in the node, and children exist for keys that fall between the remaining keys in the node. For example, if there are 4 elements, 5 pointers to children will be required.

A node of the parts tree, BTree, is defined as follows:

```
struct    BTree_node
{
  struct BTree_node    * parent;
  int                    no_of_elements;
  ELEMENT                elements[MAX_NODE];
  struct BTree_node    * children[MAX_NODE+1];
};

typedef   struct BTree_node        BTREE_NODE;

typedef   BTREE_NODE          *    BTREE_PTR;
```

Each node of type BTREE_NODE has a pointer to its parent, a count of the number of elements currently in the node, an array to contain elements (part records) of type ELEMENT up to twice the defined order, and an array to contain pointers to children of the node up to twice the defined order plus one additional. The pointer of type BTREE_PTR to the parent of a node is used for backtracking. MAX_NODE is two times the order, ORDER, of the BTree.

To maintain balance, new elements are always inserted at a leaf node of the BTree at the appropriate node. If a node does not exist, a new root node is created. If adding an element to a node causes an overflow in the node, the node is split into two independent nodes, each containing an order number of elements with the middle or separating element being passed up to the parent node with pointers to each of the split nodes. If inserting the middle node into the parent node causes an overflow, the process continues until no more overflows occur or a new root node is created.

Elements to be deleted, to maintain balance, are always removed from the leaf of a BTree. If an element to be deleted is in a nonleaf node, the element is replaced by its successor in an inorder traversal, or the smallest element in the leftmost node of the node's right subtree. The replaced element is then deleted from the leaf node. If deleting an element causes an underflow in a node, an element is borrowed from a left or right neighbor if available, otherwise the node is combined with its left or right neighbor along with the element separating the two nodes in the parent node. If taking an element from the parent nodes causes an underflow, the process continues until no more underflows occur or the root node is reached. If the root node contains less than one element, its right child becomes the new root node.

Description of Parts B-Tree Functions

Create_node() allocates memory for a new node in a BTree. The function calls malloc() to obtain a pointer to allocate memory for a new node. If NULL is returned by malloc(), the function prints an error message to the screen and the program is terminated. The function initializes the new node's parent pointer to NULL and sets the node's number of elements equal to zero. A pointer to the new node is returned to the calling function.

Search_btree() finds an element in a BTree given the element's search key. A pointer to the root of the tree, the search key of the element to find, the address of a location to receive a pointer to a located node, and the address of a location to receive an index of the element within the node are passed to the function. The BTree is searched iteratively, starting with the root node. If the root node is not empty, the node is searched starting with index zero and continuing until the search key is no greater than the current element in the node's element array or the index is equal to the number of elements. If the search key is equal to the current element, a pointer to the node and the current index is stored in the requested addresses and control is returned to the calling function. Otherwise, the root pointer is set equal to the child pointer stored in the node's child pointer array at the current index and the iterative loop is repeated.

Find_index() finds the index in a node's element array to insert a new element. A pointer to the node to search and the search key of the new element are passed to the function. The function uses an iterative loop, starting at zero and continuing until the node's number of elements is reached. When the loop finds the index where the search key is less than the current element, the function returns an integer containing the found index in which the new element should be inserted within the requested node.

Split_elements() inserts a new element into a full node by splitting the node in half and inserting the new element into the appropriate half. The pointer to the existing node location, the pointer to the new node location, the new element to insert, the new element's left child, and the insertion index of the new element are passed to the function. The function first builds the new or left node using elements and children from the existing node or using the new element along with its left child as required. If the children of the existing node are not equal to NULL, the children's parent pointers are updated to point to the new node. The function then builds the middle element from an element in the existing node or from the new element as required. The function finally rebuilds the existing or right node using the remaining elements and children from the existing node or using the new element along with its left child as required. If the children of the existing node are not equal to NULL, the children's parent pointers are updated to point to the existing node. The midelement is returned to the calling function.

Insert_element() inserts a new element into a BTree. The address of the root node, the pointer to the node location where the new element is to be inserted, the new element to insert, the left child of the new element, and the right child of the new element are passed to the function. If the requested node does not exist, a new root node is created by calling create_node(), the new element is inserted as the only element in the node, the root node of the BTree is updated, and control is returned to the calling function. Otherwise, the index of the appropriate place to insert the new element within the node is found by calling find_index(). If the number of elements in the node is less than MAX, the element is inserted into the node at the found index. Otherwise, a new node is created by calling create_node(), the new node is initialized, and the existing node is split with the new node by calling split_elements(). The returned middle element is inserted into the node's parent by recursively calling insert_element().

`Insert_btree()` adds a new element to a `BTree`. The address of the root pointer and the new element to add are passed to the function. If the element already exists in the `BTree`, found by calling `search_btree()`, control is returned to the calling function. The leaf node where the new element is to be inserted is found iteratively and `insert_element` is called once the appropriate leaf node is located.

`Combine_nodes()` is used to combine two nodes into one. The pointer to the left node, the pointer to the right node, the pointer to the parent node, and the index of the element within the parent node separating left and right nodes are passed to the function. A new node is created by calling `create_node()`. The function copies elements and children from the left node to the new node, then copies the separating element from the parent node to the new node, and finally copies elements and children from the right node to the new node. If the children of the new node are not equal to NULL, the children's parent pointers are updated to point to the new node. The parent pointer of the new node is set to the parent pointer of the left and right nodes, and the parent pointer's right child is set to point to new node. Memory containing left and right nodes is returned to the system.

`Delete_element()` deletes an element from a node. The address of the root pointer, the pointer to the node from which the element is to be deleted, and the index of the element to delete are passed to the function. The function deletes the requested element and the corresponding child pointer by shifting the arrays left the appropriate number of times. If the node is the root pointer, it is set equal to its right child pointer if all of the elements have been deleted. If the node still has a sufficient number of elements, control is returned to the calling function. If there are not enough elements, the function tries to borrow an element from the node's left or right neighbor. If the left neighbor has extra elements, the last element in the left neighbor's array is borrowed and inserted as the first element in the node. If the right neighbor has extra elements, the first element in the right neighbor's array is borrowed and inserted as the last element in the node. If no elements can be borrowed, the node is combined with its right or left neighbor by calling `combine_nodes` and the element separating the combined nodes is deleted by recursively calling `delete_element()`.

`Replace_element()` is used to replace an element by the smallest element in the leftmost node of the element's right subtree. The address of the node in which the element is to be replaced and the address of the element's index are passed to the function. The function finds the smallest element in the leftmost node of the element's right subtree, and overwrites the current element with the found element. The function then sets the address of the node pointer to node in which the smallest element was found and sets the address of the element's index to the smallest element.

`Delete_btree()` is used to delete an element from a `BTree`. The address of the root pointer and the key of the element to be deleted are passed to the function. If the element is not found by calling `search_btree()`, control is returned to the calling function. If the element to be deleted is not in a leaf node, it is replaced by the smallest element in the leftmost node of the element's right subtree by calling `replace_element()`. The element is then deleted from the leaf node by calling `delete_element()`.

The implementations of the above functions are presented in Example 11.1.

11.3 Implementation Restrictions and Issues

In the above implementation of the Parts Inventory Application System, we will use the following limitations:

1. Names are defined as an array of characters. Storage can be saved if pointers are used instead.
2. There is no checking for the following situations when a user tries to load the database from disk into memory more than once or tries to save data from memory buffer into the database file on disk.

The C-language implementation of the parts database as a B-tree is given below. The disk copy of the database file name is "PartTree.dat." The file is opened to read its records in a block-by-block manner, and the part records are placed into the database manager's memory buffer by the read_part_btree() routine. The newly created and updated part records are written into the parts database disk file "PartTree.dat" using fwrite() by the function, save_part_btree().

We provide an output of this program in the output section.

Example 11.1

Code Section

```
/* ************************************************************ *
 *              PARTS  INVENTORY  CONTROL  DATABASE  PROGRAM    *
 *                                                             *
 *   Program Name:   parts_db.c    (Using B-Trees)            *
 *                                                             *
 *   Compiled using Borland's Turbo C Version 2.0             *
 *                                                             *
 * ************************************************************ */

#include <stdio.h>
#include <stdlib.h>
#include <math.h>
#include <conio.h>          /*  For clrscr() call  */

#define   MALLOC(x)   ( (x *) malloc( sizeof(x) ) )
#define   FOREVER   1
#define   YES   1
#define   NO   0
#define   BELL   "\007"    /*  ascii code for tone  */
#define   ESC   27    /*  ascii code for ESC key  */
#define   ORDER   2
#define   MAX_NODE   2 * ORDER

typedef long   KEY_TYPE;

struct element_def
{
  KEY_TYPE   key;                      /*  part number  */
  char       part_name[15],
```

```
                part_rev_level[4],
                part_vendor_name[11],
                part_vendor_phone[12],
                part_description[60];
  long        part_quantity;
  float       part_unit_price;
};

typedef struct element_def    ELEMENT;

struct    BTree_node
{
  struct BTree_node    *parent;    /*  Used for back-tracking  */
  int                  no_of_elements;
  ELEMENT              elements[MAX_NODE];
  struct BTree_node    *children[MAX_NODE+1];
};

typedef struct BTree_node     BTREE_NODE;
typedef BTREE_NODE            *BTREE_PTR;

/*
 *   create_node():
 *      Function to allocate memory space for a BTree node,
 *      initialize the node, and return a pointer to the
 *      node.  If no memory space is available, an error
 *      message is printed and the program is exited.
 */

BTREE_PTR    create_node ()
{
  BTREE_PTR    new_node_ptr;

  /*
   *   request memory for new node - exit if no memory
   *   is available.
   */
  if ( ( new_node_ptr = MALLOC ( BTREE_NODE ) ) == NULL )
  {
    printf ("\n\nError:  No Memory Available!\n\n");
    exit ( 1 );
  }
  else   /*  initialize the node and return pointer  */
  {
    new_node_ptr->parent = NULL;
    new_node_ptr->no_of_elements = 0;
    return ( new_node_ptr );
  }
}

/*
 *   search_btree():
 *      Function to search for an element in a BTree.
```

```
 *      Root pointer, key of search element, address of
 *      location to receive pointer to located node, and
 *      address of location to receive index of located
 *      node are passed to the function.  If node is not found,
 *      node pointer and index are set to NULL.
 */

void    search_btree ( BTREE_PTR    root_ptr, KEY_TYPE    search_key,
                       BTREE_PTR    *node_ptr, int    *index )
{
  int    i, size;

  while ( root_ptr != NULL )
  {
    size = root_ptr->no_of_elements;
    i = 0;
    while ( i < size && search_key > root_ptr->elements[i].key )
      ++i;

    if ( search_key == root_ptr->elements[i].key && i < size )
    {
      *node_ptr = root_ptr;
      *index = i;
      return;
    }

    root_ptr = root_ptr->children[i];
  }

  *node_ptr = NULL;
  *index = 0;
}

/*
 *  find_index ():
 *     Function to find index in a node's element array
 *     to insert a new element.  Node pointer to insert
 *     and search key of new element are passed to the function.
 *     Function returns an integer index to calling function.
 */

int    find_index ( BTREE_PTR    node_ptr, KEY_TYPE    search_key )
{
  int    i, size = node_ptr->no_of_elements;

  for ( i = 0; i < size; i++ )
    if ( search_key < node_ptr->elements[i].key )
      return ( i );

  return ( size );
}

/*
 *  split_elements ():
```

```
 *     Function to insert a new element into a full node.
 *     Function splits full node's element array and children
 *     array in half, inserts new element into the proper half,
 *     and returns the middle element value to calling function.
 *     Pointer to existing node location, pointer to new node
 *     location, the new element to insert, the new element's
 *     left child, and insertion index of new element are passed
 *     to function.
 */

ELEMENT    split_elements ( BTREE_PTR    location_ptr,
                            BTREE_PTR    new_location_ptr,
                            ELEMENT      new_element,
                            BTREE_PTR    left_child, int index )
{
   int        i = 0, j = 0, mid_element_inserted = NO;
   ELEMENT    mid_element;

   /*
    * build new/left node and insert new element
    * if appropriate
    */
   while ( i < ORDER )
   {
     if ( mid_element_inserted == NO && j == index )
     {
       new_location_ptr->elements[i] = new_element;
       new_location_ptr->children[i] = left_child;
       ++i;
       mid_element_inserted = YES;
     }
     else
     {
       new_location_ptr->elements[i] = location_ptr->elements[j];
       new_location_ptr->children[i] = location_ptr->children[j];
       ++i;
       ++j;
     }
   }

   /*
    * establish mid element and use new element
    * if appropriate
    */
   if ( mid_element_inserted == NO && j == index )
   {
     mid_element = new_element;
     new_location_ptr->children[i] = left_child;
     mid_element_inserted = YES;
   }
   else
   {
     mid_element = location_ptr->elements[j];
```

```
      new_location_ptr->children[i] = location_ptr->children[j];
      ++j;
    }

  /*  update parent pointers in children if required  */
  if ( new_location_ptr->children[0] != NULL )
    for ( i = 0; i <= ORDER; i++ )
      new_location_ptr->children[i]->parent = new_location_ptr;

  /*
   *  update existing/right node and insert new element
   *  if appropriate
   */
  i = 0;
  while ( i < ORDER )
  {
    if ( mid_element_inserted == NO && j == index )
    {
      location_ptr->elements[i] = new_element;
      location_ptr->children[i] = left_child;
      ++i;
      mid_element_inserted = YES;
    }
    else
    {
      location_ptr->elements[i] = location_ptr->elements[j];
      location_ptr->children[i] = location_ptr->children[j];
      ++i;
      ++j;
    }
  }
  location_ptr->children[i] = location_ptr->children[j];

  /*  update parent pointers in children if required  */
  if ( location_ptr->children[0] != NULL )
    for ( i = 0; i <= ORDER; i++ )
      location_ptr->children[i]->parent = location_ptr;

  return ( mid_element );
}

/*
 *  insert_element():
 *     Function to insert a new element into a BTree.  If
 *     a node does not exist, a new root node is created.
 *     If the element causes overflow in the node, the node is
 *     split and the middle element is inserted into the parent
 *     node.  Address of root node, pointer to node location,
 *     new element to insert, left child of new element, and
 *     right child of new element are passed to function.
 *     If a new root is created, root pointer is updated.
 */
```

```
void    insert_element ( BTREE_PTR    *root_ptr,
                         BTREE_PTR    location_ptr,
                         ELEMENT      new_element,
                         BTREE_PTR    left_child,
                         BTREE_PTR    right_child )
{
  BTREE_PTR    new_location_ptr;
  ELEMENT      mid_element;
  int          index, i, size;

  /*  if node does not exist, create new root node  */
  if ( location_ptr == NULL )
  {
    new_location_ptr = create_node ();
    new_location_ptr->elements[0] = new_element;
    new_location_ptr->children[0] = left_child;
    new_location_ptr->children[1] = right_child;
    if ( left_child != NULL && right_child != NULL )
      left_child->parent = right_child->parent = new_location_ptr;

    new_location_ptr->no_of_elements = 1;
    *root_ptr = new_location_ptr;
    return;
  }

  index = find_index ( location_ptr, new_element.key );
  if ( location_ptr->no_of_elements < MAX_NODE )
  {
    /*  insert new element  */
    size = location_ptr->no_of_elements;
    /*  move right most child pointer  */
    location_ptr->children[size+1] = location_ptr->children[size];
    /*
     *  move elements and left children to make room
     *  for new element
     */
    for ( i = size; i > index; i-- )
    {
      location_ptr->elements[i] = location_ptr->elements[i-1];
      location_ptr->children[i] = location_ptr->children[i-1];
    }

    location_ptr->elements[index] = new_element;
    location_ptr->children[index] = left_child;
    location_ptr->children[index+1] = right_child;
    location_ptr->no_of_elements += 1;
  }
  else   /*  split node  */
  {
    new_location_ptr = create_node ();
    new_location_ptr->parent = location_ptr->parent;
    new_location_ptr->no_of_elements = ORDER;
```

```
        location_ptr->no_of_elements = ORDER;
        mid_element = split_elements ( location_ptr, new_location_ptr,
                                     new_element, left_child, index );
        insert_element ( root_ptr, location_ptr->parent, mid_element,
                         new_location_ptr, location_ptr );
    }
}


/*
 *  insert_btree ():
 *     Function to add a new element to a BTree.  Address
 *     of root pointer and new element to add are passed
 *     to function.  If element already exists, the
 *     function returns.
 */

void    insert_btree ( BTREE_PTR    *root_ptr, ELEMENT    new_element )
{
  BTREE_PTR    node_ptr;
  int          index, i, size;

  /*  see if element already exists  */
  search_btree ( *root_ptr, new_element.key, &node_ptr, &index );
  if ( node_ptr != NULL )
    return;

  /*  find node where new element is to be inserted  */
  node_ptr = *root_ptr;
  while ( node_ptr != NULL )
  {
    size = node_ptr->no_of_elements;
    i = 0;
    while ( i < size && new_element.key > node_ptr->elements[i].key )
      ++i;

    if ( node_ptr->children[i] != NULL )
      node_ptr = node_ptr->children[i];
    else
      break;
  }

  insert_element ( root_ptr, node_ptr, new_element, NULL, NULL );
}


/*
 *   combine_nodes ():
 *      Function to combine two nodes.  A new node is created,
 *      elements from the left node are added, the separating
 *      element from the parent node is added, and elements from
 *      the right node are added. The new node replaces the right
 *      node and vacated memory is released.  Pointer to left node,
 *      pointer to right node, pointer to parent node, and index
 *      within parent node are passed to the function.
 */
```

```
void    combine_nodes ( BTREE_PTR    left_ptr, BTREE_PTR    right_ptr,
                        BTREE_PTR    parent_ptr, int    index )
{
  BTREE_PTR    combined_ptr;
  int          i, j, size;

  combined_ptr = create_node ();
  size = left_ptr->no_of_elements;
  /*  add left node elements   */
  for ( i = 0; i < size; i++ )
  {
    combined_ptr->elements[i] = left_ptr->elements[i];
    combined_ptr->children[i] = left_ptr->children[i];
  }

  /*  add separating element from parent node   */
  combined_ptr->elements[i] = parent_ptr->elements[index];
  combined_ptr->children[i] = left_ptr->children[i];
  ++i;
  size = right_ptr->no_of_elements;
  /*  add right node elements   */
  for ( j = 0; j < size; j++, i++ )
  {
    combined_ptr->elements[i] = right_ptr->elements[j];
    combined_ptr->children[i] = right_ptr->children[j];
  }
  combined_ptr->children[i] = right_ptr->children[j];

  /*  update parent pointers in children if required   */
  if ( combined_ptr->children[0] != NULL )
    for ( i = 0; i <= MAX_NODE; i++ )
      combined_ptr->children[i]->parent = combined_ptr;

  combined_ptr->parent = parent_ptr;
  combined_ptr->no_of_elements = MAX_NODE;
  parent_ptr->children[index+1] = combined_ptr;
  free ( left_ptr );
  free ( right_ptr );
}

/*
 *   delete_element ():
 *      Function to delete an element from a node.   If a
 *      node is the root pointer, it is adjusted if all
 *      elements have been deleted, otherwise function returns.
 *      If a node other than the root pointer underflows, an element
 *      is borrowed from left or right neighbor if sufficient
 *      elements exist, otherwise the node is combined with left or
 *      right neighbor.   Address of root pointer, pointer to
 *      node, and index of element to delete are passed to
 *      the function.
 */
```

```
void    delete_element ( BTREE_PTR  *root_ptr,
                         BTREE_PTR  node_ptr, int    index )
{
  BTREE_PTR    neighbor_ptr, parent_ptr;
  int          i, size;

  /*  remove element from node  */
  node_ptr->no_of_elements -= 1;
  size = node_ptr->no_of_elements;
  for ( i = index; i < size; i++ )
  {
    node_ptr->elements[i] = node_ptr->elements[i+1];
    node_ptr->children[i] = node_ptr->children[i+1];
  }
  node_ptr->children[i] = node_ptr->children[i+1];

  /*  determine if node is the root node  */
  if ( node_ptr == *root_ptr )
  {
    /*  adjust root pointer if root node is empty  */
    if ( node_ptr->no_of_elements == 0 )
    {
      *root_ptr = node_ptr->children[1];
      (*root_ptr)->parent = NULL;
      free ( node_ptr );
    }
    return;
  }

  /*  determine if node has enough elements  */
  if ( node_ptr->no_of_elements >= ORDER )
    return;

  /*  try to borrow an element from a neighbor  */
  parent_ptr = node_ptr->parent;
  i = 0;
  size = parent_ptr->no_of_elements;
  while ( i <= size && parent_ptr->children[i] != node_ptr )
    ++i;

  if ( i > 0 &&
       parent_ptr->children[i-1]->no_of_elements > ORDER )
  {
    /*  left neighbor  */
    neighbor_ptr = parent_ptr->children[i-1];
    size = neighbor_ptr->no_of_elements;
    insert_element ( root_ptr, node_ptr,
                     parent_ptr->elements[i-1],
                     neighbor_ptr->children[size],
                     node_ptr->children[0] );
    if ( node_ptr->children[0] != NULL )
      node_ptr->children[0]->parent = node_ptr;
    parent_ptr->elements[i-1] = neighbor_ptr->elements[size-1];
    neighbor_ptr->no_of_elements -=1;
```

```
      return;
   }
   else if ( i < size &&
               parent_ptr->children[i+1]->no_of_elements > ORDER )
   {
      /*  right neighbor  */
      neighbor_ptr = parent_ptr->children[i+1];
      size = node_ptr->no_of_elements;
      insert_element ( root_ptr, node_ptr,
                       parent_ptr->elements[i],
                       node_ptr->children[size],
                       neighbor_ptr->children[0] );
      if ( node_ptr->children[size+1] != NULL )
        node_ptr->children[size+1]->parent = node_ptr;
      parent_ptr->elements[i] = neighbor_ptr->elements[0];
      delete_element ( root_ptr, neighbor_ptr, 0 );
      return;
   }
   else    /*  combine two nodes  */
   {
      if ( i > 0 )
      {
         /*  left neighbor  */
         neighbor_ptr = parent_ptr->children[i-1];
         combine_nodes ( neighbor_ptr, node_ptr, parent_ptr, i - 1 );
         delete_element ( root_ptr, parent_ptr, i - 1 );
         return;
      }
      else    /*  i < size  */
      {
         /*  right neighbor  */
         neighbor_ptr = parent_ptr->children[i+1];
         combine_nodes ( node_ptr, neighbor_ptr, parent_ptr, i );
         delete_element ( root_ptr, parent_ptr, i );
         return;
      }
   }
}


/*
 *   replace_element ():
 *      Function to replace an element by the smallest element
 *      in the leftmost node of the nodes's right subtree.
 *      Address of node to be replace and address of index of
 *      element to be replaced are passed to the function.  Function
 *      updates node to contain pointer of leaf node used to
 *      replace element and updates index to contain element's
 *      index.
 */

BTREE_PTR   replace_element ( BTREE_PTR   *node_ptr, int   *index )
{
   BTREE_PTR   replace_ptr = (*node_ptr)->children[*index+1];
```

```
    while ( replace_ptr->children[0] != NULL )
      replace_ptr = replace_ptr->children[0];

    (*node_ptr)->elements[*index] = replace_ptr->elements[0];
    *node_ptr = replace_ptr;
    *index = 0;
}

/*
 *  delete_btree():
 *     Function to delete an element from a BTree.  Function
 *     returns if the element is not found.  If element is not
 *     in a leaf node, element is replace by the smallest element
 *     in the leftmost node of the nodes's right subtree.
 *     Address of root pointer and key of element to delete are
 *     passed to function.
 */

void   delete_btree ( BTREE_PTR   *root_ptr, KEY_TYPE   delete_key )
{
  BTREE_PTR    node_ptr;
  int          index;

    search_btree ( *root_ptr, delete_key, &node_ptr, &index );
    if ( node_ptr == NULL )   /* element not found */
      return;

    /*
     *  if element to delete is not in a leaf node - replace
     *  it by the smallest element in the left most node of
     *  its right subtree
     */
    if ( node_ptr->children[index] != NULL )
      replace_element ( &node_ptr, &index );

    /* delete element from leaf */
    delete_element ( root_ptr, node_ptr, index );
}

/*
 *  display_menu():
 *     Function to display main operator interface menu.
 */

void   display_menu ()
{
  clrscr ();
  printf ("\n\n");
  printf ("\nParts Inventory Control Database Program");
  printf ("\nEnter Choice or ESC to Quit!");
  printf ("\n");
  printf ("\nA.  Add a Part to Database");
  printf ("\nE.  Erase a Part from Database");
```

```
  printf ("\nM.  Modify a Part in Database");
  printf ("\nD.  Display a Part in Database");
  printf ("\nS.  Save Database to Disk");
  printf ("\nR.  Read Database from Disk");
  printf ("\nP.  Print Part Numbers in Database");
  printf ("\n\n");
}

/*
 *  key_to_continue ():
 *    Function to continue if any key is pressed.
 */

void   key_to_continue ()
{
  printf ("\n\nPress any key to continue!  ");
  if ( getch () == 0 )    /*  read extended ascii code  */
    getch ();
}

/*
 *  add_an_element ():
 *    Function to add an element into a BTree.  Address
 *    of the root pointer is passed to function.
 */

void   add_an_element ( BTREE_PTR   *root_ptr )
{
  ELEMENT       new_element;
  char          buffer[81];

  clrscr ();
  printf ("\n\nAdd a Part to Database");
  printf   ("\n--------------------");
  printf ("\n\nPart Number:  ");
  gets ( buffer );
  new_element.key = atol ( buffer );
  printf ("Part Name:  ");
  gets ( new_element.part_name );
  printf ("Part Revision Level:  ");
  gets ( new_element.part_rev_level );
  printf ("Part Vendor Name:  ");
  gets ( new_element.part_vendor_name );
  printf ("Part Vendor Phone:  ");
  gets ( new_element.part_vendor_phone );
  printf ("Part Description:  ");
  gets ( new_element.part_description );
  printf ("Part Quantity:  ");
  gets ( buffer );
  new_element.part_quantity = atol ( buffer );
  printf ("Part Unit Price:  ");
  gets ( buffer );
  new_element.part_unit_price = atof ( buffer );
```

```
    insert_btree ( root_ptr, new_element );
}

/*
 *   delete_an_element ():
 *      Function to delete an element from a BTree.   Address
 *      of root pointer is passed to function.
 */

void    delete_an_element ( BTREE_PTR    *root_ptr )
{
  char    buffer[81];

  clrscr ();
  printf ("\n\nErase a Part from Database");
  printf    ("\n------------------------");
  printf ("\n\nPart Number:   ");
  gets ( buffer );

  delete_btree ( root_ptr, atol ( buffer ) );
}

/*
 *   get_string ():
 *      Function to get a string from keyboard and to
 *      update string if required.   Pointer to string
 *      must be passed to function.
 */

void    get_string ( char    *string )
{
  char    buffer[81];

  gets ( buffer );
  if ( buffer[0] != '\0' )
    strcpy ( string, buffer );
}

/*
 *   modify_an_element ():
 *      Function to modify an element in a BTree.   Root
 *      pointer is passed to function.
 */

void    modify_an_element ( BTREE_PTR    root_ptr )
{
  BTREE_PTR    node_ptr;
  int          index;
  char         buffer[81];

  clrscr ();
  printf ("\n\nModify a Part in Database");
  printf    ("\n------------------------");
```

```
    printf ("\n\nPart Number to Modify:   ");
    gets ( buffer );

    search_btree ( root_ptr, atol ( buffer ), &node_ptr, &index );
    if ( node_ptr == NULL )
    {
      printf ("\nPart Not Found in Database");
      key_to_continue ();
      return;
    }

    printf ("\nModify Part Number %ld",
              node_ptr->elements[index].key);
    printf ("\nEnter a New Value or <Return> to Keep Old Value");
    printf ("\n-----------------------------------------------");
    printf ("\nPart Name [%s]:   ",
              node_ptr->elements[index].part_name);
    get_string ( node_ptr->elements[index].part_name );
    printf ("Part Revision Level [%s]:   ",
              node_ptr->elements[index].part_rev_level);
    get_string ( node_ptr->elements[index].part_rev_level );
    printf ("Part Vendor Name [%s]:   ",
              node_ptr->elements[index].part_vendor_name);
    get_string ( node_ptr->elements[index].part_vendor_name );
    printf ("Part Vendor Phone [%s]:   ",
              node_ptr->elements[index].part_vendor_phone);
    get_string ( node_ptr->elements[index].part_vendor_phone );
    printf ("Part Description [%s]:   ",
              node_ptr->elements[index].part_description);
    get_string ( node_ptr->elements[index].part_description );
    printf ("Part Quantity [%ld]:   ",
              node_ptr->elements[index].part_quantity);
    gets ( buffer );
    if ( buffer[0] != '\0' )
      node_ptr->elements[index].part_quantity = atol ( buffer );
    printf ("Part Unit Price [$%5.2f]:   ",
              node_ptr->elements[index].part_unit_price);
    gets ( buffer );
    if ( buffer[0] != '\0' )
      node_ptr->elements[index].part_unit_price = atof ( buffer );
}

./*
 *  display_an_element ():
 *     Function to display an element in a BTree.  Root
 *     pointer is passed to function.
 */

void   display_an_element ( BTREE_PTR   root_ptr )
{
  BTREE_PTR   node_ptr;
  int         index;
  char        buffer[81];
```

```
    clrscr ();
    printf ("\n\nDisplay a Part in Database");
    printf    ("\n------------------------");
    printf ("\n\nPart Number to Display:   ");
    gets ( buffer );

    search_btree ( root_ptr, atol ( buffer ), &node_ptr, &index );
    if ( node_ptr == NULL )
    {
      printf ("\nPart Not Found in Database");
      key_to_continue ();
      return;
    }

    printf ("\nPart Name:   %s",
                node_ptr->elements[index].part_name);
    printf ("\nPart Revision Level:   %s",
                node_ptr->elements[index].part_rev_level);
    printf ("\nPart Vendor Name:   %s",
                node_ptr->elements[index].part_vendor_name);
    printf ("\nPart Vendor Phone:   %s",
                node_ptr->elements[index].part_vendor_phone);
    printf ("\nPart Description:   %s",
                node_ptr->elements[index].part_description);
    printf ("\nPart Quantity:   %ld",
                node_ptr->elements[index].part_quantity);
    printf ("\nPart Unit Price:   $%5.2f",
                node_ptr->elements[index].part_unit_price);
    key_to_continue ();
}


/*
 *  write_to_disk():
 *      Function to recursively traverse BTree and write
 *      elements to disk.  Root pointer and file pointer
 *      are passed to function.
 */

void   write_to_disk ( BTREE_PTR   root_ptr, FILE   *file_ptr )
{
    int   i;

    if ( root_ptr == NULL )
      return;

    for ( i = 0; i < root_ptr->no_of_elements; i++ )
      fwrite ( &root_ptr->elements[i],
                sizeof ( root_ptr->elements[i] ), 1, file_ptr );

    for ( i = 0; i <= root_ptr->no_of_elements; i++ )
      write_to_disk ( root_ptr->children[i], file_ptr );
}
```

```c
/*
 *   save_part_btree ():
 *      Function to save elements in a BTree to disk file
 *      PartTree.dat.  Root pointer is passed to function.
 */

void    save_part_btree ( BTREE_PTR    root_ptr )
{
  FILE    *file_ptr;

  if ( root_ptr == NULL )
  {
    printf ("\n\nError:   Current BTree is Empty!");
    key_to_continue ();
    return;
  }

  if ( ( file_ptr = fopen ( "PartTree.dat", "wb" ) ) == NULL )
  {
    printf ("\n\nError:   File Could Not Be Opened!");
    key_to_continue ();
    return;
  }

  write_to_disk ( root_ptr, file_ptr );
  fclose ( file_ptr );
}

/*
 *   read_part_btree ():
 *      Function to read a BTree from disk file "PartTree.dat".
 *      Address of root pointer is passed to function.  If
 *      the root pointer is not NULL, function returns.
 */

void    read_part_btree ( BTREE_PTR    *root_ptr )
{
  FILE        *file_ptr;
  ELEMENT     new_element;

  if ( *root_ptr != NULL )
  {
    printf ("\n\nError:   Current BTree is Not Empty!");
    key_to_continue ();
    return;
  }

  if ( ( file_ptr = fopen ( "PartTree.dat", "rb" ) ) == NULL )
  {
    printf ("\n\nError:   File Could Not Be Opened!");
    key_to_continue ();
    return;
  }
```

```
  while ( fread ( &new_element, sizeof ( new_element ),
          1, file_ptr ) == 1 )
    insert_btree ( root_ptr, new_element );

  fclose ( file_ptr );
}

/*
 *  print_part_btree():
 *    Function to vertically print key's of elements in
 *    a BTree.  Root pointer is passed to the function.
 */

void    print_part_btree ( BTREE_PTR    root_ptr )
{
  int    i;

  if ( root_ptr == NULL )
    return;

  printf ("\n");
  for ( i = 0; i < root_ptr->no_of_elements; i++ )
    printf ("%d ", root_ptr->elements[i].key);

  for ( i = 0; i <= root_ptr->no_of_elements; i++ )
    print_part_btree ( root_ptr->children[i] );
}

/*
 *  main():
 *    Main test driver for Parts Inventory Control
 *    Database System.
 */

main ()
{
  BTREE_PTR    root_ptr = NULL;

  while ( FOREVER )
  {
    display_menu ();
    switch ( getch () )
    {
      case 0:          /*  read extended code  */
        getch ();
        printf ( BELL );
        break;

      case 'a':
      case 'A':    /*  add a record to database  */
        add_an_element ( &root_ptr );
        break;
```

```
       case 'e':
       case 'E':    /*  erase a record from database   */
         delete_an_element ( &root_ptr );
         break;

       case 'm':
       case 'M':    /*  modify a record in database   */
         modify_an_element ( root_ptr );
         break;

       case 'd':
       case 'D':    /*  display a record in database   */
         display_an_element ( root_ptr );
         break;

       case 's':
       case 'S':    /*  save btree to disk   */
         save_part_btree ( root_ptr );
         break;

       case 'r':
       case 'R':    /*  read btree from disk   */
         read_part_btree ( &root_ptr );
         break;

       case 'p':
       case 'P':    /*  print keys of database   */
         clrscr ();
         printf    ("Part Numbers in Database");
         printf ("\n-----------------------\n");
         print_part_btree ( root_ptr );
         key_to_continue ();
         break;

      case ESC:    /*  quit   */
         clrscr ();
         exit ( 0 );
         break;

     default:
         printf ( BELL );
         break;
   }
  }
}
```

Output Section

Here is the output of the run on the IBM PC-DOS system:

```
       Parts Inventory Control Database Program
       Enter Choice or ESC to Quit!
```

```
A.   Add a Part to Database
E.   Erase a Part from Database
M.   Modify a Part in Database
D.   Display a Part in Database
S.   Save Database to Disk
R.   Read Database from Disk
P.   Print Part Numbers in Database

a

Add a Part to Database
----------------------

Part Number:  50
Part Name:  System Unit
Part Revision Level:  2.1
Part Vendor Name:  IBM
Part Vendor Phone:  555-1212
Part Description:  Main 386 Computer System Unit
Part Quantity:  30
Part Unit Price:  3000

Parts Inventory Control Database Program
Enter Choice or ESC to Quit!

A.   Add a Part to Database
E.   Erase a Part from Database
M.   Modify a Part in Database
D.   Display a Part in Database
S.   Save Database to Disk
R.   Read Database from Disk
P.   Print Part Numbers in Database

a

Add a Part to Database
----------------------

Part Number:  100
Part Name:  Keyboard
Part Revision Level:  1.5
Part Vendor Name:  IBM
Part Vendor Phone:  555-1212
Part Description:  386 Computer Keyboard
Part Quantity:  30
Part Unit Price:  100

Parts Inventory Control Database Program
Enter Choice or ESC to Quit!

A.   Add a Part to Database
E.   Erase a Part from Database
```

```
M.   Modify a Part in Database
D.   Display a Part in Database
S.   Save Database to Disk
R.   Read Database from Disk
P.   Print Part Numbers in Database

a

Add a Part to Database
----------------------

Part Number:  25
Part Name:  Monitor
Part Revision Level:  6.5
Part Vendor Name:  IBM
Part Vendor Phone:  555-1212
Part Description:  VGA Video Monitor
Part Quantity:  30
Part Unit Price:  1000


Parts Inventory Control Database Program
Enter Choice or ESC to Quit!

A.   Add a Part to Database
E.   Erase a Part from Database
M.   Modify a Part in Database
D.   Display a Part in Database
S.   Save Database to Disk
R.   Read Database from Disk
P.   Print Part Numbers in Database

a

Add a Part to Database
----------------------

Part Number:  75
Part Name:  Harddisk
Part Revision Level:  5.1
Part Vendor Name:  IBM
Part Vendor Phone:  555-1212
Part Description:  80 Meg Hard Drive
Part Quantity:  30
Part Unit Price:  600


Parts Inventory Control Database Program
Enter Choice or ESC to Quit!

A.   Add a Part to Database
E.   Erase a Part from Database
M.   Modify a Part in Database
D.   Display a Part in Database
```

```
S.   Save Database to Disk
R.   Read Database from Disk
P.   Print Part Numbers in Database


p


Part Numbers in Database
------------------------


25 50 75 100


Press any key to continue!


Parts Inventory Control Database Program
Enter Choice or ESC to Quit!


A.   Add a Part to Database
E.   Erase a Part from Database
M.   Modify a Part in Database
D.   Display a Part in Database
S.   Save Database to Disk
R.   Read Database from Disk
P.   Print Part Numbers in Database


a


Add a Part to Database
----------------------


Part Number:   125
Part Name:   Mouse
Part Revision Level:   1.0
Part Vendor Name:   IBM
Part Vendor Phone:   555-1212
Part Description:   Rollar Ball Mouse
Part Quantity:   30
Part Unit Price:   75


Parts Inventory Control Database Program
Enter Choice or ESC to Quit!


A.   Add a Part to Database
E.   Erase a Part from Database
M.   Modify a Part in Database
D.   Display a Part in Database
S.   Save Database to Disk
R.   Read Database from Disk
P.   Print Part Numbers in Database


p
```

```
Part Numbers in Database
------------------------

75
25 50
100 125

Press any key to continue!

Parts Inventory Control Database Program
Enter Choice or ESC to Quit!

A.   Add a Part to Database
E.   Erase a Part from Database
M.   Modify a Part in Database
D.   Display a Part in Database
S.   Save Database to Disk
R.   Read Database from Disk
P.   Print Part Numbers in Database

s

Parts Inventory Control Database Program
Enter Choice or ESC to Quit!

A.   Add a Part to Database
E.   Erase a Part from Database
M.   Modify a Part in Database
D.   Display a Part in Database
S.   Save Database to Disk
R.   Read Database from Disk
P.   Print Part Numbers in Database

m

Modify a Part in Database
------------------------

Part Number to Modify:   100
Modify Part Number 100
Enter a New Value or <Return> to Keep Old Value
-----------------------------------------------
Part Name [Keyboard]:
Part Revision Level [1.5]:   1.7
Part Vendor Name [IBM]:
Part Vendor Phone [555-1212]:
Part Description [386 Computer Keyboard]:
Part Quantity [30]:
Part Unit Price [$100.00]:


Parts Inventory Control Database Program
Enter Choice or ESC to Quit!
```

```
A.    Add a Part to Database
E.    Erase a Part from Database
M.    Modify a Part in Database
D.    Display a Part in Database
S.    Save Database to Disk
R.    Read Database from Disk
P.    Print Part Numbers in Database


d

Display a Part in Database
------------------------

Part Number to Display:   100
Part Name:  Keyboard
Part Revision Level:  1.7
Part Vendor Name:   IBM
Part Vendor Phone:   555-1212
Part Description:   386 Computer Keyboard
Part Quantity:   30
Part Unit Price:   $100.00


Press any key to continue!

Parts Inventory Control Database Program
Enter Choice or ESC to Quit!

A.    Add a Part to Database
E.    Erase a Part from Database
M.    Modify a Part in Database
D.    Display a Part in Database
S.    Save Database to Disk
R.    Read Database from Disk
P.    Print Part Numbers in Database


p

Part Numbers in Database
-----------------------

75
25 50
100 125


Press any key to continue!

Parts Inventory Control Database Program
Enter Choice or ESC to Quit!

A.    Add a Part to Database
E.    Erase a Part from Database
M.    Modify a Part in Database
```

```
D.   Display a Part in Database
S.   Save Database to Disk
R.   Read Database from Disk
P.   Print Part Numbers in Database

e

Erase a Part from Database
-------------------------

Part Number:   75

Parts Inventory Control Database Program
Enter Choice or ESC to Quit!

A.   Add a Part to Database
E.   Erase a Part from Database
M.   Modify a Part in Database
D.   Display a Part in Database
S.   Save Database to Disk
R.   Read Database from Disk
P.   Print Part Numbers in Database

p

Part Numbers in Database
-----------------------

25 50 100 125

Press any key to continue!

Parts Inventory Control Database Program
Enter Choice or ESC to Quit!

A.   Add a Part to Database
E.   Erase a Part from Database
M.   Modify a Part in Database
D.   Display a Part in Database
S.   Save Database to Disk
R.   Read Database from Disk
P.   Print Part Numbers in Database

e

Erase a Part from Database
-------------------------

Part Number:   50

Parts Inventory Control Database Program
Enter Choice or ESC to Quit!
```

```
A.   Add a Part to Database
E.   Erase a Part from Database
M.   Modify a Part in Database
D.   Display a Part in Database
S.   Save Database to Disk
R.   Read Database from Disk
P.   Print Part Numbers in Database

e

Erase a Part from Database
--------------------------

Part Number:   100

Parts Inventory Control Database Program
Enter Choice or ESC to Quit!

A.   Add a Part to Database
E.   Erase a Part from Database
M.   Modify a Part in Database
D.   Display a Part in Database
S.   Save Database to Disk
R.   Read Database from Disk
P.   Print Part Numbers in Database

e

Erase a Part from Database
--------------------------

Part Number:   25

Parts Inventory Control Database Program
Enter Choice or ESC to Quit!

A.   Add a Part to Database
E.   Erase a Part from Database
M.   Modify a Part in Database
D.   Display a Part in Database
S.   Save Database to Disk
R.   Read Database from Disk
P.   Print Part Numbers in Database

e

Erase a Part from Database
--------------------------

Part Number:   125

Parts Inventory Control Database Program
Enter Choice or ESC to Quit!
```

```
A.    Add a Part to Database
E.    Erase a Part from Database
M.    Modify a Part in Database
D.    Display a Part in Database
S.    Save Database to Disk
R.    Read Database from Disk
P.    Print Part Numbers in Database


p


Part Numbers in Database
-----------------------


Press any key to continue!

Parts Inventory Control Database Program
Enter Choice or ESC to Quit!

A.    Add a Part to Database
E.    Erase a Part from Database
M.    Modify a Part in Database
D.    Display a Part in Database
S.    Save Database to Disk
R.    Read Database from Disk
P.    Print Part Numbers in Database


r


Parts Inventory Control Database Program
Enter Choice or ESC to Quit!

A.    Add a Part to Database
E.    Erase a Part from Database
M.    Modify a Part in Database
D.    Display a Part in Database
S.    Save Database to Disk
R.    Read Database from Disk
P.    Print Part Numbers in Database


p


Part Numbers in Database
-----------------------

75
25 50
100 125


Press any key to continue!

Parts Inventory Control Database Program
Enter Choice or ESC to Quit!
```

```
A.    Add a Part to Database
E.    Erase a Part from Database
M.    Modify a Part in Database
D.    Display a Part in Database
S.    Save Database to Disk
R.    Read Database from Disk
P.    Print Part Numbers in Database

ESC
```

11.4 A Small SQL Preprocessor

In this section, we attempt to demonstrate a database application using structured query language (SQL). A small SQL preprocessor (SSQLPP) that converts a SQL program into a C program will be described. Its coding is left as an exercise. This section refers to the parts database, `parts_db_f1`, and the program in Section 5.6.

Once you create a database and store data in it, you can request information from that database. The query language is a high-level English-like language in which your request can be specified. Most commercial relational database systems provide a query language. The language can be procedural or nonprocedural. In a procedural language, your instructions are specified by a sequence of operations on the database that lead to obtaining the result. In a nonprocedural language, the desired information is described without specifying the specific operations. The SQL contains the characteristics of both these languages. For detailed discussion, see Korth and Silberschatz (1986).

Some of the features of SQL are:

1. Creating a database
2. Defining the structure (table) for data
3. Altering the structure (table) for data
4. Querying a database
5. Retrieving and updating data in the database
6. Inserting data in the database
7. Deleting data from the database
8. Displaying data in a specified form
9. Granting access-privilege to ensure security.

For our implementation of a small SQL preprocessor (SSQLPP), we use the following keywords:

Keyword	Description
DATABASE	Specify the target database
INSERT	Insert data in a database
SELECT	For querying a database

In SSQLPP, we specify simple syntax of the above keywords. We use semicolon as the delimiter of each SQL statement. Identifiers written within the angle brackets must be specified by the user. Any number of spaces between the keywords and the user-supplied identifiers are allowed. No comments are allowed. The uppercase letters denote the keywords. Items listed within square brackets are optional.

Keyword	Description
DATABASE	DATABASE <database name>;
INSERT	INSERT INTO <table name> VALUES (<value list>);
SELECT	SELECT <select attributes> FROM <table name> WHERE <condition1> [AND <condition2>];

Assume our database in reference is stored in `parts_db_fl`. As each PART_ RECORD structure has fields, `part_name`, `part_rev_level`, `part_ serial_no`, `part_vendor_name`, `part_vendor_phone`, etc. An example of an INSERT statement can be shown as:

```
INSERT INTO PART_RECORD
    VALUES ("SNA", "A-1", "SNA-342", "Plexus Computers",
            "313-223-9090", "SNA Communications board",
            200, 1529.95 );
```

The SQL program, `sample.sql`, shown in Figure 11-2 generates a query for a part by the key, `part_name`.

```
DATABASE  parts_db_fl;

SELECT
    FROM   PART_RECORD
        WHERE  part_name = iAPX-80386;
```

Figure 11-2 A Small SQL Program for SSQLPP.

The preprocessor SSQLPP translates the program into a C program suitable for compilation by the C compiler. You then execute this program. The translated form, `sample.c`, looks like that shown in Figure 11-3.

```
extern load_db_disk( char * );
extern search_display_part ( char [] );

main()
{

    load_db_from_disk( "parts_db_fl" );

    srch_display_part( "iAPX-80386" );

}
```

Figure 11-3 C program generated by SSQLPP.

This assumes some modifications of the functions `load_db_from_disk()` and `srch_display_part()` to pass arguments. Compile `sample.c` and link it

with the compiled version of parts_db.c without main(). The disadvantage of
the code in Figure 11-2 is that each time we use SELECT, it loads the database from
disk into memory buffer. This can be avoided by incorporating a menu for SSQLPP
and compilation of the C program. This is what is done in commercial applications.
As mentioned earlier, the coding of SSQLPP is left as an exercise.

Exercises

11-1 In the given example, add a menu "Move data from one part record to
another," and the associated routine.

11-2 *Programming project:* In this project, write a program to implement
the small SQL preprocessor (SSQLPP), as discussed in Section 11.5.
SSQLPP is table-driven; the table will contain the keywords and the
pointers to the associated functions. It parses each SQL statement from
left to right in the SQL program. It checks the correct syntax of each
SQL statement. It then generates a C program. For further information, see Chapter 13. Test your program using the SQL program in Figure 11-3 as the input and the C program in Figure 11-3 as the output.

11-3 Redo Exercise 11-2 for the parts database, PartTree.dat, developed in Section 11.4.

CHAPTER 12

Applications for Science and Engineering

In this chapter we will develop several applications in engineering and statistics to demonstrate the uses of arrays and recursion.

12.1 Engineering Application

In this section we will show how to apply the concept and techniques of data structure in solving engineering problems. The pipe temperature problem that we will implement in C, was originally implemented by Carnahan *et al.* (1969) in FORTRAN. The plate temperature problem described in Carnahan *et al.* (1969) is quoted as follows: Find the steady-state temperature distribution in a square plate, one side of which is maintained at 100 degrees Centigrade(C), with the other sides maintained at 0 degree Centigrade."

This problem is solved using Laplace's equation:

$$T_{xx} + T_{yy} = 0$$

subject to the boundary conditions

$$T(x,n) = 0, \qquad T(n,y) = 0$$
$$T(x,0) = 100, \qquad T(0,y) = 0$$

where T_{xx} and T_{yy} respectively mean second-order partial derivatives of temperature $T[x,y(x)]$ with respect to variables x and y.

To solve this problem numerically, we divide the region into rectangles by partitioning each x and y side into n subintervals. The corner of each rectangle is called a *grid point,* represented by a dot (.) in Figure 12-1. The corners of rectangles at the boundaries are also grid points. Our goal is to calculate the approximate value of the temperature at these grid points.

The program will solve the problem by storing and manipulating data at these grid points. The number of these points may be huge if n, the number of partitions, is large. Structuring these data as a two-dimensional array will solve such a problem. This approach used is to iteratively approximate the temperature at each in-

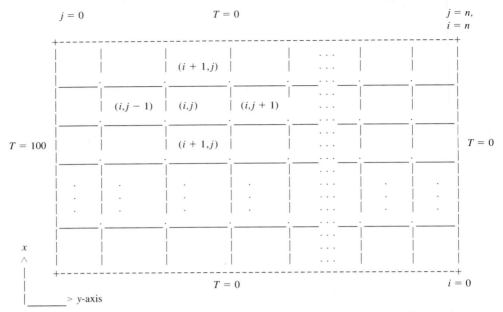

Figure 12-1 Solution of a temperature problem by grid-point arrangement and manipulation of data.

terior grid point (i,j) from the average of the surrounding grid points using the following equation:

$$T_{i,j} = \frac{T_{i-1,j} + T_{i+1,j} + T_{i,j-1} + T_{i,j+1}}{4}$$

where $i = 1, 2, \ldots, n - 1$
$\qquad j = 1, 2, \ldots, n - 1$

These equations will form a system of $(n - 1) \times (n - 1)$ simultaneous linear equations, with temperatures at the interior grid points as the unknowns. We will use the Gauss–Seidel iterative method to solve this system of equations.

During the iterative process, a new approximation to T is calculated, and the previous approximation is discarded if the new approximation is better than the previous one. The iterative process continues until all grid points are used.

For further discussion, see Carnahan *et al.* Here is the C implementation of the solution.

Example 12.1

Code Section

```
/* Program:  Laplace_heat.c  ( STEADY-STATE )
 * Purpose:  The mathematical form of the heat equation is
 *
 *              2
 *           ∇ T(x, y) = 0, with boundary conditions
 *                              (fixed edge temperatures),
 *           also known as Laplace's equation (or Partial
 *           Differential Equation or Boundary Value Problem),
 *           where T (temperature) is a function of x and y.
 *
```

```
*              To solve this problem using a computer, we do the
*              following steps:
*
*                 1. Set up a rectangular region covering the plate
*                    and the given boundaries.
*
*                 2. Divide the region into small rectangles. The
*                    corners of each rectangle will be called "grid"
*                    or "mesh" points.
*
*                 3. Using the "Finite Element Method" at these grid
*                    points including the boundary points, we will
*                    arrive at a System of Linear equations, whose
*                    coefficient matrix will have most of its elements
*                    zero. In each row nonzero coefficients will occur
*                    in this pattern:
*                         -1, -1, 4, -1, and -1.
*                    This is because each equation in this system of
*                    Linear Equations has exactly five nonzero
*                    coefficients:
*                         -1, -1, 4, -1, and -1.
*
*                 In other words,
*
*       - 1T_{i-1,i} - 1T_{i+1,i} + 4T_{i,j} - 1T_{i,j-1} - 1T_{i,j+1} = 0
*
*
*                 4. Iteratively solve the system using Gauss-Seidel's
*                    Iterative method.
*
*                 5. The solution will approximate temperature,
*                    satisfying the Heat equation subject to the
*                    conditions at the edges of the region.
*/

#define absolute( a )  ( ((a) < 0 ) ? -(a) : (a) )

#define    EPSILON    1.0e-4  /* Tolerance used in main()              */
/* Define ITERATION_MAX to safeguard the Iterative process
 * from infinite looping.
 */
#define    ITERATION_MAX  150

#define    ROWS  9          /* No of rows of grid_temper[] [] matrix */
#define    COLS  9          /* No of cols of grid_temper[] [] matrix */
                            /* n = 0 .. 8 */

/* ************************************************************** *
 * main ():  STEADY-STATE HEAT CONDUCTION IN A SQUARE PLATE       *
 * ************************************************************** */
main()
{
    /*  Declare Matrix of Plate temperatures at grid points;
     *  previous:          Previous approx temperature;
```

```
         *   total_residual: Total of differences between
         *                   previous & new approximations.
         */
        float    grid_temper[ROWS][COLS],
                 previous,
                 total_residual;
        int    i, j,
                 iteration = 0;
        /* n = (Input) Number of partitions of each edge in
         *       x- and y-directions.
         */
        int    n = 8;

        printf("\n ** STEADY-STATE HEAT %s ** \n",
               "CONDUCTION IN A SQUARE PLATE" );

/* ***************************************************************  *
 *  Initialize the coefficient (temperature) matrix at the grid  *
 *  points using given boundary (surface and edge) temperatures  *
 *  ***************************************************************  */
        for ( i = 0; i <= n; i++ )
            {
            grid_temper[ i ][ 0 ] = 100.0;

            for ( j = 1; j <= n; j++ )
                 grid_temper[ i ][ j ] = 0.0;
            }

/* ***************************************************************  *
 * Perform iteration to successively calculate temperatures at   *
 * grid points using GAUSS-SEIDEL METHOD. Stop the iterative     *
 * process                                                       *
 *    if     total_residual <  EPSILON                           *
 *    or     iteration = ITERATION_MAX                           *
 * ***************************************************************  */
        for ( iteration = 0; iteration < ITERATION_MAX; iteration++ )
            {
            total_residual = 0.0;

            for ( i = 1; i < n; i++ )
                {
                for ( j = 1; j < n; j++ )
                    {
                    previous = grid_temper[ i ][ j ];
                    grid_temper[i][j] = ( grid_temper[i ][ j+1] +
                                          grid_temper[ i][ j-1] +
                                          grid_temper[ i+1 ][j] +
                                          grid_temper[ i-1][j] )/4.0;

                    total_residual += absolute( grid_temper[ i][ j ]
                                                - previous );
                    }
                }
```

```
        if (  total_residual <  EPSILON )
          {
            /*
             *  total_residual <  EPSILON ,
             *  so print temperatures at grid points
             */
            printf("\n For EPSILON = %10.5f  %s %d  iterations \n",
                        EPSILON, "Convergence attained in ",
                        iteration );
            printf(" The Temperatures %s \n\n",
                    "at Boundaries and interior are:");

            for ( i = 0;  i <= n;  i++ )
              {
                for ( j = 0;  j <= n;  j++ )
                    printf(" %5.2f ", grid_temper[ i ][ j ]);
                printf( "\n" );
              }
            exit ( 0 );

          }
      }   /* --- End of 'for ( iteration = 0,  ... )    ---      */

    printf("\n LAPLACE: %s %d  iterations \n",
            "Convergence not attained in", ITERATION_MAX );

}
```

Output Section

** STEADY-STATE HEAT CONDUCTION IN A SQUARE PLATE **

For EPSILON =   0.00010 Convergence attained in 89 iterations

The Temperatures at Boundaries and interior are:

```
100.00    0.00    0.00    0.00    0.00    0.00    0.00    0.00    0.00
100.00   48.26   26.93   16.36   10.29    6.44    3.77    1.74    0.00
100.00   66.10   43.11   28.20   18.38   11.69    6.89    3.20    0.00
100.00   73.05   51.18   34.97   23.35   15.03    8.93    4.15    0.00
100.00   74.93   53.61   37.14   25.00   16.17    9.63    4.48    0.00
100.00   73.05   51.18   34.97   23.35   15.03    8.93    4.15    0.00
100.00   66.10   43.11   28.20   18.38   11.69    6.89    3.20    0.00
100.00   48.26   26.93   16.36   10.29    6.44    3.77    1.74    0.00
100.00    0.00    0.00    0.00    0.00    0.00    0.00    0.00    0.00
```

12.2 **Statistical Application**

We often deal with the collection and the analysis of a large set of discrete data to solve real-world problems. Statistics is the method of collecting and analyzing data. Because many professionals, including engineers, are engaged in such activites, it is necessary for them to use statistics to analyze data in the presence of variation and perturbation. In designing any program, we must consider some key items:

1. How much memory is available on the system?
2. How fast is the system (in millions of instructions per second)?
3. How efficient must our program be, in order to
   (a) Conserve memory and CPU time?
   (b) Reach a reliable solution in the shortest time possible?

We will structure our data and algorithms with these design constraints in mind. In Example 12.2, we will calculate the basic statistical measures Mean, Variance, and Standard Deviation, structuring the data items as a one-dimensional array. To conserve memory and time, we will write functions, passing the array as a function argument. We will return the values of Mean and Standard Deviation as fields of a structure. (Note this convenience of returning a structure in order to process a related variable; we add that variable as a field in the original structure. This does not require change in the calling routine.)

Example 12.3, on simple linear regression, uses the numerical data in Ward (1985) for the verification of the result produced by our C program.

For more detail, see Ward (1985) and Hogg and Ledolter (1987).

Example 12.2

Code Section

```
/*  Program:   statistics.c
 *  Purpose:   Calculate the Mean, Variance and Standard
 *             Deviation of 'Number_items' data items
 *             using the Statistical method.
 *
 *  To Compile: cc -O statistics.c   -o statistics /lib/libm.a
 */

#include <math.h>              /* For sqrt() in library
                                  /lib/libm.a           */
#define   n         10         /* Number of data items  */

typedef   float       item_type;
typedef   item_type Data_ary[n]; /* Array of item_type   */
struct    Mean_Std_Dev
          {
            float     Mean;       /* Calculated Mean      */
            float     Variance;   /* Variance             */
            float     Std_Dev;    /* Standard Deviation   */
          };

/* ******************************************************* *
 * Calculate_stats(): Calculate Mean & Standard Dev       *
 * float    Mean   :         Output: Calculated Mean      *
 * float    Std_Dev:         Output: Standard Deviation   *
 * ******************************************************* */
struct Mean_Std_Dev  Calculate_stats ( Data_ary   A,
                                        int   Number_items )
{
```

```
    int         i;              /* Array index              */
    item_type   sum;            /* Accumulated sum of Items */
    struct      Mean_Std_Dev temp;   /* To store results    */

    if ( Number_items == 0 )
      { printf("\n Calculate_stats: ERROR: No items \n");
        exit( 1 );
      }
    else
      { /* Calculate Mean and Standard Deviation        */
        sum = 0;
        for ( i = 0; i < Number_items; ++i )
           sum += A[ i ];

        temp.Mean = sum / Number_items;             /* Mean */
        /* === Proceed to calculate Standard Deviation == */
        sum = 0;                        /* Reinitialize sum  */
        for ( i = 0; i < Number_items; ++i )
           sum += ( A[ i ] - temp.Mean ) *
                  ( A[ i ] - temp.Mean );

        temp.Variance = sum / (Number_items - 1);
        temp.Std_Dev  = sqrt( temp.Variance );
      }

    return ( temp );
}

/* ***************************************************** *
 * print_stats(): Print Data's, Mean & Standard Dev    *
 * ***************************************************** */
void   print_stats ( Data_ary  A, int  Number_items,
                     struct     Mean_Std_Dev  Results )
{
   int  i;          /* Index for array A  */

   printf("\n The Given Data items are: \n");
   for ( i = 0; i < Number_items; ++i )
     {
       if ( i % 5 == 0 ) printf( "\n");   /* Print 5 items
                                        per line       */
       printf(" %10.2f  ", A[ i ] );
     }
   printf("\n");
   printf("\n Mean              = %10.5f ", Results.Mean );
   printf("\n Variance          = %10.5f ", Results.Variance );
   printf("\n Standard Deviation = %10.5f ", Results.Std_Dev );
}

/* ***************************************************** *
 * main(): STATISTICAL BASICS - MEAN & STANDARD DEV     *
 * ***************************************************** */
main()
{                               /* Initialize data items  */
```

```
static   Data_ary   A =   { 19.2,  23.5,  50.0,  24.5,  52.2,
                             62.6,  72.5,  51.3,  10.9,  47.1 };
int                  Number_items = 10;

struct               Mean_Std_Dev  Results;

printf ("\n **** STATISTICAL BASICS **** \n");
Results = Calculate_stats ( A, Number_items );
print_stats      ( A, Number_items, Results);
printf ("\n\n **** End of STATISTICAL BASICS **** \n");
}
```

Output Section

```
**** STATISTICAL BASICS ****

The Given Data items are:

        19.20           23.50           50.00           24.50           52.20
        62.60           72.50           51.30           10.90           47.10

Mean               =      41.38000
Variance           =     418.53952
Standard Deviation =      20.45824

**** End of STATISTICAL BASICS ****
```

12.3 Least-Squares Application

Given a set of n observed data (x,y), get a model of these observations by curve fitting using the linear least-squares method. That is, using this method, to predict y values for the given values of x, we want to fit a straight line

$$y = a + bx$$

where

$$b = \frac{\text{sum } (x_i * y_i) - n * (x\text{-bar}) * (y\text{-bar})}{\text{sum } (x_i \wedge 2) - n * (x\text{-bar} \wedge 2)}$$

where "sum" represents summation for $i = 1, 2, \ldots, n$ and

$$a = y\text{-bar} - b(x\text{-bar})$$

where x-bar = mean of x-values
     y-bar = mean of y-values
We must note:

1. The above expressions for a and b are, in fact, their minimum values obtained through the least-squares method.
2. The linear least-squares method can be used in finding the simple linear regression model.

Here is the example.

Example 12.3

Code Section

```
/*  Program:  least_squares.c
 */


#define  n            10              /* Number of data items   */

typedef  float      item_type;
typedef  item_type Data_ary[n];  /* Array of item_type       */

/* ************************************************** *
 * Least_squares() : CURVE FITTING USING LEAST SQUARES *
 * INPUTS:                                           *
 *    Data_ary   X:          X-values array          *
 *              Y:           Y-values array          *
 *    int  Number_items:     Number of data items    *
 *                                                   *
 * OUTPUTS:                                          *
 *    float      *a_min:     1st coeff of line equation *
 *              *b_min:      2nd coeff of line eqnuation *
 * ************************************************** *
 */
Least_squares( Data_ary  X,       Data_ary  Y,
              int        Number_items,
              float      *a_min, float *b_min )
{
   int          i;             /* Array index                 */
   item_type    sum_x =0,     /* Accumulated sum of X-values */
                sum_y =0,     /* Accumulated sum of Y-values */
                sum_xy=0,     /* Accumulated sum of X*Y-values*/
                sum_sqx=0,    /* Accumulated sum of X*Y-values*/
                x_bar,        /* Mean of X-values             */
                y_bar;        /* Mean of Y-values             */

   if ( Number_items == 0 )
     { printf("\n Least_squares(): ERROR: No items \n");
       exit( 1 );
     }
   else
     {  /* Calculate Mean for X-values, Mean for Y-values
           accumulated sum of the product X[i] and Y[i]
           and accumulated sum of squares of X[i].        */

        for ( i = 0; i < Number_items; ++i )
          {
            sum_x    += X[ i ];
            sum_y    += Y[ i ];
            sum_xy   += X[ i ] * Y[ i ];
```

```
                    sum_sqx  += X[ i ] * X[ i ];
                }

        x_bar     = sum_x / Number_items;   /* Mean of X's  */
        y_bar     = sum_y / Number_items;   /* Mean of Y's  */

        *b_min    = ( sum_xy  - Number_items * x_bar * y_bar ) /
                    ( sum_sqx - Number_items * x_bar * x_bar );

        *a_min    = y_bar - *b_min * x_bar;
    }
}     /* ******  end of Least_squares()      ******        */

/* ******************************************************** *
 * print_stats(): Print Least Square values                *
 * ******************************************************** */
void    print_stats ( Data_ary  A,      Data_ary  B,
                       int       Number_items,
                       float     a_min, float b_min )
{
    int     i;                  /* Index for array A          */

    printf("\n The Given ( X, Y ) Data items are: \n");
    for ( i = 0; i < Number_items; ++i )
        {
          printf("\n %10.2f  %10.2f ", A[ i ], B[ i ] );
        }
    printf("\n\n Least Squares Linear %s \n",
              "Regression Equation y = a + b * x ");
    printf("\n   Minimum Value of a = %10.5f ", a_min );
    printf("\n   Minimum Value of b = %10.5f ", b_min );
}

/* ******************************************************** *
 * main(): STATISTICAL BASICS - MEAN & STANDARD DEV         *
 * ******************************************************** */
main()
{                               /* Initialize data items  */
    static  Data_ary  X = { 3.4, 3.8, 4.1, 2.2, 2.6,
                            2.9, 2.0, 2.7, 1.9, 3.4  };

    static  Data_ary  Y = { 5.5, 5.9, 6.5, 3.3, 3.6,
                            4.6, 2.9, 3.6, 3.1, 4.9  };

    int       Number_items = 10;
    float     a_min,        /* Output: 1st coeff of line eqn*/
              b_min;        /* Output: 2nd coeff of line eqn*/

    printf("\n **** LEAST-SQUARES METHOD **** \n");
    Least_squares    ( X, Y, Number_items, &a_min, &b_min );

    print_stats      ( X, Y, Number_items, a_min, b_min );
    printf("\n\n **** End of LEAST-SQUARES METHOD **** \n");
}
```

Output Section

```
**** LEAST-SQUARES METHOD ****

The Given ( X, Y ) Data items are:

        3.40        5.50
        3.80        5.90
        4.10        6.50
        2.20        3.30
        2.60        3.60
        2.90        4.60
        2.00        2.90
        2.70        3.60
        1.90        3.10
        3.40        4.90

Least Squares Linear Regression Equation y = a + b * x

   Minimum Value of a =    -0.36310
   Minimum Value of b =     1.63900

**** End of LEAST-SQUARES METHOD ****
```

Using another set of values not included in the above main (), we give the output below.

Output Section

```
**** LEAST-SQUARES METHOD ****

The Given ( X, Y ) Data items are:

        2.50        4.32
        3.00        4.83
        3.50        5.27
        4.00        5.74
        4.50        6.26

Least Squares Linear Regression Equation y = a + b * x

   Minimum Value of a =     1.93101
   Minimum Value of b =     0.95800

**** End of LEAST-SQUARES METHOD ****
```

Exercise

12-1 Write program to compute the temperatures in the interior of a square pipe. The state of the pipe is described as: "It is half immersed in ice water at 0 degree centigrade; the top surface is held at 100 degrees centigrade; the temperature along the tops of the sides varies linearly from 0 to 100 degrees; a fluid at 200 degrees is flowing through the pipe" [McCracken (1984)]. Graphically display the temperatures. (*Hint:* Follow Example 12.1.)

CHAPTER 13

Compiler and Editor Applications

In previous chapters we discussed several ADT structures. In this chapter we want to show small applications of the ADT stack, and then the uses of ADT strings and lists. We do not intend to present the complete solutions of these applications. We also included a brief discussion of a finite-state machine simulator that has practical uses in the lexical analyzer, one function of a compiler. At the end, we presented a line-oriented editor.

An application on a cross-reference generator is left as an exercise. It will require a parser, input and output files, and a binary search tree structure.

An application of SSQLPP, a small SQL preprocessor, is discussed in Chapter 11. It will require a parser, input and output files, and a code generator. It is left as an exercise in Chapter 11.

13.1 Application: Compiler

To show the uses of stacks and their operations by a compiler, we will discuss the compilation process, such components as the lexical analyzer, the parser, the parser symbol table, the code generator, grammar, and state stack and stack operations of a table-driven compiler. We used conventional nomenclature as used in Dr. Dobb (1986). For a thorough and nice discussion see Holub (1990).

13.1.1 Overview of the Compilation Process

A compiler takes a text file (the source) and produces an executable object file (the program). The major stages of this process are diagrammed in Figure 13-1.

A source file's contents are presented to the compiler's lexical analyzer (also called scanner) character-by-character. The analyzer converts recognized character strings (like keywords) into tokens (representing predefined language objects) and passes through unrecognized character strings (like variable names) as is. The compiler's parser (also called syntax analyzer) takes these tokens and strings and produces statement–parse trees connected together as one large structure, the parse tree

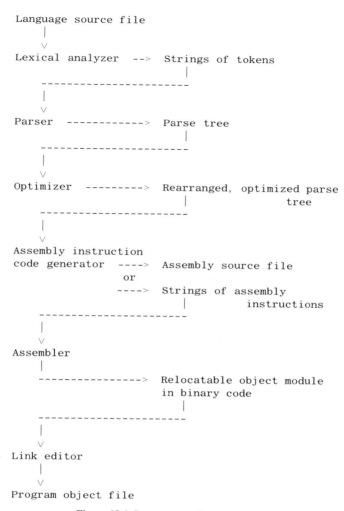

Figure 13-1 Program compilation sequence.

(which is a tree form of data type). The parse tree is passed through the compiler's optimizer to achieve some efficiencies, which results in a rearranged, optimized parse tree. This tree is passed to the compiler's code generator, which takes the tree and produces strings of assembly language instructions in an assembly source file (usually temporary). The assembler is called by the compiler to convert the instructions into a binary machine code module, stored in a temporary file, with internal address references relative to start of module and external address references left unresolved. The compiler then calls the link-loader, which links the specified number of relocatable modules and library routine modules together, resolves the external address and the intermodule address references to the beginning of the object file, and produces the executable object file (the program).

The C compiler is usually implemented as table-driven (using a table to match language patterns with actions), but it may also be built by recursive descent (pattern/action conversions done explicitly in code). In either case, many kinds of stacks, lists, arrays, structs, and trees are used.

We'll look first at a table-driven version, then briefly discuss recursive descent. The code and output of a simple recursive descent parser are given in Chapter 7.

13.1.2 The Lexical Analyzer

In the lexical analyzer, a language keyword table is used to define tokens that are recognized, predefined elements of the language. The table is a struct and its declaration and initialization are shown in Figure 13-2.

```
static struct Key_Word_Table
{
    char *key_name;
    int   key_value;                    /*  value */
} Key_Word_Table[]  =
    {
        "while",      TOK_WHILE,
        "if",         TOK_IF,
        "else",       TOK_ELSE,

           .

           .

        "int",        TOK_INT,
        "short",      TOK_SHORT,
        "long",       TOK_LONG,
        "char",       TOK_CHAR
    };
```

Figure 13-2 The keyword pattern/action table.

A table is static and the size is constant. The contents are also often constant. The table of pattern (keyword/ID number) pairs in Figure 13-2 is turned into a table within the lexical analyzer used to generate the token (an int!) on recognition of a keyword.

13.1.3 The Parser

The parser is a stack machine. Its elements are a large stack to hold current states (expression beginning, subexpression found, expression accepted, etc.), a transition matrix to obtain a new state for each possible pair of current state and the next symbol, a table of user-defined actions, and an interpreter of those actions to produce final output. The parser's primary function calls the lexical analyzer, which reads the next character from standard input or designated source files and returns the next token or character string.

The current state on top of the stack is used with the next symbol to locate an operation in the transition table as shown in Figure 13-3.

13.1.4 The Parser Symbol Table

The primary data structure of the parser is the symbol table, some global pointers to the type, and the access/processing routines. During the compilation process, when a symbol (a string of characters) is encountered in the source program, it

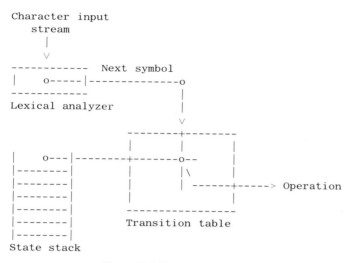

Figure 13-3 The transition table.

is searched in the symbol table. If the symbol is not found in the table, its record is added to the symbol table. The record of a symbol typically contains the symbol name, symbol length, symbol type (e.g., integer, real, string, a simple variable, a pointer, a structure, an array, a function), number of function parameters, and the symbol address (location) in the main memory. It is not necessary to keep the length of a symbol in some computer languages. User-defined symbols go into the symbol table and the stack. The stack is used to keep track of block levels in case of nesting and recursion. The keywords also go into the symbol table if they are not reserved (prohibited to be reused) in a language. Several stages in the compilation process use the information in the symbol table requiring the following operations:

1. Search for a symbol in the symbol table
2. Add a new symbol to the symbol table
3. Delete a symbol from the symbol table
4. Retrieve information for a symbol specified by its name
5. Add new information for a symbol specified by its name
6. Initializing a symbol table
7. Deleting a symbol table

The data structures to implement the symbol table are an array of records, a singly or doubly linked list, a hash table, and various forms of trees (e.g., binary search tree, AVL tree). In the abstract sense, each record is a pair (symbol name, information), where information contains the remaining attributes about the symbol. It is imperative to consider the performance issues for operations like adding, deleting, and searching symbols in order to select the appropriate and efficient data structure for the symbol table.

Implementing the Symbol Table Using a Doubly Linked List

Assuming the doubly linked list structure for a symbol table, a glimpse for the symbol table-entry data-type definitions and global pointers is shown in Figure 13-4.

```
typedef struct symbol_table
{
   char * sym_name;
   int     sym_type;
   int     nest_level;              /*  nesting level  */
   union
   {
      int       int_value;
      short     short_value;
      long      long_value;
   } sym_val;
   union
   {
      int  parm_num;               /*  number of parameters  */
      struct symbol_table * parm_list;
   } func_parm;
   struct symbol_table * next;   /*  next symbol */
   struct symbol_table * prev;   /*  previous symbol  */

}  SYMBOL_TABLE, * SYM_TABL_PTR;

/*  The possible values of sym_type are: */
#define   INT              0
#define   CHAR             1
#define   SHORT            2
#define   LONG             3
#define   STRUCTURE        4

#define   VARIABLE         5
#define   POINTER          6
#define   LABEL            7    /*  used for GOTO   */
#define   ARRAY            8
#define   FUNCTION         9
#define   UNDECLARED      10
#define   NOT_FUNCTION    11

/*  Global pointers and access functions  */

SYM_TABL_PTR
      sym_head,                   /*  pointer to the first record
                                      in the symbol table */
      create_sym(char *),      /*  create a symbol   */
      search_sym(char *),      /*  search for a specified symbol */
      get_sym(char *);         /*  get information for a symbol   */

void  init_symtab(),             /*  initialize a symbol table list */
      add_sym(char *, int ),     /*  add a new symbol */
      delete_sym(char * ),       /*  delete a specified symbol */
      add_info();                /*  add information for a specified symbol */
```

Figure 13-4 The symbol table and functions using it.

The symbol table access function definitions and implementations are shown in Figure 13-5.

```
SYM_TABL_PTR   create_sym( char * new_sym_name )
{
    SYM_TABL_PTR   new_sym_ptr;
```

Figure 13-5 Functions to create, add, delete, search, and initialize the symbol table. *(continues)*

```
        new_sym_ptr = (SYM_TABL_PTR) calloc( 1, sizeof( SYMBOL_TABLE) );
        if ( new_sym_ptr == NULL )
        {
           printf("\n create_sym: No memory for symbol \n");
           return( NULL );
        }
        new_sym_ptr -> sym_name = new_sym_name;
        new_sym_ptr -> sym_type = UNDECLARED;
        return( new_sym_ptr );
}

/*
 *   is_symtab_empty() : Check whether the doubly linked list of
 *                       symbols is empty.
 */
int is_symtab_empty( SYM_TABL_PTR sym_head )
{
        return( sym_head == NULL );
}

/*
 *   add_sym() :   Add a new symbol at the front of the list
 *                 if it is not already in the symbol table.
 */
void add_sym( char * new_sym_name, int new_sym_type )
{
        SYM_TABL_PTR  new_sym_ptr;

        /*
         *  Check the given symbol is already in the table.
         *  If it is in the table, return.
         */
        new_sym_ptr = search_sym( new_sym_name );
        if ( new_sym_ptr != NULL )
          return;

        /*
         *  Allocate memory space for the new symbol.
         */
        new_sym_ptr = create_sym( new_sym_name );
        if ( new_sym_ptr == NULL )
          return;

        new_sym_ptr -> sym_name = new_sym_name;
        new_sym_ptr -> sym_type = new_sym_type;
        new_sym_ptr -> next = NULL;
        new_sym_ptr -> prev = NULL;

        /* Is the doubly linked list of symbols empty?  */
        if ( is_symtab_empty( sym_head ) )
          sym_head = new_sym_ptr;

        /* Add the new symbol at the front of the list of symbols. */
        sym_head -> prev = new_sym_ptr;
        new_sym_ptr -> next = sym_head;
        sym_head = new_sym_ptr;
}
```

Figure 13-5 *(continues)*

```
/*
 *   delete_sym() :   Delete a symbol specified by its name
 */
void   delete_sym( char * sym_name )
{
    SYM_TABL_PTR   sym_ptr, temp_ptr;

    sym_ptr = search_sym( sym_name );
    /*  If it is not found, return  */
    if ( sym_ptr == NULL )
      return;

    /*  Is the symbol to be deleted the head of the list?  */
    if ( sym_ptr == sym_head )
    {
      if ( sym_head -> next == NULL )
        free( sym_head );
      else
      {
        temp_ptr = sym_head -> next;
        free( sym_head );
        sym_head = temp_ptr;
        sym_head -> prev = NULL;
      }
    }
    else
    {
      /*  The symbol to be deleted is found; unlink it  */
      sym_ptr -> prev -> next = sym_ptr -> next;
      sym_ptr -> next -> prev = sym_ptr -> prev;
      free( sym_ptr );
    }
}

/*
 *   search_sym() :   Search for a symbol specified by a symbol name
 */
SYM_TABL_PTR   search_sym( char * srch_sym_name )
{
    SYM_TABL_PTR   search_sym_ptr = sym_head;

    while ( search_sym_ptr != NULL )
    {
      if ( strcmp( srch_sym_name, search_sym_ptr -> sym_name )
                == NULL )
        return( search_sym_ptr );

      search_sym_ptr = search_sym_ptr -> next;
    }
    /*  Search failed; Specified symbol is not found in the list */
    return( NULL );
}

/*
 *   init_symtab() :   Initialize the symbol table.
 */
void   init_symtab()
{
    sym_head = create_sym( "main" );
```

Figure 13-5 *(continues)*

```
    if ( sym_head != NULL )
        sym_head -> sym_type = NOT_FUNCTION;
}
```

Figure 13-5 *(continued)*

Implementing the Symbol Table Using Hash Strategy

The hash table with chaining is now used to implement the symbol table. The hash symbol table, hsymtab, is an array of pointers to the chains of symbol records (entries). The chaining of symbol records uses a doubly linked list. This allows handling overflow, symbol–name collision, and easier deletion of any symbol in a chain.

The declarations for this hash symbol table are shown in Figure 13-6.

```
#define HASH_TABL_SIZ   200

typedef struct symbol_record       /*  record of symbol  */
{
    unsigned char  * sym_name;
    int              sym_type;
    int              nest_level; /*  nesting level  */
    union
    {
        int      int_value;
        short    short_value;
        long     long_value;
    } sym_val;
    union                          /*  if sym_type == FUNCTION */
    {

        int      parm_num;      /*  number of parameters  */
        struct symbol_record * parm_list;
    } func_parm;

    struct symbol_record * next;  /*  next symbol in chain */
    struct symbol_record * prev;  /*  previous symbol */

} SYMBOL, * SYMBOL_PTR;

typedef SYMBOL_PTR  HASH_SYM_TABLE[ HASH_TABL_SIZ ];

HASH_SYM_TABLE  hsymtab;

/*  The possible values of sym_type are: */
#define  INT          0
#define  CHAR         1
#define  SHORT        2
#define  LONG         3
#define  STRUCTURE    4

#define  VARIABLE     5
#define  POINTER      6
#define  LABEL        7     /*  used for GOTO  */
#define  ARRAY        8
#define  FUNCTION     9
#define  UNDECLARED   10
#define  NOT_FUNCTION 11
```

Figure 13-6 Definition for a symbol table with hash.

Figure 13-7 shows a hash function hash_sym() for a simple symbol-table implementation. It uses a symbol's name, sym_name, as the key, adds integer value of each character in the name, and takes the modulus with hash_tab_size, which is returned as the hash value.

```
/*
 *  hash_sym() :   hash function for the symbol hash table
 *                 with chaining.
 */
unsigned int  Hash_sym( char * sym_name, int hash_tab_size )
{
    unsigned int  hash_value = 0;

    while ( *sym_name != '\0' )
        hash_value +=  *sym_name++;

    return( hash_value % hash_tab_size );
}
```

Figure 13-7 Hash function for a simple symbol table.

The management functions for this hashed symbol table are:

```
SYMBOL_PTR
    hash_create_sym(),     /*  create a symbol */
    hash_search_sym(),     /*  search for a specified symbol in
                               the hash symbol table  */
    hash_get_sym();        /*  get information for a symbol  */

void init_hash_symtab(),   /*  initialize hashed symbol table  */
    hash_add_sym(),        /*  add a new symbol in the hash symbol
                               table */
    hash_delete_sym(),     /*  delete a symbol from the hash symbol
                               table */
    hash_add_info();       /*  add information for a specified symbol
                               in the hash symbol table */
```

Implementations of these functions are analogous to the functions described for hashing with chaining in Chapter 9.

13.1.5 The Code Generator

The code generator is the final phase of the compilation process. It assumes that the source program has been lexically and syntactically analyzed and that the type-checks were completed. Then the code generator takes the parse tree and generates strings of assembly language instructions for a target computer system. Designing a code generator requires the prior knowledge of the target computer and its instruction set. The fundamental issues in designing a code generator are:

1. State of input (e.g., error-free parse tree) to the code generator
2. Format of the output of the code generator; for example, absolute addressing machine language, relocatable addressing language, or assembly language

3. Memory allocation and mapping of variable names and labels to the addresses in the main memory
4. Allocation and usage of central processing unit (CPU) registers registers are temporary storage areas)
5. Selection of assembler instructions (e.g., ADD, SUB, MOV, etc.) and their speeds
6. Use of operator precedence in expression evaluations
7. Generation of optimized and correct code for the target computer

For simplicity we assume that the target computer system uses Intel microprocessor iAPX-80386 as the CPU, and our code generator uses its registers AX and BX for operands. The equivalent assembly language codes for the arithmetic and logical operations and other declarations (e.g., int, short, long, char) are stored in an array, `asm_codes[N_PSUEDO_CODES]`. The necessary declarations and mnemonics for a simple and small code generator are shown in Figure 13-8. The code for the code generator is not included.

```
#define   N_PSUEDO_CODES   400
char *    asm_codes[ N_PSUEDO_CODES ];

/*  Some selected keyword (token) types  */
#define   Tok_Assign    1    /*  Token  =  */
#define   Tok_Plus      2    /*  Token  +  */
#define   Tok_Minus     3    /*  Token  -  */
#define   Tok_Times     4    /*  Token  *  */
#define   Tok_Divide    5    /*  Token  /  */

#define   Tok_Lt        6    /*  Token  <  */
#define   Tok_Le        7    /*  Token  <= */
#define   Tok_Eq        8    /*  Token  == */
#define   Tok_Ne        9    /*  Token  != */
#define   Tok_Ge       10    /*  Token  >= */
#define   Tok_Gt       11    /*  Token  >  */
#define   Tok_Or       12    /*  Token  || */
#define   Tok_And      13    /*  Token  && */
#define   Tok_Not      14    /*  Token  !  */

#define   Tok_Tilde    15    /*  Token Bitwise complement  ~  */
#define   Tok_Bit_And  16    /*  Token Bitwise AND    &   */
#define   Tok_Bit_Or   17    /*  Token Bitwise OR     |   */
#define   Tok_Sft_Lft  18    /*  Token Shift Left    <<   */
#define   Tok_Sft_Rgt  19    /*  Token Shift Right   >>   */

#define   Tok_Auto_Plus   20 /*  Token ++ */
#define   Tok_Auto_Minus  21 /*  Token -- */

#define   Tok_IF       22    /*  Token  if     */
#define   Tok_ELSE     23    /*  Token  else   */
#define   Tok_CASE     24    /*  Token  case   */
#define   Tok_SWITCH   25    /*  Token  switch */
#define   Tok_WHILE    26    /*  Token  while  */

#define   Tok_INT      27    /*  Token  int    */
#define   Tok_SHORT    28    /*  Token  short  */
```

Figure 13-8 Mnemonics for the code generator. *(continues)*

```
#define  Tok_LONG    29    /*  Token  long  */
#define  Tok_CHAR    30    /*  Token  char  */

/*  Equivalent assembly language codes    */
asm_codes[Tok_Assign] = "MOV AX, BX \n";
asm_codes[Tok_Plus ]  = "ADD AX, BX \n";
asm_codes[Tok_Minus]  = "SUB AX, BX \n";
asm_codes[Tok_Times]  = "XOR DX, DX \nMUL BX \n";
                              /*  DX:AX = AX * BX  */
asm_codes[Tok_Divide] = "XOR DX, DX \nDIV BX \n";
                              /*  BX divides AX; remainder in DX */


/*  ....  */

asm_codes[Tok_Tilde]       = "NOT AX \n";
asm_codes[Tok_Bit_And]     = "AND AX, BX \n";
asm_codes[Tok_Sft_Lft]     = "SHL AX, 1 \n";
asm_codes[Tok_Sft_Rgt]     = "SHR AX, 1 \n";
asm_codes[Tok_Auto_Plus]   = "INC AX \n";
asm_codes[Tok_Auto_Minus]  = "DEC AX \n";

asm_codes[Tok_CHAR]        = "DB  ";   /*  1 byte  */
asm_codes[Tok_INT]         = "DW  ";   /*  1 word  */
```

Figure 13-8 *(continued)*

13.2 Application: A Small Editor

Most computer systems provide a text editor. Text editors are useful for producing program source files and text data files for programs, letters, books, and manuals. Creation of such files involves string manipulation and operations like insertion, deletion, update, and search within the text file. If the text file does not exist, the editor will have to create one, and save data created in the memory buffer into the file on disk. Note that the data in a text file is basically a collection of characters.

In this section, we present a small line-oriented editor, applying the data structure concepts we learned in the previous chapters. The main concepts used here are files, strings, pointers, structures (struct), and singly or doubly linked lists.

13.2.1 Specification of a Small Line-Oriented Editor

The features of a line-oriented editor are described below:

```
Command format:
     ledit <filename>
         If <filename> exists, it is brought into the
             editor's buffer.
         If <filename> does not exist, then it will be
             created when the file is written.
         If <filename> is not specified, then the file name
             will be set to "noname.led".

Edit commands:
         l <range>   - to list a range of lines
         d <range>   - to delete a range of lines
```

```
          w <filename>- to write the edited file to
                        <filename> If <filename> is not
                        specified, it is written to the name
                        used on the initial command.
          i <lineno>  - to begin inserting lines after
                        <lineno>

          s [<range>] <search_value> - to search (forward)
                        for a string within a range.
          r <range>   - to replace a range of lines

          m <range>   - to modify a range of lines at the
                        current cursor position with the
                        following subcommands:
                        i)    i for Character Insertion
                        ii)   d for Character Deletion
                        iii)  r for Character Replacement
                        iv)   <DEL> to exit from Modify mode

          h <command> - to display Help for editor command(s)
          q           - to exit from the editor

      where <range> = [lower line [,upper line]]
                          or
                      <null> which implies the current
                          line

            <search_value> is a delimited string
                        described by <delim><string><delim>,
                        e.g., /Green/ to find an occurrence
                        of "Green" in the file.

      <ESC> terminates an "input" operation.
```

Our approach to design and implement such an editor is based on dynamically creating and deleting a line in the editor buffer. The basic data that a line-oriented editor deals with is a line. We can view each line as an element of a singly linked list-type structure as follows:

```
typedef struct an_edit_line LINE;

struct an_edit_line
   {
     LINE  *line_next;    /* Pointer to next line */
     char  line_text[MAX_LINE];
   };
```

The field line_text of the an_edit_line structure is an array of characters to hold actual data of a line. The other LINE-type pointer field is used to point to the next line. The detailed implementation and sample run are given in Example 13.1. While running the editor, the editing session was captured using Unix's 'tee' utility.

13.2.2 Source Code for the Small Editor

Example 13.1

Code Section

```
/*
 * Program Name     : ledit.c    LINE-ORIENTED EDITOR
 *
 * Program Description :
 *    The program "ledit" implements a simple text line editor.
 *
 *   Instructions to Compile this program ledit.c :
 *      On Unix:   cc  -D UNIX   -O ledit.c -o ledit
 *
 *      On MSDOS: Define 'MSDOS' because command line
 *                may differ from MS-C, QUICK-C
 *
 */


#include <stdio.h>
#include <ctype.h>            /*  Calling case conversion routines
                                  declared in this header file     */


/* ****   Start of declaration of GLOBAL VARIABLES     ****    */

#define MAX_LINE 80          /*  Size of maximum line            */

#define LIST     'l'         /*  Abbreviation for List command    */
#define DELETE   'd'         /*  Abbreviation for Delete command  */
#define REPLACE  'r'         /*  Abbreviation for Replace command */
#define WRITE    'w'         /*  Abbreviation for Write command    */
#define SEARCH   's'         /*  Abbreviation for Search command  */
#define INSERT   'i'         /*  Abbreviation for Insert command  */
#define QUIT     'q'         /*  Abbreviation for Quit command    */

#define ESC      0x1B        /*  Terminates input                */
#define NL       '\n'        /*  New Line                        */
#define CR       '\r'        /*  Carriage Return                 */

/* Define LINE as a single linked list structured data type   */
typedef struct an_edit_line LINE;

        struct an_edit_line {
                LINE   *line_next;
                char   line_text[MAX_LINE];
        };

        LINE *insert_line();  /*  Function to insert line    */
        LINE *locate_line();  /*  Function to locate a line */

        int  linelow  = 0,
        linehi    = 0,
        curline   = 0,
```

```
               linelast  = 0;
               char *search_string;
               char *subst_string;
               int  cursor;
               char cmd_line[80]; /*  Command input line      */
               LINE line_zero;   /*  the zeroth line         */
               FILE *fp;  /*  the handle for edited file*/
               char filename[64]; /*  Edited file name        */

/* End of declaration of GLOBAL VARIABLES    */

/*
 * main(): main for LINE ORIENTED EDITOR
 */
main( int argc, char **argv )
{

#ifdef  UNIX
       system( "clear" ); /* Clear Screen */
#endif

    printf("\n \t\t\t   LINE-ORIENTED EDITOR   V1.0 \n\n");

        /* Set up "noname.led" as a default file name */
        strcpy(filename,"noname.led");
        line_zero.line_next = NULL;
        curline = 1;
        linelast = 0;

    /*  Decide next phase of work based on how many
     *  arguments were passed as command line arguments.
     */

        switch (argc)
          {
            case 2:
                     strcpy(filename,*(++argv));
                     break;
            case 1:
                     break;
            default:
                     printf("usage: ledit <filename> \n");
                     exit(-1);
          }
        if ((fp = fopen(filename,"r")) == NULL)
          {
                printf("ledit: file \"%s\" not found.",
                               filename);
                printf(" Assumed to be new. \n");
          }
        else
          {
```

```
                        printf("ledit: file \"%s\" is taken as \
                                    default.\n", filename);
                        read_file( fp, &line_zero );
                }
        do_edit();
}


/*
 * read_file() :   It is called if file already exists
 *
 *          read_file( fp, line_zero )
 *              reads file from fp into the editor after the
 *              line pointed to by line_zero
 */
read_file(  FILE *fp, LINE *line_zero )
{
        LINE *curr_line = line_zero;
        char inline[MAX_LINE+1];

        while ( fgets( inline,MAX_LINE+1,fp) )
        {
                curr_line = insert_line( inline, curr_line );
                linelast++;
        }
        fclose(fp);
}


/*
 * do_edit(): Do       LINE ORIENTED EDITING
 *
 *          do_edit
 *                  Loop which processes edit commands until
 *                  quit command is entered.
 *
 */
do_edit()
{
        char command;

        while ( get_cmd( cmd_line, sizeof(cmd_line) ) )
          {
                cursor = 0;
                /*          skip over any spaces, tabs, etc */
                skip_space();
                command = tolower(cmd_line[cursor]);
                cursor++;   /* move cursor to next char */

                switch ( command )
                  {
                    case LIST  :
                        if (get_range() > 0)
                                do_list();
                        break;
```

```
                        case DELETE:
                            if (get_range() > 0)
                                    do_delete();
                            break;
                        case REPLACE:
                            if (get_range() > 0)
                                    do_replace();
                            break;
                        case WRITE :
                            skip_space();
                            if ( cmd_line[ cursor ] )
                                    do_write( &cmd_line[ cursor ]);
                            else
                                    do_write( filename );
                            break;
                        case SEARCH:
                            if (get_range() > 0)
                                    do_search();
                            break;
                        case INSERT:
                            if (get_range() > 0)
                                    do_insert();
                            break;
                        case QUIT  :
                            return(0);
                            break;
                        default:
                            printf("\n ledit: Unrecognized \
                                                command\n");

                }
        }
}
/*
 * get_cmd(): Prints LEDIT and waits to get command
 */
get_cmd( char *line, int len )
{
        printf("LEDIT: ");
        return( (int) gets(line,len) );
}

/*
 * skip_space() : Skip spaces to move cursor in editing line
 */
skip_space()
{
        while (isspace(cmd_line[cursor]) && cmd_line[cursor])
                cursor++;
}

/*
 * get_range():
 *
```

```
 *          get_range:
 *              sets linelow, linehi from current line number.
 *              if there is a numeric range value specified,
 *              it sets linelow and linehi from the values
 *              specified.
 *
 */
get_range()
{
        char *linep;

        skip_space();
        linep = &cmd_line[cursor];

        linelow = curline;
        linehi  = curline;
        if ( isdigit(*linep) )
          {
            linelow = 0;
            while (isdigit(*linep))
              {
                    linelow = linelow * 10 + *linep - '0';
                linep++;
              }
            curline = linelow;
            linehi  = linelow;
            /*        Check for high line number           */
            if (*linep == ',')
              {
                    linehi = 0;
                    linep++;
                    while (isdigit(*linep))
                      {
                        linehi = linehi * 10 + *linep - '0';
                        linep++;
                      }
              }
          }

        if ((linelow <= linehi) && (linelow > 0))
                return(linelow);
        else
          {
                printf("invalid line number range\n");
                return(-1);
          }
}


/*
 * insert_line():
 *
 *          insert_line(line_text, curr_line)
 *              inserts a line containing "line_text" between
 *              curr_line and the line which follows it.
```

```
*              Returns a pointer to the line allocated
*          ( Lines are structured as a Single Linked list
*            It calls 'malloc()' to allocate memory
*            LINE-type structured data
*
*/

LINE   *insert_line( char   *line_text, LINE   *curr_line )
{
        int line_len;
        LINE *new_line;

    /*
     *   Compute the size of this line element as size of the
     *   text plus size of the LINE structure, minus the size
     *   of the defined text portion of the LINE struct
     *   (MAX_LINE)
     */
        line_len = strlen(line_text) - MAX_LINE + sizeof(LINE);

        new_line = (LINE *) malloc( line_len );

        if ( new_line == NULL )
          {
            printf("\n insert_line: ERROR - No memory space \n");
            return( NULL );
          }
        new_line->line_next = curr_line->line_next;
        curr_line->line_next = new_line;
        strcpy(new_line->line_text, line_text);
        return(new_line);
}


/*
 * delete_line(): Search for line number. If found, delete
 *               the line by readjusting the pointers in
 *               the single linked list, and finally
 *               releasing the memory space doing free( )
 *               system call.
 */

delete_line( int lineno )
{
        LINE *plinep, *clinep;
        /* locate the line prior to the one to delete     */
        plinep = locate_line(lineno-1);
        clinep = plinep->line_next;
        /* Point prior line to deleted line's successor  */
        plinep->line_next = clinep->line_next;
        /* Free the deleted line */
        free(clinep);
}
```

```
/*
 * locate_line(): Searches for the specified line number.
 *                Note that the lines are constructed as a
 *                Singly Linked list.
 *
 *   locate_line(lineno)
 *        locates the line structure for the <lineno>th line
 *        If the lineno is not found, it returns NULL
 */
LINE   *locate_line( int lineno )
{
        LINE *linep;
        linep = &line_zero; /* Point at the first line */
        while (lineno--)
           if ((linep = linep->line_next) == NULL) break;
        return(linep);
}


/*
 * do_list(): First calls locate_line(); If fond, displays
 *            the line(s) on the screen.
 */
do_list()
{
        LINE *linep;
        for (curline = linelow; curline <= linehi ; curline++)
          {
            if (linep = locate_line(curline))
                printf("%d: %s", curline, linep->line_text);
            else
                break;
          }
}


/*
 * do_replace(): Replace a character in a line or range
 *               (Not implemented for Exercise )
 */
do_replace()
{
    /*  Left as an exercise  */
}


/*
 * do_search (): Search  a character in a line or range
 *               (Not implemented for Exercise )
 */
do_search()
{
    /*  Left as an exercise  */
}
```

```
/*
 * do_insert (): Insert  new line(s) in a line or range
 */
do_insert()
{
        LINE *linep;

        if (curline > linelast)
                curline = linelast;
        linep = locate_line(curline);
        while (get_input(curline+1, cmd_line, sizeof(cmd_line)))
          {
             linep = insert_line(cmd_line, linep);
             linelast++;
             curline++;
          }
}


/*
 * do_delete (): Delete one and/or range of lines to
 *               execute the 'd' command
 *
 *       do_delete
 *               delete lines from high line number back to
 *               low line number
 *
 */
do_delete()
{
        while (linehi >= linelow)
          {
             delete_line(linehi--);
             linelast--;                  /* Drop last line count */
          }
        curline = linelow;
}


/*
 * get_input () : Get the input line character by character
 *               until <ESC> character
 */
get_input( char lineno, char * line, int len )
{
        char ch;

        printf("%d: ", lineno);

#ifdef  MSDOS
        while ((ch = getche() ) != ESC)
          {
             if (ch == CR) /* If new line before ESC, stop */
#endif
```

```
#ifdef   UNIX

        while ((ch = getchar() ) != ESC)
          {
            if (ch == NL)   /* If new line before ESC, stop */
#endif
                break;
            else
              {
                *line = ch;
                line++;
              }
          }
        *line = '\n';        /* Add new line to terminate   */
        *(++line) = '\0';    /* Terminate string            */
        printf("\n");        /* Move to next line           */
        if (ch == ESC)
                return(0);
        else
                return(1);

}


/*
 * do_write(): Execute Write (W) command
 *
 *        do_write(fname)
 *          Save editor buffer contents into disk by writing
 *          editor buffer contents to file named "fname"
 *
 */
do_write( char *fname )
{
        LINE *clinep;              /* Current Line Pointer   */

        if (fp = fopen(fname,"w")) /* Open file as writable  */
          {
                /*          get first line         */
                clinep = line_zero.line_next;
                while (clinep)
                  {
                    fputs(clinep->line_text, fp);
                    clinep = clinep->line_next;
                  }
                fclose(fp);        /* Close the file now      */
          }
        else
          {
                printf("do_write: unable to open file %s\n",
                                                fname);
          }

}
```

Output Section

Here is the sample editing session with this line-oriented editor.

```
                        LINE-ORIENTED EDITOR    V1.0
 ledit: file "ledit.txt" not found. Assumed to be new.
LEDIT:
 ledit: Unrecognized command
LEDIT: i
 1:
 2:
 3:
 4:
 5:
LEDIT: w
LEDIT: l 1,4
 1: This text is being created by using "ledit" editor
 2: to demonstrate that it does some text processing.
 3:
 4: This ends the session.
LEDIT: q
```

Note that at the `write` (w) command the editor saves the content of the edit
buffer into a file `ledit.txt`, the default name. Here is the content of the file
`"ledit.txt"`:

```
This text is being created by using the "ledit" editor
to demonstrate that it does some text processing.

This ends the session.
```

Exercises

13-1 Write a program to implement a cross-reference generator, also known
as mapper. It does the following:

1. Reads an input file in C.
2. Inserts line numbers for each line, and creates an output file.
3. Parses the output file and forms a binary search tree in a lexicographic ascending order; each node contains a token, and
   the line numbers where the token is found. (The number of
   lines in which a token may be found, is not fixed.)
4. Prints the output file, followed by the tokens, and their associated line numbers. For example:

break:	2	10	15
continue:	16	35	99
temp:	4	15	20

   The words "break," "continue," and "temp" are tokens.
5. Print out all c-reserved keywords and user-defined symbols.
   Also filter out all commented texts.

13-2 With reference to the program on line-oriented editing in Example 13.1, write programs to implement the following commands and integrate them with `ledit.c`:

```
s [<range>] <search_value> - to search (forward)
                                for a string within
                                a range.
r <range>    - to replace a range of lines

h <command> - to display help of command(s)

m <range>    - to modify a range of lines at the
               current cursor position with following
               subcommands:
                    i)    i for Character Insertion
                    ii)   d for Character Deletion
                    iii)  r for Character Replacement
                    iv)   <DEL> to exit from Modify mode

where <range> = [lower line [,upper line]]
                    or
      <null> which implies the current line.

      <search_value> is a delimited string described
      by <delim><string><delim>, e.g.,
      /Green/ to find an occurrence
      of "Green" in the file.

<ESC> terminates an "input" operation.
```

Applications for Windowing

In this chapter we will demonstrate the uses of data structures like struct, stacks, and trees in the area of window-based applications development. Window-based applications provide such unique advantages as easy user interface, graphic representation of data, shared display, data interchange between applications, sharp look of the application, and display of information in an elegant, attractive, and organized style. Some window applications are based on packages like X-Window, Microsoft Window, and Unix Curses library.

A window is conceptually a rectangular area, that is, a two-dimensional array of characters displayed on the screen of a video display terminal. A window has a length and width. The image of the terminal screen, also known as *screen image*, is maintained by the character array. There is one character in that array corresponding to each place (point) on the screen. Each point on the screen will have (x,y) coordinates. A bit-mapped terminal possesses an area of memory with each bit corresponding to a pixel on the screen. Each pixel has various types of intensity and display resolution such as high, low, and reverse video. The screen image is initially filled with blank characters.

The physical structure of a window is in general characterized by a record consisting of many attributes as follows:

1. Current (x,y) position of the cursor relative to the current window
2. Beginning values of x and y coordinates—that is, the upper left corner of the window relative to the upper left corner of the screen
3. Maximum height and width of a window
4. Color of points in a window
5. Previous normal color of a window
6. Style flags such as Overlapped, Popup, Child, Subwindow, Fullwindow, Box, and Border
7. State flags such as Iconic, Visible, Hidden, Disabled, and Scroll—Vertical/Horizontal
8. Title of a window
9. Uniqueness of a window
10. Address or pointer of the character array that contains the screen image of a window

11. Efficient organization of windows such as an array of window records, a singly linked list, a doubly linked list, or a tree

This list of attributes is not complete and may vary from application to application, and from canned packages. While working with windows, one (root) window may create one or more child(ren) window(s). Such windows when displayed may overlap entirely or partially on the currently displayed window. The basic operations and functions related to a window are:

1. Define structure of a window
2. Initialize a window
3. Allocate memory for a window
4. Create a window
5. Position and/or move cursor anywhere inside a window
6. Insert, delete, and move characters and/or text anywhere inside a window
7. Display a window; if overlapped, do not destroy the previous window
8. Draw border around a window
9. Set or change attributes of a window
10. Refresh a window
11. Delete, destroy, and/or close one window
12. Delete, destroy, and/or close all windows
13. Move characters between windows
14. Move a window to icon area
15. Partition the screen into subwindows
16. Handle each window independently
17. Scroll a window in any one of the four directions
18. Create a subwindow
19. Delete, destroy, and/or close subwindow(s)
20. Clean up and exit

In the following section, we will discuss the data structure and develop our stand-alone window routines and a small window applications. The routines can be used or modified to write any other application.

14.1 Stand-Alone Window Applications

In this section, we will implement some basic operations on a window. To implement the operations, it is essential to look into the WINDOW structure as shown below:

```
/* *********************************************** *
 * DATA STRUCTURE 'FIELD' FOR Template in a WINDOW        *
 * (FIELD structures will be maintained as a Double Linked *
 *  List using two FIELD-type structure pointers 'fnxt'   *
 *  'fprv'.                                               *
 * *********************************************** */
typedef struct field
    {                           /* data entry field description */
      char *fmask;              /* field data entry mask        */
```

```
        char *fprot;              /* field protection            */
        char *fbuff;              /* field buffer                */
        int ftype;                /* field type                  */
        int frow;                 /* field row                   */
        int fcol;                 /* field column                */
        void (*fhelp)();          /* field help function         */
        char *fhwin;              /* field help window           */
        int flx, fly;             /* help window location        */
        int (*fvalid)();          /* field validation function   */
        struct field *fnxt;       /* next field on template      */
        struct field *fprv;       /* previous field on template  */

    } FIELD;

/* ************************************************************ *
 * Main DATA STRUCTURE 'WINDOW' FOR WINDOW                      *
 * (includes fields '_nx' and '_pv' to form a Double Linked     *
 *    List of Windows.)                                         *
 * ************************************************************ */

typedef struct _wnd
  {
        int _wv;                  /* true if window is visible   */
        int _hd;                  /* true if window was hidden   */
        char *_ws;                /* points to window save block */
        char *_tl;                /* points to window title      */
        int _wx;                  /* new x coordinate            */
        int _wy;                  /* new y coordinate            */
        int _ww;                  /* window width                */
        int _wh;                  /* window height               */
        int _wsp;                 /* scroll pointer              */
        int _sp;                  /* selection pointer           */
        int _cr;                  /* cursor x location           */
        int btype;                /* border type                 */
        int wcolor[4];            /* colors for window           */
        int _pn;                  /* previous normal color       */
        struct _wnd *_nx;         /* points to next window       */
        struct _wnd *_pv;         /* points to previous window   */
        FIELD *_fh;               /* points to 1st data entry fld */
        FIELD *_ft;               /* points to last data entry fld */

    }  WINDOW;

/* ************************************************************ *
 * DATA STRUCTURE 'MENU' FOR MENU in a WINDOW                   *
 * ************************************************************ */

typedef struct w_menu
  {
        char *mname;              /* Menu name (description)     */
        char **mselcs;            /* Pointer to menu selection   */
        void (**func)();
  } MENU;
```

Note that in the WINDOW structure, most of the window attributes as noted in the
first few paragraphs of this chapter, are included. Moreover, it includes two pointers, _fh and _ft, pointing to the first and last FIELD-type structure data-entry
fields, respectively. The members _nx and _pv, respectively as pointers to the next
and previous WINDOW-type structures will enable us to organize the windows as a
doubly linked list. As a result, window operations such as create, add, and delete a
window will simply follow their counterpart procedures in case of a doubly linked
list structure. The specific work is to change or supply the data content of the list
element. Inclusion of the FIELD-type pointer members fnxt and fprv will allow
us to organize the list of FIELD-type structures as a doubly linked list. *fbuff is
the pointer to the character buffer that contains the screen image.

The doubly linked list structure of WINDOW-type structures is:

```
        Window 1          Window 2                          Last window
                                        Previous
                                        link
       ---------         ---------                          ---------
      |  NULL   | <---|-*  _pv  |      . . .      <---|-*  _pv  |
      |-------  |      |------- |                          |------- |
      |    .    |      |    .    |                          |    .    |
      |    .    |      |    .    |                          |    .    |
      |    .    |      |    .    |                          |    .    |
      |------- |      |------- |                          |------- |
      |  _nx  *-|--->  |  _nx  *-|--->  . . .             |  NULL   |
       ---------         ---------       Next link           ---------
```

The steps in creating a new window are:

    Step 1. Allocate physical memory for a WINDOW-type structure using the
            malloc () system call. If successful, it returns a pointer to memory
            block of size of WINDOW structure.
    Step 2. Initialize the attribute fields of the WINDOW structure.
    Step 3. Insert the window in the doubly linked list of windows. This is simi-
            lar to inserting an element in a doubly linked list by adjusting '_nx'
            and '_pv' pointers.
    Step 4. Return the WINDOW-type pointer pointing to the newly created
            window.

The steps in deleting a window are:

    Step 1. Search for the window in the doubly linked list of windows. If it is
            not found, stop. If it is found, proceed to step 2.
    Step 2. Remove the window by adjusting pointers with the pointers of the
            specified window's two adjacent neighbors—next and previous
            windows.
    Step 3. Release memory space allocated to the window using the free ()
            library function call.

In window. c, we implemented the following window operations in ANSI C on an
IBM-PC/Compatible with DOS operating system:

Description	Function in C
1. Create a window	WINDOW *establish_window(int, int, int, int)

2. Set border of a window	`void set_border(WINDOW *, int);`
3. Set color of a window	`void set_colors(WINDOW *, int, int,` `int, int)`
4. Set intensity	`void set_intensity(WINDOW *, int)`
5. Set title of a window	`void set_title(WINDOW *, char *)`
6. Display a window	`void display_window(WINDOW *)`
7. Delete a window	`void delete_window(WINDOW *)`
8. Clear a window	`void clear_window(WINDOW *)`
9. Hide a window	`void hide_window(WINDOW *)`
10. Write inside a window	`void wprintf(WINDOW *, char * )`
11. Write a char inside a window	`void wputchar(WINDOW *, int)`
12. Close and delete all window	`void close_all(void)`
13. Position cursor inside a window	`void wcursor(WINDOW *, int x,` `int y)`
14. Create a window and display an error message inside it	`void error_message(char *)`
15. Clear the window for error message	`void clear_message(void)`

Implementations of these window routines and their use in a calling C application are given in Example 14-1. This application is a simple menu-driven process management program. A window is created with the title "PROCESS MANAGEMENT MENU" and seven menus are displayed inside the window. The program continuously runs, waiting for menu selection from the user.

Examples

Example 14-1

Code Section

```
/* ************************************************************ *
 * window.h  :  Header file defining data structure to        *
 *              create stand-alone window routines.           *
 *              This is intended to build own window routines *
 *              without using any built-in window package     *
 * ************************************************************ */

#define RED    4
#define GREEN  2
#define BLUE   1
#define WHITE  (RED+GREEN+BLUE)
#define YELLOW (RED+GREEN)
#define AQUA   (GREEN+BLUE)
#define MAGENTA (RED+BLUE)
#define BLACK   0
#define BRIGHT  8
#define DIM     0
```

```
#define BORDER  0
#define TITLE   1
#define ACCENT  2
#define NORMAL  3
#define ALL     4

#define FALSE   0
#define TRUE    ~FALSE
#define ERROR   -1
#define OK      0

/* *********************************************************   *
 * DATA STRUCTURE 'FIELD' FOR Template in a WINDOW             *
 * (FIELD structures will be maintained as a Doubly Linked     *
 *  List using two FIELD-type structure pointers 'fnxt'        *
 *  'fprv'.                                                    *
 * *********************************************************   */
typedef struct field
    {                           /* data entry field description */
        char *fmask;            /* field data entry mask        */
        char *fprot;            /* field protection             */
        char *fbuff;            /* field buffer                 */
        int ftype;              /* field type                   */
        int frow;               /* field row                    */
        int fcol;               /* field column                 */
        void (*fhelp)();        /* field help function          */
        char *fhwin;            /* field help window            */
        int flx, fly;           /* help window location         */
        int (*fvalid)();        /* field validation function    */
        struct field *fnxt;     /* next field on template       */
        struct field *fprv;     /* previous field on template   */

    } FIELD;

/* *********************************************************   *
 * Main DATA STRUCTURE 'WINDOW' FOR WINDOW                     *
 * (includes fields '_nx' and '_pv' to form a Doubly Linked    *
 *   List of Windows.)                                         *
 * *********************************************************   */

typedef struct _wnd
    {
        int _wv;                /* true if window is visible    */
        int _hd;                /* true if window was hidden    */
        char *_ws;              /* points to window save block  */
        char *_tl;              /* points to window title       */
        int _wx;                /* new x coordinate             */
        int _wy;                /* new y coordinate             */
        int _ww;                /* window width                 */
        int _wh;                /* window height                */
        int _wsp;               /* scroll pointer               */
        int _sp;                /* selection pointer            */
        int _cr;                /* cursor x location            */
        int btype;              /* border type                  */
```

```
        int wcolor[4];          /* colors for window            */
        int _pn;                /* previous normal color        */
        struct _wnd *_nx;       /* points to next window        */
        struct _wnd *_pv;       /* points to previous window    */
        FIELD *_fh;             /* points to 1st data entry fld */
        FIELD *_ft;             /* points to last data entry fld */

   }  WINDOW;

/* ********************************************************** *
 * DATA STRUCTURE 'MENU' FOR MENU in a WINDOW                *
 * ********************************************************** */

typedef struct w_menu
   {
        char *mname;            /* Menu name (description)      */
        char **mselcs;          /* Pointer to menu selection    */
        void (**func)();
   } MENU;

/* ********************************************************** *
 * Define MACROS for defining and accessing WINDOW attributes*
 * ********************************************************** */

#define SAV        (wnd->_ws)
#define WTITLE     (wnd->_tl)
#define COL        (wnd->_wx)
#define ROW        (wnd->_wy)
#define WIDTH      (wnd->_ww)
#define HEIGHT     (wnd->_wh)
#define SCROLL     (wnd->_wsp)
#define SELECT     (wnd->_sp)
#define WCURS      (wnd->_cr)
#define WBORDER    (wnd->wcolor[BORDER])
#define WTITLEC    (wnd->wcolor[TITLE])
#define WACCENT    (wnd->wcolor[ACCENT])
#define WNORMAL    (wnd->wcolor[NORMAL])
#define PNORMAL    (wnd->_pn)
#define BTYPE      (wnd->btype)
#define NEXT       (wnd->_nx)
#define PREV       (wnd->_pv)
#define WCOLOR     (wnd->wcolor)
#define VISIBLE    (wnd->_wv)
#define HIDDEN     (wnd->_hd)
#define FHEAD      (wnd->_fh)
#define FTAIL      (wnd->_ft)

#define NW         (wcs[wnd->btype].nw)      /* North West      */
#define NE         (wcs[wnd->btype].ne)      /* North East      */
#define SE         (wcs[wnd->btype].se)      /* South East      */
#define SW         (wcs[wnd->btype].sw)      /* South West      */
#define SIDE       (wcs[wnd->btype].side)
#define LINE       (wcs[wnd->btype].line)
```

```
/* *************************************************** *
 * Declaring General purpose external cursor management    *
 * routines (implemented in cursrman.c)                    *
 * *************************************************** */
void clear_screen(void);
int vmode(void);
void cursor(int, int);
void curr_cursor(int *, int *);
int cursor_type(void);
void set_cursor_type(int);
int get_char(void);
int scroll_lock(void);
void vpoke(unsigned, unsigned, unsigned);
int vpeek(unsigned, unsigned);


/* *************************************************** *
 * Declaring routines for operations on WINDOWs            *
 * (These are implemented in WINDOW.c)                     *
 * *************************************************** */

WINDOW *establish_window(int, int, int, int);
void set_border(WINDOW *, int);
void set_colors(WINDOW *, int, int, int, int);
void set_intensity(WINDOW *, int);
void set_title(WINDOW *, char *);
void display_window(WINDOW *);
void delete_window(WINDOW *);
void clear_window(WINDOW *);
void hide_window(WINDOW *);
void wprintf(WINDOW *, char *);
void wputchar(WINDOW *, int);
void close_all(void);
void wcursor(WINDOW *, int x, int y);
void error_message(char *);
void clear_message(void);


/* *************************************************** *
 * Define MACROS for defining and accessing WINDOW attributes*
 * *************************************************** */

#define reverse_video(wnd)  wnd->wcolor[3]=wnd->wcolor[2]
#define normal_video(wnd)  wnd->wcolor[3]=wnd->_pn
#define rmove_window(wnd,x,y)  repos_wnd(wnd, x, y, 0)
#define move_window(wnd,x,y)  repos_wnd(wnd, COL-x, ROW-y, 0)
#define forefront(wnd)  repos_wnd(wnd, 0, 0, 1)
#define rear_window(wnd)  repos_wnd(wnd, 0, 0, -1)

void accent(WINDOW *);
void deaccent(WINDOW *);
void scroll(WINDOW *, int);
void repos_wnd(WINDOW *, int, int, int);
void acline(WINDOW *, int);
```

```
#define accent(wnd)        acline(wnd, WACCENT)
#define deaccent(wnd) acline(wnd, WNORMAL)
#define clr(bg,fg,in)  ((fg)|(bg<<4)|(in))
#define vad(x,y)  ((y)*160+(x)*2)
void displ(WINDOW *wnd, int x, int y, int ch, int at);


/* ******************************************************* *
 * End of GLOBAL VARIABLES AND STRUCTURES for WINDOW Program *
 * ******************************************************* */


/* ******************************************************* *
 * keys.h   Define keys for IBM-PC DOS-based keyboard      *
 * ******************************************************* */


#define HT              9       /* Horizontal Tab            */
#define RUBOUT          8       /* Rub Out                   */
#define BELL            7       /* Bell                      */
#define ESC             27      /* Escape                    */
#define SHIFT_HT        143     /* Shift with Horizontal Tab */
#define CTRL_T          20      /* Control - T               */
#define CTRL_B          2       /* Control - B               */
#define CTRL_D          4       /* Control - D               */
#define ALT_D           160     /* Alt     - D               */

#define F1              187
#define F2              188
#define F3              189
#define F4              190
#define F5              191
#define F6              192
#define F7              193
#define F8              194
#define F9              195
#define F10             196

#define HOME            199     /* HOME                      */
#define UP              200     /* Up Arrow                  */
#define PGUP            201     /* Page Up                   */
#define BS              203     /* Back Space                */
#define FWD             205     /* Forward (Right arrow)     */
#define END             207     /* END                       */
#define DN              208     /* Down Arrow                */
#define PGDN            209     /* Page Down                 */
#define INS             210     /* Insert                    */
#define DEL             211     /* Delete                    */

#define CTRL_HOME       247     /* Control - Home            */
#define CTRL_BS         243     /* Control - Backspace       */
#define CTRL_FWD        244     /* Control - Forward         */
#define CTRL_END        245     /* Control - End             */

/* ******    End of keys.h      ***********              */
```

```
/* ******************************************************** *
 * Program Name:  menu_application.c                        *
 *                                                          *
 * Purpose:       Write a simple Menu-driven application     *
 *                using stand-alone Window-based routines in *
 *                window.c. The menu will be displayed inside *
 *                a window, and ask the user for selecting a  *
 *                menu.                                       *
 * System:        IBM-PC/Compatible with DOS Operating System *
 *                                                          *
 * ******************************************************** */

#include <stdio.h>
#include <stdlib.h>
#include <bios.h>
#include <ctype.h>
#include <conio.h>
#include "window.h"
#include "keys.h"

WINDOW *mnwnd;                              /* Pointer to Menu window */
void process_menu();                        /* Simple Menu            */

/* ******************************************************** *
 * Program Name:  main()  to demonstrate WINDOW-based       *
 *                Application.                               *
 * ******************************************************** */
main()
{
    process_menu();
}


/* ******************************************************** *
 * process_menu()  : Create a window, display the window    *
 *                   with a title                           *
 *                       "PROCESS MANAGEMENT MENU"          *
 *                   and display following seven choices    *
 *                       Settime, Gettime, Run, Delay,      *
 *                       Wakeup, Interrupt, Quit.           *
 *                   inside the window.                     *
 *                   It does not call or implement any of   *
 *                   the choices.                           *
 * ******************************************************** */

void process_menu()
{
    int key, id, tm;

    /* ----  Create a window             */
    mnwnd = establish_window(19, 16, 10, 26);
    /* ----  Set title, colors           */
    set_title(mnwnd, " PROCESS MANAGEMENT MENU ");
```

```
set_colors(mnwnd, ALL, RED, AQUA, BRIGHT);
set_colors(mnwnd, ACCENT, WHITE, BLACK, DIM);
/* ---- Write menus inside the window */
wprintf(mnwnd,"      Settime \n");
wprintf(mnwnd,"      Gettime \n");
wprintf(mnwnd,"      Run \n");
wprintf(mnwnd,"      Delay \n");
wprintf(mnwnd,"      Wakeup \n");
wprintf(mnwnd,"      Interrupt \n");
wprintf(mnwnd,"      Quit \n");
/* ---- Display the window          */
display_window( mnwnd );

/* ---- Wait for choice selection.   */

while ( 1 )
   {
     wcursor(mnwnd,0,7);
     wprintf(mnwnd," Pick first letter ?      ");
     wcursor(mnwnd,21,7);

     key = toascii(bioskey(0));
     putch(key);
     switch(key)
        {
           case 'r':             /* Run a Process     */
              wprintf(mnwnd," Run Menu is not implemented");
              break;

           case 'd':             /* Delay a Process   */
              wprintf(mnwnd," Delay Menu is not implemented");
              break;
           case 's':             /* Set System time   */
              wprintf(mnwnd," Settime Menu is not implemented");
              break;

           case 'g':             /* Get System time   */
              wprintf(mnwnd," Gettime Menu is not implemented");
              break;

           case 'w':             /* Wakeup a process   */
              wprintf(mnwnd," Wakeup Menu is not implemented");
              break;

           case 'i':             /* Interrupt a process */
              wprintf(mnwnd," Run Menu is not implemented");
              break;

           case 'q':             /* Quit               */
              break;
           default:
              wprintf(mnwnd," Invalid choice");
              break;
```

```
        }                                    /*  end  switch()      */
    }                                        /*  end  while(1)      */

}

/* ********************************************************* *
 * Program:  cursrman.c                                      *
 *           Implement cursor management routines for an IBM *
 *           PC DOS-based compatible system.                 *
 * ********************************************************* */

#pragma inline
#include <dos.h>
static union REGS rg;

/* ********************************************************* *
 *  cursor(): For defining cursor position                   *
 * ********************************************************* */

void cursor(int x, int y)
{
    rg.x.ax = 0x0200;
    rg.x.bx = 0;
    rg.x.dx = ((y << 8) & 0xff00) + x;
    int86(16, &rg, &rg);
}

/* ********************************************************* *
 *  curr_cursor(): Determining cursor position.              *
 * ********************************************************* */

void curr_cursor(int *x, int *y)
{
    rg.x.ax = 0x0300;
    rg.x.bx = 0;
    int86(16, &rg, &rg);
    *x = rg.h.dl;
    *y = rg.h.dh;
}

/* ********************************************************* *
 *  set_cursor_type(): To set cursor type.                   *
 * ********************************************************* */

void set_cursor_type(int t)
{
    rg.x.ax = 0x0100;
    rg.x.bx = 0;
    rg.x.cx = t;
    int86(16, &rg, &rg);
}

char attrib = 7;
```

```c
/* ********************************************************** *
 *   clear_screen(): Generic clear screen.                  *
 * ********************************************************** */

void clear_screen()
{
    cursor(0, 0);
    rg.h.al = ' ';
    rg.h.ah = 9;
    rg.x.bx = attrib;
    rg.x.cx = 2000;
    int86(16, &rg, &rg);
}

/* ********************************************************** *
 *   vmode(): To determine the video mode.                  *
 * ********************************************************** */

int vmode()
{
    rg.h.ah = 15;
    int86(16, &rg, &rg);
    return rg.h.al;
}

/* ********************************************************** *
 *   scroll_lock(): Test for scroll lock. (scroll key)      *
 * ********************************************************** */

int scroll_lock()
{
    rg.x.ax = 0x0200;
    int86(0x16, &rg, &rg);
    return rg.h.al & 0x10;
}

void (*helpfunc)();
int helpkey = 0;
int helping = 0;

/* ********************************************************** *
 *   get_char(): Get a keyboard character.                  *
 * ********************************************************** */

int get_char()
{
    int c;

    while (1)
    {
        rg.h.ah = 1;
        int86(0x16, &rg, &rg);
```

```
        if (rg.x.flags & 0x40)
        {
                int86(0x28, &rg, &rg);
                continue;
        }
        rg.h.ah = 0;
        int86(0x16, &rg, &rg);
        if (rg.h.al == 0)
                c = rg.h.ah | 128;
        else
                c = rg.h.al;
        if (c == helpkey && helpfunc)
        {
            if (!helping)
            {
                helping = 1;
                (*helpfunc)();
                helping = 0;
                continue;
            }
        }
        break;
    }
    return c;
}

/* ******         End of cursrman.c      ***************** */

/* **********************************************************  *
 * Program Name:   window.c                                   *
 *                                                            *
 * Purpose:        Implement necessary Input/Output routines  *
 *                 in order to develop stand-alone Window-based *
 *                 application.                               *
 * System:         IBM-PC/Compatible with DOS Operating System *
 *                                                            *
 * **********************************************************  */

#include <stdio.h>
#include <ctype.h>
#include <stdarg.h>
#include <dos.h>
#include <mem.h>
#include <alloc.h>
#include <stdlib.h>
#include <string.h>
#include "window.h"
#include "keys.h"

#define TABS        4
#define SCRNHT      25          /* 25 rows per display screen */
#define SCRNWIDTH   80          /* 80 cols per display screen */
```

```
#define ON          1
#define OFF         0
#define ERROR      -1

/*  Initializing structure   */
struct
 {
    int nw, ne, se, sw, side, line;
 } wcs[] = {
    {218,191,217,192,179,196},          /* single line              */
    {201,187,188,200,186,205},          /* double line              */
    {214,183,189,211,186,196},          /* single top, double side  */
    {213,184,190,212,179,205},          /* double top, single side  */
    {194,194,217,192,179,196}           /* pop-down menu            */
};

WINDOW *listhead = NULL;            /* start of window link list */
WINDOW *listtail = NULL;            /* end of window link list   */
int VSG;                    /* video segment address      */

/* ********************************************************** *
 * establish_window():                                        *
 *                                                            *
 *   DESCRIPTION : This creates a Window by allocating        *
 *                 memory space and setting all attributes    *
 *                 of the window.                             *
 *   INPUT :       The starting point in the screen and width *
 *                 and height.                                *
 *   OUTPUT :      pointer of type WINDOW.                     *
 * ********************************************************** */

WINDOW *establish_window(int x, int y, int h, int w)
{
    WINDOW *wnd;

    VSG = (vmode() == 7 ? 0xb000 : 0xb800);
    if ((wnd = (WINDOW *) malloc(sizeof (WINDOW))) == NULL)
          return NULL;
    WTITLE  = "";                       /* Window Title is blank */
    HEIGHT  = min(h, SCRNHT);
    WIDTH   = min(w, SCRNWIDTH);
    COL     = max(0, min(x, SCRNWIDTH-WIDTH));
    ROW     = max(0, min(y, SCRNHT-HEIGHT));
    WCURS   = 0;
    SCROLL  = 0;
    SELECT  = 1;
    BTYPE   = 0;
    VISIBLE = 0;
    HIDDEN  = 0;
    PREV    = NULL;
    NEXT    = NULL;
```

```
    FHEAD    = NULL;
    FTAIL    = NULL;

    WBORDER = clr(BLACK, WHITE, BRIGHT);
    WNORMAL = clr(BLACK, WHITE, BRIGHT);
    PNORMAL = clr(BLACK, WHITE, BRIGHT);
    WTITLEC = clr(BLACK, WHITE, BRIGHT);
    WACCENT = clr(WHITE, BLACK, DIM);

    if ((SAV = malloc(WIDTH * HEIGHT * 2)) == (char *) 0)
        return NULL;
    setmem(SAV, WIDTH * HEIGHT * 2, ' ');

    add_list(wnd);   /* Insert/add this newly created window
                        in the Double Linked list              */
    return (wnd);

}

/* ****************************************************** *
 * set_border() :                                         *
 *  DESCRIPTION : This sets the border to a different type *
 *                ( 5 types ) of a window                 *
 *  INPUT : A pointer to a window and type ( 1 to 5 )     *
 *  OUTPUT : none                                         *
 * ****************************************************** */

void set_border(WINDOW *wnd, int btype)
{
    if (verify_wnd(&wnd))
      {
        BTYPE = btype;             /* Set Border type of window */
        redraw( wnd );             /* Redraw the window         */
      }
}

/* ****************************************************** *
 * set_colors() :                                         *
 *  DESCRIPTION : It sets the colors for the window.      *
 *  INPUT :                                               *
 *    1) pointer to a window                              *
 *    2) the area ( ALL, BORDER, TITLE, ACCENT, NORMAL )  *
 *    3) bg and fg ( RED, GREEN, BLUE, WHITE, YELLOW, AQUA,*
 *                   MAGENTA, BLACK)                      *
 *    4) inten ( BRIGHT , DIM )                           *
 *  OUTPUT : none                                         *
 * ****************************************************** */
void set_colors(WINDOW *wnd, int area, int bg, int fg, int inten)
{
    if (vmode() == 7)
      {
        if (bg != WHITE && bg != BLACK)
            return;
```

```
              if (fg != WHITE && fg != BLACK)
                 return;
          }
       if (verify_wnd(&wnd))
          {
            if (area == ALL)
              while (area)
                WCOLOR [--area] = clr(bg, fg, inten);
            else
                WCOLOR [area] = clr(bg, fg, inten);
            redraw(wnd);
          }
   }

/* *********************************************************** *
 * set_intensity() :                                           *
 *                                                             *
 *   DESCRIPTION : It sets the window intensity.               *
 *   INPUT       : pointer to window and intensity             *
 *   OUTPUT      : none                                        *
 * *********************************************************** */

void set_intensity(WINDOW *wnd, int inten)
{
    int area = ALL;
    if (verify_wnd(&wnd))
       {
         while (area)
            {
              WCOLOR [--area] &= ~BRIGHT;
              WCOLOR [area]  |= inten;
            }
         redraw(wnd);
       }
}

/* *********************************************************** *
 * void set_title()  :                                         *
 *                                                             *
 *   DESCRIPTION : This puts  a title on the window.           *
 *   INPUT       : ptr to window and ptr to string             *
 *   OUTPUT      : none                                        *
 * *********************************************************** */

void set_title(WINDOW *wnd, char *title)
{
    if (verify_wnd(&wnd))
       {
         WTITLE = title;
         redraw(wnd);
       }
}
```

```
/* ********************************************************* *
 * static redraw(WINDOW *wnd) :                              *
 *   DESCRIPTION : Draws the window.                         *
 *   INPUT       : window                                    *
 *   OUTPUT      : none                                      *
 * ********************************************************* */

static redraw(WINDOW *wnd)
{
    PNORMAL = WNORMAL;
}

/* ********************************************************* *
 * void display_window(WINDOW *wnd) :                        *
 *   DESCRIPTION : Shows the window.                         *
 *   INPUT       : window                                    *
 *   OUTPUT      : none                                      *
 * ********************************************************* */

void display_window(WINDOW *wnd)
{
    if (verify_wnd(&wnd) && !VISIBLE)
      {
        VISIBLE = 1;
        clear_window(wnd);
        wframe(wnd);
      }
}

/* ********************************************************* *
 * void close_all() :                                        *
 *   DESCRIPTION : Clears all the windows (clears the screen )*
 *                 This calls delete_window() to delete all  *
 *                 windows in the double linked list. Start  *
 *                 deleting from the last (tail) of the list.*
 *   INPUT       : none                                      *
 *   OUTPUT      : none                                      *
 * ********************************************************* */

void close_all()
{
    WINDOW *sav, *wnd = listtail;

    while (wnd)
      {
        sav = PREV;
        delete_window(wnd);
        wnd = sav;
      }
}
```

```
/*  *************************************************************  *
 *  void delete_window(WINDOW *wnd)                               *
 *   DESCRIPTION : Removes a window. Release the alloacated       *
 *                 space by free() system call.                   *
 *   INPUT       : window                                         *
 *   OUTPUT      : none                                           *
 *  *************************************************************  */

void delete_window(WINDOW *wnd)
{
    WINDOW *SAV;

    if (verify_wnd(&wnd))
      {
        SAV  = wnd;
        hide_window(wnd);
        free(SAV);
        remove_list(wnd);              /* remove window from list */
        free(wnd);
      }
}


/*  *************************************************************  *
 *  void hide_window(WINDOW *wnd)                                 *
 *   DESCRIPTION : Hides the window and uses the one saved        *
 *                 as output.                                     *
 *   INPUT       : window                                         *
 *   OUTPUT      : none                                           *
 *  *************************************************************  */

void hide_window(WINDOW *wnd)
{
    if (verify_wnd(&wnd) && VISIBLE)
      {
        HIDDEN  = 1;
        VISIBLE = 0;
        vrstr(wnd);
      }
}


/*  *************************************************************  *
 *  void clear_window(WINDOW *wnd)                                *
 *   DESCRIPTION : Clears the window area.                        *
 *   INPUT       : window                                         *
 *   OUTPUT      : none                                           *
 *  *************************************************************  */

void clear_window(WINDOW *wnd)
{
    register int x1, y1;

    if (verify_wnd(&wnd))
```

```
        for (y1 = 1; y1 < HEIGHT-1; y1++)
            for (x1 = 1; x1 < WIDTH-1; x1++)
                {
                    displ(wnd,x1, y1, ' ', WNORMAL);
                }
}

/* *********************************************************** *
 * static wframe(WINDOW *wnd)                                  *
 * DESCRIPTION : Develops the window frame.                    *
 * INPUT       : window                                        *
 * OUTPUT      : none                                          *
 * *********************************************************** */

static wframe(WINDOW *wnd)
{
    register int x1, y1;

    if (!verify_wnd(&wnd) && (!VISIBLE))
        return;
    displ(wnd,0, 0, NW, WBORDER);
    dtitle(wnd);
    displ(wnd,WIDTH-1, 0, NE, WBORDER);
    for (y1 = 1; y1 < HEIGHT-1; y1++)
        {
            displ(wnd,0, y1, SIDE, WBORDER);
            displ(wnd,WIDTH-1, y1, SIDE, WBORDER);
        }
    displ(wnd,0, y1, SW, WBORDER);
    for (x1 = 1; x1 < WIDTH-1; x1++)
        displ(wnd,x1, y1, LINE, WBORDER);
    displ(wnd,x1, y1, SE, WBORDER);

}  /*  ---   End of wframe()        ---              */

/* *********************************************************** *
 * static dtitle(WINDOW *wnd)                                  *
 * DESCRIPTION : Puts the title on the window.                 *
 * INPUT       : window                                        *
 * OUTPUT      : none                                          *
 * *********************************************************** */

static dtitle(WINDOW *wnd)
{
    int x1 = 1, i, ln;
    char *s = WTITLE;

    if (!verify_wnd(&wnd))
        return;
    if (s)
        {
        ln = strlen(s);
        if (ln > WIDTH-2)
            i = 0;
```

```
                else
                    i = ((WIDTH-2-ln) / 2);
                    if (i > 0)
                        while (i--)
                            displ(wnd, x1++, 0, LINE, WBORDER);
                        while (*s && x1 < WIDTH-1)
                            displ(wnd, x1++, 0, *s++, WTITLEC);
            }
        while (x1 < WIDTH-1)
            displ(wnd, x1++, 0, LINE, WBORDER);

}

/* ************************************************************ *
 * void wprintf(WINDOW *wnd, char *ln )                         *
 * DESCRIPTION : printf string inside the window.               *
 * INPUT        : window, and what you would put in printf.     *
 * OUTPUT       : none                                          *
 * ************************************************************ */

void wprintf(WINDOW *wnd, char *ln )
{
    char dlin [100], *dl = dlin;

    if (verify_wnd(&wnd))
      {
        va_list ap;
        va_start(ap, ln);
        vsprintf(dlin, ln, ap);
        va_end(ap);

        while (*dl)
            {
                wputchar(wnd, *dl++);
            }
      }
}

/* ************************************************************ *
 * void wputchar(WINDOW *wnd, int c)                            *
 * DESCRIPTION : Similar to putchar putting character           *
 *               inside the window.                             *
 * INPUT        : window  and the character                     *
 * OUTPUT       : none                                          *
 * ************************************************************ */

void wputchar(WINDOW *wnd, int c)
{
    if (!verify_wnd(&wnd))
        return;
    switch (c)
      {
        case '\n':
```

```
                        if (SCROLL == HEIGHT-3)
                            scroll(wnd, UP);
                        else
                            SCROLL++;
                        WCURS = 0;
                        break;
            case '\t':
                        do displ(wnd, (WCURS++)+3, SCROLL+1, ' ',WNORMAL);
                            while ((WCURS%TABS) && (WCURS+1) < WIDTH-1);
                        break;
            default:
                        if ((WCURS+1) < WIDTH-1)
                          {
                            displ(wnd, WCURS+1, SCROLL+1, c, WNORMAL);
                            WCURS++;
                          }
                        break;
        }
}


/* *********************************************************** *
 * void wcursor(WINDOW *wnd, int x, int y)                     *
 *  DESCRIPTION : Puts the cursor inside the window            *
 *  INPUT       : window, and point                            *
 *  OUTPUT      : none                                         *
 * *********************************************************** */

void wcursor(WINDOW *wnd, int x, int y)
{
    if (verify_wnd(&wnd) && x < WIDTH-1 && y < HEIGHT-1)
      {
        WCURS = x;
        SCROLL = y;
        cursor(COL+x+1, ROW+y+1);
      }
}



/* *********************************************************** *
 * void scroll(WINDOW *wnd, int dir)                           *
 *  DESCRIPTION : Scroll contents in the window                *
 *  INPUT       : window and direction                         *
 *  OUTPUT      : none                                         *
 * *********************************************************** */

void scroll(WINDOW *wnd, int dir)
{
    union REGS rg;
    int row = HEIGHT-1, col, chat;

    if (!verify_wnd(&wnd))
        return;
    if (NEXT == NULL && HEIGHT > 3 && VISIBLE)
      {
```

```
                    rg.h.ah = dir == UP ? 6 : 7;
                    rg.h.al = 1;
                    rg.h.bh = WNORMAL;
                    rg.h.cl = COL + 1;
                    rg.h.ch = ROW + 1;
                    rg.h.dl = COL + WIDTH - 2;
                    rg.h.dh = ROW + HEIGHT - 2;
                    int86(16, &rg, &rg);
                    return;
                 }
          if (dir == UP)
             {
               for (row = 2; row < HEIGHT-1; row++)
                  for (col = 1; col < WIDTH-1; col++)
                     {
                       chat = dget(wnd, col, row);
                       displ(wnd, col, row-1, chat&255, (chat>>8)&255);
                     }
               for (col = 1; col < WIDTH-1; col++)
                  displ(wnd, col, row-1, ' ', WNORMAL);
             }
          else
             {
               for (row = HEIGHT-2; row > 1; --row)
                  for (col = 1; col < WIDTH-1; col++)
                     {
                       chat = dget(wnd, col, row);
                       displ(wnd,col,row+1,chat&255, (chat>>8)&255);
                     }
               for (col = 1; col < WIDTH-1; col++)
                  displ(wnd, col, row+1, ' ', WNORMAL);
             }

}


/* **********************************************************  *
 * static int *waddr(WINDOW *wnd, int x, int y)               *
 *  DESCRIPTION : Computes address of window's display        *
 *                character                                   *
 *  INPUT       : window , (x,y)-coordinates of a point in    *
 *                the window                                  *
 *  OUTPUT      : none                                        *
 * **********************************************************  */

static int *waddr(WINDOW *wnd, int x, int y)
{
   WINDOW *nxt = NEXT;
   int *vp;

   if (!VISIBLE)
      return (int *) (SAV+y*(WIDTH*2)+x*2);
   x += COL;
   y += ROW;
```

```
      while (nxt)
        {
          if (nxt->_wv)
          if (x >= nxt->_wx && x <= nxt->_wx + nxt->_ww-1)
            if (y >= nxt->_wy &&
                y <= nxt->_wy + nxt->_wh-1)
              {
                x -= nxt->_wx;
                y -= nxt->_wy;
                vp = (int *) ((nxt->_ws) +y*(nxt->_ww*2)+x*2);
                return( vp );
              }
          nxt = nxt->_nx;
        }
      return( NULL );
  }

/* ********************************************************** *
 * void displ(WINDOW *wnd, int x, int y, int ch, int at)    *
 *   DESCRIPTION : Displays a character in the window        *
 *   INPUT       : window, point in the window, the          *
 *                 character, and attribute                  *
 *   OUTPUT      : none                                      *
 * ********************************************************** */

void displ(WINDOW *wnd, int x, int y, int ch, int at)
{
    int *vp;
    int vch = ( ch & 255 ) | ( at << 8 );

    if ((vp = waddr(wnd, x, y)) != NULL)
      *vp = vch;
    else
      vpoke(VSG, vad(x + COL, y + ROW), vch);
}

/* ********************************************************** *
 * static int dget(WINDOW *wnd, int x, int y)               *
 *   DESCRIPTION : Gets a displayed character from the window *
 *   INPUT       : window, and the point in the window       *
 *   OUTPUT      : none                                      *
 * ********************************************************** */

static int dget(WINDOW *wnd, int x, int y)
{
    int *vp;

    if ((vp = waddr(wnd, x, y)) != NULL)
        return( *vp );
    return( vpeek(VSG, vad( x + COL, y + ROW )));
}
```

```
/* ************************************************************ *
 * static vswap (WINDOW *wnd)                                   *
 * DESCRIPTION : swaps with the saved window                    *
 * INPUT       : window                                         *
 * OUTPUT      : none                                           *
 * ************************************************************ */

static vswap(WINDOW *wnd)
{
    int x, y, chat;
    int *bf = (int *) SAV;

    for (y = 0; y < HEIGHT; y++)
       for (x = 0; x < WIDTH; x++)
          {
            chat = *bf;
            *bf++ = dget(wnd, x, y);
            displ(wnd, x, y, chat&255, (chat>>8)&255);
          }
}


/* ************************************************************ *
 * static vsave (WINDOW *wnd)                                   *
 * DESCRIPTION : Saves the window.                              *
 * INPUT       : window                                         *
 * OUTPUT      : none                                           *
 * ************************************************************ */

static vsave(WINDOW *wnd)
{
    int x, y;
    int *bf = (int *) SAV;

    for (y = 0; y < HEIGHT; y++)
       for (x = 0; x < WIDTH; x++)
          *bf++ = vpeek(VSG, vad(x+COL, y+ROW));
}


/* ************************************************************ *
 * static vrstr (WINDOW *wnd)                                   *
 * DESCRIPTION : Restore the saved window.                      *
 * INPUT       : window                                         *
 * OUTPUT      : none                                           *
 * ************************************************************ */

static vrstr(WINDOW *wnd)
{
    int x, y;
    int *bf = (int *) SAV;

    for (y = 0; y < HEIGHT; y++)
       for (x = 0; x < WIDTH; x++)
          vpoke(VSG, vad(x+COL, y+ROW), *bf++);
}
```

```
/* ********************************************************* *
 * void acline(WINDOW *wnd, int set)                         *
 *  DESCRIPTION : accent or deaccent the line where SELECT   *
 *                points                                     *
 *  INPUT       : window and current setting                 *
 *  OUTPUT      : none                                       *
 * ********************************************************* */

void acline(WINDOW *wnd, int set)
{
    int x, ch;

    if (!verify_wnd(&wnd))
       return;
    for (x = 1; x < WIDTH - 1; x++)
       {
         ch = dget(wnd, x, SELECT) & 255;
         displ(wnd, x, SELECT, ch, set);
       }
}

/* ********************************************************* *
 * static add_list(WINDOW *wnd)                              *
 *  DESCRIPTION : Adds a window at the end of the Doubly     *
 *                Linked list of windows.                    *
 *  INPUT : window                                           *
 *  OUTPUT : none                                            *
 * ********************************************************* */

static add_list(WINDOW *wnd)
{
    if (listtail)
      {
         PREV = listtail;
         listtail->_nx = wnd;
      }
    listtail = wnd;
    if (!listhead)
      listhead = wnd;
}

/* ********************************************************* *
 * static remove_list(WINDOW *wnd)                           *
 *  DESCRIPTION : Removes a window from the end of the       *
 *                Doubly Linked list, and adjust 'prev' and  *
 *                'next' pointers.                           *
 *  INPUT       : window                                     *
 *  OUTPUT      : none                                       *
 * ********************************************************* */

static remove_list(WINDOW *wnd)
{
    if (NEXT)
        NEXT->_pv = PREV;
```

```
        if  (PREV)
            PREV->_nx = NEXT;
        if  (listhead == wnd)
            listhead = NEXT;
        if  (listtail == wnd)
            listtail = PREV;
        NEXT = NULL;
        PREV = NULL;
}


/* ****************************************************** *
 * static verify_wnd(WINDOW **w1)                        *
 * DESCRIPTION : This verifies if the window exists in the *
 *               Doubly Linked list of Windows.          *
 * INPUT        : window                                 *
 * OUTPUT       : window                                 *
 * ****************************************************** */

static verify_wnd(WINDOW **w1)
{
    WINDOW *wnd;

    if  (*w1 == NULL)
      {
        *w1 = listtail;
      }
    else
      {
        wnd = listhead;
        while (wnd != NULL)
          {
            if  (*w1 == wnd)
                break;
            wnd = NEXT;
          }
      }
    return *w1 != NULL;

}


WINDOW *ewnd = NULL;

/* ****************************************************** *
 * void error_message(char *s)                           *
 * DESCRIPTION : Creates a window, and then displays an  *
 *               error message inside the window.        *
 *               Also gives a BELL                       *
 * INPUT        : The string s.                          *
 * OUTPUT       : none                                   *
 * ****************************************************** */

void error_message(char *s)
{
    ewnd = establish_window(50, 22, 3, max(10, strlen(s)+11));
```

```
    set_title(ewnd, " Press ESC ");
    display_window(ewnd);
    wprintf(ewnd, " ERROR : %s",s);
    putchar(BELL);
}

/* ************************************************************ *
 * void clear_message() :                                      *
 *   DESCRIPTION : Clears the window area.                     *
 *   INPUT       : none                                        *
 *   OUTPUT      : none                                        *
 * ************************************************************ */

void clear_message()
{
    if (ewnd)
      delete_window(ewnd);
    ewnd = NULL;  }

/*     ---    End of routines for Window operations   ---      */
```

Output Section

Because the program is based on the terminal display, the output could not be captured to include here.

CHAPTER 15

Applications for Mathematics

In this chapter we will show applications for complex numbers and numerical analysis.

15.1 ADT Complex Numbers and Implementations in C

Complex numbers play an important role in the applications of sciences, engineering, and mathematics. A complex number is of the form

$$a + bi$$

where a and b are real numbers and $i = \overline{V - 1}$. The numbers a and b are respectively called the *real* and *imaginary parts of the complex number*. In this section we will discuss how to deal with complex number data in C.

The C language does not provide a built-in type declaration for complex numbers. A complex number may be viewed as a structured pair (a, b) object. We will be able to define such structured-type data in a static or dynamic form in the following section.

15.1.1 Static and Dynamic Implementations of Complex Numbers in C

The static representations of Complex Numbers uses array or struct.

Form I

```
typedef float   COMPLEX[ 2 ];
COMPLEX  A;                 /* Declare complex identifier  */
```

A[0] is used to access the real part of A, and A[1] is used to access the imaginary part of A. The drawback is that there is no visible name to differentiate the real and imaginary components.

Form II

```
typedef struct_COMPLEX
     {
       float    real;
       float    imaginary;
     } COMPLEX;

     COMPLEX    A;              /* Declare complex identifier */
```

A. real is used to access the real part of A, and A. imaginary is used to access the imaginary part of A. Now the component name differentiates the elements of the object.

The pointer representation of complex numbers uses pointers to a C structure as follows.

Form III

```
     struct Complex_struct
        {
          float    real;
          float    imaginary;
        };

     typedef struct Complex_struct   Complex_type;

     /*   Define COMPLEX type as a pointer to the
      *   Complex_struct.
      */
     typedef struct Complex_struct *COMPLEX;

     COMPLEX    A;
```

A -> real is used to access the real part of A, and A -> imaginary is used to access the imaginary part of A. Again the component names allow for differentiation.

In the case of pointer (dynamic) representation, declaring identifiers does not allocate memory space. Before we use them we must allocate memory, using the system call malloc (), which returns a pointer to a memory location that can hold this complex data type. Below are examples of a function to create the object, and a function to dispose of the object:

```
/*
 *   create_complex( ):
 */

  COMPLEX create_Complex ()
  {
     COMPLEX   temp_complex;

     if ( (temp_complex = (COMPLEX) malloc (
                          sizeof (Complex_type) )) == NULL )
        printf ("\n create_complex: malloc failed for Complex \n");
```

```
    /*  A return value of NULL implies malloc failure. */
    return ( temp_complex );
}

/*
 *  free_complex():
 *      Release the memory space acquired through 'malloc'.
 *      It uses the routine 'free()' to release the
 *      allocated area.
 */
free_complex ( COMPLEX   Complex_pointer )
{
    free( Complex_pointer );
}
```

15.1.2 Implementations of Standard Operations on Complex Numbers

Given two complex numbers $A = a + bi$ and $B = c + di$, we obtain the following:

Operations	Result	Our implementation in C
Addition: A + B	$(a + c) + (b + d)i$	complex_add (A, B)
Subtract: A - B	$(a - c) + (b - d)i$	complex_sub (A, B)
Multiply: A * B	$(ac - bd) + (ad + bc)i$	complex_mult (A, B)
Division: A / B	$((ac + bd) + (bc - ad)i)$ $/(cc + dd)$	complex_div (A, B)
Negate: -A	$-a - bi$	complex_neg (A)
Print A:		print_complex (A complex_var_name)

As none of the standard arithmetical operations on complex numbers are defined in C, we implemented them using the struct and pointer forms for complex numbers in Example 15.1. Each of these functions will return a COMPLEX type. In order to use these implementations, the reader may wish to create a library, and declare the related operations as extern in the calling programs. Finally, it is necessary to link the calling program with the library containing these complex arithmetic functions.

15.1.3 Complex Function Evaluation

When we use complex numbers for the variables in a complex function, we generally get a complex number as the result. In C, we will replace all real arithmetic operations by their complex arithmetic counterparts [e.g., complex_add(), complex_sub()]. The functions will return COMPLEX-type data.

```
/*
 *  complex_f():
 *      Assuming the Form III type declaration,
 *      evaluate complex function f
 *          f ( A, B ) = A*A + B,
 *      where the arguments A & B are complex numbers
 */
```

```
COMPLEX   complex_f ( COMPLEX   A, COMPLEX B )
{
    return ( complex_add ( complex_mult( A, A ), B );
}
```

15.1.4 Examples of Complex Arithmetic

Example 15.1

Code Section

```
/*
 *   Program Name: ptr_complx_ops.c
 *                 ( Pointer Implementation of Complex number
 *                   Arithmetic in C )
 *
 *   Purpose:    1) Declare Complex as a Pointer structure
 *               2) Define Complex_add, Complex_sub, Complex_mult,
 *                        Complex_div, Complex_power, Complex_neg
 */

#define NULL          0

typedef struct Complex_struct
   {
      float  real;          /* a for the Complex number a + bi */
      float  imaginary;     /* b for the Complex number a + bi */
   };

typedef        struct Complex_struct     Complex_type;

/* type COMPLEX is defined at this line. */
typedef   struct Complex_struct    *COMPLEX_PTR;

#define CPLX_NULL   (COMPLEX_PTR) NULL

/*
 * create_Complex() : Dynamically allocate memory for a
 *                     Complex number. It will try to get a
 *                     memory allocation to store a Complex-
 *                     type data, and if successful, will
 *                     return a COMPLEX_PTR pointer.
 */

COMPLEX_PTR create_Complex ()
{
   COMPLEX_PTR    temp_complex;

   if ( (temp_complex = (COMPLEX_PTR)
                   malloc ( sizeof (Complex_type) ))
            == CPLX_NULL )
       printf ("\n create_Complex: malloc failed  \n");
```

```
        /* A return value of CPLX_NULL indicates malloc failure */
        return ( temp_complex );
}


/*
 * complex_add ():    A + B and returns COMPLEX_PTR pointer
 */
COMPLEX_PTR complex_add ( COMPLEX_PTR  A,  COMPLEX_PTR  B )
{
    COMPLEX_PTR              temp_complex,   create_Complex();

    if ((temp_complex = create_Complex()) != CPLX_NULL )
       {
         temp_complex -> real      = A -> real  + B -> real;
         temp_complex -> imaginary = A -> imaginary +
                                         B -> imaginary;
       }
    return ( temp_complex );
}


/*
 *  complex_neg ( A ):   Negate A and return COMPLEX_PTR
 *                       pointer
 *    - A = ( - A_Real, - A_imagn )  for A = ( A_Real, A_imagn)
 */
COMPLEX_PTR complex_neg ( COMPLEX_PTR  A )
{
    COMPLEX_PTR   temp_complex,  create_Complex();

    if ((temp_complex = create_Complex()) != CPLX_NULL )
       {
         temp_complex -> real      = - A -> real;
         temp_complex -> imaginary = - A -> imaginary;
       }
    return ( temp_complex );
}


/*
 *  complex_sub ():  A - B and returns COMPLEX_PTR pointer
 *
 *      A - B = ( A_Real - B_Real, A_imagn - B_imagn )
 *              where  A = ( A_Real, A_imagn )
 *              and    B = ( B_Real, B_imagn )
 */

COMPLEX_PTR    complex_sub ( COMPLEX_PTR  A,  COMPLEX_PTR  B )
{
    COMPLEX_PTR   temp_complex,  create_Complex();

    if ((temp_complex = create_Complex()) != CPLX_NULL )
       {
         temp_complex -> real      = A -> real - B -> real;
```

```
                temp_complex -> imaginary = A -> imaginary -
                                        B -> imaginary;
        }
    return ( temp_complex );


}


/*
 *  complex_mult (): A * B and returns COMPLEX_PTR pointer
 *
 *    A * B = ( A_Real * B_Real  - A_imagn * B_Real,
 *              A_Real * B_imagn + A_imagn * B_Real )
 */
COMPLEX_PTR  complex_mult ( COMPLEX_PTR   A, COMPLEX_PTR          B
{
    COMPLEX_PTR  temp_complex,  create_Complex();

    if ((temp_complex = create_Complex()) != CPLX_NULL )
      {
        temp_complex -> real = A -> real * B -> real -
                            A -> imaginary * B -> imaginary;

        temp_complex -> imaginary = A -> real * B -> imaginary +
                            A -> imaginary * B -> real;
      }
    return ( temp_complex );
}

/*
 *  complex_div ():    A / B and returns COMPLEX_PTR pointer
 */
COMPLEX_PTR   complex_div ( COMPLEX_PTR  A, COMPLEX_PTR          B )
{
    COMPLEX_PTR   temp_complex, create_Complex();
    double        temp1, temp2, temp3;

    /* Is the divisor  B = 0 ? */
    if ( B -> real != 0 && B -> imaginary != 0 )
      {
        /* Divisor complex number B is non-zero     */

        temp1       =    A -> real  * B -> real +
                         A -> imaginary * B -> imaginary;
        temp2       =    A -> imaginary * B -> real -
                         A -> real * B -> imaginary;
        temp3       =    B -> real  * B -> real +
                         B -> imaginary * B -> imaginary;
        if ((temp_complex = create_Complex()) != CPLX_NULL )
          {
            temp_complex -> real      = temp1 / temp3;
            temp_complex -> imaginary = temp2 / temp3;
      }
```

```
            return ( temp_complex );
        }
    else
        {
            printf("\n complex_div: ERROR: Division by %s \n",
                    "a Complex number ZERO is not allowed ");
            exit( 2 );
        }
}

/*
 *    print_complex() : Print a complex number
 */
void   print_complex ( COMPLEX_PTR   A,  char   *Complex_var_name )
{
    printf("\n Complex %s      =     %10.3f +   %10.3f * i  \n",
                                    Complex_var_name,
                                    A -> real, A -> imaginary );
}

/*
 *    main(): POINTER IMPLEMENTATION OF COMPLEX ARITHMETIC
 */
main()
{
    COMPLEX_PTR       C, D, Complex_result;

    printf("\n ***  POINTER IMPLEMENTATION OF %s \n",
            "OF COMPLEX  ARITHMETIC *** ");

    if ((C  =  create_Complex()) == CPLX_NULL )
        exit(1);
    C -> real   = 10.0;
    C -> imaginary = 12.0;

    if ((D  =  create_Complex()) == CPLX_NULL )
        exit(1);
    D -> real   = - 5.0;
    D -> imaginary = 15;

    print_complex ( C, "C" );
    print_complex ( D, "D" );

    if ((Complex_result =  create_Complex()) == CPLX_NULL)
        exit(1);
    Complex_result = complex_add( C, D );
    print_complex ( Complex_result, "C + D" );

    Complex_result = complex_sub( C, D );
    print_complex ( Complex_result, "C - D" );
```

```
    Complex_result = complex_mult( C, D );
    print_complex ( Complex_result, "C * D" );

    Complex_result = complex_div( C, D );
    print_complex ( Complex_result, "C / D" );

    Complex_result = complex_neg( C );
    print_complex ( Complex_result, "- C  " );

    free( C );
    free( D );
    free( Complex_result );
}
```

Output Section

```
    ***  POINTER  IMPLEMENTATION OF  COMPLEX  ARITHMETIC  ***

    Complex C    =        10.000 +        12.000 * i

    Complex D    =        -5.000 +        15.000 * i

    Complex C + D    =       5.000 +       27.000 * i

    Complex C - D    =      15.000 +       -3.000 * i

    Complex C * D    =    -230.000 +       90.000 * i

    Complex C / D    =       0.520 +       -0.840 * i

    Complex - C      =     -10.000 +      -12.000 * i
```

15.2 Applications in Numerical Analysis in C

In this section we will present implementations of some algorithms in numerical analysis. We have chosen this topic because numerical methods are widely used to solve, by approximation, wide ranges of problems. Moreover, solving a problem numerically requires manipulating a large amount of data. How should these data be organized efficiently in terms of computer time and storage requirements? Such problems can be efficiently handled using arrays. Pointers and doubly linked lists can be used to represent a sparse matrix to save storage. Note that when performing swapping of rows, it is necessary (and more efficient) to use pointers because this approach avoids the need to physically move data around. Instead we can simply interchange values of pointers holding the addresses of the rows.

We implemented the following numerical methods in C:

Numerical Method/Algorithm	Description
1. Bisection	To approximate root of $f(x) = 0$
2. Newton–Raphson	To approximate root of $f(x) = 0$

3. Lagrange interpolation	Interpolate a function given a discrete set of (x,y) values
4. Simpson	To numerically integrate $f(x)$
5. Runge–Kutta (4th-order)	To approximate solution of a first-order differential equation
6. Gaussian elimination with partial pivoting and backward substitution	To numerically approximate solution of n linear equations of the form $Ax = b$, A being a coefficient matrix
7. LU Decomposition	To numerically solve $Ax = b$
8. Gauss–Seidel iterative method	Iterative approach to numerically solve $Ax = b$, given initial approximation

As described in Burden *et al.* (1978), the description of each of these methods is included in the programs. Burden's book is recommended for further information. For clarity and completeness of source listing, we are including main() with output in the following subsections.

15.2.1 C Code of Bisection Algorithm for Root Finding

Code Section

```
/*   Program Name: bisect.c
 *
 *   Purpose:   To find root of f(x) = 0 given that the function f
 *              is continuous over the interval [ A, B ], using the
 *              Bisection Algorithm. We are not assuming that f(A)
 *              and f(B) have opposite signs.
 */

#define EPSILON_1    1.0e-5    /* Tolerance  on function value */
#define EPSILON_2    1.0e-9    /* Tolerance  on width
                                  of interval */
/* Absolute value */
#define absolute(x)  ( (x < 0 ) ? - ( x ) : ( x ) )

float function(x)
float x;
{
        /*     f (x) = x ** 3 + 2 * X + 4         */
        return ( x * ( x * x + 2.0 ) + 4.0 );
}

float bisect (float (*f) (), float A, float B,
              float epsilon_1, float epsilon_2 )
{
    float       mid_point;
    float       f_at_A, f_at_B, f_at_mid;

    /* First check whether [ A, B ] contains any root   */
    /* For efficiency, save these values   */
```

```
        f_at_A =   (*f)  (A);
        f_at_B =   (*f)  (B);

        if ( f_at_A * f_at_B > 0.0 )
            {
              printf("\n bisect:   [ %10f, %10f ] %s \n",
                    "does not contain any root ", A,  B );
              exit ( 1 );
            }
        else
          {
            /* Mid point of the interval [A, B] */
            mid_point = ( A + B ) * 0.5;

            f_at_mid  =  (*f) (mid_point);
            if ( ( absolute ( f_at_mid ) < epsilon_1) ||
                 ( absolute ( B - A ) < epsilon_2 ) )
                    return ( mid_point );
                    /* current mid_point is a root    */
            else if ( f_at_A * f_at_mid < 0.0 )
              return ( bisect (f, A, mid_point, epsilon_1, epsilon_2 ) );
            else
              return ( bisect (f, mid_point, B, epsilon_1, epsilon_2 ) );
          }
}

main()
{
 float       root;
 float       A = -3.0,   B = 4.0;

 printf("\n **** Root finding method: BISECTION   **** \n");
 root = bisect ( function, -3.0, 4.0, EPSILON_1, EPSILON_2 );
 printf("\n For the interval [ %5f, %5f ] \n %s %10.5f \n %s %10.5f\
        A, B, " Function value : ",
        function( root ), " Computed root  : ", root );
}
```

Here we have two outputs for two different inputs.

Output Section

```
        **** Root finding method: BISECTION   ****

        For the interval [ -3.000000, 4.000000 ]
         Function value :    0.00001
         Computed root  :    -1.17951
```

Output Section

```
**** Root finding method: BISECTION   ****

bisect:   [   3.000000,    4.000000 ] does not contain any root
```

15.2.2 C Code of Newton–Raphson Algorithm for Root Finding

Code Section

```
/*   Program Name: newton.c
 *                    ( Recursive Version )
 *
 *   Purpose:   To numerically approximate a root of f(x) = 0 given
 *              f(x) continuously differentiable at an initial
 *              approximation x0 using Newton-Raphson method.
 *              The steps are as follows:
 *
 *       Step 1:   prev_x = x0
 *       Step 2:   If f'( prev_x ) = 0, STOP reporting ERROR.
 *       Step 3:   next_x = prev_x - f( prev_x ) / f'( prev_x )
 *       Step 4:   If | f(next_x) | < Tolerance_1
 *                          or
 *                 if | next_x - prev_x | < Tolerance_2,
 *                 RETURN next_x as the root
 *       Step 5:   Otherwise, set x0 = next_x, and goto Step 1
 */


#define EPSILON_1   1.0e-5   /*  Tolerance  on function value   */
#define EPSILON_2   1.0e-9   /*  Tolerance  on diff between
                                 new and old approximations      */
/* Absolute value */
#define absolute(x)  ( (x < 0 ) ? - ( x ) : ( x ) )


/*
 * function(x): Given function
 */
float function(x)
float x;
{
        /*    f(x) = x ** 3 + 2 * x + 4   */
        return ( x * ( x * x + 2.0 ) + 4.0 );
}


/*
 * derivative_f(x): Derivative of the given function
 */
float derivative_f(x)
float x;
{
        /*    f'(x) = 3* x ^ 2 + 2   */
        return ( 3.0 * x * x + 2.0 );
}


/*
 * newton(): Implements Newton-Raphson method as a Recursive
 *           function. Returns result as a floating point number.
 */
```

```c
float newton(float (*f)(), float (*deriv_f)(),
             float initial_x, float epsilon_1, float epsilon_2)
{
    float   next_x, /* Holding area for next approximation */
            prev_x, /* Holding area for prev approximation */
            deriv_f_x,   /* Derivative value of f at x */
            f_new;   /* Value of f at the new approx next_x */

    /* First check whether f'(x) is zero at initial_x */
    deriv_f_x = (*deriv_f)(initial_x);

    if ( absolute( deriv_f_x ) == 0 )
       {
         printf("\n newton: Failss to find a root because %s \n",
                          " f'(x) is zero " );
         exit ( 1 );
       }
    else
     {
         prev_x = initial_x;
         /*  Calculate next approximation using Newton-Raphson
          *  method
          */

         next_x = prev_x - (*f)(prev_x) / deriv_f_x;

         f_new  = (*f)( next_x );      /* Evaluate f() at next_x  */
         if ( ( absolute ( f_new ) < epsilon_1) ||
              ( absolute ( next_x - prev_x ) < epsilon_2 ) )
                 return ( next_x );/* next_x is a root */
         else                          /* Call newton(), i.e,itself */
               return (newton(f, deriv_f, next_x,
                                 epsilon_1, epsilon_2 ));
     }
}


/*
 * main(): NEWTON-RAPHSON METHOD FOR APPROXIMATING
 *          ROOT OF f(x) = 0 *
 */
main()
{
    float    root;
    float    initial_x = 0; /* Initial Approximation to root  */

    printf("\n ==  Root finding method: NEWTON-RAPHSON   == \n");
    root = newton ( function, derivative_f, initial_x,
                    EPSILON_1, EPSILON_2 );

    printf("\n %24s : %5f \n %17s %10.5f \n  %17s  %10.5f \n",
              "For initial approximation",  initial_x,
              " Function value : ", function( root ),
              " Computed root  : ", root );
}
```

Output Section

```
  ==  Root finding method: NEWTON-RAPHSON   ==

  For initial approximation : 0.000000
     Function value :      0.00000
     Computed root  :     -1.17951
```

15.2.3 C Code of Lagrange Interpolation

Code Section

```
/*  Program: lagrange.c
 *
 *  Purpose: Implement Lagrange Interpolation Method, described
 *                as in Burden et al. (1978)
 *
 *      If x , x , ..., x  are (n+1) distinct numbers and f() is
 *         0   1       n
 *      a function whose values are given at these numbers, then
 *      there exists a unique Polynomial P of degree n with the
 *      property that
 *      f(x )  =  P(x )     for each j = 0, 1, ..., n.
 *         j        j
 *      The polynomial P(x), approximating f(x), is
 *
 *      P(x) = f(x ) * L   (x) + ... + f(x ) * L   (x)
 *                0     n,0              n     n,n
 *
 *      where
 *
 *                    (x-x )(x-x )  ... (x-x   )(x-x   )...(x-x )
 *                        0     1          j-1     j+1         n
 *      L   (x) = ---------------------------------------------------
 *       n,j          (x -x )(x -x ) ... (x -x   )(x -x   )...(x -x )
 *                      j  0   j  1        j  j-1   j  j+1      j  n
 *
 *
 *      Note: (1) P(x) is called Lagrange Interpolating Polynomial.
 *      (2) This method is used when you do not have the
 *      mathematical form of the function f(x) except the
 *      (n+1) distinct pairs (x , f(x )), j = 0,..., n.
 *                             j     j
 */


/*
 * Lagrange ( x, y, n, at_x ) : LAGRANGE Polynomial
 *                               approximation at x
 *       Returns floating point number as result
 */
float   Lagrange ( float   x[ ], float  y[ ],
                   int     n,    float  at_x )
{
    int   i, j;
    float Lagrange_poly, L_numerator, L_denominator;
```

```
    /* Check whether x[i]'s are distinct   */
    for ( i = 0; i < n ; i++ )
      {
        if ( x[i] == x[ i + 1 ] )
          {
            printf("\n Lagrange: ERROR: Given x[i]'s %s \n",
                    "are not distinct");
            exit ( 1 );
          }
      }
    /* Calculate Lagrange factors L   */

    L_numerator    = 1;
    L_denominator  = 1;
    Lagrange_poly  = 0;           /* Initialize before sum    */

    for ( j = 0; j < n; j++ )
      {
        for ( i = 0; (i != j && i < n ); i++ )
          {
            L_numerator    *= ( at_x    - x [ i ] );
            L_denominator  *= ( x[ j ]  - x [ i ] );
          }

      Lagrange_poly += (L_numerator / L_denominator) * y[j];
      }
    return ( Lagrange_poly );

}


/*
 * main(): POLYNOMIAL APPROXIMATION BY LAGRANGE METHOD
 */
main()
{
   /* Initial x-values          */
   static  float   x[ ] = { 2.0, 2.5, 4.0 };
   /* Initial f(),y-values    */
   static  float   y[ ] = { 0.5, 0.4, 0.25 };
   int     n = 3;              /* Number of given points */
   float   at_x = 3,           /* Find approx of f() at x */
           approx_value_at_x;

   printf("\n === POLYNOMIAL APROX %s \n",
          "Using LAGRANGE INTERPOLATION  ===");
   approx_value_at_x = Lagrange ( x, y, n, at_x );

   printf("\n Lagrange approximation to f(%5f ) : %10.5f \n",
           at_x, approx_value_at_x );

}
```

Output Section

```
===   POLYNOMIAL APROX Using LAGRANGE INTERPOLATION  ===

Lagrange approximation to f(3.000000) :    1.38333
```

15.2.4 C Code of Simpson Algorithm for Integration

Code Section

```c
/* Program: simpson.c
 *
 * Purpose: To approximate the integral of f(x) over the interval
 *          [a, b] using Simpson's Composite Algorithm:
 *
 *          h * [f(a)+f(b)+2*Sum(f(a + i*h))+4*Sum(f(a + i*h)) / 3
 *                i even,              i odd,
 *                i= 2,...,n-2         i = 1,..., n-1
 *          where h = (b - a)/n, and n is even.
 *
 */

float Simpson(float (*f)(), float a, float b, int n)
{
    int       i;
    float     h;  /* Width of each subinterval      */
    float     even_sum, odd_sum, x;

    /* Check whether the given 'n' is even  */
    if ( n % 2 != 0 )
       {
       printf("\n Simpson: ERROR: Input n (# of %s \n",
               "subintervals) is not even ");
       exit( 1 );
       }
    else
       {
       h = ( b - a ) / n; /* Set width of each subinterval */

       even_sum = 0;
       odd_sum  = 0;

       for ( i = 1; i < n; i++)
          {
          x = a + i * h;   /* Partition points in [a, b] */
          if ( i % 2 == 0 ) /* Check whether  i is even */
             even_sum += f( x );   /* i is even */
          else                     /* i is odd  */
             odd_sum  += f( x );
          }

       return(h*(f(a)+f(b)+2.0*even_sum+4.0*odd_sum ) / 3.0);
       }
}
```

```
float    f(x)
float x;
{
    return ( x * x * x );
}

main()
{
    float    a = 0, b = 2, approx_integral;
    int      n = 4;

    printf("\n ===  SIMPSON'S RULE for %s \n",
           "for NUMERICAL INTEGRATION  === ");
    approx_integral = Simpson ( f, a, b, n );
    printf("\n For f(x) = x^3 over [ %2f, %2f ]: \n", a, b);
    printf("\n   Simpson's integral approximation = %10.5f \n",
           approx_integral );
}
```

Output Section

```
        ===  SIMPSON'S RULE for NUMERICAL INTEGRATION   ===

        For f(x) = x^3 over [ 0.000000, 2.000000 ]:

        Simpson's integral approximation =    4.00000
```

15.2.5 C Code of Runge–Kutta for a Differential Equation

Code Section

```
/* Program:  To numerically approximate the solution of the
 *           First Order Differential Equation (in particular,
 *           Initial Value Problem):
 *
 *               y' = f( x, y ), a <= x <= b, y( a ) = y0,
 *
 *           at (n + 1) equally spaced numbers in the interval
 *           [a, b].
 */


/*
 *     RUNGE-KUTTA FOURTH-ORDER METHOD for O.D.E.
 */

float   Runge_Kutta(float (*f)(), float initial_x,
                    float initial_y, float end_x, float h,
                    float y[], int * n )

/* where (*f)()     Function at right hand side of y' = f(x, y)
 *       initial_x Input: initial condition of x (i.e., a  )
 *       initial_y Input: initial condition of y (i.e., y0 )
 *       end_x     Input: End value of x (i.e., b )
```

```
*          h              Input: Step size to get next x in x-direction
*          *n             Number of sub-intervals in x-direction
*          y[ ]           Output: array of size n containing the
*                                 corresponding solutions of x ,
*                                                              i
*                         where  x   =  x    + h
*                                 i      i-1
*/
{
    float    k1, k2, k3, k4, /* Steps in the y-direction */
             next_y,         /* Next approximation for y */
             x;              /* Starts with initial_x,
                                initial_x + h, ..., end_x       */
    int      i;

    *n       = ( end_x - initial_x ) / h;
    x        = initial_x;
    y[0]  = initial_y;
    next_y = initial_y;

    for ( i = 1;  i <= *n + 2;  i++ )
       {
         k1 = h * (*f) ( x, next_y );
         k2 = h * (*f) ( x + h / 2, next_y + k1 / 2 );
         k3 = h * (*f) ( x + h / 2, next_y + k2 / 2 );
         k4 = h * (*f) ( x + h      , next_y + k3       );

         /* Compute the approximate solution y corresponding
          * to current x
          */

         y[i]  = x + ( k1 + 2.0 * k2 + 2.0 * k3 + k4 )/ 6.0;

         x += h;  /* x = x + h (i.e, next x) */
         next_y = y[ i ]; /* Use current y to compute next */
       }
}

/*
 *  Function f ( x, y ) of the ODE y' = f ( x, y )
 */
float  f(x, y)
float x, y;
{
    return( -y + x + 1);     /* y' = -y+x+1, 0<=x<=1, y(0)=1 */
}

/*
 * main(): RUNGE-KUTTA METHOD TO NUMERICALLY SOLVE the
 *         ODE y' = f ( x, y )
 */
```

```
main()
{
     float    initial_x = 0, initial_y = 1, end_x = 1,
              y[ 30 ], h = 0.2;
     int      i, n;

     char *diff_equation =
              " y' = -y + x + 1, 0 <= x <= 1, y(0) = 1 \n";

     printf("\n =  RUNGE-KUTTA FOURTH ORDER METHOD  = \n\n");
     printf( diff_equation );
     printf("\n x-values \t   y-values \n");

     Runge_Kutta ( f, initial_x, initial_y, end_x, h, y, &n );

     for ( i = 0; i <= n + 2; ++i )
        printf(" %5f \t  %5f \n", initial_x + i * h, y[ i ] );
}
```

Output Section

```
            =  RUNGE-KUTTA FOURTH ORDER METHOD  =

       y' = -y + x + 1, 0 <= x <= 1, y(0) = 1

       x-values              y-values
       0.000000              1.000000
       0.200000              0.018733
       0.400000              0.432858
       0.600000              0.594044
       0.800000              0.801080
       1.000000              0.999804
       1.200000              1.200035
```

15.2.6 C Code of Gaussian Elimination for $Ax = b$

Code Section

```
/* Program: Gauss.c
 *
 * Purpose: Use the Gaussian Elimination with Maximal Pivoting
 *          method to numerically solve a system of n linear
 *          equations:
 *          Ax = b  ................................. ( 1 )
 *          where A = ( a[i, j] ), i, j = 0, ..., n - 1
 *                                             T
 *          x = ( x[0], ..., x[n-1]),   T means Transpose,
 *                                     T
 *          b = ( b[0], ..., b[n-1])
 *
 *          Programming goal:
 *              1. Find maximal pivot in each column from i-th to
 *                 n-th row
```

```
*                  2.  Exchange row if necessary to place the pivot
*                      element at the diagonal position
*                  3.  Using the diagonal element, eliminate all the
*                      elements below in the same column in the
*                      augmented matrix [ A | b ] (Note: Augmented
*                      matrix is considered as the best Data Structure
*                      in this approach. )
*                  4.  Through elimination, transform ( 1 ) as an
*                      Upper Triangular form:
*                          Ux = v     .............. ( 2 )
*                  5.  Solve equation ( 2 ) using Backward
*                      Substitution
*                  6.  Solutions of ( 2 ) are solutions of ( 1 )
*
*          NOTE:  If the maximal pivot element is zero, matrix A is
*                 singular.  In this case, (1) does not have a
*                 unique solution. Gaussian Elimination cannot be
*                 completed.
*/

#define   absolute(x)  ( ((x) < 0)  ?  -(x)  :  (x))
                                    /* Absolute value */
#define   ROWS      4 /* Used in main() to declare the matrix */
#define   COLUMNS   5
          /* ROWS + 1;Used in main() to declare the matrix  */

main()
{
   float  x[ ROWS ];
   static float  A[ ROWS ][ COLUMNS ] =
                          /* Augmented matrix [ A | b ]  */
      {  {  1,  -1,   2,  -1,  -8  },
                          /* Row 0 of Coeff matrix + b[0]*/
         {  2,  -2,   3,  -3,  -20 },
                          /* Row 1 of Coeff matrix + b[1]*/
         {  1,   1,   1,   0,  -2  },
                          /* Row 2 of Coeff matrix + b[2]*/
         {  1,  -1,   4,   3,   4  }  };
                          /* Row 3 of Coeff matrix + b[3]*/

/*
*    GAUSSIAN ELIMINATION   METHOD TO SOLVE   A'x = b,
*                                             A = [ A' | b ]
*/

/* Gaussian_elimination   ( A, x, b, n )
* float  A[ ][ ];       Input: Augmented matrix [ A' | b ] with
*                                n-rows & (n + 1)-columns
* float       x[ ];     Output: Solution vector of size n
* float       b[ ];     Input: Solution vector of size n
*/
   int       n = ROWS;
          /* Input: number of unknowns or Problem dimension   */
```

```
int          i, j, k, pivot_index;
float        pivot, temp;
double       multiplier, sum;

/* Step 1: Do elimination for i = 0, ..., n - 2  */
for ( i = 0; i < n - 1; i++ )
  {
    /* Step 2: Search for maximal pivot element in rows i
     * through n - 1
     */
    pivot       = absolute( A[ i ][ i ] );
    pivot_index = i;
    for ( k = i + 1; k < n; k++ )
       {
          temp = absolute( A[ k ][ i ] );
          if ( temp > pivot )
            { /* Found a new pivot element    */
               pivot       = temp;
               pivot_index = k;
            }
       }
    /*  If the pivot is zero, the matrix A is singular. */
    if ( pivot == 0 )
       {
          printf("\n Gauss_elim: ERROR: %s \n",
                 "No unique solution exists");
          exit ( 1 );
       }
    else
       { /*
          *  Found a non-zero pivot element.
          *  If the pivot element is not in i-th row,
          *  perform row interchange.
          */
          if ( pivot_index != i )
             for ( j = i; j <= n; j++ )
                {
                   temp = A[ i ][ j ];
                   A[ i ][ j ] = A[ pivot_index ][ j ];
                   A[ pivot_index ][ j ] = temp;

                }  /* Row interchange is complete  */
          /*
           *  Now compute multiplier & perform
           *  elimination on each row
           */
          for ( k = i + 1; k < n; k++ )
             {
                multiplier = (double) (A[k][i] / A[i][i] );
                for ( j = i; j <= n; j++ )
                   A[k][j] = A[k][j] - multiplier*A[i][j];
             }
       }
  }
```

```
       /*    Step 3: Check whether A[n - 1][n - 1] is zero   */
       if ( A[n - 1][n - 1] == 0 )
         {
              printf("\n Gauss_elim: ERROR: %s \n",
                     "No unique solution exists");
              exit ( 2 );
         }
       else
           { /*   Step 4: Start Backward substitution   */

            x[ n - 1 ] = A[ n - 1 ][ n ] / A[ n - 1 ][ n - 1 ];

            for ( i = n - 2; i >= 0; i-- )
               {
                 if ( A[ i ][ i ] == 0 )
                      /* Is this diagonal element zero?   */
                    {
                      printf("\n Gauss_elim: ERROR: %s \n",
                             "No unique solution exists");
                      exit ( 3 );
                    }
                 else
                    {
                      sum = 0;
                      for ( j = i + 1; j < n; j++ )
                          sum += (double) (A[ i ][ j ] * x[ j ]);
                      x[ i ] = ( A[ i ][ n ] - sum ) / A[ i ][ i ];
                    }
               }
           }
       /* End of Gaussian_elimination() */

       printf("\n ****  SOLVING SYSTEM OF %s \n",
              "LINEAR EQUATIONS USING  ");
       printf("\n   GAUSSIAN ELIMINATION %s \n",
              "WITH PARTIAL PIVOTING METHOD ****");

       printf("\n  The solution is: \n");
       for ( i = 0; i < n; i++ )
          printf("  x[ %2d ] = %10.5f \n", i, x[ i ] );
}
```

Output Section

```
  ****  SOLVING SYSTEM OF LINEAR EQUATIONS USING

     GAUSSIAN ELIMINATION WITH PARTIAL PIVOTING METHOD ****

  The solution is:
  x[  0 ] =    -7.00000
  x[  1 ] =     3.00000
  x[  2 ] =     2.00000
  x[  3 ] =     2.00000
```

15.2.7 C Code of LU-Decomposition for *Ax = b*

Code Section

```
/*   Program:     LU_decomp.c
 *
 *   Purpose:     To numerically solve a system of Linear equations
 *                           Ax = b   ......      (1)
 *                where A is an n-by-n matrix, b is an n-vector,
 *
 *                Step 1.   Compute L ( Unit Lower Triangular matrix)
 *                          & U (Upper Triangular matrix) such that
 *                              A = LU   ......      (2)
 *                Step 2.   Equation (1) can be written as:
 *                              LUx = b   or,  L( Ux ) = b
 *                          OR, a pair of two linear systems:
 *                              Lz = b   ........      (3)
 *                                             [ Lower Triangular ]
 *                          &   Ux = z   ........      (4)
 *                                             [ Upper Triangular ]
 *
 *                Step 3.   Solve (3) for z using 'Forward
 *                                       Substitution method'
 *                Step 4.   Solve (4) for x using 'Backward
 *                                       Substitution method'
 *
 *                (Note: This method is known as Direct
 *                       Factorization or LU Decomposition. )
 *                For more information, refer to Burden et al. (1978).
 */

#define     ROWS      4 /* Used in main() to declare the matrix */
#define     COLUMNS   4 /* Used in main() to declare the matrix */

main()
{
    float  x[ ROWS ], z[ ROWS ];
    static float  A[ ROWS ][ COLUMNS ] =
                            /* Coefficient matrix  A   */
        {                   /* Row 0 of Coeff matrix A */
          {  1,   1,   0,   3  },
                            /* Row 1 of Coeff matrix A */
          {  2,   1,  -1,   1  },
                            /* Row 2 of Coeff matrix A */
          {  3,  -1,  -1,   2  },
                            /* Row 3 of Coeff matrix A */
          { -1,   2,   3,  -1  }  };

    static float  b[ ROWS ] =
        { 4,  1,  -3,  4 };          /* Column 0 of vector b */

/*
 *   DIRECT FACTORIZATION OF MATRIX A as LU to solve the system
 *                Ax = b
 */
```

```
float    L[ ROWS ] [ COLUMNS ];  /* Unit Lower Triangular matrix */
float    U[ ROWS ] [ COLUMNS ];  /* Upper Triangular matrix */

    int      n = ROWS;
             /* Input:  number of unknowns or dimension  */
    int      i, j, k;
    double   sum;            /* To store accumulated sum  */

    /* Step 1: Check whether A[0] [0] is zero  */
    if ( A[ 0 ][ 0 ] == 0 )
      {
        printf("\n LU_decomp: ERROR: Direct %s \n",
               "Factorization is impossible ");
        exit ( 1 );
      }

    /* Step 2: Select L[0] [0] & U[0] [0] so that
     *                 L[0] [0]*U[0] [0]  = A[0] [0]
     */
    L[ 0 ][ 0 ] = 1;
    U[ 0 ][ 0 ] = A[ 0 ][ 0 ];

    /* Step 3: Compute i) First (0-th) row of U & ii)
     * First column of L
     */
    for ( i = 1; i < n; i++ )
       {
         U[ 0 ][ i ] =  A[ 0 ][ i ] / L[ 0 ][ 0 ];
         L[ i ][ 0 ] =  A[ i ][ 0 ] / U[ 0 ][ 0 ];
       }

    /* Step 4: For i = 1, ..., n - 2, compute remaining
     *         L's & U's
     */
    for ( i = 1; i <= n - 2; i++ )
       {  /* Step 4.1: Compute L[i] [i] & U[i] [i] */
             L[ i ][ i ]  = 1;
             sum  = 0;
             for ( k = 0; k <= i - 1; k++ )
                   sum += (double) (L[ i ][ k ] * U[ k ][ i ]);
             U[ i ][ i ] = A[ i ][ i ] - sum;
          /* Check whether A is singular  */
            if ( U[ i ][ i ] == 0 )
              {
                printf("\n LU_decomp: ERROR: Direct %s \n",
                       "Factorization is impossible ");
                exit ( 2 );
              }
          /* Step 4.2: Compute i-th row of U & i-th column of L */
            for ( j = i + 1; j < n; j++ )
               {  /* Compute i-th row of U  */
                   sum  = 0;
```

```
                    for ( k = 0; k <= i - 1; k++ )
                       sum += (double) (L[ i ][ k ] * U[ k ][ j ]);
                    U[i][j] = (A[ i ][ j ] - sum) / L[ i ][ i ];

                    /* Compute i-th column of L */
                    sum  = 0;
                    for ( k = 0; k <= i - 1; k++ )
                       sum += (double) (L[j][k] * U[k][i]);
                    L[j][i] = ( A[ j ][ i ] - sum) / U[ i ][ i ];
                 }
           }

    /* Step 5: Select L[n-1][n-1] & U[n-1][n-1] so that
     * Ln-1][n-1]*U[n-1][n-1]  =
     *                   A[n-1][n-1] - Sum(L[n-1][k] U[k][n-1])
     *                   for k = 0,..., n-2
     */

     L[ n - 1 ][ n - 1 ]  = 1;
     sum  = 0;
     for ( k = 0; k <  n - 1; k++ )
        sum += (double) (L[ n - 1 ][ k ] * U[ k ][ n - 1 ]);

     U[ n - 1 ][ n - 1 ] = A[ n - 1 ][ n - 1 ] - sum;

    /* Check whether A is singular */
       if ( U[ n - 1 ][ n - 1 ] == 0 )
          {
             printf("\n LU_decomp: ERROR: LU is done, %s \n",
                     "but A is singular");
             exit ( 3 );
          }
/* LU  Decomposition is complete */

/*
 *   FORWARD SUBSTITUTION METHOD TO SOLVE
 *     Lz = b, where L = Lower Triangular matrix
 */

/* Forward_substitution ( L, z, b, n ) ;
 * float     L[ ][ ];     Input: L is an n x n matrix
 * float         z[ ];    Output: solution vector (array) of size n
 * float         b[ ];    Input:  vector (array) of size n
 * int       n = ROWS;    Input:  number of unknowns or dimension
 */

    /* Check if the diagonal element is zero   */
    if ( L[ 0 ][ 0 ] == 0 )
       {
          printf("\n Forward_subs: ERROR: %s \n",
                  "No unique solution exists ");
          exit ( 1 );
       }
```

```
        else
           {
             z[ 0 ] = b[ 0 ] / L[ 0 ][ 0 ];

             for ( i = 1; i <= n - 1;  i++ )
                {
                  if ( L[ i ][ i ] == 0 )
                          /* Is this diagonal element zero?  */
                     {
                        printf("\n Forward_subs: ERROR: %s \n",
                                "No unique solution exists ");
                        exit ( 2 );
                     }
                  else
                     {
                        sum = 0;
                        for ( j = 0; j < i; j++ )
                            sum += (double) (L[ i ][ j ] * z[ j ]);
                        z[ i ] = ( b[ i ] - sum ) / L[ i ][ i ];
                     }
                }
           }
/* End of Forward_substitution()  */

/*
 *    BACKWARD SUBSTITUTION METHOD TO SOLVE
 *       Ux = b, where U = Upper Triangular matrix
 */

    /* Check if the diagonal element is zero  */
    if ( U[ n - 1 ][ n - 1 ] == 0 )
       {
          printf("\n Backward_subs: ERROR: %s \n",
                  "No unique solution exists ");
          exit ( 1 );
       }
    else
       {
          x[ n - 1 ] = z[ n - 1 ] / U[ n - 1 ][ n - 1 ];

          for ( i = n - 2; i >= 0; i-- )
             {
                if ( U[ i ][ i ] == 0 )
                            /* Is this diagonal element zero?  */
                   {
                      printf("\n Backward_subs: ERROR: %s \n",
                              "No unique solution exists ");
                      exit ( 2 );
                   }
                else
                   {
                      sum = 0;
```

```
                    for ( j = i + 1; j < n; j++ )
                        sum += (double) (U[ i ][ j ] * x[ j ]);
                    x[ i ] = ( z[ i ] - sum ) / U[ i ][ i ];
                }
            }
        }
    /* End of Backward_substitution()  */

    printf("\n    SOLVING SYSTEM OF LINEAR EQUATIONS USING\n");
    printf("\n    DIRECT FACTORIZATION (LU-DECOMPOSITION) METHOD n")
    printf("\n  Solution vector is:  \n");
    for ( i = 0; i < n; i++ )
        printf("  x[ %2d ] =  %5f  \n", i, x[ i ] );

}   /* End of main()  */
```

Output Section

```
        SOLVING SYSTEM OF LINEAR EQUATIONS USING

        DIRECT FACTORIZATION (LU-DECOMPOSITION) METHOD

        Solution vector is:
        x[  0 ] =  -1.000000
        x[  1 ] =   2.000000
        x[  2 ] =   0.000000
        x[  3 ] =   1.000000
```

15.2.8 C Code of Gauss–Seidel Iterative Method for $Ax = b$

Code Section

```
/*  Program:  GaussSeidel.c
 *
 *  Purpose:  Given an initial solution vector x0, iteratively
 *            solve a System of n Linear Equations
 *                Ax = b
 *            where A is an n-by-n coefficient matrix,
 *                x is an unknown vector of size n
 *                & b is a vector of size n.
 *
 *            We implement the Gauss-Seidel Iterative method
 *            as a Recursive function.
 *
 *   To compile in Unix:
 *                cc -O GaussSeidel.c -o GaussSeidel  /lib/libm.a
 */

extern      sqrt();
#define     TOLERANCE   1.0e-5 /* Stopping Criterion        */
#define     ROWS        4      /* Used in main()            */
#define     COLUMNS     4      /* Used in main()            */

typedef   float  MATRIX[ ][ COLUMNS ];
                              /* MATRIX type defined here   */
```

```
typedef    float       VECTOR[ ];
                                    /* VECTOR type defined here   */

/*
 * GAUSS-SEIDEL METHOD TO ITERATIVELY SOLVE Ax = b, given x0
 */

Gauss_Seidel ( MATRIX A, VECTOR b, VECTOR initial_x,
               int    n, float  epsilon )

/*  MATRIX   A:         A is an n-by-n coefficient matrix
 *  VECTOR   b:         Right hand side of Ax = b
 *  VECTOR   initial_x: x0 is an n-vector initial approximation
 *  int      n:         Dimension of the problem
 *  float    epsilon:   Tolerance for absolute error in x
 */


{
    int       i, j;
    float     x[ 4]; /* New approximation to the solution  */

    double lower_sum, upper_sum;   /* To store accumulated sum */
    float   vector_norm;   /* To store solution vector norm   */

    /* Step 1: Compute new approximation for i = 0, ..., n - 1 */

      for ( i = 0; i < n; i++ )
        {
            lower_sum = 0;
            for ( j = 0; j <= i - 1; j++ )
                lower_sum += (double) ( A[ i ][ j ] * x[ j ] );

            upper_sum = 0;
            for ( j = i + 1; j < n ; j++ )
                upper_sum += (double) (A[i][j] * initial_x[j]);

            x[i] = (b[i] - lower_sum - upper_sum ) / A[i][i];
        }

    /* Step 2:  Check tolerance on the vector norm  || x - x0 ||
     * Calculate vector norm for x - initial_x
     */
      lower_sum = 0;
      for ( i = 0; i < n; i++ )
        lower_sum += (x[i] - initial_x[i])*(x[i] - initial_x[i]);

      vector_norm = sqrt ( lower_sum );
            /* sqrt() defined in /lib/libm.a */

      if ( vector_norm < epsilon )
          { /*  Set up pointer to the currently computed
             *  solution x
             */
```

```
                   for ( i = 0; i < n; i++ )
                      printf(" x[ %2d ] =   %6.2f \n", i, x[ i ] );
                      exit();
               }
        else
            {
               for ( i = 0; i < n; i++ )
                   /* Set x = initial_x for next iteration  */
                   initial_x[ i ] = x[ i ];

               Gauss_Seidel ( A, b, initial_x, n, epsilon );


            }
  }


/*
 * main(): GAUSS-SEIDEL METHOD TO ITERATIVELY SOLVE Ax = b,
 *         given x0
 */
main()
{
   static float  A[ ROWS ][ COLUMNS ] =
                                  /* Row 0 of Coeff matrix A     */
         {  { 10, -1,   2,   0  },
                                  /* Row 1 of Coeff matrix A     */
            { -1, 11,  -1,   3  },
                                  /* Row 2 of Coeff matrix A     */
            {  2, -1,  10,  -1  },
                                  /* Row 3 of Coeff matrix A     */
            {  0,  3,  -1,   8  }  };

   static float  b[ ROWS ] =
           {  6, 25, -11, 15     };       /* Column b */
   static float  initial_x [ ROWS ] =
           {  0,  0,  0,  0      };       /* Initial approximation */

   printf("\n SOLVING SYSTEM OF LINEAR EQUATIONS USING  \n");
   printf("\n GAUSS-SEIDEL ITERATIVE METHOD\n");
   printf("\n  Solution vector is:  \n\n");
   Gauss_Seidel ( A, b, initial_x, ROWS, TOLERANCE);
}
```

Output Section

```
            SOLVING SYSTEM OF LINEAR EQUATIONS USING

            GAUSS-SEIDEL ITERATIVE METHOD

               Solution vector is:

            x[  0 ] =    1.00
            x[  1 ] =    2.00
            x[  2 ] =   -1.00
            x[  3 ] =    1.00
```

Exercises

15-1 Write a program to evaluate a function $f(z)$, where z is a complex number.

15-2 Write a program to add two n-dimensional complex vectors, that is, vectors whose elements are complex numbers.

15-3 Write a program to multiply two matrices whose elements are complex numbers.

Graphs

In lists, each element except the head and the tail has a unique predecessor and a unique successor. In trees, each node except the root node and the leaf nodes has a unique predecessor and a limited number of successors (children). In both cases, there is a root node, a definite direction or ordering of the nodes, and a limited number of successors of any node. In this chapter, we will develop the concept of the graph, a more general data structure. In a graph each node may be connected to many other nodes without any bounds on the number or the directions of the connections.

There are many applications of the graph data structure in mathematics, chemistry, computer networks, operations research, finding the shortest path, the "traveling salesman" problem, engineering, social sciences, linguistics, airline routing and scheduling, electrical circuit routing, and integrated circuit layout on a printed-circuit board.

In computer science, the graph is a very rich and complex subject. In this chapter we will simply discuss basic concepts and terms, present the ADT definition, explain graph traversals (breadth-first and depth-first) and representations (adjacency matrix and adjacency linked list), explain how to delete a node from a graph, and present many operations on graphs and their implementations in C.

16.1 The Concept of a Graph

A graph is a set of nodes and a set of arcs that connect pairs of nodes. The graph node is called a "vertex." The graph arc is called an "edge." If the edges of a graph have an associated direction the graph is called a "directed graph" or a "digraph." Edge direction implies an ordering of some sort.

We will use the following notational convention. If X and Y are vertices of a graph, then

(X,Y) is an undirected edge, shown as X --- Y
it means "the arc between X and Y"

$<X,Y>$ is a directed edge, shown as X --> Y
it means "the arc from X to Y"

Examples of undirected and directed edges are

(X,Y) "X and Y next to each other"—no order implied
$<X,Y>$ "X is less than Y"—an order is implied

Examples of graphs are shown below in Figure 16-1.

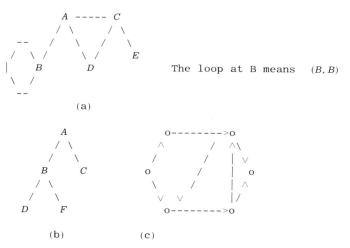

The loop at B means (B,B)

Figure 16-1 Undirected graphs (a, b) and directed graph (c).

A vertex X is "incident" to an edge E if there is a vertex Y such that E is an edge between them, so $E = (X,Y)$ or $E = (Y,X)$.

An edge E is "incident" to a vertex X if there is a vertex Y such that E is an edge between them, so $E = (X,Y)$ or $E = (Y,X)$.

The "degree" of a vertex is the number of edges incident to it. In a directed graph, the "indegree" of a vertex is the number of edges from other vertices to it, and the "outdegree" is the number of edges from it to other vertices.

Two vertices X and Y are "adjacent" to each other if there is an edge between them, (X,Y) or (Y,X).

A "relation" on a set sV of vertices is a set of ordered pairs of vertices in sV, which can be represented by a set of directed edges between the pairs of vertices. A graph can be used to represent relationships between objects. A binary search tree is a special case of the general graph. The nodes of the tree are in some defined order.

A "weighted graph" (or "network") has a numerical value associated with each edge (see Exercise 16-29).

A "path" is a sequence of edges from one vertex X to another vertex Y. We denote the path as $p(X,Y)$. Suppose X and Y are adjacent; then

$$p(X,Y) = (X,Y)   X \text{---} Y$$

Suppose there is a sequence of edges from X to T to S to Y; then

$$p(X,Y) = (X,T,) (T,S), (S,Y) X \text{---} T \text{---} S \text{---} Y$$

An edge is "reflexive" if both ends are incident on the same vertex X, so that (X,X).

A graph is "reflexive" if for each vertex X there is an edge (X,X). A graph is "irreflexive" if there is no vertex X in the graph for which the edge (X,X) exists.

A "cycle" is a path from vertex X to X. The edge (X,X) is the smallest cycle. The path (X,A), (A,B), (B,C) (C,X) is a cycle of length 3.

A "cyclic" graph contains at least one cycle. An "acyclic" graph has no cycle.

A graph is "symmetric" if for all pairs of vertices X and Y there is an edge (X,Y) and thus there is an edge (Y,X). A graph is "asymmetric" if for any two vertices X and Y for which there is an edge (X,Y) there is no edge (Y,X).

A graph is "transitive" if for any three vertices X, Y, and Z there are paths $p(X,Y)$ and $p(Y,Z)$ and thus there is a path $p(X,Z)$.

16.2 Graph Representations

A graph may be represented either by an array of vertex nodes and an array of edges, called an "adjacency matrix," or by linked lists of nodes and edges. We will first present the structures for the array approach and then discuss the concepts of path matrix and transitive closure in the light of array implementation. Finally, we will show the linked list approach. In later sections we will give details of linked list implementation and will leave array implementation as an exercise.

16.2.1 Graph Representation Using Adjacency Matrix

The array representation is based on the graph node and edge node structures and some global pointers. They are defined as shown in Figure 16-2.

```
#define MAXNODES 128
enum BOOLEAN {FALSE, TRUE};

typedef struct
{
    enum BOOLEAN adj;
    int weight;  /* associated edge weight */
} EDGE, ADJMATRIX[MAXNODES][MAXNODES];

typedef struct
{
    DATA_TYPE key;
} GNODE;

typedef struct
{
    GNODE      gnode[MAXNODES];
    ADJMATRIX  adjmatrix;
} GRAPH;

GRAPH graph;  /* the graph */
```

Figure 16-2 Array representation of a graph.

The two-dimensional array `adjmatrix` represents the edges between every possible pair of vertex nodes. For each pair of array indices I and J, g.adj `matrix[I] [J]` is either FALSE or TRUE in value. The array `adjmatrix` is called an "adjacency matrix."

Some primitive operations are

`join()`	Create an edge between two vertices
`remove()`	Remove an edge between two vertices
`adjacent()`	Is there an edge between two vertices?

These operations are quite simple:

```
join(ADJMATRIX * adjmat, GNODE * node1, GNODE * node2)
{
    adjmat[node1->key] [node2->key].adj = TRUE;
}

remove(ADJMATRIX * adjmat, GNODE * node1, GNODE * node2)
{
    adjmat[node1->key] [node2->key].adj = FALSE;
}

enum BOOLEAN
adjacent(ADJMATRIX * adjmat, GNODE * node1, GNODE * node2)
{
    return(adjmat[node1->key] [node2->key].adj);
}
```

16.2.2 Path Matrix and Transitive Closure

A graph can be constructed from an array of the vertex nodes and an two-dimensional array of boolean values that represents every possible ordered pair of vertices in the node array. In relation to our earlier terminology, If X and Y are vertices of a graph and the adjacency matrix is am, define $x = $ X.key and $y = $ Y.key:

$<X,Y>$ is equivalent to am[x] [y].adj == TRUE

If `(am[x] [y].adj && am[y] [z].adj)` has value TRUE, then there must be a path of length 2 between vertices X and Z. For the expression to have value TRUE, each of the `adjmatrix` elements `am[x] [y].adj` and `am[y] [z].adj` must be TRUE, which means that edges $<X,Y>$ and $<Y,Z>$ exist, so there is a path from X to Z of length 2.

Conversely, if there is a path of length 2 from X through Y to Z, then there is an edge $<X,Y>$ (so `am[x] [y].adj` has the value TRUE) and an edge $<Y,Z>$ (so `am[y] [z].adj` has the value TRUE). Then the expression `(am[x] [y].adj && am[y] [z].adj)` has the value TRUE.

The expression formed by all possible pairs of edges from vertex X to vertex Y through every vertex in the graph is

$p2(x,y) = $ `((am[x] [1].adj && am[1] [y].adj) ||`
`(am[x] [2].adj && am[2] [y].adj) ||`

etc.

`(am[x] [MAXNODES].adj && am[MAXNODES] [y].adj))`

where $x =$ X.key and $0 \le$ X.key $<$ MAXNODES and $y =$ Y.key and $0 \le$ Y.key $<$ MAXNODES. Also note that obviously am[z][z].adj == FALSE for the simple case of irreflexive graphs. This expression is true if and only if there is a least one path of length 2 from X to Y. The two-dimensional array, am2, formed from the set of expressions

$$\text{am2[x][y].adj} = p2(x,y)$$

for all x and y, such that $0 \le x,y <$ MAXNODES, is called the "path matrix of length 2." The original matrix, am, is then the "path matrix of length 1."

If you translate the adjacency matrix into its mathematical form, a MAX-NODES-by-MAXNODES two-dimensional matrix (call it AM_1), and take the matrix product, AM_1 X AM_1, you will discover that you have formed the MAXNODES-by-MAXNODES matrix that corresponds to the path matrix of length 2. In fact it is possible to find the path matrix of length K recursively by the following:

```
AM_2 = AM_1 X AM_1
AM_K = AM_1 X AM_(K-1)
```

To find if there is a path of length 4 from vertices X to Y, check the value of the expression

am[x][y].adj || am[x][y].adj || am[x][y].adj || am[x][y].adj

If it has value TRUE, then there is at least one path of length 4.

To find if there is a path of any length from vertices X to Y, check the value of the expression

$$P(x,y) = (\text{am[x][y].adj} \;|| $$
$$\text{am2[x][y].adj} \;|| $$
$$\text{am3[x][y].adj} \;|| $$

etc.

$$\text{amM[x][y].adj})$$

where M == MAXNODES. If $P(x,y)$ has the value TRUE, then there is at least one path from X to Y. The expression $P(x,y)$ is called the "transitive closure" of the adjacency matrix, am.

A function for calculation of the transitive closure of an adjacency matrix is given below:

```
ADJMATRIX * tclosure1(ADJMATRIX * amat, ADJMATRIX * path)
{
    int i, j, k, m, n, r;
    enum BOOLEAN res;
    ADJMATRIX * anew, * aprod;

    aprod = amat;
    path = amat;

    for (i = 0; i < MAXNODES - 1; i++)
    {
```

```
            for (m = 0; m < MAXNODES; m++)
                for (n = 0; n < MAXNODES; n++)
                {
                    res = FALSE;
                    for (r = 0; r < MAXNODES; r++)
                        res = res || (aprod[m][p].adj && amat[p][n].adj);
                    anew[m][n].adj = res;
                }

            for (j = 0; j < MAXNODES; j++)
            {
                for (k = 0; k < MAXNODES; k++)
                    path[i][k].adj = path[i][k].adj || anew[j][k].adj;
                aprod = anew;
            }
        }

        return(path);
    }
```

The function `tclosure1()` is quite inefficient. The number of loop passes is MAXNODES to the fourth power plus MAXNODES to the third power. If MAXNODES == 128, then the number of passes is 128 * 128 * 128 * (128 + 1) = 270 * 10 to the sixth. If an inner loop take 10 machine instructions at 0.01 μs per instruction, the total function execution time is about 270 s, or 4.5 min. There must be a better way.

Define the path matrix pK so that pK[x][y].adj == TRUE if and only if there is a path from node X to node Y, with x and $y \leq K$, which doesn't pass through any node with key value greater than K.

The value of pK+1[x][y].adj can be derived from that of pK[x][y].adj. If pK[x][y].adj == TRUE, then pK+1[x][y].adj must also have value TRUE, because $K+1 > K$ and there is a path from X to Y that doesn't pass through the node with key value $K+1$.

If pK[x][y].adj == FALSE, then pK+1[x][y].adj can have the value TRUE only if there is a path passing through node $K+1$ that doesn't pass through all the nodes $1 \ldots K$. So there must be a path from X to $K+1$ that passes through a subset of the nodes $1 \ldots K$, and likewise a path from $K+1$ to Y that also passes through a subset of the nodes $1 \ldots K$.

$$X \sim\sim\sim K+1 \sim\sim\sim Y \qquad \text{but not} \qquad X \sim\sim\sim Y \sim\sim\sim K+1 \text{ or}$$
$$K+1 \sim\sim\sim X \sim\sim\sim Y$$

where "$\sim\sim\sim$" means "path to."

So pK+1[x][y].adj == TRUE if and only if the expression pK[x][y].adj || (pK[x][k+1].adj == TRUE && pK[k+1][y].adj == TRUE) has value TRUE. The method for obtaining pK+1 from pK is

```
for (x = 0; x < MAXNODES; x++)
    for (y = 0; y < MAXNODES; y++)
        pK+1[x][y].adj = pK[x][y].adj ||
                        (pK[x][k+1].adj && pK[k+1][y].adj);
```

When the logic is simplified:

```
pK+1 = pK;
 for (x = 0; x < MAXNODES; x++)
     if (pK[x,k+1].adj == TRUE)
         for (y = 0; y < MAXNODES; y++)
             pK+1[x][y].adj = pK[x][y].adj || pK[k+1][y].adj;
```

Clearly p0 is the adjacency matrix, since for all nodes *X* and *Y* the only path directly from *X* to *Y* is (*X,Y*). Also pMAXNODES-1 is the transitive closure path matrix, since for all *X* and *Y* the paths from *X* to *Y* through all the other nodes are contained in it.

The improved function, tclosure2(), for calculation of the transitive closure is shown below. Its algorithm is called "Warshall's algorithm."

```
ADJMATRIX * tclosure1(ADJMATRIX * amat, ADJMATRIX * path)
{
    int i, j, k;
    enum BOOLEAN res;
    ADJMATRIX * anew, * aprod;

    path = amat;

    for (k = 0; k < MAXNODES; k++)
        for (i = 0; i < MAXNODES; i++)
            if (path[i][k].adj == TRUE)
                for (j = 0; j < MAXNODES; j++)
                    path[i][j].adj = path[i][j].adj || path[k][j].a

    return(path);
}
```

16.2.3 Graph Representation Using Linked Adjacency List

The linked list representation has as its basis the graph node and edge node structures and some global pointers. They are defined as shown in Figure 16-3.

The first members of the edge node, key1 and key2, identify the graph vertex nodes that the edge connects. The second member, edge_next, is a pointer to the next element of the edge node list.

The first member of the graph node, key, is used to identify the node quickly. The key might be a unique value derived from the next member, data. The third member, visit_status, is used for keeping track of whether the node is visited. It may be TRUE or FALSE. The fourth and fifth members, next and prev, are respectively forward and backward pointers to the graph node list elements. The sixth and seventh members, edge_head_ptr and edge_tail_ptr, are pointers to the front and rear of the associated singly linked edge list.

To illustrate the use of the structures, let us use a graph with six vertices, *A, B, C, D, E,* and *F*. The graph is shown in Figure 16-4. The edges are undirected. The graph node data will be character strings.

```
struct edge_node
{
    KEY_TYPE              key1;
    KEY_TYPE              key2;
    struct edge_node  *  edge_next;
};

typedef struct edge_node * EDGE_LIST_PTR;

struct  graph_node        /*  Vertex  */
{
    KEY_TYPE              key;
    DATA_TYPE             data;
    VISIT_STATUS          visit_status;
    struct graph_node  *  next;
    struct graph_node  *  prev;
    EDGE_LIST_PTR         edge_head_ptr;
    EDGE_LIST_PTR         edge_tail_ptr;
};

typedef struct graph_node * GNODE_LIST_PTR;

/*  Global variables: the list head and tail pointers  */
GNODE_LIST_PTR  ghead_ptr, gtail_ptr;
```

Figure 16-3 The basic graph node types.

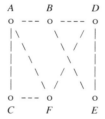

Figure 16-4 A six node graph.

The graph has eight edges and six nodes. The graph node list is shown in Figure 16-5.

```
ghead_ptr                          gtail_ptr

   |                                  |
   V                                  V

(A)  ->  (B)  ->  (C)  ->  (D)  ->  (E)  ->  (F)

(A) graph node:                 (D) graph node:
    A.key = a                       D.key = d
    A.data = "alpha"                D.data = "delta"
    A.next = &(B)                   D.next = &(E)
    A.prev = NULL                   D.prev = &(C)
    A.edge_head_ptr = &(A,B)        D.edge_head_ptr = &(D,B)
    A.edge_head_ptr = &(A,F)        D.edge_tail_ptr = &(D,F)
```

Figure 16-5 The graph node list.

The edge node lists for graph nodes *A* and *D* are shown in Figure 16-6.

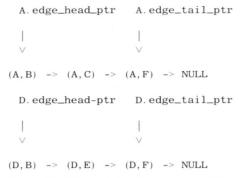

Figure 16-6 Edge node lists for vertices *A* and *D*.

A more general linked adjacency list representation is shown in Figure 16-7. Its implementation is shown in Example 16-1.

16.3 The Abstract Data Type Graph

An ADT graph has a collection of vertices and edges together with the following operations:

Function name	Operation
init_graph()	Initializing a graph
is_glist_empty()	Checking whether the list of graph nodes is empty
create_gnode()	Creating a graph node
insert_gnode()	Inserting a graph node at the end of the the list of graph nodes
create_graph()	Creating a graph
delete_graph()	Deleting the entire graph
print_graph()	Printing the entire graph
search_gnode()	Searching for a graph node in the list
delete_gnode()	Deleting a graph node from the list
create_edge_elt()	Creating an edge element
insert_edge()	Inserting an edge at the end of the list of edge elements
search_edge()	Searching for an edge element in the edge list
delete_edge()	Deleting an edge element from the edge list
is_adjacent_node()	Checking whether two graph nodes are adjacent
retrieve_gnode()	Retrieving a graph node
update_gnode()	Updating a graph node
find_path()	Finding a path between two graph nodes
print_path()	Printing a path between two graph nodes
Breadth_first_trav()	Breadth-first traversing a graph
Depth_first_trav()	Depth-first traversing a graph

The vertex of an ADT graph is as abstract as possible. For example, it may be a city's name, molecule, etc. It contains a key that may be used to establish its relationship (connection) with one or more other nodes. The connection between two nodes is indicated by the edge. The edge may have an associated weight.

For the graph to be fully abstract, the structure defining it must include point-

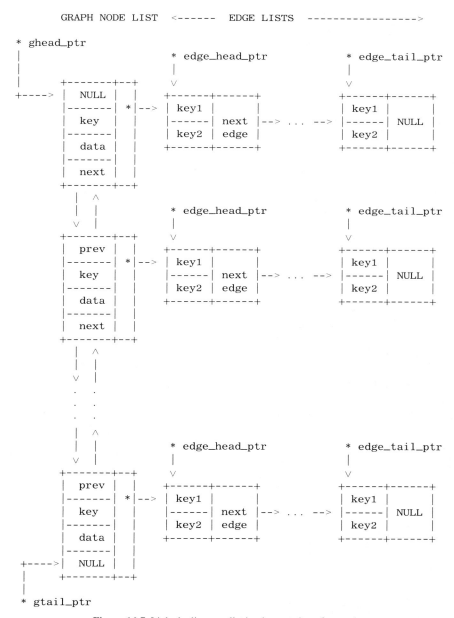

```
GRAPH NODE LIST  <------   EDGE LISTS   ----------------->

* ghead_ptr
|                               * edge_head_ptr         * edge_tail_ptr
|                               |                       |
|        +-------+--+           V                       V
+----->  | NULL  |  |     +------+------+         +------+------+
         |-------| *|-->  | key1 |      |         | key1 |      |
         | key   |  |     |------| next |--> ... --> |------| NULL |
         |-------|  |     | key2 | edge |         | key2 |      |
         | data  |  |     +------+------+         +------+------+
         |-------|  |
         | next  |  |
         +-------+--+
            |  ^
            |  |                 * edge_head_ptr         * edge_tail_ptr
            V  |                 |                       |
         +-------+--+            V                       V
         | prev  |  |     +------+------+         +------+------+
         |-------| *|-->  | key1 |      |         | key1 |      |
         | key   |  |     |------| next |--> ... --> |------| NULL |
         |-------|  |     | key2 | edge |         | key2 |      |
         | data  |  |     +------+------+         +------+------+
         |-------|  |
         | next  |  |
         +-------+--+
            |  ^
            |  |
            V  |
            .  .
            .  .
            .  .
            |  ^
            |  |                 * edge_head_ptr         * edge_tail_ptr
            V  |                 |                       |
         +-------+--+            V                       V
         | prev  |  |     +------+------+         +------+------+
         |-------| *|-->  | key1 |      |         | key1 |      |
         | key   |  |     |------| next |--> ... --> |------| NULL |
         |-------|  |     | key2 | edge |         | key2 |      |
         | data  |  |     +------+------+         +------+------+
         |-------|  |
+----->  | NULL  |  |
|        +-------+--+
|
* gtail_ptr
```

Figure 16-7 Linked adjacency list implementation of a graph.

ers to functions with generic names that are the implementations of the above operations. Below is an example of such a structure.

```
struct DATA
  {
   char datatype[8];
   union
     {
      int     Ibuf[128];
```

```
            char      Cbuf [512] ;
            double    Dbuf [64] ;

            /*  etc ...    */

        } buffer;
    };

struct Vertex
    {
      struct Vertex * edges;    /* pointer to a list of vertices */
      DATA * data;              /* pointer to data buffer */
    };

struct Graph
    {
      char datatype [8] ;
      ADJMAT   adjmatrix;

      void (* init_graph) () ;
      int (* is_glist_empty) () ;
      GNODE_LIST_PTR (* create_gnode) () ;
      void (* insert_gnode) () ;
      void (* create_graph) () ;
      void (* delete_graph) () ;
      void (* print_graph) () ;
      GNODE_LIST_PTR (* search_gnode) () ;
      void (* delete_gnode) () ;
      EDGE_LIST_PTR (* create_edge_elt) () ;
      void (* insert_edge) () ;
      EDGE_LIST_PTR (* search_edge) () ;
      void (* delete_edge) () ;
      int (* is_adjacent_node) () ;
      GNODE_LIST_PTR (* retrieve_gnode) () ;
      void (* update_gnode) () ;
      void (* Breadth_first_trav) () ;
      void (* Depth_first_trav) () ;
      int (* find_path) () ;
      void (* print_path) () ;
    };
```

The structure of the linked list version of the adjacency matrix is left as an exercise.

16.4 Traversal of Graphs

Traversing a graph is movement through the graph. Graph traversals are used for determining the connectivity of two nodes, finding the shortest path between two nodes for a weighted graph, building a spanning tree, etc. As with trees, there are several ways of traversing a graph. The two most common methods are breadth-first traversal and depth-first traversal. Breadth-first traversal is roughly analogous to in-order traversal for trees; depth-first traversal is roughly analogous to preorder traversal for trees. Since a graph is a collection of a finite number of vertex nodes and edges, a node must be visited exactly once in order to avoid cycles. For example, see the graph shown in Figure 16-8.

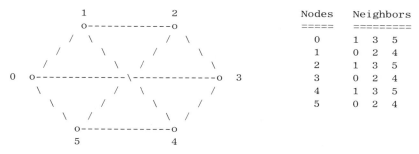

Figure 16-8 An undirected graph.

Starting traversal from node 0, the sequence in which the nodes are visited is shown below:

Traversal	Order of visiting the nodes
Depth-first traversal	0 1 2 3 4 5
Breadth-first traversal	0 1 3 5 2 4

The graph in Figure 16-8 is used in Example 16-1 in order to demonstrate the graph operations.

A graph is a general form of a tree in which more than one edge may come into or go out of a node. This may lead to visiting the same node "multiple times." For a connected graph, multiple visits of the same node may lead to an infinite loop of traversal. In order to avoid the possibility of multiple visits of the same node, we cannot use the assumptions made for tree traversal. It is necessary to maintain the information about whether a node has been visited. Before visiting a node, we must check the status to ensure that the node has not been visited previously. For an unconnected graph, special work is required to ensure visits of all nodes.

16.4.1 Breadth-First Traversal

Breadth-first traversal of a graph, also called "breadth-first search," is roughly analogous to inorder traversal for trees. Suppose we start breadth-first traversal with a node N, whose adjacent nodes are $N_1, N_2, \ldots, N_k$. We first visit N and all of its neighbors N_i ($i = 1, \ldots, k$), putting all the neighbors of each N_i in a queue. Then we skip visiting N_1 because it has been visited previously. We proceed to visit all the neighbors of N_1. Once all the neighbors of each neighbor of N_1 that have been waiting in the queue are visited, the breadth-first traversal continues visiting the neighbors of N_i ($i = 2, \ldots, k$) in the same manner.

In short, in a breadth-first traversal, after a node N is visited, all the neighboring nodes (that is, nodes adjacent to it) are visited before any other nodes.

Algorithm of Breadth-First Traversal

Step 1. (Initialization step.) For all nodes k ($k = 1, \ldots, n$) in the graph, set `visit_status[ k ]` to FALSE.

Step 2. Initialize a queue Q.
Step 3. For each node, say k, ($k = 1, \ldots, n$) in the graph, do steps 4 through 10.
Step 4. If visit_status [k] is FALSE, then proceed to visit node k in step 5.
Step 5. Enqueue node k in the queue Q.
Step 6. While the queue Q is not empty, do steps 7 through 10.
Step 7. Get a node, say N, from the queue Q.
Step 8. Set the visit_status [N] to TRUE.
Step 9. Visit (e.g., print) the node N.
Step 10. For all neighbors (that is, adjacent nodes) of N, if not yet visited, enqueue them in the queue Q.

Note that a queue is needed for breadth-first traversal.

To illustrate the breadth-first traversal algorithm, consider the graph in Figure 16-8.

Breadth-first traversal starts out by printing node 0. Since node 0 has the neighboring nodes 1, 3, and 5, it prints all of them before visiting any of the neighboring nodes of these neighbors. The neighboring nodes of node 1 are 0, 2, and 4. Since node 0 has been visited previously, it prints the remaining neighboring nodes 2 and 4. The breadth-first traversal then finds that the neighbors 1, 3, and 5 of node 2 have been visited. It proceeds to visit the neighbors 1, 3, and 5 of node 4, the neighbor of node 2. Since these are found to have been visited previously, this completes the visits of the neighbors of the neighbors of the neighboring node 2 for the node 1. Then the breadth-first traversal turns to visit the neighbors of the neighbor 4 for the node 1 in the similar manner. The final order of the breadth-first traversal for the above graph is 0, 1, 3, 5, 2, and 4.

16.4.2 Depth-First Traversal

Depth-first traversal of a graph, also called "depth-first search," is roughly analogous to preorder traversal for trees. It is also called "backtracking," because it returns to the nodes previously visited to continue visit of the next node.

Suppose we start depth-first traversal with a node N, whose adjacent nodes are $N_1, N_2, \ldots, N_k$. We first visit N, and visit N_1 and pushing the remaining neighbors N_i ($i = 2, \ldots, k$) of N in a stack. Then we proceed to visit all the neighbors of N_1. Once all the neighbors of each neighbor of N_1 that have been waiting in the stack are visited, the depth-first traversal returns to visit the neighbors N_i ($i = 2, \ldots, k$) of N in the same manner.

Algorithm for Depth-First Traversal

Step 1. (Initialization step.) For all nodes k ($k = 1, \ldots, n$) in the graph, set visit_status [k] to FALSE.
Step 2. Initialize a stack Q.
Step 3. For each node, say k, ($k = 1, \ldots, n$) in the graph, do steps 4 through 10.
Step 4. Visit (e.g., print) one node, say k, if not visited previously; set visit_status [k] to TRUE.
Step 5. If node k has any neighbors (adjacent nodes), visit one adjacent

node, say *M*, if not visited previously; set `visit_status[ M ]` to TRUE.

Step 6. Push the remaining neighbors of *k* in a stack *S*.

Step 7. If node *M* has any neighbors (adjacent nodes), visit one adjacent node, say *P*, if not visited previously; set `visit_status[ P ]` to TRUE.

Step 8. Push the remaining neighbors of *M* in the stack *S*.

Step 9. If node *P*, just visited, does not have any neighbors, pop the stack *S*.

Step 10. Repeat steps 3 through 9.

Note that steps 4 through 10 of the depth-first algorithm may be done conveniently using a recursive procedure. A stack is needed for depth-first traversal.

To illustrate the breadth-first traversal algorithm, consider the graph in Figure 16-8.

Depth-first traversal first visits node 0 and prints it. Node 0 has three neighbors, nodes 1, 3, and 5. Since node 1 has not been visited previously, it prints 1, and keeps 3 and 5 in the stack for later visit. Since node 1 has the neighbors nodes 0, 2, and 4, and since the neighboring node 0 has been visited previously, it visits node 2, and keeps the other neighboring node, node 4, in the stack. It then proceeds to visit the neighbors, nodes 1, 3, and 5, of node 2. Since its neighboring node, node 1, has been visited previously, it prints node 3, and keeps node 5 in the stack. Proceeding to visit the neighbors, nodes 0, 2, and 4, of node 3, it is found that nodes 0 and 2 have been visited previously. It prints node 4. The neighbors of node 4 include nodes 1, 3, and 5. Since nodes 1 and 3 have been visited previously, it prints node 5. The neighbors, nodes 0, 2, and 4, of node 5 have already been visited. Thus all the neighbors of the neighboring node 1 for node 0 are now visited. Then the depth-first traversal turns to visit the neighbors, nodes 3 and 5, of node 0 in a similar manner. The final order of the depth-first traversal for the above graph is 0, 1, 2, 3, 4, and 5.

16.5 Graph Operations

The operations on a graph are shown in `graph.c`, a linked adjacency list implementation of an ADT undirected graph. The graph vertex list is implemented as a doubly linked list. The graph edge list is implemented as a singly linked list. The package contains the ADT graph operations listed in Section 16.3.

The primary data objects are the vertex and graph structures:

```
typedef   struct  edge_node
{
     KEY_TYPE                 key1,   key2;
     struct edge_node    *  edge_next;

}  EDGE_NODE,  * EDGE_LIST_PTR;

typedef   struct   graph_node              /*   Vertex   */
{
     KEY_TYPE                 key;
     DATA_TYPE                data;
     VISIT_STATUS             visit_status;
```

```
        struct graph_node  *  next;
        struct graph_node  *  prev;
        EDGE_LIST_PTR          edge_head_ptr;
        EDGE_LIST_PTR          edge_tail_ptr;

    }  GRAPH_NODE, * GNODE_LIST_PTR;

    /*  Global variables  */
    GNODE_LIST_PTR  ghead_ptr, gtail_ptr;
```

The first function, init_graph() of type void, initializes the global list headers of the graph vertices by setting them to NULL:

```
        ghead_ptr      = NULL;
        gtail_ptr      = NULL;
```

The second function, is_glist_empty() of type int, checks whether the doubly linked list of graph vertices is empty. It returns the value of the test:

```
        ( ghead_ptr == NULL )
```

The third function, create_gnode(), creates a new vertex of the graph. It returns a pointer of type GNODE_LIST_PTR. It allocates memory for the new graph vertex using a call to the standard library routine calloc().

The fourth function, insert_gnode(), adds the new graph node at the end of the graph node doubly linked list. The function is of type void. It takes as arguments the new key, KEY_TYPE new_key, the new data, DATA_TYPE new_data, the head pointer, GNODE_LIST_PTR ghead_ptr, and the tail pointer GNODE_LIST_PTR gtail_ptr. It calls create_gnode() to allocate memory space for the new graph node of type GRAPH_NODE. It updates the new vertex structure fields: key, next, prev, edge_head_ptr, and edge_tail_ptr. If the graph node list is empty, then the new vertex (node) is the first of the list, so ghead_ptr and gtail_ptr are set to its location.

The fifth function, create_graph(), is used by the demonstration function, main(). Create_graph() creates an undirected graph with six nodes (see Figure 16-8). This is the initial form of the graph, and it is represented by an incidence matrix, Incidenc_mat[][], where

$$\text{Incidence\_mat[i][j]} = \begin{cases} 1 & \text{if there is an edge incident to node } i \text{ from node } j \\ 0 & \text{otherwise} \end{cases}$$

Create_graph() is of type void. Calling insert_gnode(), it creates the doubly linked list of six graph nodes. Then calling insert_edge(), it creates the singly linked edge list for each graph node.

The sixth function, delete_graph() of type void, destroys the entire graph by the iterative method. It takes the graph list pointer GNODE_LIST_PTR ghead_ptr as an argument. It calls delete_edge_list() to remove the edges iteratively and finally frees the head pointer.

The seventh function, count_graph_size(), reports the graph's size, the total of all graph nodes, plus all edges. The function takes a pointer to the graph, `ghead_ptr`, as its argument and it returns an int. It uses an interative method. The limitation of this function is that it counts the edges $<i,j>$, $<j,i>$ as in the case of a directed graph. Its modification for an undirected graph is left as an exercise.

The eighth function, `print_graph()`, prints the nodes and edges of the entire graph by an iterative method. It takes a pointer to the graph, `ghead_ptr`, as its argument.

The ninth function, `search_gnode()`, searches for the graph node specified by the key, `search_key`, using an iterative method. It takes the search key and a pointer to the graph as its arguments and returns a pointer of type GNODE_LIST_PTR to a node. If it does not find the match in the graph node list, it returns a NULL pointer.

The tenth function, `delete_gnode()`, deletes a node from the graph's node list. The node to be deleted is searched by its key. It is the most complex operation for a graph. The complexity arises because it is necessary to find its reference in other nodes' edge lists and delete all those edges incident to this node. The function takes the key, the addresses of the pointers, `ghead_ptr` and `gtail_ptr`, respectively, to the graph head and to the graph tail as its arguments. It calls `search_gnode()` to search for the graph node to be deleted, and if the match is found, it deletes the node's associated edge list and frees the node's space.

The eleventh function, `create_edge_elt()`, creates a memory space for a new edge in the edge list. It returns a pointer of type EDGE_LIST_PTR. It allocates memory for the new edge of the graph vertex.

The twelfth function, `delete_edge_list()`, deletes the singly linked list of edges by an iterative method. It takes a pointer to the edge list as an argument and checks whether the associated singly linked edge list is empty. If the list is not empty, it calls the library function, `free()`, to free the space for each edge in the edge list.

The thirteenth function, `insert_edge()`, appends a new edge (`new_key1`, `new_key2`) to the edge list for the node `key1`. Because the graph is considered undirected, the edge (`new_key2`, `new_key1`) can be optimally appended to the edge list for the node `key2`. The function takes two keys and pointers, `ehead_ptr` and `etail_ptr`, respectively, to the head and tail of the edge list as arguments. It calls `create_edge_elt()` to create a new edge element and updates its fields from the arguments. If the edge list is empty, then this is the first element; otherwise link the new edge after the edge currently at the last position, pointed to by `etail_ptr`, of the edge list.

The fourteenth function, `search_edge()`, searches for an edge specified by the keys `key1` and `key2` and a pointer to the graph. It uses a linear iterative method. If the vertex is not found, return a NULL pointer. If one vertex with key `key1` is found, then it does a linear traversal of the singly linked edge list to find a match for the pair (`key1`, `key2`). If the match is not found, it returns NULL; otherwise it returns a pointer to the edge.

The fifteenth function, `search_prev_edge()`, searches for the edge previous to a given edge (`key1`, `key2`) in a singly linked edge list. It uses a recursive method. It calls the function `search_gnode`. If the first vertex is not found, it returns NULL. If `key1` is found, then it does a linear traversal of the singly linked edge list to find a match for the pair of vertices, (`key1`, `key2`). It returns a pointer to the edge list element if found; otherwise it returns NULL.

The sixteenth function, delete_edge(), deletes an edge specified by its vertices (key1, key2), from the singly linked edge list. It takes the vertices, a pointer to the graph, and the graph type as arguments. It first checks to see if the edge (key1, key2) is the first one in the edge list, and if so, it needs a pointer to the node with key1, so it calls search_gnode(key1, ghead_ptr). Then it does a search for the edge (key1, key2) in the graph and if the result is NULL, it returns. If the match is found, it then searches for the edge previous to it in the list calling the function search_prev_edge(key1, key2, ghead_ptr), and if that is found, it adjusts the pointers of the previous edge and the next edge. If the node to be deleted is the tail of the list, then free the space; otherwise unlink and then free. For the graph of type UNDIRECTED, since the edges (key1, key2) and (key2, key1) are the same, both of these edges must be deleted. To do this, delete_edge() calls itself directly.

The seventeenth function, is_adjacent_node(), determines whether there is an edge between two vertices specified by key1 and key2. It takes the keys and a pointer to the graph as arguments and returns YES or NO depending on whether an edge is found in the edge list. It calls search_edge() to find an edge between the two vertices.

The eighteenth function, retrieve_gnode(), takes a key as its argument and returns a pointer to a vertex node if the key is found in the graph. The implementation is left as an exercise.

The nineteenth function, update_gnode(), takes a key and a data item, new_data, and a pointer, ghead_ptr, to the graph as arguments and updates the designated vertex node.

The twentieth function, find_path(), takes two vertices as arguments and tries to find a path between them. The implementation is left as an exercise.

The twenty-first function, Depth_first_trav(), takes a pointer, ghead_ptr of type GNODE_LIST_PTR, to the graph as an argument. It performs a depth-first traversal on an undirected graph. It calls the recursive function, visit_node(). Visit_node() visits (i.e., prints) each node of the graph node if the node has not been visited previously. This is checked by testing the node's visit status field, visit_status, with FALSE. If the status is FALSE, it prints the key value of the node, and sets its visit_status to TRUE. Note that when a new graph node is created from insert_gnode(), the visit_status field is initialized to FALSE. However, if we want to call of Depth_first_trav() later on, it is necessary to reinitialize the field for each graph node.

The twenty-second function, Breadth_first_trav(), takes a pointer, ghead_ptr of type GNODE_LIST_PTR, to the graph as an argument. It performs a breadth-first traversal on an undirected graph. The implementation is left as an exercise.

The final function, main(), is a driver for a demonstration of the graph and its operations. It calls init_graph() to set up the graph head and tail pointers, calls create_graph() to make the demonstration graph, calls print_graph() to print the graph, performs a depth-first traversal using Depth_first _trav(), does a search for a node using search_gnode(), calls is_adjacent_node() to check whether two nodes are adjacent, deletes an edge using delete_edge(), deletes a graph node calling delete_gnode(), and then prints the result by calling print_graph() again, and finally prints the graph statistics using count_graph_size().

When an undirected graph of n nodes is implemented using the linked adjacency list, the worst-case time complexities of some of the above graph operations are as noted below:

Operations	Worst-case performance
search_gnode()	$O(n)$
insert_gnode()	$O(1)$
create_gnode()	$O(1)$
delete_gnode()	$O(n)$
search_edge()	$O(n)$
insert_edge()	$O(1)$
create_edge_elt()	$O(1)$
delete_edge()	$O(n)$

16.6 Spanning Trees

Sometimes it is necessary to know that there is at least one path between any two nodes (vertices) in a graph. For example, consider five towns as vertices and paths connecting them. During bad weather, it is necessary to ensure a path from one town to any other town. A spanning tree will be useful in this case.

A spanning tree of graph G is a subgraph of G, which is a tree containing all the vertices of G. A graph G is connected when there is a path between any two vertices of G. If a graph G has a spanning tree, it is connected. Conversely, if a graph is connected, it has a spanning tree. However, the trees of a graph are not unique because any one of the vertices of G may be considered to build a spanning tree.

Building a spanning tree can be done by either deleting the redundant edges or adding edges. Two common approaches to build a spanning tree of a graph are based on the depth-first and breadth-first traversals. These traversal methods add edges to a vertex in order to build a spanning tree.

16.6.1 Building a Spanning Tree of a Graph Using Depth-First Traversal

We illustrate this method using graph G shown in Figure 16-9.

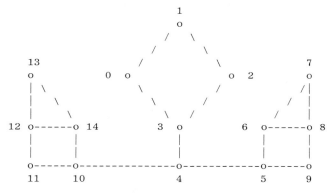

Figure 16-9 A simple graph G.

We start a depth-first traversal from node 4 of G. This will be the root of a spanning tree that is being built (see Figure 16-10).

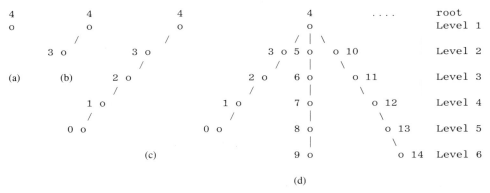

Figure 16-10 A spanning tree for graph G in Figure 16-9 using depth-first traversal.

The depth-first traversal adds the edge with node 4 and node 3, in Figure 16-10(b). It then successively adds edges from neighbors of neighbors of node 4, if these vertices have not been visited previously. This yields a path with nodes 4, 3, 2, 1, and 0 in Figure 16-10(c). Since node 0 has no neighbor, we backtrack to node 1. Since node 1 has no neighbor, we backtrack to node 2. Proceeding similarly, we backtrack to node 4. Its neighbors, nodes 5 and 10, are in the stack, not yet visited. Considering node 5, we add edges in the tree for the neighbors of neighbors of 5. Finally, using the depth-first traversal for node 10, we build the path adding edges for nodes 10, 11, 12, 13, and 14. Backtrackings from nodes 14 to 13, from 13 to 12, from 12 to 11, and from 11 to 10 show that all nodes have been visited previously. This completes the depth-first traversal of the entire graph G. This yields the spanning tree of G in Figure 16-10(d).

16.6.2 Building a Spanning Tree of a Graph Using Breadth-First Traversal

In Figure 16-11 we illustrate the method of building a spanning tree for graph G in Figure 16-9. We start a depth-first traversal from the node 4 of G. This will be the root of a spanning tree that is being built.

Since node 4 has the neighboring nodes 3, 5, and 10, we add all edges incident to these nodes 3, 5, and 10 in level 3 of the tree. We keep the neighbors of 3, 5, and 10 in the queue for later visit. Since the neighboring nodes of 3 are 0 and 2, which have not been visited previously, we add the edges (3, 0) and (3, 2) in level 3. Since the nodes 5 and 10 in level 2 have respective neighbors { 6, 9 } and { 11, 14 } that have not been visited previously, we add the edges (5, 6), (5, 9), (10, 11), (10, 14) in level 3 of the tree. Now we add the edges incident to nodes 0, 2, 6, 9, 11, and 14 that have not already been added in the tree. The edges (0, 1), (6, 7), (6, 8), (11, 12), and (14, 13) are added in level 4. This yields the final form of a spanning tree in Figure 16-11(d).

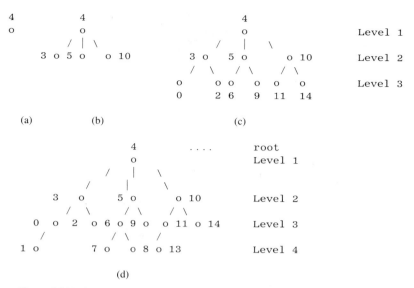

```
4                 4                            4
o                 o                            o                         Level 1
               / | \                       /  |  \
      3 o 5 o     o 10            3 o    5 o       o 10                  Level 2
                               / \  / \    / \
                              o    o o    o  o    o                     Level 3
                              0    2 6    9  11   14

   (a)            (b)                         (c)
```

```
                    4        . . . .       root
                    o                       Level 1
                 /  |  \
              /     |     \
       3   o     5 o        o 10            Level 2
          / \     / \      / \
     0  o   2   o 6 o 9  o   o 11 o 14      Level 3
       /           / \    /
     1 o         7 o    o 8 o 13            Level 4

                    (d)
```

Figure 16-11 A spanning tree for graph G in Figure 16-9 using breadth-first traversal.

16.7 Application: Computing the Shortest Path

In this section we will discuss Dijkstra's Distance Algorithm that computes the shortest path between two vertices (nodes in a weighted and directed graph. Its implementation is left as Exercise 16-33.

Consider a weighted digraph with no particular order of weights. Each directed edge $<X,Y>$ has a weight, $W(X,Y)$, associated with it. (The weight might represent cost, time duration, capacity, distance, resistance, etc.) Given two vertices X and Y in the graph, we might want to find a path, $p(X,Y)$ that satisfies some given condition. For example, suppose the weights represent distance and the condition is that the path be the least distance between X and Y. In the example below, all the edges have equal weights equal to 1. The shortest path from X to D is

$$\text{MINpath}(X, D) \; == \; \{ \; <X, B>, \; <B, D> \; \}$$

and its distance is 2.

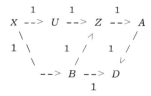

```
        1       1       1
   X --> U --> Z --> A
     \             ↗       /
    1  \       1  /   1  /
        \      /       ↓
         --> B --> D
              1
```

Figure 16-12 A weighted digraph.

Dijkstra developed an algorithm to compute the minimum distance between pairs of vertices in a graph. It attaches a label, $L(Z)$, to each vertex Z on any given path from X to Y, which represents the distance of the shortest path from X to Z. The algorithm modifies the labels as it continues through the graph so that the value of the labels of vertices are being reduces toward a final value for $L(Y)$ When $Z ==$ Y, $L(Z)$ represents the value of the shortest distance. As each vertex is visited, if it has the minimum label, it is removed from the working set of vertices.

The Dijkstra Distance Algorithm is as follows:

Step 1. Initializations:
> The graph vertex set Gv = {X, X1, X2, . . . , Xm, Y}.
>
> MAXNODES = the maximum number of vertices in the graph.
> MAXWEIGHT = the maximum vertex weight in the graph.
> HUGE = 100 * MAXNODES * MAXWEIGHT.
>
> X and Y are the start and end vertices in the graph.
>
> For all Xi in Vw, L (Xi = HUGE.
> L (X) = 0 (which makes X the first minimum label vertex).
> The working vertex set Sv = Gv.

Step 2. Loop:
> Find vertex Z in Sv with the minimum label L (Z) . Take the first one found if there are more than one.

Step 3. If Z == Y then exit loop (done!).

Step 4. For all edges out of Z, Ei = <Z, Xi>,
> if Xi is in Sv and L (Xi) > L (Z) + weight (Ei)
> > where weight () yields the weight of edge Ei)
> > then L (Xi) = L (Z) + weight (Ei) .

Step 5. Remove Z from Sv: Sv = Sv - {Z}.

Step 6. Go to step 2.

Step 7. Return the result: L (Y) .

To illustrate the algorithm, we will find the minimum distance from vertex A to vertex I in the graph shown below.

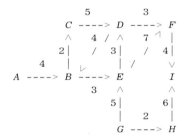

Figure 16-13 A weighted digraph for the calculation.

The sequence of steps leading to the solution is as follows:

Step 1. Initializations:
> The graph vertex set Gv = {A, B, C, D, E, F, G, H, I}.
> MAXNODES = 9 (the number of vertices in the graph).
> MAXWEIGHT = 10.
> HUGE = 9000 (100 * 9 * 10).
> A and I are the start and end vertices in the graph.

For all Xi in Gv, L (Xi) = HUGE.

L (A) = 0 (which makes A the first minimum label vertex).

The working vertex set Sv = Gv.

Step 2. Sv == {A, B, C, D, E, F, G, H, I}.

Find vertex Z in Sv with the minimum label L (Z) .

Z = A, since L (A) == 0, and the rest are 9000.

Step 3. A ! = I (so don't exit the loop).

Step 4. All edges out of A == <A, B>.

$$9000 == L (B) > L (A) + W (<A, B>) == 0 + 4,$$
$$\text{so} \quad L (B) = 4.$$

Step 5. Remove A from Sv: Sv = Sv − {A} == {B, C, D, E, F, G, H, I}.

Step 6. Go to step 2.

Step 2. Sv == {B, C, D, E, F, G, H, I}.

Find vertex Z in Sv with the minimum label L (Z) .

Z = B, since L (B) == 4, and the rest are 9000.

Step 3. B ! = I.

Step 4. All edges out of B == <B, C>, <B, E>.

$$9000 == L (C) > L (B) + W (<B, C>) == 4 + 2,$$
$$\text{so} \quad L (C) = 6.$$
$$9000 == L (E) > L (B) + W (<B, E>) == 4 + 3,$$
$$\text{so} \quad L (E) = 7.$$

Step 5. Remove B from Sv: Sv = Sv − {B} == {C, D, E, F, G, H, I}.

Step 6. Go to step 2.

Step 2. Sv == {C, D, E, F, G, H, I}.

Find vertex Z in Sv with the minimum label L (Z) .

Z = C, since L (C) == 6, L (E) == 7, and the rest are 9000.

Step 3. C ! = I.

Step 4. All edges out of C == <C, D>.

$$9000 == L (D) > L (C) + W (<C, D>) == 6 + 5,$$
$$\text{so} \quad L (D) = 11.$$

Step 5. Remove C from Sv: Sv = Sv − {C} == {D, E, F, G, H, I}.

Step 6. Go to step 2.

Step 2. Sv == {D, E, F, G, H, I}.

Find vertex Z in Sv with the minimum label L (Z) .

Z = E, since L (E) == 7, L (D) == 11, and the rest are 9000.

Step 3. E ! = I.

Step 4. All edges out of E == <E, D>, <E, F>, <E, G>.

$$11 == L (D) > L (E) + W (<E, D>) == 7 + 3,$$
$$\text{so} \quad L (D) = 10.$$
$$9000 == L (F) > L (E) + W (<E, F>) == 7 + 7,$$
$$\text{so} \quad L (F) = 14.$$
$$9000 == L (G) > L (E) + W (<E, G>) == 7 + 5,$$
$$\text{so} \quad L (F) = 12.$$

Step 5. Remove E from Sv: Sv = Sv − {E} == {D, F, G, H, I}.

Step 6. Go to step 2.

Step 2. Sv == {D, F, G, H, I}

Find vertex Z in Sv with the minimum label L (Z) .

Z = D, since L (D) == 10, L (F) == 14, L (G) = 12,

and the rest are 9000.

Step 3. D != I.
Step 4. All edges out of D == <D, F>.
            14 == L (F) > L (D) + W (<D, F>) == 10 + 3,
              so   L (F) = 13.
Step 5. Remove D from Sv: Sv = Sv - {D} == {F, G, H, I}.
Step 6. Go to step 2.
Step 2. Sv == {F, G, H, I}
            Find vertex Z in Sv with the minimum label L (Z).
            Z = G, since L (G) == 12, L (F) == 13,
              and the rest are 9000.
Step 3. G != I.
Step 4. All edges out of G == <G, H>.
            9000 == L (H) > L (G) + W (<G, H>) == 12 + 2,
              so   L (H) = 14.
Step 5. Remove G from Sv: Sv = Sv - {G} == {F, H, I}.
Step 6. Go to step 2.
Step 2. Sv == {F, H, I}
            Find vertex Z in Sv with the minimum label L (Z).
            Z = F, since L (F) == 13, L (H) == 14, and L (I) == 9000.
Step 3. F != I.
Step 4. All edges out of F == <F, I>
            9000 == L (I) > L (F) + W (<F, I>) == 13 + 4,
              so   L (I) = 17.
Step 5. Remove F from Sv: Sv = Sv - {F} == {H, I}.
Step 6. Go to step 2.
Step 2. Sv == {H, I}
            Find vertex Z in Sv with the minimum label L (Z).
            Z = H, since L (H) == 14, L (I) == 17.
Step 3. H != I.
Step 4. All edges out of H == <H, I>.
            17 == L (I) <= L (H) + W (<H, I>) == 14 + 6,
              so   L (I) remains == 17.
Step 5. Remove H from Sv: Sv = Sv - {H} == {I}.
Step 6. Go to step 2.
Step 2. Sv == {I}
            Find vertex Z in Sv with the minimum label L (Z).
            Z = I, since I is the only vertext left.
Step 3. I == I, so exit from the loop.
Step 7. Return the result L (I) : 17.

Example

Example 16-1

Code Section

```
/*
 *  graph. c
 *
 *    Linked Adjacency List Implementation of ADT Undirected Graph.
 *    Graph node list is implemented as a doubly linked list.
```

```
*      Graph edge list is implemented as a singly linked list.
*
*      The graph in Figure 16-8 is used to create the graph,
*      and test the operations on it.
*
*   This package contains the following ADT Graph Operations:
*
*      init_graph()
*      is_glist_empty()
*      create_gnode()
*      insert_gnode()
*      create_graph()
*      delete_graph()
*      count_graph_size()
*      print_graph()
*      search_gnode()
*      delete_gnode()
*      create_edge_elt()
*      delete_edge_list()
*      insert_edge()
*      search_edge()
*      search_prev_edge()
*      delete_edge()
*      is_adjacent_node()
*      retrieve_gnode()
*      update_gnode()
*      find_path()
*      print_path()
*      Depth_first_trav()
*      Breadth_first_trav()
*/

#include <stdio.h>

#define    YES      1
#define    NO       0

typedef    enum     { DIRECTED, UNDIRECTED } GRAPH_TYPE;
typedef    enum     { TRUE, FALSE } VISIT_STATUS;

typedef    int      KEY_TYPE;       /*  Vertex's key value  */
typedef    char     DATA_TYPE;

typedef    struct edge_node
{
    KEY_TYPE               key1, key2;
    struct edge_node   *   edge_next;

}  EDGE_NODE, * EDGE_LIST_PTR;

typedef    struct  graph_node          /*  Vertex  */
{
    KEY_TYPE                  key;
```

```
    DATA_TYPE                    data;
    VISIT_STATUS                 visit_status;
    struct graph_node    *  next;
    struct graph_node    *  prev;
    EDGE_LIST_PTR                edge_head_ptr;
    EDGE_LIST_PTR                edge_tail_ptr;

}  GRAPH_NODE, * GNODE_LIST_PTR;

/* Global variables */
GNODE_LIST_PTR  ghead_ptr, gtail_ptr;

GNODE_LIST_PTR  search_gnode( KEY_TYPE, GNODE_LIST_PTR );
void  delete_edge_list( EDGE_LIST_PTR );
void  insert_edge ( KEY_TYPE,           KEY_TYPE,
                    EDGE_LIST_PTR *,   EDGE_LIST_PTR * );
void  delete_edge( KEY_TYPE,            KEY_TYPE   key2,
                    GNODE_LIST_PTR,    GRAPH_TYPE );

/*
 *  init_graph() :  Initialize list of graph nodes
 */
void  init_graph()
{
    ghead_ptr       = NULL;
    gtail_ptr       = NULL;
}


/*
 *   is_glist_empty() :  Check whether the doubly linked
 *                       list of graph nodes is empty.
 */
int  is_glist_empty( GNODE_LIST_PTR   ghead_ptr )
{
    return( ghead_ptr == NULL );
}


/*
 *   create_gnode() : Create a new node of the graph
 */

GNODE_LIST_PTR  create_gnode()
{
    GNODE_LIST_PTR  new_gnode_ptr;

    /* Allocate memory for the new graph node  */

    new_gnode_ptr = (GNODE_LIST_PTR) calloc( 1, sizeof( GRAPH_NODE) )
    if (new_gnode_ptr == NULL )
        printf("\n create_gnode: calloc failed \n\n");
    return( new_gnode_ptr );
}
```

```
/*
 *    insert_gnode()  :  Add the new graph node at the end of
 *                       the list.
 */

void  insert_gnode( KEY_TYPE   new_key,   DATA_TYPE   new_data,
                    GNODE_LIST_PTR  *   ghead_ptr,
                    GNODE_LIST_PTR  *   gtail_ptr )
{
    GNODE_LIST_PTR   new_gnode_ptr;

    new_gnode_ptr = create_gnode();
    if ( new_gnode_ptr == NULL )
      return;

    /*  Assign the new values  */
    new_gnode_ptr -> key  = new_key;
    new_gnode_ptr -> data = new_data;
    new_gnode_ptr -> visit_status = FALSE;
    new_gnode_ptr -> next = NULL;
    new_gnode_ptr -> prev = NULL;
    new_gnode_ptr -> edge_head_ptr = NULL;

    /*  Is the doubly linked list of graph nodes empty?  */
    if ( is_glist_empty( *ghead_ptr ) )
      {
        *ghead_ptr = new_gnode_ptr;
        *gtail_ptr = new_gnode_ptr;
      }
    else
      {
        /*
         *  Link the new node after the node currently at
         *  the last position of the list.
         */
        (*gtail_ptr) -> next   = new_gnode_ptr;
        new_gnode_ptr -> prev = *gtail_ptr;
        *gtail_ptr  = new_gnode_ptr;
      }
}

/*
 *    create_graph()  :  Create an undirected graph with 6 nodes.
 *                       This is the initial form of the graph
 *                       in Figure 16-8.
 */

void  create_graph()
{
    GNODE_LIST_PTR      gnode_ptr;
    EDGE_LIST_PTR       elist_ptr;
    KEY_TYPE            key1,  key2;
```

```
        int   i, j;

        /*  Input Data  for graph nodes and nodes' edges  */

        static  int gnodes[6] = { 0, 1, 2, 3, 4, 5 };

        /*
         *  For the graph in Figure 16-8, the
         *  nodes's edges are shown using a boolean
         *  Adjacent matrix (called Incidence matrix).
         */

        static int Incidence_mat[6][6]  =
          { { 0, 1, 0, 1, 0, 1 },      /*  Edges for node 0  */
            { 1, 0, 1, 0, 1, 0 },      /*  Edges for node 1  */
            { 0, 1, 0, 1, 0, 1 },      /*  Edges for node 2  */
            { 1, 0, 1, 0, 1, 0 },      /*  Edges for node 3  */
            { 0, 1, 0, 1, 0, 1 },      /*  Edges for node 4  */
            { 1, 0, 1, 0, 1, 0 } };    /*  Edges for node 5  */

        /*  Create the doubly linked list of six graph nodes  */
        for ( i = 0; i < 6; i++ )
              insert_gnode( i, gnodes[i], &ghead_ptr, &gtail_ptr );

        /*  Create the edge list for each graph node  */
        for ( i = 0; i < 6; i++ )
           {
              /*  Search for the graph node with key i  */
              key1 = (KEY_TYPE) i;
              gnode_ptr = search_gnode( key1, ghead_ptr );

              for ( j = 0; j < 6; j++ )
              {
                 key2 = (KEY_TYPE) j;
                 /*
                  *  If the node i has an edge, say j,
                  *  Incidence_mat[ i, j ] = 1. Then insert
                  *  the edge <i, j> in the edge list for node i.
                  */
                 if ( Incidence_mat[ i ][ j ] ==  1 )
                   insert_edge( key1, key2,
                              &(gnode_ptr->edge_head_ptr),
                              &(gnode_ptr->edge_tail_ptr) );
              }
           }
}


/*
 *   delete_graph()   :  Destroy the entire graph.
 *                       (Iterative method)
 */
void  delete_graph( GNODE_LIST_PTR  ghead_ptr )
{
     GNODE_LIST_PTR   gnext_ptr;
```

```
        if ( is_glist_empty( ghead_ptr ) )
          return;                    /*  List is empty  */

        while ( ghead_ptr != NULL )
          {
             gnext_ptr = ghead_ptr -> next;
             delete_edge_list( ghead_ptr -> edge_head_ptr );
             free( ghead_ptr );                    /*  Free memory  */
             ghead_ptr = gnext_ptr;
          }
}

/*
 *    count_graph_size()   :   Count graph's size, the total of all
 *                             graph nodes plus all edges.
 */

int   count_graph_size( GNODE_LIST_PTR   ghead_ptr )
{
        GNODE_LIST_PTR   glist_ptr = ghead_ptr;   /* Graph list pointer */
        EDGE_LIST_PTR    elist_ptr;
        int              node_count = 0,     /* Total graph nodes */
                         edge_count = 0;     /* Total edges */

        if ( is_glist_empty( ghead_ptr ) )
            return( 0 );

        while ( glist_ptr != NULL )
        {
           node_count++;

           elist_ptr = glist_ptr -> edge_head_ptr;

           while ( elist_ptr != NULL )
           {
             edge_count++;       /*  edge_count = edge_count + 1  */

             elist_ptr = elist_ptr -> edge_next;
           }
           glist_ptr = glist_ptr -> next;
        }

        /*  Return graph size = node_count + edge_count  */
        return( node_count + edge_count );
}

/*
 *    print_graph()   :   Print the entire graph (Iterative method)
 */
void  print_graph( GNODE_LIST_PTR   ghead_ptr )
{
        GNODE_LIST_PTR   glist_ptr = ghead_ptr;   /* Graph list pointer */
        EDGE_LIST_PTR    elist_ptr;
```

```
        printf("\n\n GRAPH NODES          EDGE LISTS  \n");
        printf(" ==========          ==========  \n\n");

        if ( is_glist_empty( ghead_ptr ) )
            printf( " NULL \n" );

        while ( glist_ptr != NULL )
        {
            elist_ptr = glist_ptr -> edge_head_ptr;

            printf(" %d : ",  glist_ptr -> key );

            while ( elist_ptr != NULL )
            {
                printf(" (%d, %d) ->",  elist_ptr -> key1,
                            elist_ptr -> key2 );

                elist_ptr = elist_ptr -> edge_next;
            }
            printf( " NULL \n" );
            glist_ptr = glist_ptr -> next;
        }
}

/*
 *   search_gnode()   :   Search for the graph node specified by
 *                        the key, search_key. (Iterative method)
 */

GNODE_LIST_PTR   search_gnode ( KEY_TYPE           search_key,
                                GNODE_LIST_PTR   ghead_ptr )
{
        GNODE_LIST_PTR   glist_ptr = ghead_ptr;   /* Graph list pointer *

        if ( is_glist_empty( ghead_ptr ) )
            return( NULL );

        while ( glist_ptr != NULL )
        {
            if ( glist_ptr -> key == search_key )
                return( glist_ptr );

            glist_ptr = glist_ptr -> next;
        }

        /* Searched key is not found */
        return( NULL );
}

/*
 *   delete_gnode() :   Delete a node from the graph's node
 *                      list. The node to be deleted is specified
 *                      by its key "delete_node_key". All the edges
 *                      to and from this node must be deleted.
 */
```

```
void  delete_gnode(  KEY_TYPE              delete_node_key,
                     GNODE_LIST_PTR * ghead_ptr,
                     GNODE_LIST_PTR * gtail_ptr )
{
    GNODE_LIST_PTR   search_ptr,  temp_ptr;
    EDGE_LIST_PTR    edge_hd_ptr, next_ptr;

    /*  Search for the graph node to be deleted  */
    search_ptr = search_gnode( delete_node_key, *ghead_ptr );
    if ( search_ptr == NULL )     /*  node is not found  */
      {
        printf("\n delete_gnode: Node to be deleted %s \n",
               "is not found" );
        return;
      }
    /*
     *  Graph node is found. Delete the list of edges for this
     *  node.
     */
    edge_hd_ptr = search_ptr -> edge_head_ptr;

    /*  Delete the associated edge list  */
    delete_edge_list ( edge_hd_ptr );

    /*
     *  The associated edge list is either empty or deleted.
     *  Now drop the link.
     */

    /*  Is the node to be deleted the head of the list?  */
    if ( search_ptr == *ghead_ptr )
      {
        temp_ptr = (*ghead_ptr) -> next;
        if ( *gtail_ptr == *ghead_ptr )
            *gtail_ptr = temp_ptr;
        free( ghead_ptr );             /*  Free memory  */
        *ghead_ptr = temp_ptr;
        (*ghead_ptr) -> prev = NULL;
        return;
      }

    /*  Is the node to be deleted the tail of the list?  */
    if ( search_ptr == *gtail_ptr )
      {
        *gtail_ptr = search_ptr -> prev;
        free( search_ptr );            /*  Free memory  */
        return;
      }

    /*
     *    The node to be deleted is not the head of the list.
     *    Adjust the links of the next and previous nodes.
     */
    search_ptr -> prev -> next = search_ptr -> next;
```

```
        search_ptr -> next -> prev = search_ptr -> prev;
        free( search_ptr );

        /*
         *  Delete all the edges to and from node with 'key'.
         *  Search for these edges in all the edge lists for
         *  each node in the graph.
         */

        temp_ptr = *ghead_ptr;

        while ( temp_ptr != NULL )
          {

            delete_edge( temp_ptr -> key, delete_node_key,
                         temp_ptr, DIRECTED );
            /*
             *  Remove the edge(s) to and from delete_node_key
             *  in the next node's edge list.
             */
            temp_ptr = temp_ptr -> next;
          }
}

/*
 *    create_edge_elt() :   Create a memory space for a new
 *                          edge in the edge list.
 */

EDGE_LIST_PTR   create_edge_elt()
{
  EDGE_LIST_PTR   new_edge_ptr;

    /*  Allocate memory for the new edge of a graph node  */

    new_edge_ptr = (EDGE_LIST_PTR) calloc( 1, sizeof( EDGE_NODE) );
    if  (new_edge_ptr == NULL )
        printf("\n create_edge_elt: calloc failed \n\n");
    return( new_edge_ptr );
}

/*
 *  delete_edge_list():  Delete the singly linked list of edges.
 *                       (Iterative method)
 */
void  delete_edge_list( EDGE_LIST_PTR  edge_hd_ptr )
{
  EDGE_LIST_PTR   next_ptr;

    /*  Is the associated singly linked edge list empty ?  */
    while ( edge_hd_ptr != NULL )
      {
        next_ptr = edge_hd_ptr -> edge_next;
        free( edge_hd_ptr );                       /*  Free memory  */
```

```
            edge_hd_ptr = next_ptr;
        }
}

/*
 *    insert_edge ()  :  Append a new edge <new_key1, new_key2> to the
 *                       edge list for the node key1. Because the
 *                       graph is considered undirected, the
 *                       edge <new_key2, new_key1> can be optimally
 *                       appended to the edge list for the node key2.
 */

void  insert_edge ( KEY_TYPE  new_key1,  KEY_TYPE   new_key2,
                    EDGE_LIST_PTR  *   ehead_ptr,
                    EDGE_LIST_PTR  *   etail_ptr )
{
    EDGE_LIST_PTR  new_edge_ptr;

    new_edge_ptr = create_edge_elt ();
    if ( new_edge_ptr == NULL )
      return;

    /*  Assign the new values  */
    new_edge_ptr -> key1  = new_key1;
    new_edge_ptr -> key2  = new_key2;
    new_edge_ptr -> edge_next = NULL;

    /*  Is the doubly linked list of graph nodes empty?  */
    if ( *ehead_ptr == NULL )
      {
         *ehead_ptr = new_edge_ptr;
         *etail_ptr = new_edge_ptr;
      }
    else
      {
        /*
         *  Link the new edge after the edge currently at
         *  the last position of the edge list.
         */
        (*etail_ptr) -> edge_next   = new_edge_ptr;
        *etail_ptr  = new_edge_ptr;
      }
}

/*
 *    search_edge ()  :  Search for an edge specified by the keys
 *                       (vertices) key1, and key2.
 *                       (Linear Iterative method)
 */
EDGE_LIST_PTR  search_edge ( KEY_TYPE  key1, KEY_TYPE  key2,
                             GNODE_LIST_PTR  ghead_ptr )
{
    GNODE_LIST_PTR  search_gnode_ptr;
    EDGE_LIST_PTR   edge_list_ptr;
```

```
    /*  Find the graph node with the key, key1, in node list  */
    search_gnode_ptr  =  search_gnode( key1, ghead_ptr );

    /*  If it is not found, return  */
    if ( search_gnode_ptr == NULL )
      return( NULL );

    /*
     *  One node with key, key1, is found. Now linearly traverse
     *  the singly linked edge list to find a match for the pair
     *  of keys (vertices) <key1, key2>
     */
    edge_list_ptr = search_gnode_ptr -> edge_head_ptr;

    while  ( edge_list_ptr != NULL )
       {
           if ( ( edge_list_ptr -> key1 == key1 )  &&
                ( edge_list_ptr -> key2 == key2 ) )
              return( edge_list_ptr );

              edge_list_ptr = edge_list_ptr -> edge_next;
       }

    /*  Search failed; Edge is not found in the Edge list ! */
    return( NULL );
}

/*
 *  search_prev_edge() :   Search for the edge previous to a
 *                         given edge <key1, key2> in a singly
 *                         linked edge list. (Recursive method)
 */

EDGE_LIST_PTR  search_prev_edge( KEY_TYPE  key1,  KEY_TYPE  key2,
                                 GNODE_LIST_PTR  ghead_ptr )
{
    GNODE_LIST_PTR  search_gnode_ptr;
    EDGE_LIST_PTR   edge_list_ptr;

    /*  Find the graph node with the key, key1, in node list  */
    search_gnode_ptr  =  search_gnode( key1, ghead_ptr );

    /*  If it is not found, return  */
    if ( search_gnode_ptr == NULL )
      return( NULL );

    /*
     *  One node with a key, key1, is found. Now linearly traverse
     *  the singly linked edge list to find a match for the pair
     *  of keys (vertices) <key1, key2>
     */
    edge_list_ptr = search_gnode_ptr -> edge_head_ptr;
```

```
        while  ( edge_list_ptr != NULL )
          {
              if ( ( edge_list_ptr -> edge_next -> key1 == key1 )  &&
                   ( edge_list_ptr -> edge_next -> key2 == key2 ) )
                  return( edge_list_ptr );

                  edge_list_ptr = edge_list_ptr -> edge_next;
          }
      /*  Search failed  */
      return( NULL );
}

/*
 *   delete_edge ()   :   Delete an edge specified by its key
 *                        vertices <key1, key2>, from the singly
 *                        linked edge list.
 */
void  delete_edge( KEY_TYPE   key1,  KEY_TYPE   key2,
                   GNODE_LIST_PTR   ghead_ptr,
                   GRAPH_TYPE       graph_type )
{
    GNODE_LIST_PTR   search_node_ptr;
    EDGE_LIST_PTR    delete_edge_ptr, prev_edge_ptr;

    /*
     *  Check to see if the edge <key1, key2> is the first one
     *  in the edge list; if so, we need a pointer to the node
     *  with key1.
     */

    search_node_ptr = search_gnode( key1, ghead_ptr );
    if ( search_node_ptr == NULL )
        return;

    /*  Search for the edge <key1, key2> in the graph  */
    delete_edge_ptr = search_edge( key1, key2, ghead_ptr );

    if ( delete_edge_ptr == NULL )
      return;       /*  Specified edge is not in the graph  */

    /*
     *  Check to see if the edge <key1, key2> is the first
     *  one in the edge list.
     */
    if ( search_node_ptr -> edge_head_ptr == delete_edge_ptr )

        search_node_ptr -> edge_head_ptr = delete_edge_ptr->edge_next;

    else
      {
        /*  Now search for the edge previous to it in the list  */
        prev_edge_ptr = search_prev_edge( key1, key2, ghead_ptr );
```

```
                /*  Adjust the pointers of the prev edge & the next edge  */
                prev_edge_ptr -> edge_next = delete_edge_ptr -> edge_next;
            }

        free( delete_edge_ptr );

        if ( graph_type == UNDIRECTED )

            /*
             *  For an undirected graph, edges <key1, key2> and
             *  <key2, key1> must be deleted.
             */
            delete_edge( key2, key1, ghead_ptr, graph_type );
    }

/*
 *   is_adjacent_node() :  Determine whether there is an edge
 *                         between two vertices specified by
 *                         key1 and key2.
 */
int   is_adjacent_node( KEY_TYPE  key1, KEY_TYPE  key2,
                        GNODE_LIST_PTR  ghead_ptr )
{
    /*
     *  Check whether there exists an edge between two vertices:
     *  <key1, key2> or <key2, key1>
     */

    if ( ( search_edge( key1, key2, ghead_ptr ) != NULL ) )
       return( YES );

    if ( ( search_edge( key2, key1, ghead_ptr ) != NULL ) )
       return( YES );

    /*  The vertices (nodes) are not adjacent.  */
    return( NO );
}

/*
 *   retrieve_gnode()
 */

GNODE_LIST_PTR  retrieve_gnode( KEY_TYPE  srch_key )
{

    /*  Left as an exercise  */
}

/*
 *   update_gnode() : Update a graph node, specified by the
 *                    key "key", by the new data, new_data.
 */
```

```
void update_gnode ( KEY_TYPE   key,      DATA_TYPE   new_data,
                    GNODE_LIST_PTR    ghead_ptr )
{
    GNODE_LIST_PTR   search_ptr;

    /*  Search for the graph node by its key  */
    search_ptr = search_gnode ( key,  ghead_ptr );

    if ( search_ptr != NULL )
        search_ptr -> data = new_data;
}


/*
 *   Depth_first_trav () : Perform Depth-First Traversal on an
 *                         undirected graph (Depth-First Search).
 *                         It calls visit_node (), a recursive function.
 */
void  visit_node ( GNODE_LIST_PTR    gnode_ptr )
{
    GNODE_LIST_PTR   neighbor_node_ptr;
    EDGE_LIST_PTR    elist_ptr;

    elist_ptr = gnode_ptr -> edge_head_ptr;

    /*  Check whether this graph node is visited previously */
    if ( gnode_ptr -> visit_status == FALSE )
      {
        gnode_ptr -> visit_status = TRUE;
        printf (" %3d ", gnode_ptr -> key );
      }

     while ( elist_ptr != NULL )
       {
         /*  Search for its neighbor identified by "key2"  */
         neighbor_node_ptr = search_gnode ( elist_ptr -> key2,
                                            gnode_ptr );
         if ( neighbor_node_ptr != NULL )
            /*  Visit the neighbors of its neighbors  */
            visit_node ( neighbor_node_ptr );

         elist_ptr = elist_ptr -> edge_next;
       }
}

void  Depth_first_trav ( GNODE_LIST_PTR  ghead_ptr )
{
    GNODE_LIST_PTR  glist_ptr = ghead_ptr;  /* Graph list pointer */
    EDGE_LIST_PTR   elist_ptr;

    printf ("\n\n DEPTH-FIRST TRAVERSAL OF GRAPH:  \n");

    if ( is_glist_empty ( ghead_ptr ) )
        printf ( " NULL \n" );
```

```
    while ( glist_ptr != NULL )
    {
       if ( glist_ptr -> visit_status == FALSE )
         {
            printf(" %3d ", glist_ptr -> key );
            /*  Set that this node is visited  */
            glist_ptr -> visit_status = TRUE;
         }

       /*  Visit the neighbors of its neighbors  */
       visit_node( glist_ptr );

       glist_ptr = glist_ptr -> next;
    }
}

/*
 *   Breadth_first_trav() : Perform Breadth-First Traversal on an
 *                          undirected graph (Breadth-First Search).
 */
void  Breadth_first_trav( GNODE_LIST_PTR  ghead_ptr )
{

    /*  Left as an exercise  */

}

/*
 *   find_path() : Find a path between two nodes identified
 *                 node1_key, node2_key.
 */

find_path( KEY_TYPE  node1_key,  KEY_TYPE  node2_key )
{

    /*  Left as an exercise  */
}

/*
 *   main():  Test driver for ADT Undirected Graph.
 */
main()
{

   printf("\n ***  EXAMPLE OF AN ADT UNDIRECTED GRAPH  *** \n");

   init_graph();
   create_graph();
   print_graph( ghead_ptr );
   printf("\n\n The Graph size is: %d \n",
          count_graph_size( ghead_ptr ) );
   Depth_first_trav( ghead_ptr );
```

```
   printf("\n\n Searching for graph node 4 ... \n");
   if ( search_gnode( 4, ghead_ptr ) != NULL )
      printf("\n Search for graph node 4 succeeded \n");

   if ( search_edge( 1, 4, ghead_ptr ) != NULL )
      printf("\n Search for graph edge %s \n",
              "between nodes 1 & 4 succeeded ");

   if ( is_adjacent_node( 2, 5, ghead_ptr ) == YES )
      printf("\n Nodes 2 and 5 are adjacent. \n");
   else
      printf("\n Nodes 2 and 5 are not adjacent. \n");

   delete_edge(2, 3, ghead_ptr, UNDIRECTED );
   printf("\n Graph after deleting the edge (2, 3):\n");
   print_graph( ghead_ptr );

   printf("\n Graph after deleting the node 4:\n");
   delete_gnode( 4, &ghead_ptr, &gtail_ptr );
   print_graph( ghead_ptr );
   printf("\n\n The Graph size is: %d \n",
           count_graph_size( ghead_ptr ) );
}
```

Output Section

```
   ***   EXAMPLE OF AN ADT UNDIRECTED GRAPH   ***

   GRAPH NODES          EDGE LISTS
   ===========          ==========

   0 :   (0, 1) -> (0, 3) -> (0, 5) -> NULL
   1 :   (1, 0) -> (1, 2) -> (1, 4) -> NULL
   2 :   (2, 1) -> (2, 3) -> (2, 5) -> NULL
   3 :   (3, 0) -> (3, 2) -> (3, 4) -> NULL
   4 :   (4, 1) -> (4, 3) -> (4, 5) -> NULL
   5 :   (5, 0) -> (5, 2) -> (5, 4) -> NULL

   The graph size is: 24

   DEPTH-FIRST TRAVERSAL OF GRAPH:
      0    1    2    3    4    5

   Searching for graph node 4 ...

   Search for graph node 4 succeeded

   Search for graph edge between nodes 1 & 4 succeeded

   Nodes 2 and 5 are adjacent.

   Graph after deleting the edge (2, 3):
```

```
GRAPH NODES          EDGE LISTS
===========          ==========

0 :    (0, 1)  ->  (0, 3)  ->  (0, 5)  -> NULL
1 :    (1, 0)  ->  (1, 2)  ->  (1, 4)  -> NULL
2 :    (2, 1)  ->  (2, 5)  -> NULL
3 :    (3, 0)  ->  (3, 4)  -> NULL
4 :    (4, 1)  ->  (4, 3)  ->  (4, 5)  -> NULL
5 :    (5, 0)  ->  (5, 2)  ->  (5, 4)  -> NULL
```

Graph after deleting the node 4:

```
GRAPH NODES          EDGE LISTS
===========          ==========

0 :    (0, 1)  ->  (0, 3)  ->  (0, 5)  -> NULL
1 :    (1, 0)  ->  (1, 2)  -> NULL
2 :    (2, 1)  ->  (2, 5)  -> NULL
3 :    (3, 0)  -> NULL
5 :    (5, 0)  ->  (5, 2)  -> NULL
```

The graph size is: 15

Exercises

16-1 (a) Describe adjacency matrix representation of an ADT graph.

     (b) What are its advantages and disadvantages?

16-2 (a) Described linked adjacency list representation of an ADT graph.

     (b) What are its advantages and disadvantages?

16-3 Find a spanning tree for each of the following undirected graphs:

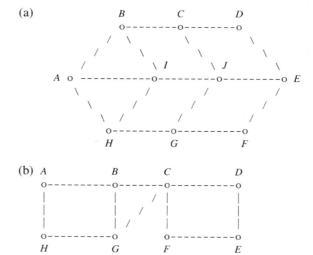

16-4 Using a breadth-first traversal, find a spanning tree for each of the following undirected graphs:

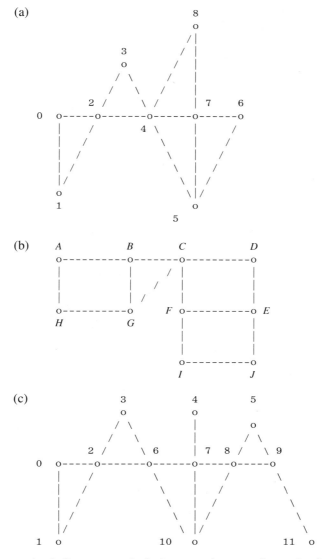

16-5 Using a depth-first traversal, find a spanning tree for each of the undirected graphs in Exercise 16-4.

16-6 When an ADT graph, directed or undirected, is implemented by the
adjacency matrix, write a function `init_graph()` that initializes an
ADT graph.

16-7 When an ADT graph, directed or undirected, is implemented by the
adjacency matrix, write a function `is_graph_empty()` that checks
whether an ADT graph is empty.

16-8 When an ADT graph, directed or undirected, is implemented by the
adjacency matrix, write a function `create_gnode()` that creates an
ADT graph node.

16-9 When an ADT graph, directed or undirected, is implemented by the adjacency matrix, write a function `insert_gnode()` that inserts an ADT graph node in the adjacency matrix.

16-10 When an ADT graph, directed or undirected, is implemented by the adjacency matrix, write a function `create_graph()` that creates the adjacency matrix for an ADT graph.

16-11 When an ADT graph, directed or undirected, is implemented by the adjacency matrix, write a function `delete_graph()` that deletes the entire graph.

16-12 When an ADT graph, directed or undirected, is implemented by the adjacency matrix, write a function `print_graph()` that prints the entire graph.

16-13 When an ADT graph, directed or undirected, is implemented by the adjacency matrix, write a function `search_gnode()` that searchs for an ADT graph node in the matrix.

16-14 When an ADT graph, directed or undirected, is implemented by the adjacency matrix, write a function `delete_gnode()` that deletes an ADT graph node from the matrix.

16-15 When an ADT graph, directed or undirected, is implemented by the adjacency matrix, write a function `insert_edge()` that verifies the parameters of an edge and inserts the edge in the adjacency matrix.

16-16 When an ADT graph, directed or undirected, is implemented by the adjacency matrix, write a function `search_edge()` that searchs for an edge element in the matrix.

16-17 When an ADT graph, directed or undirected, is implemented by the adjacency matrix, write a function `delete_edge()` that deletes an edge element from the matrix by setting the associated weight to unused. It must check the validity of parameters.

16-18 When an ADT graph, directed or undirected, is implemented by the adjacency matrix, write a function `is_adjacent_node()` that checks whether two graph nodes are adjacent, that is, whether there is an edge from one node to the other.

16-19 When an ADT graph, directed or undirected, is implemented by the adjacency matrix, write a function `retrieve_gnode()` that retrieves an ADT graph node.

16-20 When an ADT graph, directed or undirected, is implemented by the adjacency matrix, write a function `update_gnode()` that updates an ADT graph node.

16-21 When an ADT graph, directed or undirected, is implemented by the adjacency matrix, write a function `Breadth_first_trav()` that performs a breadth-first traversal of an ADT graph.

16-22 When an ADT graph, directed or undirected, is implemented by the adjacency matrix, write a function `Depth_first_trav()` that performs a depth-first traversal of an ADT graph.

16-23 When an ADT graph, directed or undirected, is implemented by the adjacency matrix, write a function `find_path()` that finds a path between two graph nodes.

16-24 When an ADT graph, directed or undirected, is implemented by the adjacency matrix, write a function `print_path()` that prints a path between two graph nodes.

16-25 When an ADT graph, directed or undirected, is implemented by the adjacency matrix, write a function `count_hops()` that counts the total number of hops (edges) on a path between two graph nodes.

16-26 When an ADT graph is implemented by the linked adjacency list (see Example 16-1), write a function `retrieve_gnode()` that returns a pointer to a graph node if a match of its key is found.

16-27 When an ADT graph is implemented by the linked adjacency list (see Example 16-1), write a function `find_path()` that finds a path between two graph nodes.

16-28 When an ADT graph is implemented by the linked adjacency list (see Example 16-1), write a function `count_hops()` that counts the total number of hops (edges) on a path between two graph nodes.

16-29 When an ADT graph is implemented by the linked adjacency matrix, write a function `Breadth_first_trav()` that performs a breadth-first traversal of an ADT graph.

16-30 When a connected undirected graph is implemented by the adjacency matrix, write a program that finds and prints a spanning tree for this graph using a depth-first traversal.

16-31 When a connected undirected graph is implemented by the adjacency matrix, write a program that finds and prints a spanning tree for this graph using a depth-first traversal.

16-32 Study the following directed and weighted computer network:

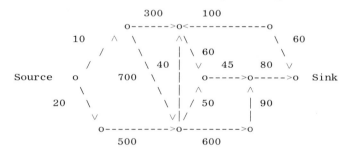

16-33 *Programming project* (the shortest-path problem). For a directed and weighted graph, implemented by the adjacency matrix, find the shortest path from the single source to a destination. Use Dijkstra's algorithm (see Gould, 1988).

Important C-Language Information

A.1 Form of a Simple Program in C

```
main()                    /* This is the main entry in a C program  */
/* Purpose: To demo the use of pointer '*' & address '&'            */
{                                      /* Begin main                 */
   int a, *pntr_to_a, b;               /* Identifier declaration     */
   a = 10;                             /* Value 10 is assigned to a  */
   pntr_to_a = &a;                     /* pntr_to_a holds address of a*/
   b = *pntr_to_a;                     /* Now b = a                  */
   printf(" a = %d  b = %d , a, b );        /* Write on display      */
   printf(" Enter a = " );
   scanf("%d", &a );                   /* Read 'a' from keyboard     */
   printf(" a = %d  b = %d , a, b );        /* Write on display      */
}    /* End of main */
```

A.2 28 Reserved Words in C

The combination of the formal C syntax and the following reserved words forms the
C programming language:

auto	double	if	static
break	else	int	struct
case	enum	long	switch
char	extern	register	typedef
continue	float	return	union
default	for	sizeof	unsigned
do	goto	short	while

A.3 Special Characters Reserved in C

```
+     -     *     /     %     +=    -=    *=    /=    %=
++    --    **    [  ]     (   )     {   }      ;
```

```
/*   */   ,    != >    <    == >= <=   !
&&   ||   &    |    ^    ~    << >> >>   :
>>=  <<=  &=   |=   ^=   ?    \t \n \r \b
```

A.4 Built-in Data Types in C

A.4.1 Basic Integer Data Types in Standard C

There are nine groups presented in columns in the order of their increasing guaranteed size.

Least size	Medium size	Maximum size
Group I	Group II	Group III
Signed char	Char	Unsigned char
Group IV		Group V
Short		Unsigned short
Short int		Unsigned short int
Signed short		
Signed short int		
Group VI		Group VII
Int		Unsigned
Signed int		Unsigned int
Group VIII		Group IX
Long		Unsigned long
Long int		Unsigned long int
Signed long		
Signed long int		

A.4.2 Other Integer Types as Bitfields

These are of three forms:

Plain bitfield
Signed bitfield
Unsigned bitfield

For example:

```
struct status_bits
  {
    int          state0:3;   /* basic bitfield    */
    signed int   state1:4;   /* signed bitfield   */
    unsigned int state2:6;   /* unsigned bitfield */
  } process_0;
```

A.4.3 Floating-Point Types

The following floating types are defined in Standard C:

Float
Double
Long double

For example:

char	character	1 byte
int	integer	2 or 4 bytes
float	floating point	4 bytes
double	double-precision floating point	8 bytes

The relative precision and range requirements are:

Float precision	<= double precision
Float range	<= double range
Double precision	<= long double precision
Double range	<= long double range

A.4.4 Enumeration Types

The keyword enum is used to declare enumeration types of data. It provides a means of naming a finite set. For example,

```
enum objects { computer, house, car };    /* template   */

/*  Allocates space for obj1 and obj2 of type objects  */
enum obj1, obj2;
```

A.5 Casting in C

Casting in C forces an expression to be of a specific type. Its form is

(type) expression

e.g., sum = (double) (a + b);

Casts are considered as unary operators. Its precedence is the same as any other unary operators.

A.6 Identifiers in C

The identifiers are user-defined alphanumeric names. They may be variable names, function names, derived data types, etc. In most implementations, there is no restriction on the number of alphanumeric characters forming the identifier.

A.7 Arithmetic Operators in C

A.7.1 Standard Binary Operators

Operator	Description
+	Addition
–	Subtraction
*	Multiplication
/	Division
%	Remainder

A.7.2 Auto Increment and Decrement Operators

Operator	Description	Meaning
++	Increment assignment	a++ means a = a + 1
--	Decrement assignment	a-- means a = a - 1

The variable a is assumed to be an integer in the above examples. Any one of these can be used as a prefix or a suffix to a variable.

A.8 Relational Binary Operators in C

Operator	Description
>	Greater than
<	Less than
==	Equal to
>=	Greater than or equal to
<=	Less than or equal to
!=	Not equal to

A.9 Logical Operators in C

Operator	Description
!	Logical NOT
&&	Logical AND
||	Logical OR

A.10 Bitwise Operators in C

Operator	Description	Meaning
&	Bitwise AND	0110 & 1010 = 0010
|	Bitwise inclusive OR	0110 | 1010 = 1110
∧	Bitwise exclusive OR	0110 ∧ 1010 = 1100
~	Bitwise complement	~ 0110 = 1001
<<	Shift left	0110 << 2 = 1000
>>	Shift right (unsigned)	0110 >> 3 = 0001
>>	Shift right (signed) (machine-dependent)	0110 >> 3 = 1111

A.11 Assignment Operators in C

Operator	Description	Meaning
=	Simple assignment	a = b;
+=	Addition assignment	a += b means a = a + b
-=	Subtraction assignment	a -= b means a = a - b

*=	Multiplication assignment	a *= b means a = a * b
/=	Division assignment	a /= b means a = a / b
%=	Remainder assignment	a %= b means a = a % b
&=	Bitwise AND assignment	
|=	Bitwise inclusive OR assignment	
∧=	Bitwise exclusive OR assignment	
<<=	Shift-left assignment	
>>=	Shift-right assignment	

Note that b may be an expression.

A.12 Operators' Precedence and Associativity in C

The following table shows precedence level from the highest to the lowest. The operators in the same precedence level are shown with at least one space in between them. Associativity implies order of evaluation. In case of uncertainty or to guarantee evaluation, one must use parentheses.

Precedence	Operators	Associativity
1	() [] . ->	Left to right
2	- ~ ! * & ++ --	
	sizeof (type)	Right to left
3	* / %	Left to right
4	+ -	Left to right
5	<< >>	Left to right
6	< > <= >=	Left to right
7	== !=	Left to right
8	&	Left to right
9	∧	Left to right
10	|	Left to right
11	&&	Left to right
12	||	Left to right
13	exp1?exp2:exp3	Right to left
14	= += -= *= /= %= >>=	
	<<= &= |= ∧=	Right to left
15	,	Left to right

A.13 Arrays in C

There is no built-in data type in C. Arrays are declared using [ ] brackets. For example:

```
char string [ 80 ];    /* Single dimensional array   */
int matrix[ 6 ][ 7 ];  /* Two dimensional array      */
```

A.14 Records in C

A record is a composite of related but different types of members. A record in C is defined using struct, e.g.:

```
struct customer
  {
     char   cust_name[ 20 ];    /* Customer Name      */
     int    cust_no;            /* Customer number    */
     float  old_balance;
     float  new_balance;
     float  payment;
  } x, y;                       /* Identifiers x and y  */
```

A.15 Pointers in C

A pointer variable contains the address of another variable. It is declared with a *
prefixed. For example:

```
int    a,  b,    *pntr;
pntr = &a;       /* Assigns the address
                    of 'a' to 'pntr'.    */
```

A.16 Statement Formats of Each Key Word in C

Statement	Description
break;	Cancels execution of the smallest enclosing do, for, switch, or while statement in which it appears

{
 [declaration];
 . . .
 [statement];
 }
	C program body with begin and end

continue;	Continues to the next iteration
do { statement_1; . . . statement_n; } while (expression);	Executes the loop until expression becomes 0
[expression];	Evaluates the expression; the expression may be empty

for ([init] ; [condition] ; [increment])
 { statement_1;
 . . .
 statement_n;
 }
	Statements 1 through *n* are executed until the condition becomes false

goto step; . . . step: statement;	Jumps directly to the statement specified by the label step

```
if ( expression  )                          Statements 1 through m are
  {  statement_1;                           executed if expression is
     . . .                                  nonzero; otherwise, statements n
     statement_m;                           through z are executed if else
  }                                         clause is present; otherwise
else                                        executes the next statement
  {  statement_n;
     . . .
     statement_z;
  }


  return[expression];                       Terminates the execution of the
                                            function; returns control and the
                                            value of expression to the
                                            calling function


  switch(expression )                       Executes the statement associated
  {                                         with the value of the
    case value:                             expression
      statement;
    case value:
      statement;

    . . .
    default:
      statement;
  }

while (expression )                         Statements 1 through n are
  {                                         executed until expression
     statement_1;                           becomes 0
     . . .
     statement_n;
  }
```

A.17 Input/Output Basics in C

To read input from the standard-in (stdin) (e.g., keyboard), use scanf() function. To write output to the standard-out (stdout) (e.g., screen), use printf() function. For example:

```
scanf("%d", &integer );   /* Formatted Read  */
printf("%d", integer );   /* Formatted Write */
```

A.18 File-Based Input/Output in C

FILE I/O routines are not part of the formal C language. They are provided with the operating system. To access these routines in your program, include the following line in the beginning of your of your program:

```
#include <stdio.h>
```

To read input from a file, use the fscanf() function. To write output to a file, use the fprintf() function. For example:

```
FILE    *inp_fl, *out_fl;                    /* Declaration      */
inp_fl = fopen("input_file_name", "r"); /* Open  read */
out_fl = fopen("output_file_name", "w");/* Write read */
fscanf(inp_fl,"%d", &integer );   /* Read from file   */
fprintf(out_fl,"%d", integer );   /* Write to file    */

fclose( inp_fl );                             /* Close file       */
fclose( out_fl );                             /* Close file       */
```

A.19 Common Preprocessor Directives in C

Directive	Example
#define identifier #ifndef identifier	#define SQR(x) ((x) * (x)) #ifndef BOOLEAN #define TRUE 0xff #define FALSE 0 #endif
#include " [path]file" #include < [path]file>	#include "my_prog.h" #include <stdio.h>
#undef identifier	#undef TEST /* TEST was defined earlier */

#ifdef identifier	#ifdef DEBUG
	    printf("loader: base_addr = %lx ,
	                                base_addr);
	#endif

#if expression
   [statement]
#elif expression
   [statement]
#else
   [statement]
#endif
	#if MOTOROLA_68020
	#define PROCR_OFF 0x100000
	#elif MOTOROLA_68000
	#define PROCR_OFF 0x80000
	#else
	#define PROCR_OFF 0x60000
	#endif

A.20 Creating an Executable File for a C Program

A.20.1 Unix Environment

Step 1. Create your program using an editor (e.g., vi, ed)
Step 2. Create an executable file, type:

```
        make file_name
OR      cc -O file_name.c -o file_name [path]/library
```

A.20.2 IBM PC/MS–DOS Environment

Step 1. Create your program using an editor (e.g., vi, edlin)
Step 2. Assuming you are using Microsoft C, create an object, typing:

```
    msc  file_name.c /I A: INCLUDE /I B: INCLUDE
```

Step 3. To create an executable (. EXE) file, run the interactive linker:

```
                        LINK
```

Standard C Library Functions for Handling Strings

The string handling functions are not part of the C language. They are provided in a library that is packaged with the compiler. Because these functions are useful and relevant to our discussion, they are given below.

Function syntax	Description
1. `int strlen(s)` `char *s;`	Returns number of characters excluding \0

2. `int strcmp (s1, s2)`
   `char *s1;`
   `char*s2;`
	Lexically compares s1 and s2; returns –1 if s1 < s2, 0 if s1 = s2, 1 if s1 > s2

3. `int strncmp (s1, s2, n)`
   `char *s1, *s2;`
   `int n;`
	Lexically compares at most *n* characters of s1 and s2; returns values similar to `strcmp ()`

4. `char *index(s, c)`
   `char *s;`
   `char c;`
	Searches for character c starting from left; returns pointer to the leftmost first occurrence of c in s, or NULL if not found in the string s

5. `char *rindex(s, c)`
   `char *s;`
   `char c;`
	Searches for character c starting from right; returns pointer to the rightmost first occurrence of c in s, or NULL if not found in the string s

6. `char *strcpy(s1, s2)` `char *s1, *s2;`	Copies string s2 over s1 until \0, assuming `length(s1) >= length(s2)`; returns pointer to s1

7. `char *strncpy(s1, s2, n)`
   `char *s1, *s2;`
   `int n;`
	Copies at most *n* characters of string s2 over s1 until \0; if `length(a2) < n`, \0 used for padding; if `length(s2) >= n`, s1 may not terminate at NULL; returns pointer to s1

8. `char *strcat(s1, s2)` `char *s1, *s2;`	Concatenates (appends) s2, including \0 to the end of s1; returns pointer to s1

9. `char *strncat(s1, s2, n)`
   `char *s1, *s2;`
   `int n;`
	Concatenates (appends) at most *n* characters of s2 plus \0 to the end of s1; returns pointer to s1

Bibliography

Adel'son-Vel'skii, G. M., and Landis, E. M. (1962). *Doklady Akademii Nauk SSSR* **146;** English translation in *Soviet Mathematics* (*Providence*) **3,** 1259–1263.

Bentley, J. (1986). "Programming Pearls." Addison-Wesley, Reading, Massachusetts.

Bentley, J. (1988). "More Programming Pearls—Confessions of a Coder." Addison-Wesley, Reading, Massachusetts.

Burden, R. J., *et al.* (1978). "Numerical Analysis." Prindle, Weber & Schmidt, Boston.

Carnahan, B., *et al.* (1969). "Applied Numerical Methods." Wiley, New York.

Comer, D. (1979). The ubiquitous B-tree, *ACM* **11**(2).

Cox, B. J. (1988). "Object Oriented Programming: An Evolutionary Approach." Addison-Wesley, Reading, Massachusetts.

Deitel, H. M. (1984). "An Introduction to Operating Systems." Addison-Wesley, Reading, Massachusetts.

Dr. Dobb's Journal Staff (1986). "Dr. Dobb's Toolbook of C." Prentice-Hall, Englewood Cliffs, New Jersey.

Gettys, J., Newman, R., and Fera T. D. (1986). Xlib—C Language Interface Protocol Version 10, January.

Gonnet, G. (1984). "Handbook of Algorithms and Data Structures." Addison-Wesley, Reading, Massachusetts.

Gould, R. (1988). "Graph Theory." Benjamin–Cummings, Menlo Park, California.

Hansen, E. R. (1969). "Topics in Interval Analysis." Oxford Univ. Press, New York.

Hogg, R. V., and Ledolter, J. (1987). "Engineering Statistics." Macmillan, New York.

Holub, A. I. (1990). "Compiler Design in C." Prentice-Hall, Englewood Cliffs, New Jersey.

Holub, A. (1987). "C Companion." Prentice-Hall. Englewood Cliffs, New Jersey.

Intel (1987). "80386 System Software Writer's Guide." Intel, Santa Clara, California.

Jaeschke, G. (1981). Reciprocal hashing—A method for generating minimal perfect hashing functions, *Communications of the ACM* **24**(12).

Kelly, A., and Pohl, I. (1984). "An Introduction to Programming in C." Bejamin–Cummings, Menlo Park, California.

Kernighan, B. W., and Ritchie, D. M. (1978). "The C Programming Language." Prentice-Hall, Englewood Cliffs, New Jersey.

Knuth, D. E. (1973). "The Art of Computer Programming: Fundamental Algorithms," Vol. 1, 2nd ed. Addison-Wesley, Reading, Massachusetts.

Knuth, D. E. (1973). "The Art of Computer Programming: Sorting and Searching," Vol. 3, Addison-Wesley, Reading, Massachusetts.

Knuth, D. E., Morris, J. H., and Pratt, V. R. (1977). Fast pattern matching in strings, *SIAM Journal on Computing*, June, pp. 323–349.

Korth, H. F., and Silberschatz, A. (1986). "Database System Concepts." McGraw-Hill, New York.

Lafore, R. (1987). "Turbo C Programming for the IBM." The Waite Group,

Larson, P. (1982). Expected worst-case performance of hash files, *Computer Journal,* **25,** 347–352.

Leestma, S., and Nyhoff, L. (1987). "PASCAL Programming and Problem Solving." Macmillan, New York.

Lippman, S. B. (1989). "C++ Primer." Addison-Wesley, Reading, Massachusetts.

Liskov, B. H., and Zilles, S. N. (1975). Specification techniques for data structures, *IEEE Transactions on Software Engineering* **1**(1).

McCracken, D. D. (1984). "Computing for Engineers and Scientists with Fortran 77," pp. 241–261. Wiley, New York.

Microsoft Corporation (1987). Advanced Windows Programming.

Moore, R. E. (1966). "Interval Analysis." Prentice-Hall, Englewood Cliffs, New Jersey.

Parsaye, K., *et al.* (1989). "Intelligent Databases—Object-Oriented, Deductive Hypermedia Technologies." Wiley, New York.

Plauger, P. J. (1988). Types play central role in new standard C, *The C Users Journal,* March/April, pp. 17–23.

Plum, T. (1986). "Programming in C." Plum-Hall, Cardiff, New Jersey.

Ramakrishna, M. W. (1989). Practical performance of Bloom filters and parallel free-text searching, *Communications of the ACM* **32**(10).

Reingold, E. M., and Hansen, W. J. (1983). "Data Structures." Little, Brown & Co., Boston.

Scheifer, R. W., and Gettys, J. (1986). The X Window System, July.

Schreiner, A., and Friedman, H. G. (1987). "Compiler Construction in Unix." Prentice-Hall, Englewood Cliffs, New Jersey.

Sedgewick, R. (1983). "Algorithms." Addison-Wesley, Reading, Massachusetts.

Standish, T. A. (1980). "Data Structure Techniques." Addison-Wesley, Reading, Massachusetts.

Strang, J. (1986). "Programming with Curses." O'Reilly & Associates, Newton, Massachusetts.

Stroustrup, B. (1986). "The C++ Programming Language." Addison-Wesley, Reading, Massachusetts.

Stubbs, D. F., and Webre, N. W. (1985). "Data Structures with Abstract Data Types and Pascal." Wadsworth, Belmont, California.

Tanenbaum, A. (1981). "Data Structures Using Pascal." Prentice-Hall, Englewood Cliffs, New Jersey.

Tanenbaum, A. S. (1987). "Operating Systems Design and Implementation." Prentice-Hall, Englewood Cliffs, New Jersey.

Ward, T. (1985). "Probability and Statistics Exam File." Engineering Press, San Jose, California.

Wiener, R. S., and Pinson, L. J. (1989). "An Introduction to Object-Oriented Programming and C++." Addison-Wesley, Reading, Massachusetts.

Index

Abstract data structure, 4
Abstract data type
  arrays, 62, 76
  AVL trees, 281
  B-trees, 292
  binary search trees, 262
  binary trees, 250
  circular lists, 141
  circular queues, 200
  complex numbers, 5, 8, 539
  definition, 4
  double stacks, 187
  file, 9
  general trees, 269
  graph, 576
  image, 4
  interval numbers, 8
  lists, 109
  matrix, 8
  natural numbers, 8
  polynomial, 9
  queues, 196
  rational numbers, 8
  set, 8
  stacks, 181
  string, 7, 83
  window, 9
  window pop-up menu, 9
Abstraction, 4
ADT, 4
Algorithm, 3
Analysis
  binary search tree, 359
  bubble sort, 382
  hash search, 375
  insertion sort, 384
  interpolation search, 356

  linear search, 352, 353
  merge sort, 389
  quick sort, 386
  selection sort, 381
ANSI C, 7
Arrays
  multidimensional
    address translation, 67
    ADT definition, 76
    as function argument, 66
    concept, 64
    initialization, 65
    operations
      creating, 77
      init(), 77
      retrieve(), 78
      store(), 78
  one-dimensional
    address translation, 60
    ADT definition, 62
    as function argument, 61
    concept, 57
    initialization, 59
    operations
      creating, 62
      delete(), 64
      init(), 62
      insert(), 63
      store(), 63
      update(), 63
AVL tree
  ADT definition, 281
  concept, 280
  deleting a node, 288
  inserting a node, 283
  operations
    AVL_Create(), 323

AVL tree, operations (*continued*)
    `AVL_InOrder()`, 326
    `AVL_Insert()`, 286, 325
    `AVL_PostOrder()`, 327
    `AVL_PreOrder()`, 327
    `AVLdelete_tree()`, 326
    `create_node()`, 324
    `hPrint_AVLtree()`, 327
    `Rotate_Left()`, 324
    `Rotate_Right()`, 324
  pointer implementation, 282
  rebalancing, 283, 289
  rotating left, 289
  rotating right, 289

B-tree
  ADT definition, 292
  concept, 290
  deleting a node, 296
  inserting a node, 292
B$^+$-tree, 299
B*-tree, 299
Backtracking, 107
Balanced binary search tree, 280
Big Oh notation, 349
Binary search tree
  ADT definition, 262
  building a BST, 266
  deleting a node, 267
  linked implementation, 262
  operations
    `BST_Create()`, 263, 266, 317
    `BST_InOrder()`, 263, 319
    `BST_PostOrder()`, 263, 320
    `BST_PreOrder()`, 263, 320
    `BST_Search()`, 263, 264, 317
    `BSTdelete_tree()`, 263, 318
    `BSTdelete_subtree()`, 263, 318
    `BSTinit_tree()`, 263, 315
    `BST_Insert_node()`, 263, 265, 316
    `BSTretrieve_node()`, 263, 316
    `BSTsearch_parent()`, 263, 318
    `BSTupdate_node()`, 263, 316
    `create_node()`, 263, 315
    `is_BST_empty()`, 263, 315
Binary tree
  ADT definition
  array implementation, 250
  building a binary tree, 256
  linked implementation, 254
  operations
    `create_node()`, 258, 259, 308
    `delete_subtree()`, 258, 261, 311
    `delete_tree()`, 258, 261, 310
    `init_tree()`, 258, 259, 308
    `insert_node()`, 258, 259, 309
    `is_tree_empty()`, 258, 308
    `retrieve_node()`, 258, 259, 309

    `search_parent()`, 258, 259, 310
    `Traverse_InOrder()`, 258, 261, 311
    `Traverse_PostOrder()`, 258, 261, 312
    `Traverse_PreOrder()`, 258, 261, 312
    `update_node()`, 258, 259, 308
  traversal algorithms
    inorder, 249, 257
    postorder, 249, 257
    preorder, 249, 257
Binomial coefficient, 103
BIOS, 86
Bitfields, 33
BST, 262
Buffer queue, 203

C++, 4, 422
Circle
  class, 424
  list, 425
  procedures
    `append_obj()`, 425, 426, 429
    `Circle_list()`, 425, 428
    `~Circle_List()`, 425, 426, 428
    `Circle_obj()`, 433
    `count_circle_objs()`, 425, 426, 432
    `delete_obj()`, 425, 426, 431
    `display_menu()`, 433
    `get_obj()`, 425, 432
    `init_list()`, 425
    `insert_obj()`, 425, 429
    `is_list_empty()`, 425
    `print_list()`, 425, 426, 432
    `process_choice()`, 433
    `search_obj()`, 425, 426, 430
    `search_previous()`, 425, 426, 430
    `user_interface()`, 435
Class
  AVL tree, 441
  B-tree, 441
  binary expression tree, 440
  binary search tree, 441
  binary tree, 440
  of circle objects, 424
  complex, 439
  definition, 422, 423
  hexagon, 439
  matrix, 439
  polygon, 439
  polynomial, 439
  queue, 440
  rectangle, 439
  RPN, 440
  sparse matrix, 440
  spreadsheet, 441
  stack, 440
  string, 439
  triangle, 439
CLI, 91

Compiler
  code generator, 496–498
    mnemonics, 497
  compilation, 488
  lexical analyzer, 488, 489
  overview, 488
  parser, 488, 489
  recursive descent, 301, 304, 490
  table driven, 490
  symbol table, 490
    data structure, 492, 495
    declaration, 492
    functions, 491
      add_info(), 492
      add_sym(), 492, 493
      create_sym(), 492
      delete_sym(), 492, 494
      get_sym(), 492
      hash_add_info(), 496
      hash_add_sym(), 496
      hash_create_sym(), 496
      hash_delete_sym(), 496
      hash_get_sym(), 496
      hash_search_sym(), 496
      hash_sym(), 496
      init_hash_symtab(), 496
      init_symtab(), 492, 494
      is_symtab_empty(), 493
      search_sym(), 492, 494
    implementations
      hash strategy, 495
      linked list, 491
  translation table, 491
Complex numbers
  ADT definition, 539
  array implementation, 539
  pointer implementation, 540
    operations
      complex_add(), 541, 542
      complex_div(), 541, 544
      complex_mult(), 541, 544
      complex_neg(), 541, 542
      complex_sub(), 541, 542
      create_Complex(), 540, 542
      free_complex(), 541
      print_complex(), 545
  struct implementation, 540
Cross-reference generator, 509
Customer database, 330

Data structure
  definition, 2
  dynamic, 3
  static, 3
Data types
  atomic, 5
  fixed-structured, 5
  variable-structured, 5

Database, parts inventory control
  definition, 158, 442
  implementation
    using B-trees, 442
    using doubly linked list, 159
  restrictions, 161
  schema, 157, 442
Deque, 245
Dequeue, 246
Disk schedulings
  FCFS, 209, 246
  SCAN, 246
  SSTF, 207–217
Double stack, 187
Dynamic binding, 421

Employee database
  add_empl(), 52
  delete_empl(), 52
  display_menu(), 50
  modify_empl(), 53
  process_choice(), 51
  quit_db(), 54
  search_empl(), 51,
  srch_display_empl(), 53
Encapsulation, 4
Engineering, Laplace heat equation, 478
Enqueue, 246
Expression
  infix, 188, 192
  postfix, 188, 189, 192
  prefix, 245
Expression evaluator, 189, 299–306
Expression tree
  concept, 299
  evaluation, 301
  traversals
    inorder, 300
    postorder, 300
    preorder, 300

Factorial()
  iterative, 99
  recursive, 100
FCFS, 209
Fibonacci_no()
  improved, 98
  recursive, 101
FIFO, 203
File
  access, 334, 335
  data structure programming, 340
  FILE type, 336
  raw-mode I/O, 334
  streams-mode I/O, 335, 338
  tree-structured application, 342
    functions
      Filltree(), 343

File, tree-structured application, functions (*cont.*)
    `Dumptree()`, 344
    `Nalloc()`, 342
    `Nestlev()`, 342
    `Sumtree()`, 344
File system, 91, 269

Graph
  adjacent, 569
  ADT definition, 576
  cycle, 570
  cyclic, 570
  degree, 569
  directed graph, 568
  edge, 568
  incident, 569
  operations, graph
    `Breadth_first_trav()`, 576, 604
    `Depth_first_trav()`, 576, 603
    `count_graph_size()`, 576, 595
    `create_edge_elt()`, 576, 598
    `create_gnode()`, 576, 592
    `create_graph()`, 576, 593
    `delete_edge()`, 576, 601
    `delete_edge_list()`, 576, 598
    `delete_gnode()`, 576, 596
    `delete_graph()`, 576, 594
    `find_path()`, 576, 604
    `init_graph()`, 576, 592
    `insert_edge()`, 576, 599
    `insert_gnode()`, 576, 592
    `is_adjacent_node()`, 576, 602
    `is_glist_empty()`, 576, 592
    `print_graph()`, 576, 595
    `print_path()`, 576
    `retrieve_gnode()`, 576, 602
    `search_edge()`, 576, 599
    `search_gnode()`, 576, 596
    `search_prev_edge()`, 576, 600
    `update_gnode()`, 576, 602
  path, 569, 571
  performance, operations, 585
  reflexive, 569
  representations, graph
    adjacency matrix, 570
    incidence matrix, 582, 594
    linked adjacency matrix, 574
    transitive closure, 571
  shortest path, 587
  spanning tree, 585
  symmetric, 570
  transitive, 570
  traversals
    breadth-first, 579, 604
    depth-first, 579, 580, 603
  vertex, 568
  weighted, 569
Greatest common divisor, 101

General tree
  building a general tree, 273
  concept, 269
  examples
    corporate organization, 2, 269
    file system, 269
    pop-up menu, 270
  operations
    `Build_Tree()`, 277
    `Print_Tree()`, 278
    `t_postorder()`, 273
  pointer implementation, 270, 274

Hash
  concept, 360
  function
    bloom filters, 365
    digit conversion, 364
    modulus, 363
    key points, 378
  search
  linear search
    algorithm, 367
    `Hash_Linear_Search()`, 367
  operators for hash chain
    `Create_Hash_Node()`, 372
    `Hash_Chain_Delete()`, 374
    `Hash_Chain_Init()`, 372
    `Hash_Chain_Insert()`, 373
    `Hash_Chain_Search()`, 371
    search algorithm, 371
    worst-case performance, 375
  table
    bucket, 361
    chaining, 362, 364
    collision, 366
    heap, 377
    insertion, 366
    interval analysis, 376
    overflow, 366
Heap
  `Adjust_Heap()`, 396, 397
  concept, 391
  `Create_Heap()`, 394
  creating a heap, 392
  sort
    algorithm, 397
    `Heap_Sort()`, 399
  structure
    array, 392
    tree, 392

Infix notation, 188, 192
Infix-to-postfix
  concept, 188
  conversion
    algorithm, 192

priority(), 193
  in_to_post(), 190
evaluation
  algorithm, 189
  Evaluate_Postfix(), 190
Inheritance, 421
Interval, 35, 376

Least squares, 484
Least_squares(), 485
Lexical analyzer, action table, 490
LIFO, 181
Line-oriented editor
  delete_line(), 505
  do_delete(), 507
  do_edit(), 502
  do_insert(), 507
  do_list(), 506
  do_replace(), 506
  do_search(), 506
  do_write(), 508
  get_cmd(), 503
  get_input(), 507
  get_range(), 503
  insert_line(), 504
  line structure, 499
  locate_line(), 506
  read_file(), 502
  skip_space(), 503
  specification, 498
List
  ADT definition, 109
  array implementation
    approach, 110
    operations, 113
  pointer implementation, 118
List, circular
  doubly linked, 157
  operations
    cir_create_list(), 141, 142, 145
    cir_delete_list(), 141, 142, 145
    count_element(), 141, 143, 150
    create_element(), 141, 142, 144
    delete_element(), 141, 142, 147
    init_list(), 141, 144
    is_list_empty(), 141, 142, 144
    modify_element(), 141, 142
    print_list(), 141, 143, 149
    search_element(), 141, 142, 146
  singly linked, 140
List, doubly linked
  algorithms
    deleting an element, 132
    inserting an element, 131
  operations
    count_elt(), 134, 135, 139
    create_elt(), 134, 136
    create_list(), 134, 135, 137

delete_list(), 134, 135, 138
    dispose_elt(), 134, 135, 137
    forw_print_list(), 134, 135, 139
    init_list(), 134, 136
    is_list_empty(), 134, 136
    retrieve_elt(), 134, 135, 138
    rev_print_list(), 134, 135, 139
    search_elt(), 134, 135, 138
  structure, 131
List, linked, 118
List, singly linked
  algorithms
    creating a list, 122
    deleting an element, 123
    inserting an element, 123
  operations
    count_elt(), 125, 126, 129
    create_elt(), 124, 125, 127
    create_list(), 124, 125, 127
    delete_list(), 124, 125, 126, 128
    dispose_elt(), 124, 125, 128
    init_list(), 124, 125, 127
    is_list_empty(), 124, 125, 127
    print_list(), 125, 126, 129
    retrieve_elt(), 124, 126, 129
    search_elt(), 124, 126, 128
  structure, 5–12

Machine storage
  data types, 2
  sizes, 2
Matrix
  ADT definition, 8, 70, 76
  array implementation, 70
    address translation, 67
    initializing a matrix, 65, 77
    operations
      matrix_add(), 70
      matrix_mult(), 70
      print_matrix(), 71
    passing as an argument, 66
  pointer implementation, 45
    operations
      Assign_ptr_to_mat(), 46
      matrix_add(), 46
      matrix_mult(), 46
      print_matrix(), 47
Maze
  ADT definition, 108
  operations, 108
Multitasking, 18, 208

Numerical analysis
  Bisection, bisect(), 547
  Gaussian elimination, 556
  Gauss–Seidel, Gauss_Seidel(), 564
  Lagrange, Lagrange(), 551

Numerical analysis (*continued*)
  LU-decomposition, 560
  Newton–Raphson, newton(), 549
  Runge–Kutta, Runge_Kutta(), 554
  Simpson, Simpson(), 553

O notation, 349
Object identity, 421
Object-oriented programming
  abstract data typing, 421
  dynamic binding, 421
  fundamental aspects, 421
  inheritance, 421
  key points, 421
  object identity, 421

Parser, 84, 107, 488, 490
Parts database using B-tree
  functions
    add_an_element(), 459
    combine_nodes(), 447, 454
    create_node(), 445, 449
    delete_an_element(), 460
    delete_btree(), 447, 458
    delete_element(), 447, 455
    display_an_element(), 461
    display_menu(), 458
    find_index(), 446, 450
    get_string(), 460
    insert_btree(), 447, 454
    insert_element(), 446, 452
    key_to_continue(), 459
    modify_an_element(), 460
    print_part_btree(), 464
    read_part_btree(), 463
    replace_element(), 447, 457
    save_part_btree(), 463
    search_btree(), 446, 449
    split_elements(), 446, 450
    write to disk(), 462
  user interface, 443
Parts database using doubly linked list
  functions
    add_part(), 165
    create_part_record(), 164
    delete_part(), 166
    display_menu(), 163
    exit_db(), 168
    get_input(), 166
    load_db_from_disk(), 169
    modify_part(), 167
    pause_screen(), 171
    print_menu_hdr(), 168
    process_choice(), 163
    save_db_to_disk(), 169
    search_part(), 164
    srch_display_part(), 167

    user_confirm(), 168
  schema, 159
Pascal triangle, 89
Pointer in C
  arithmetic operations, 11
  concept, 10
  decrement, 12
  as function argument, 13
  to functions, 13
  increment, 12
  operators, 11
  to structures, 23
Polymorphic, 6
Polynomial, 9, 178
Pop(), 182, 185, 218, 222
Postfix notation, 188, 189, 192
Prefix notation, 245
Preprocessor, 474–476
Priority, 192, 193, 207, 244, 246
Priority queue, 207, 244, 246
Programming
  classical, 419
  database, 50, 158, 442
  object-oriented, 421
Push(), 182, 185, 218, 222

Queens
  eight, 104
  four, 107
Queue
  ADT definition, 196
  array implementation, 196
    operations
      qadd(), 196, 198, 228
      qcreate(), 196
      qempty(), 196, 228
      qinit(), 196, 198, 228
      qremove(), 196, 198, 228
  front of queue, 197, 199
  linked implementation, 199
    operations
      qadd(), 196, 200, 232
      qcreate(), 196
      qempty(), 196, 222
      qinit(), 196, 200, 232
      qremove(), 196, 200, 234
  rear of queue, 197, 199
Queue, circular
  array implementation, 200
    operations
      qadd(), 201, 202, 239
      qcreate(), 201
      qempty(), 201, 239
      qfull(), 201, 239
      qinit(), 201, 202, 239
      qremove(), 201, 202, 240
  linked implementation, 203

Queue, message, 203
Queue, priority, 244

Recursion
  C-stack, 95
  definition, 93
  function calls, 95
  steps, 94
Reverse polish notation, 188
ROM BIOS, 86
RPN, 188

Search
  analysis, 351
  best-case, 351
  binary, 351, 354
  binary search tree, 357
  `binary_search()`, 403
  `BST_Search()`, 317, 404
  comparisons, 351
  Fibonacci, 356
  Hash, 360
  `Hash_Chain_Search()`, 371
  interpolation, 351, 355
  linear of an array, 351
  linear of a linked list, 352
  linear of an ordered array, 353
  linear of an ordered list, 354
  `linear_srch()`, 401
  performance, 351
  `search_elt()`, 402
  worst-case, 351
Search path, 279
Segment descriptor, iAPX286, 19
Sort
  analysis, 379
  external storage, 379
  internal storage, 379
  best-case, 379
  binary search tree, 391
  bubble, 379, 381
  `bubble()`, 408
  comparisons, 379
  concatenate, 391
  `concat_ordr()`, 414
  heap, 379, 391
  `Heap_Sort()`, 399
  `insert_sort()`, 410
  insertion, 379, 383
  insertion for a linked list, 379, 384
  merge, 379, 386
  quick, 379, 385
  `quick_sort()`, 413
  `select_sort()`, 406
  selection, 379, 380
  shell, 379
  performance, 379
  worst-case, 379

Sparse matrix, 178
SQL, 474–476
SQL preprocessor, 474–476
SSTF, 207–246
Stack
  ADT definition, 181
  array implementation, 183
    operations
      `clear_stk()`, 182, 219
      `create_stk()`, 182, 220
      `get_top()`, 182, 220
      `init_stk()`, 181, 185, 218
      `is_stk_empty()`, 181, 218
      `pop()`, 182, 185, 219
      `print_stk()`, 182, 220
      `push()`, 182, 185, 219
  bottom of stack, 182
  linked implementation, 185
    operations
      `clear_stk()`, 182, 225
      `create_elt()`, 187, 222
      `create_stk()`, 182, 224
      `get_top()`, 182, 224
      `init_stk()`, 182, 222
      `is_stk_empty()`, 181, 222
      `pop()`, 182, 187, 223
      `print_stk()`, 182, 224
      `push()`, 182, 223
  top of stack, 182
Stack, double
  ADT definition, 187
  array sharing, 188
  concerns, 187
Statistics, 482
  mean, 482
  `Mean_Std_Dev()`, 482
  standard deviation, 482
  variance, 482
Strings
  ADT definition, 83
  array of, 81
  array implementation, 78
  array of pointers to, 82
  interchange, 83
  memory storage, 81
  operations
    `Append_Str()`, 84
    `max_Str()`, 84, 85
    `numeric_compare()`, 84, 85
    `Parse_Str()`, 84
    `position_Str()`, 84, 85
    `strlen()`, 80, 84
  pointer implementation, 79
Structure in C
  assignment, 23
  components, 18, 21
  defining, 16
  entering data into, 28
  initializing, 22

Structure in C (*continued*)
  need for, 16
  operators, 21, 24
  passing an argument, 24
  return value, 26
  structure of, 26

Traversals, tree
  inorder, 249
  LNR, 249
  LRN, 249
  NLR, 249
  NRL, 249
  postorder, 249
  preorder, 249
  RLN, 249
  RNL, 249
Tree
  AVL, 279
  B-tree, 290
  B$^+$-tree, 299
  B*-tree, 299
  binary, 247
  binary search, 262
  expression, 299
  general, 269

Union in C, 28

Virtual memory, 18

Window
  ADT definition, 9
  C structure, 512
  characteristics, 511
  functions
    acline(), 536
    add_list(), 536
    clear_message(), 538
    clear_screen(), 523
    clear_window(), 529

    close_all(), 528
    curr_cursor(), 522
    cursor(), 522
    delete_window(), 529
    dget(), 534
    displ(), 534
    display_window(), 528
    dtitle(), 530
    error_message(), 537
    establish_window(), 525
    hide_window(), 529
    redraw(), 528
    remove_list(), 536
    scroll(), 532
    scroll_lock(), 523
    set_border(), 526
    set_colors(), 526
    set_cursor_type(), 522
    set_intensity(), 527
    set_title(), 527
    verify_wnd(), 537
    vmode(), 523
    vrstr(), 535
    vsave(), 535
    vswap(), 535
    waddr(), 533
    wcursor(), 532
    wframe(), 530
    wprintf(), 531
    wputchar(), 531
  macros
    forefront(), 518
    move_window(), 518
    normal_video(), 518
    rear_window(), 518
    reverse_video(), 518
    rmove_window(), 518
  operations, 512, 514
Word processor
  features, 86
  implementation, 87

X-window, 20